COMPACT
WORLD
ATLAS

A DORLING KINDERSLEY BOOK
www.dk.com

EDITOR-IN-CHIEF
Andrew Heritage

SENIOR MANAGING ART EDITOR
Philip Lord

SENIOR CARTOGRAPHIC MANAGER
David Roberts

SENIOR CARTOGRAPHIC EDITOR
Simon Mumford

PROJECT CARTOGRAPHER
Iorwerth Watkins

PROJECT DESIGNER
Karen Gregory

PROJECT EDITOR
Debra Clapson

SYSTEMS CO-ORDINATOR
Philip Rowles

PRODUCTION
Wendy Penn

First published in Great Britain in 2001
by Dorling Kindersley Limited
80 Strand, London WC2R 0RL

A CIP catalogue record for this book is available from the British Library

ISBN 1-4053-1021-9

Printed and bound in China by Toppan Printing Co. (Shenzhen) Ltd.

For the very latest information, visit:
www.dk.com and click on the Maps & Atlases icon

KEY TO MAP SYMBOLS

PHYSICAL FEATURES

Elevation

- 4,000m/13,124ft
- 2,000m/6,562ft
- 1,000m/3,281ft
- 500m/1,640ft
- 250m/820ft
- 100m/328ft
- 0
- Below sea level

△ Mountain

▽ Depression

◬ Volcano

)(Pass/tunnel

▨ Sandy desert

DRAINAGE FEATURES

Major perennial river

Minor perennial river

- - - Seasonal river

Canal

| Waterfall

Perennial lake

Seasonal lake

Wetland

ICE FEATURES

Permanent ice cap/ice shelf

Winter limit of pack ice

Summer limit of pack ice

BORDERS

Full international border

- - - Disputed *de facto* border

· · · · · Territorial claim border

x x x Cease-fire line

- - - Undefined boundary

Internal administrative boundary

COMMUNICATIONS

Major road

Minor road

Rail

✈ International airport

SETTLEMENTS

⊡ Over 500,000

◉ 100,000 - 500,000

○ 50,000 - 100,000

○ Less than 50,000

● National capital

● Internal administrative capital

MISCELLANEOUS FEATURES

+ Site of interest

⏛ Ancient wall

GRATICULE FEATURES

Line of latitude/longitude/ Equator

- - Tropic/Polar circle

25° Degrees of latitude/ longitude

NAMES

Physical features

Andes

Sahara   Landscape features

Ardennes

Land's End   Headland

Mont Blanc 4,807m   Elevation/volcano/pass

Blue Nile   River/canal/waterfall

Ross Ice Shelf   Ice feature

PACIFIC OCEAN

     Sea features

Sulu Sea

Palk Strait

Chile Rise   Undersea feature

Regions

FRANCE   Country

JERSEY (to UK)   Dependent territory

KANSAS   Administrative region

Dordogne   Cultural region

Settlements

PARIS   Capital city

SAN JUAN   Dependent territory capital city

Chicago

Kettering   Other settlements

Burke

INSET MAP SYMBOLS

Urban area

City

Park

▪ Place of interest

▫ Suburb/district

CONTENTS

The Political World 6-7

The Physical World 8-9

Time Zones 10

THE WORLD ATLAS

NORTH & CENTRAL AMERICA

North & Central America 12-13
Western Canada & Alaska 14-15
Eastern Canada 16-17
USA: The Northeast 18-19
USA: The Southeast 20-21
  Bermuda
USA: Central States 22-23
USA: The West 24-25
  Los Angeles & Hawaii
USA: The Southwest 26-27
Mexico .28-29
Central America 30-31
The Caribbean 32-33
  Jamaica, St. Lucia, & Barbados

SOUTH AMERICA

South America 34-35
Northern South America 36-37
Western South America 38-39
  Galapagos Islands
Brazil 40-41
Southern South America 42-43

The Atlantic Ocean 44-45

AFRICA

Africa 46-47
Northwest Africa 48-49
Northeast Africa 50-51
West Africa 52-53
Central Africa 54-55
  Sao Tome & Principe
Southern Africa 56-57

EUROPE

Europe .58-59
The North Atlantic 60-61
Scandinavia & Finland 62-63
The Low Countries 64-65
The British Isles 66-67
  London
France, Andorra, & Monaco . . .68-69
  Paris, Andorra, & Monaco
Spain & Portugal 70-71
  Azores & Gibraltar
Germany & the Alpine States . .72-73
  Liechtenstein

EUROPE *continued*

Italy 74-75
  San Marino & Vatican City
Central Europe 76-77
Southeast Europe 78-79
  Bosnia & Herzegovina
The Mediterranean 80-81
  Malta & Cyprus . . . .
Bulgaria & Greece 82-83
The Baltic States
  & Belarus 84-85
Ukraine, Moldova,
  & Romania 86-87
European Russia 88-89

NORTH & WEST ASIA

North & West Asia 90-91
Russia & Kazakhstan 92-93
Turkey & the Caucasus 94-95
The Near East 96-97
  West Bank
The Middle East 98-99
Central Asia 100-101

SOUTH & EAST ASIA

South & East Asia 102-103
Western China & Mongolia . .104-105
Eastern China & Korea 106-107
  Hong Kong (Xianggang)
Japan 108-109
  Tōkyō & Nansei-Shotō
South India & Sri Lanka 110-111

North India, Pakistan,
  & Bangladesh 112-113
Mainland Southeast Asia 114-115
Maritime Southeast Asia 116-117
  Singapore

The Indian Ocean 118-119

AUSTRALASIA & OCEANIA

Australasia & Oceania 120-121
The Southwest Pacific 122-123
Western Australia 124-125
Eastern Australia 126-127
  Sydney
New Zealand 128-129

The Pacific Ocean 130-131

Antarctica 132

The Arctic Ocean 133

INDEX – GAZETTEER

Overseas Territories
  & Dependencies 134-135

Countries Factfile 135-151

Geographical Comparisons . .152-153

Index 154-192

THE POLITICAL WORLD

ABBREVIATIONS

AFGH.
Afghanistan

ALB.
Albania

AUT.
Austria

AZ. OR AZERB.
Azerbaijan

B. & H.
Bosnia &
Herzegovina

BELA.
Belarus

BELG.
Belgium

BOTS.
Botswana

BULG.
Bulgaria

CAMB.
Cambodia

C.A.R.
Central African
Republic

CRO.
Croatia

CZ. REP.
Czech Republic

DOM. REP.
Dominican
Republic

EST.
Estonia

EQ. GUINEA
Equatorial
Guinea

HUNG.
Hungary

KYRG.
Kyrgyzstan

LAT.
Latvia

LIECH.
Liechtenstein

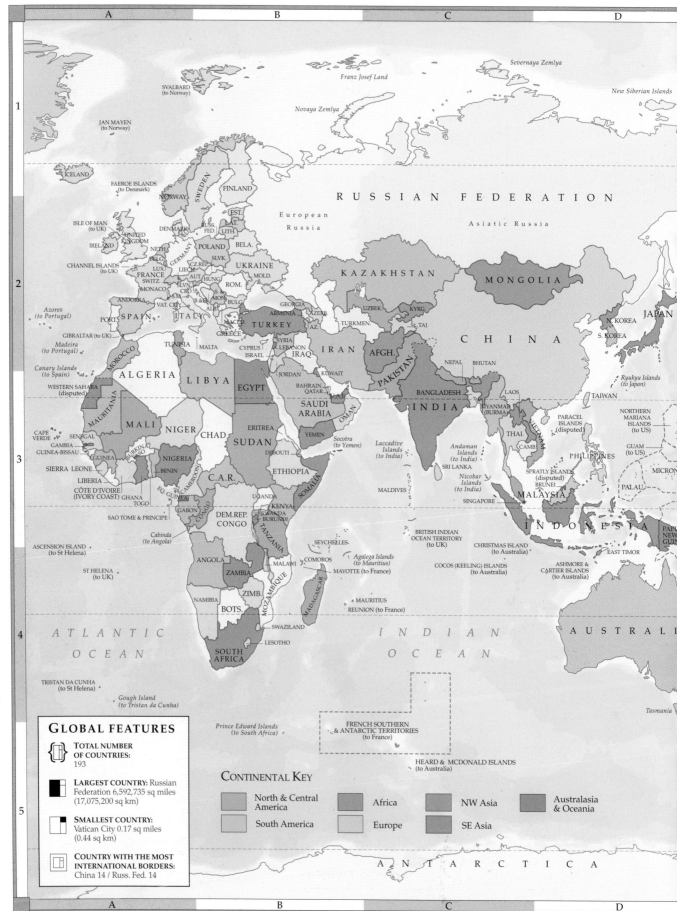

GLOBAL FEATURES

TOTAL NUMBER OF COUNTRIES:
193

LARGEST COUNTRY: Russian Federation 6,592,735 sq miles (17,075,200 sq km)

SMALLEST COUNTRY: Vatican City 0.17 sq miles (0.44 sq km)

COUNTRY WITH THE MOST INTERNATIONAL BORDERS: China 14 / Russ. Fed. 14

CONTINENTAL KEY

North & Central America

South America

Africa

Europe

NW Asia

SE Asia

Australasia & Oceania

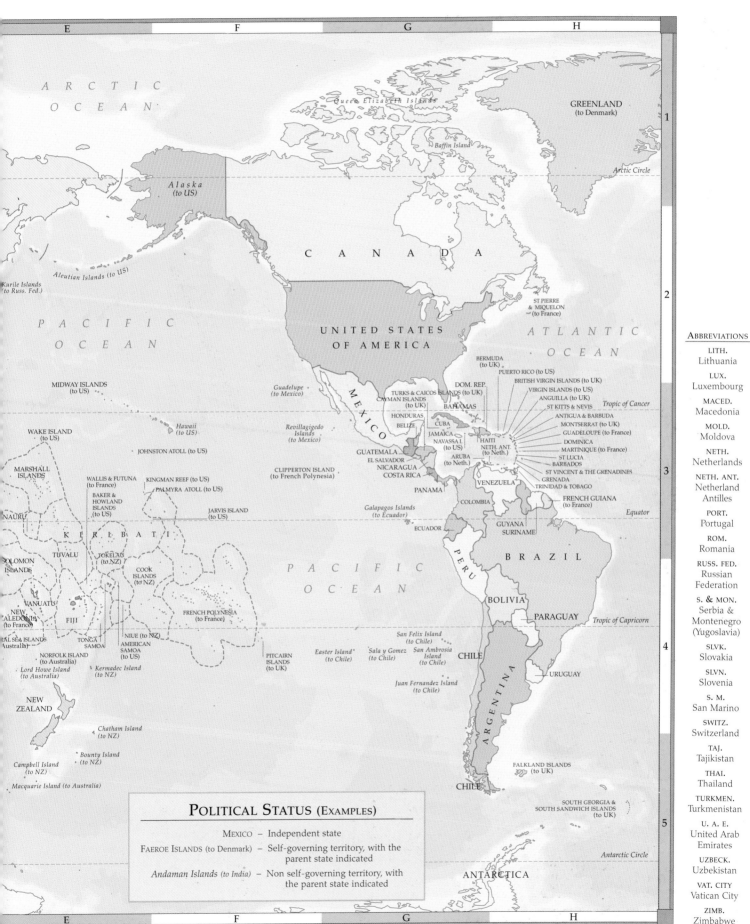

POLITICAL STATUS (EXAMPLES)

MEXICO – Independent state

FAEROE ISLANDS (to Denmark) – Self-governing territory, with the parent state indicated

Andaman Islands (to India) – Non self-governing territory, with the parent state indicated

ABBREVIATIONS

LITH.
Lithuania

LUX.
Luxembourg

MACED.
Macedonia

MOLD.
Moldova

NETH.
Netherlands

NETH. ANT.
Netherland Antilles

PORT.
Portugal

ROM.
Romania

RUSS. FED.
Russian Federation

S. & MON.
Serbia & Montenegro (Yugoslavia)

SLVK.
Slovakia

SLVN.
Slovenia

S. M.
San Marino

SWITZ.
Switzerland

TAJ.
Tajikistan

THAI.
Thailand

TURKMEN.
Turkmenistan

U. A. E.
United Arab Emirates

UZBECK.
Uzbekistan

VAT. CITY
Vatican City

ZIMB.
Zimbabwe

THE PHYSICAL WORLD

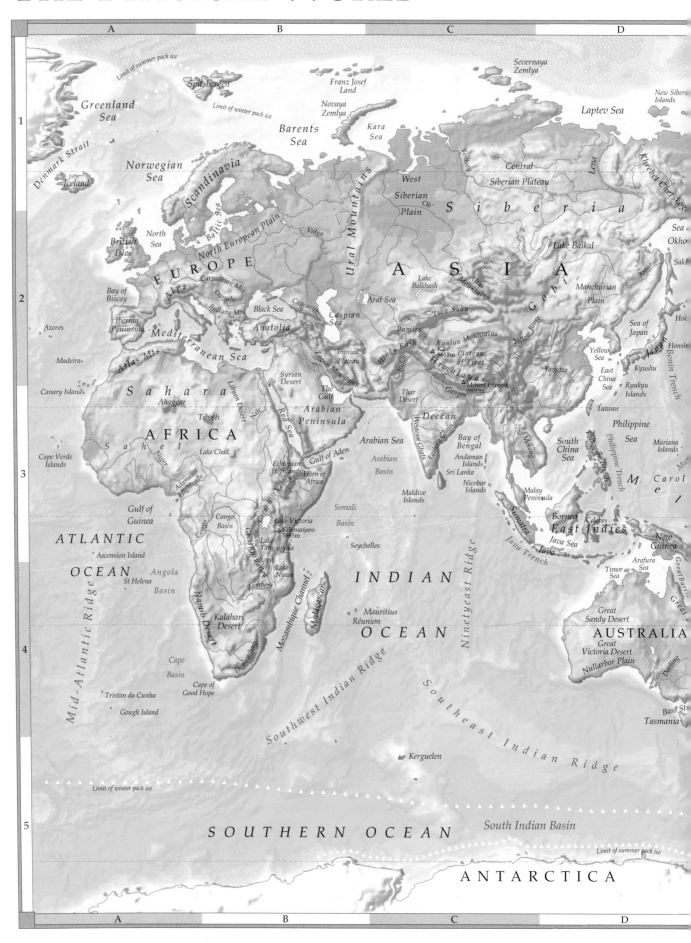

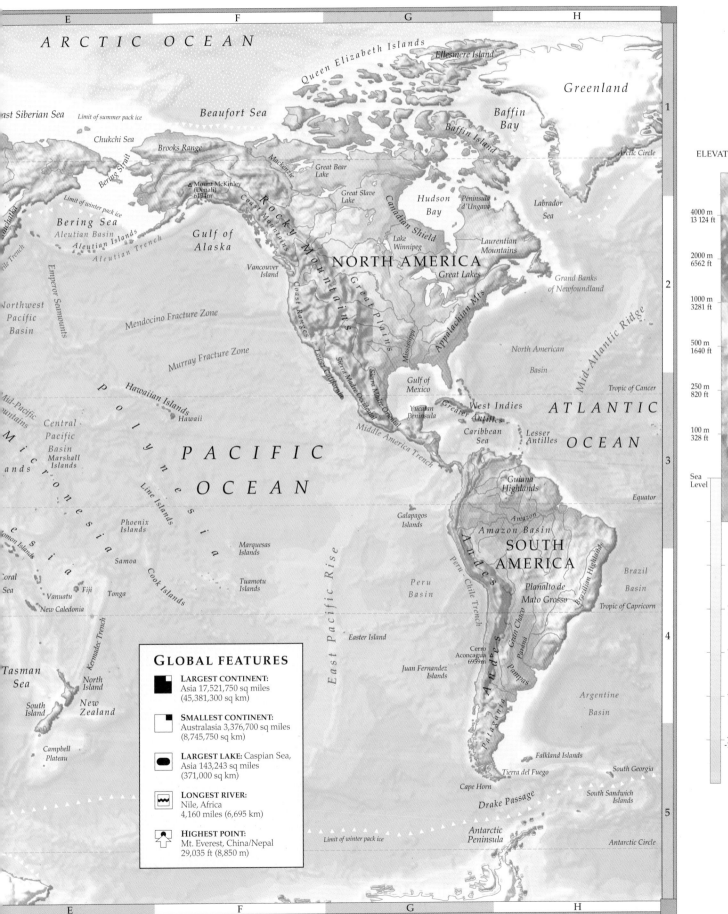

TIME ZONES

The numbers represented thus: +2/-2, indicate the number of hours ahead or behind GMT (Greenwich Mean Time) of each time zone.

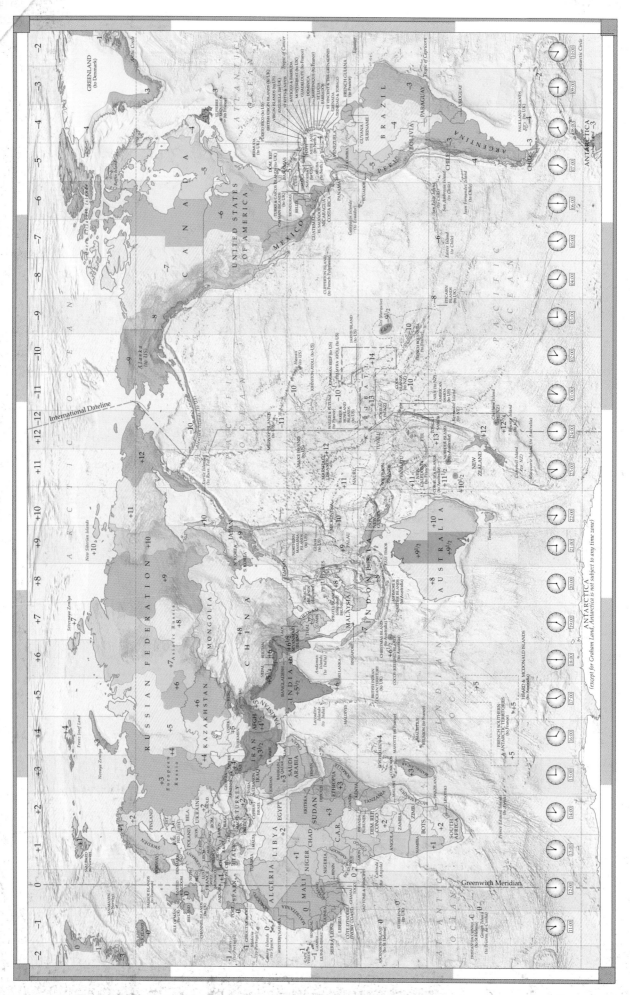

THE
WORLD
ATLAS

THE WORLD ATLAS

POPULATION

- ▣ Over 500,000
- ◉ 100,000 - 500,000
- ○ 50,000 - 100,000
- ○ Less than 50,000
- ● National capital

EUROPE

Barents Sea

Mohns Ridge

Greenland Sea

SVALBARD (to Norway)

JAN MAYEN (to Norway)

Iceland

Denmark Strait

Reykjanes Basin

North Atlantic Mid-Ocean Canyon

Newfoundland

St. John's

Grand Banks of

Kong Frederik VI Kyst

Kong Christian IX Land

GREENLAND (to Denmark)

Kong Christian X Land

Kong Frederik VIII Land

NUUK

Labrador Basin

Labrador Sea

Limit of winter pack ice

Wandel Sea

Kap Morris Jesup

Lincoln Sea

Davis Strait

Labrador

Nansen Basin

Nansen Cordillera

North Pole

Makarov Basin

Lomonosov Ridge

Alpha Cordillera

Ellesmere Island

Baffin Bay

Baffin Island

Smallwood Reservoir

Labrador Mountains

Queen Elizabeth Islands

Lancaster Sound

Péninsule d'Ungava

Ungava Bay

Foxe Basin

ARCTIC OCEAN

ASIA

East Siberian Sea

Mendeleyev Ridge

Canada Basin

Prince of Wales Island

Gulf of Boothia

Southampton Island

Hudson Strait

James Bay

Belcher Islands

Hudson Bay

Lake Nipigon

Laptev Sea

Chukchi Plateau

Chukchi Sea

Wrangel Island

Banks Island

Victoria Island

Great Bear Lake

Reindeer Lake

Lake Winnipeg

Winnipeg

Beaufort Sea

Great Slave Lake

Lake Athabasca

Saskatoon

Regina

Bering Strait

Limit of summer pack ice

Mackenzie Mountains

Mackenzie

CANADA

Saint Lawrence Island

Nunivak Island

Brooks Range

Arctic Circle

Athabasca

Calgary

Edmonton

Bering Sea

Norton Sound

Yukon

Mount McKinley (Denali) 6194m

Alaska Range

Alaska (to US)

Rocky Mountains

Coast Mountains

Vancouver

Aleutian Basin

Bristol Bay

Kodiak Island

Anchorage

Juneau

Mount Logan 5959m

Snake

Vancouver Island

Seattle

Mount Rainier 4392m

Victoria

Cascadia Basin

Cascade Range

Eugene

Boise

Aleutian Islands

Aleutian Range

Aleutian Trench

Gulf of Alaska

Alexander Archipelago

Queen Charlotte Islands

PACIFIC OCEAN

58

90

91

131

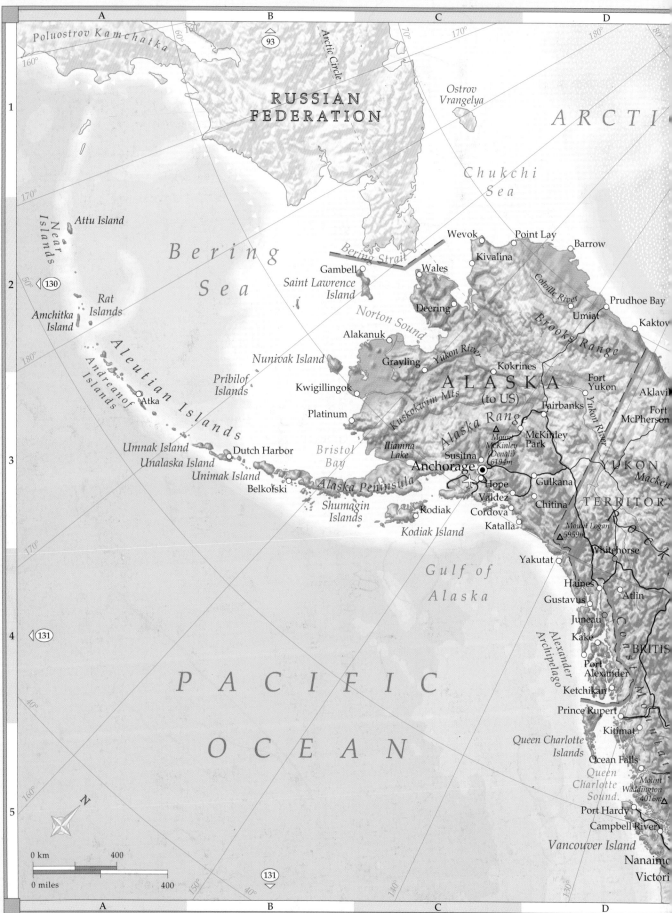

Poluostrov Kamchatka

RUSSIAN
FEDERATION

Arctic Circle

Ostrov
Vrangelya

A R C T I

Chukchi
Sea

Bering
Sea

Near
Islands

Attu Island

Rat
Islands

Amchitka
Island

Aleutian Islands

Andreanof
Islands

Atka

Umnak Island
Unalaska Island
Unimak Island

Dutch Harbor

Belkofski

Pribilof
Islands

Nunivak Island

Kwigillingok

Platinum

Bristol
Bay

Alaska Peninsula

Shumagin
Islands

Saint Lawrence
Island

Gambell

Norton Sound

Alakanuk

Grayling

Wevok
Wales

Deering

Point Lay
Kivalina

Barrow

Colville River

Umiat

Prudhoe Bay

Kaktov

Brooks Range

Yukon River

Kokrines

A L A S K A
(to US)

Kuskokwim Mts

Iliamna
Lake

Susitna

Anchorage

Hope
Valdez

Kodiak

Cordova
Katalla

Kodiak Island

Fort
Yukon

Fairbanks

McKinley
Park

Mount
McKinley
(Denali)
6194m

Alaska Range

Gulkana

Chitina

Aklavi

Fort
McPherson

Yukon River

Y U K O N

Macken

T E R R I T O R

Mount Logan
5959m

Whitehorse

Gulf of
Alaska

Yakutat

Haines

Gustavus
Juneau

Kake

Atlin

BRITIS

Port
Alexander

Alexander
Archipelago

Ketchikan

Prince Rupert

Kitimat

Queen Charlotte
Islands

Ocean Falls

Queen
Charlotte
Sound

Mount
Waddington
4016m

Port Hardy

Campbell River

P A C I F I C

O C E A N

Vancouver Island

Nanaimo

Victori

N

0 km   400

0 miles   400

GREENLAND
(to Denmark)

Knud Rasmussen Land

Alert

133

Ellesmere Island

Axel Heiberg Island

Queen Elizabeth Islands

Ellef Ringnes Island
Isachsen

Amund Ringnes Island

Prince Patrick Island

OCEAN

Baffin Bay

Arctic Circle

60

Bathurst Island
Cornwallis Island

Mould Bay

Melville Island

Devon Island

Resolute

Viscount Melville Sound

Banks Island

Somerset Island

Brodeur Peninsula

Baffin Island

Beaufort Sea

McClintock Channel

Prince of Wales Island

Boothia Peninsula

Gulf of Boothia

Igloolik

Cumberland Sound

achs Harbour

Amundsen Gulf

Holman

Victoria Island

King William Island

Pelly Bay

Melville Peninsula

Nettilling Lake

Davis Strait

iktoyaktuk

Foxe Basin

Iqaluit

Paulatuk

Cambridge Bay

Gjoa Haven

Amadjuak Lake

Fort Good Hope

Kugluktuk

Repulse Bay

Southampton Island

Hudson Strait

Mackenzie

Great Bear Lake

Echo Bay

Burnside

NUNAVUT

Coral Harbour

Péninsule d'Ungava

Back

Garry Lake

Baker Lake

NORTHWEST
TERRITORIES

Coats Island

Mansel Island

QUÉBEC

Rankin Inlet

Edzo

Yellowknife

Reliance

Dubawnt

Whale Cove

ELEVATION

Fort Simpson

Lutselk'e

Great Slave Lake

Arviat

HUDSON

Fort Providence

Fort Liard

Hay River

Fort Smith

Hudson Bay

James Bay

Belcher Islands

16

Fort Nelson

Lake Athabasca

Churchill

ONTARIO

Fort Vermilion

Reindeer Lake

LUMBIA

C A   N   A   D   A

Fort St. John

ALBERTA

Fort McMurray

Fox Mine

Southern Indian Lake

Nelson

Grande Prairie

Buffalo Narrows

SASKATCHEWAN

Thompson

rince George

Athabasca

Flin Flon

Athabasca

Lake Winnipeg

Edmonton

North Saskatchewan

The Pas

MANITOBA

Mount Robson
3954 m

Leduc

Saskatchewan

Prince Albert

Red Deer

Saskatoon

amloops

Calgary

Kindersley

Yorkton

Lake Manitoba

Kelowna

Medicine Hat

Regina

Qu'Appelle

Winnipeg

Lake Superior

Lake Huron

Cranbrook

Brandon

Weyburn

Lake of the Woods

Lake Michigan

ncouver

Lethbridge

Melita

23

Milk River

Estevan

U N I T E D   S T A T E S   O F   A M E R I C A

4000 m 13 124 ft	
2000 m 6562 ft	
1000 m 3281 ft	
500 m 1640 ft	
250 m 820 ft	
100 m 328 ft	
Sea Level	Sea Level
	-250 m -820 ft
	-500 m -1640 ft
	-1000 m -3281 ft
	-2000 m -6562 ft
	-3000 m -9843 ft
	-4000 m -13 124 ft

EASTERN CANADA

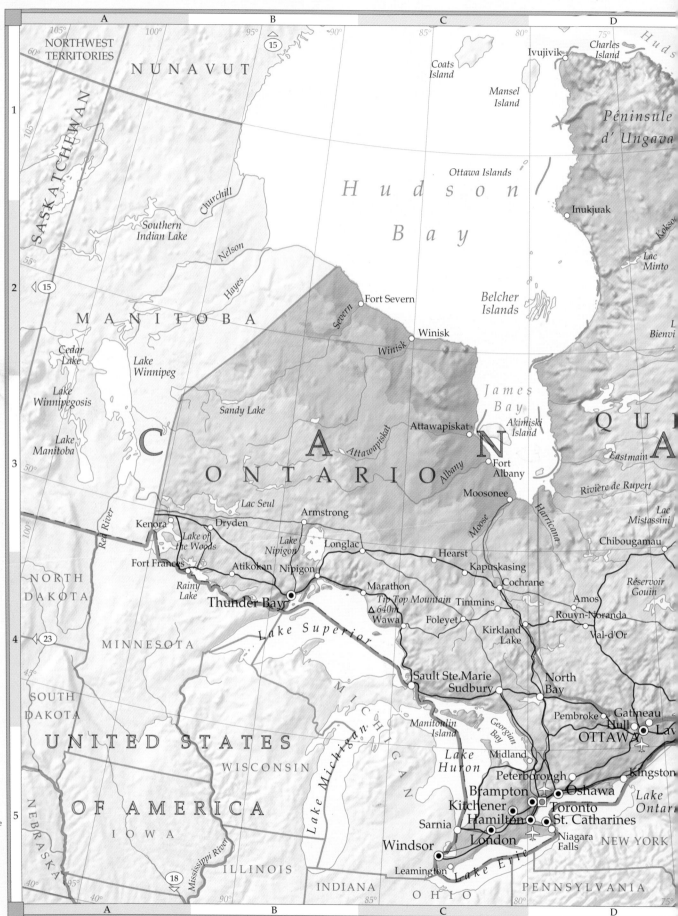

POPULATION

- ◉ Over 500,000
- ◉ 100,000 - 500,000
- ○ 50,000 - 100,000
- ○ Less than 50,000
- ● National capital
- ● Internal administrative capital

NORTHWEST TERRITORIES

NUNAVUT

SASKATCHEWAN

MANITOBA

Churchill

Southern Indian Lake

Nelson

Hayes

Cedar Lake

Lake Winnipeg

Lake Winnipegosis

Lake Manitoba

Sandy Lake

C A N A D A

O N T A R I O

Coats Island

Mansel Island

Ivujivik

Charles Island

Péninsule d' Ungava

Hudson Bay

Ottawa Islands

Inukjuak

Belcher Islands

Lac Minto

James Bay

Akimiski Island

QU

Bienvi

Fort Severn

Winisk

Severn

Winisk

Attawapiskat

Attawapiskat

Fort Albany

Albany

Moosonee

Moose

Hurricana

Eastmain

Rivière de Rupert

Lac Mistassini

Chibougamau

Réservoir Gouin

Lac Seul

Armstrong

Kenora

Dryden

Lake of the Woods

Lake Nipigon

Longlac

Hearst

Kapuskasing

Cochrane

Amos

Rouyn-Noranda

Val-d'Or

Red River

Fort Frances

Atikokan

Nipigon

Marathon

Tip Top Mountain △640m

Wawa

Timmins

Foleyet

Kirkland Lake

Rainy Lake

Thunder Bay

Lake Superior

NORTH DAKOTA

MINNESOTA

SOUTH DAKOTA

NEBRASKA

UNITED STATES

OF AMERICA

WISCONSIN

IOWA

ILLINOIS

MICHIGAN

Lake Michigan

Lake Huron

Manitoulin Island

Georgian Bay

Sault Ste.Marie

Sudbury

North Bay

Pembroke

Gatineau

Hull

OTTAWA

Lav

Midland

Peterborough

Brampton

Kitchener

Hamilton

Sarnia

London

Windsor

Leamington

Toronto

Oshawa

St. Catharines

Niagara Falls

Kingston

Lake Ontar

Lake Erie

NEW YORK

PENNSYLVANIA

OHIO

INDIANA

Mississippi River

60°

55°

50°

45°

40°

105°

100°

95°

90°

85°

80°

75°

ELEVATION

4000 m
13 124 ft

2000 m
6562 ft

1000 m
3281 ft

500 m
1640 ft

250 m
820 ft

100 m
328 ft

Sea
Level

Sea
Level

-250 m
-820 ft

-500 m
-1640 ft

-1000 m
-3281 ft

-2000 m
-6562 ft

-3000 m
-9843 ft

-4000 m
-13 124 ft

0 km   400
0 miles   400

Labrador Sea

Baffin
Island

Resolution
Island

Button Islands

trait

Akpatok
Island

*Ungava
Bay*

uujjuaq

Rivière à la Baleine

Nain

Hopedale   Makkovik

Cape Harrison

Cartwright

NEWFOUNDLAND

Caniapiscau

Schefferville

*Smallwood
Reservoir*

Lake Melville

Churchill

*Réservoir de
aniapiscau*

St.Anthony

& LABRADOR

Strait of Belle Isle

Gander

Grand Falls   St.John's

Corner Brook

Newfoundland

Havre-St-Pierre

Île d'Anticosti

Cape Race

E   C

D

A

Laurentian Mountains

*Réservoir
Manicouagan*

Sept-Îles

Baie-Comeau

St.Lawrence

*Péninsule de
Gaspé*

Gaspé

*Gulf of
St. Lawrence*

Channel-Port
aux Basques

**ST PIERRE
& MIQUELON**
(to France)

Cabot Strait

*Lac
Jean*

Chicoutimi

Matane

Rimouski

*Îles de la
Madeleine*

Glace Bay

Sydney

uière

Rivière-du-Loup

Edmundston

Bathurst

PRINCE
EDWARD
ISLAND

*Cape Breton
Island*

a Tuque

Charlesbourg

NEW
BRUNSWICK

Moncton

Charlottetown

Amherst

New Glasgow

Québec

Oromocto

Truro

Trois-
Rivières

St-Georges

Fredericton

NOVA SCOTIA

Drummondville

Saint John

Dartmouth

Sable Island

ntréal

Halifax

Sherbrooke

MAINE

Bay of Fundy

Liverpool

VERMONT

NEW
HAMPSHIRE

Yarmouth

ATLANTIC

ASSACHUSETTS

Cape Cod

OCEAN

CONNECTICUT

RHODE ISLAND

N

USA: The Northeast

POPULATION

- ▣ Over 500,000
- ◉ 100,000 – 500,000
- ○ 50,000 – 100,000
- ○ Less than 50,000
- ● National capital
- ◉ Internal administrative capital

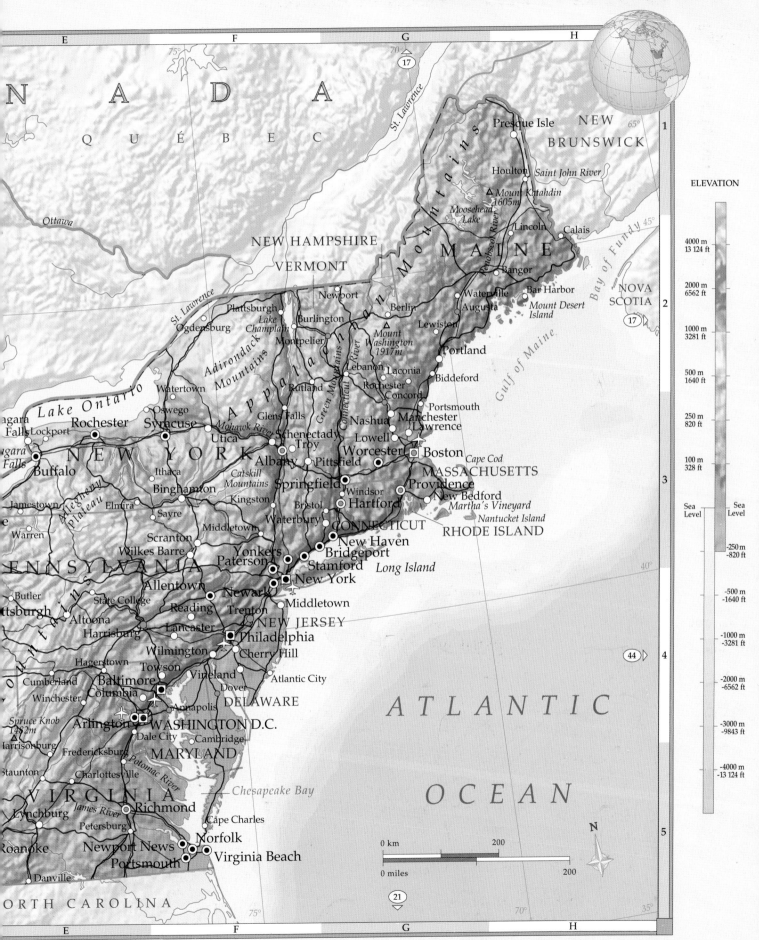

N A D A

Q U É B E C

NEW
BRUNSWICK

Presque Isle

Ottawa

Houlton   *Saint John River*

St. Lawrence

△ Mount Katahdin
1605m

M A I N E

*Moosehead
Lake*

Lincoln   Calais

NEW HAMPSHIRE

Bangor

Bay of Fundy 45°

NOVA
SCOTIA

VERMONT

Newport   Berlin

Waterville   Bar Harbor

Plattsburgh

Burlington

Augusta

*Mount Desert
Island*

Ogdensburg

*Lake
Champlain*

Montpelier

△ *Mount
Washington*
1917m

Lewiston

St. Lawrence

Lebanon

Portland

Gulf of Maine

*Adirondack
Mountains*

Rutland

Laconia

Rochester

Biddeford

Watertown

Glens Falls

Concord

Portsmouth

Oswego

Utica

Schenectady

Nashua

Manchester

Rochester

Syracuse

Troy

Lowell

Lawrence

Niagara
Falls   Lockport

N E W   Y O R K

Albany   Pittsfield

Worcester   Boston

Cape Cod

Niagara
Falls

Buffalo

Ithaca

*Catskill
Mountains*

Springfield

Windsor

Providence

MASSACHUSETTS

Mohawk River

Green Mountains

Connecticut River

Binghamton

Kingston

Bristol   Hartford

New Bedford

Jamestown

*Allegheny
Plateau*

Elmira

Sayre

Waterbury

CONNECTICUT

Martha's Vineyard

Nantucket Island

Warren

Middletown

New Haven

RHODE ISLAND

Scranton

Yonkers   Bridgeport

Wilkes Barre

Paterson   Stamford

Long Island

P E N N S Y L V A N I A

Allentown

New York

Butler

State College

Newark

Altoona

Reading   Middletown

Pittsburgh

Harrisburg

Trenton

NEW JERSEY

Lancaster

Philadelphia

Wilmington

Cherry Hill

Cumberland

Towson

Vineland

Atlantic City

Winchester

Baltimore

Dover

Columbia

Spruce Knob
1482m △

Annapolis

DELAWARE

Arlington   WASHINGTON D.C.

Harrisonburg

Dale City   Cambridge

MARYLAND

Fredericksburg

Potomac River

Chesapeake Bay

Staunton

Charlottesville

V I R G I N I A

Richmond

James River

Lynchburg

Cape Charles

Petersburg

Roanoke

Newport News   Norfolk

Danville

Portsmouth   Virginia Beach

N O R T H   C A R O L I N A

A T L A N T I C

O C E A N

ELEVATION

	4000 m 13 124 ft
	2000 m 6562 ft
	1000 m 3281 ft
	500 m 1640 ft
	250 m 820 ft
	100 m 328 ft
Sea Level	Sea Level
	-250 m -820 ft
	-500 m -1640 ft
	-1000 m -3281 ft
	-2000 m -6562 ft
	-3000 m -9843 ft
	-4000 m -13 124 ft

0 km   200

0 miles   200

N

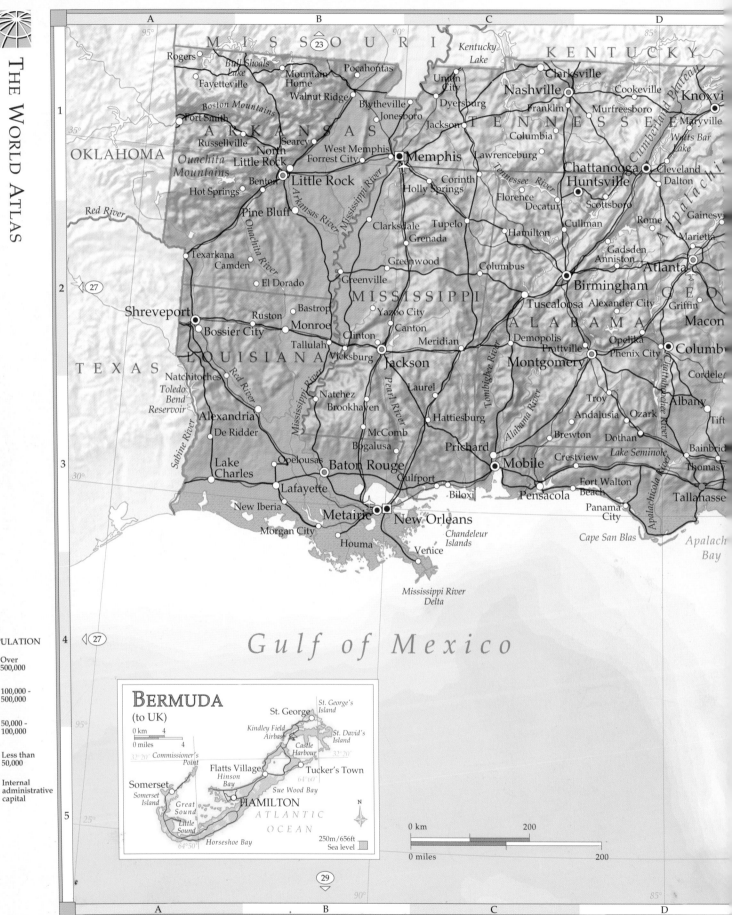

A B C D

MISSOURI
23

KENTUCKY

Kentucky Lake

Rogers
Bull Shoals Lake
Mountain Home
Pocahontas
Clarksville
Union City
Nashville
Cookeville
Knoxvi

Fayetteville
Walnut Ridge
Dyersburg
Franklin
Murfreesboro
Maryville

1

Fort Smith
Blytheville
Jonesboro
Jackson
TENNESSEE
Columbia
Watts Bar Lake

Boston Mountains
Searcy
West Memphis
Lawrenceburg
Chattanooga
Cleveland

Russellville
North Little Rock
Forrest City
Memphis
Corinth
Florence
Huntsville
Dalton

OKLAHOMA
ARKANSAS
Decatur
Scottsboro
Gainesv

Ouachita Mountains
Benton
Little Rock
Holly Springs
Hamilton
Cullman
Rome

Hot Springs
Clarksdale
Tupelo
Gadsden
Anniston
Marietta

Red River
Pine Bluff
Grenada
Columbus
Atlanta

Arkansas River
Greenwood
Birmingham
GEO

Texarkana
Mississippi River
Greenville
MISSISSIPPI
Tuscaloosa
Alexander City
Griffin

2

Camden
Ouachita River
Greenville
Columbus
Macon

El Dorado
Yazoo City
Demopolis
Opelika
Columb

Shreveport
Ruston
Bastrop
Canton
Prattville
Phenix City

Bossier City
Monroe
Clinton
Meridian
Montgomery
Cordele

LOUISIANA
Tallulah
Vicksburg
Jackson
Alabama River
Albany

TEXAS
Natchitoches
Red River
Natchez
Laurel
Troy
Tift

Toledo Bend Reservoir
Brookhaven
Andalusia
Ozark

Alexandria
Pearl River
Hattiesburg
Brewton
Dothan
Bainbrid

De Ridder
McComb
Tombigbee River

3

Sabine River
Opelousas
Bogalusa
Prichard
Crestview
Fort Walton Beach
Thomasv

Lake Charles
Baton Rouge
Gulfport
Mobile
Lake Seminole

Lafayette
Biloxi
Pensacola
Apalachicola River
Tallahasse

New Iberia
Metairie
New Orleans
Panama City

Morgan City
Houma
Chandeleur Islands
Cape San Blas
Apalach Bay

Venice
Mississippi River Delta

4

Gulf of Mexico

POPULATION

■ Over 500,000
◉ 100,000 - 500,000
○ 50,000 - 100,000
○ Less than 50,000
● Internal administrative capital

BERMUDA
(to UK)

0 km 4
0 miles 4

St. George's Island
St. George
Kindley Field Airbase
St. David's Island
Commissioner's Point
Castle Harbour
Flatts Village
Tucker's Town
Hinson Bay
Sue Wood Bay
Somerset
Somerset Island
HAMILTON
Great Sound
Little Sound
ATLANTIC OCEAN
Horseshoe Bay
250m/656ft
Sea level
N

0 km 200
0 miles 200

5

29

A B C D

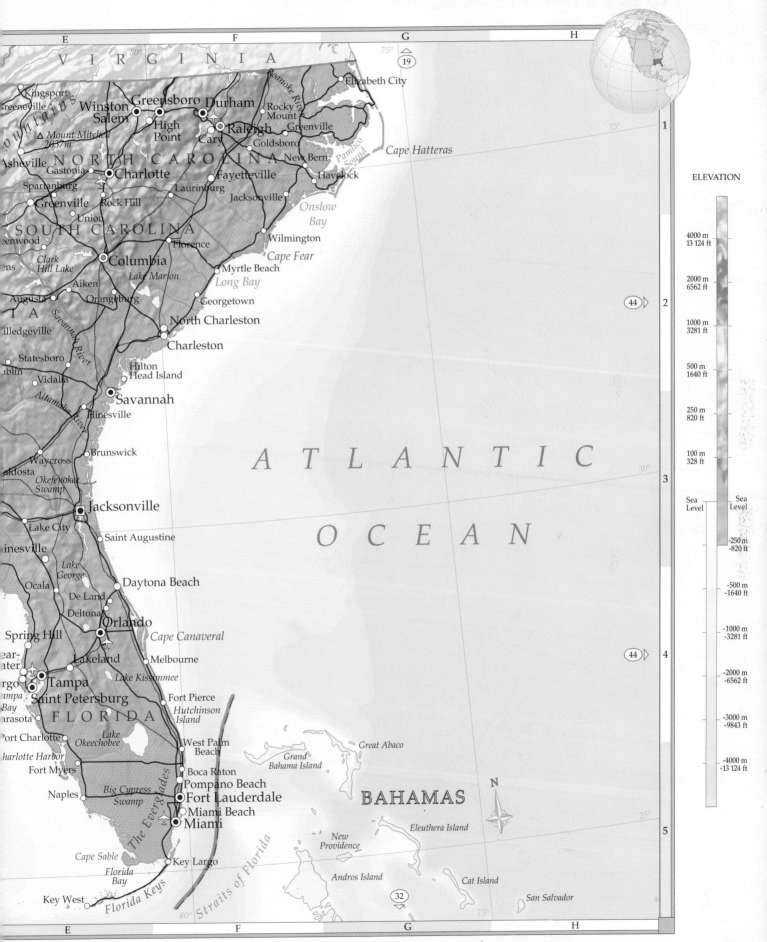

E F G H

VIRGINIA

Kingsport
Greeneville
Winston Greensboro Durham
Salem Rocky
High Mount
Point Cary Raleigh Greenville
△ Mount Mitchell Goldsboro
2037m New Bern
Asheville **NORTH CAROLINA** Havelock
Gastonia Charlotte Fayetteville
Spartanburg Laurinburg Jacksonville
Greenville Rock Hill
Union **SOUTH CAROLINA**
Florence Wilmington
Columbia Myrtle Beach
Aiken Lake Marion
Orangeburg Georgetown
North Charleston
Charleston
Hilton
Head Island

Elizabeth City
Roanoke River
35° 1
Cape Hatteras
Pamlico Sound
Onslow Bay
Cape Fear
Long Bay
44 2

ELEVATION

Greenwood
Clark
Hill Lake
Augusta
Milledgeville Savannah River
Statesboro
Vidalia
Dublin Altamaha River
Savannah
Hinesville

Waycross
Valdosta Brunswick
Okefenokee Swamp

A T L A N T I C

30° 3

Jacksonville
Lake City
Saint Augustine
Gainesville

Lake George
Ocala Daytona Beach
De Land
Deltona
Orlando Cape Canaveral
Spring Hill
Clear- Lakeland Melbourne
water Lake Kissimmee
Largo Tampa
Tampa Saint Petersburg
Bay **FLORIDA**
Sarasota Fort Pierce
Port Charlotte Hutchinson Island
Charlotte Harbor Lake Okeechobee
Fort Myers West Palm Beach
Naples Big Cypress Boca Raton
Swamp Pompano Beach
Fort Lauderdale
Miami Beach
The Everglades Miami
Cape Sable
Key Largo
Florida
Bay Florida Keys
Key West Straits of Florida

O C E A N

Great Abaco
Grand
Bahama Island
44 4

BAHAMAS N

Eleuthera Island
25° 5
New
Providence
Andros Island Cat Island
32 San Salvador
80° 75°

E F G H

4000 m
13 124 ft

2000 m
6562 ft

1000 m
3281 ft

500 m
1640 ft

250 m
820 ft

100 m
328 ft

Sea Sea
Level Level

-250 m
-820 ft

-500 m
-1640 ft

-1000 m
-3281 ft

-2000 m
-6562 ft

-3000 m
-9843 ft

-4000 m
-13 124 ft

75°
19

THE WORLD ATLAS

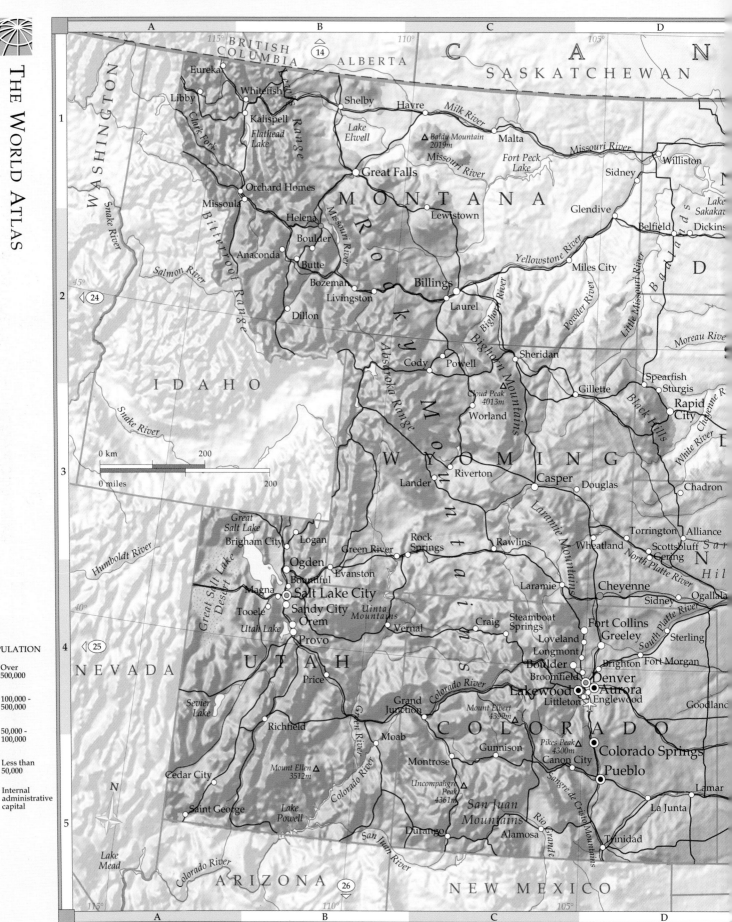

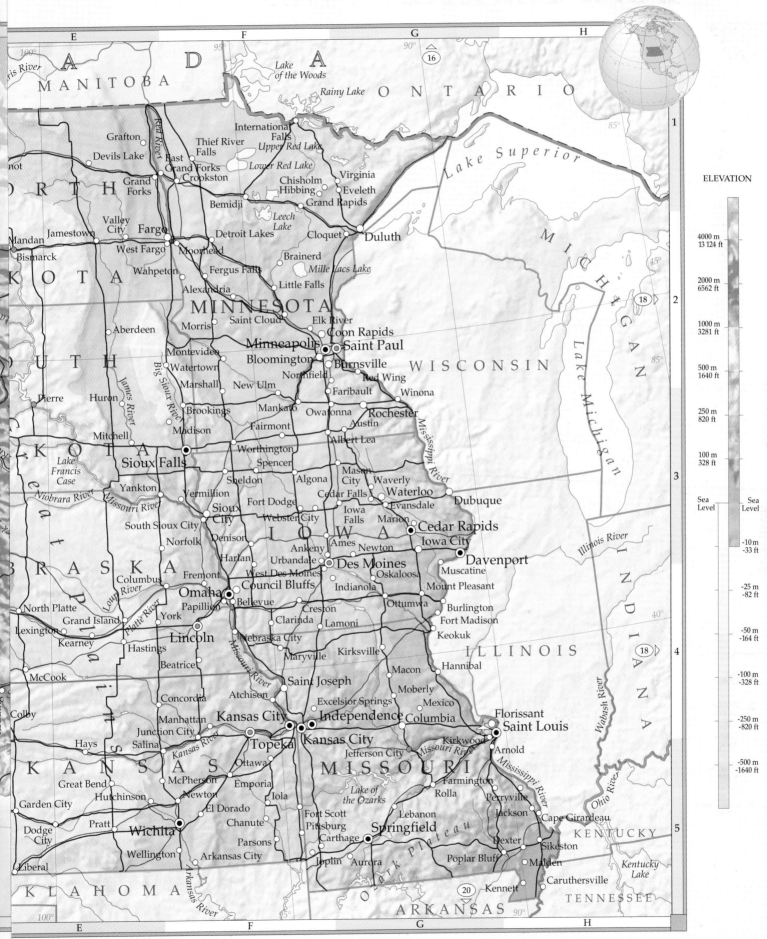

ELEVATION

4000 m
13 124 ft

2000 m
6562 ft

1000 m
3281 ft

500 m
1640 ft

250 m
820 ft

100 m
328 ft

Sea Level

Sea Level

-10 m
-33 ft

-25 m
-82 ft

-50 m
-164 ft

-100 m
-328 ft

-250 m
-820 ft

-500 m
-1640 ft

Labels on map:

MANITOBA · ONTARIO · Lake of the Woods · Rainy Lake · Lake Superior · MICHIGAN · Lake Michigan

Grafton · Devils Lake · East Grand Forks · Thief River Falls · Upper Red Lake · Lower Red Lake · International Falls · Virginia · Eveleth · Chisholm · Hibbing · Grand Rapids · Crookston · Grand Forks

NORTH DAKOTA · Valley City · Jamestown · Mandan · Bismarck · West Fargo · Fargo · Moorhead · Wahpeton · Fergus Falls · Detroit Lakes · Bemidji · Leech Lake · Cloquet · Duluth · Brainerd · Mille Lacs Lake · Little Falls · Alexandria

MINNESOTA · Aberdeen · Morris · Saint Cloud · Elk River · Coon Rapids · Minneapolis · Saint Paul · Montevideo · Watertown · Bloomington · Burnsville · Marshall · New Ulm · Northfield · Red Wing · WISCONSIN

SOUTH DAKOTA · Pierre · Huron · Big Sioux River · James River · Faribault · Winona · Brookings · Mankato · Owatonna · Rochester · Austin · Madison · Fairmont · Albert Lea · Mitchell · Lake Francis Case · Sioux Falls · Worthington · Spencer · Sheldon · Mason City · Waverly · Waterloo · Dubuque · Mississippi River

Yankton · Vermillion · Algona · Cedar Falls · Evansdale · Niobrara River · Missouri River · Sioux City · Fort Dodge · Iowa Falls · Marion · Cedar Rapids · South Sioux City · Webster City · IOWA · Ames · Iowa City · Norfolk · Denison · Ankeny · Newton · Davenport · Harlan · Urbandale · Des Moines · Muscatine

NEBRASKA · Columbus · Loup River · Fremont · West Des Moines · Oskaloosa · Mount Pleasant · Council Bluffs · Indianola · North Platte · Grand Island · Platte River · Omaha · Papillion · Bellevue · Ottumwa · Burlington · York · Creston · Fort Madison · Lexington · Kearney · Lincoln · Clarinda · Lamoni · Keokuk · Hastings · Nebraska City · Beatrice · Maryville · Kirksville · ILLINOIS · McCook · Missouri River · Macon · Hannibal · Concordia · Saint Joseph · Atchison · Moberly · Mexico · Colby · Manhattan · Excelsior Springs · Columbia · Florissant · Saint Louis · Junction City · Kansas City · Independence · Kirkwood · Hays · Salina · Kansas River · Kansas City · Topeka · Jefferson City · Missouri River · Arnold

KANSAS · Ottawa · MISSOURI · Farmington · Great Bend · McPherson · Emporia · Lake of the Ozarks · Rolla · Perryville · Hutchinson · Newton · Iola · Lebanon · Jackson · Garden City · El Dorado · Chanute · Fort Scott · Springfield · Cape Girardeau · Dodge City · Pratt · Wichita · Parsons · Pittsburg · Carthage · Dexter · Sikeston · KENTUCKY · Wellington · Arkansas City · Joplin · Aurora · Poplar Bluff · Malden · Liberal · Caruthersville · Kennett · TENNESSEE · OKLAHOMA · Arkansas River · ARKANSAS · Ozark Plateau · Kentucky Lake

Illinois River · INDIANA · Wabash River · Ohio River

USA: THE SOUTHWEST

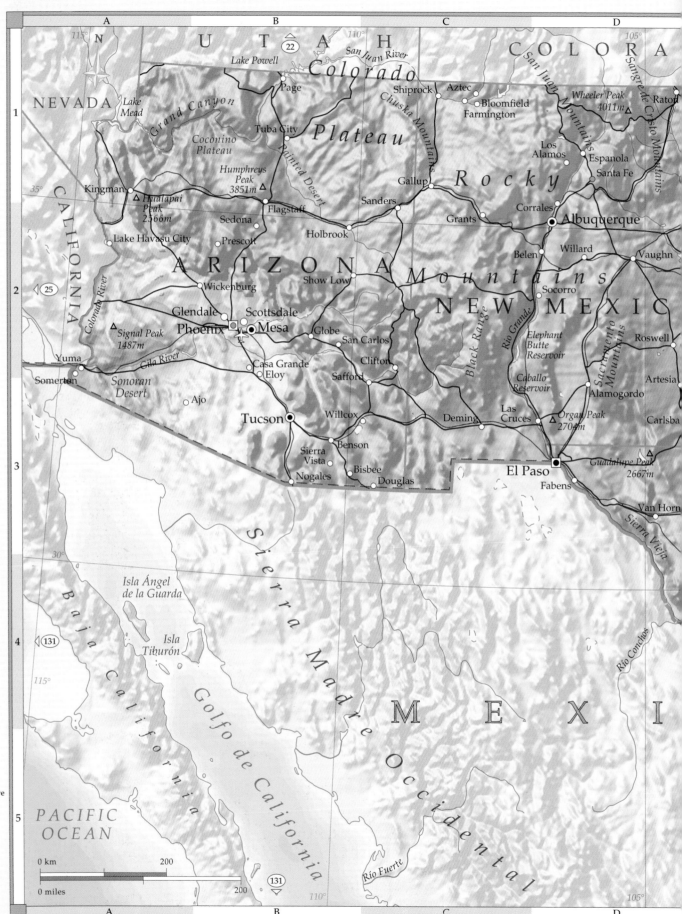

POPULATION

- ◉ Over 500,000
- ◉ 100,000 – 500,000
- ○ 50,000 – 100,000
- ○ Less than 50,000
- ● Internal administrative capital

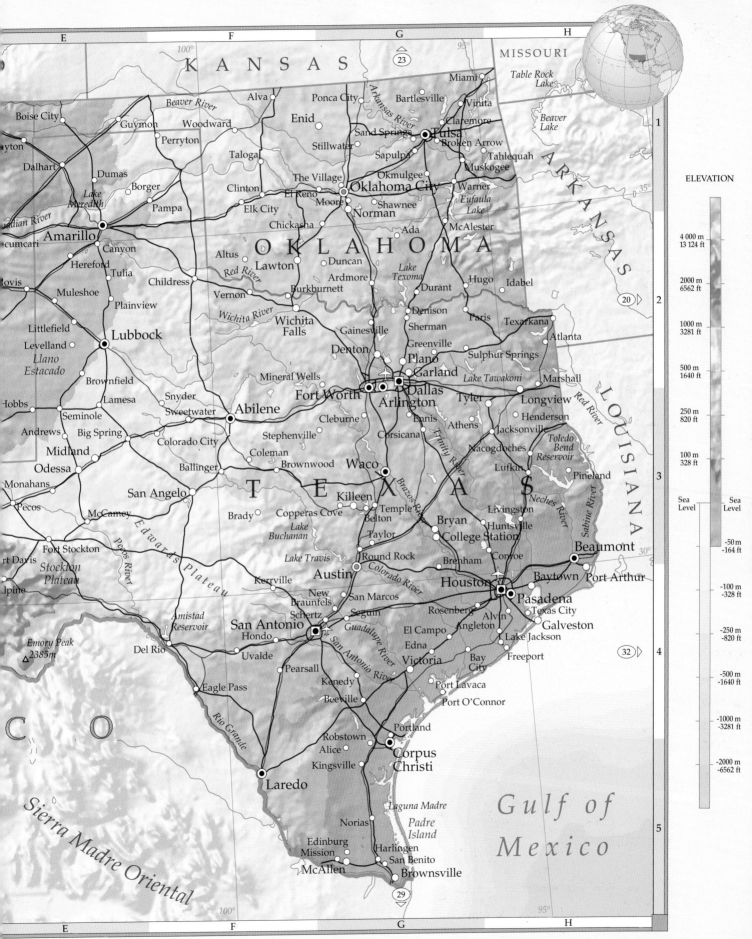

ELEVATION

4 000 m 13 124 ft	
2000 m 6562 ft	
1000 m 3281 ft	
500 m 1640 ft	
250 m 820 ft	
100 m 328 ft	
Sea Level	Sea Level
-50 m -164 ft	
-100 m -328 ft	
-250 m -820 ft	
-500 m -1640 ft	
-1000 m -3281 ft	
-2000 m -6562 ft	

Mexico

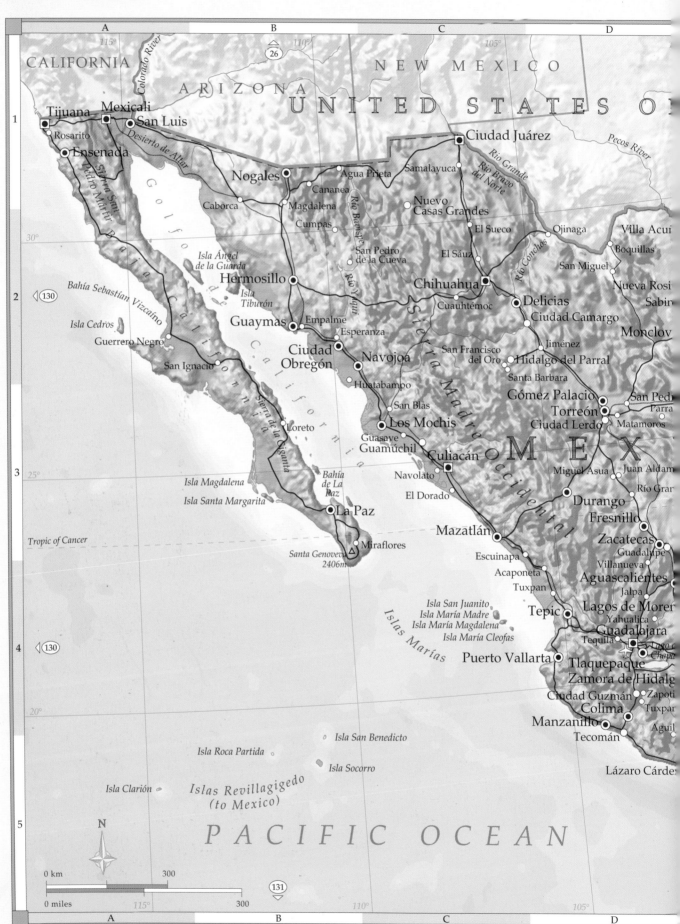

CALIFORNIA
ARIZONA
NEW MEXICO
UNITED STATES O
Colorado River
26
115°
110°
105°
Pecos River

1
Tijuana
Rosarito
Mexicali
San Luis
Ensenada
Desierto de Altar
Ciudad Juárez
Río Grande
del Norte
Río Bravo

Nogales
Agua Prieta
Samalayuca
Cananea
Caborca
Magdalena
Cumpas
Nuevo
Casas Grandes
El Sueco
Ojinaga
Villa Acuí
Boquillas

Río Bavispe
30°
Isla Ángel
de la Guarda
San Pedro
de la Cueva
El Sáuz
San Miguel
Nueva Rosi
Sabin

Bahía Sebastián Vizcaíno
130
Hermosillo
Chihuahua
Cuauhtémoc
Delicias
Ciudad Camargo
Monclov

2
Isla
Tiburón
Río Yaqui
San Francisco
del Oro
Jiménez
Ciudad Camargo

Isla Cedros
Guaymas
Empalme
Esperanza
Hidalgo del Parral
Santa Barbara

Guerrero Negro
Ciudad
Obregón
Navojoa
Gómez Palacio
San Pedí
Parra

San Ignacio
Huatabampo
Torreón
Ciudad Lerdo
Matamoros

San Blas
Los Mochis
Guasave
Guamúchil
M E X

Loreto
Culiacán
Miguel Asua
Juan Aldam
Río Grar

3
25°
Isla Magdalena
Isla Santa Margarita
Bahía
de La
Paz
Navolato
El Dorado
Durango
Fresnillo

La Paz
Mazatlán
Zacatecas
Guadalupe
Villanueva

Tropic of Cancer
Miraflores
Escuinapa
Aguascalientes
Jalpa

Santa Genoveva
2406m
Acaponeta
Tuxpan
Lagos de Morer
Yahualica

Isla San Juanito
Isla María Madre
Isla María Magdalena
Isla María Cleofas
Tepic
Guadalajara
Tequila
Lago c
Chapa

Islas Marías
Puerto Vallarta
Tlaquepaque
Zamora de Hidalg
Ciudad Guzmán
Zapoti

4
130
Colima
Tuxpar

20°
Manzanillo
Aguil

Isla San Benedicto
Tecomán

Isla Roca Partida
Isla Socorro
Lázaro Cárde

Isla Clarión
Islas Revillagigedo
(to Mexico)

5
N
PACIFIC OCEAN

POPULATION

- ▣ Over 500,000
- ◉ 100,000 – 500,000
- ○ 50,000 – 100,000
- ∘ Less than 50,000
- ● National capital

0 km   300
0 miles   300
115°
131
110°
105°

A   B   C   D

28

ELEVATION

4000 m
13 124 ft

2000 m
6562 ft

1000 m
3281 ft

500 m
1640 ft

250 m
820 ft

100 m
328 ft

Sea Level — Sea Level

-250 m
-820 ft

-500 m
-1640 ft

-1000 m
-3281 ft

-2000 m
-6562 ft

-3000 m
-9843 ft

-4000 m
-13 124 ft

ALABAMA
FLORIDA
MISSISSIPPI
LOUISIANA

Brazos River
Red River
Sabine River
Mississippi River

AMERICA
T E X A S
Colorado River

Mississippi River Delta

Gulf of Mexico

Piedras Negras
Río Grande
Nuevo Laredo
Sabinas Hidalgo
Ciudad Miguel Alemán
Reynosa
Río Bravo
Matamoros
Monterrey
Montemorelos
Linares
Laguna Madre
Padre Island

Ciudad Victoria

Sierra Madre Oriental

Ciudad Mante
Ciudad Madero
n Luis
Pánuco
Tampico
otosí
Ciudad Valles
ío Verde
Tamazunchale
Dolores Hidalgo
Tuxpán
Laguna de Tamiahua
Guanajuato
Poza Rica
rapuato
Querétaro
Papantla
Pachuca
Tulancingo
orelia
Teziutlán
MÉXICO
Perote
Xalapa
(MEXICO CITY)
Tlaxcala
Veracruz
Toluca
Puebla
Alvarado
Cuernavaca
Córdoba
Popocatépetl 5452m
Zacatepec
Tehuacán
San Andrés
Coatzacoalcos
Taxco
Cuautla
Tuxtepec
Tuxtla
Minatitlán
esa del fiernillo
Iguala
Huajuapan
Istmo de Tehuantepec
Teapa
o Balsas
Sierra Madre del Sur
Chilpancingo
Oaxaca
Ocozocuautla
Tuxtla
Chiapa de Corzo
San Cristóbal de Las Casas
xtapa
Tecpan
Ixtepec
Matías Romero
Comitán
Acapulco
Pinotepa Nacional
Tehuantepec
Juchitán
Arriaga
Presa de la Angostura
Miahuatlán
Salina Cruz
Pijijiapán
Puerto Escondido
Puerto Angel
Golfo de Tehuantepec
Escuintla
Huixtla
Tapachula
Ciudad Hidalgo
GUATEMALA
HONDURAS
EL SALVADOR

Yucatan Channel
Río Lagartos
Cancún
Progreso
Tizimín
Isla Cozumel
Motul
Mérida
Umán
Valladolid
Ticul
Peto
Oxkutzcab
Teka
Felipe Carrillo Puerto
Campeche
Yucatan Peninsula
Champotón
Laguna de Términos
Chetumal
Frontera
Fransisco Escárcega
Comalcalco
Carmen
Villahermosa
BELIZE
Macuspana
Río Usumacinta
Gulf of Honduras

Tropic of Cancer
Bahía de Campeche

CENTRAL AMERICA

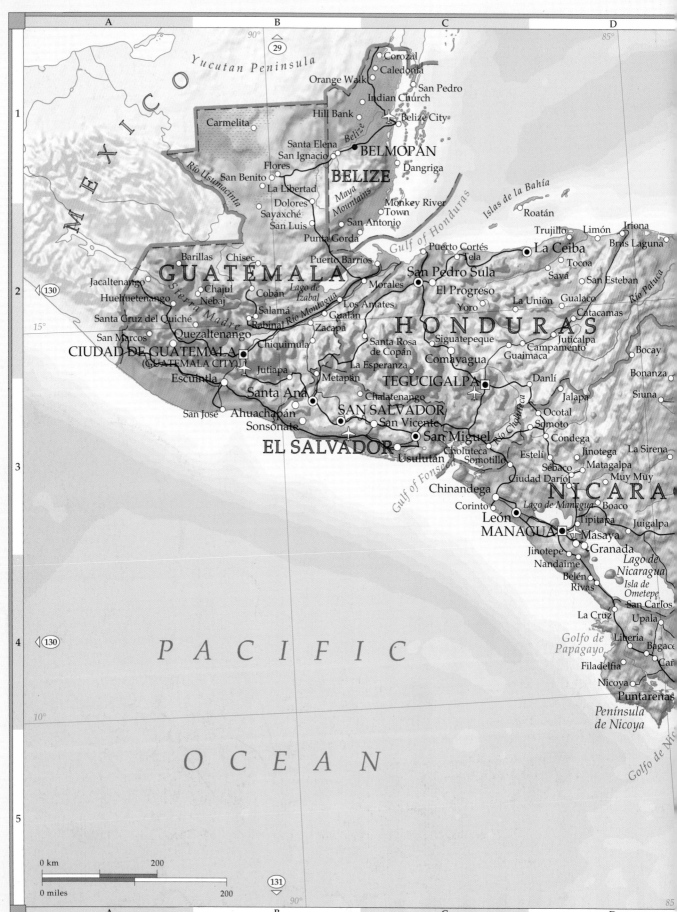

POPULATION

- ◉ Over 500,000
- ◉ 100,000 – 500,000
- ○ 50,000 – 100,000
- ○ Less than 50,000
- ● National capital

MEXICO

Yucatan Peninsula

Corozal
Caledonia
Orange Walk
San Pedro
Indian Church
Hill Bank
Belize City
Carmelita
Santa Elena
San Ignacio
BELMOPAN
Flores
San Benito
BELIZE
Dangriga
La Libertad
Dolores
Sayaxché
San Luis
San Antonio
Monkey River Town
Punta Gorda
Gulf of Honduras
Islas de la Bahía
Roatán

Barillas
Chisec
Puerto Barrios
Puerto Cortés
Tela
La Ceiba
Trujillo
Limón
Iriona
Brus Laguna

GUATEMALA
Jacaltenango
Chajul
Cobán
Lago de Izabal
Morales
San Pedro Sula
El Progreso
Tocoa
Savá
San Esteban

Huehuetenango
Nebaj
Salamá
Rabinal
Río Montagua
Gualán
Zacapa
Los Amates
Yoro
La Unión
Gualaco
Catacamas
Río Patuca

Santa Cruz del Quiché
HONDURAS

San Marcos
Quezaltenango
Chiquimula
Santa Rosa de Copán
Siguatepeque
Juticalpa
Campamento
Bocay

CIUDAD DE GUATEMALA
(GUATEMALA CITY)
Jutiapa
La Esperanza
Comayagua
Guaimaca
Bonanza

Escuintla
Metapán
TEGUCIGALPA
Danlí
Siuna

Santa Ana
Chalatenango
Jalapa

San José
Ahuachapán
SAN SALVADOR
San Vicente
Ocotal
Condega

Sonsonate
San Miguel
Somoto
Jinotega
La Sirena

EL SALVADOR
Usulután
Choluteca
Somotillo
Estelí
Matagalpa

Gulf of Fonseca
Ciudad Darío
Muy Muy

Chinandega
NICARA

Corinto
Lago de Managua
Boaco

León
Tipitapa
Juigalpa

MANAGUA
Masaya

Jinotepe
Granada
Lago de Nicaragua

Nandaime
Isla de Ometepe

Belén
Rivas
San Carlos

La Cruz
Upala

Golfo de Papagayo
Liberia
Bagace
Cañ

PACIFIC
Filadelfia

Nicoya
Puntarenas

Península de Nicoya

OCEAN

Golfo de Nic

Sierra Madre

Maya Mountains

Río Usumacinta

Río Chaluteca

0 km   200
0 miles   200

E · F · G · H

N

32

Bajo Nuevo
(to Colombia)

Cayo de Serranilla
(to Colombia)

15°

as Santanilla
Honduras)

na de Caratasca

Puerto Lempira

Coco

spam

Cayo de Serrana
(to Colombia)

33

75°

Tuapi

Cayos Miskitos

Puerto Cabezas

ablis

C a r i b b e a n

Prinzapolka

Isla de Providencia
(to Colombia)

Barra de Río Grande

S e a

A

Laguna de Perlas

Isla de San Andrés
(to Colombia)

Rama

Islas del Maíz

Bluefields

Mosquito Coast

Punta Gorda

San Juan del Norte

10°

San Juan
to

36

ejo

COSTA RICA

esada

Istmo de Panamá

El Porvenir

ela

Siquirres

Heredia

Portobelo

Ailigandí

SAN JOSÉ

Limón

Colón

Cordillera de San Blas

Gulf of

Darien

Cartago

Guabito

Cristóbal

Cerro Chirripó

Almirante

Panama Canal

Lago Bayano

Grande
3819m

Cordillera de Talamanca

Laguna
de Chiriquí

Golfo de los
Mosquitos

Lago Gatún

Balboa

San Miguelito

Serranía del Darién

Puerto Obaldía

os

Buenos Aires

PANAMÁ

Chimán

Cortés

Volcán Barú 3475m

(PANAMA CITY)

Palmar Sur

Capira

La Palma

Yaviza

Boquete

Cordillera Central

Penonomé

Archipiélago
de las Perlas

El Real

Bahía
Coronado

La Concepción

David

Aguadulce

P A N A M Á

Isla
del Rey

Garachiné

nínsula de Osa

Golfo Dulce

Santiago

Chitré

Golfo

Golfo
de Chiriquí

Guarumal

Ocú

Las Tablas

de Panamá

Jaqué

Isla de Coiba

Isla
Cébaco

Península de
Azuero

131

80°

E · F · G · H

COLOMBIA

ELEVATION

4000 m
13 124 ft

2000 m
6562 ft

1000 m
3281 ft

500 m
1640 ft

250 m
820 ft

100 m
328 ft

Sea
Level

Sea
Level

-250 m
-820 ft

-500 m
-1640 ft

-1000 m
-3281 ft

-2000 m
-6562 ft

-3000 m
-9843 ft

-4000 m
-13 124 ft

1

2

3

4

5

The Caribbean

N

85° 80° ②①

Gulf of Mexico

The Everglades

UNITED STATES OF AMERICA

25° 1

Florida Keys

Straits of Florida

Tropic of Cancer

Cay Sal

Bimini Islands

Berry Islands

Nicholls Town

Andros Town

Andros Island

Grand Bahama Island

Freeport

Marsh Harbour

Great Abaco

Northeast Providence Channel

NASSAU

New Providence

Eleuthera Island

Rock Sound

Cat Island

San Salvador

George Town

Rum Cay

BAHAMAS

LA HABANA (HAVANA)

Guanabacoa

Artemisa

Cárdenas

Matanzas

Sagua la Grande

Pinar del Río

La Fé

Consolación del Sur

Santa Clara

Cienfuegos

Placetas

Nueva Gerona

Cayo Largo

Isla de la Juventud

Archipiélago de los Canarreos

Bahía de Cochinos

Sancti Spíritus

Morón

Ciego de Ávila

CUBA

Great Exuma Island

Exuma Cays

Exuma Sound

Anguilla Cays

Archipiélago de Camagüey

Ragged Island Range

Camagüey

20° Archipiélago de los Jardines de la Reina

Las Tunas

Manzanillo

Bayamo

Nuevitas

Holguín

Clarence Town

Long Island

Acklins Island

Crooked Island Passage

Crooked Island

Mayaguana Passage

Mayaguana

Little Inagua

Lake Rosa

Matthew Town

Great Inagua

Palma Soriano

Santiago de Cuba

Guantánamo

Guantánamo Bay (to US)

Windward Passage

Cap-Haïtien

Gonaïves

HAI

Little Cayman

Cayman Brac

GEORGE TOWN

Grand Cayman

CAYMAN ISLANDS (to UK)

NAVASSA ISLAND (to US)

Jérémie

PORT-AU-PRINCE

Cayes

Jacm

Montego Bay

Spanish Town

Portmore

KINGSTON

JAMAICA

Pedro Cays

G r e a t e r

Jamaica Channel

C a r i b b e a n

HONDURAS

15° ③⓪

NICARAGUA

COSTA RICA

10° ③①

85° 80° 75°

POPULATION

- ◉ Over 500,000
- ● 100,000 - 500,000
- ○ 50,000 - 100,000
- ○ Less than 50,000
- ● National capital

JAMAICA

N

78° 77°

Caribbean Sea

Montego Bay

Lucea

Falmouth

Runaway Bay

St Ann's Bay

Ocho Rios

Annotto Bay

Buff Bay

Port Antonio

Cambridge

The Cockpit Country

Christiana

Ewarton

Savanna-La-Mar

Mandeville

Spanish Town

Blue Mountain Peak △ 2258m

18°

Black River

May Pen

Old Harbour

KINGSTON

Portmore

Morant Bay

Portland Bight

Caribbean Sea

78° 77°

0 km 20

0 miles 20

2000m/6562ft
1000m/3281ft
500m/1640ft
200m/656ft
Sea level

0 km 200

0 miles 200

32

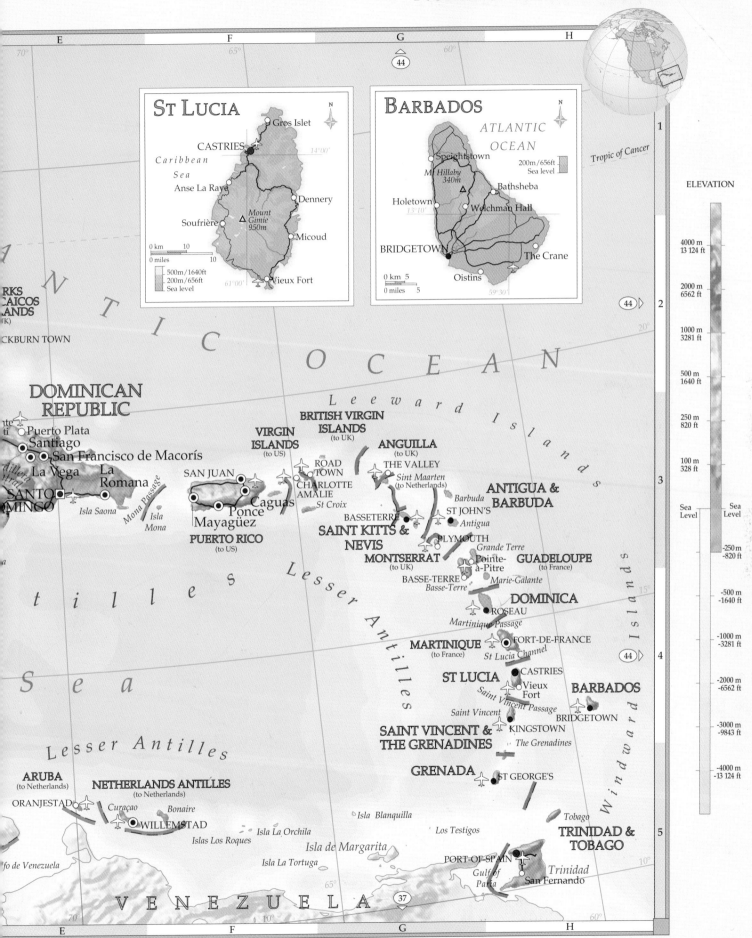

ST LUCIA

N

Gros Islet

CASTRIES

Caribbean Sea

14°00'

Anse La Raye

Dennery

Soufrière

△ Mount Gimie 950m

Micoud

0 km 10
0 miles 10

500m / 1640ft
200m / 656ft
Sea level

61°00'

Vieux Fort

BARBADOS

N

ATLANTIC OCEAN

Speightstown

Mt Hillaby 340m △

200m / 656ft
Sea level

Bathsheba

Holetown

13°10'

Welchman Hall

BRIDGETOWN

The Crane

0 km 5
0 miles 5

Oistins

59°30'

Tropic of Cancer

ELEVATION

4000 m
13 124 ft

2000 m
6562 ft

1000 m
3281 ft

500 m
1640 ft

250 m
820 ft

100 m
328 ft

Sea Level | Sea Level

-250 m
-820 ft

-500 m
-1640 ft

-1000 m
-3281 ft

-2000 m
-6562 ft

-3000 m
-9843 ft

-4000 m
-13 124 ft

RKS
AICOS
ANDS
(K)

CKBURN TOWN

A T L A N T I C   O C E A N

Leeward Islands

DOMINICAN REPUBLIC

tte
ti
Puerto Plata
Santiago
San Francisco de Macorís
La Vega
La Romana
SANTO MINGO
Isla Saona
Mona Passage
Isla Mona

SAN JUAN
Caguas
Ponce
Mayagüez
St Croix

PUERTO RICO (to US)

VIRGIN ISLANDS (to US)

BRITISH VIRGIN ISLANDS (to UK)

ROAD TOWN
CHARLOTTE AMALIE

ANGUILLA (to UK)

THE VALLEY
Sint Maarten (to Netherlands)

Barbuda

ST JOHN'S

Antigua

ANTIGUA & BARBUDA

BASSETERRE

SAINT KITTS & NEVIS

PLYMOUTH

MONTSERRAT (to UK)

BASSE-TERRE
Basse-Terre

Pointe-à-Pitre

GUADELOUPE (to France)

Marie-Galante

DOMINICA

ROSEAU

Martinique Passage

MARTINIQUE (to France)

FORT-DE-FRANCE

St Lucia Channel

ST LUCIA

CASTRIES

Vieux Fort

BARBADOS

BRIDGETOWN

Saint Vincent Passage

Saint Vincent

SAINT VINCENT & THE GRENADINES

KINGSTOWN

The Grenadines

GRENADA

ST GEORGE'S

tilles

Lesser Antilles

Sea

Sea

Lesser Antilles

ARUBA (to Netherlands)

ORANJESTAD

NETHERLANDS ANTILLES (to Netherlands)

Curaçao
Bonaire
WILLEMSTAD
Islas Los Roques
Isla La Orchila
Isla Blanquilla
Isla de Margarita
Los Testigos

Tobago

TRINIDAD & TOBAGO

fo de Venezuela
Isla La Tortuga
Gulf of Paria
PORT-OF-SPAIN
Trinidad
San Fernando

V E N E Z U E L A

Windward Islands

SOUTH AMERICA

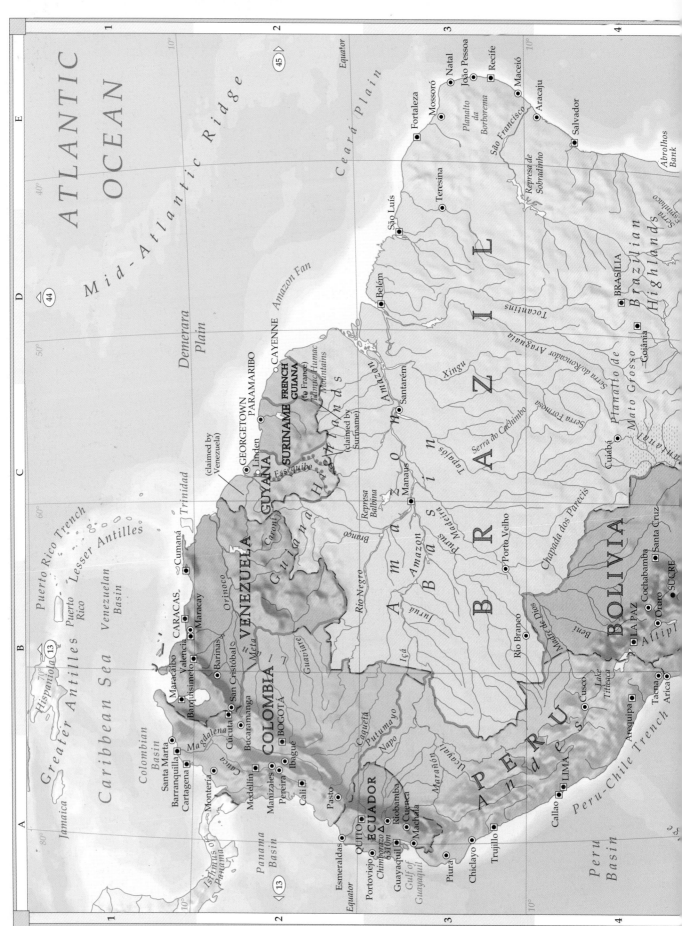

POPULATION

◙	Over 500,000
◉	100,000 – 500,000
○	50,000 – 100,000
○	Less than 50,000
●	National capital

ATLANTIC OCEAN

Mid-Atlantic Ridge

Demerara Plain

Amazon Fan

Ceará Plain

Equator

Mossoró
Natal
João Pessoa
Recife
Maceió
Aracaju
Fortaleza
Planalto da Borborema
São Francisco
Salvador
Represa de Sobradinho
Abrolhos Bank
Serra do Espinhaço

Teresina
São Luís
Belém
BRASÍLIA
Brazilian Highlands
Tocantins
Goiânia
Araguaia
Serra do Roncador
Planalto de Mato Grosso
Ibiapaba

B R A Z I L

Xingu
Amazon
Santarém
Serra do Cachimbo
Tapajós
Cuiabá
Chapada dos Parecis

CAYENNE
PARAMARIBO
FRENCH GUIANA (to France)
SURINAME
Tumuc Humac Mountains
GEORGETOWN
GUYANA
Linden
Essequibo
(claimed by Venezuela)
(claimed by Suriname)
Guiana Highlands

Represa Balbina
Manaus
Rio Negro
Branco
Amazon
Madeira
A m a z o n   B a s i n
Içá
Japurá

Porto Velho
Rio Branco
Madre de Dios
BOLIVIA
Santa Cruz
Cochabamba
SUCRE
LA PAZ
Oruro
Altiplano
Lake Titicaca
Beni

Puerto Rico Trench
Greater Antilles
Lesser Antilles
Puerto Rico
Venezuelan Basin
Caribbean Sea
Jamaica
Hispaniola
Trinidad
Cumaná
CARACAS
Maracay
Valencia
Barcelona
Maracaibo
Barquisimeto
VENEZUELA
Orinoco
Barinas
San Cristóbal
Meta
Caroní
Guaviare
Colombian Basin
Santa Marta
Barranquilla
Cartagena
Montería
Medellín
Manizales
Pereira
Cali
Magdalena
Cauca
Cúcuta
Bucaramanga
COLOMBIA
BOGOTÁ
Ibagué
Pasto
Putumayo
Caquetá
Napo
Marañón
Ucayali
Juruá

ECUADOR
QUITO
Esmeraldas
Portoviejo
Chimborazo 6310m
Guayaquil
Gulf of Guayaquil
Riobamba
Cuenca
Machala

P E R U
LIMA
Callao
Cusco
Arequipa
Tacna
Arica
Chiclayo
Trujillo
Piura
Andes
Peru-Chile Trench
Peru Basin

Isthmus of Panama
Panama Basin

Equator

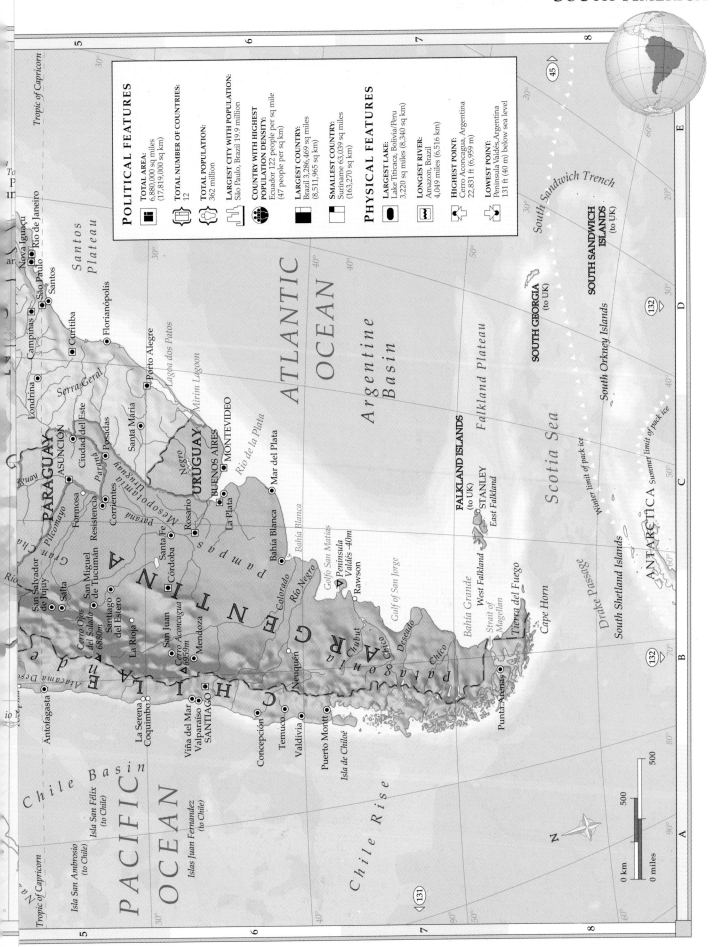

WESTERN SOUTH AMERICA

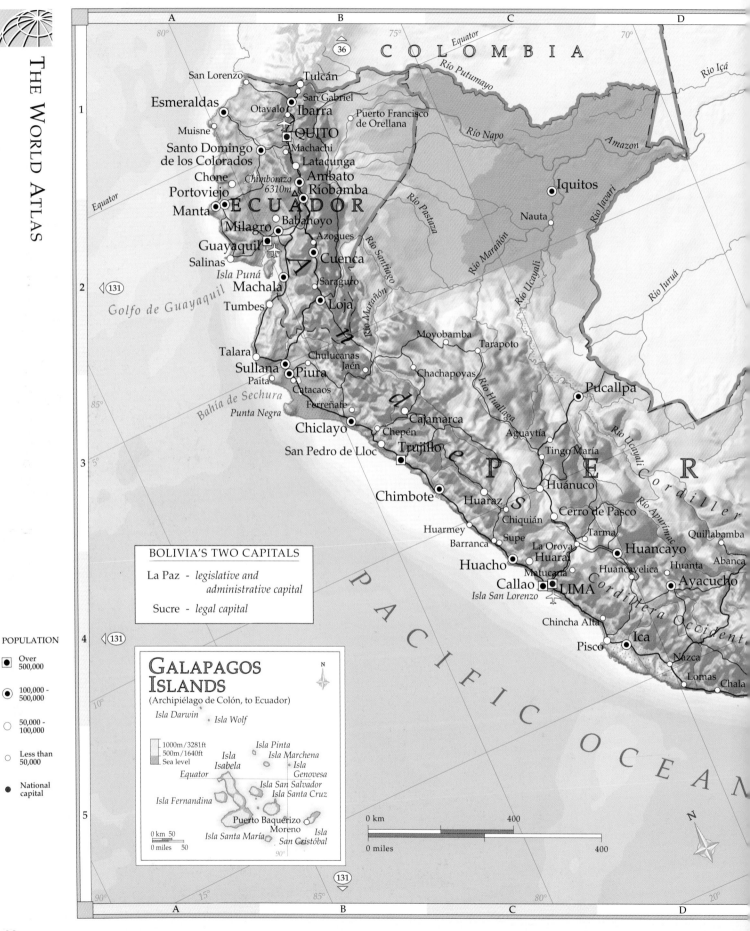

COLOMBIA

San Lorenzo
Tulcán
Esmeraldas
San Gabriel
Otavalo
Ibarra
Muisne
Puerto Francisco de Orellana
QUITO
Machachi
Santo Domingo de los Colorados
Latacunga
Chone
Chimborazo
6310m
Ambato
Riobamba
Portoviejo
ECUADOR
Manta
Milagro
Babahoyo
Guayaquil
Azogues
Salinas
Cuenca
Isla Puná
Saraguro
Machala
Loja
Tumbes
Golfo de Guayaquil
Talara
Chulucanas
Jaén
Sullana
Piura
Paita
Catacaos
Bahía de Sechura
Ferreñafe
Punta Negra
Cajamarca
Chiclayo
Chepén
San Pedro de Lloc
Trujillo
Chimbote
Huaraz
Chiquián
Huarmey
Cerro de Pasco
Barranca
Supe
Tarma
La Oroya
Huancayo
Huaral
Huánuco
Matucana
Huancavelica
Huanta
Abanca
Huacho
LIMA
Callao
Isla San Lorenzo
Ayacucho
Chincha Alta
Quillabamba
Pisco
Ica
Nazca
Lomas
Chala

Iquitos
Nauta
Moyobamba
Tarapoto
Chachapoyas
Pucallpa
Aguaytía
Tingo María

Río Putumayo
Río Napo
Amazon
Río Içá
Río Jacari
Río Juruá
Río Pastaza
Río Marañón
Río Santiago
Río Ucayali
Río Huallaga
Río Apurímac

PERU

Cordillera Occidental

PACIFIC OCEAN

Equator

BOLIVIA'S TWO CAPITALS

La Paz - legislative and administrative capital

Sucre - legal capital

POPULATION

- ▣ Over 500,000
- ◉ 100,000 - 500,000
- ○ 50,000 - 100,000
- ○ Less than 50,000
- ● National capital

GALAPAGOS ISLANDS

(Archipiélago de Colón, to Ecuador)

Isla Darwin • Isla Wolf

	1000m/3281ft
	500m/1640ft
	Sea level

Isla Pinta
Isla Marchena
Isla Isabela
Isla Genovesa
Equator
Isla San Salvador
Isla Fernandina
Isla Santa Cruz
Puerto Baquerizo Moreno
Isla San Cristóbal
Isla Santa María

0 km 50
0 miles 50

0 km 400
0 miles 400

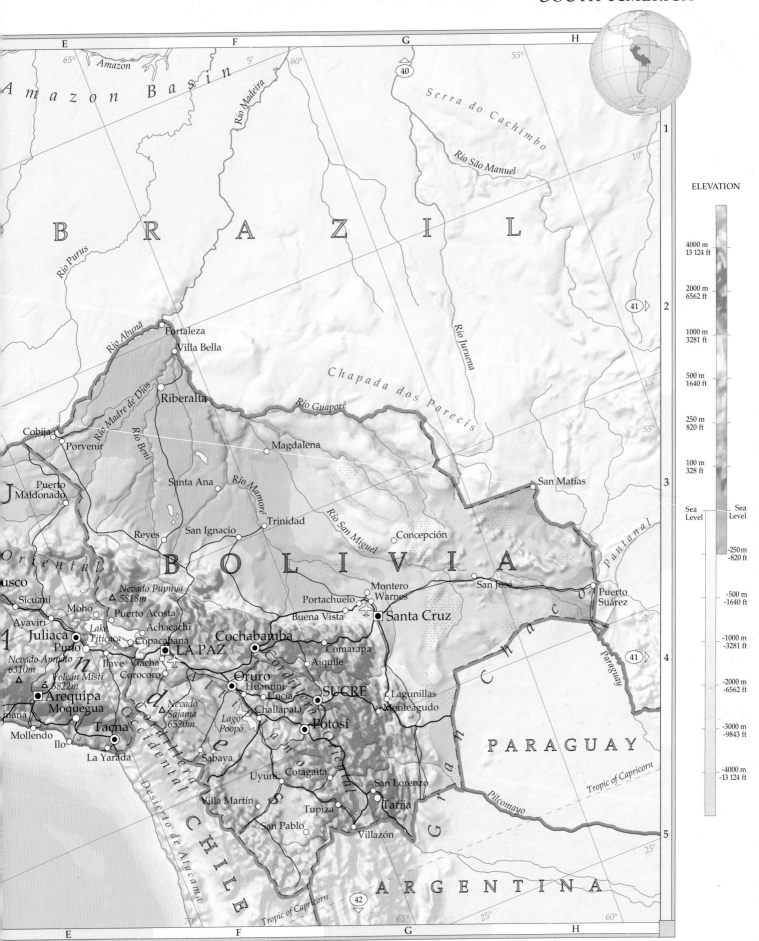

E 65° *Amazon* 5° F 60° G 55° H

⬆ 40

Serra do Cachimbo

Rio Madeira

Rio São Manuel

1

10°

A m a z o n   B a s i n

ELEVATION

B R A Z I L

4000 m
13 124 ft

Rio Purus

41 ▷ 2

2000 m
6562 ft

Rio Abunã Fortaleza
Villa Bella

1000 m
3281 ft

Rio Madre de Dios Riberalta

500 m
1640 ft

15°

Chapada dos Parecis

Rio Guaporé

55°

Cobija
Porvenir Magdalena

250 m
820 ft

Rio Beni

San Matías 3

100 m
328 ft

J Puerto
Maldonado Santa Ana *Rio Mamoré*

Reyes San Ignacio Trinidad *Rio San Miguel* Concepción

Sea
Level Sea
Level

B O L I V I A

–250 m
–820 ft

Oriental

usco
Sicuani Nevado Pupuya
△ 5818m Montero
Portachuelo Warnes San José Puerto
Suárez

–500 m
–1640 ft

Moho Puerto Acosta Buena Vista ⊞ Santa Cruz

Ayaviri Achacachi

Juliaca *Lake*
Titicaca Copacabana Cochabamba Comarapa

41 ▷ 4

20°

Puno Aiquile

–1000 m
–3281 ft

Nevado Ampato
6310m Ilave Viacha ⊞ LA PAZ

△ Corocoro Oruro

Volcán Misti
△ *5822m* Huanuni Lagunillas

–2000 m
–6562 ft

◻ Arequipa Uncia SUCRE
Moquegua Challapata Monteagudo

maná Nevado
△ *Sajama*
6520m Potosí

–3000 m
–9843 ft

Mollendo Tacna *Lago*
Poopó P A R A G U A Y

Ilo

La Yarada Sabaya

–4000 m
–13 124 ft

Uyuni Cotagaita

Villa Martín San Lorenzo Tropic of Capricorn

Tupiza Tarija

San Pablo

C H I L E Villazón *Pilcomayo*

25°

Desierto de Atacama *Gran Chaco* 5

A R G E N T I N A

Tropic of Capricorn ⬇ 42

70° F 65° G 25° H 60°

E F G H

BRAZIL

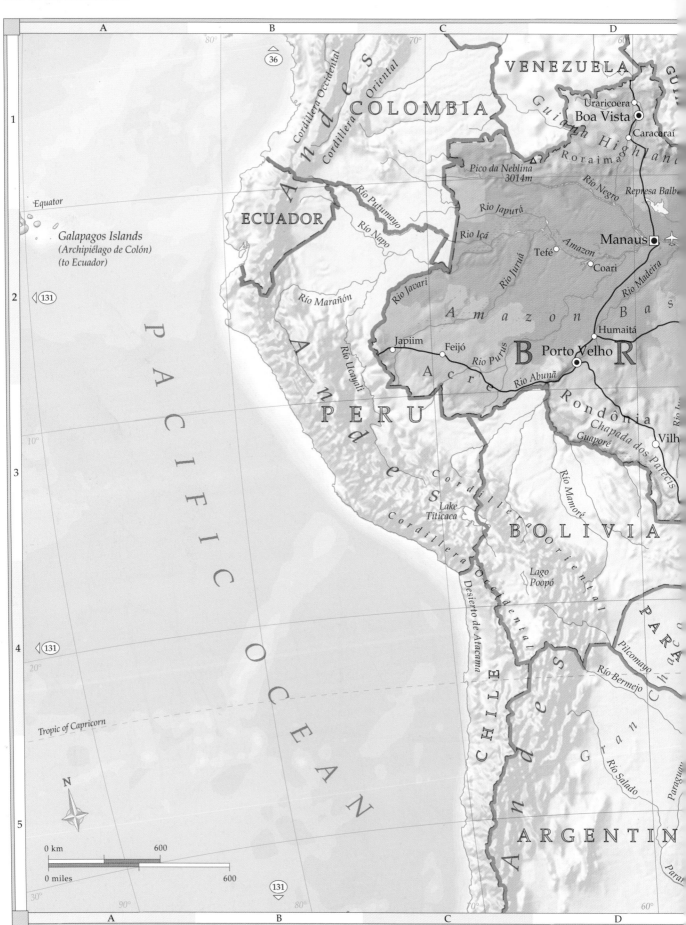

VENEZUELA

COLOMBIA

Cordillera Occidental

Cordillera Oriental

A n d e s

GUI

Uraricoera

Boa Vista

Caracaraí

ECUADOR

Roraima

Pico da Neblina
3014m

Rio Putumayo

Guiana Highl

Rio Napo

Rio Negro

Represa Balb

Rio Japurá

Rio Içá

Amazon

Manaus

Equator

Tefé

Coari

Galapagos Islands
(Archipiélago de Colón)
(to Ecuador)

Rio Marañón

Rio Javari

Rio Juruá

Rio Madeira

A m a z o n

B a s

Humaitá

131

A n d e s

Japiim

Feijó

B Porto Velho **R**

Rio Purus

A c r e

Rio Abunã

Rondônia

Rio I

PERU

Río Ucayali

Chapada dos Parecis

Guaporé

Vilh

Cordillera

Río Mamoré

10°

Cordillera Oriental

Lake
Titicaca

BOLIVIA

P A C I F I C

Lago
Poopó

P A R A

Desierto de Atacama

Cordillera Occidental

Pilcomayo

20°

Río Bermejo

Tropic of Capricorn

CHILE

A n d e s

g a n

G

Río Salado

Paraguay

O C E A N

N

POPULATION

◉ Over
500,000

◉ 100,000 –
500,000

○ 50,000 –
100,000

○ Less than
50,000

● National
capital

ARGENTIN

Para

0 km   600

0 miles   600

131

80°

90°

70°

60°

ELEVATION

4000 m / 13 124 ft
2000 m / 6562 ft
1000 m / 3281 ft
500 m / 1640 ft
250 m / 820 ft
100 m / 328 ft
Sea Level / Sea Level
-250 m / -820 ft
-500 m / -1640 ft
-1000 m / -3281 ft
-2000 m / -6562 ft
-3000 m / -9843 ft
-4000 m / -13 124 ft

FRENCH GUIANA (to France)
RINAME
Tumuc Humac Mountains
Amapá
Macapá
Ilha Caviana de Fora
Baía de Marajó
Mouths of the Amazon
Alenquer
Amazon
Santarém
Altamira
Ilha de Marajó
Belém
Baía de São Marco
São Luís
Parnaíba
Camocim
Itaituba
Rio Tapajós
Represa de Tucuruí
Bacabal
Piripiri
Fortaleza
Atol das Rocas
San Fernando de Noronha (to Brazil)
Rio Xingu
Marabá
Imperatriz
Teresina
Mossoró
Açu
Cabo de São Roque
Pará
Maranhão
Ceará
Rio Grande do Norte
Natal
Serra do Cachimbo
Carolina
Floriano
Juazeiro do Norte
João Pessoa
Balsas
Picos
Piauí
Campina Grande
Represa de Sobradinho
Pernambuco
Alagoas
Recife
São Manuel
Chapada Diamantina
Juazeiro
Maceió
Rio São Franscisco
Tocantins
Rio Tocantins
Aracaju
Estância
Taguatinga
Bahia
Feira de Santana
Salvador
Cuiabá
Planalto
Baía de Todos os Santos
BRASÍLIA
Itabuna
ndonópolis
Anápolis
Central
Jananba
Vitória da Conquista
Mato Grosso
Jataí
Goiás
Montes Claros
Canavieiras
Goiânia
Minas
Araçuai
Araguari
Gerais
Mato Grosso do Sul
Uberlândia
Uberaba
Governador Valadares
antal
Espírito Santo
Campo Grande
Belo Horizonte
Aquidauana
Ribeirão Preto
Divinópolis
Vitória
Presidente Epitácio
Juiz de Fora
Campos
Marília
Campinas
Londrina
São Paulo
Nova
Maringá
São Paulo
Iguaçu
Rio de Janeiro
Paraná
Santos
AY
Ponta Grossa
Represa de Itaipú
Curitiba
Salto do Iguaçu
Rio Iguaçu
Joinville
Paraná
Blumenau
Santa Catarina
Florianópolis
Passo Fundo
Rio Negro
nta Maria
do Sul
Canoas
Rio Grande
Porto Alegre
Bagé
Lagoa dos Patos
RUGUAY
Rio Grande
Mirim Lagoon

ATLANTIC OCEAN

Equator
Tropic of Capricorn

A
Z
I
L

44
45
45
45

50°
40°
30°
10°
20°
30°

1
2
3
4
5

E
F
G
H

POPULATION

- Over 500,000
- 100,000 – 500,000
- 50,000 – 100,000
- Less than 50,000
- National capital

Planalto de Mato Grosso

B R A Z I L

Pantanal

Pedro Juan Caballero

Tropic of Capricorn

Represa de Itaipú

Ciudad del Este

Eldorado

Encarnación

Posadas

Rivera

Lagoa dos Patos

Mirim Lagoon

Chuy

MONTEVIDEO

BUENOS AIRES

Coronel Oviedo

Villarrica

Caazapá

Yuty

San Juan Bautista

Santo Tomé

Artigas

Tacuarembó

Río Negro

Melo

Concepción

Paraguay

PARAGUAY

Rosario

ASUNCIÓN

Pilar

Formosa

Corrientes

Mercedes

Paraná

Santo Tomé

Salto

Paysandú

Mercedes

Florida

Trinidad

Río de la Plata

La Plata

Lomas de Zamora

Capitán Pablo Lagerenza

Fuerte Olimpo

General Eugenio A. Garay

Mariscal Estigarribia

BOLIVIA

Las Lomitas

Río Bermejo

Resistencia

Reconquista

Vera

Goya

Monte Caseros

Concordia

Paraná

Rosario

Gualeguaychú

Dolores

Zárate

Junín

Cordillera Oriental

Lago Poopó

Pilcomayo

C h a c o

San Ramón de la Nueva Orán

San Salvador de Jujuy

Metán

San Miguel de Tucumán

Santiago del Estero

Añatuya

Frías

Río Salado

Laguna Mar Chiquita

Rafaela

Santa Fe

Santa María

Deán Funes

Córdoba

Villa María

Río Cuarto

Rufino

Pergamino

Realicó

P a m p a s

Cordillera Occidental

La Quiaca

Nevado de Chañi 6200m

Salta

Cafayate

Cerro Galán 6600m

San Fernando del Valle de Catamarca

La Rioja

Jesús María

San Luis

Villa Mercedes

General Alvear

San Rafael

Chuquicamata

Calama

Cerro Ojos del Salado 6882m

Cerro Aconcagua 6959m

San Juan

Mendoza

Godoy Cruz

La Calera

SANTIAGO

Rancagua

PERU

Arica

Iquique

Lagunas

Tocopilla

Mejillones

Antofagasta

Taltal

Chañaral

Caldera

Copiapó

Vallenar

Domeyko

La Serena

Coquimbo

Ovalle

Monte Patria

Illapel

Salamanca

La Ligua

Viña del Mar

Valparaíso

San Antonio

Pichilemu

Curicó

Talca

Desierto de Atacama

C H I L E

A R G E N T I N A

U R U G U A Y

P A C I F I C   O C E A N

Tropic of Capricorn

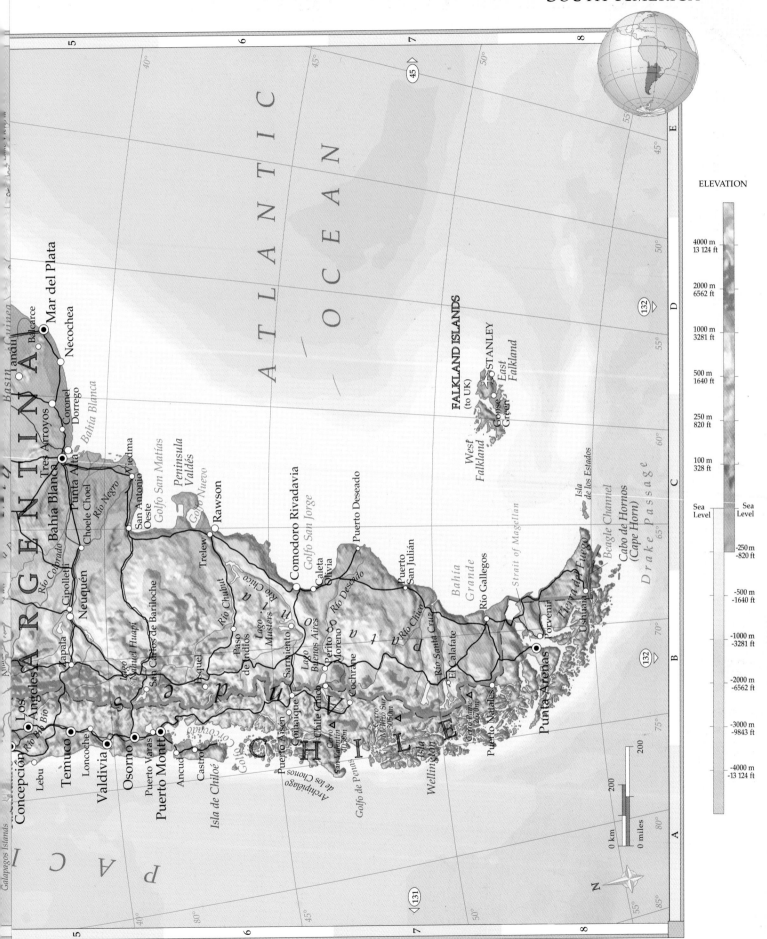

ATLANTIC

OCEAN

PACIFIC

ELEVATION

4000 m	13 124 ft
2000 m	6562 ft
1000 m	3281 ft
500 m	1640 ft
250 m	820 ft
100 m	328 ft
Sea Level	Sea Level
-250 m	-820 ft
-500 m	-1640 ft
-1000 m	-3281 ft
-2000 m	-6562 ft
-3000 m	-9843 ft
-4000 m	-13 124 ft

ARGENTINA

CHILE

FALKLAND ISLANDS
(to UK)

STANLEY
Goose Green
East Falkland
West Falkland

Mar del Plata
Balcarce
Necochea
Coronel Dorrego
Tres Arroyos
Punta Alta
Bahía Blanca
Choele Choel
Viedma
San Antonio Oeste
Rawson
Trelew
Cipolletti
Neuquén
Zapala
San Carlos de Bariloche
Esquel
Paso de Indios
Sarmiento
Comodoro Rivadavia
Caleta Olivia
Puerto Deseado
Puerto San Julián
Río Gallegos
El Calafate
Puerto Natales
Cochrane
Chile Chico
Coihaique
Puerto Aisén
Punta Arenas
Porvenir
Ushuaia

Concepción
Los Ángeles
Lebu
Temuco
Loncoche
Valdivia
Osorno
Puerto Varas
Puerto Montt
Ancud
Castro

Galápagos Islands

Península Valdés
Golfo San Matías
Golfo Nuevo
Golfo San Jorge
Bahía Grande
Strait of Magellan
Beagle Channel
Cabo de Hornos (Cape Horn)
Drake Passage
Tierra del Fuego
Isla de los Estados
Isla de Chiloé
Archipiélago de los Chonos
Golfo de Penas
Isla Wellington

Río Negro
Río Colorado
Río Chubut
Río Chico
Río Deseado
Río Chico
Río Santa Cruz
Bío Bío

Lago Nahuel Huapi
Lago Musters
Lago Buenos Aires
Perito Moreno

43

AFRICA

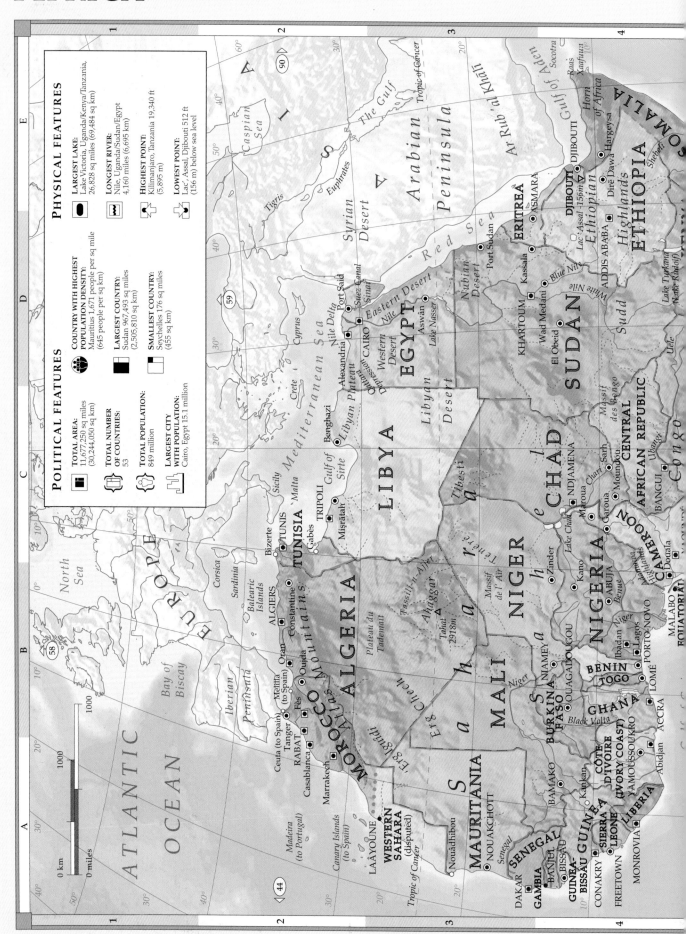

POLITICAL FEATURES

- **TOTAL AREA:**
11,677,250 sq miles
(30,244,050 sq km)

- **TOTAL NUMBER OF COUNTRIES:**
53

- **TOTAL POPULATION:**
849 million

- **LARGEST CITY WITH POPULATION:**
Cairo, Egypt 15.1 million

- **COUNTRY WITH HIGHEST POPULATION DENSITY:**
Mauritius 1,671 people per sq mile (645 people per sq km)

- **LARGEST COUNTRY:**
Sudan 967,493 sq miles (2,505,810 sq km)

- **SMALLEST COUNTRY:**
Seychelles 176 sq miles (455 sq km)

PHYSICAL FEATURES

- **LARGEST LAKE:**
Lake Victoria, Uganda/Kenya/Tanzania, 26,828 sq miles (69,484 sq km)

- **LONGEST RIVER:**
Nile, Uganda/Sudan/Egypt 4,160 miles (6,695 km)

- **HIGHEST POINT:**
Kilimanjaro, Tanzania 19,340 ft (5,895 m)

- **LOWEST POINT:**
Lac' Assal, Djibouti 512 ft (156 m) below sea level

POPULATION

- Over 500,000
- 100,000 – 500,000
- 50,000 – 100,000
- Less than 50,000
- National capital

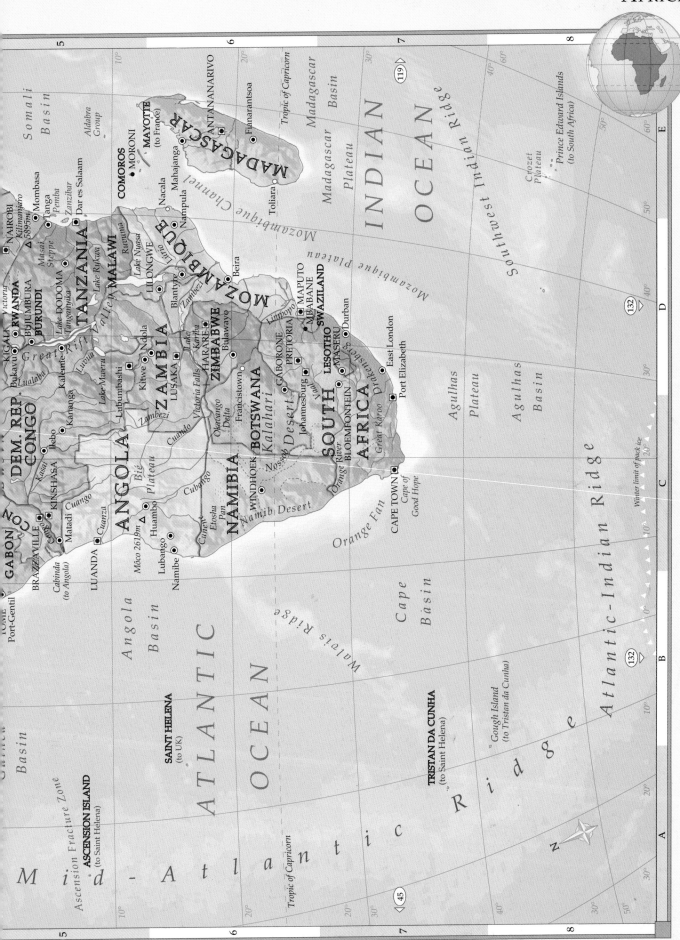

Somali Basin

Aldabra Group

NAIROBI
Kilimanjaro 5895m

COMOROS
MORONI

MAYOTTE
(to France)

Mombasa
Tanga
Pemba
Zanzibar
Dar es Salaam

ANTANANARIVO

119

Fianarantsoa

Tropic of Capricorn

Madagascar Basin

INDIAN OCEAN

Prince Edward Islands
(to South Africa)

Crozet Plateau

Southwest Indian Ridge

RWANDA
KIGALI
Bukavu
BUJUMBURA
BURUNDI

Victoria

Masai Steppe

TANZANIA
DODOMA
Lake
Tanganyika

Ruvuma

Nacala
Nampula

MALAWI

Madagascar Plateau

MADAGASCAR

Toliara

Mahajanga

KINSHASA

DEM. REP. CONGO

Lualaba

Kalemie
Lake Mweru
Kananga
Kasai

Lubumbashi

Lake Rukwa

Luvua

Lake Nyasa

LILONGWE

Blantyre

Zambezi

MOZAMBIQUE

Beira

Mozambique Channel

Mozambique Plateau

CONGO
GABON
BRAZZAVILLE
Port-Gentil

ANGOLA

Cabinda
(to Angola)
Matadi
LUANDA
Cuanza

Cuango

Bié Plateau
Môco 2619m
Huambo
Lubango
Namibe

Kwango

Kasai

Lake Kariba
HARARE

Ndola
Kitwe
ZAMBIA
LUSAKA

ZIMBABWE
Bulawayo

Victoria Falls
Cuando
Zambezi

BOTSWANA
Kalahari
GABORONE
Francistown

Okavango Delta
Cubango
Cunene

NAMIBIA
WINDHOEK

Etosha Pan

Namib Desert

Nossob

Limpopo

PRETORIA
MBABANE
SWAZILAND
MAPUTO

Johannesburg
Vaal
BLOEMFONTEIN
LESOTHO
MASERU

SOUTH AFRICA

Orange River

Great Karoo

Drakensberg

Durban

East London
Port Elizabeth

Cape of Good Hope
CAPE TOWN

Orange Fan

Agulhas Plateau

Agulhas Basin

Angola Basin

ATLANTIC OCEAN

SAINT HELENA
(to UK)

Walvis Ridge

Cape Basin

ASCENSION ISLAND
(to Saint Helena)

Ascension Fracture Zone

TRISTAN DA CUNHA
(to Saint Helena)

Gough Island
(to Tristan da Cunha)

Atlantic-Indian Ridge

Winter limit of pack ice

Mid-Atlantic Ridge

Tropic of Capricorn

45

132

N

132

47

NORTHWEST AFRICA

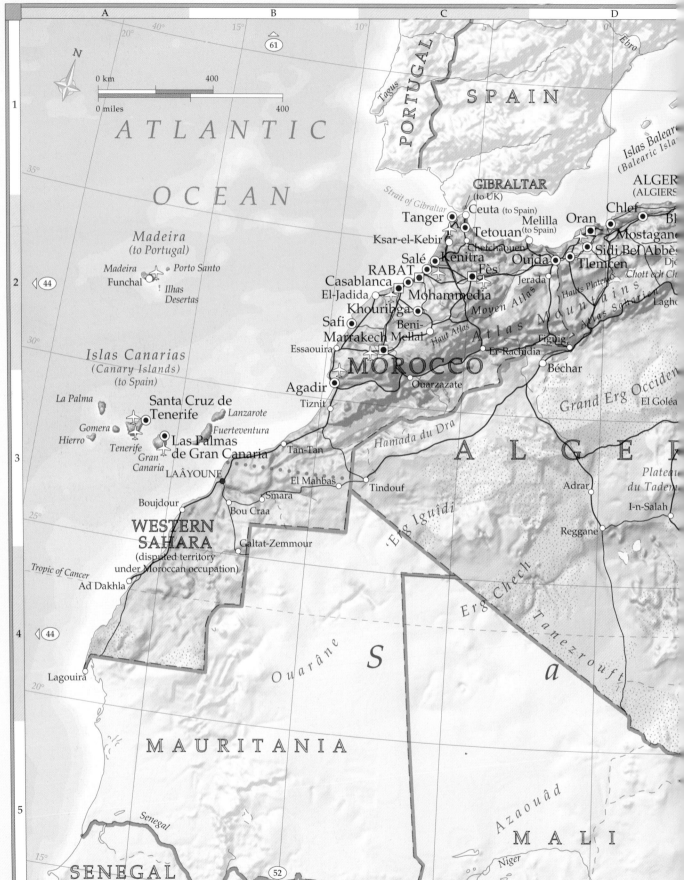

ATLANTIC

OCEAN

Madeira
(to Portugal)

Madeira • *Porto Santo*
Funchal
Ilhas
Desertas

Islas Canarias
(Canary Islands)
(to Spain)

La Palma

Gomera

Hierro

Tenerife

Santa Cruz de
Tenerife

Lanzarote

Fuerteventura

Las Palmas
de Gran Canaria

Gran
Canaria

LAÂYOUNE

Boujdour

**WESTERN
SAHARA**
(disputed territory
under Moroccan occupation)

Tropic of Cancer

Ad Dakhla

Lagouira

MAURITANIA

Senegal

SENEGAL

PORTUGAL

Tagus

SPAIN

Ebro

Islas Baleare
(Balearic Isl

ALGER
(ALGIERS

Strait of Gibraltar

GIBRALTAR
(to UK)

Ceuta (to Spain)

Tanger

Tetouan

Melilla
(to Spain)

Oran

Chlef

El

Mostagan

Ksar-el-Kebir

Chefchaouen

Sidi Bel Abbè

Salé

Kenitra

Oujda

Tlemcen

RABAT

Fès

Dje

Casablanca

El-Jadida

Mohammedia

Jerada

Chott ech Ch

Khouribga

Hauts Plateaux

Lagho

Safi

Beni-

Moyen Atlas

Marrakech Mellal

Figuig

Essaouira

Haut Atlas

Er-Rachidia

Atlas *Mountains*

Atlas Saharien

MOROCCO

Béchar

Agadir

Ouarzazate

Tiznit

Grand Erg Occiden

El Goléa

Hamada du Dra

Tan-Tan

ALGE

Plateau
du Tadem

El Mahbas

Tindouf

Adrar

Smara

I-n-Salah

Bou Craa

Erg Iguîdi

Reggane

Galtat-Zemmour

Erg Chech

S

a

Ouarâne

Tanezrouft

Azaouâd

MALI

Niger

POPULATION

- Over 500,000
- 100,000 – 500,000
- 50,000 – 100,000
- Less than 50,000
- National capital

0 km   400

0 miles   400

N

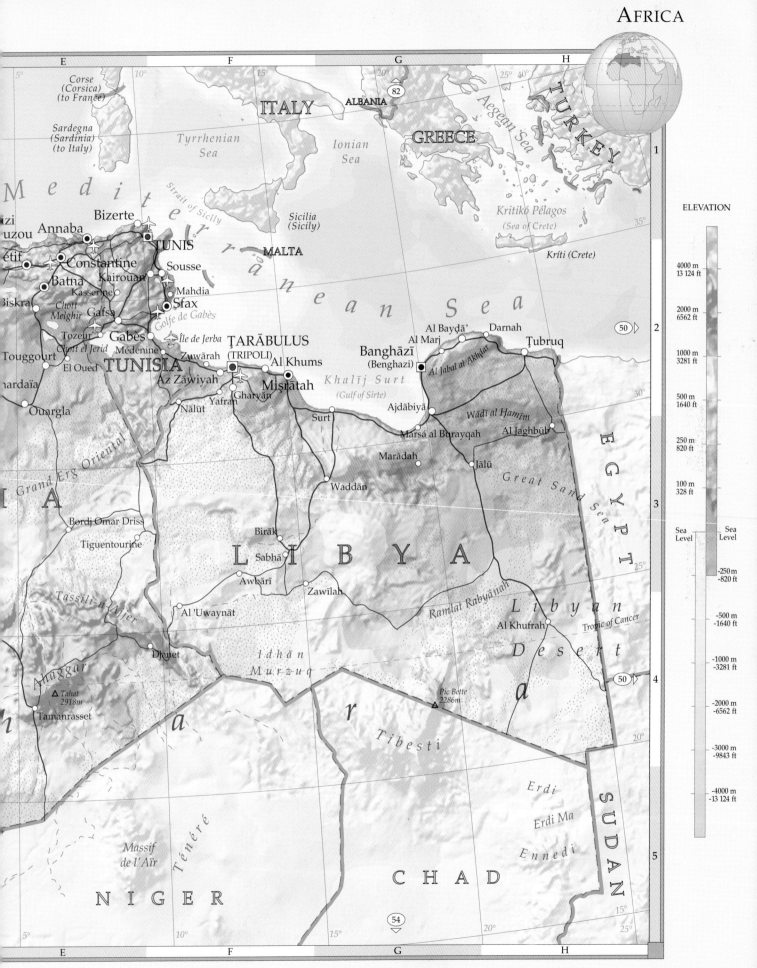

ELEVATION

4000 m
13 124 ft

2000 m
6562 ft

1000 m
3281 ft

500 m
1640 ft

250 m
820 ft

100 m
328 ft

Sea
Level

Sea
Level

-250 m
-820 ft

-500 m
-1640 ft

-1000 m
-3281 ft

-2000 m
-6562 ft

-3000 m
-9843 ft

-4000 m
-13 124 ft

Corse
(Corsica)
(to France)

Sardegna
(Sardinia)
(to Italy)

ITALY

ALBANIA

82

GREECE

TURKEY

Tyrrhenian
Sea

Ionian
Sea

Aegean Sea

Kritikó Pélagos
(Sea of Crete)

Kríti (Crete)

M e d i t e r r a n e a n   S e a

Strait of Sicily

Sicilia
(Sicily)

MALTA

Bizerte

Annaba

TUNIS

Sousse

izi

uzou

étif

Constantine

Batna

Kasserine

Kairouan

Mahdia

Sfax

Biskra'

Chott
Melrhir

Gafsa

Golfe de Gabès

Île de Jerba

Al Baydā'

Al Marj

Darnah

Ţubruq

Ţouggourt

Tozeur

Gabes

Médenine

Chott el Jerid

Zuwārah

TARĀBULUS
(TRIPOLI)

Al Khums

Banghāzī
(Benghazi)

Al Jabal al Akhḍar

50

El Oued

TUNISIA

Az Zāwiyah

Misrātah

Khalīj Surt
(Gulf of Sirte)

hardaïa

Ouargla

Nālūt

Yafran

Gharyān

Surt

Ajdābiyā

Wādī al Hamīm

Al Jaghbūb

I A

I Grand Erg Oriental

Marsá al Burayqah

Marādah

Jālū

Great Sand Sea

EGYPT

Bordj Omar Driss

Waddān

Tiguentourine

Birāk

L I B Y A

Sabhā

Tassili-n-Ajjer

Awbārī

Zawīlah

Ramlat Rabyānah

L i b y a n

Al 'Uwaynāt

Al Khufrah

Tropic of Cancer

50

Hoggar

Djanet

Idhān
Murzuq

r

D e s e r t

a

Tahat
2918m

Pic Bette
2286m

Tamanrasset

h

a

r

Tibesti

Erdi

Erdi Ma

Ennedi

SUDAN

Massif
de l'Aïr

Ténéré

N I G E R

CHAD

54

5°

10°

15°

20°

25°

40°

35°

30°

25°

20°

15°

25°

E

F

G

H

1

2

3

4

5

NORTHEAST AFRICA

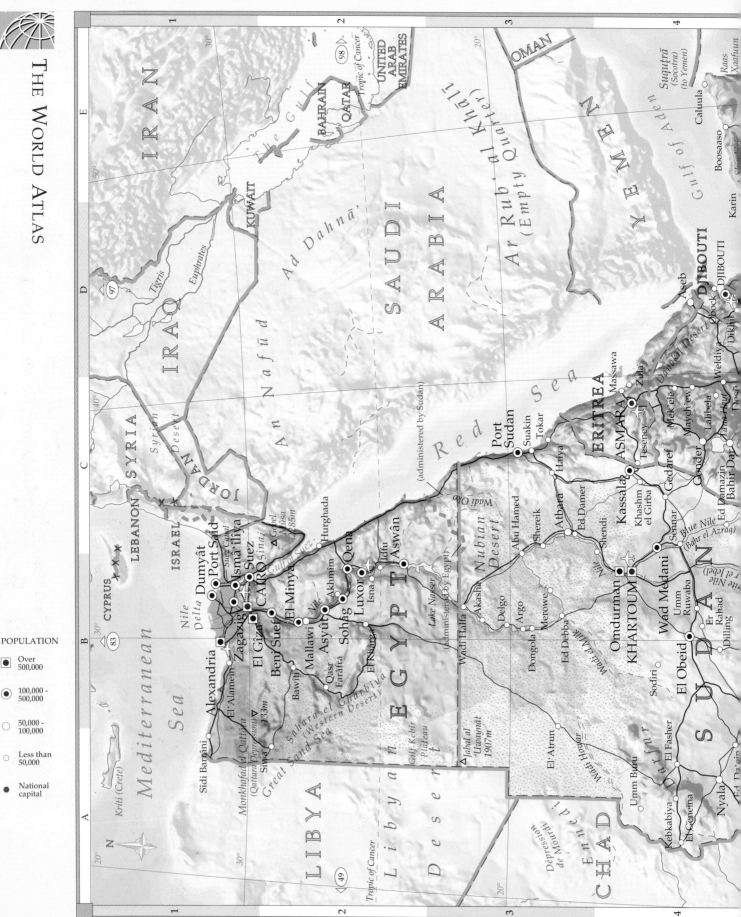

POPULATION

- ▣ Over 500,000
- ◉ 100,000 – 500,000
- ○ 50,000 – 100,000
- ∘ Less than 50,000
- ● National capital

IRAN

IRAQ

SYRIA

LEBANON

ISRAEL

JORDAN

CYPRUS

Kriti (Crete)

Mediterranean Sea

KUWAIT

BAHRAIN

QATAR

UNITED ARAB EMIRATES

OMAN

SAUDI ARABIA

Ar Rub' al Khālī (Empty Quarter)

An Nafūd

Ad Dahnā'

Tigris

Euphrates

Syrian Desert

Tropic of Cancer

YEMEN

Gulf of Aden

Suquṭrā (Socotra) (to Yemen)

Raas Xaafuun

Catuula

Boosaaso

Karin

DJIBOUTI

DJIBOUTI

Aseb

Obock

Weldiya

Dikhil

ERITREA

ASMARA

Massawa

Zula

Danakil Desert

Mek'elē

Maych'ew

Lalibela

Desē

Bahir Dar

Ed Damazin

Gonder

Gedaref

Teseney

Kassala

Khashm el Girba

Haiya

Suakin

Tokar

Port Sudan

Red Sea

Abu Hamed

Shereik

Atbara

Ed Damer

Shendi

Sennar

Blue Nile (Bahr el Azraq)

Wad Medani

Omdurman

KHARTOUM

White Nile (Bahr el Jebel)

Umm Ruwaba

Er Rahad

El Obeid

Dilling

Ed Debba

Merowe

Argo

Dongola

Delgo

Akasha

Wadi Halfa

(administered by Egypt)

Nubian Desert

Wadi Oko

Lake Nasser

(administered by Sudan)

Aswân

Idfu

Isna

Luxor

Qena

Akhmîm

Sohâg

Asyût

El Khârga

Mallawi

El Minya

Beni Suef

Qasr Farâfra

Bawîti

Sahara el Gharbiya (Western Desert)

Gilf Kebir Plateau

Jabal al Uwaynāt 1907m

El'Atrun

Wadi Howar

Sodiri

Umm Badr

Kebkabiya

El Fasher

El Geneina

Nyala

Dilling

DARFUR

S U D A N

CHAD

Ennedi

Dépression de Mourdi

E G Y P T

L i b y a n   D e s e r t

LIBYA

Sîdi Barrâni

El'Alamein

Alexandria

Zagazig

El Gîza

CAIRO

Suez

Isma'iliya

Port Said

Dumyât

Nile Delta

Gulf of Suez

Sinai

Gebel Sinai

Gebel Misa 2285m

Hurghada

Monkhafad el Qattâra (Qattara Depression) 133m

Siwa

Great Sand Sea

Nile

Tropic of Cancer

N

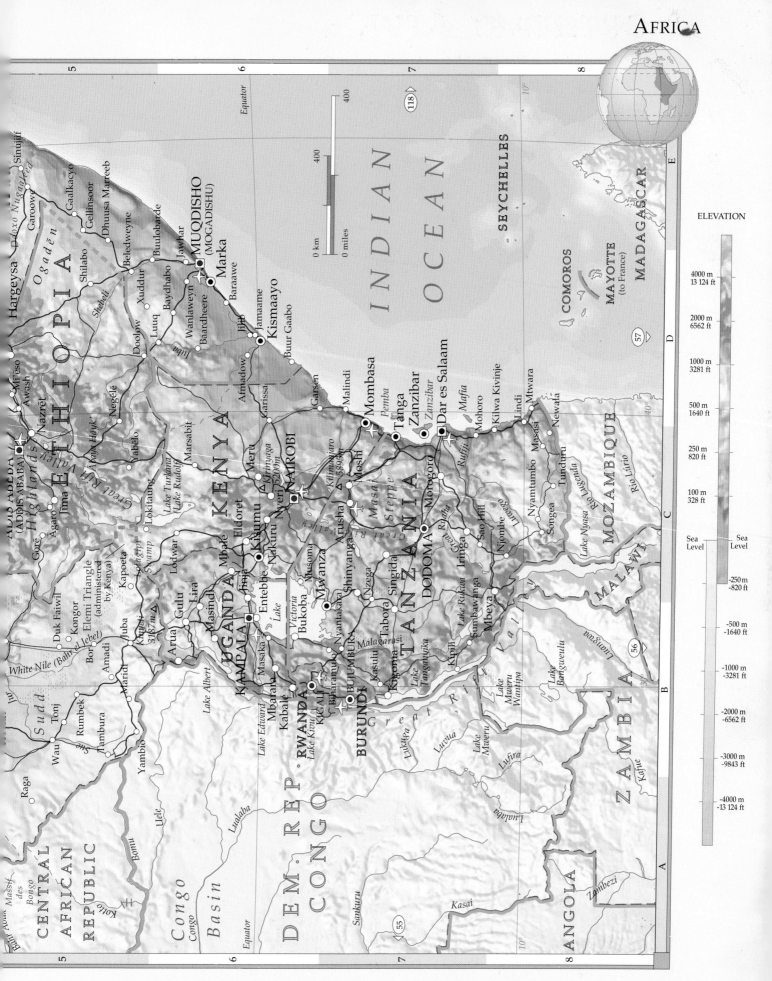

5   6   7   8

Sinujiif
Bari Awe Nugaaleed
Hargeysa   Doxo Nugaaleed
Miʻeso   Garoowe
Awash   Gaalkacyo
Nazrēt   Shilabo   Gellinsoor
Dhuusa Marreeb
Ogadēn   Beledweyne
Negēlē   Xuddur   Buulobarde
Jawhar
Highlands   Luuq   Baydhabo   MUQDISHO (MOGADISHU)
ADDIS ABEBA (ADDIS ABABA)
ETHIOPIA   Doolow   Wanlaweyn   Marka
Agaro   Shebeli   Baardheere   Baraawe
Gorē   Jīma   Yabēlo   Afmadow   Jilib   Jamaame   Kismaayo
Abaya Hāyk'   Jubba   Buur Gaabo

Great Rift Valley

INDIAN OCEAN

Equator

400   118

SEYCHELLES

COMOROS
MAYOTTE (to France)
MADAGASCAR   57

400
400

0 km
0 miles

ELEVATION

Marsabit   Garissa   Garsen
Lake Turkana / Lake Rudolf   Meru   Malindi
Lodwar   Nyeri   Mombasa   Pemba
Lokitaung   Kirinyaga 5200m   NAIROBI   Tanga
Lotagipi Swamp   Eldoret   Kilimanjaro 5895m   Zanzibar   Zanzibar
Kapoeta   Nakuru   Moshi   Dar es Salaam
Elemi Triangle (administered by Kenya)   Kisumu   Arusha   Mafia
KENYA   Masai Steppe   Mohoro
Mbale   Musoma   Morogoro   Kilwa Kivinje
Mwanza   Rufiji   Lindi
Jinja   Bukoba   Shinyanga   Kidatu   Mtwara
Kitgum 3187m   Gulu   Entebbe   Nzega   Ruaha   Masasi   Newala
Lira   Lake Victoria   Nyantakara   Singida   DODOMA   Sao Hill   Tunduru
Masindi   KAMPALA   Tabora   Iringa   Njombe   Songea
Duk Faiwil   Kongor   Arua   Masaka   Nyamtumbo
Kotido   UGANDA   Bujumbura   Kasulu   Njombe   Lake Nyasa / Lake Malawi
White Nile (Baḥr el Jebel)   Lake Albert   Kabale   RWANDA   Kigoma   Sumbawanga   Rio Lúrio
Bor   Amadi   Lake Edward   Mbarara   KIGALI   BURUNDI   Lake Tanganyika   Mbeya   MOZAMBIQUE
Maridi   Lake Kivu   Biharamulo   Malagarasi   Kipili   MALAWI
Yambio   Sudd   Great Rift Valley   Lake Rukwa   Rio Lugenda

CENTRAL AFRICAN REPUBLIC

Raga   Tonj   Rumbek
Tambura   Wau
Uele   Bomu
Kotto

Congo Basin   Lualaba   Congo
DEM. REP. CONGO

Sankuru   Kasai   Lualaba

55

ANGOLA   ZAMBIA

Lake Mweru   Luvua   Lufira   Lake Bangweulu   Luangwa
Lake Mweru Wantipa   56
Zambezi   Kafue

Equator

A   B   C   D   E

4000 m / 13 124 ft
2000 m / 6562 ft
1000 m / 3281 ft
500 m / 1640 ft
250 m / 820 ft
100 m / 328 ft
Sea Level   Sea Level
-250 m / -820 ft
-500 m / -1640 ft
-1000 m / -3281 ft
-2000 m / -6562 ft
-3000 m / -9843 ft
-4000 m / -13 124 ft

51

WEST AFRICA

WESTERN SAHARA
(disputed territory
under Moroccan occupation)

Tropic of Cancer

Aïn Ben Tili

Bîr Mogreïn

Fdérik   Zouérat
Touâjil

Nouâdhibou

Choûm

Akchâr

Atâr   Chinguetti
Akjoujt   Oujeft

**CAPE
VERDE**

Ilhas de Barlavento

Santo
Antão   Mindelo
São   Pedra Lume
Vicente   São   Sal
Nicolau   Boa Vista

Santiago
Fogo   Maio

PRAIA

Ilhas de Sotavento

NOUAKCHOTT   Idîni

Boutilimit

Rkîz

Rosso   Aleg
Richard Toll   Dagana
Saint Louis

Louga

DAKAR   Mékhé
Thiès   Mbaké
Mbour   Diourbel
Sokone   **Kaolack**
BANJUL   **GAMBIA**
Bignona   Kolda
Ziguinchor   Sédhiou
Bafatá

BISSAU   Gaoual
**GUINEA-
BISSAU**   Boké   Labé
Kindia
Mamou
CONAKRY
Makeni
**SIERRA
LEONE**
FREETOWN   Bo   Kenema
Nzérékoré

Tubmanburg
Harbel
MONROVIA   Zwedru
Buchanan   **LIBERIA**

Harper

M A U R I T A N I A

Tidjikja   Tîchît

Magta
Lahjar   Boûmdeïd   Oualâta
Tâmchekket   'Ayoûn el 'Atroûs   Néma
Kaédi   Kiffa   Kobenni   Timbedgha   Amourj
Matam   Sélibabi   Bassikou
Nioro
Kayes   Ténenkou
Toukoto   Kolokani
Kita   Ségou
Koulikoro
BAMAKO
Koutia
Dinguiraye   Siguiri   Bougouni   Sika
Pita
Faranah   Kankan   Odienné   Ferkéssédou
Tokounou   Tengréla   Boundiali   Korh
Kissidougou   **CÔTE
D'IVOIRE**
Beyla   (IVORY COAST)
Katiola
Danané
Gbanga   **YAMOUSSOUKRO**
Gagnoa
Divo
Sassand
San-Pédro

El Hank

El Mreyyé

Aoukâr

POPULATION

▣ Over
500,000

◉ 100,000 -
500,000

○ 50,000 -
100,000

○ Less than
50,000

● National
capital

0 km   400

0 miles   400

52

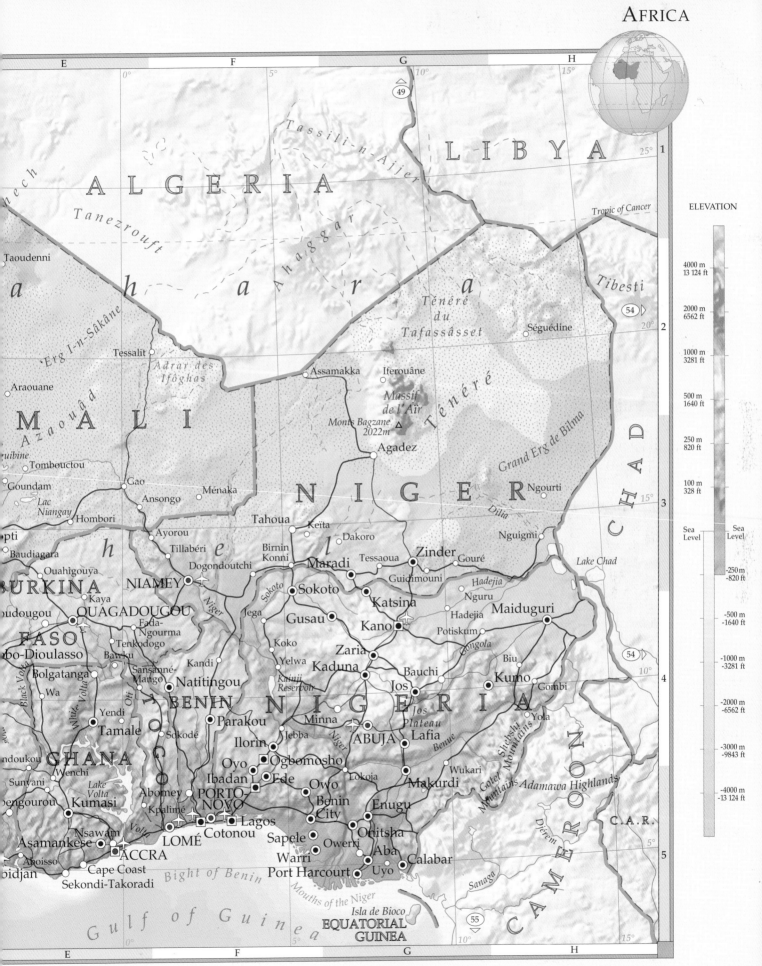

AFRICA

ELEVATION

4000 m	13 124 ft
2000 m	6562 ft
1000 m	3281 ft
500 m	1640 ft
250 m	820 ft
100 m	328 ft
Sea Level	Sea Level
-250 m	-820 ft
-500 m	-1640 ft
-1000 m	-3281 ft
-2000 m	-6562 ft
-3000 m	-9843 ft
-4000 m	-13 124 ft

LIBYA

ALGERIA

Tanezrouft

Tassili-n-Ajjer

Ahaggar

S a h a r a

Tibesti

Tropic of Cancer

Taoudenni

'Erg I-n-Sâkâne

Tessalit

Adrar des Ifôghas

Assamakka

Iferouâne

Ténéré du Tafassâsset

Séguédine

Araouane

MALI

Azaouâd

Massif de l'Aïr

Monts Bagzane 2022m

Ténéré

Grand Erg de Bilma

CHAD

uibine

Tombouctou

Gao

Ménaka

Agadez

Ngourti

Goundam

Ansongo

NIGER

Lac Niangay

Hombori

Tahoua

Keïta

Dakoro

Dilia

Nguigmi

pti

Baudiagara

Ayorou

Tillabéri

Birnin Konni

Maradi

Tessaoua

Zinder

Gouré

Lake Chad

Ouahigouya

Dogondoutchi

Hadejia

BURKINA

NIAMEY

Sokoto

Sokoto

Guidimouni

Nguru

Kaya

Jega

Katsina

Hadejiá

Maiduguri

udougou

QUAGADOUGOU

Gusau

Kano

Potiskum

Gongola

Biu

FASO

Fada-Ngourma

Koko

Zaria

bo-Dioulasso

Tenkodogo

Bawku

Kandi

Yelwa

Kaduna

Bauchi

Kumo

Gombi

Bolgatanga

Sansanné-Mango

Kainji Reserboir

Jos

Wa

Natitingou

NIGERIA

Jos Plateau

Yola

Yendi

BENIN

Minna

Shebshi Mountains

Tamale

Sokodé

Ilorin

Jebba

ABUJA

Lafia

Benue

Adamawa Highlands

ndoukou

GHANA

Oyo

Ogbomosho

Lokoja

Wukari

Gotel Mountains

Wenchi

Ibadan

Ede

Owo

Makurdi

C.A.R.

Sunyani

Abomey

PORTO-NOVO

Benin City

Enugu

engourou

Kumasi

Kpalimé

Onitsha

Djérem

Nsawam

Cotonou

Sapele

Owerri

Aba

Calabar

Asamankese

LOMÉ

Warri

Uyo

boisso

ACCRA

Port Harcourt

Cape Coast

Bight of Benin

CAMEROON

bidjan

Sekondi-Takoradi

Mouths of the Niger

Lake Volta

Volta

Sanaga

Gulf of Guinea

Isla de Bioco

EQUATORIAL GUINEA

53

CENTRAL AFRICA

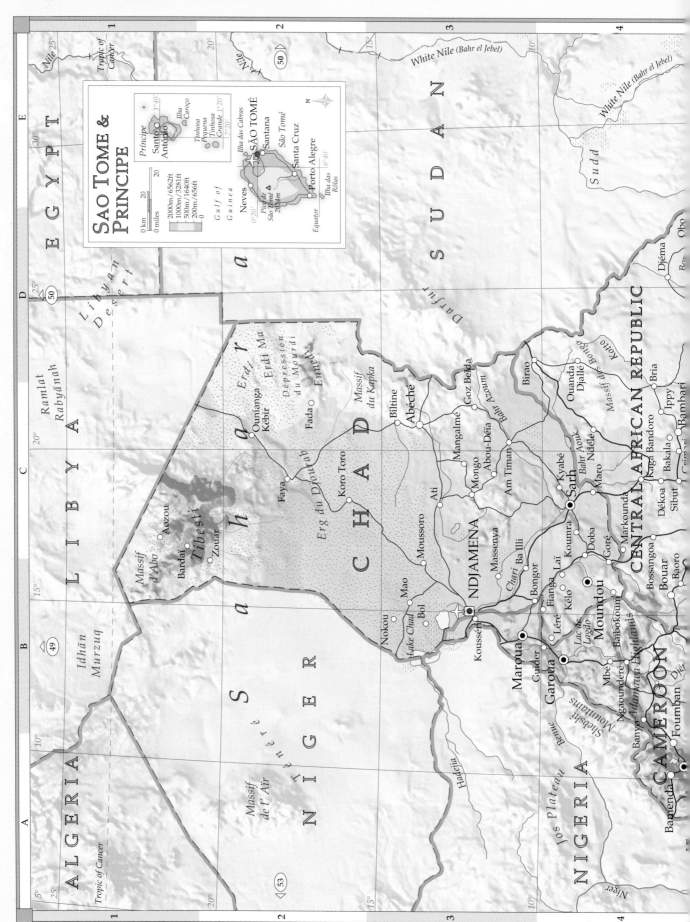

SAO TOME & PRINCIPE

Príncipe
Santo
António
Ilha das Cabras
SÃO TOMÉ
Santana
São Tomé
Santa Cruz
Neves
Pico de
São Tomé
2024m
Porto Alegre
Ilha das
Rôlas
Equator

Tinhosa
Pequena
Tinhosa
Grande

Ilha
Caroço

Gulf of Guinea

0 km 20
0 miles 20

2000m/6562ft
1000m/3281ft
500m/1640ft
200m/656ft
0

EGYPT

Nile
Tropic of Cancer

Libyan
Desert

Ramlat
Rabyānah

LIBYA

Idhān
Murzuq

ALGERIA
Tropic of Cancer

NIGER

Massif
de l' Aïr

Ténéré

SUDAN

Sudd

Darfur

White Nile (Bahr el Jebel)

White Nile (Bahr el Jebel)

Djéma

Obo

Kotto

Massif des Bongo

CENTRAL AFRICAN REPUBLIC

Ouanda
Djallé
Bria
Ippy
Bambari
Raga
Bandoro
Bakala
Ndélé
Bangui

Birao

Goz Beïda

Bahr Azoum

Mangalmé
Abou-Déia
Am Timan

Massif
du Kapka

Biltine
Abéché

Aïr

Erdi Ma
Dépression
du Mourdi
Ennedi

Erdi

Sahara

Ounianga
Kébir
Fada

Koro Toro

Faya

 Erg du Djourab

Aozou
Tibesti
Bardaï
Zouar
Massif
d'Abo

CHAD

Ati
Mongo
Mao
Moussoro
Nokou
Bol
Lake Chad

NDJAMENA
Kousséri
Maroua
Garoua
Guider

Massenya
Chari Ba Illi
Bongor
Fianga
Kélo
Léré
Lac de
Léré
Lai
Koumra
Doba
Goré
Markounda
Bossangoa
Bouar
Baoro

Sarh
Kyabé
Bahr Aouk
Maro
Ndélé
Dékoa
Sibut

Moundou
Baïbokoum
Ngaoundéré
Shebshi Mountains
Adamawa Highlands
Mbé
Foumban

CAMEROON

Benue
Jos Plateau
NIGERIA
Hadejia
Niger
Banyo
Bamenda

POPULATION

▣ Over 500,000

◉ 100,000 – 500,000

○ 50,000 – 100,000

○ Less than 50,000

● National capital

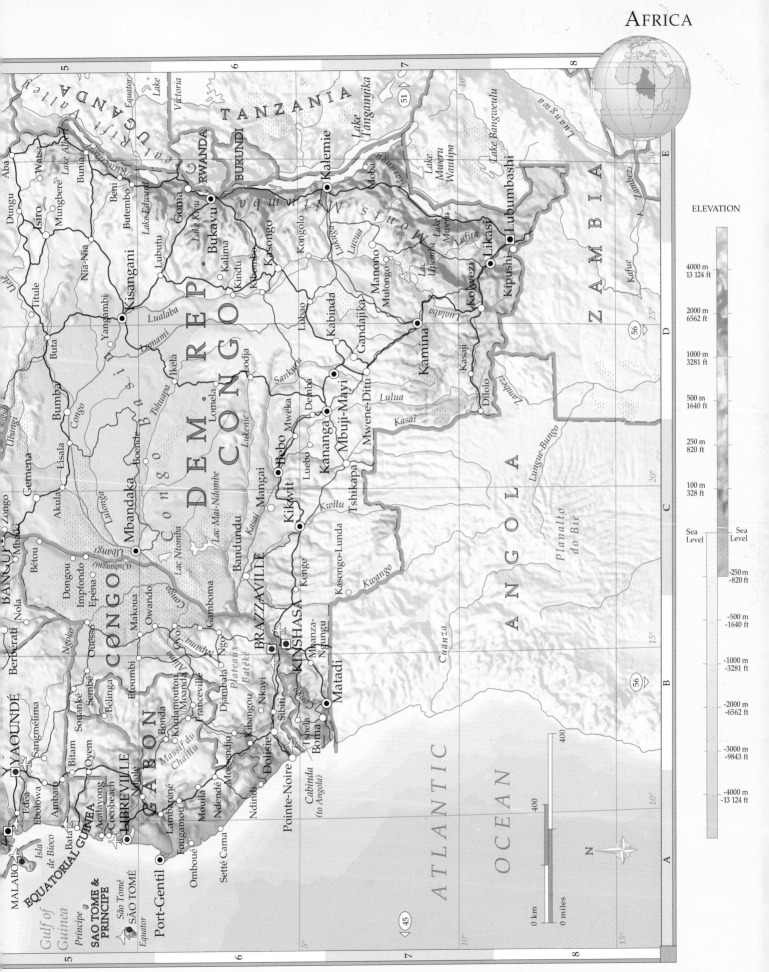

ELEVATION

4000 m	13 124 ft
2000 m	6562 ft
1000 m	3281 ft
500 m	1640 ft
250 m	820 ft
100 m	328 ft
Sea Level	Sea Level
-250 m	-820 ft
-500 m	-1640 ft
-1000 m	-3281 ft
-2000 m	-6562 ft
-3000 m	-9843 ft
-4000 m	-13 124 ft

SOUTHERN AFRICA

CONGO

CABINDA
(to Angola)
Cabinda

M'Banza Congo

Uíge

Ambriz
Caxito

LUANDA

Dondo
Cuanza

Gabela

Sumbe

Camabatela

N'Dalatando

Malanje

Lóvua

Chitato

Lucapa

Saurimo

DEM. REP. CONGO

Lake Tanganyika

Lake Mweru

Mbala

Kasama

Iso

Mansa   Samfya

Mp

ANGOLA

Lobito
Benguela

Cubal

Camacupa
Môco 2610m

Caála
Huambo

Caconda

Cubango

Kuito

Planalto do Bie

Luena

Lunge-Bungo

Zambezi

Solwezi

Chililabombwe

Chingola
Kitwe

Mufulira
Ndola

Luanshya

Lubango

Namibe

Tombua

Menongue

Cubango

Cuito

Zambezi

Kaoma

Mongu

Kafue

ZAMBIA

Serenje

Chipa

Kabwe

Nambala
Mazabuka

LUSAKA

Monze
Choma

Kafue

Zambezi

Albufeira de Cahora Bass

Vila do Zumbo

Kunene

Olifa

Oshikango

Etosha Pan

Rundu

Katima Mulilo

Caprivi Strip

Victoria Falls

Livingstone

Kariba

Lake Kariba

HARARE

Nyamapand

Tsumeb
Otavi

Grootfontein

Okavango

Hwange

Victoria Falls

Kadoma

Kwekwe

Chitungwiza

Inyangani 2592

Mutare

Huila Plateau

N'Giva

Otjiwarongo

Okavango Delta

Maun

Boteti

Nata

ZIMBABWE

Masving

Brandberg 2573m

NAMIBIA

Ghanzi

Bulawayo

Zvishavane

Francistown

Shashe

Gwanda

Wlotzkasbaken
Swakopmund
Walvis Bay

Karibib

Gobabis

Mamuno

BOTSWANA

Serowe
Palapye

Limpopo

Musina
(Messina)

Kalahari

Mahalapye

Polokwane
(Pietersburg)

WINDHOEK

Rehoboth

Fish

Mariental

Nosob

Jwaneng

GABORONE

Mochudi

Kanye

Werda

Lobatse

Desert

Módimolle
(Nylstroom)

PRETORIA

MAPUTO

Tropic of Capricorn

Auob

Molopo

Mmabatho

Soweto

Johannesburg

MBABANE

Keetmanshoop

Lüderitz

Aus

Klein Karas

Karasburg

Groot Karasberg

SOUTH

Klerksdorp

Kroonstad

SWAZILAND

Dundee

Vaal

Bethlehem

LESOTHO

Welkom

Oranjemund

Orange River

Upington

Kimberley

BLOEMFONTEIN

Prieska

AFRICA

MASERU

Pietermaritzburg

Durban

Kokstad

De Aar

Colesberg

Drakensberg

Umtata

Queenstown

Mdantsane

St Helena Bay

Beaufort West

Cradock

Mdantsane
East London

Port Alfred

Bellville

Worcester

George

Uitenhage

CAPE TOWN

Mosselbaai

Port Elizabeth

Cape of Good Hope

POPULATION

- ⊙ Over 500,000
- ◉ 100,000 – 500,000
- ○ 50,000 – 100,000
- ○ Less than 50,000
- ● National capital

SOUTH AFRICA'S THREE CAPITALS

Pretoria – *administrative capital*

Cape Town – *legislative capital*

Bloemfontein – *judicial capital*

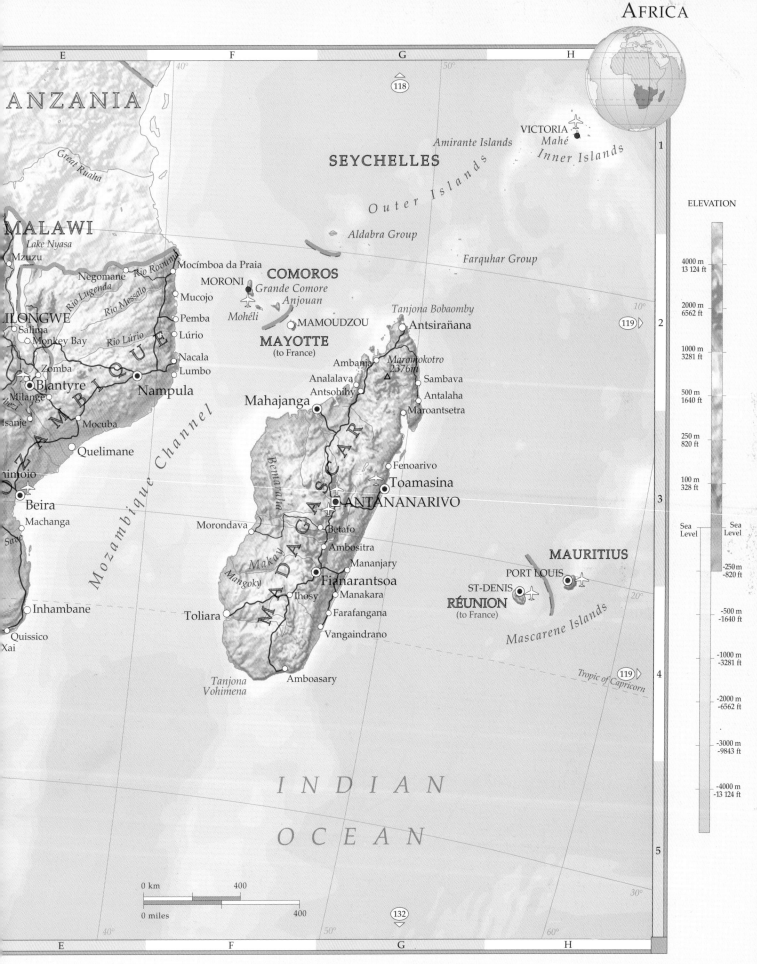

ANZANIA

MALAWI
Lake Nyasa
Mzuzu
Negomane   Rio Rovuma
MILONGWE   Rio Lugenda
Salima   Rio Messalo
Monkey Bay   Rio Lúrio
Zomba
Blantyre
Milange
Isanje   Mocuba
Quelimane
himoio
Beira
Machanga

Inhambane

Quissico
Xai

MOZAMBIQUE

Mocímboa da Praia
Mucojo
Pemba
Lúrio
Nacala
Lumbo
Nampula

Mozambique Channel

SEYCHELLES

Amirante Islands

Outer Islands

Aldabra Group

Farquhar Group

COMOROS
MORONI
Grande Comore
Anjouan
Mohéli
MAMOUDZOU
MAYOTTE
(to France)

Ambanja
Analalava
Antsohihy

Mahajanga

Bemaraha

MADAGASCAR

Makay

Mangoky

Morondava

Tanjona Bobaomby
Antsirañana

Maromokotro
2876m

Sambava
Antalaha
Maroantsetra

Fenoarivo
Toamasina
ANTANANARIVO
Betafo
Ambositra
Mananjary
Fianarantsoa
Manakara
Ihosy
Farafangana

Toliara

Vangaindrano

Tanjona
Vohimena   Amboasary

VICTORIA
Mahé
Inner Islands

Tanjona Bobaomby

MAURITIUS
PORT LOUIS
ST-DENIS
RÉUNION
(to France)

Mascarene Islands

Tropic of Capricorn

INDIAN

OCEAN

ELEVATION

4000 m
13 124 ft

2000 m
6562 ft

1000 m
3281 ft

500 m
1640 ft

250 m
820 ft

100 m
328 ft

Sea   Sea
Level   Level

-250 m
-820 ft

-500 m
-1640 ft

-1000 m
-3281 ft

-2000 m
-6562 ft

-3000 m
-9843 ft

-4000 m
-13 124 ft

118

119

119

132

0 km   400

0 miles   400

Europe

POLITICAL FEATURES

TOTAL AREA:
4,809,200 sq miles
(12,456,000 sq km)

TOTAL NUMBER OF COUNTRIES:
43

TOTAL POPULATION:
707 million

LARGEST CITY WITH POPULATION:
Moscow, European Russia 15.5 million

COUNTRY WITH HIGHEST POPULATION DENSITY:
Monaco 42,840 people per sq mile
(16,477 people per sq km)

LARGEST COUNTRY:
European Russia 1,527,341 sq miles
(3,955,818 sq km)

SMALLEST COUNTRY:
Vatican City, Italy 0.17 sq miles
(0.44 sq km)

PHYSICAL FEATURES

LARGEST LAKE:
Lake Lagoda, European Russia
7,100 sq miles (18,390 sq km)

LONGEST RIVER:
Volga, European Russia
2,290 miles (3,688 km)

HIGHEST POINT:
El'brus, Caucasus, European Russia
18,510ft (5,642 m)

LOWEST POINT:
Volga Delta, Caspian Sea, European
Russia 92 ft (28m) below sea level

POPULATION

- ■ Over 500,000
- ◉ 100,000 – 500,000
- ○ 50,000 – 100,000
- ○ Less than 50,000
- ● National capital

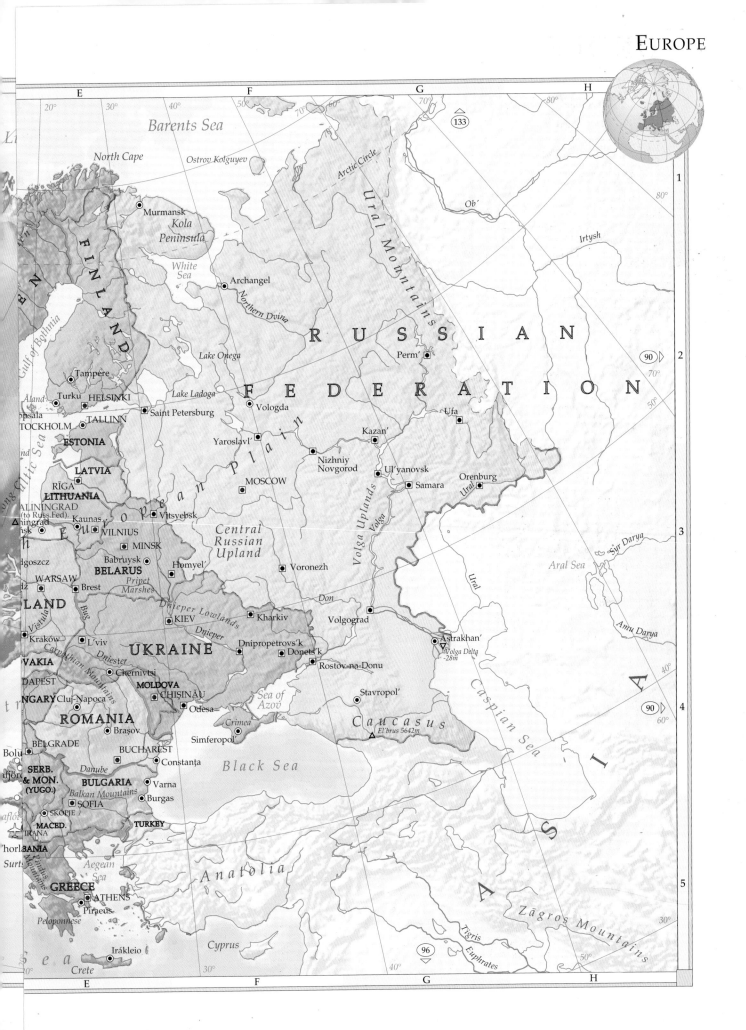

E   F   G   H

20°   30°   40°   50°   70°   60°   70°   80°

Barents Sea

North Cape   *Ostrov Kolguyev*   Arctic Circle   80°

133

Ob'   1

Irtysh

● Murmansk   *Kola Peninsula*

White Sea

● Archangel   *Northern Dvina*   **R U S S I A N**

Lake Onega   Perm' □   90   2

70°

F E D E R A T I O N   50°

Gulf of Bothnia   ● Tampere   *Lake Ladoga*   Vologda ●   Ufa □

Åland   Turku ●   **HELSINKI**   Yaroslavl' □   Kazan' □

psala   ● **TALLINN**   ● Saint Petersburg   Nizhniy Novgorod □   Ul'yanovsk □   Orenburg □

STOCKHOLM   **ESTONIA**   Samara ●

nd   **LATVIA**   MOSCOW □   *Ural*

RĪGA ●   3

LITHUANIA

ALININGRAD   Vitsyebsk ●   *Central Russian Upland*   *Aral Sea*

(to Russ.Fed.)   Kaunas ●   **Syr Darya**

ningrad   **VILNIUS** ●

sk   ● **MINSK**   *Amu Darya*

lgoszcz   Babruysk ●   Homyel' ●   *Ural*

WARSAW ●   **BELARUS**   *Pripet Marshes*   Voronezh □

z   ● Brest   *Dnieper Lowlands*

LAND   *Bug*   Kharkiv ●   Volgograd □

● Kraków   ● L'viv   **KIEV** □   *Dnieper*   Don

VAKIA   *Carpathian Mountains*   **UKRAINE**   Dnipropetrovs'k □   Astrakhan' ●   40°

● Chernivtsi   *Dniester*   Donets'k □   *Volga Delta -28m*

DAPEST   **MOLDOVA**   Rostov-na-Donu ●

NGARY Cluj-Napoca   ● **CHIŞINĂU**   *Sea of Azov*   Stavropol' ●   90   4

tr   ● Odesa   60°

ROMANIA   ● Braşov   *Crimea*   *Caucasus*

BELGRADE   Simferopol' ●   El'brus 5642m △   *Caspian Sea*

Bolu   **BUCHAREST**   ● Constanţa   *Black Sea*

SERB. & MON.   *Danube*

 njor   **(YUGO.)**   **BULGARIA**   ● Varna   **TURKEY**

Balkan Mountains   ● Burgas

aflo   ● **SKOPJE**   ● **SOFIA**

MACED.   **TIRANA**

horl   **BANIA**   *Pindus Mountains*

Surt   *Aegean Sea*   *Anatolia*   *Zagros Mountains*   30°   5

GREECE

● **ATHENS**

Piraeus ●

Peloponnese

Sea   Irákleio ●   96

Crete   *Cyprus*   *Tigris*   *Euphrates*   50°

20°   30°   40°   50°

E   F   G   H

POPULATION

- ■ Over 500,000
- ◉ 100,000 - 500,000
- ○ 50,000 - 100,000
- ○ Less than 50,000
- ● National capital

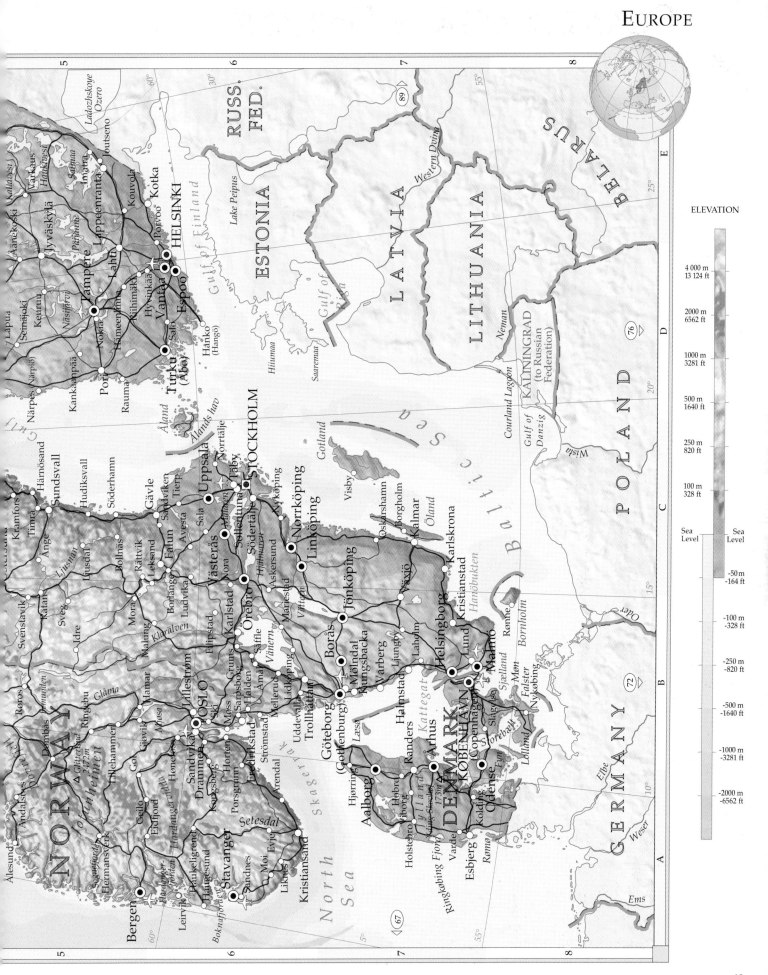

ELEVATION

4 000 m
13 124 ft

2000 m
6562 ft

1000 m
3281 ft

500 m
1640 ft

250 m
820 ft

100 m
328 ft

Sea Level | Sea Level

-50 m
-164 ft

-100 m
-328 ft

-250 m
-820 ft

-500 m
-1640 ft

-1000 m
-3281 ft

-2000 m
-6562 ft

RUSS. FED.

BELARUS

ESTONIA

LATVIA

LITHUANIA

KALININGRAD
(to Russian
Federation)

POLAND

GERMANY

NORWAY

DENMARK

Finland

Gulf of Finland

Ladozhskoye Ozero

Joutseno

Varkaus
Kallavesi
Hankasalmi
Imatra
Lappeenranta
Kouvola
Kotka
Porvoo
HELSINKI
Jyväskylä
Keuruu
Päijänne
Lahti
Kiihimäki
Hyvinkää
Vantaa
Espoo
Äänekoski
Tampere
Nokia
Hämeenlinna
Salo
Hanko (Hangö)
Lapua
Seinäjoki
Näsijärvi
Turku (Åbo)
Narpes
Kankaanpää
Pori
Rauma
Lake Peipus
Hiiumaa
Saaremaa
Neman
Western Dvina
Gulf of Riga
Courland Lagoon
Gulf of Danzig
Wisła
Oder

Åland
Ålands hav

Härnösand
Sundsvall
Hudiksvall
Söderhamn
Gävle
Sandviken
Tierp
Norrtälje
Uppsala
Täby
STOCKHOLM
Nyköping
Kramfors
Timrå
Ange
Bollnäs
Rättvik
Leksand
Falun
Avesta
Sala
Sollentuna
Södertälje
Gotland
Visby
Oskarshamn
Borgholm
Kalmar
Öland
Karlskrona
Svenstavik
Kätan
Sveg
Idre
Mora
Malung
Borlänge
Ludvika
Nora
Västerås
Eskilstuna
Katrineholm
Askersund
Linköping
Norrköping
Vättern
Mariestad
Jönköping
Växjö
Ljungby
Kristianstad
Hanöbukten
Ronne
Bornholm
Klarälven
Filipstad
Karlstad
Örebro
Säffle
Grums
Vänern
Lidköping
Skövde
Borås
Mölndal
Kungsbacka
Varberg
Halmstad
Laholm
Helsingborg
Lund
Malmö
Sjælland
Møn
Falster
Nykøbing
Lolland
Røros
Åmot
Andalsnes
Dombås
Ringebu
Gol
Gjøvik
Hamar
Mjøsa
Lillehammer
Glåma
Lillestrøm
OSLO
Ski
Moss
Sarpsborg
Halden
Mellerud
Trollhättan
Uddevalla
Göteborg (Gothenburg)
Läsø
Frederikstad
Strömstad
Åmal
Vänersborg
Kattegat
Randers
Århus
Fyn
Odense
Svendborg
Storebælt
KØBENHAVN (Copenhagen)
Slagelse
Alesund
Sognefjorden
Hermansverk
Galdhøpiggen 2472m
Jotunheimen
Geilo
Eidfjord
Hardangerfjorden
Honefoss
Kongsberg
Drammen
Sandvika
Horten
Porsgrunn
Arendal
Setesdal
Skagerrak
Hjørring
Aalborg
Hobro
Viborg
Holstebro
Jylland
Ringkøbing Fjord
Varde
Esbjerg
Kolding
Rømø
Bergen
Leirvik
Haukeligrend
Haugesund
Hardangervidda
Stavanger
Sandnes
Moi
Eviè
Liknes
Kristiansand
North Sea
Weser
Elbe
Ems
Boknafjorden

Baltic Sea

63

THE LOW COUNTRIES

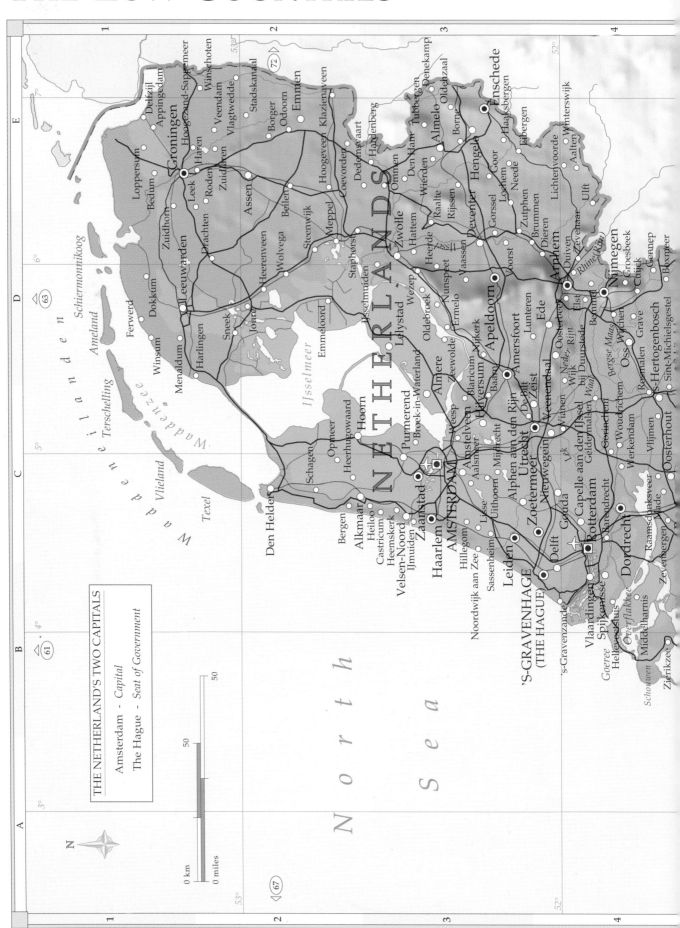

THE NETHERLAND'S TWO CAPITALS

Amsterdam - *Capital*
The Hague - *Seat of Government*

POPULATION

- ◍ Over 500,000
- ◉ 100,000 – 500,000
- ○ 50,000 – 100,000
- ○ Less than 50,000
- ● National capital

N

0 km 50
0 miles 50

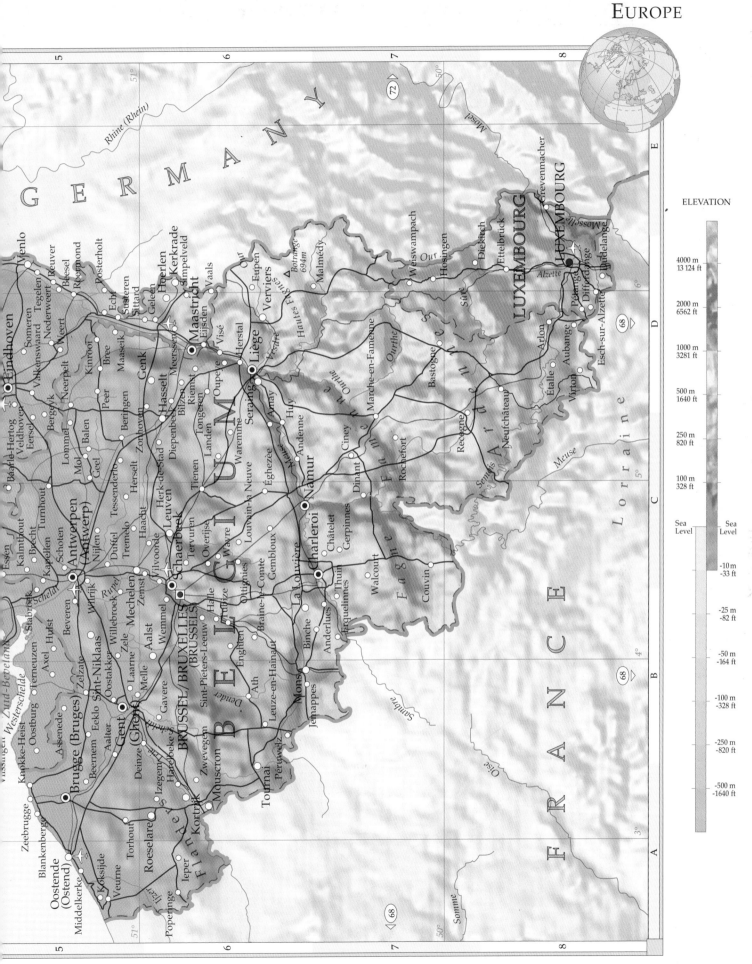

EUROPE

ELEVATION

4000 m
13 124 ft

2000 m
6562 ft

1000 m
3281 ft

500 m
1640 ft

250 m
820 ft

100 m
328 ft

Sea
Level

Sea
Level

-10 m
-33 ft

-25 m
-82 ft

-50 m
-164 ft

-100 m
-328 ft

-250 m
-820 ft

-500 m
-1640 ft

GERMANY

LUXEMBOURG

BELGIUM

FRANCE

Rhine (Rhein)

Mosel

Venlo
Reuver
Roermond
Tegelen
Nederweert
Weert
Echt
Susteren
Sittard
Geleen
Heerlen
Kerkrade
Simpelveld
Vaals
Maastricht
Eijsden
Visé
Herstal
Eupen
Verviers
Liège
Seraing
Oupeye
Amay
Huy
Andenne

Eindhoven
Someren
Veldhoven
Eersel
Baarle-Hertog
Bergeyk
Neerpelt
Lommel
Mol
Balen
Geel
Herentals
Beringen
Zonhoven
Hasselt
Diepenbeek
Genk
Maaseik
Bree
Kinrooi
Peer
Bilzen
Tongeren
Riemst
Landen
Waremme
Tienen
Éghezée
Gembloux
Namur
Ciney
Dinant
Rochefort
Marche-en-Famenne

Bastogne
Recogne
Neufchâteau
Étalle
Arlon
Aubange
Virton
Esch-sur-Alzette
Dudelange
Pétange
Differdange
LUXEMBOURG
Grevenmacher
Ettelbrück
Diekirch
Hosingen
Weiswampach
Malmédy
Botrange
694m

Antwerpen
(Antwerp)
Schoten
Brecht
Essen
Kalmthout
Kapellen
Stabroek
Beveren
Sint-Niklaas
Zele
Aalst
Mechelen
Duffel
Nijlen
Lier
Willebroek
Wemmel
Schaerbeek
BRUSSEL / BRUXELLES
(BRUSSELS)
Halle
Wavre
Leuven
Haacht
Overijse
Louvain-la-Neuve
Ottignies
Nivelles
Braine-le-Comte
Enghien
La Louvière
Binche
Anderlues
Charleroi
Châtelet
Gerpinnes
Thuin
Walcourt
Couvin

Brugge (Bruges)
Knokke-Heist
Zeebrugge
Blankenberge
Oostende
(Ostend)
Middelkerke
Koksijde
Veurne
Diksmuide
Torhout
Roeselare
Ieper
Poperinge
Kortrijk
Mouscron
Zwevegem
Izegem
Harelbeke
Deinze
Gavere
Eeklo
Maldegem
Aalter
Beernem
Gent (Ghent)
Laarne
Melle
Wetteren
Ninove
Geraardsbergen
Ath
Leuze-en-Hainaut
Péruwelz
Tournai
Mons
Jemappes
Frameries

Westerschelde
Zuid-Beveland
Vlissingen
Terneuzen
Axel
Hulst
Assenede
Oostburg

65

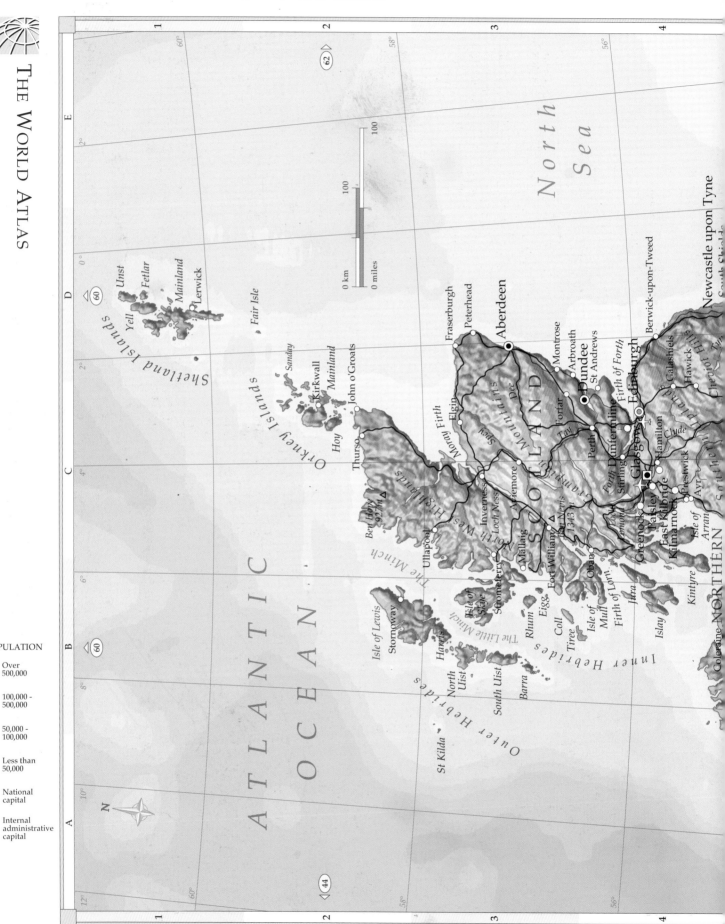

North Sea

ATLANTIC OCEAN

Shetland Islands

Unst
Yell
Fetlar
Mainland
Lerwick

Fair Isle

Sanday
Orkney Islands
Kirkwall
Mainland
Hoy

John o'Groats

Thurso

Ben Hope
927 m

North West Highlands

Ullapool

The Minch

Isle of Lewis
Stornoway

Harris

The Little Minch

North Uist
South Uist
Barra

Outer Hebrides

St Kilda

Isle of Skye
Stromeferry
Rhum
Eigg
Coll
Tiree
Isle of Mull

Mallaig
Fort William
Ben Nevis
1343 m

Oban
Firth of Lorn
Jura

Islay

Inner Hebrides

Kintyre
Isle of Arran

Fraserburgh
Peterhead
Aberdeen

Elgin
Moray Firth
Spey
Dee
Grampian Mountains

Inverness
Loch Ness
Aviemore

Montrose
Arbroath
Dundee
St Andrews
Forfar
Tay
Firth of Forth
Perth
Dunfermline
Stirling
Forth
Loch Lomond
Greenock
Paisley
Glasgow
Hamilton
Clyde
East Kilbride
Kilmarnock
Prestwick
Ayr

Edinburgh
Galashiels
Hawick
Southern Uplands
Cheviot Hills

Berwick-upon-Tweed

Newcastle upon Tyne

NORTHERN
Coleraine

SCOTLAND

N

POPULATION

- ⊙ Over 500,000
- ◉ 100,000 - 500,000
- ○ 50,000 - 100,000
- ○ Less than 50,000
- ● National capital
- ● Internal administrative capital

0 km   100
0 miles   100

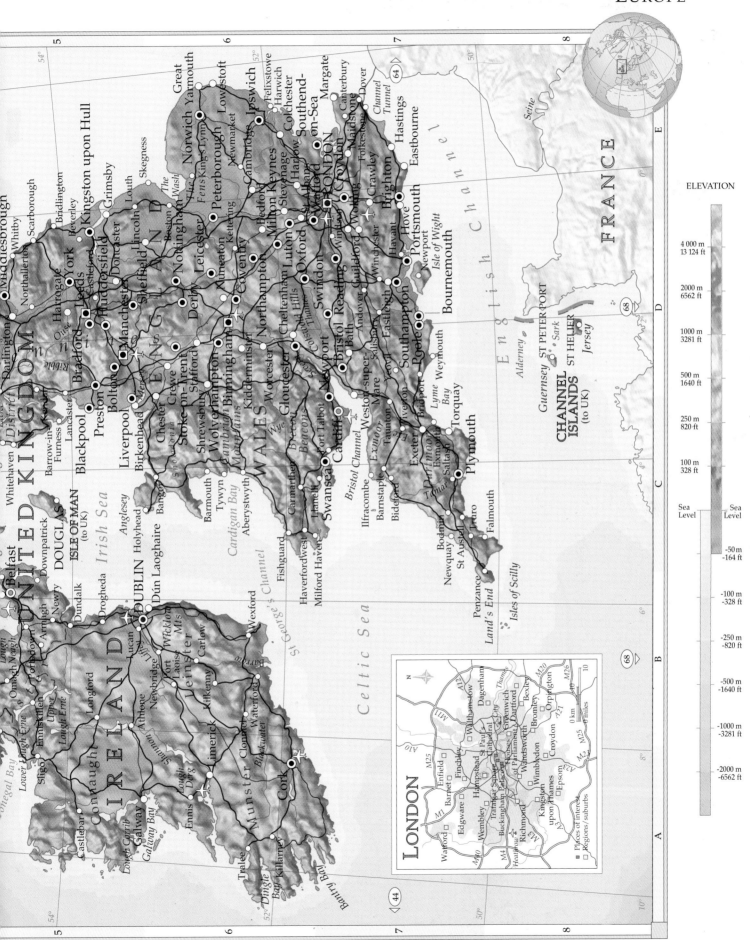

ELEVATION

4 000 m
13 124 ft

2000 m
6562 ft

1000 m
3281 ft

500 m
1640 ft

250 m
820 ft

100 m
328 ft

Sea Level — Sea Level

-50 m
-164 ft

-100 m
-328 ft

-250 m
-820 ft

-500 m
-1640 ft

-1000 m
-3281 ft

-2000 m
-6562 ft

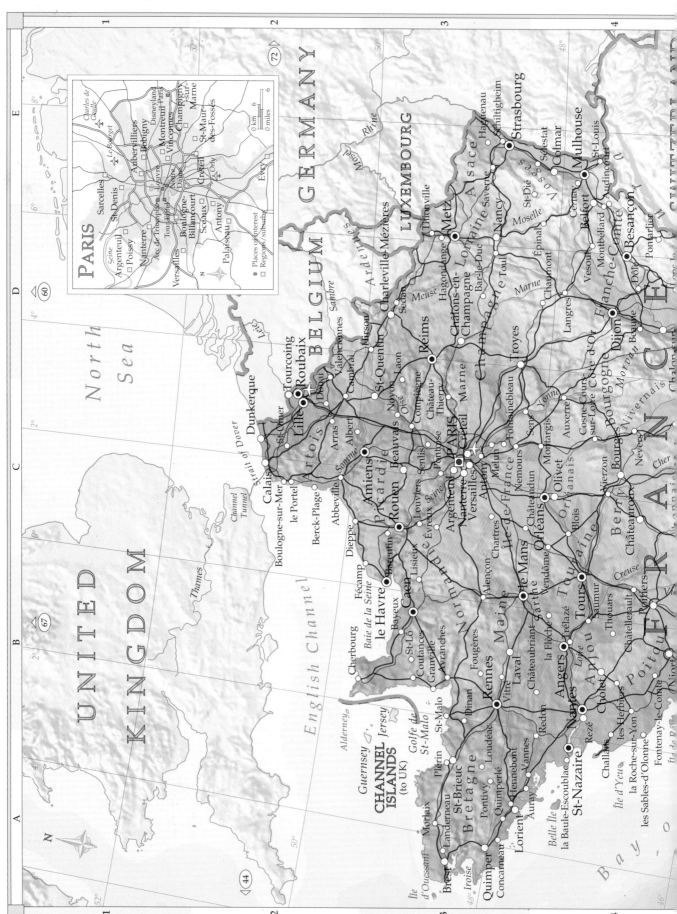

PARIS

Sarcelles
St-Denis
Argenteuil
Poissy
Nanterre
Arc de Triomphe
Tour Eiffel
Notre-Dame
Versailles
Boulogne-Billancourt
Sceaux
Antony
Palaiseau
Le Bourget
Aubervilliers
Disneyland
Bobigny
Montreuil-Paris
Vincennes
Louvre
Champigny-sur-Marne
St-Maur-des-Fossés
Créteil
Orly
Evry
Charles de Gaulle
Seine

Places of interest
Regions / suburbs

0 km 6
0 miles 6

GERMANY
LUXEMBOURG
BELGIUM
UNITED KINGDOM

North Sea

Strait of Dover
Channel Tunnel
English Channel

CHANNEL ISLANDS (to UK)
Guernsey
Alderney
Jersey
Golfe de St-Malo

Bay of

FRANCE

Dunkerque
Tourcoing
Roubaix
Lille
St-Omer
Calais
Boulogne-sur-Mer
le Portel
Berck-Plage
Abbeville
Dieppe
Fécamp
Baie de la Seine
le Havre
Bayeux
Caen
Cherbourg
St-Lô
Coutances
Granville
Avranches
Barentin
Lisieux
Rouen
Louviers
Évreux
Seine
Amiens
Picardie
Beauvais
Senlis
Pontoise
Compiègne
Noyon
Oise
Laon
Château-Thierry
St-Quentin
Cambrai
Valenciennes
Douai
Arras
Albert
Somme
Artois
Hirson
Charleville-Mézières
Sedan
Ardennes
Sambre
Meuse
Thionville
Hagondange
Metz
Châlons-en-Champagne
Bar-le-Duc
Toul
Nancy
Lunéville
Verdun
Reims
Épernay
Marne
Châteaudun
Troyes
Chaumont
Langres
St-Dié
Sarrebourg
Saverne
Lorraine
Moselle
Épinal
Vosges
Haguenau
Schiltigheim
Strasbourg
Sélestat
Colmar
Mulhouse
St-Louis
Audincourt
Cernay
Belfort
Montbéliard
Vesoul
Franche-Comté
Besançon
Pontarlier
Dole
Beaune
Dijon
Bourgogne
Nivernais
Morvan
Côte d'Or
Auxerre
Sens
Yonne
Montargis
Cosne-Cours-sur-Loire
Nevers
Bourges
Vierzon
Berry
Cher
Châteauroux
Creuse
Poitou
PARIS
Argenteuil
Nanterre
Créteil
Versailles
Antony
Melun
Île-de-France
Fontainebleau
Nemours
Montereau
Chartres
Orléans
Orléanais
Olivet
Blois
Vendôme
Touraine
Tours
Trélazé
Saumur
Thouars
Châtellerault
Poitiers
Fontenay-le-Comte
le Mans
Sarthe
Maine
Alençon
Laval
Fougères
Vitré
Rennes
Châteaubriant
la Flèche
Angers
Anjou
Loire
Cholet
les Herbiers
la Roche-sur-Yon
les Sables-d'Olonne
Île d'Yeu
Challans
Redon
Nantes
Rezé
St-Nazaire
la Baule-Escoublac
Bretagne
Loudéac
Pontivy
Hennebont
Lorient
Vannes
Auray
Belle Île
Quimperlé
Concarneau
Quimper
Douarnenez
Châteaulin
Carhaix-Plouguer
Morlaix
St-Brieuc
Plérin
Dinan
St-Malo
Landerneau
Brest
Île d'Ouessant
Iroise

POPULATION

- ◉ Over 500,000
- ◉ 100,000 – 500,000
- ○ 50,000 – 100,000
- ○ Less than 50,000
- ● National capital

N

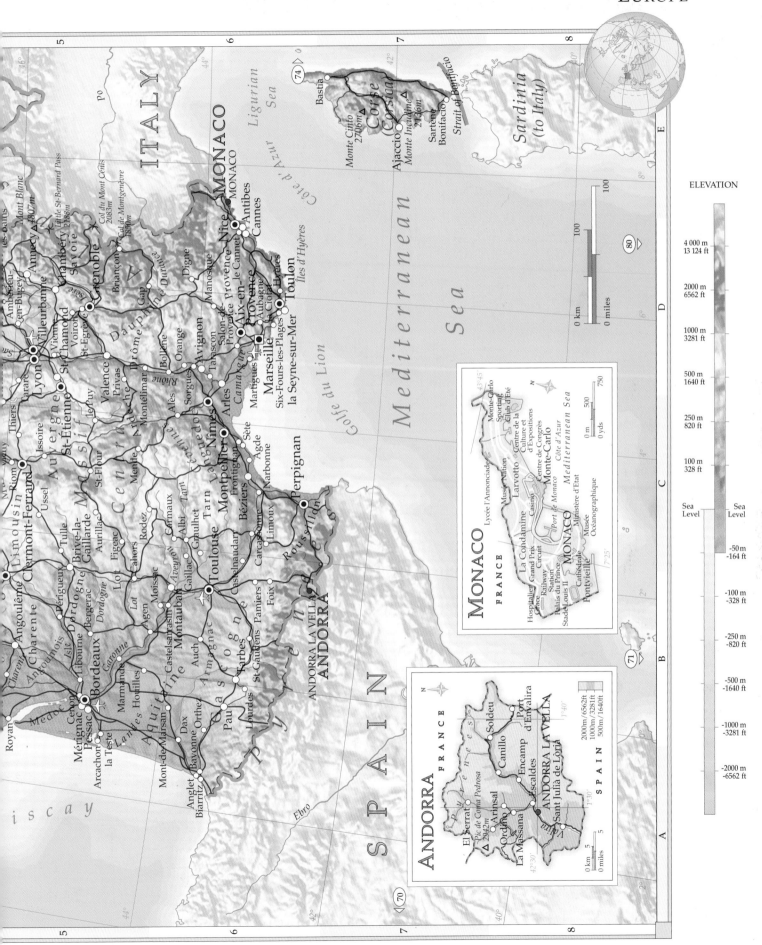

ITALY

Po

Ligurian Sea

MONACO
MONACO

Côte d'Azur

Mont Blanc
4807m
Col du Mont Cenis
2083m
Col du Petit St-Bernard Pass
Col de Montgenèvre
1850m
Little St-Bernard Pass
2188m
les-Bains
Ambérieu-
en-Bugey
Annecy
Chambéry
Savoie
Grenoble
Villeurbanne
Lyon
St-Chamond
Vienne
Voiron
St-Égrève
Tarare
Gap
Briançon
Digne
Durance
Dauphiné
Isère
Romans
le Puy
Valence
Privas
Montélimar
Drôme
Orange
Bollène
Avignon
Sorgues
Ardèche
Alès
Nîmes
Tarascon
Arles
Camargue
Salon-de-
Provence
Aix-en-
Provence
Aubagne
la Ciotat
Martigues
Marseille
Six-Fours-les-Plages
la Seyne-sur-Mer
Toulon
Hyères
Îles d'Hyères
Manosque
Provence
le Cannet
Antibes
Cannes
Nice

Golfe du Lion

Mediterranean Sea

Rhône
Thiers
Riom
Clermont-Ferrand
Issoire
St-Étienne
St-Flour
Auvergne
Ussel
Tulle
Aurillac
Brive-la-
Gaillarde
Massif
Central
Périgueux
Bergerac
Dordogne
Figeac
Rodez
Cahors
Millau
Tarn
Carmaux
Albi
Gaillac
Castres
Aveyron
Lot
Moissac
Castelnaudary
Agen
Montauban
Castelsarrasin
Toulouse
Narbonne
Béziers
Agde
Sète
Frontignan
Montpellier
Languedoc
Mende
Carcassonne
Limoux
Foix
Pamiers
Perpignan
Roussillon

Angoulême
Charente
Limousin
Angoumois
Isle
Libourne
Bordeaux
Cenon
Pessac
Mérignac
Médoc
Royan
Arcachon
la Teste
Landes
Dax
Mont-de-Marsan
Orthez
Bayonne
Anglet
Biarritz
Pau
Lourdes
Tarbes
Auch
St-Gaudens
Gascogne
Armagnac
Garonne
Marmande
Aquitaine
Gironde
Dordogne
Lot

Pyrénées

SPAIN

Ebro

Biscay

ANDORRA LA VELLA
ANDORRA

Corse
(Corsica)
Bastia
Monte Cinto
2706m
Ajaccio
Monte Incudine
2136m
Sartène
Bonifacio
Strait of Bonifacio

Sardinia
(to Italy)

MONACO

FRANCE

Monte-Carlo
Sporting Club d'Été
Larvotto
Musée National
Centre de Culture et d'Expositions
Centre de Congrès
Lycée l'Annonciade
Monte-Carlo
Casino
Grace
Hospital
Railway Station
La Condamine
Grand Prix Circuit
Port de Monaco
Palais du Prince
Stade Louis II
Pontvieille
Cathédrale
Musée Océanographique
Ministère d'État
MONACO

Mediterranean Sea

ANDORRA

FRANCE

Pyrénées

Soldeu
Canillo
Port d'Envalira
El Serrat
Pic de Coma Pedrosa
2942m
Ordino
Arinsal
La Massana
Encamp
Escaldes
ANDORRA LA VELLA
Sant Julià de Lòria
Valira

SPAIN

2000m/6562ft
1000m/3281ft
500m/1640ft

69

SPAIN & PORTUGAL

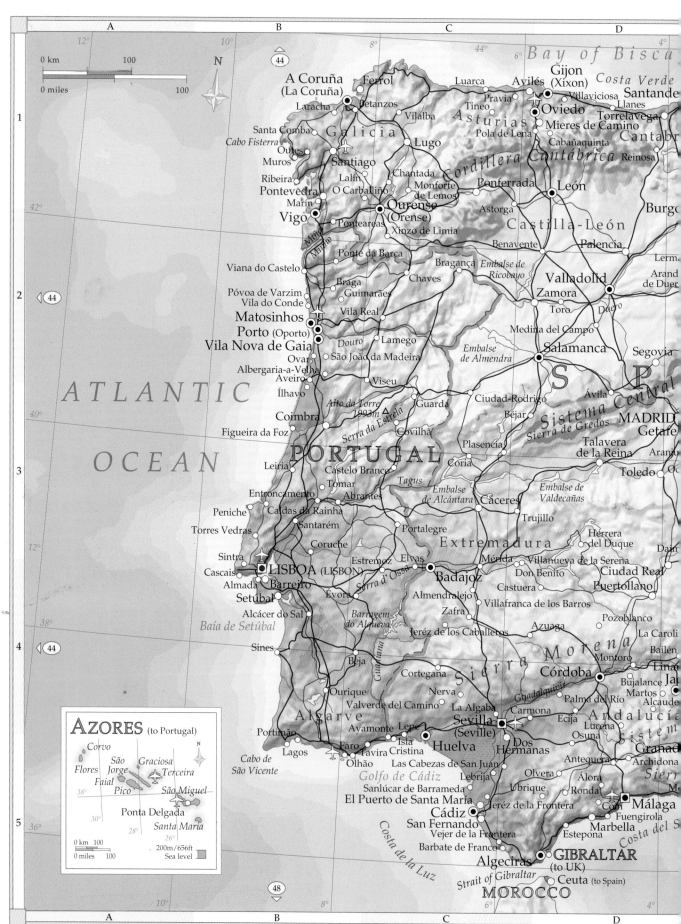

POPULATION

- ◉ Over 500,000
- ◉ 100,000 – 500,000
- ○ 50,000 – 100,000
- ○ Less than 50,000
- ● National capital

AZORES (to Portugal)

Corvo
Flores
São Jorge   Graciosa
Faial   Terceira
Pico
São Miguel
Ponta Delgada
Santa Maria

0 km 100
0 miles 100

200m/656ft
Sea level

FRANCE

Golfe du Lion

ELEVATION

4000 m
13 124 ft

2000 m
6562 ft

1000 m
3281 ft

500 m
1640 ft

250 m
820 ft

100 m
328 ft

Sea Level — Sea Level

-250 m
-820 ft

-500 m
-1640 ft

-1000 m
-3281 ft

-2000 m
-6562 ft

-3000 m
-9843 ft

-4000 m
-13 124 ft

edo · Bermeo
Zarautz
Eibar
Donostia-San Sebastián
Irún
lbao · Tolosa
Bergara
País Vasco · Pamplona (Iruña)
Vitoria-Gasteiz
Miranda de Ebro
Estella
Logroño
Arnedo · Calahorra
La Rioja
Tudela
Tarazona
Soria
Sistema Ibérico
Navarra
Jaca
Monte Perdido 3348m
La Seu d'Urgell
Berga
Manlleu
Huesca
Barbastro
Monzón
Ejea de los Caballeros
Ebro
Zaragoza
Lleida (Lérida)
Cervera
Balaguer
Tàrrega
Fraga
Aragón
Calatayud
Daroca
Alcañiz
Medinaceli
El Burgo de Osma
Guadalajara
Alcalá de Henares
rrejón de Ardoz
Sierra de Guadarrama
Tajo
Teruel
Javalambre 2020m △
Cuenca
Tarancón
Castilla-La Mancha
Mota del Cuervo
Campo de Criptana
Socuéllamos
Tomelloso
La Roda
Manzanares
La Solana
depeñas
Villanueva de los Infantes
Albacete
Almansa
Ontinyent
Villena
Jumilla
Hellín
Segura
Beas de Segura
Moratalla
Villacarrillo
beda
Cazorla
Béticos
Murcia
Huéscar
Baza
Guadix
Mulhacén 3481m
Nevada
Berja
Adra
Almería
Mojácar
Aguilas
Lorca
Totana
Murcia
Elche (Elx)
Orihuela
Callosa de Segura
La Unión
Cartagena
Costa Blanca
Monóvar
San Juan de Alicante
Alicante (Alacant)
Elda
Villajoyosa
Benidorm
Alcoy
Dénia
Oliva
Gandía
Xàtiva
Cullera
Algemesí
Sueca
Catarroja
Torrent
Valencia
Sagunto
Burjassot
Vall d' Uxó
Burriana
Castelló de la Plana
Onda
Costa del Azahar
Golfo de Valencia
Vinaròs
Sant Carles de la Ràpita
Amposta
Tortosa
Costa Dorada
Reus
Tarragona
El Vendrell
Sitges
Valls
Vilafranca del Penedès
L'Hospitalet de Llobregat
Barcelona
Mataró
Arenys de Mar
Terrassa
Sabadell
Vic
Cataluña
Banyoles
Blanes
Palamós
Palafrugell
Girona (Gerona)
Figueres
Ripoll
ANDORRA
Costa Brava

Eivissa (Ibiza)
Eivissa
Formentera

Islas Baleares (Balearic Islands)

Cabrera
Mallorca (Majorca)
Palma
Llucmajor
Manacor
Felanitx
Sa Pobla
Pollença

Ciutadella de Menorca
Menorca (Minorca)
Mahón

Mediterranean Sea

ALGERIA

68

74

75

49

SPAIN

GIBRALTAR (to UK)

N
5° 21'
SPAIN
Gibraltar Airport
North Mole
Gibraltar Harbour
Bay of Gibraltar
Catalan Bay
The Rock
Catalan Bay
36° 8'
Summit 426m △
Sandy Bay
Rosia
Rosia Bay
Buena Vista
Little Bay
Europa Point
Strait of Gibraltar

200m/656ft
Sea level
0 km   1
0 mile   1

71

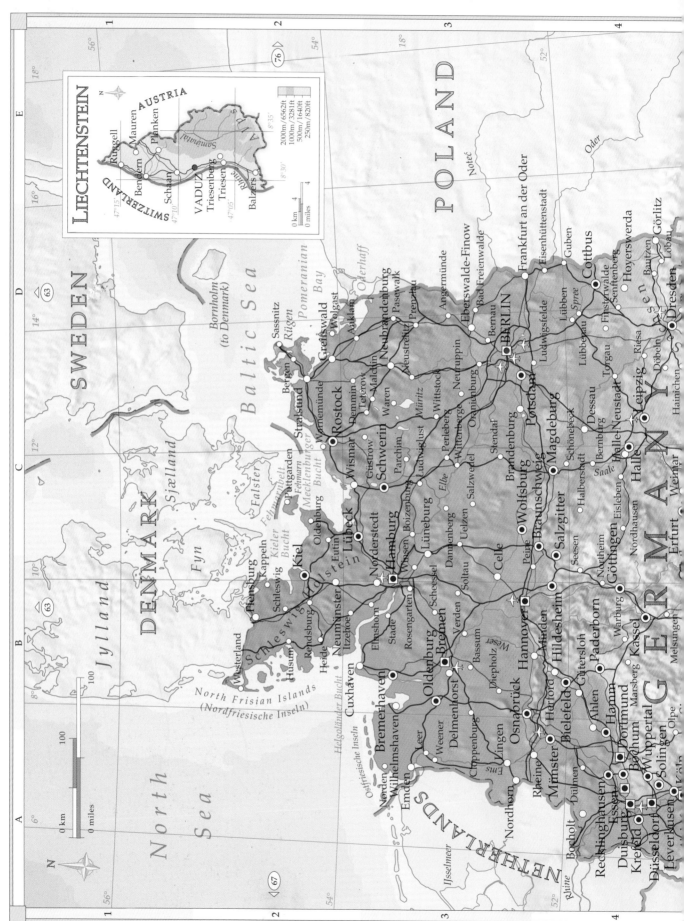

LIECHTENSTEIN

AUSTRIA

SWITZERLAND

Ruggell
Mauren
Planken
Benders
Schaan
VADUZ
Triesenberg
Triesen
Balzers

2000m / 6562ft
1000m / 3281ft
500m / 1640ft
250m / 820ft

0 km
0 miles

POLAND

Oder

Notec

POPULATION

- Over 500,000
- 100,000 – 500,000
- 50,000 – 100,000
- Less than 50,000
- National capital

SWEDEN

DENMARK

Jylland

Sjælland

Fyn

Falster

Bornholm (to Denmark)

Baltic Sea

Rügen

Pomeranian Bay

Sassnitz
Bergen
Stralsund
Greifswald
Wolgast
Oderhaff
Warnemünde
Rostock
Wismar
Demmin
Teterow
Maldin
Anklam
Neubrandenburg
Ueckermünde
Pasewalk
Prenzlau
Angermünde
Eberswalde-Finow
Bad Freienwalde
Frankfurt an der Oder
Eisenhüttenstadt
Guben
Cottbus
Hoyerswerda
Görlitz
Löbau
Bautzen
Dresden
Döbeln
Riesa
Torgau
Leipzig
Halle
Weimar
Erfurt
Nordhausen
Eisleben
Halle-Neustadt
Bernburg
Dessau
Schönebeck
Halberstadt
Magdeburg
Brandenburg
Potsdam
BERLIN
Oranienburg
Neuruppin
Wittenberg
Perleberg
Wittstock
Müritz
Neustrelitz
Waren
Parchim
Schwerin
Güstrow
Ludwigslust
Boizenburg
Lüneburg
Wittenberge
Salzwedel
Stendal
Wolfsburg
Braunschweig
Salzgitter
Seesen
Göttingen
Warburg
Kassel
Marsberg
Paderborn
Gütersloh
Bielefeld
Herford
Minden
Hildesheim
Hannover
Celle
Peine
Uelzen
Soltau
Dannenberg
Verden
Bassum
Diepholz
Osnabrück
Rheine
Münster
Ahlen
Hamm
Dortmund
Bochum
Essen
Recklinghausen
Duisburg
Krefeld
Düsseldorf
Solingen
Leverkusen
Wuppertal
Dülmen
Bocholt
Nordhorn
Lingen
Cloppenburg
Meppen
Weener
Leer
Emden
Norden
Wilhelmshaven
Delmenhorst
Oldenburg
Bremen
Bremerhaven
Cuxhaven
Stade
Elmshorn
Buxtehude
Rosengarten
Scheessel
Wümme
Soltau
Hamburg
Norderstedt
Lübeck
Eutin
Oldenburg
Kiel
Kappeln
Schleswig
Flensburg
Husum
Heide
Rendsburg
Neumünster
Itzehoe
Westerland
Holstein
Schleswig
Kieler Bucht
Fehmarn
Poltgarden
Mecklenburger Bucht
Fehmarnbelt
Helgoländer Bucht

Helgoland
Ostfriesische Inseln

North Frisian Islands (Nordfriesische Inseln)

NETHERLANDS

Rhine
Ems
Weser
Elbe
Saale
IJsselmeer

North Sea

GERMANY

0 km 100
0 miles 100

N

CZECH REPUBLIC

SLOVAKIA

HUNGARY

AUSTRIA

SLOVENIA

CROATIA

ITALY

SWITZERLAND

FRANCE

BELGIUM

LUX.

Hessen

Bayern

Tirol

LIECHTENSTEIN

WIEN (VIENNA)

Mistelbach an der Jaya
Hollabrunn
Tulln
Perchtoldsdorf
Traiskirchen
Bad Vöslau
Wiener Neustadt
Eisenstadt
Neusiedler See
Neusiedl
Sankt Pölten
Zwettl
Mürzzuschlag
Leoben
Judenburg
Graz
Mur
Maribor
Ptuj
Drava
Murska Sobota
Velenje
Celje
Trbovlje
Novo mesto
Krško
Kočevje
San
LJUBLJANA
Jesenice
Kranj
Klagenfurt
Loibl Pass 1367m
Wolfsberg
Villach
Tolmin
Nova Gorica
Postojna
Koper
Istra
Gulf of Venice

Linz
Danube (Donau)
Wels
Hauzenberg
Passau
Deggendorf
Ried im Innkreis
Vöcklabruck
Steyr
Enns
Salzburg
Ebensee
Bad Ischl
Traun
Hohe Tauern
Grossglockner 3798m
Gesäuse
Lienz
Plöcken Pass 1357m

Plauen
Hof
Suhl
Fulda
Giessen
Wetzlar
Marktredwitz
Münchberg
Bayreuth
Lichtenfels
Kronach
Coburg
Bamberg
Schweinfurt
Würzburg
Forchheim
Erlangen
Fürth
Nürnberg (Nuremberg)
Schwandorf
Regenstauf
Regensburg
Straubing
Landshut
Pocking
Inn
München (Munich)
Rosenheim
Schwaz
Innsbruck
Brenner Pass 1374m
Kufstein
Kitzbühel
Zell am See

Bohemian Forest
Danube (Donau)
Elbe

Marburg
Fulda
Frankfurt am Main
Main
Offenbach
Bad Homburg vor der Höhe
Darmstadt
Aschaffenburg
Pfungstadt
Mannheim
Heidelberg
Ludwigshafen
Worms
Neustadt an der Weinstrasse
Heilbronn
Sinsheim
Ludwigsburg
Stuttgart
Sindelfingen
Göppingen
Aalen
Heidenheim an der Brenz
Weissenburg in Bayern
Ingolstadt
Donauwörth
Augsburg
Mindelheim
Memmingen
Kaufbeuren
Kempten
Füssen
Friedrichshafen
Lake Constance
Konstanz
Bregenz
Sankt Gallen
VADUZ
St Moritz
Klosters

Aachen
Andernach
Koblenz
Boppard
Wiesbaden
Mainz
Rhine (Rhein)
Bingen
Bad Kreuznach
Kaiserslautern
Neunkirchen
Saarbrücken
Karlsruhe
Pforzheim
Baden-Baden
Kehl
Offenburg
Reutlingen
Tübingen
Rottweil
Villingen
Schwenningen
Lahr
Emmendingen
Freiburg im Breisgau
Bad Krozingen
Müllheim
Lörrach
Basel
Schaffhausen
Singen
Stockach
Schwäbische Alb
Ulm
Neu-Ulm
Donau
Neckar
Vosges
Schwarzwald
Rhine (Rhein)

Trier
Bitburg
Wittlich
Birkenfeld
Merzig
Eifel
Rheinisches Schiefergebirge
Blankenheim

Winterthur
Bülach
Zürich
Zürichsee
Uster
Schwyz
Zug
Luzern
BERN
Thun
Thuner See
Sion
Montreux
Neuchâtel
Lac de Neuchâtel
La Chaux-de-Fonds
Lausanne
Lake Geneva
Genève (Geneva)
Onex
Rhône
Biel/Bienne
Aare
Berner Alpen
Berner Oberland
Pennine Alps
Matterhorn 4478m
Monte Rosa
Brig
Great Saint Bernard Pass 2469m
Simplon Pass 2005m
Locarno
Bellinzona
Lugano
Lake Maggiore

San Gottardo
Reuss
Chur

Po Valley
Po

ELEVATION

4000 m	13 124 ft
2000 m	6562 ft
1000 m	3281 ft
500 m	1640 ft
250 m	820 ft
100 m	328 ft
Sea Level	Sea Level
-10 m	-33 ft
-25 m	-82 ft
-50 m	-164 ft
-100 m	-328 ft
-250 m	-820 ft
-500 m	-1640 ft

ITALY

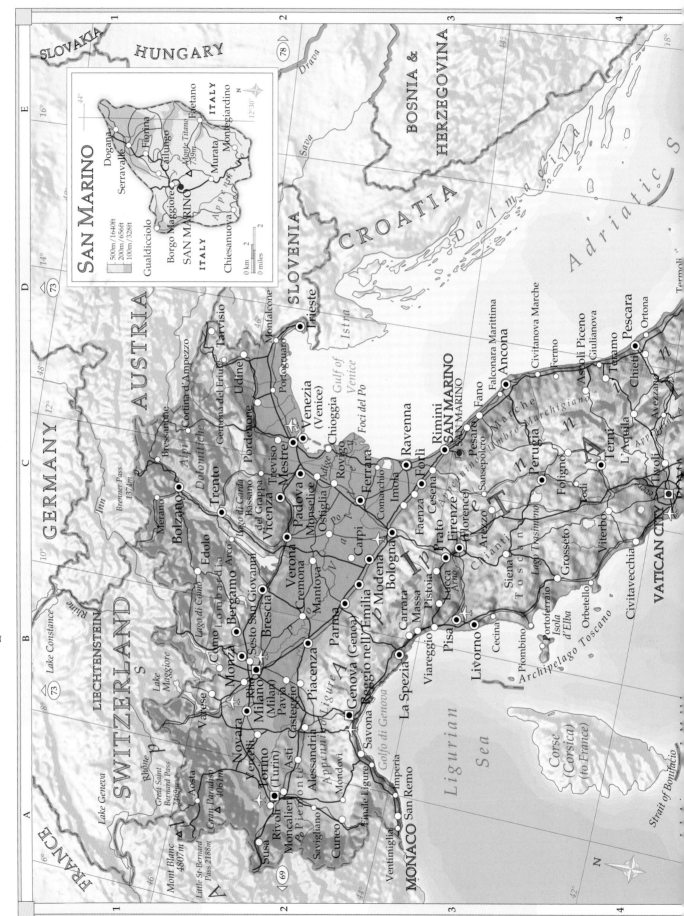

SAN MARINO

500m/1640ft	
200m/656ft	
100m/328ft	

Dogana
Serravalle
Fiorina
Gualdicciolo
Borgo Maggiore
Montegiardino
Faetano
Monte Titano 739m
Murata
SAN MARINO
ITALY
Chiesanuova

ITALY

0 km   2
0 miles   2

POPULATION

- ◉ Over 500,000
- ⊙ 100,000 – 500,000
- ○ 50,000 – 100,000
- ○ Less than 50,000
- ● National capital

SLOVAKIA
HUNGARY
AUSTRIA
GERMANY
SWITZERLAND
LIECHTENSTEIN
FRANCE
MONACO
SLOVENIA
CROATIA
Bosnia & Herzegovina
Adriatic Sea
Ligurian Sea

Lake Geneva
Lake Constance
Lake Maggiore
Lago di Como
Lago di Garda

Mont Blanc 4807m
Gran Paradiso 4061m
Great Saint Bernard Pass 2469m
Little St-Bernard Pass 2188m
Brenner Pass 1374m

Trieste
Monfalcone
Portogruaro
Tarvisio
Udine
Gemona del Friuli
Pordenone
Cortina d'Ampezzo
Bressanone
Merano
Bolzano
Trento
Dolomitiche
Alpi
Edolo
Arco
Bassano del Grappa
Treviso
Mestre
Venezia (Venice)
Chioggia
Gulf of Venice
Foci del Po
Vicenza
Padova
Monselice
Ostiglia
Rovigo
Adige
Comacchio
Ravenna
Ferrara
Imola
Faenza
Forlì
Cesena
Rimini
SAN MARINO
Pesaro
Fano
Falconara Marittima
Ancona
Civitanova Marche
Fermo
Ascoli Piceno
Giulianova
Teramo
Pescara
Ortona
Chieti
Termoli
Avezzano
Tivoli
VATICAN CITY
Viterbo
Orbetello
Civitavecchia
Grosseto
Siena
Arezzo
Sansepolcro
Perugia
Foligno
Todi
Terni
L'Aquila
Lago Trasimeno
Chianti
Toscana
Firenze (Florence)
Prato
Pistoia
Lucca
Arno
Pisa
Viareggio
Livorno
Cecina
Piombino
Portoferraio
Isola d'Elba
Archipelago Toscano
Corse (Corsica) (to France)
Strait of Bonifacio
Carrara
Massa
La Spezia
Golfo di Genova
Savona
Finale Ligure
Imperia
San Remo
Ventimiglia
Genova (Genoa)
Reggio nell'Emilia
Parma
Piacenza
Pavia
Castèggio
Alessandria
Asti
Torino (Turin)
Moncalieri
Rivoli
Susa
Savigliano
Cuneo
Mondovì
Appennino Ligure
Appennino Piemonte
Novara
Vercelli
Varese
Como
Lombardia
Bergamo
Sesto San Giovanni
Monza
Milano (Milan)
Brescia
Cremona
Mantova
Verona
Modena
Bologna
Carpi
Appennino Emilia
Aosta

Inn
Rhône
Rhine
Drava
Sava
Po
Istra
Gulf of Venice
Marche
Umbro Marchigiano
Appennino Tosco
Dalmacija

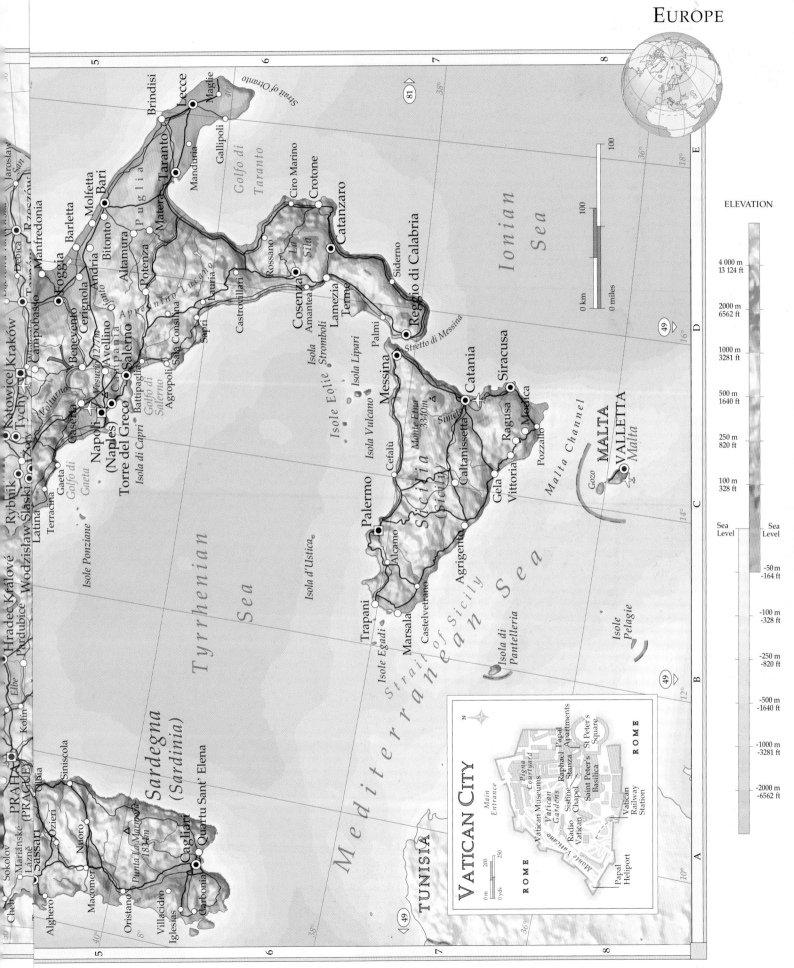

EUROPE

ELEVATION

4 000 m	13 124 ft
2000 m	6562 ft
1000 m	3281 ft
500 m	1640 ft
250 m	820 ft
100 m	328 ft
Sea Level	Sea Level
-50 m	-164 ft
-100 m	-328 ft
-250 m	-820 ft
-500 m	-1640 ft
-1000 m	-3281 ft
-2000 m	-6562 ft

Map labels

Jarosław
San
Rzeszów
Dębica
Tarnów
Kraków
Katowice
Rybnik
Żory
Tychy
Wodzisław Śląski

Sokolov
Cheb
Mariánské Lázně
Hradec Králové
Pardubice
PRAHA (PRAGUE)
Kolín
Elbe

Brindisi
Lecce
Maglie
Taranto
Manduria
Gallipoli
Strait of Otranto
Golfo di Taranto

Molfetta
Bari
Barletta
Manfredonia
Bitonto
Andria
Cerignola
Altamura
Matera
Foggia
Benevento
Campobasso
Avellino
Potenza
Puglia
Appenino Lucano
Basento
Agri
Sinni

Ciro Marino
Crotone
Catanzaro
Rossano
La Sila
Castrovillari
Cosenza
Amantea
Lamezia Terme
Siderno
Reggio di Calabria
Sapri
Sala Consilina

Napoli (Naples)
Caserta
Salerno
Battipaglia
Golfo di Salerno
Agropoli
Torre del Greco
Vesuvio 1277m
Campania
Volturno
Gaeta
Golfo di Gaeta
Terracina
Latina
Isole Ponziane

Isola di Capri
Isola d'Ustica
Isole Eolie
Isola Stromboli
Isola Lipari
Isola Vulcano

Stretto di Messina
Messina
Monte Etna 3340m
Catania
Siracusa
Simeto
Caltanissetta
Enna
Ragusa
Modica
Pozzallo
Cefalù
Palermo
Alcamo
Sicilia (Sicily)
Gela
Vittoria
Agrigento
Castelvetrano
Marsala
Trapani
Isole Egadi

Malta Channel
Gozo
MALTA
VALLETTA
Malta

Ionian Sea

Tyrrhenian Sea

Mediterranean Sea

Strait of Sicily

Isola di Pantelleria
Isole Pelagie

TUNISIA

Sardegna (Sardinia)
Siniscola
Olbia
Ozieri
Sassari
Nuoro
Macomer
Alghero
Oristano
Villacidro
Iglesias
Carbonia
Cagliari
Quartu Sant' Elena
Punta La Marmora 1834m

Vatican City inset

VATICAN CITY

N

Main Entrance
Vatican Museums
Pigna Courtyard
Raphael Stanza
Sistine Chapel
Radio Vatican
Papal Apartments
Saint Peter's Basilica
St Peter's Square
Vatican Railway Station
Monte Vaticano
Papal Heliport

ROME

0 m   200
0 yds   250

75

SOUTHEAST EUROPE

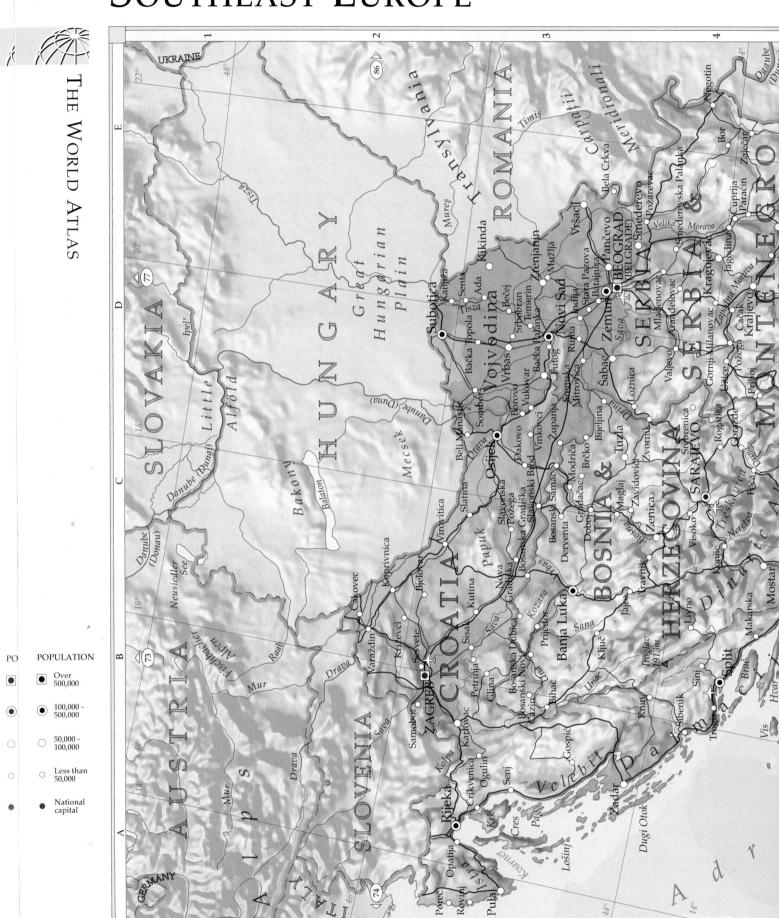

POPULATION

- ● Over 500,000
- ◉ 100,000 – 500,000
- ○ 50,000 – 100,000
- ○ Less than 50,000
- ● National capital

BULGARIA

(YUGOSLAVIA)

MACEDONIA

GREECE

ALBANIA

ITALY

MONTENEGRO

KOSOVO

SKOPJE

TIRANË (TIRANA)

Pirot
Vlasotince
Surdulica
Leskovac
Vranje
Južna Morava
Bujanovac
Preševo
Gnjilane
Kumanovo
Kratovo
Kočani
Štip
Radoviš
Strumica
Bregalnica
Strumešnica
Vardar
Kavadarci
Gevgelija
Negotino
Prilep
Crna Reka
Bitola
Lake Prespa
Lake Ohrid
Ohrid
Struga
Pogradec
Devollit
Korçë
Kičevo
Veles
Gostivar
Tetovo
Uroševac
Prizren
Priština
aonik
Leskovac
Podujevo
Vučitrn
Kosovska Mitrovica
Kosovo Polje
Peć
Orahovac
Berane
North
Albanian Alps
Bajram Curri
2558m
Đakovica
Drenica
Kukës
Drini
Peshkopi
Burrel
Debar
Black Drim
Elbasan
Lumi i Shkumbinit
Librazhd
Kavajë
Kuçovë
Berat
Lumi Osumit
Fier
Lushnjë
Lumi i Devollit
Tepelenë
Gjirokastër
Lumi i Vjosës
Vlorë
Sarandë
Konispol
Përmet
Durrës
Laç
Krujë
Lezhë
Shkodër
Lake Scutari
Bar
Podgorica
Cetinje
Kotor
Nikšić
Trebinje
Dubrovnik
Mljet
Palagruža

Píndos (Píndus Mountains)
Pineiós
Aegean Sea
Thermaïkós Kólpos
Strymónas
Évvoia (Euboea)

Ionian Sea
Iónioi Nísoi (Ionian Islands)
Kérkyra (Corfu)
Lefkáda
Kefallinía
Strait of Otranto

Adriatic Sea

Golfo di Taranto
Appennino Lucano

82
83
81
75

ELEVATION

4 000 m	13 124 ft
2000 m	6562 ft
1000 m	3281 ft
500 m	1640 ft
250 m	820 ft
100 m	328 ft
Sea Level	Sea Level
-50 m	-164 ft
-100 m	-328 ft
-250 m	-820 ft
-500 m	-1640 ft
-1000 m	-3281 ft
-2000 m	-6562 ft

100 km
100 miles
0 km
0 miles

N

BOSNIA & HERZEGOVINA

CROATIA
SERBIA
SERB. & MON. (YUGO.)
MONTENEGRO
CROATIA

Bihać
Banja Luka
Bosna
Sava
Brčko
Tuzla
Drina
Sarajevo
Goražde
Mostar
Split
Dubrovnik
Adriatic Sea

Territorial extent
Republika Srpska
Federacija Bosna i Hercegovina

50 km
50 miles

THE MEDITERRANEAN

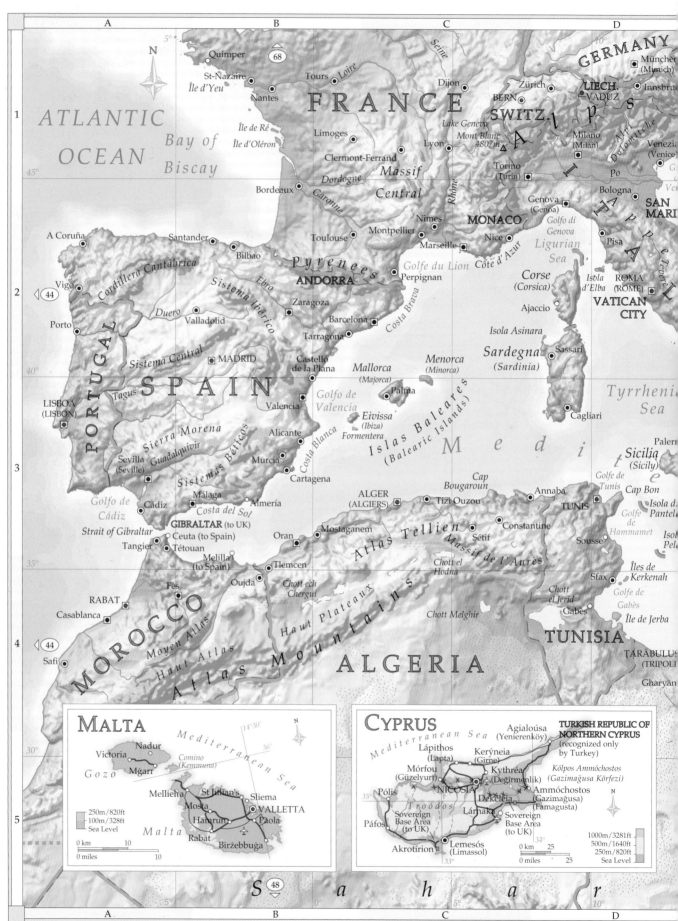

POPULATION

- ◼ Over 500,000
- ◉ 100,000 – 500,000
- ○ 50,000 – 100,000
- ○ Less than 50,000
- ● National capital

MALTA

Mediterranean Sea

Gozo

Victoria
Nadur
Comino (Kemmuna)
Mġarr

Mellieħa
St Julian's
Sliema
Mosta
VALLETTA
Ħamrun
Paola
Rabat
Birżebbuġa

Malta

250m/820ft
100m/328ft
Sea Level

0 km 10
0 miles 10

CYPRUS

Mediterranean Sea

Agialoúsa (Yenierenköy)

TURKISH REPUBLIC OF NORTHERN CYPRUS
(recognized only by Turkey)

Lápithos (Lapta)
Kerýneia (Girne)
Mórfou (Güzelyurt)
Kythréa (Degirmenlik)
Pólis
NICOSIA
Dekélcia
Ammóchostos (Gazimağusa / Famagusta)
Kólpos Ammóchostos (Gazimağusa Körfezi)
Páfos
Troódos
Lárnaka
Sovereign Base Area (to UK)
Sovereign Base Area (to UK)
Akrotírion
Lemesós (Limassol)

1000m/3281ft
500m/1640ft
250m/820ft
Sea Level

0 km 25
0 miles 25

ELEVATION

4000 m	13 124 ft
2000 m	6562 ft
1000 m	3281 ft
500 m	1640 ft
250 m	820 ft
100 m	328 ft
Sea Level	Sea Level
-250 m	-820 ft
-500 m	-1640 ft
-1000 m	-3281 ft
-2000 m	-6562 ft
-3000 m	-9843 ft
-4000 m	-13 124 ft

SLOVAKIA
WIEN (VIENNA)
Danube
BUDAPEST
Satu Mare
Carpathian Mountains
Bâlti
86
UKRAINE
Kakhovs'ka Vodoskhovyshche
HUNGARY
Great Hungarian Plain
Târgu Mures
Tisza
MOLD.
CHIŞINĂU
Dniester
Odesa
Dnieper
Berdyans'k
Sea of Azov
ROMANIA
Carpaţii Meridonali
ZAGREB
CROATIA
Novi Sad
Galaţi
Kerch
RUSS. FED.
Kryms'kyy Pivostrov
Sava
BOSNIA & HERZ.
BEOGRAD (BELGRADE)
BUCUREŞTI (BUCHAREST)
Danube
Constanţa
Sevastopol'
Novorossiysk
SARAJEVO
Dalmacija
SERBIA & MONTENEGRO (YUGOSLAVIA)
BULGARIA
Varna
Black Sea
Adriatic Sea
Priština
Balkan Mountains
Burgas
SOFIYA (SOFIA)
SKOPJE
MACED.
Rhodope Mountains
Edirne
İstanbul Boğazi (Bosporus)
95
Küre Dağları
TIRANË (TIRANA)
Bari
ALBANIA
İstanbul
Zonguldak
Samsun
Ordu
Naples
Lecce
Strait of Otranto
Pindos (Pindus) Mts
Thessaloniki (Salonica)
Límnos
Marmara Denizi
Bursa
ANKARA
Kizil Irmak
Vesuvio 1277m
Kérkyra (Corfu)
Ionian Sea
GREECE
Lárisa
Aegean Sea
Balıkesir
TURKEY
Cosenza
Golfo di Taranto
Catanzaro
Kefallinía
Chíos
İzmir
Tuz Gölü
Kayseri
Monte Etna 3340m
ATHÍNA (ATHENS)
Sámos
Kykládes (Cyclades)
Dodekánisos (Dodecanese)
Toros Dağları
Gaziantep
Catania
Zákynthos
Mirtóo Pelagos
Antalya
Adana
Siracusa
Kýthira
Kritikó Pélagos (Sea of Crete)
Ródos (Rhodes)
Antalya Körfezi
İskenderun Körfezi
Halab (Aleppo)
MALLETTA
MALTA
Kárpathos
NICOSIA
CYPRUS
Lárnaka
SYRIA
Euphrates
Irákleio
Kríti (Crete)
Lemesós (Limassol)
LEBANON
BEYROUTH (BEIRUT)
DIMASHQ (DAMASCUS)
97
Hefa
ISRAEL
Tel Aviv-Yafo
AMMĀN
Darnah
Misrātah
Banghāzi (Benghazi)
JERUSALEM
Gaza
Dead Sea
Khalīj Surt (Gulf of Sirte)
Libyan Plateau
Alexandria
Nile Delta
Port Said
Suez Canal
JORDAN
Surt
Ajdābiyā
Great Sand Sea
Monkhafad al Qattāra (Qattāra Depression)
CAIRO
Suez
Elat
Al 'Aqabah
Waddān
El Gîza
Sinai
SAUDI ARABIA
LIBYA
Libyan Desert
EGYPT
Nile
Sahara el Sharqīya (Eastern Desert)
Gulf of Suez
Red Sea
50

0 km 400
0 miles 400

81

BULGARIA & GREECE

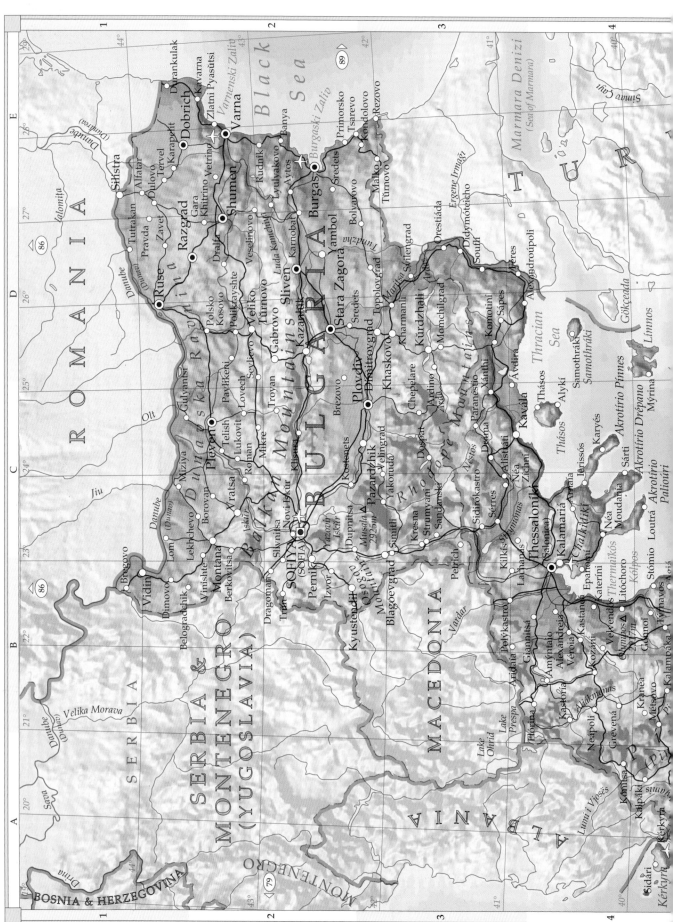

POPULATION

- ▣ Over 500,000
- ◉ 100,000 – 500,000
- ○ 50,000 – 100,000
- ○ Less than 50,000
- ● National capital

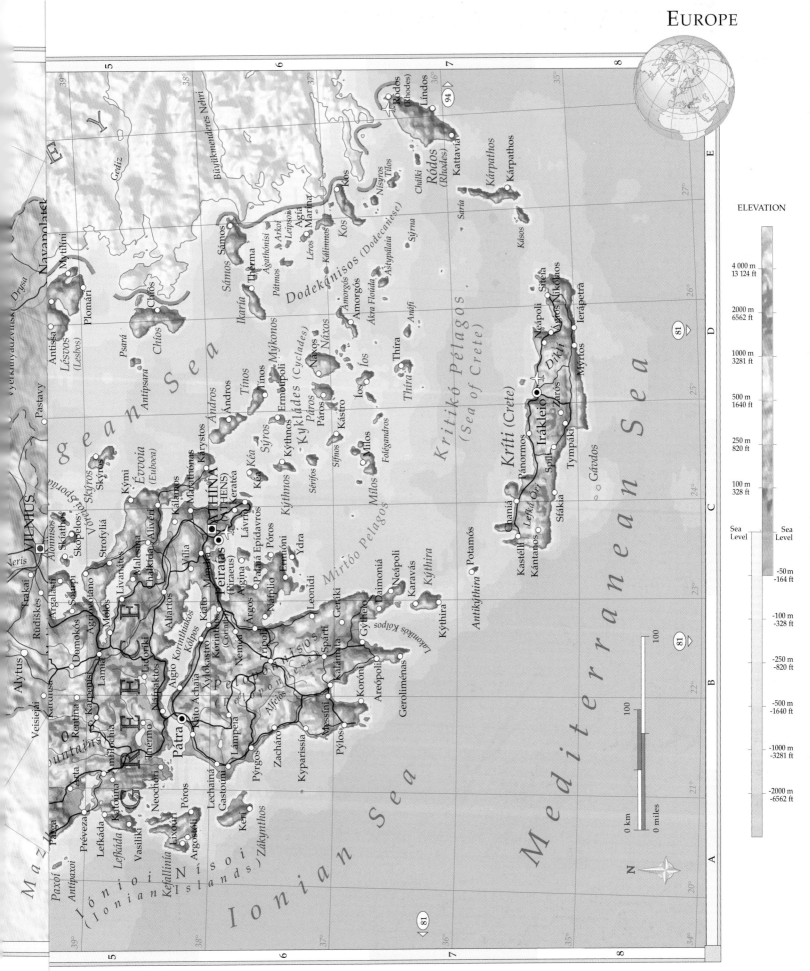

EUROPE

ELEVATION

4 000 m
13 124 ft

2000 m
6562 ft

1000 m
3281 ft

500 m
1640 ft

250 m
820 ft

100 m
328 ft

Sea
Level

Sea
Level

-50 m
-164 ft

-100 m
-328 ft

-250 m
-820 ft

-500 m
-1640 ft

-1000 m
-3281 ft

-2000 m
-6562 ft

Mediterranean Sea

Ionian Sea

Aegean Sea

Kritikó Pélagos (Sea of Crete)

Mírtóo Pélagos

Kríti (Crete)

Ródos (Rhodes)

Dodekánisos (Dodecanese)

Kykládes (Cyclades)

GREECE

Peloponnisos

Athína (Athens)

UKRAINE, MOLDOVA & ROMANIA

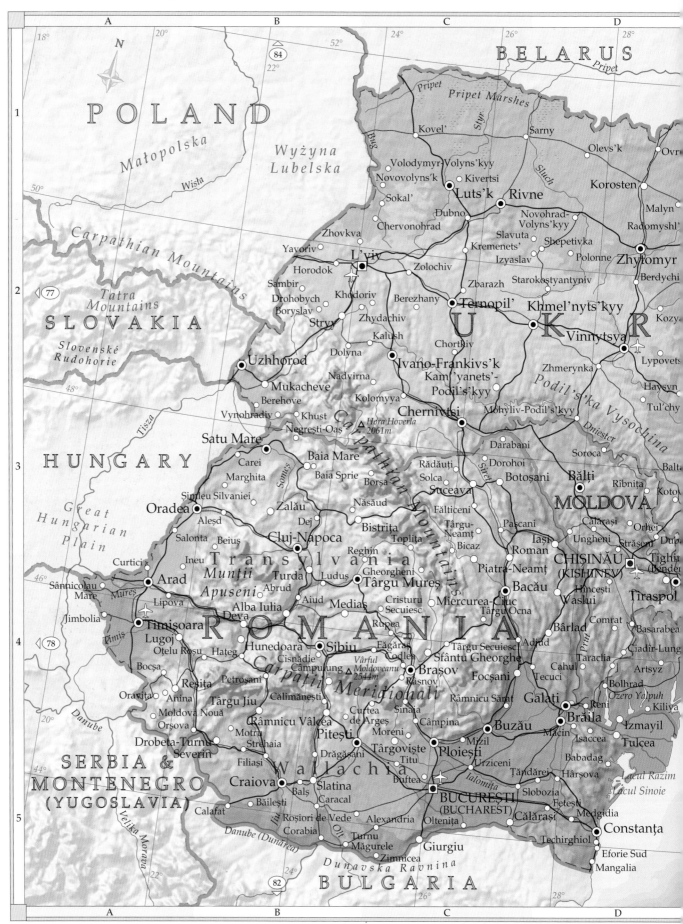

POPULATION

- ◉ Over 500,000
- ◉ 100,000 – 500,000
- ○ 50,000 – 100,000
- ○ Less than 50,000
- ● National capital

ELEVATION

4 000 m	13 124 ft
2000 m	6562 ft
1000 m	3281 ft
500 m	1640 ft
250 m	820 ft
100 m	328 ft
Sea Level	Sea Level
-50 m	-164 ft
-100 m	-328 ft
-250 m	-820 ft
-500 m	-1640 ft
-1000 m	-3281 ft
-2000 m	-6562 ft

RUSSIAN FEDERATION

Srednerusskaya Vozvyshennost'

Don

Horodnya
Shchors
Shostka
Krolevets'
Hlukhiv
Chernihiv
Konotop
Bakhmach
Nizhyn
Romny
Sumy
Nosivka
Oster
Lebedyn
Pryluky
Okhtyrka
Zolochiv
Brovary
Yahotyn
Pyryatyn
Derhachi
Vasyl'kiv
Hrebinka
Lubny
Myrhorod
Lyubotyn
Kharkiv
astiv
Bila Tserkva
Kaniv
Merefa
Bohuslav
Zolotonosha
Hlobyne
Poltava
Izyum
Starobil's'k
Horodyshche
Cherkasy
Donets
Kreminna
Rubizhne
Zvenyhorodka
Smila
Chyhyryn
Kremenchuts'ke Vodoskhovyshche
Slov''yans'k
Syeverodonets'k
Shpola
Svitlovods'k
Kramators'k
Lysychans'k
Tal'ne
Oleksandrivka
Kremenchuk
Kostyantynivka
Zolote
Luhans'k
Mala Vyska
Znam''yanka
Oleksandriya
Dniprodzerzhyns'ke Vodoskhovyshche
Novomoskovs'k
Horlivka
Stakhanov
Holovanivs'k
Dniprodzerzhyns'k
Pavlohrad
Yenakiyeve
Krasnodon
Kirovohrad
Zhovti Vody
Dnipropetrovs'k
Synel'nykove
Makiyivka
Krasnyy Luch
Ulyanivka
Vil'shanka
P''yatykhatky
Pokrovs'ke
Torez
Pervomays'k
Bobrynets
Kryvyy Rih
Donets'k
Amvrosiyivka
Kryve Ozero
Arbyzynka
Inhulets'
Zaporizhzhya
Orikhiv
Volnovakha
Dokuchayevs'k
Novyy Buh
Nikopol
Marhanets
Polohy
Novoazovs'k
Voznesens'k
Ordzhonikidze
Dniprorudne
Tokmak
Kam''yanka-Dniprovs'ka
Kakhovs'ka Vodoskhovyshche
Molochans'k
Mariupol'
Mykolayiv
Dnieper (Dnipro)
Melitopol'
Gulf of Taganrog
Zhovtneve
Kakhovka
Akinovka
Prymors'k
Berdyans'k
Yeya
Kherson
Tsyurupyns'k
Novotroyits'ke
Ochakiv
Hola Prystan'
Chaplynka
Odesa
Kalanchak
Heniches'k
Illichivs'k
Armyans'k
Sea of Azov

RUSSIAN FEDERATION

Krasnoperekops'k
Rozdol'ne
Dzhankoy
Kerch Strait
Karkinits'ka Zatoka
Krasnohvardiys'ke
Zatoka Syvash
Kerch
Chornomors'ke
Nyzhn'ohirs'kyy
Kuban'
Yevpatoriya
Kryms'kyy Pivostriv
Lenine
Saky
Simferopol'
Feodosiya
Bakhchysaray
Sevastopol'
Kryms'ki Hory
Alushta
Yalta
Alupka

Black Sea

0 km	100
0 miles	100

THE WORLD ATLAS

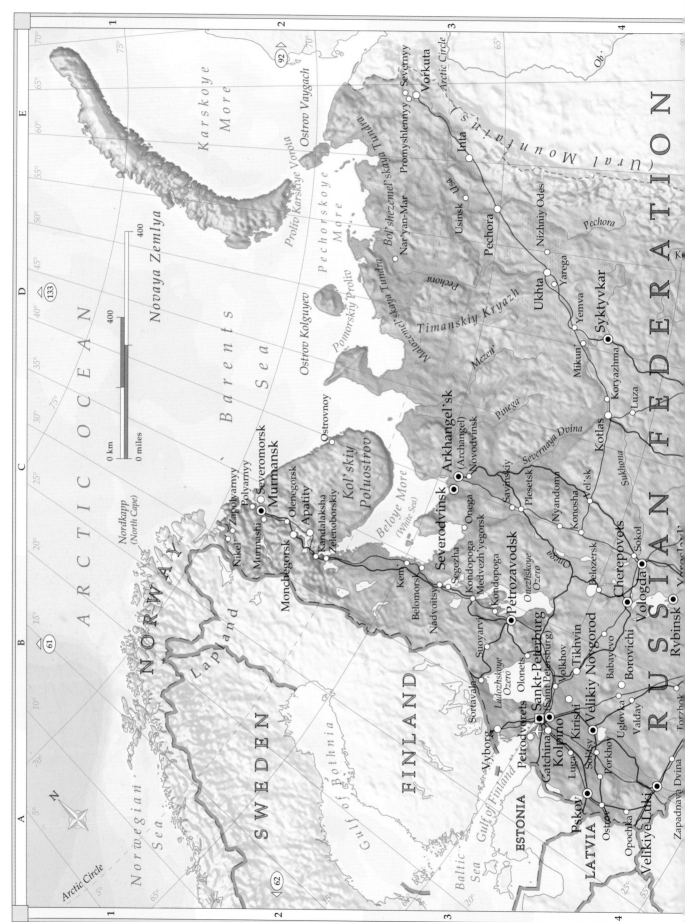

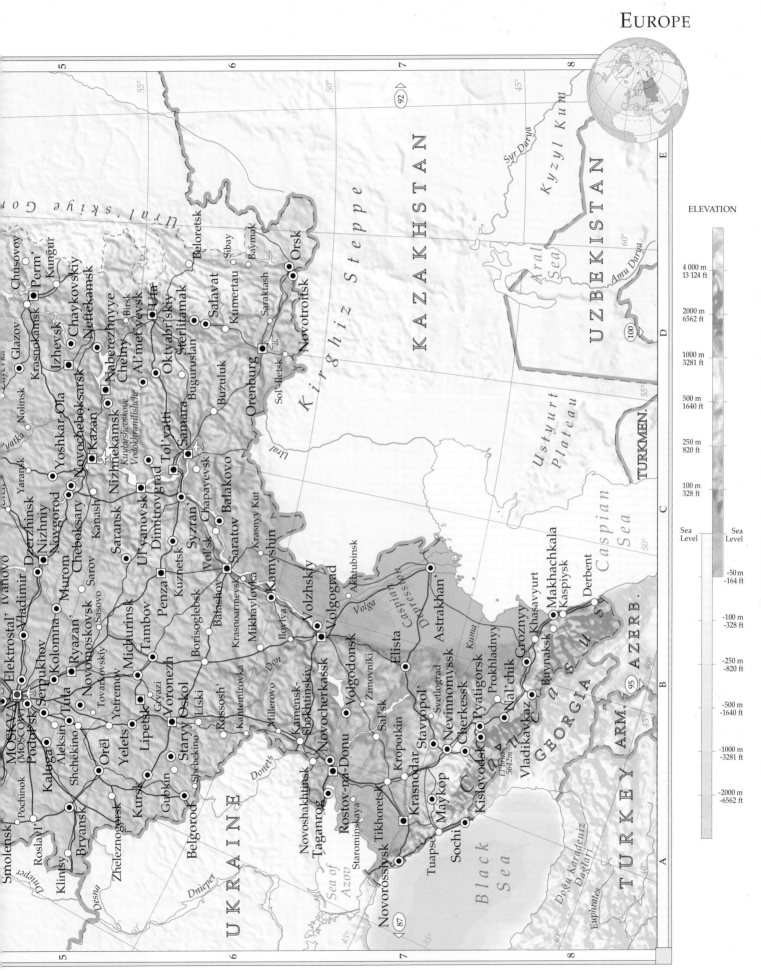

ELEVATION

4 000 m
13 124 ft

2000 m
6562 ft

1000 m
3281 ft

500 m
1640 ft

250 m
820 ft

100 m
328 ft

Sea
Level

Sea
Level

-50 m
-164 ft

-100 m
-328 ft

-250 m
-820 ft

-500 m
-1640 ft

-1000 m
-3281 ft

-2000 m
-6562 ft

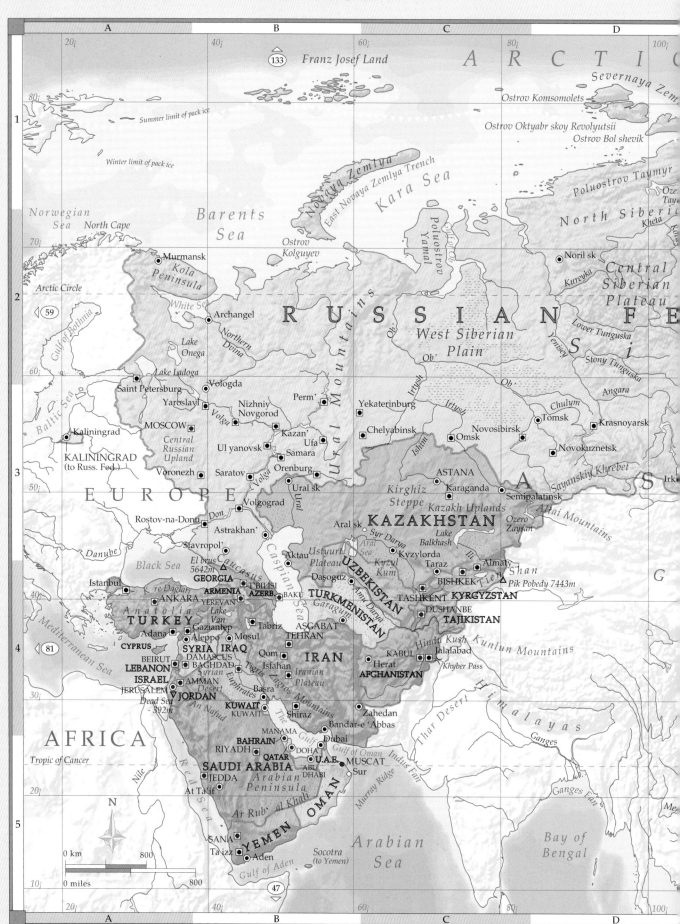

ARCTIC

133

Franz Josef Land

Ostrov Komsomolets

Severnaya Zem

Ostrov Oktyabr skoy Revolyutsii
Ostrov Bol shevik

Summer limit of pack ice

Winter limit of pack ice

Poluostrov Taymyr

Oze
Tay

Kheta

North Siberi

Novaya Zemlya

East Novaya Zemlya Trench

Kara Sea

Norwegian
Sea   North Cape

Barents
Sea

Ostrov
Kolguyev

Poluostrov
Yamal

RUSSIAN FE

Murmansk

Kola
Peninsula

Noril sk

Central
Siberian
Plateau

Arctic Circle

59

White Sea

Archangel

West Siberian
Plain

Kureyka

Lower Tunguska

Ural Mountains

Ob

Ob'

Ob'

Irtysh

Yenisey

Stony Tunguska

Angara

Lake
Onega

Northern
Dvina

Lake Ladoga

Vologda

Perm'

Yekaterinburg

Chulym

Tomsk

Krasnoyarsk

Irk

Saint Petersburg

Yaroslavl

Nizhniy
Novgorod

Chelyabinsk

Novosibirsk

Omsk

Novokuznetsk

MOSCOW

Volga

Kazan'

Ufa

Irtysh

Ishim

Ul yanovsk

Samara

Kaliningrad

Baltic Sea

Central
Russian
Upland

KALININGRAD
(to Russ. Fed.)

Voronezh

Saratov

Orenburg

Ural sk

ASTANA

Sayanskiy Khrebet

A

Karaganda

S

Kirghiz
Steppe

Kazakh Uplands

Semipalatinsk

Altai Mountains

EUROPE

Volga

Ural

Volgograd

Don

Aral sk

KAZAKHSTAN

Ozero
Zaysan

Rostov-na-Donu

Astrakhan'

Syr Darya

Lake
Balkhash

Stavropol'

El brus
5642m

Caucasus

Aktau

Ustyurt
Plateau

Aral
Sea

Kyzylorda

Ili

Almaty

G

Danube

Black Sea

Caspian Sea

Kyzyl
Kum

Taraz

BISHKEK

Tien Shan

Pik Pobedy 7443m

Istanbul

re Daglari

GEORGIA

T BILISI

ARMENIA

AZERB.

BAKU

Dasoguz

UZBEKISTAN

Amu Darya

TASHKENT

KYRGYZSTAN

ANKARA

YEREVAN

Lake
Van

TURKMENISTAN

Garagum

DUSHANBE

Anatolia

Gaziantep

Tabriz

TEHRAN

ASGABAT

TAJIKISTAN

TURKEY

Adana

Aleppo

Mosul

Qom

IRAN

KABUL

Hindu Kush

Kunlun Mountains

CYPRUS

SYRIA IRAQ

Isfahan

Herat

Jalalabad

Khyber Pass

LEBANON

DAMASCUS

BAGHDAD

Syrian
Desert

Tigris

Iranian
Plateau

AFGHANISTAN

Himalayas

BEIRUT

ISRAEL

AMMAN

Euphrates

Basra

Zagros Mountains

Zahedan

Thar Desert

Ganges

JERUSALEM

JORDAN

Dead Sea
- 392m

An Nafud

KUWAIT

KUWAIT

Shiraz

The Gulf

Bandar-e 'Abbas

Ganges Fan

AFRICA

Nile

Tropic of Cancer

MANAMA

Dubai

Gulf of Oman

Indus Fan

Mer

BAHRAIN

RIYADH

DOHA

U.A.E.

MUSCAT

Murray Ridge

QATAR

ABU
DHABI

Sur

SAUDI ARABIA

JEDDA

Arabian
Peninsula

OMAN

Arabian
Sea

Bay of
Bengal

At Ta'if

Ar Rub' al Khali

N

SANA

Red Sea

YEMEN

Socotra
(to Yemen)

Ta izz

Aden

Gulf of Aden

47

81

0 km   800

0 miles   800

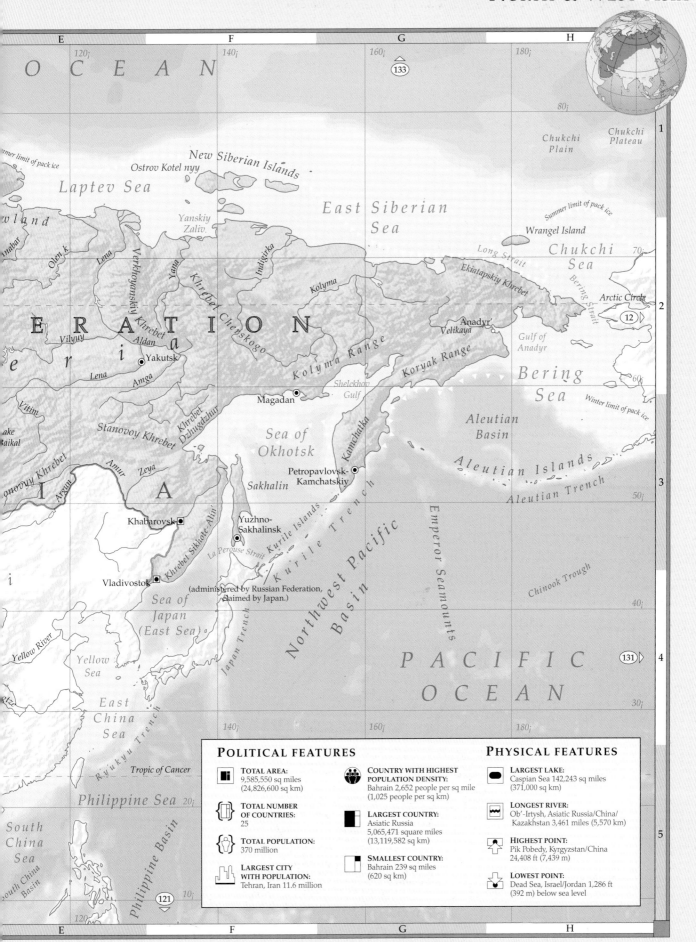

O C E A N

Summer limit of pack ice

Chukchi
Plain

Chukchi
Plateau

80j

1

Laptev Sea

New Siberian Islands

Ostrov Kotel nyy

*East Siberian
Sea*

Summer limit of pack ice

Wrangel Island

Yanskiy
Zaliv

Long Strait

Chukchi
Sea

70

owland

Anabar

Olen k

Lena

Verkhoyanskiy Khrebet

Yana

Khrebet Chenskogo

Indigirka

Kolyma

Ekiatapskiy Khrebet

Bering Strait

Arctic Circle

12

2

E R A T I O N

eria

Vilyuy

Aldan

Kolyma Range

Anadyr'

Velikaya

Gulf of
Anadyr

Yakutsk

Koryak Range

60

Lena

Amga

Shelekhov
Gulf

*Bering
Sea*

Vitim

Stanovoy Khrebet

Khrebet Dzhugdzhur

Magadan

Kamchatka

*Aleutian
Basin*

Winter limit of pack ice

ake
aikal

onovoy Khrebet

Amur

Zeya

Argun

Sea of
Okhotsk

Aleutian Islands

50

3

I A

Khabarovsk

Sakhalin

Petropavlovsk-
Kamchatskiy

Aleutian Trench

Yuzhno-
Sakhalinsk

Kurile Islands

Kurile Trench

*Northwest Pacific
Basin*

Emperor Seamounts

Chinook Trough

Vladivostok

Khrebet Sikhote-Alin'

La Perouse Strait

(administered by Russian Federation,
claimed by Japan.)

40

Sea of
Japan
(East Sea)

Japan Trench

P A C I F I C

131

4

Yellow River

Yellow
Sea

O C E A N

30

atzi

i

East
China
Sea

140j

160j

180j

Ryukyu Trench

Tropic of Cancer

Philippine Sea

20j

South
China
Sea

5

South China
Basin

Philippine Basin

121

10j

120

E　　　　　F　　　　　G　　　　　H

POLITICAL FEATURES

TOTAL AREA:
9,585,550 sq miles
(24,826,600 sq km)

**TOTAL NUMBER
OF COUNTRIES:**
25

TOTAL POPULATION:
370 million

**LARGEST CITY
WITH POPULATION:**
Tehran, Iran 11.6 million

**COUNTRY WITH HIGHEST
POPULATION DENSITY:**
Bahrain 2,652 people per sq mile
(1,025 people per sq km)

LARGEST COUNTRY:
Asiatic Russia
5,065,471 square miles
(13,119,582 sq km)

SMALLEST COUNTRY:
Bahrain 239 sq miles
(620 sq km)

PHYSICAL FEATURES

LARGEST LAKE:
Caspian Sea 142,243 sq miles
(371,000 sq km)

LONGEST RIVER:
Ob'-Irtysh, Asiatic Russia/China/
Kazakhstan 3,461 miles (5,570 km)

HIGHEST POINT:
Pik Pobedy, Kyrgyzstan/China
24,408 ft (7,439 m)

LOWEST POINT:
Dead Sea, Israel/Jordan 1,286 ft
(392 m) below sea level

RUSSIA & KAZAKHSTAN

NETH.
NORWAY
DENMARK
GERMANY
SWEDEN
KALININGRAD
(to Russ. Fed.)
Kaliningrad
POLAND
LITH. LAT. EST.
Sankt-Peterburg
BELARUS
Pskov
Velikiy
Novgorod
Smolensk
UKRAINE
MOLDOVA
Bryansk
MOSKVA
(MOSCOW)
Tver'
Tula
Belgorod
Ryazan'
Voronezh
Tambov
Mikhaylovka
Rostov-na-
Donu
Krasnodar
Sochi
Stavropol'
Nal'chik
Vladikavkaz
Groznyy
Makhachkala
GEORGIA
ARM.
AZERBAIJAN
IRAN

FINLAND
Arctic Circle
Murmansk
Kandalaksha
Petrozavodsk
Cherepovets
Vologda
Yaroslavl'
Kineshma
Vladimir
Nizhniy Novgorod
Kirov
Penza
Kazan'
Glazov
Ul'yanovsk
Izhevsk
Tol'yatti
Naberezhnyye
Chelny
Saratov
Samara
Ufa
Balakovo
Volgograd
Ural'sk
Sterlitamak
Orenburg
Astrakhan'
Magnitogorsk
Aktobe
Orsk
Alga
Atyrau
Emba
Aktau
Fort-Shevchenko
Zhanaozen
Shalkar
KAZAKHSTAN
Ustyurt
Plateau
Aral
Sea
Aral'sk
Ayteke Bi
UZBEKISTAN
TURKMENISTAN
Dzhusaly
Kyzylorda
Turkestan
Kentau
Arys'
Karatau
Shymkent
Taraz
Shu
AFGHANISTAN
TAJIKISTAN
KYRGYZSTAN

SVALBARD
(to Norway)
Winter limit of pack ice
Summer limit of pack ice
Zemlya Frantsa
Iosifa
Nordkapp
(North Cape)
Barents
Sea
ARCTI
Novaya Zemlya
Karskoye More
Severodvinsk
Arkhangel'sk
Ostrov
Kolguyev
Ostrov Belyy
Dikson
Nar'yan-Mar
Pechora
Poluostrov Yamal
Kotlas
Syktyvkar
Ukhta
Vorkuta
Salekhard
Ob'
Talna
Noril'sk
Igarka
Solikamsk
Nadym
Perm'
Serov
Nyagan'
Zapadno-
Lesnoy
Khanty-Mansiysk
Sibirskaya
Yekaterinburg
Surgut
Nizhnevartovsk
Tyumen'
Ravnina
Chelyabinsk
Tobol'sk
RUSSIAN
Ishim
Chulym
Petropavlovsk
Omsk
Seversk
Tomsk
Strel
Rudnyy
Kostanay
Novosibirsk
Krasnoyar
Kokshetau
Atbasar
Shchuchinsk
Kemerovo
ASTANA
Barnaul
Pavlodar
Novokuznetsk
Temirtau
Saran'
Karaganda
Semipalatinsk
Abak
Zhezkazgan
Kazakhskiy
Melkosopochnik
Shar
Leninogorsk
Zyryanovsk
Ky
Gora Belukha
4506m
Balkhash
Ayagoz
Ozero
Zaysan
Altai Mountains
Ust'-Kamenogorsk
Ozero
Balkhash
Taldykorgan
Tokeli
Almaty
(Alma-Ata)
Tien Shan
CHINA

POPULATION

- Over 500,000
- 100,000 - 500,000
- 50,000 - 100,000
- Less than 50,000
- National capital

92

E   F   G   H

180° 80°   170°   70°

0 km   800

0 miles   800

△ 14

Chukchi Sea

ALASKA (to US)

Bering Strait

Arctic Circle

Proliv Longa

Ostrov Vrangelya

Vostochno-Sibirskoye More

Pevek

Ekiatapskiy Khrebet

Anadyrskiy Zaliv

Anadyr

O C E A N

Ostrov Komsomolets

Ostrov Oktyabr'skoy Revolyutsii
Severnaya Zemlya

trov 'shevik

Novosibirskiye Ostrova

Ostrov Novaya Sibir'

Ostrov Kotel'nyy

Ostrov Bol'shoy Lyakhovskiy

Ambarchik
Cherskiy

Alazeya

Indigirka

Kolyma

Anadyr'

Koryakskoye Nagor'ye

Bering Sea

180°

130° ▷

Ossora

170°

Ostrov Karaginskiy

More Laptevykh

Ostrov Taymyr

Ozero Taymyr

Ust'-Olenëk

Tiksi

Kazach'ye

Yana

Khrebet Cherskogo

Adycha

Susuman

Zaliv Shelikhova

Ust'-Kamchatsk

Vulkan Klyucheyskaya Sopka 4750m

Atlasovo

o-Sibirskaya Nizmennost'

Kheta

Kotuy

Anabar

Olenëk

Olenëk

Atka
● Magadan

Poluostrov Kamchatka

Mil'kovo

ato rana

SRednesibirskoye Ploskogor'ye

Nyurba

Vilyuy

Yakutsk

Lena

Anga

Okhotsk

Petropavlovsk-Kamchatskiy

50°

160°

S I B I R

nyaya Tunguska

(S I B E R I A)

Chunya

Mirnyy

Suntar

Olëkminsk

Lena

Aldan

Khrebet Dzhugdzhur

Okhotskoye More

Shantarskiye Ostrova

Ostrov Paramushir

Pervyy Kuril'skiy Proliv

F E D E R A T I O N

Olëkma

Neryungri

Ostrov Sakhalin

150°

Ostrov Urup

Angara

Ust'-Ilimsk

Bodaybo

Lena

Vitim

Tynda

Skovorodino

Amur

Komsomol'sk-na-Amure

Amur

Khrebet Sikhote-Alin'

Ostrov Iturup

Kuril'sk

Kuril'skiye Ostrova (Kurile Islands)

130° ▷

ansk

Ust'-Kut

Bratsk

Tulun

Ozero Baykal

Shilka

Svobodnyy

Khabarovsk

Yuzhno-Sakhalinsk

La Pérouse Strait

Usol'ye-Sibirskoye

Angarsk

Yablonovyy Khrebet

Chita

Blagoveshchensk

Birobidzhan

Khor

Bikin

(administered by Russian Federation, claimed by Japan)

40°

Irkutsk

Ulan-Ude

Olovyannaya

Amur

stern Sayan

Kyakhta

Krasnokamensk

Zabaykal'sk

C H I N A

Ussuriysk

Vladivostok

Nakhodka

J A P A N

M O N G O L I A

G o b i

N

Sea of Japan (East Sea)

140°

NORTH KOREA

△ 106

120°

40°

110°

100°

130°

E   F   G   H

ELEVATION

4000 m 13 124 ft	
2000 m 6562 ft	
1000 m 3281 ft	
500 m 1640 ft	
250 m 820 ft	
100 m 328 ft	
Sea Level	Sea Level
-250 m -820 ft	
-500 m -1640 ft	
-1000 m -3281 ft	
-2000 m -6562 ft	
-3000 m -9843 ft	
-4000 m -13 124 ft	

1

2

3

4

5

Turkey & The Caucasus

POPULATION

- Over 500,000
- 100,000 – 500,000
- 50,000 – 100,000
- Less than 50,000
- National capital

0 km   200

0 miles   200

94

RUSSIAN

FEDERATION

Caucasus

Caspian

Sea

Gagra
Gudaut'a
Sokhumi
Och'amch'ire
Abkhazia
Enguri
Mestia
Kazbek 5047m
South
Ossetia
Xaçmaz
Samtredia
K'ut'aisi
GEORGIA
Zaqatala
Quba
Siyäzän
P'ot'i
Gori
Tsalka
T'BILISI
Şäki
Greater Caucasus
K'obulet'i
Akhalts'ikhe
Rust'avi
Mingäçevir
Märäzä
Bat'umi
Ajaria
Artvin
Vanadzor
Gäncä
Yevlax
Sumqayıt
Hopa
Lesser
Kura
BAKI
(BAKU)
Trabzon
Pazar
Rize
Of
Dağları
Gyumri
Sevan
AZERBAIJAN
40°
Giresun
Dogu
Karadeniz
Art'ik
Kars
ARMENIA
Qazimämmäd
Äli Bayramı
müşhane
Sarıkamış
YEREVAN
Sevana Lich
Nagorno-
Karabakh
Imişli
İspir
Çoruh Nehri
Aras
Büyükağrı Dağı
Artashat
Xankändi
Biläsuvar
hiye
Pasinler
Horasan
(Mount Ararat)
5137m
Goris
Askale
Ağrı
AZERBAIJAN
Länkäran
Erzincan
Erzurum
Kura
rrat Nehri)
Doğubayazıt
Naxçivan
Aras
Kemah
Patnos
Muradiye
E Y
Tercan
Erciş
Bingöl
Muş
Van Gölü
Daryācheh-ye Orūmīyeh
Keban Baraji
Elazığ
Tatvan
Van
alatya
Bitlis
Gevaş
Silvan
Siirt
IRAN
Ataürk Baraji
Diyarbakır
Batman
T o r o s
diyaman
Silverek
Şırnak
Kurdistan
Şanlıurfa
Viranşehir
Mardin
Ceylanpınar
Nusaybin
Tigris
RIA
Al Jazīrah
Jabal Bishrī
Euphrates
IRAQ
Buhayrat ath Tharthār
hayrat Asad

Reshteh-ye Kühhä-ye Alborz
(Elburz Mountains)

Kühhä-ye Zagros
(Zagros Mountains)

ELEVATION

4 000 m 13 124 ft
2000 m 6562 ft
1000 m 3281 ft
500 m 1640 ft
250 m 820 ft
100 m 328 ft
Sea Level
-50 m -164 ft
-100 m -328 ft
-250 m -820 ft
-500 m -1640 ft
-1000 m -3281 ft
-2000 m -6562 ft

THE NEAR EAST

THE WORLD ATLAS

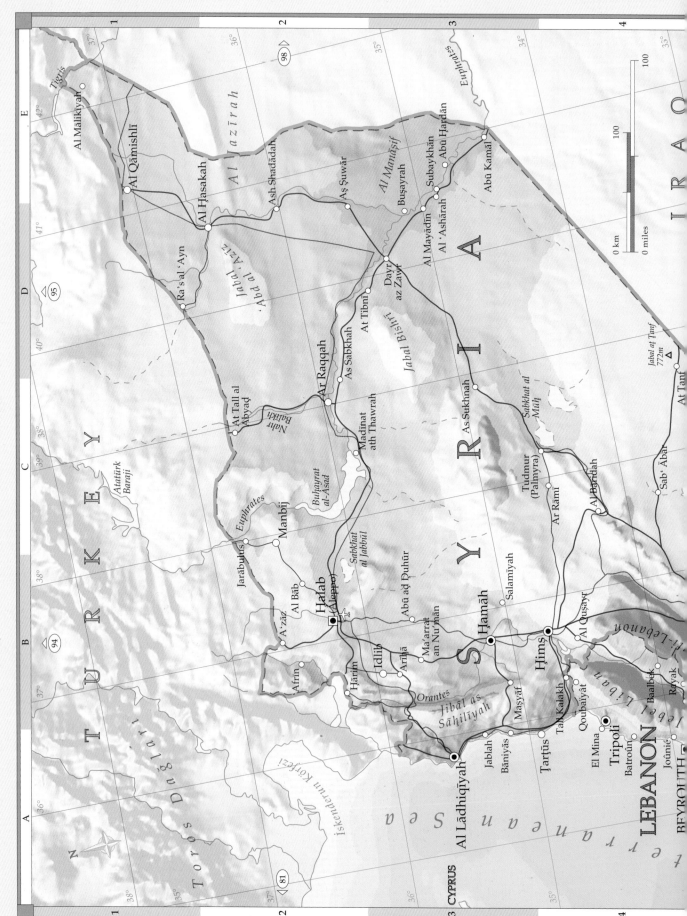

POPULATION

- ⬣ Over 500,000
- ◉ 100,000 – 500,000
- ○ 50,000 – 100,000
- ○ Less than 50,000
- ● National capital

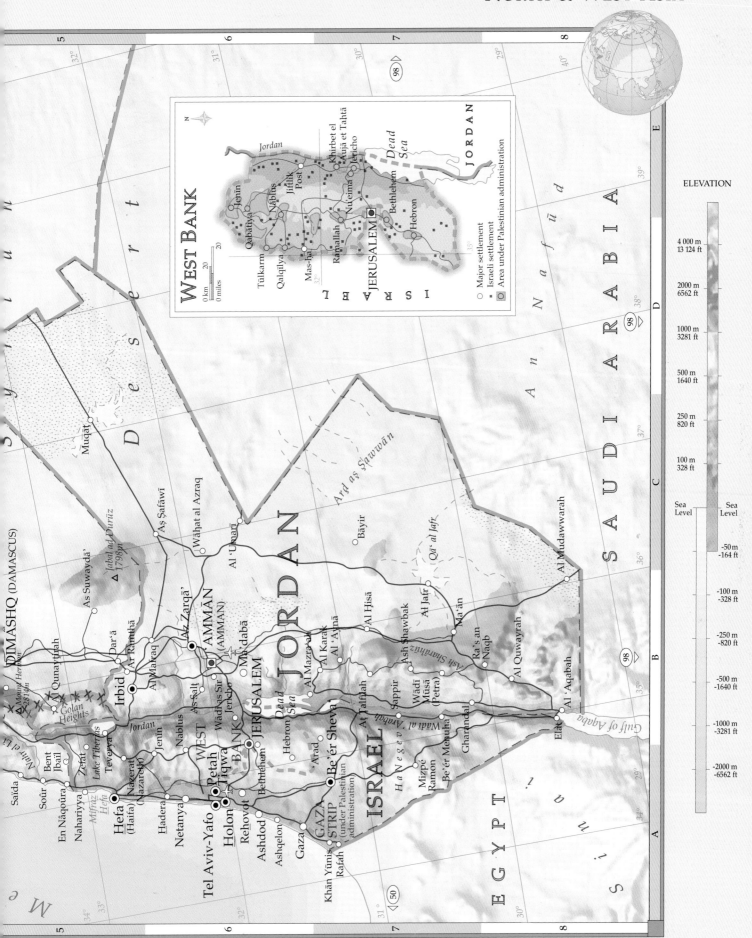

WEST BANK

N

Jordan

Khirbet el
'Auja et Tahtā
Jericho

Dead Sea

Jiftlik
Post

Jenin

Nāblus

Nu'eima

JORDAN

Qabātiya

Bethlehem

Hebron

JERUSALEM

Ramallah

Tulkarm

Qalqīlya

Mas-ha

0 km   20
0 miles 20

ISRAEL

○ Major settlement
■ Israeli settlement
◉ Area under Palestinian administration

ELEVATION

4 000 m
13 124 ft

2000 m
6562 ft

1000 m
3281 ft

500 m
1640 ft

250 m
820 ft

100 m
328 ft

Sea Level   Sea Level

-50 m
-164 ft

-100 m
-328 ft

-250 m
-820 ft

-500 m
-1640 ft

-1000 m
-3281 ft

-2000 m
-6562 ft

Syrian Desert

An Nafūd

SAUDI ARABIA

JORDAN

DIMASHQ
(DAMASCUS)

Muqāt

As Şafāwī

Wāhat al Azraq

Al 'Unarī

Ard aş Şawwān

Bāyir

Qā' al Jafr

As Suwaydā'

△ Jabal ad Durūz
1798m

Az Zarqā'

AMMAN
('AMMĀN)

Al Hīsā

Ash Shawbak

Al Jafr

Ma'ān

Al Mudawwarah

Al Quwayrah

Al Qunayţiah

Dar'ā

At Ramthā

Al Mafraq

As Salt

Mādabā

Al Karak

Al 'Aynā

Al Mazra'ah

Ra's an
Naqb

Al 'Aqabah

Elat

Gulf of Aqaba

Irbid

Al 'Amarī

Jericho

Wādi as Sir

JERUSALEM

Dead Sea

At Tafīlah

Qappir

Wadi Mūsā
(Petra)

Ash Sharāh

Mount Hermon
△ 2814m

*Golan
Heights*

Teverya

Jordan

Jenin

Nablus

WEST
BANK

Hebron

Gharandal

Bent Jbail

Zefat

Lake Tiberias

Naẕerat
(Nazareth)

Bethlehem

Arad

Be'ér Sheva'

Wādī al 'Araba

En Nāqoūra

Nahariyya

Hefa
(Haifa)

Hadera

Petah
Tiqwa

Hebron

HaNegev

Mizpé
Ramon

Be'ér Menuha

Saïda

Soûr

Nahr el Li

*Mifraz
Hefa*

Netanya

Tel Aviv-Yafo

Holon

Rehovot

GAZA
STRIP

Khān Yūnis

Rafah

Ashdod

Ashqelon

Gaza

ISRAEL

(under Palestinian
administration)

Me

EGYPT

THE MIDDLE EAST

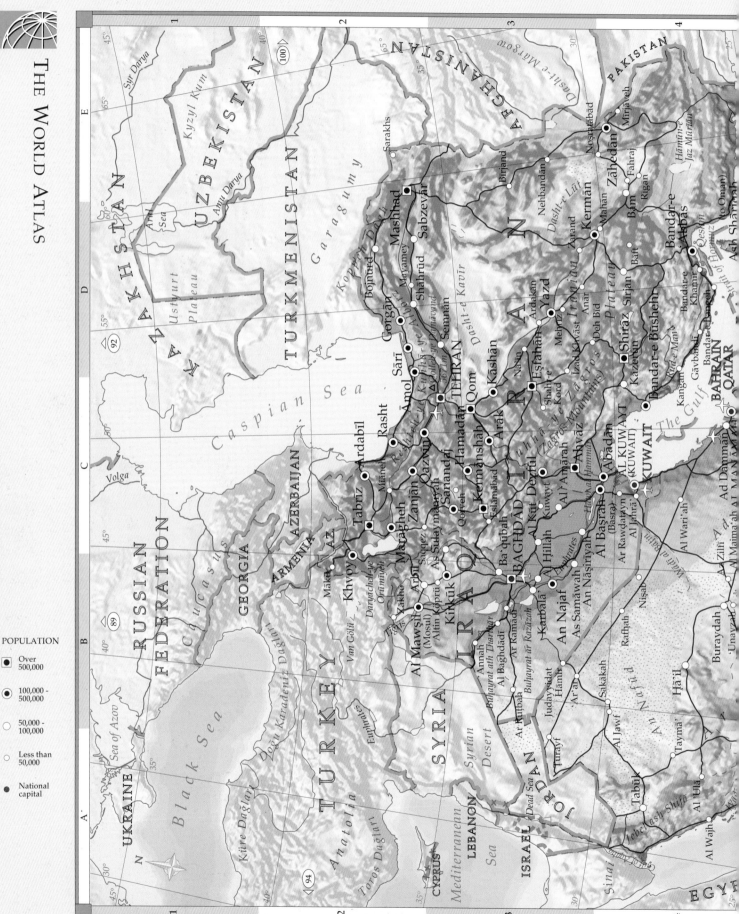

POPULATION

- ■ Over 500,000
- ◉ 100,000 – 500,000
- ○ 50,000 – 100,000
- ○ Less than 50,000
- ● National capital

North & West Asia

5 · 6 · 7 · 8

65° · 20° · 15° · 10° · 60° · 55°

E

ELEVATION

400

400

0 km
0 miles

INDIAN

OCEAN

Arabian
Sea

118

118

D

SAUDI ARABIA'S TWO CAPITALS

Ar Riyaḍ -   *Capital*
Jiddah   -   *Seat of Government*

4000 m
13 124 ft

2000 m
6562 ft

1000 m
3281 ft

500 m
1640 ft

250 m
820 ft

100 m
328 ft

Sea
Level

Sea
Level

-250 m
-820 ft

-500 m
-1640 ft

-1000 m
-3281 ft

-2000 m
-6562 ft

-3000 m
-9843 ft

-4000 m
-13 124 ft

(MUSCAT)
Ṣūr
Ar Rustāq
Ramla
Al Waḥibah
Jazīrat
Maṣīrah

Al Ghābah

O M A N

Khalīj
Maṣīrah

Duqm

Jazīrat
Maṣīrah

Ḥāsik
Al Ghaydah

Shawqirah

Thamarīt
Ṣalālah

Juzur al Ḥalāniyāt

Damqawt

UNITED ARAB
EMIRATES

(ABU DHABI)

Ko

Y E M E N

Al Maḥrah

Sayḥūt

Suquṭrā
(Socotra)
(to Yemen)

Raas Xaafuun

Sanāw

Ash Shiḥr
Al Mukallā

Gulf of Aden

SAUDI ARABIA

Ar Rub' al Khālī
(Empty Quarter)

Wuday'ah

Tarīm
Say'ūn

Ḥaḍramawt

SOMALIA

P
e
n
i
n
s
u
l
a

Laylā

Shuqrah

A
r
a
b
i
a
n

As Sulayyil

Ramlat
as Sab'atayn

Ramlat Dahm

SAN'Ā'
(SANA)

Adan
(Aden)

Ogaden

Najrān

Ta'izz

(RIYADH)
الرياض

Khamīs Mushayt

Ṣa'dah

Bab el Mandeb

Tathlīth

Qal 'at Bīshah

Zalim

Wādī Bīshah

Turabah

Abhā

Ṣabyā

Jīzān

Zabīd

DJIBOUTI

At Ṭā'if

Al Bāḥah

Jazā'ir
Farasān

Al Ḥudaydah
(Hodeida)

ERITREA

E
T
H
I
O
P
I
A

(Medina)

Ḥarrat Rahaṭ

Al Lith

Danakil Desert

Ethiopian
Highlands

Great Rift Valley

Makkah
(Mecca)

JIDDAH
(JEDDA)

Red
Sea

Nubian
Desert

SUDAN

C

B

A

5 · 6 · 7 · 8

35° · 15° · 10° · 5°

50°

45°

40°

20°

99

SOUTH & EAST ASIA

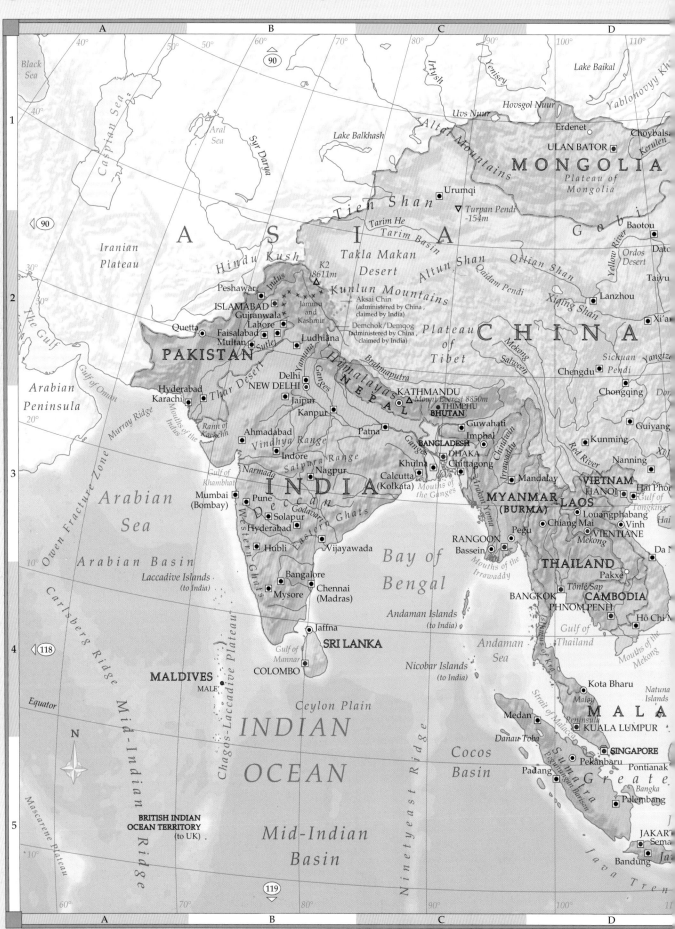

POPULATION

- ◉ Over 500,000
- ◉ 100,000 - 500,000
- ○ 50,000 - 100,000
- ○ Less than 50,000
- ● National capital

A · S · I · A

Black Sea

Caspian Sea

Aral Sea

Syr Darya

Lake Balkhash

Irtysh

Yenisey

Lake Baikal

Uvs Nuur

Hovsgol Nuur

Altai Mountains

Yablonovyy

Erdenet

Choybals

ULAN BATOR

MONGOLIA

Plateau of Mongolia

Kerulen

Iranian Plateau

Hindu Kush

Tien Shan

Urumqi

Turpan Pendi -154m

Gobi

Baotou

Datc

Takla Makan Desert

Tarim He

Tarim Basin

Altun Shan

Qilian Shan

Ordos Desert

Yellow River

Xiqing Shan

Taiyu

K2 8611m

Kunlun Mountains

Qaidam Pendi

Lanzhou

Xi'a

Peshawar

Indus

Aksai Chin (administered by China, claimed by India)

CHINA

ISLAMABAD

Jammu and Kashmir

Demchok/Demqog (administered by China, claimed by India)

Plateau of Tibet

Mekong

Salween

Chengdu

Sichuan Pendi

Yangtze

Gujranwala

Lahore

Quetta

Faisalabad

Multan

Sutlej

Ludhiana

Plateau of Tibet

Chongqing

Do

PAKISTAN

The Gulf

Yamuna

Ganges

Himalayas

Brahmaputra

KATHMANDU

N E P A L

Mount Everest 8850m

Guiyang

Hyderabad

Karachi

Thar Desert

NEW DELHI

Delhi

Jaipur

Kanpur

THIMPHU

BHUTAN

Guwahati

Imphal

Chindwin

Kunming

Nanning

Xi

Arabian Peninsula

Gulf of Oman

Murray Ridge

Rann of Kachchh

Ahmadabad

Vindhya Range

Patna

Ganges

BANGLADESH

DHAKA

Khulna

Chittagong

Mandalay

Irrawaddy

Arakan Yoma

VIETNAM

HANOI

Hai Pho

Gulf of Tongking

Gulf of Khambhat

Indore

Satpura Range

Nagpur

Calcutta (Kolkata)

Mouths of the Ganges

MYANMAR (BURMA)

Red River

LAOS

Louangphabang

Vinh

Mumbai (Bombay)

Narmada

Pune

Solapur

Godavari

I N D I A

Eastern Ghats

Chiang Mai

VIENTIANE

Mekong

Da

Arabian Sea

Deccan

Hyderabad

Western Ghats

Hubli

Vijayawada

RANGOON

Bassein

Pegu

THAILAND

Pakxe

Arabian Basin

Laccadive Islands (to India)

Bay of Bengal

Mouths of the Irrawaddy

Tônlé Sap

CAMBODIA

Bangalore

Mysore

Chennai (Madras)

BANGKOK

Andaman Islands (to India)

PHNOM PENH

Hô Chi

Carlsberg Ridge

Jaffna

Gulf of Mannar

SRI LANKA

Andaman Sea

Gulf of Thailand

Mouths of the Mekong

MALDIVES

MALE

COLOMBO

Nicobar Islands (to India)

Kota Bharu

Natuna Islands

Chagos-Laccadive Plateau

Ceylon Plain

Ninetyeast Ridge

M A L A

Equator

INDIAN

Medan

Strait of Malacca

KUALA LUMPUR

Mid-Indian Ridge

N

Cocos Basin

Danau Toba

SINGAPORE

Pekanbaru

Pontianak

Padang

Sumatra

G r e a t e

BRITISH INDIAN OCEAN TERRITORY (to UK)

OCEAN

Bangka

Palembang

Mid-Indian Basin

JAKAR

Sema

Mascarene Plateau

Java Tren

Bandung

Qiqihar
Manchuria
Plain
Harbin
Changchun
Liao He
Shenyang
BEIJING
Tianjin
Dandong
Dalian
Jinan
Qingdao
Nanjing
Shanghai
Wuhan
Hangzhou
Nanchang
Fuzhou
Wuyi Shan
TAIPEI
TAIWAN
Kaohsiung
Hong Kong (Xianggang)
Macao
Aomen
Guangzhou
South China Sea

Great Khingan Range
Amur
Lake Khanka
Yalu
Bo Hai
Yellow Sea
Korea Strait
East China Sea
Taiwan Strait
Luzon Strait

Sapporo
Hokkaido
JAPAN
Sendai
NORTH KOREA
PYONGYANG
SEOUL
SOUTH KOREA
Sea of Japan (East Sea)
Honshu
Nagoya
Kyoto
Osaka
TOKYO
Yokohama
Fuji-san 3776m
Hiroshima
Shikoku
Kitakyushu
Kyushu

Sakhalin
Kurile Islands
Kurile Trench
Japan Trench
Northwest Pacific Basin
Shatskiy Rise

Ryukyu Islands
Ryukyu Trench
Shikoku Basin
Kyushu-Palau Ridge

PACIFIC OCEAN

Philippine Sea
Philippine Basin

West Mariana Basin
Mariana Trench

PARACEL ISLANDS
(disputed)
Baguio
Luzon
MANILA
Mindoro
PHILIPPINES
Panay
Samar
SPRATLY ISLANDS
(disputed)
Bacolod
Cebu
Negros
Palawan
Sulu Sea
Zamboanga
Mindanao
Davao

Micronesia
Eauripik Rise
Yap Trench

BRUNEI
BANDAR SERI BEGAWAN
MALAYSIA
Celebes Sea
Manado
Halmahera
Borneo
Makassar Strait
Balikpapan
Moluccas
Seram
Ambon
Buru
INDONESIA
Banjarmasin
Ujungpandang
Celebes
Banda Sea
Flores Sea
Bali
Lesser Sunda Islands
Flores
Surabaya
Malang
Sumba
Timor
Timor Sea
Timor Trough
DILI
EAST TIMOR

Jayapura
Pegunungan Maoke
New Guinea
Arafura Sea

Bismarck Archipelago
Solomon Islands
Ontong Java Rise
Melanesia
Solomon Sea

Equator

AUSTRALIA
Coral Sea

POLITICAL FEATURES

TOTAL AREA:
7,936,200 sq miles
(20,554,700 sq km)

TOTAL NUMBER OF COUNTRIES:
24

TOTAL POPULATION:
3,483 million

LARGEST CITY WITH POPULATION:
Tokyo, Japan 33.9 million

COUNTRY WITH HIGHEST POPULATION DENSITY:
Singapore 18,200 people per sq mile
(7,049 people per sq km)

LARGEST COUNTRY:
China 3,705,386 sq miles
(9,596,960 sq km)

SMALLEST COUNTRY:
Maldives 116 sq miles
(300 sq km)

PHYSICAL FEATURES

LARGEST LAKE:
Tônlé Sap, Cambodia
1,000 sq miles (2,850 sq km)

LONGEST RIVER:
Chang Jiang (Yangtze), China
3,965 miles (6,380 km)

HIGHEST POINT:
Mount Everest, China/Nepal
29,035 ft (8,850 m)

LOWEST POINT:
Turpan Pendi (Turfan Basin), China
505 ft (154 m) below sea level

0 km 1000

0 miles 1000

WESTERN CHINA & MONGOLIA

POPULATION

- ■ Over 500,000
- ◉ 100,000 – 500,000
- ○ 50,000 – 100,000
- ○ Less than 50,000
- ● National capital
- ● Internal administrative capital

Map labels:

RUSSIAN FED

KAZAKHSTAN

Kazakhskiy Melkosopochnik

Kulunda Steppe

Ozero Balkhash

Zapadnyy Sayan

Yenisey

Hövsgöl Nuur

Uvs Nuur

Ulaangom

Ölgiy

Altay

Charus Nuur

Hyargas Nuur

Har Nuur

Hovd

Hangayn Nuruu

Tsetserleg

Mörö

M O N

Altay

Bayanhongor

Aj Bogd Uul 3802m

Atas Bogd 2702m

G

Ulungur Hu

Karamay

Gurbantünggüt Shamo

Kuytun

Bohoro Shan

Yining

Shihezi

Fukang

Jimsar

Qitai

Ürümqi

Turpan

Turpan Pendi

Hami

Xingxingxia

Ejin Qi

KYRGYZSTAN

Ozero Issyk-Kul'

Tien Shan

Pik Pobedy 7443m

Korla

Bosten Hu

Kuruktag

GANSU

Qilian Shan

Kashi

Tarim He

Tarim Basin

Lop Nur

Qinghai Hu

TAJIKISTAN

AFGH.

Yengisar

Shache

XINJIANG UYGUR ZIZHIQU

Ruoqiang

Altun Shan

Danghe Nanshan

PAKISTAN

Karakoram Range

Yecheng (claimed by India)

Pishan

Moyu

Taklimakan Shamo

Qaidam Pendi

Golmud

Burhan Budai Shan

Dulan

Kashmir

Hotan

Qira

Kunlun Shan

CH

Indus

K2 8611m

AKSAI CHIN

AKSAI CHIN (administered by China, claimed by India)

QINGHAI

Anyêmaqên Sh

JAMMU AND KASHMIR

Rutög

Qingzang Gaoyuan (Plateau of Tibet)

Tongtian He

Bayan Har Sha

DEMCHOK/DÊMQOG (administered by China, claimed by India)

Gar

Zanda

XIZANG ZIZHIQU (Tibet)

Nyima

Tanggula Shan

Siling Co

Amdo

Yushu

Mekong

Tangra Yumco

Gyaring Co

Nam Co

Nagqu

Qamdo

Salween

Ngangzê Co

Damxung

Yamuna

Ganges

Brahmaputra

NEPAL

Nyainqêntanglha Shan

Lhazê

Xigazê

Maizhokunggar

Lhasa

ARUNACHAL PRADESH (claimed by China)

Jinsha Jiang

Hengduan Shan

Mount Everest 8850m

Gonggar

Gyangzê

H i m a l a y a s

INDIA

BHUTAN

INDIA

MYANMAR (BURMA)

104

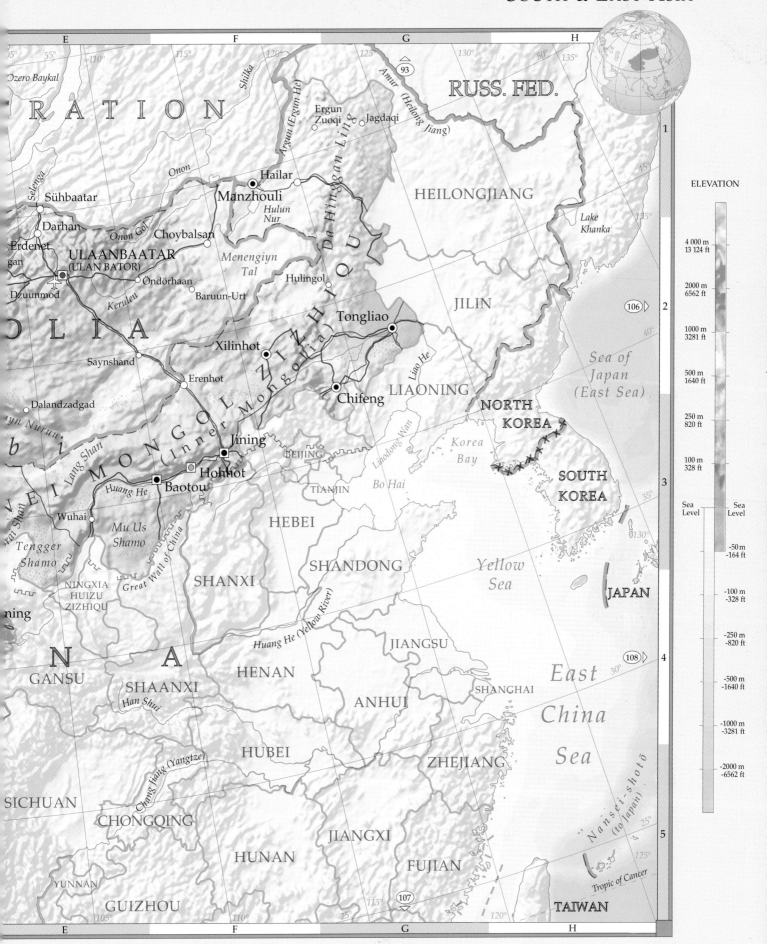

RUSS. FED.

Ozero Baykal

RATION

Shilka

Amur (Heilong Jiang)

93

HEILONGJIANG

Lake Khanka

Onon

Argun (Ergun He)

Ergun Zuoqi

Jagdaqi

Hailar

Manzhouli

Hulun Nur

Sühbaatar

Darhan

Onon Gol

Choybalsan

Menengiyn Tal

JILIN

Erdenet

gan

ULAANBAATAR
(ULAN BATOR)

Öndörhaan

Hulingol

106

Sea of
Japan
(East Sea)

Dzuunmod

Kerulen

Baruun-Urt

OLIA

Tongliao

Liao He

Xilinhot

Saynshand

Erenhot

Chifeng

LIAONING

NORTH
KOREA

Dalandzadgad

yn Nuruu

b

Jining

BEIJING

Liadong Wan

Korea
Bay

SOUTH
KOREA

EI

Lang Shan

Hohhot

Baotou

TIANJIN

Bo Hai

JAPAN

Wuhai

Huang He

HEBEI

SHANDONG

Yellow
Sea

Tengger
Shamo

Mu Us
Shamo

Great Wall of China

NINGXIA
HUIZU
ZIZHIQU

SHANXI

ning

N

A

Huang He (Yellow River)

JIANGSU

East

GANSU

HENAN

108

China

SHAANXI

Han Shui

ANHUI

SHANGHAI

Sea

HUBEI

ZHEJIANG

SICHUAN

Chang Jiang (Yangtze)

CHONGQING

JIANGXI

Nansei-shotō (to Japan)

HUNAN

FUJIAN

Tropic of Cancer

YUNNAN

107

GUIZHOU

TAIWAN

Qin Ling

Da Hinggan Ling

Nei Mongol Zizhiqu (Inner Mongolia)

EASTERN CHINA & KOREA

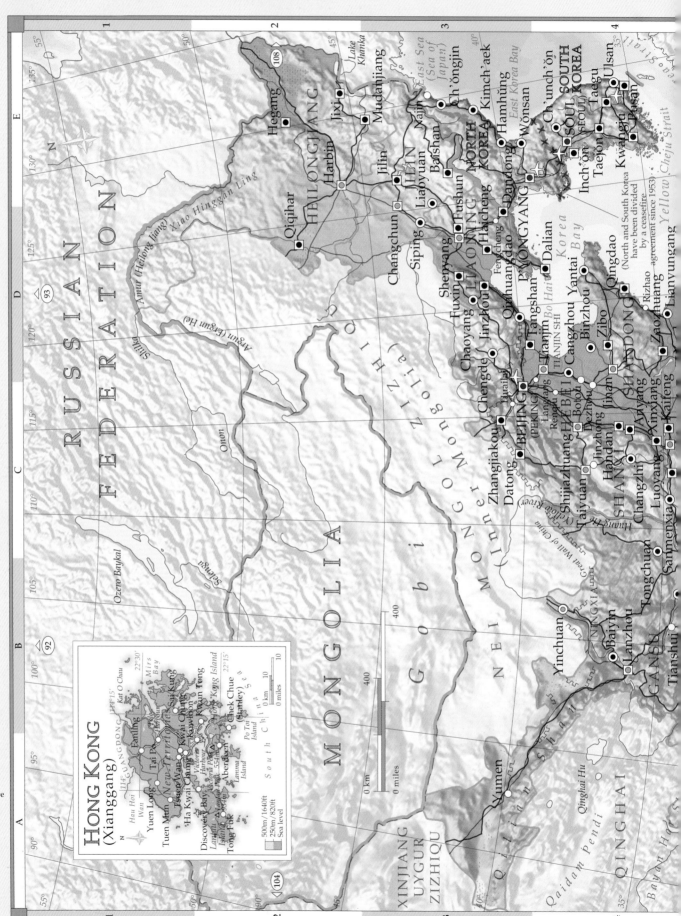

POPULATION

- ◉ Over 500,000
- ◉ 100,000 – 500,000
- ○ 50,000 – 100,000
- ○ Less than 50,000
- ● National capital
- ● Internal administrative capital

HONG KONG (Xianggang)

ELEVATION

4 000 m
13 124 ft

2000 m
6562 ft

1000 m
3281 ft

500 m
1640 ft

250 m
820 ft

100 m
328 ft

Sea Level — Sea Level

-50 m
-164 ft

-100 m
-328 ft

-250 m
-820 ft

-500 m
-1640 ft

-1000 m
-3281 ft

-2000 m
-6562 ft

JAPAN

East China Sea

Okinawa

N a n s e i - s h o t o (part of Japan)

Tropic of Cancer

PACIFIC OCEAN

PHILIPPINES

Luzon Strait

TAIWAN

(China and Taiwan claim all of each other's territory)

Chilung
TAIPEI
T'aichung
Chiai
T'ainan
Kaohsiung
Shantou

Taiwan Strait

Shanghai
Suzhou
Wuxi
Jiaxing
Ningbo
Wenzhou
Hangzhou
Jinhua
Shangrao
Nanjing
Hefei
Wuhu
Anqing
ANHUI
ZHEJIANG
Huangshi
Wuhan
HUBEI
Xinyang
Nanyang
Xiangfan
Yichang
Jingdezhen
Nanchang
JIANGXI
FUJIAN
Nanping
Fuzhou
Yong'an
Quanzhou
Xiamen
Zhangzhou
Ganzhou
Longyan
Shaoguan
Yueyang
Changsha
Xiangtan
HUNAN
Loudi
Hengyang
Chenzhou
Lengshuitan
Quanzhou
Guilin
Liuzhou
Guangzhou
Dongguan
Hong Kong (Xianggang)
Macao (Aomen)
Zhaoqing
Jiangmen
GUANGDONG
GUANGXI ZIZHIQU
Yulin
Maoming
Zhanjiang
Haikou
HAINAN
Nanning
Beihai
Suixi
Xuwen
Danzhou
Dongfang
Hainan Dao

South China Sea

PARACEL ISLANDS
(disputed by China, Taiwan and Vietnam)
Amphitrite Group
Crescent Group
Triton Island

SPRATLY ISLANDS
(disputed by China, Malaysia, Philippines, Taiwan and Vietnam)
Flat Island
Nanshan Island
Thitu Island
Loaita Island
Namyit Island
Len Dao
Spratly Island

Gulf of Tongking

VIETNAM

CAMBODIA

THAILAND

LAOS

Gulf of Thailand

Mekong

Red River

Gejiu
Kunming
YUNNAN
Dali
Baoshan
Wuliang Shan
Jinghong
Hengduan Shan
Salween
Mekong
Jinsha Jiang

MYANMAR (BURMA)

Tropic of Cancer

INDIA

XIZANG ZIZHIQU (TIBET)

SICHUAN
Mianyang
Chengdu
Sichuan Pendi
Ya'an
Leshan
Zigong
Neijiang
Chongqing
CHONGQING
Zunyi
Guiyang
GUIZHOU
Anshun
Wanxian
Lichuan
Utang
Mekong Jiang
Dadu He (Tong Jiang)
Xichang

Guangyuan

107

JAPAN

THE WORLD ATLAS

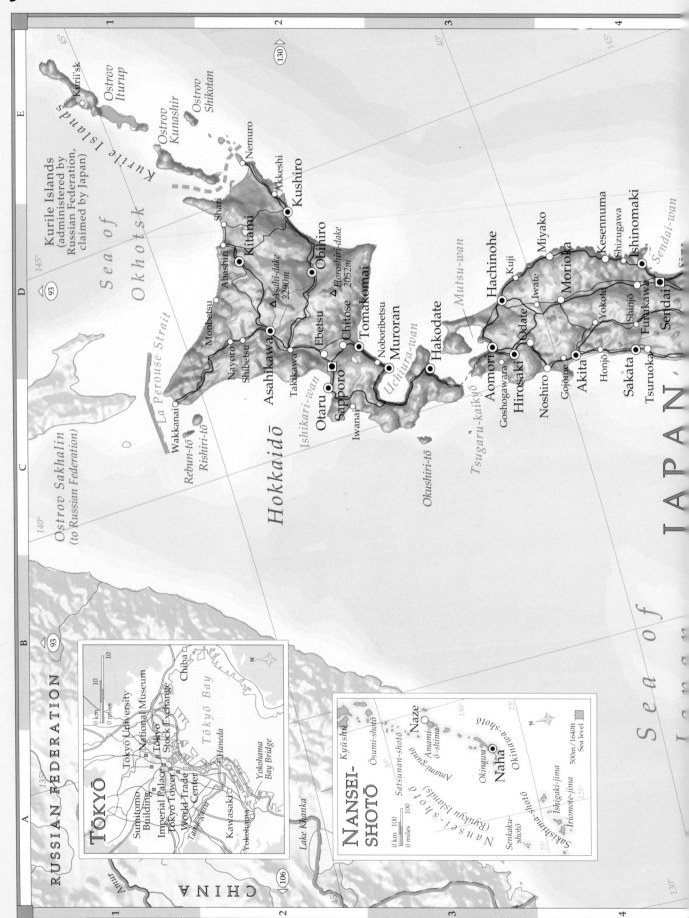

Kurile Islands
(administered by
Russian Federation,
claimed by Japan)

Kuril'sk

Ostrov
Iturup

Ostrov
Kunashir

Ostrov
Shikotan

Sea of
Okhotsk

Kurile Islands

Nemuro

Akkeshi

Kushiro

Shari

Kitami

Abashiri

Obihiro

Horoshiri-dake
2052m

Monbetsu

Asahi-dake
2290m

Tomakomai

Nayoro

Shibetsu

Ebetsu

Chitose

Noboribetsu

Muroran

Uchiura-wan

Hakodate

Takikawa

Ishikari-wan

Otaru

Asahikawa

Sapporo

Iwanai

Hokkaidō

Okushiri-tō

Wakkanai

Rebun-tō

Rishiri-tō

La Perouse Strait

Ostrov Sakhalin
(to Russian Federation)

Tsugaru-kaikyō

Tsugaru-kaikyō

Mutsu-wan

Hachinohe

Kuji

Miyako

Kesennuma

Shizugawa

Ishinomaki

Sendai-wan

Iwate

Morioka

Aomori

Goshogawara

Odate

Hirosaki

Noshiro

Gojōme

Yokota

Shinjō

Fukkawa

Sendai

Akita

Honjō

Sakata

Tsuruoka

JAPAN

Sea of

POPULATION

- Over 500,000
- 100,000 – 500,000
- 50,000 – 100,000
- Less than 50,000
- National capital

RUSSIAN FEDERATION

TŌKYŌ

Tokyo University

National Museum

Tokyo Stock Exchange

Chiba

Tōkyō Bay

Sumitomo Building

Imperial Palace

Tokyo Tower

World Trade Center

Haneda

Yokohama Bay Bridge

Kawasaki

Yokohama

Lake Khanka

CHINA

Amur

NANSEI-SHOTŌ

Kyūshū

Ōsumi-shotō

Satsunan-shotō

Naze

Amami-gunto

Amami-ō-shima

Nansei-shotō
(Ryūkyū Islands)

Okinawa

Naha

Okinawa-shotō

Senkaku-shotō

Sakishima-shotō

Ishigaki-jima

Iriomote-jima

500m/1640ft

Sea level

108

ELEVATION

4000 m 13 124 ft	
2000 m 6562 ft	
1000 m 3281 ft	
500 m 1640 ft	
250 m 820 ft	
100 m 328 ft	
Sea Level	Sea Level
-250 m -820 ft	
-500 m -1640 ft	
-1000 m -3281 ft	
-2000 m -6562 ft	
-3000 m -9843 ft	
-4000 m -13 124 ft	

Honshū

PACIFIC OCEAN

Shikoku

Kyūshū

East China Sea

(East Sea)

SOUTH KOREA

Iwaki
Hitachi
Utsunomiya
Mito
Ōyama
Kawagoe
Chōshi
Chiba
Yokohama
TOKYO
Kawasaki
Sukagawa
Maebashi
Nagaoka
Jōetsu
Nagano
Matsumoto
Toyama
Takaoka
Kanazawa
Komatsu
Fukui
Tsuruga
Nakatsugawa
Gifu
Ogaki
Nagoya
Ōtsu
Kōfu
Fuji
Shizuoka
Toyota
Hamamatsu
Okazaki
Tsu
Ise
Owase
Shingū
Kōbe
Wakayama
Gobō
Tanabe
Kyōto
Ōsaka
Himeji
Tottori
Yonago
Matsue
Okayama
Kurashiki
Fukuyama
Hiroshima
Kure
Iwakuni
Hōfu
Ube
Ōita
Nobeoka
Nobeoka
Miyazaki
Miyakonojō
Katsushiro
Sendai
Kagoshima
Kumamoto
Ōmuta
Kurume
Fukuoka
Kitakyūshū
Shimonoseki
Yamaguchi
Nagato
Sasebo
Nagasaki
Yonago
Matsuyama
Mihama
Kōchi
Tokushima
Nakamura
Sukumo
Hamada
Masuda
Gōtsu

Fuji-san 3776 m △

Fujima

Liancourt Rocks (claimed by Japan & South Korea)

Oki-shotō
Dōgo
Dōzen

Izu-shotō
Hachijō-jima
Miyake-jima
Mikura-shima
Ō-shima
Nii-jima
Kōzu-shima

Bōsō-hantō
Sagami-nada
Kashima-nada
Izu-hantō
Suruga-wan
Ise-wan

Biwa-ko
Awaji-shima
Harima-nada
Kii-suidō
Tosa-wan
Bungo-suidō
Iyo-nada

Tanega-shima
Yaku-shima
Shibushi-wan
Ōsumi-shotō
Kagoshima-wan
Koshikijima-rettō
Amakusa-nada
Gotō-rettō
Kō-saki
Iki
Tsushima

Korea Strait

Toyama-wan
Wakasa-wan
Shinano-gawa
Itoigawa

109

SOUTH INDIA & SRI LANKA

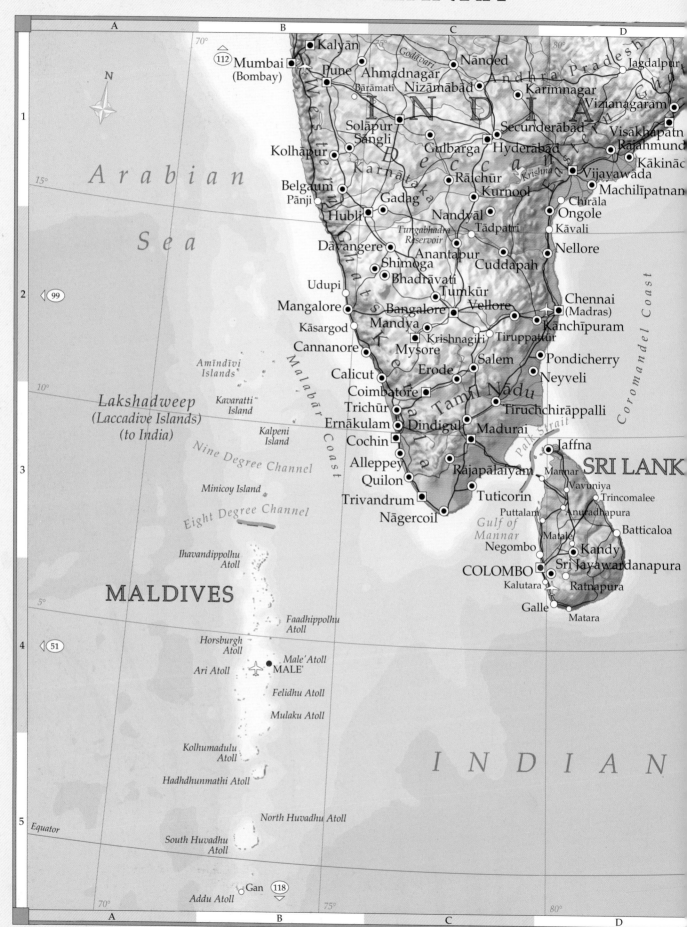

POPULATION

- ⬤ Over 500,000
- ◉ 100,000 – 500,000
- ○ 50,000 – 100,000
- ∘ Less than 50,000
- ⬤ National capital

Map labels:

Arabian Sea

Kalyān
Mumbai (Bombay)
Pune
Ahmadnagar
Bārāmati
Nizāmābād
Nānded
Karimnagar
Jagdalpur
Andhra Pradesh
Vizianagaram
Solāpur
Sangli
Secunderābād
Visākhapatn
Rājahmundry
Kolhāpur
Gulbarga
Hyderābād
Kākinād
Belgaum
Pānji
Rāichūr
Kurnool
Krishna
Vijayawāda
Machilīpatnam
Hubli
Gadag
Nandyāl
Chirāla
Ongole
Tungabhadra Reservoir
Tādpatri
Kāvali
Dāvangere
Anantapur
Cuddapah
Nellore
Shimoga
Bhadrāvati
Udupi
Tumkūr
Mangalore
Bangalore
Vellore
Chennai (Madras)
Kāsargod
Mandya
Krishnagiri
Tiruppattur
Kānchīpuram
Cannanore
Mysore
Salem
Pondicherry
Calicut
Erode
Neyveli
Coimbatore
Tamil Nādu
Trichūr
Tiruchchirāppalli
Ernākulam
Dindigul
Madurai
Cochin
Palk Strait
Jaffna
Alleppey
Rajapālaiyam
SRI LANK
Quilon
Mannar
Vavuniya
Trincomalee
Trivandrum
Tuticorin
Puttalam
Anuradhapura
Nāgercoil
Gulf of Mannar
Batticaloa
Matale
Negombo
Kandy
COLOMBO
Sri Jayawardanapura
Kalutara
Ratnapura
Galle
Matara

Coromandel Coast

Malabār Coast

Deccan
Karnātaka
INDIA

Amīndivi Islands
Lakshadweep (Laccadive Islands) (to India)
Kavaratti Island
Kalpeni Island
Nine Degree Channel
Minicoy Island
Eight Degree Channel
Ihavandippolhu Atoll

MALDIVES

Faadhippolhu Atoll
Horsburgh Atoll
Ari Atoll
Male' Atoll
MALE'
Felidhu Atoll
Mulaku Atoll
Kolhumadulu Atoll
Hadhdhunmathi Atoll

North Huvadhu Atoll
South Huvadhu Atoll

INDIAN

Equator
Addu Atoll
Gan

Godāvari

Western Ghāts

Grid references: A, B, C, D (columns); 1, 2, 3, 4, 5 (rows)

70° 75° 80° 15° 10° 5°

112 99 51 118

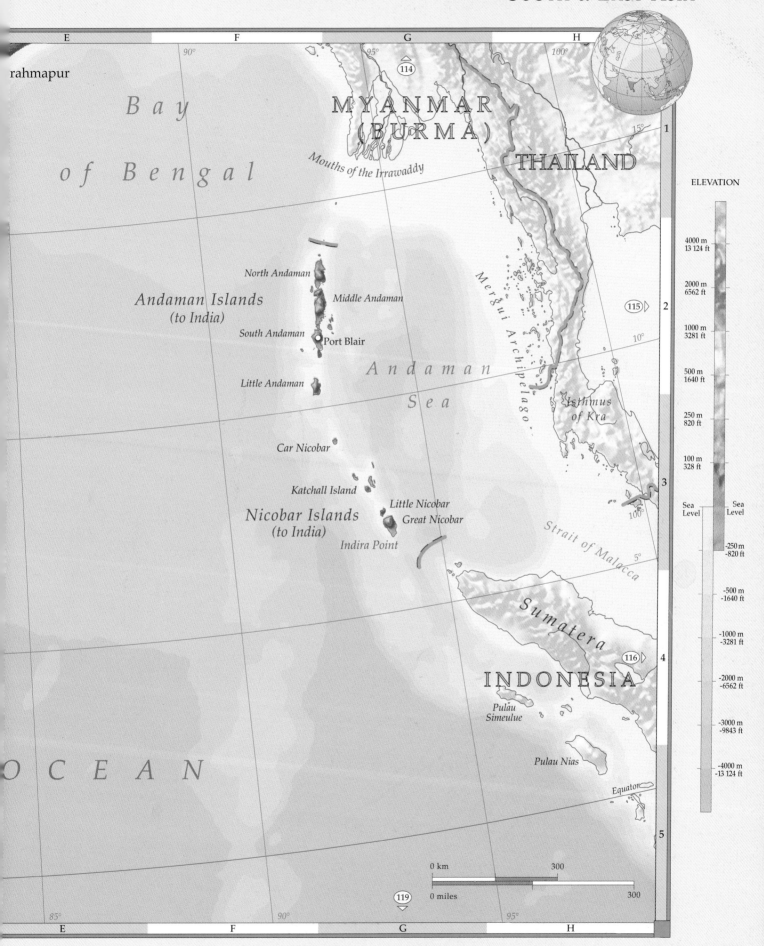

rahmapur

B a y

o f   B e n g a l

MYANMAR
(BURMA)

THAILAND

Mouths of the Irrawaddy

North Andaman

Andaman Islands
(to India)

Middle Andaman

Mergui Archipelago

South Andaman

Port Blair

Little Andaman

A n d a m a n

S e a

*Isthmus
of Kra*

Car Nicobar

Katchall Island

Little Nicobar

Nicobar Islands
(to India)

Great Nicobar

Indira Point

Strait of Malacca

S u m a t e r a

INDONESIA

*Pulau
Simeulue*

Pulau Nias

Equator

O C E A N

114

115

116

119

ELEVATION

| 4000 m 13 124 ft |
| 2000 m 6562 ft |
| 1000 m 3281 ft |
| 500 m 1640 ft |
| 250 m 820 ft |
| 100 m 328 ft |
| Sea Level | Sea Level |
| -250 m -820 ft |
| -500 m -1640 ft |
| -1000 m -3281 ft |
| -2000 m -6562 ft |
| -3000 m -9843 ft |
| -4000 m -13 124 ft |

0 km   300

0 miles   300

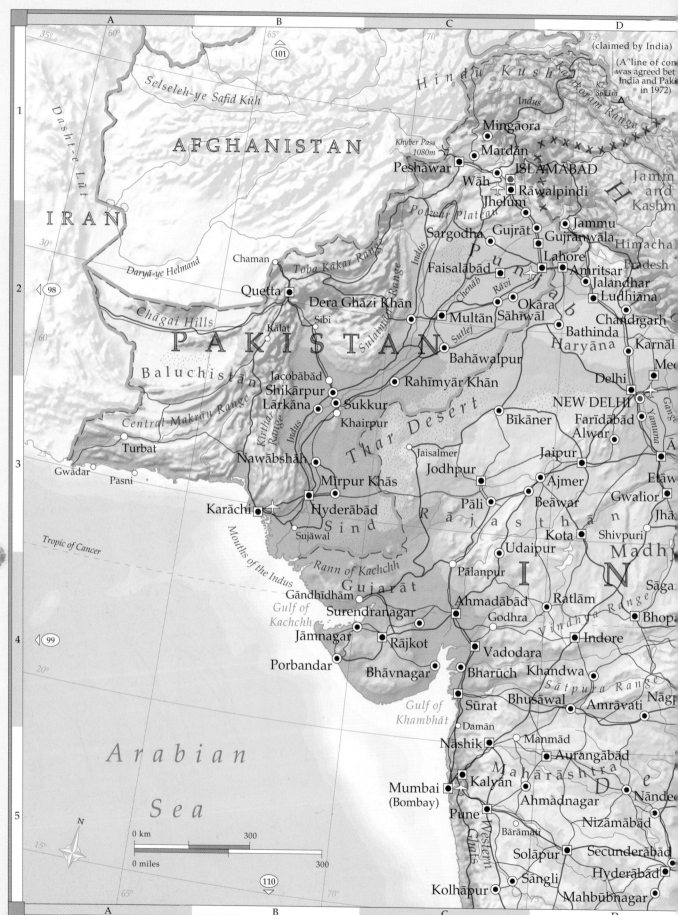

POPULATION

- Over 500,000
- 100,000 - 500,000
- 50,000 - 100,000
- Less than 50,000
- National capital

A

B

C

D

1

2

3

4

5

35°
60°
65°
70°
75°

△ 101

(claimed by India)

(A "line of con was agreed bet India and Paki in 1972)

Selseleh-ye Safid Kūh

AFGHANISTAN

Hindu Kush

Karakoram Range

Indus

K2 8611m △

Mingaora

Khyber Pass 1080m

Mardān

Peshāwar

ISLĀMĀBĀD

Wāh

Rāwalpindi

Jammu and Kashm

Dasht-e Lūt

Potwar Plateau

Jhelum

◁ 98

30°

Daryā-ye Helmand

Chaman

Toba Kākar Range

Sargodha

Gujrāt

Gujrānwāla

Jammu

Himacha Pradesh

IRAN

Indus

Lahore

Amritsar

Jalandhar

Quetta

Faisalābād

Chenāb

Rāvi

Ludhiāna

Dera Ghāzi Khān

Sibi

Okāra

Sāhīwāl

Chandīgarh

Kālat

Multān

Bathinda

Haryāna

Karnāl

Baluchistān

Bahāwalpur

Sutlej

Mee

Jacobābād

Rahīmyār Khān

Delhi

Central Makrān Range

Shikārpur

Sukkur

Bīkāner

NEW DELHI

Farīdābād

Yamuna

Ganga

Larkāna

Khairpur

Alwar

25°

Turbat

Nawābshāh

Jaisalmer

Jodhpur

Jaipur

Etāw

Gwādar

Pasni

Mīrpur Khās

Ajmer

Gwalior

Jhā

Karāchi

Hyderābād

Sind

Rā

Pāli

Beāwar

Thar Desert

j a s t h ā n

Kota

Shivpuri

Tropic of Cancer

Sujāwal

Udaipur

Madhy

Mouths of the Indus

Rann of Kachchh

Pālanpur

I

N

Gāndhīdhām

Gujarāt

Ahmadābād

Ratlām

Sāga

Gulf of Kachchh

Surendranagar

Godhra

Bhop

◁ 99

20°

Jāmnagar

Rājkot

Vadodara

Indore

Porbandar

Bhāruch

Khandwa

Bhāvnagar

Sātpura Range

Gulf of Khambhāt

Sūrat

Bhusāwal

Amrāvati

Nāg

Daman

Nāshik

Manmād

Aurangābād

A r a b i a n

Kalyān

Mahārāshtra

Mumbai (Bombay)

Ahmadnagar

Nānded

S e a

Pune

Nizāmābād

N

Bārāmati

0 km   300

Solāpur

Secunderābād

0 miles   300

Hyderābād

Kolhāpur

Sāngli

Mahbūbnagar

65°
70°
75°

△ 110

E   F   G   H

XINJIANG
Uygur Zizhiqu

Kunlun Shan

1

AKSAI CHIN
(administered by China,
claimed by India)

C H I N A

QINGHAI

Jinsha Jiang

SICHUAN

ELEVATION

Qingzang Gaoyuan
(Plateau of Tibet)

DEMCHOK/
DÊMQOG
(administered by China,
claimed by India)

Tanggula Shan

Mekong (Lancang Jiang)

4 000 m
13 124 ft

XIZANG ZIZHIQU

(Tibet)

Nyainqêntanglha Shan

**ARUNĀCHAL
PRADESH**
(claimed by China)

104

2000 m
6562 ft

2

m

Brahmaputra

1000 m
3281 ft

500 m
1640 ft

H

a

l

a

y

a

s

Dibrugarh

*Annapurna
8091m*

*Mount Everest
8850m*

*Kula Kangri
7554m*

Brahmaputra

250 m
820 ft

NEPAL

reilly

Salyan

Pokhara

THIMPHU

Bahraich

Bhaktapur

Gangtok

BHUTAN

Jorhāt

100 m
328 ft

aun

KATHMANDU

Lalitpur

Darjiling

Shiligūri

Bongaigaon

Assam

Kohīma

3

cknow

Faizābād

Gorakhpur

B i h ā r

Biratnagar

Koch Bihār

Dispur

Shillong

Sea
Level

Sea
Level

Kānpur

Mau

Chhapra

Dinajpur

Saidpur

Rangpur

Guwāhāti

M e g h ā l a y a

Silchar

Imphāl

-50 m
-164 ft

Jaunpur

Varānasi

Patna

Bhāgalpur

Jamālpur

Sylhet

Allahābād

Bihār Sharīf

Ganges

BANGLADESH

adesh

I

Gaya

Jharkhand

Rajshahi

Pabna

DHAKA

Brahmanbaria

Tropic of Cancer

-100 m
-328 ft

A

Dhanbād

Asānsol

Ganges

Comilla

MYANMAR

Murwāra

Bokāro

Bankura

Jessore

-250 m
-820 ft

Jabalpur

*Chota
Nāgpur*

Rānchi

West Bengal

Khulna

(BURMA)

Bilāspur

Korba

Jamshedpur

Hāora

Barisal

Chittagong

114

4

Raulakela

Kharagpur

**Calcutta
(Kolkata)**

Gondia

Raipur

Sambalpur

Bāleshwar

Mouths of the Ganges

-500 m
-1640 ft

Nāndgaon

Durg

Orissa

Cuttack

Mahānadi

-1000 m
-3281 ft

ndrapur

a

n

Bhubaneshwar

Irrawaddy

-2000 m
-6562 ft

Puri

imnagar

Jagdalpur

Brahmapur

*Bay of
Bengal*

Pradesh

Eastern Ghats

Godāvari

Srīkākulam

5

rangal

Vizianagaram

Visākhapatnam

Rajahmundry

*Mouths of the
Irrawaddy*

Kākināda

111

E   F   G   H

MAINLAND SOUTHEAST ASIA

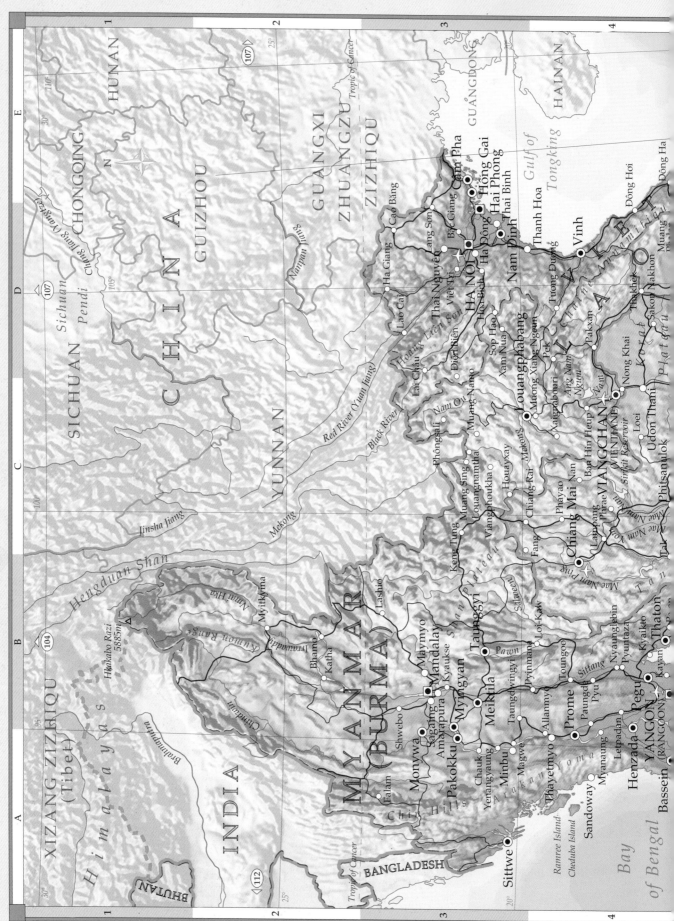

POPULATION

- ◉ Over 500,000
- ◉ 100,000 – 500,000
- ○ 50,000 – 100,000
- ○ Less than 50,000
- ● National capital

ELEVATION

4 000 m	13 124 ft
2000 m	6562 ft
1000 m	3281 ft
500 m	1640 ft
250 m	820 ft
100 m	328 ft

Sea Level	Sea Level
-50 m	-164 ft
-100 m	-328 ft
-250 m	-820 ft
-500 m	-1640 ft
-1000 m	-3281 ft
-2000 m	-6562 ft

South China Sea

Kepulauan Natuna (to Indonesia)

Côn Đao

MALAYSIA

Malay Peninsula

Strait of Malacca

INDONESIA

Sumatera (Sumatra)

Pulau Pinang

Pulau Langkawi

Pulau Simeulue

INDIAN OCEAN

Andaman Sea

Mergui Archipelago

Andaman Islands (to India)

North Andaman
Middle Andaman
South Andaman
Little Andaman

Nicobar Islands (to India)

Car Nicobar
Katchall Island
Little Nicobar
Great Nicobar

CAMBODIA

PHNUM PENH

KRUNG THEP (BANGKOK)

Gulf of Thailand

Mekong

Mouths of the Mekong

Quang Ngai
Quy Nhon
Play Cu
Virochey
Tuy Hoa
Nha Trang
Da Lat
Di Linh
Cam Ranh
Phan Rang-Thap Cham
Biên Hoa
Phan Thiêt
Hô Chi Minh
Vung Tau
My Tho
Tra Vinh
Long Xuyên
Can Tho
Soc Trăng
Bac Liêu
Ca Mau
Rach Gia
Châu Dôc
Kâmpôt
Kâmpong Spoe
Kâmpong Saôm
Ko Chang
Chanthaburi
Rayong
Pattaya
Samut Prakan
Chon Buri
Ao Krung Thep
Phetchaburi
Ban Hua Hin
Chumphon
Lang Suan
Ko Phangan
Ko Samui
Surat Thani
Sichon
Nakhon Si Thammarat
Pak Phanang
Thung Song
Phatthalung
Thale Luang
Songkhla
Pattani
Narathiwat
Yala
Hat Yai
Trang
Ko Lanta
Ko Ta Ru Tao
Phuket
Ko Phuket
Phang-Nga
Ranong
Ko Phra Thong
Zadetkyi Kyun
Tenasserim
Mergui
Daung Kyun
Letsôk-aw Kyun
Lanbi Kyun
Kadan Kyun
Mali Kyun
Tavoy
Ye

Srinagarind Reservoir

Bilauktaung Range

Isthmus of Kra

Muang Không
Muang Khôngxedôn
Pakxé
Champasak
Ubon Ratchathani
Surin
Buriram
Nakhon Ratchasima
Nakhon Savan
Lop Buri
Sara Buri
Ayutthaya
Nakhon Pathom
Ratchaburi
Tônle Sap
Phnum Dângrêk
Muang Không
Stoeng Trêng
Krâchéh
Stenăg Sên
Kâmpong Cham
Kâmpong Chhnang
Kâmpong Thum
Trapeăng Vêng
Svay Riêng
Suông
Rêânb Kesei
Chuor Phnum Krâvanh Dâmrei
Pouthisat
Môung Roessei
Batdâmbâng
Chuor Phnum Dângrêk
Siphraông
Krâlânh
Tônle Sap

Ss of the Irrawaddy

MARITIME SOUTHEAST ASIA

SINGAPORE

MALAYSIA

0 km   10
0 miles   10

Johore Strait

Causeway

Pulau Ubin

Pulau Tekong

Lim Chu Kang

Hougang New Town

Bukit Panjang

Changi

Choa Chu Kang

Bedok

Bukit Timah 176m

Queenstown

City

Bedok New Town

Jurong Industrial Estate

Telok Blangah

Sentosa

Selat Pandan

Pulau Sudong

Pulau Pawai

Strait of Singapore

Urban areas
Open areas
Nature reserves

MYANMAR (BURMA)

LAOS

VIETNAM

THAILAND

CAMBODIA

Gulf of Tongking

Hainan Dao (to China)

PARACEL ISLANDS
(disputed by China, Taiwan and Vietnam)

South Chin

Sea

Mekong

Gulf of Thailand

Mouths of the Mekong

SPRATLY ISLANDS
(disputed by China, Malaysia, Philippines, Taiwan and Vietnam)

Andaman Sea

Nicobar Islands (to India)

Isthmus of Kra

Bandaaceh

Sigli

Kota Bharu

George Town

Butterworth

Kuala Terengganu

Gunung Kinaba

Kota Kinabalu

410

Langsa

Meulaboh

Taiping

Ipoh

Dungun

BANDAR SERI BEGAWAN

Pulau Pinang

BRUNEI

Sa

Medan

Tebingtinggi

Cukai

Miri

Pematangsiantar

Klang

Kuantan

Kepulauan Natuna

Bintulu

Tav

Pulau Simeulue

KUALA LUMPUR

MALAYSIA

Strait of Malacca

PUTRAJAYA

Selat Serasan

Sibu

Batang Raja

Sarawak

Sungai Kayan

Kepulauan Banyak

Danau Toba

Melaka

Keluang

Sri Aman

Muar

Johor Bahru

Kuching

Sibolga

Batu Pahat

SINGAPORE

Sidas

Borneo

Pulau Nias

Pekanbaru

Singkawang

Equator

Solok

Rengat

Kepulauan Lingga

Pontianak

Sungai Kapuas

Pegunungan Muller

Sungai Mahakar

Padang

Batang Hari

Kualatungkal

Kalimantan

Samarinda

Pulau Siberut

Jambi

Balikpapan

Kepulauan Mentawai

Bangka

Sampit

Sungai Barito

Amuntai

Sungaipenuh

Pangkalpinang

Kandang

Palembang

Pulau Belitung

Lahat

Selat Karimata

Banjarmasin

Bengkulu

Kotabumi

I N D

Pulau Laut

Java Sea

Mak

Sumatera (Sumatra)

Bandarlampung

Cirebon

Tegal

I N D I A N

Serang

JAKARTA

Pekalongan

Semarang

Pulau Madura

Selat Sunda

Bogor

Kudus

Surabaya

Sukabumi

Probolinggo

O C E A N

Bandung

N

Tasikmalaya

Jember Matar

Jawa (Java)

Cilacap

Malang

Bali

Denpasa

Magelang

Kediri

Pulau Lombok

Yogyakarta

Madiun

Surakarta

POPULATION

⊙ Over 500,000

⊙ 100,000 – 500,000

○ 50,000 – 100,000

· Less than 50,000

● National capital

MALAYSIA'S TWO CAPITALS

Kuala Lumpur – *capital*

Putrajaya – *administrative capital*

SOUTH & EAST ASIA

Luzon Strait
Babuyan Island
Babuyan Channel
Tuguegarao
Ilagan
guio
Cordillera
Central
Luzon
Dagupan
geles
Cabanatuan
ANILA
Lucena
PHILIPPINES
tangas
Naga
Mindoro
Legaspi
Mindoro Strait
Sibuyan Sea
Calbayog
Roxas City
Samar
Panay Island
Cadiz
Tacloban
Iloilo
Leyte
Palawan
Bacolod City
Cebu
uerto rincesa
Negros
Butuan
Sulu Sea
Bohol Sea
Cagayan de Oro
Iligan
Bislig
Zamboanga
Moro Gulf
Mindanao
Basilan
Davao
dakan
Lebak
Davao Gulf
Sulu Archipelago
General Santos

Philippine Sea

NORTHERN
MARIANA
ISLANDS
(to US)

GUAM
(to US)

Yap
MICRONESIA

P A C I F I C

Babeldaob

P A L A U

O C E A N

Equator

Kepulauan Talaud

Kepulauan Sangir

Pulau Morotai
Pulau Halmahera

Celebes Sea

Manado
Bitung
Molucca Sea
Gorontalo

alu
Gulf of Tomini
Kepulauan Banggai
Sulawesi (Celebes)
Pegunungan Quarles
Danau Towuti
Kepulauan Sula

Pulau Waigeo
Halmahera Sea
Selat Dampier
Pulau Biak
Pulau Yapen
Sorong
Jazirah Doberai
Teluk Berau
Teluk Cenderawasih

Javapura

Sungai Mamberamo

Ceram Sea
Maluku (Moluccas)
Wahai
Waflia
Tifu
Pulau Buru
Ambon
Pulau Seram

N   E   S   I

Kendari
Kolaka
Pulau Buton
epare
Watampone
Ujungpandang
Bulukumba

Teluk Bone

Banda Sea

Pulau Misool

Kepulauan Kai

Puncak Jaya 5030m
Pegunungan Maoke
Papua (Irian Jaya)

A

PAPUA

NEW

New Guinea

GUINEA

Sungai Digul

Kepulauan Aru

ngkang

Flores
Tenggara
Kepulauan Alor
Pulau Wetar

DILI
Timor
EAST TIMOR
Nikiniki
Kupang

Savu Sea

at Sumba
umba
res ea

Kepulauan Leti

Kepulauan Tanimbar
Pulau Yamdena

A r a f u r a   S e a

Torres Strait

A U S T R A L I A

Timor Sea

ELEVATION

4000 m	13 124 ft
2000 m	6562 ft
1000 m	3281 ft
500 m	1640 ft
250 m	820 ft
100 m	328 ft
Sea Level	Sea Level
-250 m	-820 ft
-500 m	-1640 ft
-1000 m	-3281 ft
-2000 m	-6562 ft
-3000 m	-9843 ft
-4000 m	-13 124 ft

THE INDIAN OCEAN

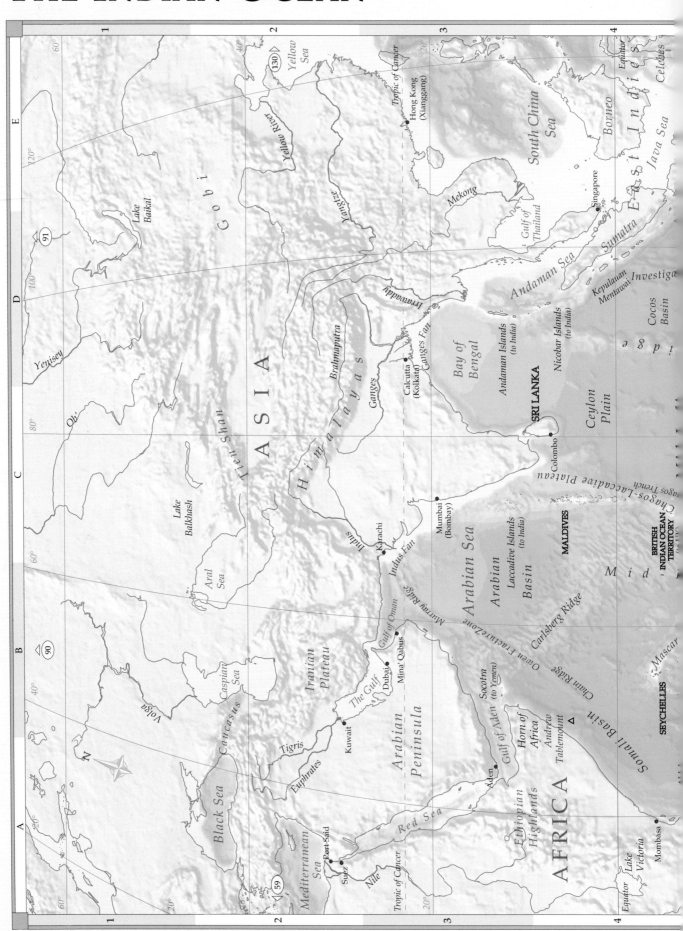

E

D

C

B

A

1   2   3   4

60°

120°

100°

80°

60°

40°

20°

20°

Yellow
Sea

Tropic of Cancer

Hong Kong
(Xianggang)

South China
Sea

Borneo

Equator

Java Sea

Celebes

Sumatra

East Indies

Singapore

Gulf of
Thailand

Mekong

Andaman Sea

Kepulauan
Mentawai

Investiga

Cocos
Basin

Gobi

Lake
Baikal

Yellow River

Yangtze

Irrawaddy

Ganges Fan

Bay of
Bengal

Andaman Islands
(to India)

Nicobar Islands
(to India)

Ceylon
Plain

ge

Yenisey

Ob'

Tien Shan

A S I A

Brahmaputra

Ganges

Calcutta
(Kolkata)

SRI LANKA

Colombo

Himalayas

Lake
Balkhash

Aral
Sea

Indus

Karachi

Indus Fan

Mumbai
(Bombay)

Arabian Sea

Arabian
Basin

Laccadive Islands
(to India)

MALDIVES

Chagos-Laccadive Plateau

agos Trench

Mid

BRITISH
INDIAN OCEAN
TERRITORY
(to UK)

Caspian
Sea

Volga

Iranian
Plateau

Gulf of Oman

Murray Ridge

Owen Fracture Zone

Carlsberg Ridge

SEYCHELLES

Mascar

Black Sea

Caucasus

The Gulf

Dubai

Mina' Qabus

Arabian
Peninsula

Socotra
(to Yemen)

Andrew
Tablemount

Chain Ridge

Somali Basin

Tigris

Euphrates

Kuwait

Gulf of Aden

Horn of
Africa

Aden

Mediterranean
Sea

Port Said

Suez

Nile

Tropic of Cancer

Red Sea

Ethiopian
Highlands

AFRICA

Equator

Lake
Victoria

Mombasa

N

90

91

59

130

1   2   3   4

North
Australian
Basin

Exmouth
Plateau

20°

5   6   7   8

AUSTRALIA

Tropic of Capricorn

Fremantle

(130)

Cuvier
Plateau

Perth
Basin

Naturaliste
Plateau

Limit of winter pack ice

Limit of summer pack ice

Antarctic Circle

140°

E

1500

80°

Diamantina Fracture Zone

Wharton

Basin

East Indian-Antarctic Ridge

1500

Broken Ridge

COCOS ISLANDS
(to Australia)

idge

Ninetyeast

Osborn
Plateau

s

INDIAN

Southeast Indian Ridge

South Indian Basin

120°

132

D

100°

0 km

0 miles

Amsterdam Island

Île St-Paul

OCEAN

SOUTHERN OCEAN

● Major port

Egeria Fracture zone

Indian Ridge

Kerguelen Plateau

FRENCH SOUTHERN &
ANTARCTIC TERRITORIES
(to France)

Bonzare
Seamounts

80°

C

ELEVATION

Argo Fracture

MAURITIUS
RÉUNION
(to France)

Kerguelen

60°

Sea
Level

ateau

Mascarene
Basin

Madagascar
Basin

Southwest

HEARD & McDONALD ISLANDS
(to Australia)

ANTARCTICA

40°

132

B

20°

Mascarene
Plain

Madagascar
Plateau

Crozet
Basin

Crozet Islands
Plateau

△ Lena Tablemount

Enderby Plain

-250 m
-820 ft

-500 m
-1640 ft

MAYOTTE
(to France)

Farafangana

MADAGASCAR

Natal
Basin

Mozambique Plateau

Indomed Fracture Zone

Ob' Tablemount △

0°

20°

-1000 m
-3281 ft

-2000 m
-6562 ft

Davie Ridge

Mozambique Channel

Prince Edward Islands
(to South Africa)

Atlantic-Indian
Basin

Antarctic Circle

-4000 m
-13 124 ft

Nyasa

Zambezi

Tropic of Capricorn

Durban ●

Africana
Seamount
△

Agulhas
Plateau

Agulhas
Basin

45

20°

80°

-6000 m
-19 686 ft

20°

A

5   6   7   8

119

AUSTRALASIA & OCEANIA

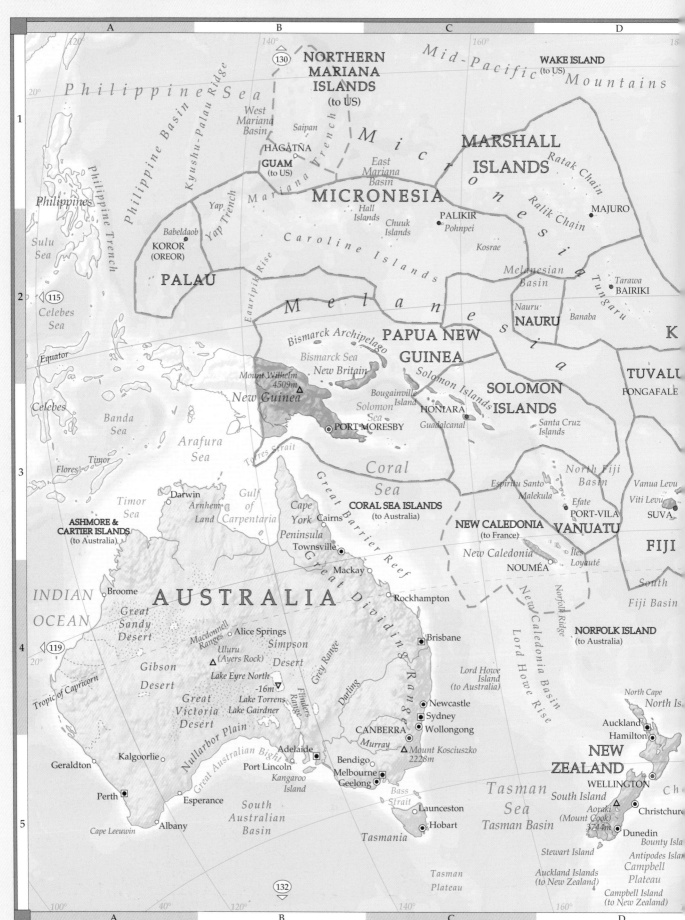

Philippine Sea

NORTHERN MARIANA ISLANDS (to US)

130

WAKE ISLAND (to US)

Mid-Pacific Mountains

West Mariana Basin

Philippine Basin

Kyushu-Palau Ridge

Philippine Trench

Saipan

HAGÁTÑA
GUAM (to US)

East Mariana Basin

MARSHALL ISLANDS

Ratak Chain

Philippine

Yap Trench

Mariana Trench

MICRONESIA

Hall Islands

Chuuk Islands

PALIKIR
Pohnpei

Ralik Chain

MAJURO

Sulu Sea

Yap

Babeldaob

KOROR (OREOR)

Caroline Islands

Kosrae

Melanesian Basin

Tarawa
BAIRIKI

115

Celebes Sea

PALAU

Eauripik Rise

Melanesia

Nauru
NAURU

Banaba

Tungaru

K

Equator

Bismarck Archipelago

PAPUA NEW GUINEA

TUVALU
FONGAFALE

Celebes

Bismarck Sea
New Britain

Mount Wilhelm 4509m

New Guinea

Banda Sea

Solomon Islands
SOLOMON ISLANDS

Bougainville Island

Solomon Sea

HONIARA

Santa Cruz Islands

North Fiji Basin

Vanua Levu

Arafura Sea

PORT MORESBY

Guadalcanal

Espiritu Santo
Malekula

Efate
PORT-VILA

Viti Levu
SUVA

Timor
Flores

Torres Strait

Coral Sea

CORAL SEA ISLANDS (to Australia)

VANUATU

FIJI

Timor Sea

Darwin

Gulf of Carpentaria

Cape York Peninsula

Cairns

NEW CALEDONIA (to France)

New Caledonia

Iles Loyauté

South Fiji Basin

ASHMORE & CARTIER ISLANDS (to Australia)

Arnhem Land

Townsville

NOUMÉA

Great Barrier Reef

Mackay

New Caledonia Ridge

Norfolk Ridge

INDIAN OCEAN

Broome

AUSTRALIA

Great Sandy Desert

Rockhampton

Lord Howe Island (to Australia)

NORFOLK ISLAND (to Australia)

119

Great Dividing Range

Brisbane

Lord Howe Basin

Lord Howe Rise

Macdonnell Ranges
Alice Springs

Simpson Desert

Gibson Desert

Uluru (Ayers Rock)

Lake Eyre North -16m

Grey Range

Darling

North Cape
North Is.

Tropic of Capricorn

Great Victoria Desert

Lake Torrens
Lake Gairdner

Flinders Range

Newcastle
Sydney
Wollongong

Auckland
Hamilton

Kalgoorlie

Nullarbor Plain

CANBERRA

Murray

Mount Kosciuszko 2228m

NEW ZEALAND

Geraldton

Adelaide

Bendigo

WELLINGTON

Perth

Great Australian Bight

Port Lincoln

Kangaroo Island

Melbourne
Geelong

Bass Strait

Tasman Sea

South Island

Aoraki (Mount Cook) 3744m

Christchurc

Esperance

South Australian Basin

Launceston

Tasman Basin

Dunedin

Albany

Hobart

Bounty Isla

Cape Leeuwin

Tasmania

Stewart Island

Antipodes Islan

Tasman Plateau

Auckland Islands (to New Zealand)

Campbell Plateau

132

Campbell Island (to New Zealand)

POPULATION

⊙ Over 500,000

◉ 100,000 – 500,000

○ 50,000 – 100,000

○ Less than 50,000

● National capital

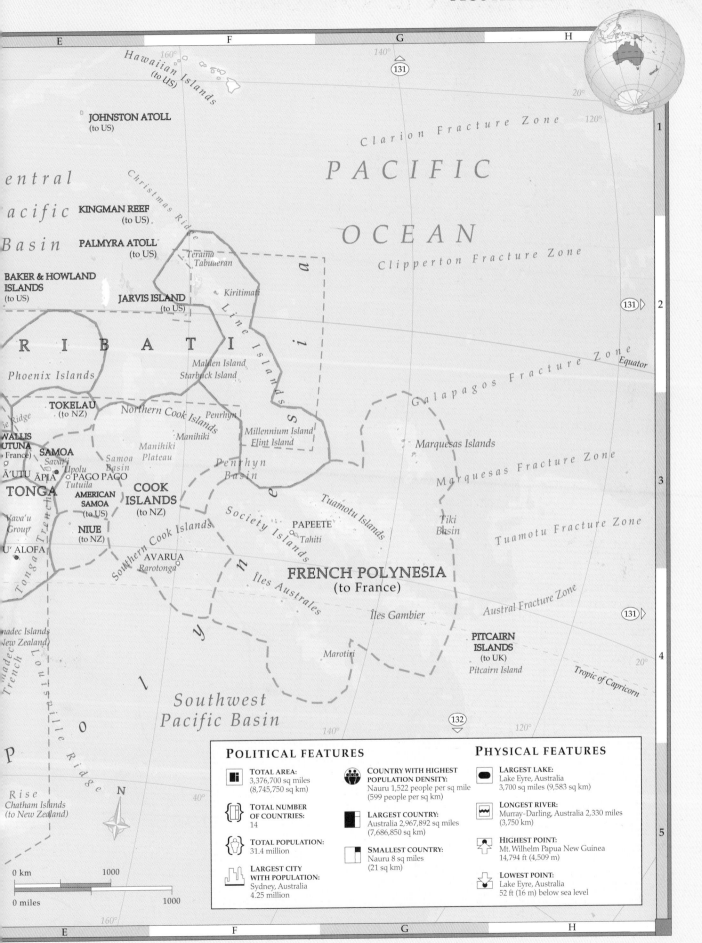

E   F   G   H

131

20°   120°

Clarion Fracture Zone

PACIFIC

JOHNSTON ATOLL
(to US)

OCEAN

Clipperton Fracture Zone

entral

acific

KINGMAN REEF
(to US)

Basin

PALMYRA ATOLL
(to US)

Teraina
Tabuaeran

BAKER & HOWLAND
ISLANDS
(to US)

Kiritimati

JARVIS ISLAND
(to US)

131

Equator

R I B A T I

Galapagos Fracture Zone

Phoenix Islands

Malden Island
Starbuck Island

Line Islands

Marquesas Fracture Zone

Ridge

TOKELAU
(to NZ)

Northern Cook Islands

Penrhyn

Millennium Island
Flint Island

Marquesas Islands

WALLIS
UTUNA
(France)

SAMOA

Savai'i

Manihiki

Manihiki
Plateau

Penrhyn
Basin

Samoa
Basin

Ā'UTU   ĀPIA

Upolu
PAGO PAGO
Tutuila

COOK
ISLANDS
(to NZ)

Tuamotu Islands

Tiki
Basin

Marquesas Fracture Zone

TONGA

AMERICAN
SAMOA
(to US)

Society Islands

PAPEETE
Tahiti

Tuamotu Fracture Zone

Vava'u
Group

NIUE
(to NZ)

U' ALOFA

AVARUA
Rarotonga

Southern Cook Islands

Îles Australes

FRENCH POLYNESIA
(to France)

Austral Fracture Zone

131

20°

madec Islands
New Zealand)

Îles Gambier

PITCAIRN
ISLANDS
(to UK)

Tropic of Capricorn

Marotiri

Pitcairn Island

Southwest
Pacific Basin

140°   132   120°

Rise
Chatham Islands
(to New Zealand)

N

40°

0 km   1000

0 miles   1000

160°

POLITICAL FEATURES

TOTAL AREA:
3,376,700 sq miles
(8,745,750 sq km)

**TOTAL NUMBER
OF COUNTRIES:**
14

TOTAL POPULATION:
31.4 million

**LARGEST CITY
WITH POPULATION:**
Sydney, Australia
4.25 million

**COUNTRY WITH HIGHEST
POPULATION DENSITY:**
Nauru 1,522 people per sq mile
(599 people per sq km)

LARGEST COUNTRY:
Australia 2,967,892 sq miles
(7,686,850 sq km)

SMALLEST COUNTRY:
Nauru 8 sq miles
(21 sq km)

PHYSICAL FEATURES

LARGEST LAKE:
Lake Eyre, Australia
3,700 sq miles (9,583 sq km)

LONGEST RIVER:
Murray-Darling, Australia 2,330 miles
(3,750 km)

HIGHEST POINT:
Mt. Wilhelm Papua New Guinea
14,794 ft (4,509 m)

LOWEST POINT:
Lake Eyre, Australia
52 ft (16 m) below sea level

E   F   G   H

THE SOUTHWEST PACIFIC

POPULATION

- ● Over 500,000
- ◉ 100,000 – 500,000
- ○ 50,000 – 100,000
- ○ Less than 50,000
- ● National capital

MARSHALL ISLANDS

Enewetak Atoll
Bikini Atoll
Rongelap Atoll
Ailuk Atoll
Ujelang Atoll
Wotje Atoll
Kwajalein Atoll
Maloelap
Namu Atoll
Majuro Atoll
Ailinglaplap Atoll
Jaluit Atoll
Mili Atoll

Ebon Atoll

Maki
Tarawa
BAIRIKI

Abemu
Nono

NAURU
Banaba

MICRONESIA

Yap

Babeldaob
**KOROR
(OREOR)**

PALAU
◁ 117

△ 130
Tinian
Saipan
Rota
**NORTHERN
MARIANA
ISLANDS**
GUAM
(to US)
HAGÁTÑA (to US)

Chuuk
Islands
PALIKIR Pohnpei

Caroline Islands
Kosrae

Equator

New Guinea

INDONESIA

Central Range
Madang
△ Mount Wilhelm
4509m
Lae
Owen Stanley Range
*Gulf of
Papua*
PORT MORESBY
Torres Strait

Admiralty
Islands
St.Matthias Group
Bismarck Archipelago
Bismarck Sea
New Ireland
PAPUA NEW GUINEA
Bougainville
Island
*New
Britain*
Solomon Sea
New
Georgia
Islands
Choiseul
Santa Isabel
**SOLOMON
ISLANDS**
Malaita
HONIARA
Guadalcanal
San Cristobal
Rennell
Santa Cruz
Islands

D'Entrecasteaux
Islands
Louisiade
Archipelago

Arafura Sea

*Arnhem
Land*
Groote
Eylandt
*Gulf of
Carpentaria*
Cape
York
Peninsula
◁ 124
Barkly Tableland

**NORTHERN
TERRITORY**
*Macdonnell
Ranges*

Great Barrier Reef
Great Dividing Range
QUEENSLAND
Tropic of Capricorn

Coral Sea
CORAL SEA ISLANDS
(to Australia)

Banks Islands
Espiritu Santo
Maéwo
Pentecost
Malekula
Ambrym
Epi
Efate
PORT-VILA
VANUATU
Erromango
Tanna
Aneityum

**NEW
CALEDONIA**
(to France)
Ouvéa
Lifou
Iles Loyauté
Maré
*New
Caledonia*
NOUMÉA

AUSTRALIA

▽ 127

122

N

International Dateline

180°   170°   160°   150°

131

0 km   750

0 miles   750

10°

ELEVATION

PACIFIC OCEAN

KINGMAN REEF
(to US)

PALMYRA ATOLL
(to US)

Teraina

Tabuaeran

131

4000 m
13 124 ft

2000 m
6562 ft

BAKER & HOWLAND
ISLANDS
(to US)

JARVIS ISLAND
(to US)

*Kiritimati
(Christmas Island)*

1000 m
3281 ft

Equator

500 m
1640 ft

aru

eru
Nikunau
ma
Arorae

K   I   R   I   B   A   T   I

Kanton

Birnie Island

Enderbury Island

McKean Island

Orona   *Manra*

Nikumaroro

Phoenix Islands

Malden Island

Line Islands

250 m
820 ft

100 m
328 ft

umea Atoll

Niutao
numaga
Nui Atoll
Nukufetau

Funafuti ● FONGAFALE
Atoll
Nukulaelae

Atafu Atoll

*Nukunonu
Atoll*

TOKELAU
(to New Zealand)

Fakaofo Atoll

Starbuck Island

P
o
l
y
n
e
s
i
a

Rakahanga   *Penrhyn*

Vostok Island   *Millennium
Island*

3

Sea
Level

Sea
Level

-250 m
-820 ft

10°

Niulakita

TUVALU

WALLIS &
FUTUNA
(to France)

Île Uvea
MATA'UTU
Île Futuna

ma

SAMOA

AMERICAN
SAMOA
(to US)

Savai'i   ĀPIA
Upolu   PAGO PAGO
Tutuila *Ta'ū*

Manihiki

*Northern Cook
Islands*

COOK
ISLANDS
(to New Zealand)

Flint Island

-500 m
-1640 ft

-1000 m
-3281 ft

Cikobia
nua Levu

di
ti ● SUVA
u

Kadavu

FIJI

Niuatoputapu

TONGA

*Vava'u
Group*

Tofua

*Ha'apai
Group*

NUKU' ALOFA
Tongatapu
'Eua
*Tongatapu
Group*

Palmerston

ALOFI

NIUE
(to New Zealand)

*Southern Cook
Islands*

Manuae

Takutea

AVARUA
Rarotonga

Mangaia

Raiatea ○ PAPEETE
Tahiti

Archipel de la Société

Îles Tuamotu

131

FRENCH POLYNESIA
(to France)

Îles Australes

-2000 m
-6562 ft

-4000 m
-13124 ft

20°

-6000 m
-19 686 ft

International Dateline

Tropic of Capricorn

Marotiri

131

180°   170°   160°   150°

E   F   G   H

5

WESTERN AUSTRALIA

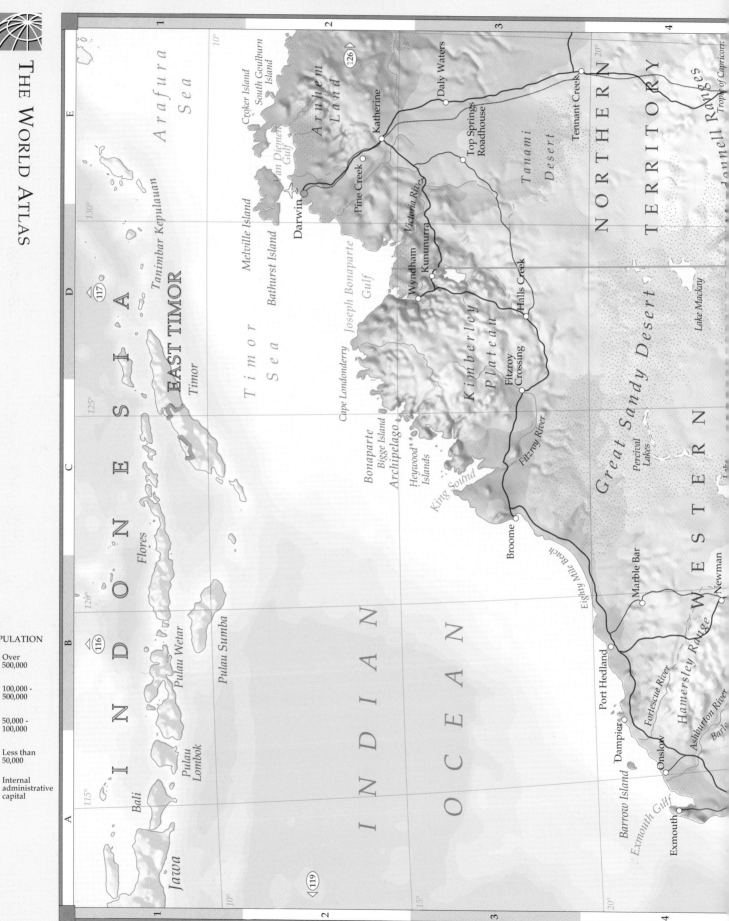

POPULATION

- ● Over 500,000
- ◉ 100,000 - 500,000
- ○ 50,000 - 100,000
- ○ Less than 50,000
- ● Internal administrative capital

Arafura Sea

Croker Island
South Goulburn Island

Arnhem Land

126

Katherine

Daly Waters

Top Springs Roadhouse

Tennant Creek

NORTHERN

Tanami Desert

TERRITORY

Tropic of Capricorn

Donnell Ranges

117

INDONESIA

EAST TIMOR

Timor

Tanimbar Kepulauan

Melville Island

Bathurst Island

Van Diemen Gulf

Darwin

Pine Creek

Wyndham
Kununurra

Victoria River

Halls Creek

Timor Sea

Cape Londonderry

Joseph Bonaparte Gulf

Kimberley Plateau

Fitzroy Crossing

Great Sandy Desert

Lake Mackay

WESTERN

Flores

Pulau Wetar

Pulau Sumba

Bonaparte Archipelago
Bigge Island

Heywood Islands

King Sound

Fitzroy River

Percival Lakes

119

Pulau Lombok

Bali

Jawa

INDIAN

OCEAN

Broome

Eighty Mile Beach

Marble Bar

Newman

Hamersley Range

Port Hedland

Dampier

Onslow

Fortescue River

Ashburton River

Barlee

Barrow Island

Exmouth Gulf

Exmouth

116

ELEVATION

4000 m
13 124 ft

2000 m
6562 ft

1000 m
3281 ft

500 m
1640 ft

250 m
820 ft

100 m
328 ft

Sea Level

Sea Level

-250 m
-820 ft

-500 m
-1640 ft

-1000 m
-3281 ft

-2000 m
-6562 ft

-3000 m
-9843 ft

-4000 m
-13 124 ft

AUSTRALIA

SOUTH AUSTRALIA

Musgrave Ranges

Uluru (Ayers Rock) 867m

Great Victoria Desert

Nullarbor Plain

Great Australian Bight

INDIAN OCEAN

Coober Pedy
Tarcoola
Lake Everard
Penong
Lake Gairdner
Ceduna
Elliston
Port Lincoln

Eucla

Reid

Zanthus
Kalgoorlie
Coolgardie
Lake Cowan
Norseman
Balladonia
Esperance

Southern Cross
Merredin
Northam
Brookton
Narrogin
Wagin
Katanning
Collie
Manjimup
Albany

Lake Carnegie
Lake Wells

Lake Carey
Lake Rebecca
Lake Barlee
Lake Moore

Robinson Range

Meekatharra
Mount Magnet
Moora
Gingin
Perth
Fremantle
Rockingham
Mandurah
Bunbury
Busselton
Augusta

Murchison River

Gascoyne River

Carnarvon
Bernier Island
Dorre Island
Shark Bay
Dirk Hartog Island
Denham
Kalbarri
Geraldton

N

Eastern Australia

POPULATION

- ◉ Over 500,000
- ◉ 100,000 - 500,000
- ○ 50,000 - 100,000
- ○ Less than 50,000
- ● National capital
- ● Internal administrative capital

SYDNEY

Broken Bay
Palm Beach
Ku-ring-gai Chase National Park
Ku-ring-gai
Manly
Port Jackson
Harbour Bridge
Opera House
Central Station
Bondi Beach
Botany
Sydney
University
Strathfield
Botany Bay
Kurnell
Cape Banks
Cronulla
Port Hacking
Tasman Sea
Sutherland
Royal National Park

Hornsby
Windsor
Penrith
St Marys
Parramatta
Ryde
Liverpool
Rockdale
Hurstville
Kogarah
Georges River
Campbell-town

Site of 2000 Olympics
Places of interest
Regions/suburby

0 km 10
0 miles 10

Coral Sea

CORAL SEA ISLANDS
(to Australia)

Great Barrier Reef

Tropic of Capricorn

INDONESIA   PAPUA NEW GUINEA

Arafura Sea

Torres Strait

Moa Island
Badu Island
Endeavour Str
Prince of Wales Island

Cape York

Cape York Peninsula

Great Dividing Range

Princess Charlotte Bay

Cooktown
Port Douglas
Mareeba   Cairns
Atherton   Innisfail
Tully
Hinchinbrook Island
Townsville
Bowen
Whitsunday Group
Mackay
Marlborough
Yeppon
Rockhampton
Curtis Island
Gladstone
Biloela

Charters Towers

Great Dividing Range

Bloomsbury
Clermont
Emerald
Springsure

Mitchell River

Gilbert River

Normanton

Gregory Range

Hughenden
Winton

Cloncurry

QUEENSLAND

Barcaldine
Longreach
Blackall

Cooper Creek

Flinders River

Selwyn Range

Mount Isa

Burketown

Gulf of Carpentaria

Mornington Island

Wellesley Islands

Sir Edward Pellew Group

Groote Eylandt

Wessel Islands

South Goulburn Island

Croker Island

Van Diemen Gulf

Darwin

Arnhem Land

Pine Creek
Katherine

Daly Waters
Top Springs Roadhouse

NORTHERN   TERRITORY

Tanami Desert

Tennant Creek

Barkly Tableland

Alice Springs

Macdonnell Ranges

Lake Amadeus
Uluru

Tropic of Capricorn

AUSTRALIA

117
122
124

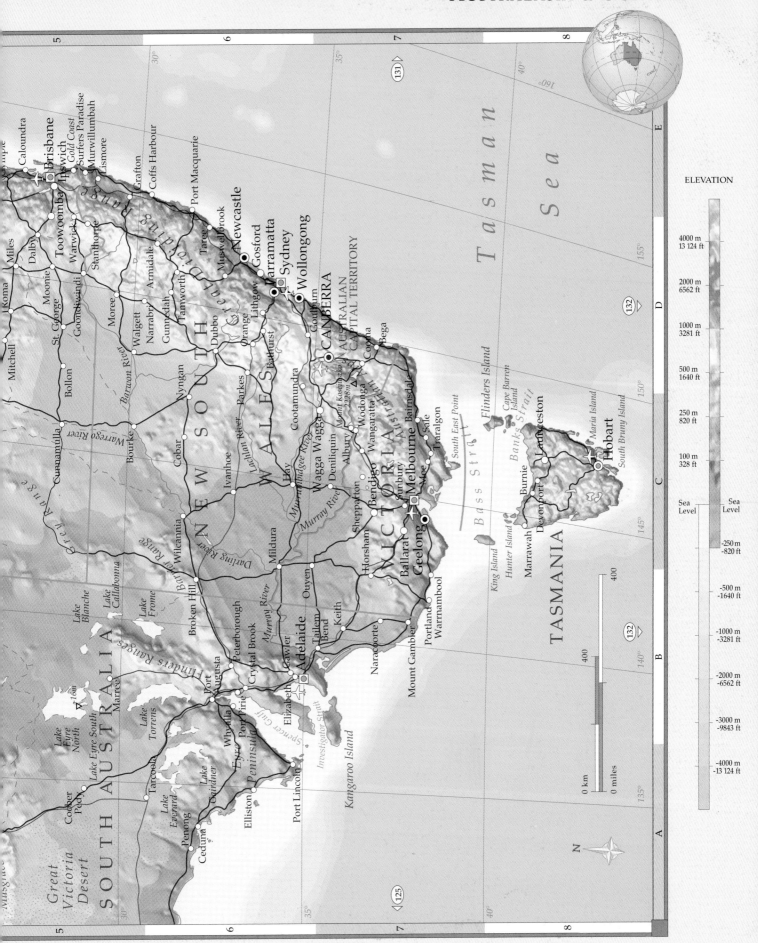

ELEVATION

4000 m	13 124 ft
2000 m	6562 ft
1000 m	3281 ft
500 m	1640 ft
250 m	820 ft
100 m	328 ft
Sea Level	Sea Level
-250 m	-820 ft
-500 m	-1640 ft
-1000 m	-3281 ft
-2000 m	-6562 ft
-3000 m	-9843 ft
-4000 m	-13 124 ft

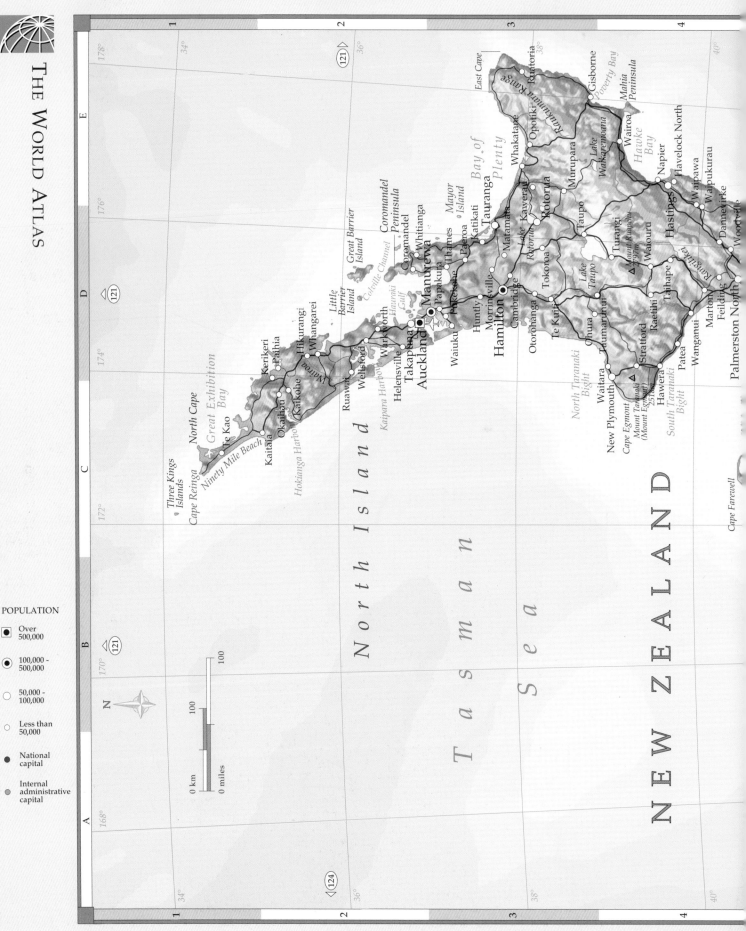

NEW ZEALAND

North Island

Tasman Sea

POPULATION

- ▣ Over 500,000
- ◉ 100,000 – 500,000
- ○ 50,000 – 100,000
- ∘ Less than 50,000
- ● National capital
- ● Internal administrative capital

N

100

100

0 km

0 miles

Three Kings Islands
Cape Reinga
North Cape
Te Kao
Great Exhibition Bay
Ninety Mile Beach
Kaitaia
Kerikeri
Pahia
Okaihau
Kaikohe
Hokianga Harbour
Hikurangi
Whangarei
Ruawai
Wellsford
Helensville
Warkworth
Takapuna
Auckland
Manurewa
Papakura
Pukekohe
Waiuku
Huntly
Morrinsville
Cambridge
Hamilton
Otorohanga
Te Kuiti
Te Awamutu
Little Barrier Island
Great Barrier Island
Coromandel Peninsula
Coromandel
Whitianga
Colville Channel
Hauraki Gulf
Kaipara Harbour
Thames
Paeroa
Mayor Island
Katikati
Tauranga
Matamata
Kawerau
Rotorua
Lake Rotorua
Tokoroa
Lake Taupo
Taupo
Turangi
Whakatane
Opotiki
Murupara
Lake Waikaremoana
Bay of Plenty
East Cape
Ruatoria
Gisborne
Poverty Bay
Mahia Peninsula
Wairoa
Hawke Bay
Napier
Havelock North
Hastings
Waipawa
Waipukurau
Dannevirke
Woodville
Raukumara Range
Ruahine Range
Waiouru
Tahape
Raetihi
Ohura
Taumarunui
Mount Ruapehu 2797m
Waitara
New Plymouth
Cape Egmont
Mount Egmont (Mount Taranaki) 2518m
North Taranaki Bight
South Taranaki Bight
Stratford
Hawera
Patea
Wanganui
Martton
Feilding
Palmerston North
Cape Farewell

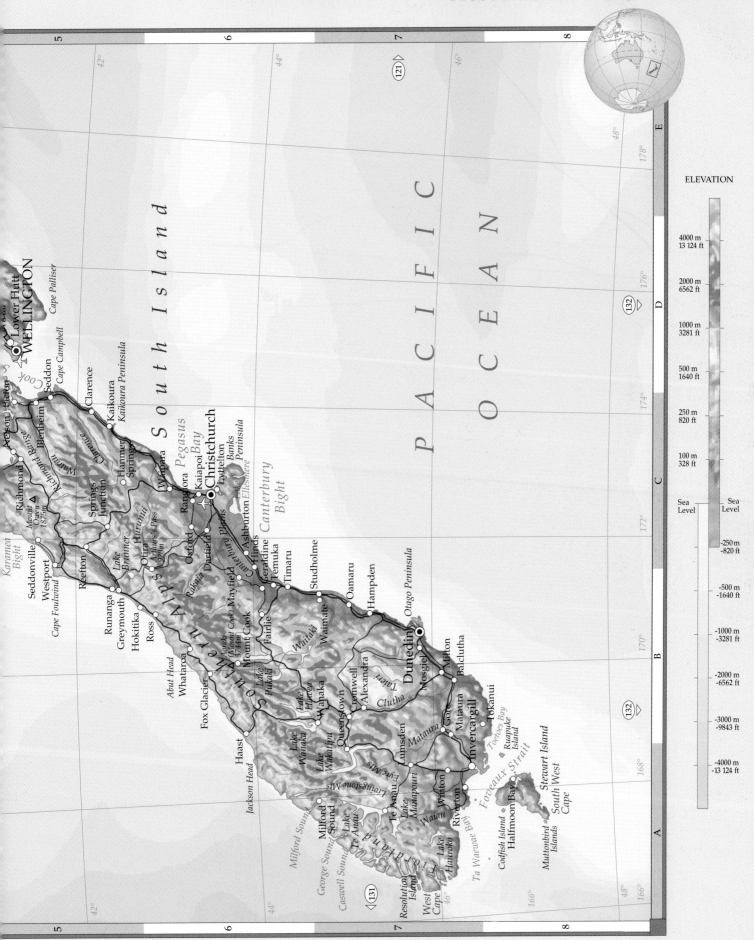

ELEVATION

4000 m
13 124 ft

2000 m
6562 ft

1000 m
3281 ft

500 m
1640 ft

250 m
820 ft

100 m
328 ft

Sea
Level

Sea
Level

-250 m
-820 ft

-500 m
-1640 ft

-1000 m
-3281 ft

-2000 m
-6562 ft

-3000 m
-9843 ft

-4000 m
-13 124 ft

PACIFIC   OCEAN

South Island

Lower Hutt
WELLINGTON
Cape Palliser
Cape Campbell
Seddon
Cape Campbell
Clarence
Kaikoura
Kaikoura Peninsula
Blenheim
Richmond
Mount Owen
1875 m
Nelson Lakes
Richmond Range
Wairau
Hanmer
Springs
Springs
Junction
Hurunui
Waipara
Rangiora
Kaiapoi
Pegasus
Bay
Christchurch
Lyttelton
Banks
Peninsula
Reefton
Lake
Brunner
Otira
Arthur's Pass
920m
Oxford
Darfield
Canterbury
Plains
Ashburton
Ellesmere
Canterbury
Bight
Runanga
Greymouth
Hokitika
Ross
Rakaia
Mayfield
Rakaia
Geraldine
Temuka
Timaru
Hinds
Studholme
Abut Head
Whataroa
Fox Glacier
Mount Cook
Aoraki
(Mount Cook)
3744m
Fairlie
Waitaki
Waimate
Oamaru
Hampden
Lake
Pukaki
Lake
Tekapo
Cromwell
Alexandra
Otago Peninsula
Haast
Jackson Head
Lake
Wanaka
Lake
Hawea
Wanaka
Queenstown
Clutha
L.Tairei
Dunedin
Mosgiel
Milton
Balclutha
Lake
Wakatipu
Lumsden
Mataura
Gore
Mataura
Invercargill
Tokanui
Milford
Sound
George Sound
Caswell Sound
Lake
Te Anau
Te Anau
Lake
Manapouri
Lake
Monowai
Winton
Riverton
Waiau
Eyre Mts
Livingstone Mts
Te Waewae Bay
Foveaux Strait
Tautuku Bay
Ruapuke
Island
Stewart Island
South West
Cape
Codfish Island
Halfmoon Bay
Muttonbird
Islands
South Cape
West
Cape
Resolution
Island
Fiordland

Karamea
Bight
Seddonville
Westport
Cape Foulwind
Southern Alps

Nelson Haven
Cook Strait

PACIFIC

THE PACIFIC OCEAN

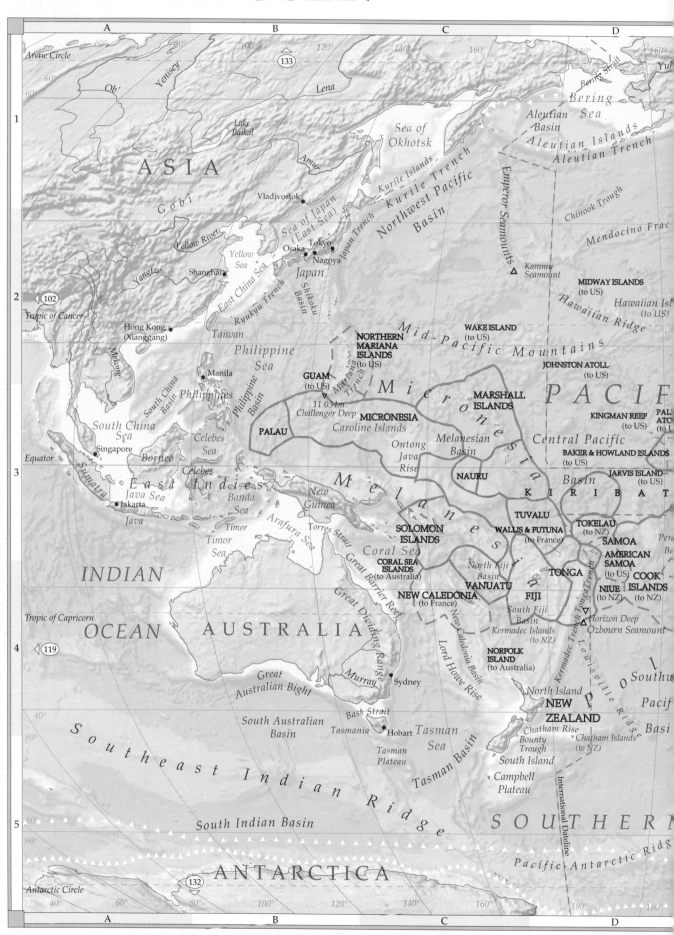

A B C D

Arctic Circle

Ob'

Yenisey

Lena

133

Bering Sea

Aleutian Basin

Aleutian Islands

Aleutian Trench

ASIA

Lake Baikal

Amur

Gobi

Sea of Okhotsk

Kurile Islands

Kurile Trench

Northwest Pacific Basin

Emperor Seamounts

Chinook Trough

Mendocino Frac

Vladivostok

Sea of Japan (East Sea)

Yellow River

Osaka Tokyo

Nagoya

Japan

Japan Trench

Kammu Seamount

MIDWAY ISLANDS (to US)

102

Tropic of Cancer

Yangtze

Shanghai

Yellow Sea

East China Sea

Shikoku Basin

Hawaiian Ridge

Hawaiian Isl (to US)

Mid-Pacific Mountains

Hong Kong (Xianggang)

Taiwan

Ryukyu Trench

WAKE ISLAND (to US)

JOHNSTON ATOLL (to US)

Philippine Sea

NORTHERN MARIANA ISLANDS (to US)

Mariana Trench

Micronesia

PACIF

Mekong

Manila

GUAM (to US)

11 034m Challenger Deep

MICRONESIA

Caroline Islands

MARSHALL ISLANDS

KINGMAN REEF (to US)

PAL ATO (to L

South China Basin

Philippines

Philippine Basin

PALAU

Melanesian Basin

Central Pacific

South China Sea

Celebes Sea

Ontong Java Rise

NAURU

BAKER & HOWLAND ISLANDS (to US)

Singapore

Borneo

Equator

Celebes

Basin

JARVIS ISLAND (to US)

East Indies

Melanesia

KIRIBAT

Java Sea

Jakarta

Banda Sea

New Guinea

TUVALU

TOKELAU (to NZ)

Java

Timor

Arafura Sea

Torres Strait

SOLOMON ISLANDS

WALLIS & FUTUNA (to France)

SAMOA

INDIAN

Timor Sea

Great Barrier Reef

Coral Sea

North Fiji Basin

TONGA

AMERICAN SAMOA (to US)

COOK ISLANDS (to NZ)

CORAL SEA ISLANDS (to Australia)

VANUATU

FIJI

NIUE (to NZ)

Per Ba

OCEAN

NEW CALEDONIA (to France)

South Fiji Basin

Kermadec Islands (to NZ)

Horizon Deep

Ozbourn Seamount

Tropic of Capricorn

AUSTRALIA

New Caledonia Basin

NORFOLK ISLAND (to Australia)

Kermadec Trench

Tonga Trench

119

Great Dividing Range

Lord Howe Rise

Louisville Ridge

Southw

Murray

Sydney

North Island

Pacif

Great Australian Bight

Bass Strait

NEW ZEALAND

Basi

South Australian Basin

Tasmania

Hobart

Tasman Sea

Chatham Rise

Chatham Islands (to NZ)

Bounty Trough

South Island

Tasman Plateau

Tasman Basin

Campbell Plateau

International Dateline

Southeast Indian Ridge

SOUTHERN

South Indian Basin

132

ANTARCTICA

Pacific-Antarctic Ridge

Antarctic Circle

A B C D

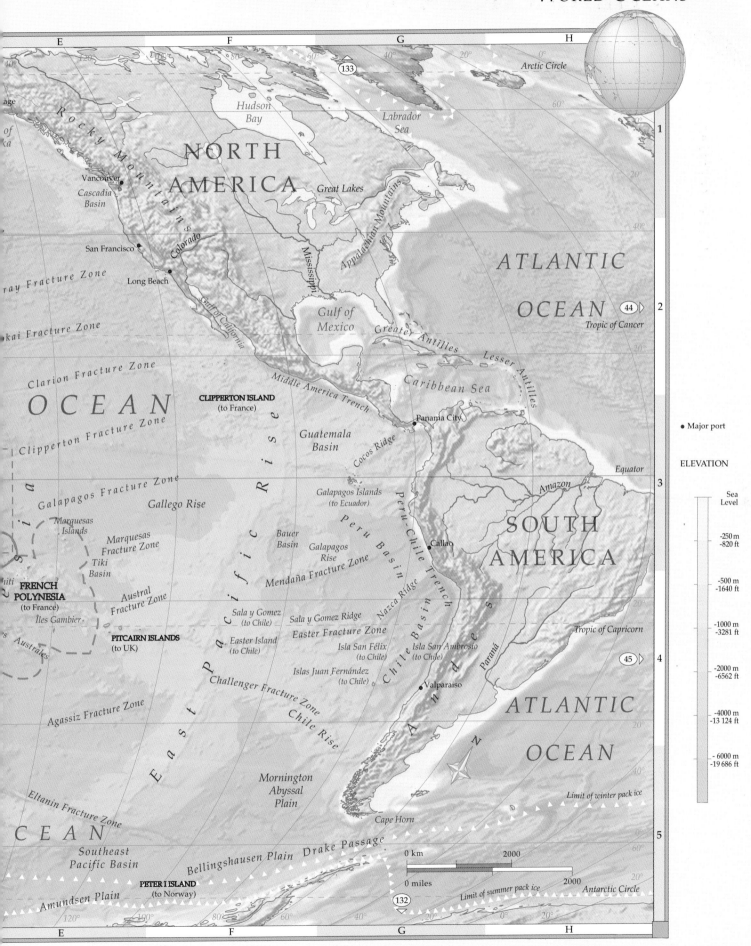

E F G H

133

Arctic Circle

1

Hudson Bay

NORTH AMERICA

Great Lakes

Labrador Sea

Rocky Mountains

Vancouver
Cascadia Basin

San Francisco

Colorado

Long Beach

ray Fracture Zone

kai Fracture Zone

Gulf of California

Mississippi

Appalachian Mountains

ATLANTIC

OCEAN

44

2

Tropic of Cancer

Clarion Fracture Zone

Gulf of Mexico

Greater Antilles

Lesser Antilles

Caribbean Sea

OCEAN

CLIPPERTON ISLAND
(to France)

Middle America Trench

Clipperton Fracture Zone

Guatemala Basin

Cocos Ridge

Panama City

• Major port

ELEVATION

Galapagos Fracture Zone

Gallego Rise

Galapagos Islands
(to Ecuador)

Equator

3

Marquesas Islands

Marquesas Fracture Zone

Bauer Basin

Galapagos Rise

Peru Basin

Peru-Chile Trench

SOUTH AMERICA

Amazon

Callao

Sea Level

-250 m
-820 ft

Tiki Basin

Mendaña Fracture Zone

FRENCH POLYNESIA
(to France)

Austral Fracture Zone

Sala y Gomez
(to Chile)

Sala y Gomez Ridge

Nazca Ridge

Chile Basin

Andes

-500 m
-1640 ft

Îles Gambier

Easter Fracture Zone

Tropic of Capricorn

-1000 m
-3281 ft

PITCAIRN ISLANDS
(to UK)

Easter Island
(to Chile)

Isla San Félix
(to Chile)

Isla San Ambrosio
(to Chile)

Paraná

45

4

Australes

Islas Juan Fernández
(to Chile)

Valparaiso

-2000 m
-6562 ft

East Pacific Rise

Challenger Fracture Zone

Chile Rise

Agassiz Fracture Zone

N

Mornington Abyssal Plain

-4000 m
-13 124 ft

-6000 m
-19 686 ft

ATLANTIC

OCEAN

Eltanin Fracture Zone

Cape Horn

Limit of winter pack ice

5

CEAN

Southeast Pacific Basin

Bellingshausen Plain

Drake Passage

0 km   2000

0 miles   2000

Limit of summer pack ice

Antarctic Circle

PETER I ISLAND
(to Norway)

Amundsen Plain

132

E F G H

ANTARCTICA

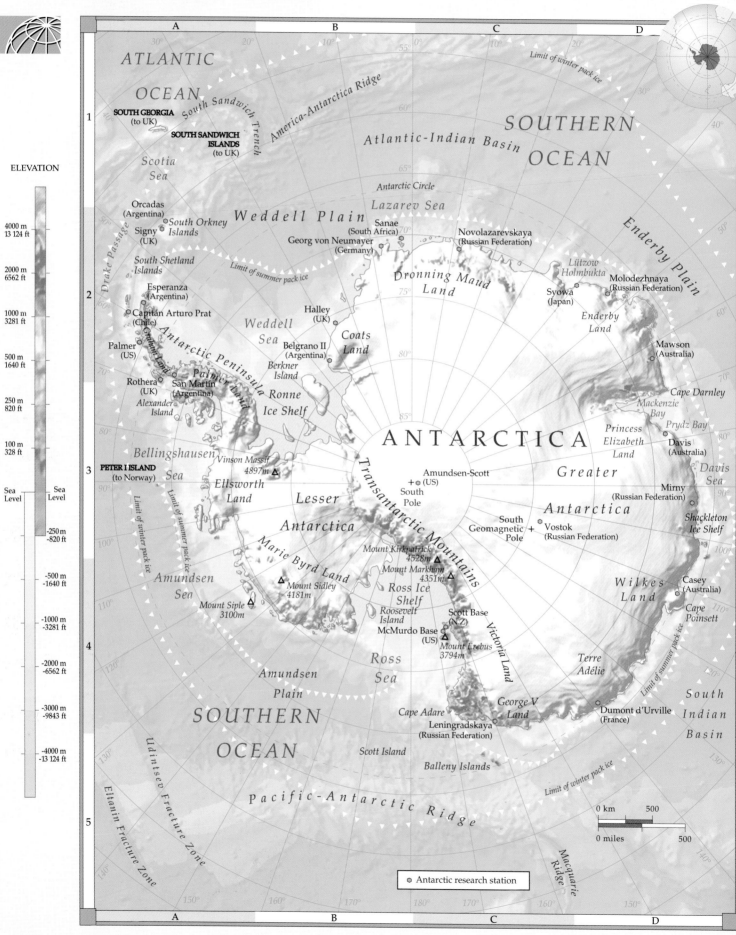

ELEVATION

4000 m	13 124 ft
2000 m	6562 ft
1000 m	3281 ft
500 m	1640 ft
250 m	820 ft
100 m	328 ft
Sea Level	Sea Level
-250 m	-820 ft
-500 m	-1640 ft
-1000 m	-3281 ft
-2000 m	-6562 ft
-3000 m	-9843 ft
-4000 m	-13 124 ft

ATLANTIC

OCEAN

SOUTH GEORGIA
(to UK)

SOUTH SANDWICH
ISLANDS
(to UK)

Scotia
Sea

South Sandwich Trench

America-Antarctica Ridge

Limit of winter pack ice

SOUTHERN
OCEAN

Atlantic-Indian Basin

Antarctic Circle

Lazarev Sea

Weddell Plain

Enderby Plain

Orcadas
(Argentina)

South Orkney
Islands

Signy
(UK)

South Shetland
Islands

Drake Passage

Limit of summer pack ice

Sanae
(South Africa)

Georg von Neumayer
(Germany)

Novolazarevskaya
(Russian Federation)

Dronning Maud
Land

Lützow
Holmbukta

Syowa
(Japan)

Molodezhnaya
(Russian Federation)

Enderby
Land

Esperanza
(Argentina)

Capitán Arturo Prat
(Chile)

Palmer
(US)

Graham Land

Antarctic Peninsula

Rothera
(UK)

San Martín
(Argentina)

Alexander
Island

Palmer Land

Halley
(UK)

Weddell
Sea

Belgrano II
(Argentina)

Berkner
Island

Ronne
Ice Shelf

Coats
Land

Mawson
(Australia)

Cape Darnley

Mackenzie
Bay

Prydz Bay

Princess
Elizabeth
Land

Davis
(Australia)

Bellingshausen
Sea

PETER I ISLAND
(to Norway)

Vinson Massif
4897m △

Ellsworth
Land

Lesser

Antarctica

Marie Byrd Land

Mount Sidley
4181m △

Mount Siple
3100m △

Limit of winter pack ice

Limit of summer pack ice

Transantarctic Mountains

ANTARCTICA

Amundsen-Scott
+ ○ (US)
South
Pole

South
Geomagnetic +
Pole

Vostok
(Russian Federation)

Greater

Antarctica

Mirny
(Russian Federation)

Davis
Sea

Shackleton
Ice Shelf

Wilkes
Land

Casey
(Australia)

Cape
Poinsett

Mount Kirkpatrick
4528m △

Mount Markham
4351m △

Ross Ice
Shelf

Roosevelt
Island

Scott Base
(N.Z.)

McMurdo Base ○
(US)

Mount Erebus
3794m △

Victoria Land

Terre
Adélie

Amundsen
Sea

Amundsen

Plain

SOUTHERN

OCEAN

Ross
Sea

Cape Adare

George V
Land

Leningradskaya
(Russian Federation)

Dumont d'Urville
(France)

South
Indian
Basin

Udintsev Fracture Zone

Eltanin Fracture Zone

Scott Island

Balleny Islands

Pacific-Antarctic Ridge

Limit of winter pack ice

Macquarie
Ridge

0 km	500
0 miles	500

○ Antarctic research station

ARCTIC OCEAN

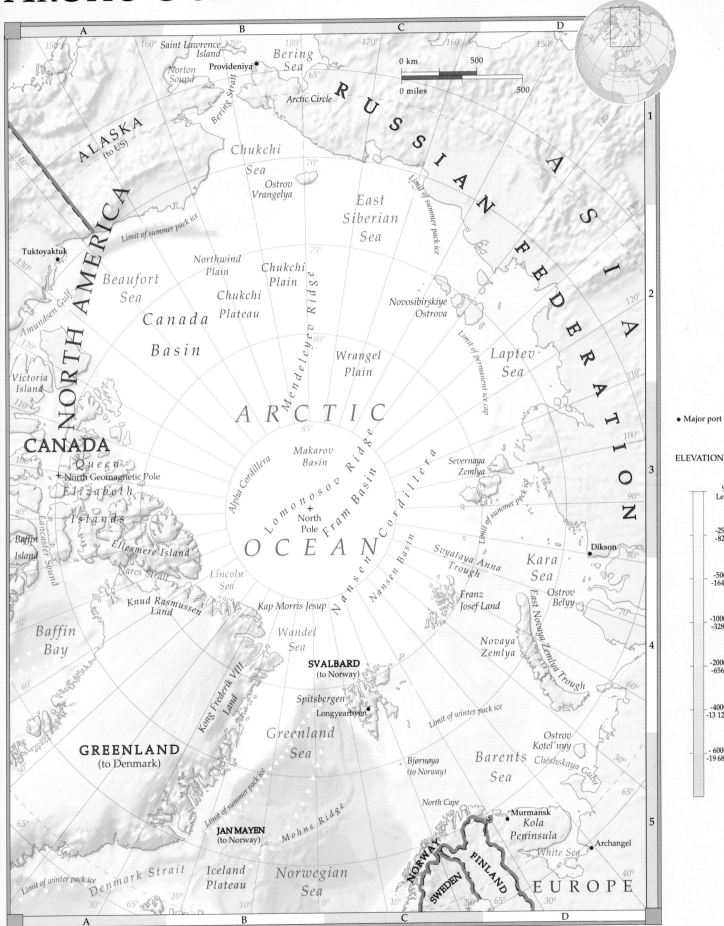

0 km   500

0 miles   500

• Major port

ELEVATION

Sea Level

-250 m
-820 ft

-500 m
-1640 ft

-1000 m
-3281 ft

-2000 m
-6562 ft

-4000 m
-13 124 ft

-6000 m
-19 686 ft

Map labels:

ALASKA (to US)

RUSSIAN FEDERATION

Saint Lawrence Island

Providzeniya

Bering Sea

Arctic Circle

Norton Sound

Bering Strait

Chukchi Sea

Ostrov Vrangelya

East Siberian Sea

NORTH AMERICA

Tuktoyaktuk

Beaufort Sea

Northwind Plain

Chukchi Plain

Chukchi Plateau

Canada Basin

Mendeleyev Ridge

Wrangel Plain

Novosibirskiye Ostrova

Limit of summer pack ice

Limit of permanent ice cap

Laptev Sea

Amundsen Gulf

Victoria Island

CANADA

ARCTIC

Queen

North Geomagnetic Pole

Elizabeth

Islands

Baffin Island

Ellesmere Island

Nares Strait

Alpha Cordillera

Makarov Basin

Lomonosov Ridge

North Pole

Fram Basin

Nansen Cordillera

Nansen Basin

Severnaya Zemlya

Svyataya Anna Trough

Franz Josef Land

Kara Sea

Ostrov Belyy

Dikson

East Novaya Zemlya Trough

Lincoln Sea

Knud Rasmussen Land

OCEAN

Kap Morris Jesup

Wandel Sea

Novaya Zemlya

Baffin Bay

SVALBARD (to Norway)

Kong Frederik VIII Land

Spitsbergen

Longyearbyen

Ostrov Kotel'nyy

Chëshskaya Guba

Greenland Sea

Bjørnøya (to Norway)

Barents Sea

GREENLAND (to Denmark)

Limit of winter pack ice

North Cape

Murmansk

Kola Peninsula

White Sea

Archangel

Limit of summer pack ice

JAN MAYEN (to Norway)

Mohns Ridge

NORWAY

FINLAND

SWEDEN

Denmark Strait

Iceland Plateau

Norwegian Sea

EUROPE

Limit of winter pack ice

133

OVERSEAS TERRITORIES AND DEPENDENCIES

DESPITE THE RAPID PROCESS of decolonization since the end of the Second World War, around 10 million people in more than 50 territories around the world continue to live under the protection of France, Australia, the Netherlands, Denmark, Norway, New Zealand, the United Kingdom or the USA. These remnants of former colonial empires may have persisted for economic, strategic or political reasons, and are administered in a variety of ways.

AUSTRALIA

ASHMORE & CARTIER ISLANDS
Indian Ocean
Status External territory
Claimed 1978
Capital *not applicable*
Population None
Area 2 sq miles (5.2 sq km)

CHRISTMAS ISLAND
Indian Ocean
Status External territory
Claimed 1958
Capital Flying Fish Cove
Population 1,275
Area 52 sq miles
(134.6 sq km)

COCOS ISLANDS
Indian Ocean
Status External territory
Claimed 1955
Capital No official capital
Population 670
Area 5.5 sq miles (14.24 sq km)

CORAL SEA ISLANDS
South Pacific
Status External territory
Claimed 1969
Capital None
Population 8 (meteorologists)
Area Less than 1.16 sq miles
(3 sq km)

HEARD & MCDONALD ISLANDS
Indian Ocean
Status External territory
Claimed 1947
Capital *not applicable*
Population None
Area 161 sq miles
(417 sq km)z

NORFOLK ISLAND
South Pacific
Status External territory
Claimed 1774
Capital Kingston
Population 2,181
Area 13.3 sq miles
(34.4 sq km)

DENMARK

FAEROE ISLANDS
North Atlantic
Status External territory
Claimed 1380
Capital Tórshavn
Population 43,382
Area 540 sq miles
(1,399 sq km)

GREENLAND
North Atlantic
Status External territory
Claimed 1380
Capital Nuuk
Population 56,076
Area 840,000 sq miles
(2,175,516 sq km)

FRANCE

CLIPPERTON ISLAND
East Pacific
Status Dependency
of French Polynesia
Claimed 1930
Capital *not applicable*
Population None
Area 2.7 sq miles   (7 sq km)

FRENCH GUIANA South America
Status Overseas department
Claimed 1817
Capital Cayenne
Population 152,300
Area 35,135 sq miles (90,996 sq km)

FRENCH POLYNESIA
South Pacific
Status Overseas territory
Claimed 1843
Capital Papeete
Population 219,521
Area 1,608 sq miles (4,165 sq km)

GUADELOUPE West Indies
Status Overseas department
Claimed 1635
Capital Basse-Terre
Population 419,500
Area 687 sq miles (1,780 sq km)

MARTINIQUE West Indies
Status Overseas department
Claimed 1635
Capital Fort-de-France
Population 381,200
Area 425 sq miles
(1,100 sq km)

MAYOTTE Indian Ocean
Status Territorial collectivity
Claimed 1843
Capital Mamoudzou
Population 131,320
Area 144 sq miles (374 sq km)

NEW CALEDONIA South Pacific
Status Overseas territory
Claimed 1853
Capital Nouméa
Population 196,836
Area 7,374 sq miles
(19,103 sq km)

RÉUNION Indian Ocean
Status Overseas department
Claimed 1638
Capital Saint-Denis
Population 697,000
Area 970 sq miles (2,512 sq km)

ST. PIERRE & MIQUELON
North America
Status Territorial collectivity
Claimed 1604
Capital Saint-Pierre
Population 6,600
Area 93.4 sq miles (242 sq km)

WALLIS & FUTUNA
South Pacific
Status Overseas territory
Claimed 1842
Capital Matā'Utu
Population 15,000
Area 106 sq miles (274 sq km)

NETHERLANDS

ARUBA
West Indies
Status Autonomous part
of the Netherlands
Claimed 1643
Capital Oranjestad
Population 88,000
Area 75 sq miles (194 sq km)

NETHERLANDS ANTILLES
West Indies
Status Autonomous part
of the Netherlands
Claimed 1816
Capital Willemstad
Population 207,175
Area 308 sq miles (800 sq km)

NEW ZEALAND

COOK ISLANDS
South Pacific
Status Associated territory
Claimed 1901
Capital Avarua
Population 20,200
Area 113 sq miles (293 sq km)

NIUE
South Pacific
Status Associated territory
Claimed 1901
Capital Alofi
Population 2,080
Area 102 sq miles (264 sq km)

TOKELAU
South Pacific
Status Dependent territory
Claimed 1926
Capital *not applicable*
Population 1,577
Area 4 sq miles (10.4 sq km)

NORWAY

BOUVET ISLAND
South Atlantic
Status Dependency
Claimed 1928
Capital *not applicable*
Population None
Area 22 sq miles (58 sq km)**JAN**

MAYEN
North Atlantic
Status Dependency
Claimed 1929
Capital *not applicable*
Population None
Area 147 sq miles (381 sq km)

PETER I ISLAND
Southern Ocean
Status Dependency
Claimed 1931
Capital *not applicable*
Population None
Area 69 sq miles (180 sq km)

SVALBARD Arctic Ocean
Status Dependency
Claimed 1920
Capital Longyearbyen
Population 3,231
Area 24,289 sq miles
(62,906 sq km)

UNITED KINGDOM

ANGUILLA
West Indies
Status Dependent territory
Claimed 1650
Capital The Valley
Population 10,300
Area 37 sq miles (96 sq km)

ASCENSION ISLAND
South Atlantic
Status Dependency of St. Helena
Claimed 1673
Capital Georgetown
Population 1,099
Area 34 sq miles (88 sq km)

BERMUDA
North Atlantic
Status Crown colony
Claimed 1612
Capital Hamilton
Population 60,144
Area 20.5 sq miles (53 sq km)

BRITISH INDIAN OCEAN TERRITORY Indian Ocean
Status Dependent territory
Claimed 1814
Capital Diego Garcia
Population 930
Area 23 sq miles (60 sq km)

BRITISH VIRGIN ISLANDS West Indies
Status Dependent territory
Claimed 1672
Capital Road Town
Population 17,896
Area 59 sq miles (153 sq km)

CAYMAN ISLANDS West Indies
Status Dependent territory
Claimed 1670
Capital George Town
Population 35,000
Area 100 sq miles (259 sq km)

FALKLAND ISLANDS South Atlantic
Status Dependent territory
Claimed 1832
Capital Stanley
Population 2,564
Area 4,699 sq miles (12,173 sq km)

GIBRALTAR Southwest Europe
Status Crown colony
Claimed 1713
Capital Gibraltar
Population 27,086
Area 2.5 sq miles (6.5 sq km)

GUERNSEY Channel Islands
Status Crown dependency
Claimed 1066
Capital St Peter Port
Population 56,681
Area 25 sq miles (65 sq km)

ISLE OF MAN British Isles
Status Crown dependency
Claimed 1765
Capital Douglas
Population 71,714
Area 221 sq miles (572 sq km)

JERSEY Channel Islands
Status Crown dependency
Claimed 1066
Capital St. Helier
Population 85,150
Area 45 sq miles (116 sq km)

MONTSERRAT West Indies
Status Dependent territory
Claimed 1632
Capital Plymouth (uninhabited)
Population 2,850
Area 40 sq miles (102 sq km)

PITCAIRN ISLANDS South Pacific
Status Dependent territory
Claimed 1887
Capital Adamstown
Population 55
Area 1.35 sq miles (3.5 sq km)

ST. HELENA South Atlantic
Status Dependent territory
Claimed 1673
Capital Jamestown
Population 6,472
Area 47 sq miles (122 sq km)

SOUTH GEORGIA & THE SOUTH SANDWICH ISLANDS South Atlantic
Status Dependent territory
Capital *not applicable*
Claimed 1775
Population No permanent residents
Area 1,387 sq miles (3,592 sq km)

TRISTAN DA CUNHA South Atlantic
Status Dependency of St. Helena
Claimed 1612
Capital Edinburgh
Population 297
Area 38 sq miles (98 sq km)

TURKS & CAICOS ISLANDS West Indies
Status Dependent territory
Claimed 1766
Capital Cockburn Town
Population 13,800
Area 166 sq miles (430 sq km)

NORWAY

AMERICAN SAMOA South Pacific
Status Unincorporated territory
Claimed 1900
Capital Pago Pago
Population 60,000
Area 75 sq miles (195 sq km)

BAKER & HOWLAND ISLANDS South Pacific
Status Unincorporated territory
Claimed 1856
Capital *not applicable*
Population None
Area 0.54 sq miles (1.4 sq km)

GUAM West Pacific
Status Unincorporated territory
Claimed 1898
Capital Hagåtña
Population 149,249
Area 212 sq miles (549 sq km)

JARVIS ISLAND South Pacific
Status Unincorporated territory
Claimed 1856
Capital *not applicabl*
Population None
Area 1.7 sq miles (4.5 sq km)

NORTHERN MARIANA ISLANDS West Pacific
Status Commonwealth territory
Claimed 1947
Capital Saipan
Population 58,846
Area 177 sq miles (457 sq km)

PALMYRA ATOLL Central Pacific
Status Unincorporated territory
Claimed 1898
Capital *not applicable*
Population None
Area 5 sq miles (12 sq km)

PUERTO RICO West Indies
Status Commonwealth territory
Claimed 1898
Capital San Juan
Population 3.8 million
Area 3,458 sq miles (8,959 sq km)

VIRGIN ISLANDS West Indies
Status Unincorporated territory
Claimed 1917
Capital Charlotte Amalie
Population 101,809
Area 137 sq miles (355 sq km)

WAKE ISLAND Central Pacific
Status Unincorporated territory
Claimed 1898
Capital *not applicable*
Population 302
Area 2.5 sq miles (6.5 sq km)

OVERSEAS TERRITORIES AND DEPENDENCIES

COUNTRY PROFILES

THIS FACTFILE IS INTENDED as a guide to a world that is continually changing as political fashions and personalities come and go. Nevertheless, all the material in these factfiles has been researched from the most up-to-date and authoritative sources to give an incisive portrait of the geographical, political, and social characteristics that make each country so unique.

There are currently 193 independent countries in the world - more than at any previous time - and 59 dependencies. Antarctica is the only land area on Earth that is not officially part of, and does not belong to, any single country.

AFGHANISTAN

Page 100 D4

In 2001, following a US-led offensive, the hard-line Muslim taliban *militia was replaced by a new interim government under* Hamid Karazi

Official name Islamic State of Afghanistan
Formation 1919
Capital Kabul
Population 23.9 million / 95 people per sq mile (37 people per sq km)
Total area 250,000 sq. miles (647,500 sq km)
Languages Pashtu, Tajik, Dari, Farsi, Uzbek, Turkmen
Religions Sunni Muslim 84%, Shi'a Muslim 15%, other 1%
Ethnic mix Pashtun 38%, Tajik 25%, Hazara 19%, other 18%
Government Transitional regime
Currency New afghani = 100 puls
Literacy rate 36%
Calorie consumption 1539 calories

135

ALBANIA

Page 79 C6

Lying at the southeastern end of the Adriatic Sea, Albania held its first multiparty elections in 1991, after nearly five decades of communism.

Official name Republic of Albania
Formation 1912
Capital Tirana
Population 3.2 million / 302 people per sq mile (117 people per sq km)
Total area 11,100 sq. miles (28,748 sq. km)
Languages Albanian, Greek
Religions Sunni Muslim 70%, Orthodox Christian 20%, Roman Catholic 10%
Ethnic mix Albanian 86%, Greek 12%, other 2%
Government Parliamentary system
Currency Lek = 100 qindarka (qintars)
Literacy rate 99%
Calorie consumption 2900 calories

ALGERIA

Page 48 C3

Algeria achieved independence from France in 1962. Today, its military-dominated government faces a severe challenge from Islamic extremists.

Official name People's Democratic Republic of Algeria
Formation 1962
Capital Algiers
Population 31.8 million / 35 people per sq mile (13 people per sq km)
Total area 919,590 sq. miles (2,381,740 sq. km)
Languages Arabic, Tamazight (Kabyle, Shawia, Tamashek), French
Religions Sunni Muslim 99%, Christian and Jewish 1%
Ethnic mix Arab 75%, Berber 24%, European and Jewish 1%
Government Presidential system
Currency Algerian dinar = 100 centimes
Literacy rate 69%
Calorie consumption 2987 calories

ANDORRA

Page 69 B6

A tiny landlocked principality, Andorra lies high in the eastern Pyrenees between France and Spain. It held its first full elections in 1993.

Official name Principality of Andorra
Formation 1278
Capital Andorra la Vella
Population 69,150 / 384 people per sq mile (149 people per sq km)
Total area 181 sq. miles (468 sq. km)
Languages Spanish, Catalan, French, Portuguese
Religions Roman Catholic 94%, other 6%
Ethnic mix Spanish 46%, Andorran 28%, French 8%, other 18%
Government Parliamentary system
Currency Euro = 100 cents
Literacy rate 99%
Calorie consumption Not available

ANGOLA

Page 56 B2

Located in southwest Africa, Angola has been in a state of civil war following its independence from Portugal, except for a brief period from 1994–98.

Official name Republic of Angola
Formation 1975
Capital Luanda
Population 13.6 million / 28 people per sq mile (11 people per sq km)
Total area 481,351 sq. miles (1,246,700 sq. km)
Languages Portuguese, Umbundu, Kimbundu, Kikongo
Religions Roman Catholic 50%, Protestant 20%, other 30%
Ethnic mix Ovimbundu 37%, other 25%, Kimbundu 25%, Bakongo 13%
Government Presidential system
Currency Readjusted kwanza = 100 lwei
Literacy rate 40%
Calorie consumption 1953 calories

ANTIGUA & BARBUDA

Page 33 H3

Lying on the Atlantic edge of the Leeward Islands, Antigua and Barbuda's area includes the uninhabited islet of Redonda.

Official name Antigua and Barbuda
Formation 1981
Capital St. John's
Population 67,897 / 399 people per sq mile (154 people per sq km)
Total area 170 sq. miles (442 sq. km)
Languages English, English patois
Religions Anglican 45%, Other Protestant 42%, Roman Catholic 10%, Rastafarian 1%, other 2%
Ethnic mix Black African 95%, other 5%
Government Parliamentary system
Currency Eastern Caribbean dollar = 100 cents
Literacy rate 87%
Calorie consumption 2381 calories

ARGENTINA

Page 43 B5

Most of the southern half of South America is occupied by Argentina. The country returned to civilian rule in 1983 after a series of military coups.

Official name Republic of Argentina
Formation 1816
Capital Buenos Aires
Population 38.4 million / 36 people per sq mile (14 people per sq km)
Total area 1,068,296 sq. miles (2,766,890 sq. km)
Languages Spanish, Italian, Amerindian languages
Religions Roman Catholic 90%, Protestant 2%, Jewish 2%, other 6%
Ethnic mix Indo-European 83%, Mestizo 14%, Jewish 2%, Amerindian 1%
Government Presidential system
Currency Argentine peso = 100 centavos
Literacy rate 97%
Calorie consumption 3171 calories

ARMENIA

Page 95 F3

Smallest of the former USSR's republics, Armenia lies in the Lesser Caucasus mountains. Territorial war with Azerbaijan ended in a 1994 ceasefire.

Official name Republic of Armenia
Formation 1991
Capital Yerevan
Population 3.1 million / 269 people per sq mile (104 people per sq km)
Total area 11,506 sq. miles (29,800 sq. km)
Languages Armenian, Azeri, Russian
Religions Armenian Apostolic Church (Orthodox) 94%, other 6%
Ethnic mix Armenian 93%, Azeri 3%, Russian 2%, other 2%
Government Presidential system
Currency Dram = 100 luma
Literacy rate 99%
Calorie consumption 1991 calories

AUSTRALIA

Page 120 A4

An island continent located between the Indian and Pacific oceans, Australia was settled by Europeans 200 years ago, but now has many Asian immigrants.

Official name Commonwealth of Australia
Formation 1901
Capital Canberra
Population 19.7 million / 7 people per sq mile (3 people per sq km)
Total area 2,967,893 sq. miles (7,686,850 sq. km)
Languages English, Italian, Cantonese, Greek, Arabic, Vietnamese, Aboriginal languages
Religions Christian 64%, Other 36%
Ethnic mix European 92%, Asian 5%, Aboriginal and other 3%
Government Parliamentary system
Currency Australian dollar = 100 cents
Literacy rate 99%
Calorie consumption 3126 calories

AUSTRIA

Page 73 D7

Bordering eight countries in the heart of Europe, Austria was created in 1920 after the collapse of the Austro-Hungarian Empire the previous year.

Official name Republic of Austria
Formation 1918
Capital Vienna
Population 8.1 million / 254 people per sq mile (98 people per sq km)
Total area 32,378 sq. miles (83,858 sq. km)
Languages German, Croatian, Slovenian, Hungarian (Magyar)
Religions Roman Catholic 78%, Nonreligious 9%, Other (including Jewish and Muslim) 8%, Protestant 5%
Ethnic mix Austrian 93%, Croat, Slovene, and Hungarian 6%, other 1%
Government Parliamentary system
Currency Euro = 100 cents
Literacy rate 99%
Calorie consumption 3799 calories

AZERBAIJAN

Page 95 G2

Situated on the western coast of the Caspian Sea, Azerbaijan was the first Soviet republic to declare independence from Moscow in 1991.

Official name Republic of Azerbaijan
Formation 1991
Capital Baku
Population 8.4 million / 251 people per sq mile (97 people per sq km)
Total area 33,436 sq. miles (86,600 sq. km)
Languages Azeri, Russian
Religions Shi'a Muslim 68%, Sunni Muslim 26%, Russian Orthodox 3%, Armenian Apostolic Church (Orthodox) 2%, other 1%
Ethnic mix Azeri 90%, Dagestani 3%, Russian 3%, Armenian 2%, other 2%
Government Presidential system
Currency Manat = 100 gopik
Literacy rate 97%
Calorie consumption 2474 calories

BAHAMAS

Page 32 C1

Located in the western Atlantic, off the Florida coast, the Bahamas comprise some 700 islands and 2,400 cays, only 30 of which are inhabited.

Official name Commonwealth of the Bahamas
Formation 1973
Capital Nassau
Population 314,000 / 81 people per sq mile (31 people per sq km)
Total area 5382 sq. miles (13,940 sq. km)
Languages English, English Creole, French Creole
Religions Baptist 32%, Anglican 20%, Roman Catholic 19%, other 17%, Methodist 6%, Church of God 6%
Ethnic mix Black African 85%, other 15%
Government Parliamentary system
Currency Bahamian dollar = 100 cents
Literacy rate 96%
Calorie consumption 2777 calories

BAHRAIN

Page 98 C4

Bahrain is an archipelago of 33 islands between the Qatar peninsula and the Saudi Arabian mainland. Only three of these islands are inhabited.

Official name Kingdom of Bahrain
Formation 1971
Capital Manama
Population 724,000 / 2652 people per sq mile (1025 people per sq km)
Total area 239 sq. miles (620 sq. km)
Languages Arabic
Religions Muslim (mainly Shi'a) 99%, other 1%
Ethnic mix Bahraini 70%, Iranian, Indian, and Pakistani 24%, Other Arab 4%, European 2%
Government Monarchy
Currency Bahraini dinar = 1000 fils
Literacy rate 89%
Calorie consumption Not available

BANGLADESH

Page 113 G3

Bangladesh lies at the north of the Bay of Bengal. It seceded from Pakistan in 1971 and, after much political instability, returned to democracy in 1991.

Official name People's Republic of Bangladesh
Formation 1971
Capital Dhaka
Population 147 million / 2837 people per sq mile (1096 people per sq km)
Total area 55,598 sq. miles (144,000 sq. km)
Languages Bengali, Urdu, Chakma, Marma (Magh), Garo, Khasi, Santhali, Tripuri, Mro
Religions Muslim (mainly Sunni) 87%, Hindu 12%, other 1%
Ethnic mix Bengali 98%, other 2%
Government Parliamentary system
Currency Taka = 100 poisha
Literacy rate 41%
Calorie consumption 2187 calories

BELGIUM

Page 65 B6

Located in northwestern Europe, Belgium's history has been marked by the division between its Flemish- and French-speaking communities.

Official name Kingdom of Belgium
Formation 1830
Capital Brussels
Population 10.3 million / 813 people per sq mile (314 people per sq mile)
Total area 11,780 sq. miles (30,510 sq. km)
Languages Dutch, French, German
Religions Roman Catholic 88%, Muslim 2%, other 10%
Ethnic mix Fleming 58%, Walloon 33%, other 6%, Italian 2%, Moroccan 1%
Government Parliamentary system
Currency Euro = 100 cents
Literacy rate 99%
Calorie consumption 3682 calories

BHUTAN

Page 113 G3

The landlocked Buddhist kingdom of Bhutan is perched in the eastern Himalayas between India and China. Gradual reforms protect its cultural identity.

Official name Kingdom of Bhutan
Formation 1656
Capital Thimphu
Population 2.3 million / 127 people per sq mile (49 people per sq mile)
Total area 18,147 sq. miles (47,000sq. km)
Languages Dzongkha, Nepali, Assamese
Religions Mahayana Buddhist 70%, Hindu 24%, other 6%
Ethnic mix Bhute 50%, Nepalese 25%, other 25%
Government Monarchy
Currency Ngultrum = 100 chetrum
Literacy rate 47%
Calorie consumption Not available

BOTSWANA

Page 56 C3

Once the British protectorate of Bechuanaland, Botswana lies landlocked in southern Africa. Diamonds provide it with a prosperous economy.

Official name Republic of Botswana
Formation 1966
Capital Gaborone
Population 1.8 million / 8 people per sq mile (3 people per sq mile)
Total area 231,803 sq. miles (600,370 sq. km)
Languages Setswana, English, Shona, San, Khoikhoi, isiNdebele
Religions Traditional beliefs 50%, Christian (mainly Protestant) 30%, Other (including Muslim) 20%
Ethnic mix Tswana 98%, other 2%
Government Presidential system
Currency Pula = 100 thebe
Literacy rate 79%
Calorie consumption 2292 calories

BARBADOS

Page 33 H4

Barbados is the most easterly of the Caribbean Windward Islands. Under British rule for 339 years, it became fully independent in 1966.

Official name Barbados
Formation 1966
Capital Bridgetown
Population 270,000 / 1627 people per sq mile (628 people per sq km)
Total area 166 sq. miles (430 sq. km)
Languages Bajan (Barbadian English), English
Religions Anglican 40%, Nonreligious 17%, Pentecostal 8%, Methodist 7%, Roman Catholic 4%, other 24%
Ethnic mix Black African 90%, other 10%
Government Parliamentary system
Currency Barbados dollar = 100 cents
Literacy rate 99%
Calorie consumption 2992 calories

BELIZE

Page 30 B1

The last Central American country to gain independence, this former British colony lies on the eastern shore of the Yucatan Peninsula.

Official name Belize
Formation 1981
Capital Belmopan
Population 256,000 / 29 people per sq mile (11 people per sq km)
Total area 8867 sq. miles (22,966 sq.km)
Languages English Creole, Spanish, English, Mayan, Garifuna (Carib)
Religions Roman Catholic 62%, Anglican 12%, Methodist 6%, Mennonite 4%, other 17%
Ethnic mix Mestizo 44%, Creole 30%, Maya 11%, Garifuna 7%, Asian Indian 4%, other 4%
Government Parliamentary system
Currency Belizean dollar = 100 cents
Literacy rate 77%
Calorie consumption 2886 calories

BOLIVIA

Page 39 F3

Bolivia lies landlocked high in central South America. Mineral riches once made it the region's wealthiest state. Today, it is the poorest.

Official name Republic of Bolivia
Formation 1825
Capital La Paz (administrative); Sucre (judicial)
Population 8.8 million / 21 people per sq mile (8 people per sq km)
Total area 424,162 sq. miles (1,098,580 sq. km)
Languages Aymara, Quechua, Spanish
Religions Roman Catholic 93%, other 7%
Ethnic mix Quechua 37%, Aymara 32%, Mixed race 13%, European 10%, other 8%
Government Presidential system
Currency Boliviano = 100 centavos
Literacy rate 87%
Calorie consumption 2267 calories

BRAZIL

Page 40 C2

Brazil covers more than half of South America and is the site of the world's largest rain forest. The country has immense natural resources.

Official name Federative Republic of Brazil
Formation 1822
Capital Brasília
Population 179 million / 55 people per sq mile (21 people per sq km)
Total area 3,286,470 sq. miles (8,511,965 sq. km)
Languages Portuguese, German, Italian, Spanish, Polish, Japanese.
Religions Roman Catholic 74%, Protestant 15%, Atheist 7%, other 4%,
Ethnic mix Black 53%, Mixed race 40%, White 6%, other 1%
Government Presidential system
Currency Real = 100 centavos
Literacy rate 86%
Calorie consumption 3002 calories

BELARUS

Page 85 B6

Formerly known as White Russia, Belarus lies landlocked in eastern Europe. The country reluctantly became independent of the USSR in 1991.

Official name Republic of Belarus
Formation 1991
Capital Minsk
Population 9.9 million / 124 people per sq mile (48 people per sq km)
Total area 80,154 sq. miles (207,600 sq. km)
Languages Belarussian, Russian
Religions Orthodox Christian 60%, Roman Catholic 8%, other 32%
Ethnic mix Belarussian 78%, Russian 13%, Polish 4%, Ukrainian 3%, other 2%
Government Presidential system
Currency Belarussian rouble = 100 kopeks
Literacy rate 99%
Calorie consumption 2925 calories

BENIN

Page 53 F4

Stretching north from the West African coast, Benin became one of the pioneers of African democratization in 1990, ending years of military rule.

Official name Republic of Benin
Formation 1960
Capital Porto-Novo
Population 6.7 million / 157 people per sq mile (61 people per sq km)
Total area 43,483 sq. miles (112,620 sq. km)
Languages Fon, Bariba, Yoruba, Adja, Houeda, Somba, French
Religions Voodoo 50%, Muslim 30%, Christian 20%
Ethnic mix Fon 47%, Adja 12%, Bariba 10%, other 31%
Government Presidential system
Currency CFA franc = 100 centimes
Literacy rate 40%
Calorie consumption 2455 calories

BOSNIA & HERZEGOVINA

Page 78 B3

At the heart of the western Balkans, Bosnia and Herzegovina was the focus of the bitter conflict surrounding the breakup of former Yugoslavia.

Official name Bosnia and Herzegovina
Formation 1992
Capital Sarajevo
Population 4.2 million / 213 people per sq mile (82 people per sq km)
Total area 19,741 sq. miles (51,129 sq. km)
Languages Serbo-Croat
Religions Muslim (mainly Sunni) 40%, Orthodox Christian 31%, Roman Catholic 15%, Protestant 4%, other 10%
Ethnic mix Bosniak 48%, Serb 38%, Croat 14%
Government Parliamentary system
Currency Marka = 100 pfeninga
Literacy rate 95%
Calorie consumption 2845 calories

BRUNEI

Page 116 D3

Lying on the northwestern coast of the island of Borneo, Brunei is surrounded and divided in two by the Malaysian state of Sarawak.

Official name Sultanate of Brunei
Formation 1984
Capital Bandar Seri Begawan
Population 358,000 / 176 people per sq mile (68 people per sq km)
Total area 2228 sq. miles (5770 sq. km)
Languages Malay, English, Chinese
Religions Muslim (mainly Sunni) 66%, Buddhist 14%, Christian 10%, other 10%
Ethnic mix Malay 67%, Chinese 16%, Indigenous 6%, other 11%
Government Monarchy
Currency Brunei dollar = 100 cents
Literacy rate 94%
Calorie consumption 2814 calories

BULGARIA

Page 82 C2

Located in southeastern Europe, Bulgaria has made slow progress toward democracy since the fall of its communist regime in 1990.

Official name Republic of Bulgaria
Formation 1908
Capital Sofia
Population 7.9 million / 185 people per sq mile (71 people per sq km)
Total area 42,822 sq. miles (110,910 sq. km)
Languages Bulgarian, Turkish, Romani
Religions Orthodox Christian 83%, Muslim 12%, other 4%, Roman Catholic 1%
Ethnic mix Bulgarian 84%, Turkish 9%, Roma 5%, other 2%
Government Parliamentary system
Currency Lev = 100 stotinki
Literacy rate 99%
Calorie consumption 2626 calories

CAMBODIA

Page 115 D5

Located in mainland Southeast Asia, Cambodia has emerged from two decades of civil war and invasion from Vietnam.

Official name Kingdom of Cambodia
Formation 1953
Capital Phnom Penh
Population 14.1 million / 207 people per sq mile (80 people per sq km)
Total area 69,900 sq. miles (181,040 sq. km)
Languages Khmer, French, Chinese, Vietnamese, Cham
Religions Buddhist 93%, Muslim 6%, Christian 1%
Ethnic mix Khmer 90%, Vietnamese 4%, Chinese 1%, other 5%
Government Parliamentary system
Currency Riel = 100 sen
Literacy rate 69%
Calorie consumption 1967 calories

CAPE VERDE

Page 52 A2

Off the west coast of Africa, in the Atlantic Ocean, lies the group of islands that make up Cape Verde, a Portuguese colony until 1975.

Official name Republic of Cape Verde
Formation 1975
Capital Praia
Population 463,000 / 298 people per sq mile (115 people per sq km)
Total area 1557 sq. miles (4033 sq. km)
Languages Portuguese Creole, Portuguese
Religions Roman Catholic 97%, other 3%
Ethnic mix Mestiço 60%, African 30%, other 10%
Government Mixed presidential–parliamentary system
Currency Cape Verde escudo = 100 centavos
Literacy rate 76%
Calorie consumption 3308 calories

CHILE

Page 42 B3

Chile extends in a ribbon down the west coast of South America. It returned to democracy in 1989 after a referendum rejected its military dictator.

Official name Republic of Chile
Formation 1818
Capital Santiago
Population 15.8 million / 55 people per sq mile (21 people per sq km)
Total area 292,258 sq. miles (756,950 sq. km)
Languages Spanish, Amerindian languages
Religions Roman Catholic 80%, other and nonreligious 20%
Ethnic mix Mixed race and European 90%, Amerindian 10%
Government Presidential system
Currency Chilean peso = 100 centavos
Literacy rate 96%
Calorie consumption 2868 calories

BURKINA FASO

Page 53 E4

Known as Upper Volta until 1984, the West African state of Burkina Faso has been under military rule for most of its post-independence history.

Official name Burkina Faso
Formation 1960
Capital Ouagadougou
Population 13 million / 123 people per sq mile (47 people per sq km)
Total area 105,869 sq. miles (274,200 sq. km)
Languages Mossi, Fulani, French, Tuareg, Dyula, Songhai
Religions Muslim 55%, Traditional beliefs 35%, Roman Catholic 9%, other Christian 1%
Ethnic mix Mossi 50%, other 50%
Government Presidential system
Currency CFA franc = 100 centimes
Literacy rate 25%
Calorie consumption 2485 calories

CAMEROON

Page 54 A4

Situated on the central West African coast, Cameroon was effectively a one-party state for 30 years. Multiparty elections were held in 1992.

Official name Republic of Cameroon
Formation 1960
Capital Yaoundé
Population 16 million /89 people per sq mile (34 people per sq km)
Total area 183,567 sq. miles (475,400 sq. km)
Languages Bamileke, Fang, Fulani, French, English
Religions Traditional beliefs 25%, Christian 53%, Muslim 22%.
Ethnic mix Cameroon highlanders 31%, Equatorial Bantu 19%, Kirdi 11%, other 21%
Government Presidential system
Currency CFA franc = 100 centimes
Literacy rate 68%
Calorie consumption 2242 calories

CENTRAL AFRICAN REPUBLIC

Page 54 C4

This landlocked country lies between the basins of the Chad and Congo rivers. Its arid north sustains less than 2% of the population.

Official name Central African Republic
Formation 1960
Capital Bangui
Population 3.9 million / 16 people per sq mile (6 people per sq km)
Total area 240,534 sq. miles (622,984 sq. km)
Languages Sango, Banda, Gbaya, French
Religions Traditional beliefs 60%, Christian 35%, Muslim 5%
Ethnic mix Baya 34%, Banda 27%, Mandjia 21%, Sara 10%, other 8%
Government Transitional regime
Currency CFA franc = 100 centimes
Literacy rate 49%
Calorie consumption 1949 calories

CHINA

Page 104 C4

This vast East Asian country was dominated by Mao Zedong, who founded the Communist republic, and Deng Xiaoping, his successor (1976–1997).

Official name People's Republic of China
Formation 960
Capital Beijing
Population 1.3 billion / 362 people per sq mile (140 people per sq km)
Total area 3,705,386 sq. miles (9,596,960 sq. km)
Languages Mandarin, Wu, Cantonese, Hsiang, Min, Hakka, Kan
Religions Nonreligious 59%, Traditional beliefs 20%, other 13%, Buddhist 6%, Muslim 2%
Ethnic mix Han 92%, other 8%,
Government One-party state
Currency Renminbi (Yuan) = 10 jiao
Literacy rate 91%
Calorie consumption 2963 calories

BURUNDI

Page 51 B7

Small, landlocked Burundi lies just south of the Equator, on the Nile-Congo watershed in Central Africa. Since 1993 it has been marked by violent ethnic conflict.

Official name Republic of Burundi
Formation 1962
Capital Bujumbura
Population 6.8 million / 687 people per sq mile (265 people per sq km)
Total area 10,745 sq. miles (27,830 sq. km)
Languages Kirundi, French, Kiswahili
Religions Christian (mainly Roman Catholic) 60%, Traditional beliefs 39%, Muslim 1%
Ethnic mix Hutu 85%, Tutsi 14%, Twa 1%
Government Transitional regime
Currency Burundi franc = 100 centimes
Literacy rate 50%
Calorie consumption 1612 calories

CANADA

Page 15 E4

Canada extends from its US border north to the Arctic Ocean. In recent years, French-speaking Quebec has sought independence from the rest of the country.

Official name Canada
Formation 1867
Capital Ottawa
Population 31.5 million / 9 people per sq mile (3 people per sq km)
Total area 3,717,792 sq. miles (9,984,670 sq. km)
Languages English, French, Chinese, Italian, German, Ukrainian, Inuktitut,
Religions Roman Catholic 44%, Protestant 29%, nonreligious 27%
Ethnic mix British origin 44%, French origin 25%, other European 20%, other 11%
Government Parliamentary system
Currency Canadian dollar = 100 cents
Literacy rate 99%
Calorie consumption 3176 calories

CHAD

Page 54 C3

Landlocked in north central Africa, Chad has been torn by intermittent periods of civil war since it gained independence from France in 1960.

Official name Republic of Chad
Formation 1960
Capital N'Djamena
Population 8.6 million / 18 people per sq mile (7 people per sq km)
Total area 495,752 sq. miles (1,284,000 sq. km)
Languages French, Sara, Arabic, Maba
Religions Muslim 55%, Traditional beliefs 35%, Christian 10%
Ethnic mix Nomads (Tuareg and Toubou) 38%, Sara 30%, other 17%, Arab 15%
Government Presidential system
Currency CFA franc = 100 centimes
Literacy rate 46%
Calorie consumption 2245 calories

COLOMBIA

Page 36 B3

Lying in northwest South America, Colombia is one of the world's most violent countries, with powerful drugs cartels and guerrilla activity.

Official name Republic of Colombia
Formation 1819
Capital Bogotá
Population 44.2 million / 110 people per sq mile (43 people per sq km)
Total area 439,733 sq. miles (1,138,910 sq. km)
Languages Spanish, Wayuu, Páez, and other Amerindian languages
Religions Roman Catholic 95%, other 5%
Ethnic mix Mestizo 58%, White 20%, other 22%
Government Presidential system
Currency Colombian peso = 100 centavos
Literacy rate 92%
Calorie consumption 2580 calories

COMOROS

Page 57 F2

In the Indian Ocean, between Mozambique and Madagascar, lie the Comoros, comprising three main islands, and a number of smaller islets.

Official name Union of the Comoros
Formation 1975
Capital Moroni
Population 768,000 /
892 people per sq mile (344 people per sq km)
Total area 838 sq. miles
(2170 sq. km)
Languages Arabic, Comoran, French
Religions Muslim (mainly Sunni) 98%, Roman Catholic 1%, other 1%
Ethnic mix Comoran 97%, other 3%
Government Presidential system
Currency Comoros franc = 100 centimes
Literacy rate 56%
Calorie consumption 1735 calories

COSTA RICA

Page 31 E4

Costa Rica is the most stable country in Central America. Its neutrality in foreign affairs is long-standing, but it has very strong ties with the US.

Official name Republic of Costa Rica
Formation 1838
Capital San José
Population 4.2 million / 213 people per sq mile (82 people per sq km)
Total area 19,730 sq. miles
(51,100 sq. km)
Languages Spanish, English Creole, Bribri, Cabecar
Religions Roman Catholic 76%, other (including Protestant) 24%
Ethnic mix Mestizo and European 96%, Black 2%, Chinese 1%, Amerindian 1%
Government Presidential system
Currency Costa Rican colón = 100 centimos
Literacy rate 96%
Calorie consumption 2761 calories

CUBA

Page 32 C

Cuba is the largest island in the Caribbean and the only Communist country in the Americas. It has been led by Fidel Castro since 1959.

Official name Republic of Cuba
Formation 1902
Capital Havana
Population 11.3 million /
264 people per sq mile (102 people per sq km)
Total area 42,803 sq. miles
(110,860 sq. km)
Languages Spanish
Religions Nonreligious 49%, Roman Catholic 40%, Atheist 6%, Protestant 1%, other 4%
Ethnic mix White 66%, European–African 22%, Black 12%
Government One-party state
Currency Cuban peso = 100 centavos
Literacy rate 97%
Calorie consumption 2643 calories

DENMARK

Page 63 A7

The country occupies the Jutland peninsula and over 400 islands in Scandinavia. Greenland and the Faeroe Islands are self-governing associated territories.

Official name Kingdom of Denmark
Formation 950
Capital Copenhagen
Population 5.4 million /
330 people per sq mile (127 people per sq km)
Total area 16,639 sq. miles
(43,094 sq. km)
Languages Danish
Religions Evangelical Lutheran 89%, Roman Catholic 1%, other 10%
Ethnic mix Danish 96%, other (including Scandinavian and Turkish) 3%, Faeroese and Inuit 1%
Government Parliamentary system
Currency Danish krone = 100 øre
Literacy rate 99%
Calorie consumption 3454 calories

CONGO

Page 55 B5

Astride the Equator in west central Africa, this former French colony emerged from 26 years of Marxist-Leninist rule in 1990.

Official name Republic of the Congo
Formation 1960
Capital Brazzaville
Population 3.7 million / 28 people per sq mile (11 people per sq km)
Total area 132,046 sq. miles
(342,000 sq. km)
Languages Kongo, Teke, Lingala, French
Religions Traditional beliefs 50%, Roman Catholic 25%, Protestant 23%, Muslim 2%
Ethnic mix Bakongo 48%, Sangha 20%, Teke 17%, Mbochi 12%, other 3%
Government Presidential system
Currency CFA franc = 100 centimes
Literacy rate 83%
Calorie consumption 2221 calories

CÔTE D'IVOIRE

Page 52 D4

One of the larger nations along the coast of West Africa, Côte d'Ivoire remains under the influence of its former colonial ruler, France.

Official name Republic of Côte d'Ivoire
Formation 1960
Capital Yamoussoukro
Population 16.6 million / 135 people per sq mile (52 people per sq km)
Total area 124,502 sq. miles
(322,460 sq. km)
Languages Akan, French, Kru, Voltaic
Religions Muslim 38%, Traditional beliefs 25%, Roman Catholic 25%, Protestant 6%, other 6%
Ethnic mix Baoulé 23%, Bété 18%, Senufo 15%, Agni-Ashanti 14%, Mandinka 11%, other 19%
Government Presidential system
Currency CFA franc = 100 centimes
Literacy rate 50%
Calorie consumption 2594 calories

CYPRUS

Page 80 C5

Cyprus lies in the eastern Mediterranean. Since 1974, it has been partitioned between the Turkish-occupied north and the Greek south.

Official name Republic of Cyprus
Formation 1960
Capital Nicosia
Population 802,000 /
225 people per sq mile (87 people per sq km)
Total area 3571 sq. miles (9250 sq. km)
Languages Greek, Turkish
Religions Orthodox Christian 78%, Muslim 18%, other 4%
Ethnic mix Greek 85%, Turkish 12%, other 3%
Government Presidential system
Currency Cyprus pound (Turkish lira in TRNC) = 100 cents (Cyprus pound); 100 kurus (Turkish lira)
Literacy rate 97%
Calorie consumption 3302 calories

DJIBOUTI

Page 50 D4

A city state with a desert hinterland, Djibouti lies in northeast Africa. Once known as French Somaliland, its economy relies on its port.

Official name Republic of Djibouti
Formation 1977
Capital Djibouti
Population 703,000 /
79 people per sq mile (30 people per sq km)
Total area 8494 sq. miles
(22,000 sq. km)
Languages Somali, Afar, French, Arabic
Religions Muslim (mainly Sunni) 94%, Christian 6%
Ethnic mix Issa 60%, Afar 35%, other 5%
Government Presidential system
Currency Djibouti franc = 100 centimes
Literacy rate 66%
Calorie consumption 2218 calories

CONGO, DEM. REP.

Page 55 C6

Straddling the Equator in east central Africa, Dem. Rep. Congo is one of Africa's largest countries. It achieved independence from Belgium in 1960.

Official name Democratic Republic of the Congo
Formation 1960
Capital Kinshasa
Population 52.8 million / 60 people per sq mile (23 people per sq km)
Total area 905,563 sq. miles
(2,345,410 sq. km)
Languages Kiswahili, Tshiluba, Kikongo, Lingala, French
Religions Roman Catholic 37%, Protestant 13%, Traditional beliefs 50%, other
Ethnic mix Bantu and Hamitic 45%, other 55%
Government Transitional regime
Currency Congolese franc = 100 centimes
Literacy rate 63%
Calorie consumption 1535 calories

CROATIA

Page 78 B2

Post-independence fighting in this former Yugoslav republic, thwarted its plans to capitalize on its prime location along the east Adriatic coast.

Official name Republic of Croatia
Formation 1991
Capital Zagreb
Population 4.4 million /
202 people per sq mile (78 people per sq km)
Total area 21,831 sq. miles
(56,542 sq. km)
Languages Croatian
Religions Roman Catholic 88%, Orthodox Christian 4%, Muslim 1%, other 7%
Ethnic mix Croat 90%, Serb 4%, Bosniak 1%, other 5%
Government Parliamentary system
Currency Kuna = 100 lipas
Literacy rate 98%
Calorie consumption 2678 calories

CZECH REPUBLIC

Page 77 A5

Once part of Czechoslovakia in eastern Europe, it became independent in 1993, after peacefully dissolving its federal union with Slovakia.

Official name Czech Republic
Formation 1993
Capital Prague
Population 10.2 million / 335 people per sq mile (129 people per sq km)
Total area 30,450 sq. miles
(78,866 sq. km)
Languages Czech, Slovak, Hungarian (Magyar)
Religions Roman Catholic 39%, Atheist 38%, Protestant 3%, Hussite 2%, other 18%
Ethnic mix Czech 81%, Moravian 13%, Slovak 6%
Government Parliamentary system
Currency Czech koruna = 100 haleru
Literacy rate 99%
Calorie consumption 3097 calories

DOMINICA

Page 33 H4

The Caribbean island Dominica resisted European colonization until the 18th century, when it first came under the French, and then, the British

Official name Commonwealth of Dominica
Formation 1978
Capital Roseau
Population 69,655 / 240 people per sq mile (93 people per sq km)
Total area 291 sq. miles
(754 sq. km)
Languages French Creole, English
Religions Roman Catholic 77%, Protestant 15%, other 8%
Ethnic mix Black 91%, Mixed race 6%, Carib 2%, other 1%
Government Parliamentary system
Currency Eastern Caribbean dollar = 100 cents
Literacy rate 76%
Calorie consumption 2995 calories

DOMINICAN REPUBLIC

Page 33 E2

The republic occupies the eastern two-thirds of the island of Hispaniola in the Caribbean. Frequent coups and a strong US influence mark its recent past.

Official name Dominican Republic
Formation 1865
Capital Santo Domingo
Population 8.7 million / 466 people per sq mile (180 people per sq km)
Total area 18,679 sq. miles (48,380 sq. km)
Languages Spanish, French Creole
Religions Roman Catholic 92%, other and nonreligious 8%
Ethnic mix Mixed race 75%, White 15%, Black 10%
Government Presidential system
Currency Dominican Republic peso = 100 centavos
Literacy rate 84%
Calorie consumption 2333 calories

EAST TIMOR

Page 116 F5

This new nation occupies the eastern half of the island of Timor. Invaded by Indonesia in 1975, it declared independence in 1999.

Official name Democratic Republic of Timor-Leste
Formation 2002
Capital Dili
Population 778,000 / 138 people per sq mile (53 people per sq km)
Total area 5756 sq. miles (14,874 sq. km)
Languages Tetum (Portuguese/Austronesian), Bahasa Indonesia, and Portuguese
Religions Roman Catholic 95%, other 5%
Ethnic mix Papuan groups approx 85%, Indonesian approx 13%, Chinese 2%
Government Parliamentary system
Currency US dollar = 100 cents
Literacy rate 59%
Calorie consumption Not available

ECUADOR

Page 38 A2

Ecuador sits high on South America's western coast. Once part of the Inca heartland, its territory includes the Galapagos Islands, to the west.

Official name Republic of Ecuador
Formation 1830
Capital Quito
Population 13 million / 122 people per sq mile (47 people per sq km)
Total area 109,483 sq. miles (283,560 sq. km)
Languages Spanish, Quechua, other Amerindian languages
Religions Roman Catholic 93%, Protestant, Jewish, and other 7%
Ethnic mix Mestizo 55%, Amerindian 25%, White 10%, Black 10%
Government Presidential system
Currency US dollar = 100 cents
Literacy rate 91%
Calorie consumption 2792 calories

EGYPT

Page 50 B2

Egypt occupies the northeast corner of Africa. Its essentially pro-Western, military-backed regime is being challenged by Islamic fundamentalists.

Official name Arab Republic of Egypt
Formation 1936
Capital Cairo
Population 71.9 million / 187 people per sq mile (72 people per sq km)
Total area 386,660 sq. miles (1,001,450 sq. km)
Languages Arabic, French, English, Berber
Religions Muslim (mainly Sunni) 94%, Coptic Christian and other 6%
Ethnic mix Eastern Hamitic 90%, Nubian, Armenian, and Greek 10%
Government Presidential system
Currency Egyptian pound = 100 piastres
Literacy rate 56%
Calorie consumption 3385 calories

EL SALVADOR

Page 30 B3

El Salvador is Central America's smallest state. A 12-year war between US-backed government troops and left-wing guerrillas ended in 1992.

Official name Republic of El Salvador
Formation 1841
Capital San Salvador
Population 6.5 million / 812 people per sq mile (314 people per sq km)
Total area 8124 sq. miles (21,040 sq. km)
Languages Spanish
Religions Roman Catholic 80%, Evangelical 18%, other 2%
Ethnic mix Mestizo 94%, Amerindian 5%, White 1%
Government Presidential system
Currency Salvadorean colón & US dollar = 100 centavos (colón); 100 cents (US dollar)
Literacy rate 80%
Calorie consumption 2512 calories

EQUATORIAL GUINEA

Page 55 A5

The country comprises the Rio Muni mainland and five islands on the west coast of central Africa. Free elections were first held in 1988.

Official name Republic of Equatorial Guinea
Formation 1968
Capital Malabo
Population 494,000 / 46 people per sq mile (18 people per sq km)
Total area 10,830 sq. miles (28,051 sq. km)
Languages Spanish, Fang, Bubi
Religions Roman Catholic 90%, other 10%
Ethnic mix Fang 85%, Bubi 4%, other 11%
Government Presidential system
Currency CFA franc = 100 centimes
Literacy rate 84%
Calorie consumption Not available

ERITREA

Page 50 C3

Lying on the shores of the Red Sea, Eritrea effectively seceded from Ethiopia in 1993, following a 30-year war for independence.

Official name State of Eritrea
Formation 1993
Capital Asmara
Population 4.1 million / 90 people per sq mile (35 people per sq km)
Total area 46,842 sq. miles (121,320 sq. km)
Languages Tigrinya, English, Tigre, Afar, Arabic, Bilen, Kunama, Nara, Saho, Hadareb
Religions Christian 45%, Muslim 45%, other 10%
Ethnic mix Tigray and Kunama 40%, Tigray 50%, Afar 4%, Saho 3%, other 3%
Government Transitional regime
Currency Nakfa = 100 cents
Literacy rate 57%
Calorie consumption 1690 calories

ESTONIA

Page 84 D2

Estonia is the smallest and most developed of the three Baltic states. It has the highest standard of living of any of the former Soviet republics.

Official name Republic of Estonia
Formation 1991
Capital Tallinn
Population 1.3 million / 75 people per sq mile (29 people per sq km)
Total area 17,462 sq. miles (45,226 sq. km)
Languages Estonian, Russian
Religions Evangelical Lutheran 56%, Orthodox Christian 25%, other 19%
Ethnic mix Estonian 62%, Russian 30%, other 8%
Government Parliamentary system
Currency Kroon = 100 senti
Literacy rate 99%
Calorie consumption 3048 calories

ETHIOPIA

Page 51 C5

Located in northeast Africa, Ethiopia was a Marxist regime from 1974–91. It has suffered a series of economic, civil, and natural crises.

Official name Federal Democratic Republic of Ethiopia
Formation 1896
Capital Addis Ababa
Population 70.7 million / 165 people per sq mile (64 people per sq km)
Total area 435,184 sq. miles (1,127,127 sq. km)
Languages Amharic, Tigrinya, Galla, Sidamo, Somali, English, Arabic
Religions Orthodox Christian 40%, Muslim 40%, other 20%
Ethnic mix Oromo 40%, Amhara 25%, Sidamo 9%, Berta 6%, other 20%
Government Parliamentary system
Currency Ethiopian birr = 100 cents
Literacy rate 42%
Calorie consumption 2037 calories

FIJI

Page 123 E5

A volcanic archipelago, Fiji comprises 882 islands in the southern Pacific Ocean. Ethnic Fijians and Indo-Fijians have been in conflict since 1987.

Official name Republic of the Fiji Islands
Formation 1970
Capital Suva
Population 839,000 / 119 people per sq mile (46 people per sq km)
Total area 7054 sq. miles (18,270 sq. km)
Languages Fijian, English, Hindi, Urdu, Tamil, Telugu
Religions Hindu 38%, Methodist 37%, Roman Catholic 9%, other 16%.
Ethnic mix Melanesian 48%, Indian 46%, other 6%
Government Parliamentary system
Currency Fiji dollar = 100 cents
Literacy rate 93%
Calorie consumption 2789 calories

FINLAND

Page 62 D4

Finland's distinctive language and national identity have been influenced by both its Scandinavian and its Russian neighbors.

Official name Republic of Finland
Formation 1917
Capital Helsinki
Population 5.2 million / 44 people per sq mile (17 people per sq km)
Total area 130,127 sq. miles (337,030 sq. km)
Languages Finnish, Swedish, Sámi
Religions Evangelical Lutheran 89%, Orthodox Christian 1%, Roman Catholic 1%, other 9%
Ethnic mix Finnish 93%, other (including Sámi) 7%
Government Parliamentary system
Currency Euro = 100 cents
Literacy rate 99%
Calorie consumption 3202 calories

FRANCE

Page 68 B4

Straddling Western Europe from the English Channel to the Mediterranean Sea, France, is one of the world's leading industrial powers.

Official name French Republic
Formation 987
Capital Paris
Population 60.1 million / 283 people per sq mile (109 people per sq km)
Total area 211,208 sq. miles (547,030 sq. km)
Languages French, Provençal, German, Breton, Catalan, Basque
Religions Roman Catholic 88%, Muslim 8%, Protestant 2%, other 2%
Ethnic mix French 90%, North African 6%, German 2%, other 2%
Government Mixed presidential–parliamentary system
Currency Euro = 100 cents
Literacy rate 99%
Calorie consumption 3629 calories

GABON

Page 55 A5

A former French colony straddling the Equator on Africa's west coast, it returned to multiparty politics in 1990, after 22 years of one-party rule.

Official name Gabonese Republic
Formation 1960
Capital Libreville
Population 1.3 million / 13 people per sq mile (5 people per sq km)
Total area 103,346 sq. miles (267,667 sq. km)
Languages Fang, French, Punu, Sira, Nzebi, Mpongwe
Religions Christian 55%, Traditional beliefs 40%, other 4%, Muslim 1%
Ethnic mix Fang 35%, other Bantu 29%, Eshira 25%, European and other African 9%, French 2%
Government Presidential system
Currency CFA franc = 100 centimes
Literacy rate 71%
Calorie consumption 2602 calories

GERMANY

Page 72 B4

Europe's strongest economic power, Germany's democratic west and Communist east were re-unified in 1990, after the fall of the east's regime.

Official name Federal Republic of Germany
Formation 1871
Capital Berlin
Population 82.5 million / 611 people per sq mile (236 people per sq km)
Total area 137,846 sq. miles (357,021 sq. km)
Languages German, Turkish
Religions Protestant 34%, Roman Catholic 33%, other 30%, Muslim 3%
Ethnic mix German 92%, other 3%, other European 3%, Turkish 2%
Government Parliamentary system
Currency Euro = 100 cents
Literacy rate 99%
Calorie consumption 3567 calories

GRENADA

Page 33 G5

The Windward island of Grenada became a focus of attention in 1983, when the US mounted an invasion to sever its growing links with Cuba.

Official name Grenada
Formation 1974
Capital St. George's
Population 89,258 / 681 people per sq mile (263 people per sq km)
Total area 131 sq. miles (340 sq. km)
Languages English, English Creole
Religions Roman Catholic 68%, Anglican 17%, other 15%
Ethnic mix Black African 82%, Mulatto (mixed race) 13%, East Indian 3%, other 2%
Government Parliamentary system
Currency Eastern Caribbean dollar = 100 cents
Literacy rate 94%
Calorie consumption 2749 calories

GUINEA-BISSAU

Page 52 B4

Known as Portuguese Guinea during its days as a colony, Guinea-Bissau is situated on Africa's west coast, bordered by Senegal and Guinea.

Official name Republic of Guinea-Bissau
Formation 1974
Capital Bissau
Population 1.5 million / 138 people per sq mile (53 people per sq km)
Total area 13,946 sq. miles (36,120 sq. km)
Languages Portuguese Creole, Balante, Fulani, Malinke, Portuguese
Religions Traditional beliefs 52%, Muslim 40%, Christian 8%
Ethnic mix Balante 25%, Mandinka 12%, Fula 20% Mandyako 11%, other 13%
Government Transitional regime
Currency CFA franc = 100 centimes
Literacy rate 40%
Calorie consumption 2481 calories

GAMBIA

Page 52 B3

A narrow state on the west coast of Africa, The Gambia was renowned for its stability until its government was overthrown in a coup in 1994.

Official name Republic of the Gambia
Formation 1965
Capital Banjul
Population 1.4 million / 363 people per sq mile (140 people per sq km)
Total area 4363 sq. miles (11,300 sq. km)
Languages Mandinka, Fulani, Wolof, Jola, Soninke, English
Religions Sunni Muslim 90%, Christian 9%, Traditional beliefs 1%
Ethnic mix Mandinka 42%, Fulani 18%, Wolof 16%, Jola 10%, Serahuli 9%, other 5%
Government Presidential system
Currency Dalasi = 100 butut
Literacy rate 38%
Calorie consumption 2300 calories

GHANA

Page 53 E5

Once known as the Gold Coast, Ghana in West Africa has experienced intermittent periods of military rule since independence in 1957.

Official name Republic of Ghana
Formation 1957
Capital Accra
Population 20.9 million / 235 people per sq mile (91 people per sq km)
Total area 92,100 sq. miles (238,540 sq. km)
Languages Twi, Fanti, Ewe, Ga, Adangbe, Gurma, Dagomba (Dagbani)
Religions Christian 69%, Muslim 16%, Traditional beliefs 9%, other 6%
Ethnic mix Ashanti and Fanti 52%, Moshi-Dagomba 16%, Ewe 12%, other 11%, Ga and Ga-adanbe 8%, Yoruba 1%
Government Presidential system
Currency Cedi = 100 psewas
Literacy rate 74%
Calorie consumption 2670 calories

GUATEMALA

Page 30 A2

The largest state on the Central American isthmus, Guatemala returned to civilian rule in 1986, after 32 years of repressive military rule.

Official name Republic of Guatemala
Formation 1838
Capital Guatemala City
Population 12.3 million / 294 people per sq mile (113 people per sq km)
Total area 42,042 sq. miles (108,890 sq. km)
Languages Quiché, Mam, Cakchiquel, Kekchí, Spanish
Religions Roman Catholic 65%, Protestant 33%, other and nonreligious 2%
Ethnic mix Amerindian 60%, Mestizo 30%, other 10%
Government Presidential system
Currency Quetzal = 100 centavos
Literacy rate 70%
Calorie consumption 2203 calories

GUYANA

Page 37 F3

The only English-speaking country in South America, Guyana gained independence from Britain in 1966, and became a republic in 1970.

Official name Cooperative Republic of Guyana
Formation 1966
Capital Georgetown
Population 765,000 / 10 people per sq mile (4 people per sq km)
Total area 83,000 sq. miles (214,970 sq. km)
Languages English Creole, Hindi, Tamil, Amerindian languages, English
Religions Christian 57%, Hindu 33%, Muslim 9%, other 1%
Ethnic mix East Indian 52%, Black African 38%, other 10%
Government Presidential system
Currency Guyana dollar = 100 cents
Literacy rate 97%
Calorie consumption 2515 calories

GEORGIA

Page 95 F2

Located on the eastern shore of the Black Sea, Georgia's northern provinces have been torn by civil war since independence from the USSR in 1991.

Official name Georgia
Formation 1991
Capital Tbilisi
Population 5.1 million / 190 people per sq mile (73 people per sq km)
Total area 26,911 sq. miles (69,700 sq. km)
Languages Georgian, Russian, Azeri, Armenian, Mingrelian, Ossetian
Religions Georgian Orthodox 65%, Muslim 11%, Russian Orthodox 10%, Armenian Orthodox 8%, other 6%
Ethnic mix Georgian 70%, Armenian 8%, Russian 6%, Azeri 6%, other 10%
Government Presidential system
Currency Lari = 100 tetri
Literacy rate 99%
Calorie consumption 2247 calories

GREECE

Page 83 A5

Greece is the southernmost Balkan nation. Surrounded by the Mediterranean, Aegean, and Ionian Seas, it has a strong seafaring tradition.

Official name Hellenic Republic
Formation 1829
Capital Athens
Population 11 million / 218 people per sq mile (84 people per sq km)
Total area 50,942 sq. miles (131,940 sq. km)
Languages Greek, Turkish, Macedonian, Albanian
Religions Orthodox Christian 98%, Muslim 1%, other 1%
Ethnic mix Greek 98%, other 2%
Government Parliamentary system
Currency Euro = 100 cents
Literacy rate 97%
Calorie consumption 3754 calories

GUINEA

Page 52 C4

Facing the Atlantic Ocean, on the west coast of Africa, Guinea became the first French colony in Africa to gain independence, in 1958.

Official name Republic of Guinea
Formation 1958
Capital Conakry
Population 8.5 million / 90 people per sq mile (35 people per sq km)
Total area 94,925 sq. miles (245,857 sq. km)
Languages Fulani, Malinke, Soussou, French
Religions Muslim 65%, Traditional beliefs 33%, Christian 2%
Ethnic mix Fulani 30%, Malinke 30%, Soussou 15%, Kissi 10%, other tribes 10%, other 5%
Government Presidential system
Currency Guinea franc = 100 centimes
Literacy rate 41%
Calorie consumption 2362 calories

HAITI

Page 32 D3

Haiti shares the Caribbean island of Hispaniola with the Dominican Republic. At independence, in 1804, it became the world's first Black republic.

Official name Republic of Haiti
Formation 1804
Capital Port-au-Prince
Population 8.3 million / 780 people per sq mile (301 people per sq km)
Total area 10,714 sq. miles (27,750 sq. km)
Languages French Creole, French
Religions Roman Catholic 80%, Protestant 16%, other (including Voodoo) 3%, Nonreligious 1%
Ethnic mix Black African 95%, Mulatto (mixed race) and European 5%
Government Transitional regime
Currency Gourde = 100 centimes
Literacy rate 52%
Calorie consumption 2045 calories

HONDURAS

Page 30 C2

Honduras straddles the Central American isthmus. The country returned to full democratic civilian rule in 1984, after a succession of military regimes.

Official name Republic of Honduras
Formation 1838
Capital Tegucigalpa
Population 6.9 million / 160 people per sq mile (62 people per sq km)
Total area 43,278 sq. miles (112,090 sq. km)
Languages Spanish, Garífuna (Carib), English Creole
Religions Roman Catholic 97%, Protestant 3%
Ethnic mix Mestizo 90%, Black African 5%, Amerindian 4%, White 1%
Government Presidential system
Currency Lempira = 100 centavos
Literacy rate 80%
Calorie consumption 2406 calories

INDIA

Page 112 D4

Separated from the rest of Asia by the Himalayan mountain ranges, India forms a subcontinent. It is the world's second most populous country.

Official name Republic of India
Formation 1947
Capital New Delhi
Population 1.07 billion / 928 people per sq mile (358 people per sq km)
Total area 1,269,338 sq. miles (3,287,590 sq. km)
Languages Hindi, English, Urdu, Bengali, Marathi, Telugu, Tamil, Bihari, Gujarati, Kanarese
Religions Hindu 83%, Muslim 11%, Christian 2%, Sikh 2%, other 1%
Ethnic mix Indo-Aryan 72%, Dravidian 25%, Mongoloid and other 3%
Government Parliamentary system
Currency Indian rupee = 100 paise
Literacy rate 61%
Calorie consumption 2487 calories

IRAQ

Page 98 B3

Oil-rich Iraq is situated in the central Middle East. Since the removal of the monarchy in 1958, it has experienced considerable political turmoil.

Official name Republic of Iraq
Formation 1932
Capital Baghdad
Population 25.2 million / 149 people per sq mile (58 people per sq km)
Total area 168,753 sq. miles (437,072 sq. km)
Languages Arabic, Kurdish, Turkic languages, Armenian, Assyrian
Religions Shi'a Muslim 62%, Sunni Muslim 33%, other (including Christian) 5%
Ethnic mix Arab 79%, Kurdish 16%, Persian 3%, Turkmen 2%
Government Transitional regime
Currency New Iraqi dinar = 1000 fils
Literacy rate 40%
Calorie consumption 2197 calories

ITALY

Page 74 B3

Projecting into the Mediterranean Sea in Southern Europe, Italy is an ancient land, but also one of the continent's newest unified states.

Official name Italian Republic
Formation 1861
Capital Rome
Population 57.4 million / 506 people per sq mile (195 people per sq km)
Total area 116,305 sq. miles (301,230 sq. km)
Languages Italian, German, French, Rhaeto-Romanic, Sardinian
Religions Roman Catholic 85%, other and nonreligious 13%, Muslim 2%
Ethnic mix Italian 94%, Sardinian 2%, other 4%
Government Parliamentary system
Currency Euro = 100 cents
Literacy rate 99%
Calorie consumption 3680 calories

HUNGARY

Page 77 C6

Hungary is bordered by seven states in Central Europe. It has changed its economic and political policies to develop closer ties with the EU.

Official name Republic of Hungary
Formation 1918
Capital Budapest
Population 9.9 million / 278 people per sq mile (107 people per sq km)
Total area 35,919 sq. miles (93,030 sq. km)
Languages Hungarian (Magyar)
Religions Roman Catholic 52%, Calvinist 16%, other 15%, Nonreligious 14%, Lutheran 3%
Ethnic mix Magyar 90%, other 7%, Roma 2%, German 1%
Government Parliamentary system
Currency Forint = 100 fillér
Literacy rate 99%
Calorie consumption 3520 calories

INDONESIA

Page 116 C4

Formerly the Dutch East Indies, Indonesia, the world's largest archipelago, stretches over 5,000 km (3,100 miles) from the Indian Ocean to the Pacific Ocean.

Official name Republic of Indonesia
Formation 1949
Capital Jakarta
Population 220 million /317 people per sq mile (122 people per sq km)
Total area 741,096 sq. miles (1,919,440 sq. km)
Languages Javanese, Sundanese, Madurese, Bahasa Indonesia, Dutch
Religions Muslim 87%, Protestant 6%, Roman Catholic 3%, other 4%
Ethnic mix Javanese 45%, other 25%, Sundanese 14%, Coastal Malays 8%, Madurese 8%
Government Presidential system
Currency Rupiah = 100 sen
Literacy rate 88%
Calorie consumption 2904 calories

IRELAND

Page 67 A6

The Republic of Ireland occupies about 85% of the island of Ireland, with the remainder (Northern Ireland) being part of the United Kingdom.

Official name Ireland
Formation 1922
Capital Dublin
Population 4 million / 150 people per sq mile (58 people per sq km)
Total area 27,135 sq. miles (70,280 sq. km)
Languages English, Irish Gaelic
Religions Roman Catholic 88%, Anglican 3%, other and nonreligious 9%
Ethnic mix Irish 93%, other 4%, British 3%
Government Parliamentary system
Currency Euro = 100 cents
Literacy rate 99%
Calorie consumption 3666 calories

JAMAICA

Page 32 C3

First colonized by the Spanish and then, from 1655, by the English, Jamaica was the first of the Caribbean island nations to achieve independence, in 1962.

Official name Jamaica
Formation 1962
Capital Kingston
Population 2.7 million / 646 people per sq mile (249 people per sq km)
Total area 4243 sq. miles (10,990 sq. km)
Languages English Creole, English
Religions Church of God 18%, Baptist 10%, Anglican 7%, other and nonreligious 45%, other Protestant 20%
Ethnic mix Black African 75%, Mulatto (mixed race) 13%, European and Chinese 11%, East Indian 1%
Government Parliamentary system
Currency Jamaican dollar = 100 cents
Literacy rate 88%
Calorie consumption 2705 calories

ICELAND

Page 61 E4

Europe's westernmost country, Iceland lies in the North Atlantic, straddling the mid-Atlantic ridge. Its spectacular, volcanic landscape is largely uninhabited.

Official name Republic of Iceland
Formation 1944
Capital Reykjavík
Population 290,000 / 7 people per sq mile (3 people per sq km)
Total area 39,768 sq. miles (103,000 sq. km)
Languages Icelandic
Religions Evangelical Lutheran 93%, Nonreligious 6%, other (mostly Christian) 1%
Ethnic mix Icelandic 94%, Danish 1%, other 5%
Government Parliamentary system
Currency Icelandic króna = 100 aurar
Literacy rate 99%
Calorie consumption 3231 calories

IRAN

Page 98 B3

Since the 1979 revolution led by Ayatollah Khomeini, which sent Iran's Shah into exile, this Middle Eastern country has become the world's largest theocracy.

Official name Islamic Republic of Iran
Formation 1502
Capital Tehran
Population 68.9 million / 109 people per sq mile (42 people per sq km)
Total area 636,293 sq. miles (1,648,000 sq. km)
Languages Farsi, Azeri, Luri, Gilaki, Mazanderani, Kurdish, Turkmen, Arabic
Religions Shi'a Muslim 93%, Sunni Muslim 6%, other 1%
Ethnic mix Persian 50%, Azari 24%, Kurdish 8%, Lur and Bakhtiari 8%, other 10%
Government Islamic theocracy
Currency Iranian rial = 100 dinars
Literacy rate 77%
Calorie consumption 2931 calories

ISRAEL

Page 97 A7

Israel was created as a new state in 1948 on the east coast of the Mediterranean. Following wars with its Arab neighbors, it has extended its boundaries.

Official name State of Israel
Formation 1948
Capital Jerusalem
Population 6.4 million / 815 people per sq mile (315 people per sq km)
Total area 8019 sq. miles (20,770 sq. km)
Languages Hebrew, Arabic, Yiddish, German, Russian, Polish, Romanian, Persian
Religions Jewish 80%, Muslim (mainly Sunni) 16%, Druze and other 2%, Christian 2%
Ethnic mix Jewish 80%, other 20%
Government Parliamentary system
Currency Shekel = 100 agorot
Literacy rate 95%
Calorie consumption 3512 calories

JAPAN

Page 108 C4

Japan comprises four principal islands and over 3,000 smaller ones. With the emperor as constitutional head, it is now the world's most powerful economy.

Official name Japan
Formation 1590
Capital Tokyo
Population 128 million / 878 people per sq mile (339 people per sq km)
Total area 145,882 sq. miles (377,835 sq. km)
Languages Japanese, Korean, Chinese
Religions Shinto and Buddhist 76%, Buddhist 16%, other (including Christian) 8%
Ethnic mix Japanese 99%, other (mainly Korean) 1%
Government Parliamentary system
Currency Yen = 100 sen
Literacy rate 99%
Calorie consumption 2746 calories

JORDAN

Page 97 B6

The kingdom of Jordan lies east of Israel. In 1993, King Hussein responded to calls for greater democracy by agreeing to multiparty elections.

Official name Hashemite Kingdom of Jordan
Formation 1946
Capital Amman
Population 5.5 million / 160 people per sq mile (62 people per sq km)
Total area 35,637 sq. miles (92,300 sq. km)
Languages Arabic
Religions Muslim (mainly Sunni) 92%, other (mostly Christian) 8%
Ethnic mix Arab 98%, Circassian 1%, Armenian 1%
Government Monarchy
Currency Jordanian dinar = 1000 fils
Literacy rate 91%
Calorie consumption 2769 calories

KAZAKHSTAN

Page 92 B4

Second largest of the former Soviet republics, mineral-rich Kazakhstan has the potential to become the major Central Asian economic power.

Official name Republic of Kazakhstan
Formation 1991
Capital Astana
Population 15.4 million / 15 people per sq mile (6 people per sq km)
Total area 1,049,150 sq. miles (2,717,300 sq. km)
Languages Kazakh, Russian, Ukrainian, Tatar, German, Uzbek, Uighur
Religions Muslim (mainly Sunni) 47%, Orthodox Christian 44%, other 9%
Ethnic mix Kazakh 53%, Russian 30%, Ukrainian 4%, Tatar 2%, German 2%, other 9%
Government Presidential system
Currency Tenge = 100 tiyn
Literacy rate 99%
Calorie consumption 2477 calories

KENYA

Page 51 C6

Kenya straddles the Equator on Africa's east coast. It became a multiparty democracy in 1992 and has been led by President Moi since 1978.

Official name Republic of Kenya
Formation 1963
Capital Nairobi
Population 32 million / 146 people per sq mile (56 people per sq km)
Total area 224,961 sq. miles (582,650 sq. km)
Languages Kiswahili, English, Kikuyu, Luo, Kalenjin, Kamba
Religions Christian 60%, Traditional beliefs 25%, Muslim 6%, other 9%
Ethnic mix Kikuyu 21%, Luhya 14%, Luo 13%, Kalenjin 11%, Kamba 11%, other 30%
Government Presidential system
Currency Kenya shilling = 100 cents
Literacy rate 84%
Calorie consumption 2058 calories

KIRIBATI

Page 123 F3

Part of the British colony of the Gilbert and Ellice Islands until independence in 1979, Kiribati comprises 33 islands in the mid-Pacific Ocean.

Official name Republic of Kiribati
Formation 1979
Capital Bairiki (Tarawa Atoll)
Population 98,549 / 360 people per sq mile (139 people per sq km)
Total area 277 sq. miles (717 sq. km)
Languages English, Kiribati
Religions Roman Catholic 53%, Kiribati Protestant Church 39%, other 8%
Ethnic mix Micronesian 96%, other 4%
Government Nonparty system
Currency Australian dollar = 100 cents
Literacy rate 99%
Calorie consumption 2922 calories

KUWAIT

Page 98 C4

Kuwait lies on the northwest extreme of the Persian Gulf. The state was a British protectorate from 1914 until 1961, when full independence was granted.

Official name State of Kuwait
Formation 1961
Capital Kuwait City
Population 2.5 million / 363 people per sq mile (140 people per sq km)
Total area 6880 sq. miles (17,820 sq. km)
Languages Arabic, English
Religions Sunni Muslim 45%, Shi'a Muslim 40%, Christian, Hindu, and other 15%
Ethnic mix Kuwaiti 45%, other Arab 35%, South Asian 9%, other 7%, Iranian 4%
Government Monarchy
Currency Kuwaiti dinar = 1000 fils
Literacy rate 83%
Calorie consumption 3170 calories

KYRGYZSTAN

Page 101 F2

A mountainous, landlocked state in Central Asia. The most rural of the ex-Soviet republics, it only gradually developed its own cultural nationalism.

Official name Kyrgyz Republic
Formation 1991
Capital Bishkek
Population 5.1 million / 67 people per sq mile (26 people per sq km)
Total area 76,641 sq. miles (198,500 sq. km)
Languages Kyrgyz, Russian, Uzbek, Tatar, Ukrainian
Religions Muslim (mainly Sunni) 70%, Orthodox Christian 30%
Ethnic mix Kyrgyz 57%, Russian 19%, Uzbek 13%, Tatar 2%, Ukrainian 2%, other 7%
Government Presidential system
Currency Som = 100 tyyn
Literacy rate 97%
Calorie consumption 2882 calories

LAOS

Page 114 D4

A former French colony, independent in 1953, Laos lies landlocked in Southeast Asia. It has been under communist rule since 1975.

Official name Lao People's Democratic Republic
Formation 1953
Capital Vientiane
Population 5.7 million / 64 people per sq mile (25 people per sq km)
Total area 91,428 sq. miles (236,800 sq. km)
Languages Lao, Mon-Khmer, Yao, Vietnamese, Chinese, French
Religions Buddhist 85%, other (including animist) 15%
Ethnic mix Lao Loum 66%, Lao Theung 30%, Lao Soung 2%, other 2%
Government One-party state
Currency New kip = 100 at
Literacy rate 66%
Calorie consumption 2309 calories

LATVIA

Page 84 C3

Situated on the east coast of the Baltic Sea, Lativa, like its Baltic neighbors, became independent in 1991. It retains a large Russian population.

Official name Republic of Latvia
Formation 1991
Capital Riga
Population 2.3 million / 92 people per sq mile (36 people per sq km)
Total area 24,938 sq. miles (64,589 sq. km)
Languages Latvian, Russian
Religions Lutheran 55%, Roman Catholic 24%, Orthodox Christian 9%, other 12%
Ethnic mix Latvian 57%, Russian 32%, Belarussian 4%, Ukrainian 3%, Polish 2%, other 2%
Government Parliamentary system
Currency Lats = 100 santims
Literacy rate 99%
Calorie consumption 2809 calories

LEBANON

Page 96 A4

Lebanon is dwarfed by its two powerful neighbors, Syria and Israel. The state started rebuilding in 1989, after 14 years of intense civil war.

Official name Republic of Lebanon
Formation 1941
Capital Beirut
Population 3.7 million / 937 people per sq mile (362 people per sq km)
Total area 4015 sq. miles (10,400 sq. km)
Languages Arabic, French, Armenian, Assyrian
Religions Muslim 70%, Christian 30%
Ethnic mix Arab 94%, Armenian 4%, other 2%
Government Parliamentary system
Currency Lebanese pound = 100 piastres
Literacy rate 87%
Calorie consumption 3184 calories

LESOTHO

Page 56 D4

The landlocked kingdom of Lesotho is entirely surrounded by South Africa, which provides all its land transportation links with the outside world.

Official name Kingdom of Lesotho
Formation 1966
Capital Maseru
Population 1.8 million / 154 people per sq mile (59 people per sq km)
Total area 11,720 sq. miles (30,355 sq. km)
Languages English, Sesotho, isiZulu
Religions Christian 90%, Traditional beliefs 10%
Ethnic mix Sotho 97%, European and Asian 3%
Government Parliamentary system
Currency Loti = 100 lisente
Literacy rate 81%
Calorie consumption 2320 calories

LIBERIA

Page 52 C5

Liberia faces the Atlantic Ocean in equatorial West Africa. Africa's oldest republic, it was established in 1847. Today, it is torn by civil war.

Official name Republic of Liberia
Formation 1847
Capital Monrovia
Population 3.4 million / 91 people per sq mile (35 people per sq km)
Total area 43,000 sq. miles (111,370 sq. km)
Languages Kpelle, Vai, Bassa, Kru, Grebo, Kissi, Gola, Loma, English
Religions Christian 68%, Traditional beliefs 18%, Muslim 14%
Ethnic mix Indigenous tribes (16 main groups) 95%, Americo-Liberians 5%
Government Transitional regime
Currency Liberian dollar = 100 cents
Literacy rate 56%
Calorie consumption 1946 calories

LIBYA

Page 49 F3

Situated on the Mediterranean coast of North Africa, Libya is a Muslim dictatorship, politically marginalized by the West for its terrorist links.

Official name Great Socialist People's Libyan Arab Jamahariyah
Formation 1951
Capital Tripoli
Population 5.6 million / 8 people per sq mile (3 people per sq km)
Total area 679,358 sq. miles (1,759,540 sq. km)
Languages Arabic, Tuareg
Religions Muslim (mainly Sunni) 97%, other 3%
Ethnic mix Arab and Berber 95%, other 5%
Government One-party state
Currency Libyan dinar = 1000 dirhams
Literacy rate 82%
Calorie consumption 3333 calories

LIECHTENSTEIN

Page 73 B7

Tucked in the Alps between Switzerland and Austria, Liechtenstein became an independent principality of the Holy Roman Empire in 1719.

Official name Principality of Liechtenstein
Formation 1719
Capital Vaduz
Population 33,145 / 535 people per sq mile (207 people per sq km)
Total area 62 sq. miles (160 sq. km)
Languages German, Alemannish dialect, Italian
Religions Roman Catholic 81%, other 12%, Protestant 7%
Ethnic mix Liechtensteiner 62%, Foreign residents 38%
Government Parliamentary system
Currency Swiss franc = 100 rappen/centimes
Literacy rate 99%
Calorie consumption Not available

LITHUANIA

Page 84 B4

The largest, most powerful and stable of the Baltic states, Lithuania was the first Baltic country to declare independence from Moscow, in 1991.

Official name Republic of Lithuania
Formation 1991
Capital Vilnius
Population 3.4 million / 135 people per sq mile (52 people per sq km)
Total area 25,174 sq. miles (65,200 sq. km)
Languages Lithuanian, Russian
Religions Roman Catholic 83%, other 12%, Protestant 5%
Ethnic mix Lithuanian 80%, Russian 9%, Polish 7%, Belarussian 2%, other 2%
Government Parliamentary system
Currency Litas (euro is also legal tender) = 100 centu
Literacy rate 99%
Calorie consumption 3384 calories

LUXEMBOURG

Page 65 D8

Making up part of the plateau of the Ardennes in Western Europe, Luxembourg is Europe's last independent duchy and one of its richest states.

Official name Grand Duchy of Luxembourg
Formation 1867
Capital Luxembourg-Ville
Population 453,000 / 454 people per sq mile (175 people per sq km)
Total area 998 sq. miles (2586 sq. km)
Languages Luxembourgish, German, French
Religions Roman Catholic 97%, Protestant, Orthodox Christian, and Jewish 3%
Ethnic mix Luxembourger 73%, Foreign residents 27%
Government Parliamentary system
Currency Euro = 100 cents
Literacy rate 99%
Calorie consumption 3701 calories

MACEDONIA

Page 79 D6

Landlocked in the southern Balkans, Macedonia has been affected by sanctions imposed on its northern trading partners and by Greek antagonism.

Official name Republic of Macedonia
Formation 1991
Capital Skopje
Population 2.02 million / 204 people per sq mile (79 people per sq km)
Total area 9781 sq. miles (25,333 sq. km)
Languages Macedonian, Albanian, Serbo-Croat
Religions Orthodox Christian 59%, Muslim 26%, Roman Catholic 4%, Protestant 1%, other 10%
Ethnic mix Macedonian 64%, Albanian 25%, Turkish 4%, Roma 3%, other 4%
Government Mixed presidential–parliamentary system
Currency Macedonian denar = 100 deni
Literacy rate 94%
Calorie consumption 2552 calories

MADAGASCAR

Page 57 F4

Lying in the Indian Ocean, Madagascar is the world's fourth largest island. Free elections in 1993 ended 18 years of radical socialist government.

Official name Republic of Madagascar
Formation 1960
Capital Antananarivo
Population 17.4 million / 77 people per sq mile (30 people per sq km)
Total area 226,656 sq. miles (587,040 sq. km)
Languages Malagasy, French
Religions Traditional beliefs 52%, Christian (mainly Roman Catholic) 41%, Muslim 7%
Ethnic mix other Malay 46%, Merina 26%, Betsimisaraka 15%, Betsileo 12%, other 1%
Government Presidential system
Currency Ariary = 5 iraimbilanja
Literacy rate 67%
Calorie consumption 2072 calories

MALAWI

Page 57 E1

A former British colony, Malawi lies landlocked in southeast Africa. Its name means "the land where the sun is reflected in the water like fire."

Official name Republic of Malawi
Formation 1964
Capital Lilongwe
Population 12.1 million / 333 people per sq mile (129 people per sq km)
Total area 45,745 sq. miles (118,480 sq. km)
Languages Chewa, Lomwe, Yao, Ngoni, English
Religions Protestant 55%, Roman Catholic 20%, Muslim 20%, Traditional beliefs 5%
Ethnic mix Bantu 99%, other 1%
Government Presidential system
Currency Malawi kwacha = 100 tambala
Literacy rate 62%
Calorie consumption 2168 calories

MALAYSIA

Page 116 B3

Malaysia's three separate territories include Malaya, Sarawak, and Sabah. A financial crisis in 1997 ended a decade of spectacular financial growth.

Official name Federation of Malaysia
Formation 1963
Capital Kuala Lumpur; Putrajaya (administrative)
Population 24.4 million / 192 people per sq mile (74 people per sq km)
Total area 127,316 sq. miles (329,750 sq. km)
Languages Bahasa Malaysia, Malay, Chinese, Tamil, English
Religions Muslim 53%, Buddhist 19%, Chinese faiths 12%, other 16%
Ethnic mix Malay 48%, Chinese 29%, Indigenous tribes 12%, other 11%
Government Parliamentary system
Currency Ringgit = 100 sen
Literacy rate 89%
Calorie consumption 2927 calories

MALDIVES

Page 110 A4

Only 200 of the more than 1,000 Maldivian small coral islands in the Indian Ocean, are inhabited. Government rests in the hands of a few influential families.

Official name Republic of Maldives
Formation 1965
Capital Male'
Population 318,000 / 2741 people per sq mile (1060 people per sq km)
Total area 116 sq. miles (300 sq. km)
Languages Dhivehi (Maldivian), Sinhala, Tamil, Arabic
Religions Sunni Muslim 100%
Ethnic mix Arab–Sinhalese–Malay 100%
Government Nonparty system
Currency Rufiyaa = 100 lari
Literacy rate 97%
Calorie consumption 2587 calories

MALI

Page 53 E2

Landlocked in the heart of West Africa, Mali held its first free elections in 1992, more than 30 years after it gained independence from France.

Official name Republic of Mali
Formation 1960
Capital Bamako
Population 13 million / 28 people per sq mile (11 people per sq km)
Total area 478,764 sq. miles (1,240,000 sq. km)
Languages Bambara, Fulani, Senufo, Soninke, French
Religions Muslim (mainly Sunni) 80%, Traditional beliefs 18%, other 2%
Ethnic mix Bambara 32%, other 26%, Fulani 14%, Senufo 12%, Soninka 9%, Tuareg 7%
Government Presidential system
Currency CFA franc = 100 centimes
Literacy rate 26%
Calorie consumption 2376 calories

MALTA

Page 80 A5

The Maltese archipelago lies off southern Sicily, midway between Europe and North Africa. The only inhabited islands are Malta, Gozo, and Kemmuna.

Official name Republic of Malta
Formation 1964
Capital Valletta
Population 394,000 / 3177 people per sq mile (1231 people per sq km)
Total area 122 sq. miles (316 sq. km)
Languages Maltese, English
Religions Roman Catholic 98%, other and nonreligious 2%
Ethnic mix Maltese 96%, other 4%
Government Parliamentary system
Currency Maltese lira = 100 cents
Literacy rate 93%
Calorie consumption 3496 calories

MARSHALL ISLANDS

Page 122 D1

A group of 34 atolls, the Marshall Islands were under US rule as part of the UN Trust Territory of the Pacific Islands until 1986. The economy depends on US aid.

Official name Republic of the Marshall Islands
Formation 1986
Capital Majuro
Population 56,429 / 806 people per sq mile (312 people per sq km)
Total area 70 sq. miles (181 sq. km)
Languages Marshallese, English, Japanese, German
Religions Protestant 90%, Roman Catholic 8%, other 2%
Ethnic mix Micronesian 97%, other 3%
Government Presidential system
Currency US dollar = 100 cents
Literacy rate 91%
Calorie consumption Not available

MAURITANIA

Page 52 C2

Situated in northwest Africa, two-thirds of Mauritania's territory is desert. A former French colony, it achieved independence in 1960.

Official name Islamic Republic of Mauritania
Formation 1960
Capital Nouakchott
Population 2.9 million / 7 people per sq mile (3 people per sq km)
Total area 397,953 sq. miles (1,030,700 sq. km)
Languages Hassaniyah Arabic, Wolof, French
Religions Sunni Muslim 100%
Ethnic mix Maure 81%, Wolof 7%, Tukolor 5%, Soninka 3%, other 4%
Government Presidential system
Currency Ouguiya = 5 khoums
Literacy rate 41%
Calorie consumption 2764 calories

MAURITIUS

Page 57 H3

Located to the east of Madagascar in the Indian Ocean, Mauritius became a republic 25 years after it gained independence. Tourism is a mainstay of its economy.

Official name Republic of Mauritius
Formation 1968
Capital Port Louis
Population 1.2 million / 1671 people per sq mile (645 people per sq km)
Total area 718 sq. miles (1860 sq. km)
Languages French Creole, Hindi, Urdu, Tamil, Chinese, English, French
Religions Hindu 52%, Roman Catholic 26%, Muslim 17%, Protestant 2%, other 3%
Ethnic mix Indo-Mauritian 68%, Creole 27%, Sino-Mauritian 3%, Franco-Mauritian 2%
Government Parliamentary system
Currency Mauritian rupee = 100 cents
Literacy rate 84%
Calorie consumption 2995 calories

MEXICO

Page 28 D3

Located between the United States of America and the Central American states, Mexico was a Spanish colony for 300 years until 1836.

Official name United Mexican States
Formation 1836
Capital Mexico City
Population 104 million / 140 people per sq mile (54 people per sq km)
Total area 761,602 sq. miles (1,972,550 sq. km)
Languages Spanish, Nahuatl, Mayan, Zapotec, Mixtec, Otomi, Totonac, Tzotzil, Tzeltal
Religions Roman Catholic 88%, Protestant 5%, other 7%
Ethnic mix Mestizo 60%, Amerindian 30%, European 9%, other 1%
Government Presidential system
Currency Mexican peso = 100 centavos
Literacy rate 91%
Calorie consumption 3160 calories

MICRONESIA

Page 122 B1

The Federated States of Micronesia, situated in the western Pacific, comprise 607 islands and atolls grouped into four main island states.

Official name Federated States of Micronesia
Formation 1986
Capital Palikir (Pohnpei Island)
Population 108,143 / 399 people per sq mile (154 people per sq km)
Total area 271 sq. miles (702 sq. km)
Languages Trukese, Pohnpeian, Mortlockese, Kosraean, English
Religions Roman Catholic 50%, Protestant 48%, other 2%
Ethnic mix Micronesian 100%
Government Nonparty system
Currency US dollar = 100 cents
Literacy rate 81%
Calorie consumption Not available

MOLDOVA

Page 86 D3

The smallest and most densely populated of the ex-Soviet republics, Moldova has strong linguistic and cultural links with Romania to the west.

Official name Republic of Moldova
Formation 1991
Capital Chisinau
Population 4.3 million / 330 people per sq mile (128 people per sq km)
Total area 13,067 sq. miles (33,843 sq. km)
Languages Moldovan, Ukrainian, Russian
Religions Orthodox Christian 98%, Jewish 2%
Ethnic mix Moldovan 65%, Ukrainian 14%, Russian 13%, Gagauz 4%, other 4%
Government Parliamentary system
Currency Moldovan leu = 100 bani
Literacy rate 99%
Calorie consumption 2712 calories

MONACO

Page 69 E6

A jet-set image and a thriving service sector define the modern identity of this tiny enclave on the Côte d'Azur in southeastern France.

Official name Principality of Monaco
Formation 1861
Capital Monaco-Ville
Population 32,130 / 42840 people per sq mile (16477 people per sq km)
Total area 0.75 sq. miles (1.95 sq. km)
Languages French, Italian, Monégasque, English
Religions Roman Catholic 89%, Protestant 6%, other 5%
Ethnic mix French 47%, Monégasque 17%, Italian 16%, other 20%
Government Monarchy
Currency Euro = 100 cents
Literacy rate 99%
Calorie consumption Not available

MONGOLIA

Page 104 D2

Lying between Russia and China, Mongolia is a vast and isolated country with a small population. Over two-thirds of the country is desert.

Official name Mongolia
Formation 1924
Capital Ulan Bator
Population 2.6 million / 4 people per sq mile (2 people per sq km)
Total area 604,247 sq. miles (1,565,000 sq. km)
Languages Khalkha Mongolian, Kazakh, Chinese, Russian
Religions Tibetan Buddhist 96%, Muslim 4%
Ethnic mix Mongol 90%, Kazakh 4%, Chinese 2%, Russian 2%, other 2%
Government Mixed presidential–parliamentary system
Currency Tugrik (tögrög) = 100 möngö
Literacy rate 98%
Calorie consumption 1974 calories

MOROCCO

Page 48 C2

A former French colony in northwest Africa, independent in 1956, Morocco has occupied the disputed territory of Western Sahara since 1975.

Official name Kingdom of Morocco
Formation 1956
Capital Rabat
Population 30.6 million / 178 people per sq mile (69 people per sq km)
Total area 172,316 sq. miles (446,300 sq. km)
Languages Arabic, Tamazight (Berber), French, Spanish
Religions Muslim (mainly Sunni) 99%, other (mostly Christian) 1%
Ethnic mix Arab 70%, Berber 29%, European 1%
Government Monarchy
Currency Moroccan dirham = 100 centimes
Literacy rate 51%
Calorie consumption 3046 calories

MOZAMBIQUE

Page 57 E3

Mozambique lies on the southeast African coast. It was torn by a civil war between the Marxist government and a rebel group from 1977–1992.

Official name Republic of Mozambique
Formation 1975
Capital Maputo
Population 18.9 million / 62 people per sq mile (24 people per sq km)
Total area 309,494 sq. miles (801,590 sq. km)
Languages Makua, Xitsonga, Sena, Lomwe, Portuguese
Religions Traditional beliefs 56%, Christian 30%, Muslim 14%
Ethnic mix Makua Lowme 47%, Tsonga 23%, Malawi 12%, Shona 11%, Yao 4%, other 3%
Government Presidential system
Currency Metical = 100 centavos
Literacy rate 47%
Calorie consumption 1980 calories

MYANMAR (BURMA)

Page 114 A3

Myanmar forms the eastern shores of the Bay of Bengal and the Andaman Sea in Southeast Asia. Since 1988 it has been ruled by a repressive military regime.

Official name Union of Myanmar
Formation 1948
Capital Rangoon (Yangon)
Population 49.5 million / 195 people per sq mile (75 people per sq km)
Total area 261,969 sq. miles (678,500 sq. km)
Languages Burmese, Shan, Karen, Rakhine, Chin, Yangbye, Kachin, Mon
Religions Buddhist 87%, Christian 6%, Muslim 4%, Hindu 1%, other 2%
Ethnic mix Burman (Bamah) 68%, Shan 9%, Karen 6%, Rakhine 4%, other 13%
Government Military-based regime
Currency Kyat = 100 pyas
Literacy rate 85%
Calorie consumption 2822 calories

NAMIBIA

Page 56 B3

Located in southwestern Africa, Namibia became free of South African control in 1990, after years of uncertainty and guerrilla activity.

Official name Republic of Namibia
Formation 1990
Capital Windhoek
Population 2 million / 6 people per sq mile (2 people per sq km)
Total area 318,694 sq. miles (825,418 sq. km)
Languages Ovambo, Kavango, English, Bergdama, German, Afrikaans
Religions Christian 90%, Traditional beliefs 10%
Ethnic mix Ovambo 50%, other tribes 16%, Kavango 9%, other 9%, Damara 8%, Herero 8%
Government Presidential system
Currency Namibian dollar = 100 cents
Literacy rate 83%
Calorie consumption 2745 calories

NAURU

Page 122 D3

Nauru lies in the Pacific, 4,000 km (2,480 miles) northeast of Australia. Phosphate deposits have made its citizens among the richest in the world.

Official name Republic of Nauru
Formation 1968
Capital None
Population 12,570 / 1552 people per sq mile (599 people per sq km)
Total area 8.1 sq. miles (21 sq. km)
Languages Nauruan, Kiribati, Chinese, Tuvaluan, English
Religions Nauruan Congregational Church 60%, Roman Catholic 35%, other 5%
Ethnic mix Nauruan 62%, other Pacific islanders 25%, Chinese and Vietnamese 8%, European 5%
Government Parliamentary system
Currency Australian dollar = 100 cents
Literacy rate 95%
Calorie consumption Not available

NEPAL

Page 113 E3

Nepal lies between India and China, on the shoulder of the southern Himalayas. The elections of 1991 ended a period of absolute monarchy.

Official name Kingdom of Nepal
Formation 1769
Capital Kathmandu
Population 25.2 million / 477 people per sq mile (184 people per sq km)
Total area 54,363 sq. miles (140,800 sq. km)
Languages Nepali, Maithili, Bhojpuri
Religions Hindu 90%, Buddhist 5%, Muslim 3%, other (including Christian) 2%
Ethnic mix Nepalese 52%, Maithili 11%, Tibeto-Burmese 10%, Bhojpuri 8%, other 19%
Government Monarchy
Currency Nepalese rupee = 100 paise
Literacy rate 44%
Calorie consumption 2459 calories

NETHERLANDS

Page 64 C3

Astride the delta of five major rivers in northwest Europe, the Netherlands has a long trading tradition. Rotterdam is the world's largest port.

Official name Kingdom of the Netherlands
Formation 1648
Capital Amsterdam; The Hague (administrative)
Population 16.1 million / 1229 people per sq mile (475 people per sq km)
Total area 16,033 sq. miles (41,526 sq. km)
Languages Dutch, Frisian
Religions Roman Catholic 36%, Protestant 27%, Muslim 3%, other 34%,
Ethnic mix Dutch 82%, Surinamese 2%, Turkish 2%, Moroccan 2%, other 12%
Government Parliamentary system
Currency Euro = 100 cents
Literacy rate 97%
Calorie consumption 3282 calories

NIGER

Page 53 F3

Niger lies landlocked in West Africa, but it is linked to the sea by the River Niger. Since 1973 it has suffered civil unrest and two major droughts.

Official name Republic of Niger
Formation 1960
Capital Niamey
Population 12 million / 25 people per sq mile (9 people per sq km)
Total area 489,188 sq. miles (1,267,000 sq. km)
Languages Hausa, Djerma, Fulani, Tuareg, Teda, French
Religions Muslim 85%, Traditional beliefs 14%, other 1%
Ethnic mix Hausa 54%, Djerma and Songhai 21%, Fulani 10%, Tuareg 9%, other 6%
Government Presidential system
Currency CFA franc = 100 centimes
Literacy rate 17%
Calorie consumption 2118 calories

NORWAY

Page 63 A5

The Kingdom of Norway traces the rugged western coast of Scandinavia. Settlements are largely restricted to southern and coastal areas.

Official name Kingdom of Norway
Formation 1905
Capital Oslo
Population 4.5 million / 38 people per sq mile (15 people per sq km)
Total area 125,181 sq. miles (324,220 sq. km)
Languages Norwegian (*Bokmål* "book language" and *Nynorsk* "new Norsk"), Sámi
Religions Evangelical Lutheran 89%, Roman Catholic 1%, other 10%
Ethnic mix Norwegian 93%, other 6%, Sámi 1%
Government Parliamentary system
Currency Norwegian krone = 100 øre
Literacy rate 99%
Calorie consumption 3382 calories

PALAU

Page 122 A2

The Palau archipelago, a group of over 200 islands, lies in the western Pacific Ocean. In 1994, it became the world's newest independent state.

Official name Republic of Palau
Formation 1994
Capital Koror
Population 19,717 / 101 people per sq mile (39 people per sq km)
Total area 177 sq. miles (458 sq. km)
Languages Palauan, English, Japanese, Angaur, Tobi, Sonsorolese
Religions Christian 66%, Modekngei 34%
Ethnic mix Micronesian 87%, Filipino 8%, Chinese and other Asian 5%
Government Nonparty system
Currency US dollar − 100 cents
Literacy rate 98%
Calorie consumption Not available

NEW ZEALAND

Page 128 A4

One of the Pacific Rim countries, New Zealand lies southeast of Australia, and comprises the North and South Islands, separated by the Cook Strait.

Official name New Zealand
Formation 1947
Capital Wellington
Population 3.9 million / 38 people per sq mile (15 people per sq km)
Total area 103,737 sq. miles (268,680 sq. km)
Languages English, Maori
Religions Anglican 24%, Presbyterian 18%, Nonreligious 16%, Roman Catholic 15%, Methodist 5%, other 22%
Ethnic mix European 77%, Maori 12%, other 6%, Pacific islanders 5%
Government Parliamentary system
Currency New Zealand dollar = 100 cents
Literacy rate 99%
Calorie consumption 3235 calories

NIGERIA

Page 53 F4

Africa's most populous state Nigeria, in West Africa, is a federation of 30 states. It adopted civilian rule in 1999 after 33 years of military government.

Official name Federal Republic of Nigeria
Formation 1960
Capital Abuja
Population 124 million / 353 people per sq mile (136 people per sq km)
Total area 356,667 sq. miles (923,768 sq. km)
Languages Hausa, English, Yoruba, Ibo
Religions Muslim 50%, Christian 40%, Traditional beliefs 10%
Ethnic mix Hausa 21%, Yoruba 21%, Ibo 18%, Fulani 11%, other 29%
Government Presidential system
Currency Naira = 100 kobo
Literacy rate 67%
Calorie consumption 2747 calories

OMAN

Page 99 D6

Situated on the eastern coast of the Arabian Peninsula, Oman is the least developed of the Gulf states, despite modest oil exports.

Official name Sultanate of Oman
Formation 1951
Capital Muscat
Population 2.9 million / 35 people per sq mile (14 people per sq km)
Total area 82,031 sq. miles (212,460 sq. km)
Languages Arabic, Baluchi, Farsi, Hindi, Punjabi
Religions Ibadi Muslim 75%, other Muslim and Hindu 25%
Ethnic mix Arab 88%, Baluchi 4%, Persian 3%, Indian and Pakistani 3%, African 2%
Government Monarchy
Currency Omani rial = 1000 baizas
Literacy rate 74%
Calorie consumption Not available

PANAMA

Page 31 F5

Southernmost of the Central American countries. The Panama Canal (returned to Panama from US control in 2000) links the Pacific and Atlantic oceans.

Official name Republic of Panama
Formation 1903
Capital Panama City
Population 3.1 million / 106 people per sq mile (41 people per sq km)
Total area 30,193 sq. miles (78,200 sq. km)
Languages English Creole, Spanish, Amerindian languages, Chibchan languages
Religions Roman Catholic 86%, Protestant 6%, other 8%
Ethnic mix Mestizo 60%, White 14%, Black 12%, Amerindian 8%, other 6%
Government Presidential system
Currency Balboa = 100 centesimos
Literacy rate 92%
Calorie consumption 2386 calories

NICARAGUA

Page 30 D3

Nicaragua lies at the heart of Central America. An 11-year war between left-wing Sandinistas and right-wing US-backed Contras ended in 1989.

Official name Republic of Nicaragua
Formation 1838
Capital Managua
Population 5.5 million / 120 people per sq mile (46 people per sq km)
Total area 49,998 sq. miles (129,494 sq. km)
Languages Spanish, English Creole, Miskito
Religions Roman Catholic 80%, Protestant Evangelical 17%, other 3%
Ethnic mix Mestizo 69%, White 14%, Black 8%, Amerindian 5%, Zambo 4%
Government Presidential system
Currency Córdoba oro = 100 centavos
Literacy rate 77%
Calorie consumption 2256 calories

NORTH KOREA

Page 106 E3

North Korea comprises the northern half of the Korean peninsula. A communist state since 1948, it is largely isolated from the outside world.

Official name Democratic People's Republic of Korea
Formation 1948
Capital Pyongyang
Population 22.7 million / 488 people per sq mile (189 people per sq km)
Total area 46,540 sq. miles (120,540 sq. km)
Languages Korean, Chinese
Religions Atheist 100%
Ethnic mix Korean 100%
Government One-party state
Currency North Korean won = 100 chon
Literacy rate 99%
Calorie consumption 2201 calories

PAKISTAN

Page 112 B2

Once a part of British India, Pakistan was created in 1947 as an independent Muslim state. Today, the country is divided into four provinces.

Official name Islamic Republic of Pakistan
Formation 1947
Capital Islamabad
Population 154 million / 516 people per sq mile (199 people per sq km)
Total area 310,401 sq. miles (803,940 sq. km)
Languages Punjabi, Sindhi, Pashtu, Urdu, Baluchi, Brahui
Religions Sunni Muslim 77%, Shi'a Muslim 20%, Hindu 2%, Christian 1%
Ethnic mix Punjabi 56%, Pathan 15%, Sindhi 14%, Mohajir 7%, other 8%
Government Presidential system
Currency Pakistani rupee = 100 paisa
Literacy rate 44%
Calorie consumption 2457 calories

PAPUA NEW GUINEA

Page 122 B3

Achieving independence from Australia in 1975, PNG occupies the eastern section of the island of New Guinea and several other island groups.

Official name Independent State of Papua New Guinea
Formation 1975
Capital Port Moresby
Population 5.7 million / 33 people per sq mile (13 people per sq km)
Total area 178,703 sq. miles (462,840 sq. km)
Languages Pidgin English, Papuan, English, Motu, 750 native languages
Religions Protestant 60%, Roman Catholic 37%, other 3%
Ethnic mix Melanesian and mixed race 100%
Government Parliamentary system
Currency Kina = 100 toeas
Literacy rate 65%
Calorie consumption 2193 calories

PARAGUAY

Page 42 D2

Landlocked in central South America. Its post-independence history has included periods of military rule. Free elections were held in 1993.

Official name Republic of Paraguay
Formation 1811
Capital Asunción
Population 5.9 million / 38 people per sq mile (15 people per sq km)
Total area 157,046 sq. miles (406,750 sq. km)
Languages Guaraní, Spanish, German
Religions Roman Catholic 96%, Protestant (including Mennonite) 4%
Ethnic mix Mestizo 90%, other 8%, Amerindian 2%
Government Presidential system
Currency Guaraní = 100 centimos
Literacy rate 92%
Calorie consumption 2576 calories

POLAND

Page 76 B3

With its seven international borders and strategic location in the heart of Europe, Poland has always played an important role in European affairs.

Official name Republic of Poland
Formation 1918
Capital Warsaw
Population 38.6 million / 328 people per sq mile (127 people per sq km)
Total area 120,728 sq. miles (312,685 sq. km)
Languages Polish
Religions Roman Catholic 93%, other and nonreligious 5%, Orthodox Christian 2%
Ethnic mix Polish 97%, Silesian 1%, other 2%
Government Parliamentary system
Currency Zloty = 100 groszy
Literacy rate 99%
Calorie consumption 3397 calories

ROMANIA

Page 86 B4

Romania lies on the Black Sea coast. Since the overthrow of its communist regime in 1989, it has been slowly converting to a free-market economy.

Official name Romania
Formation 1878
Capital Bucharest
Population 22.3 million / 251 people per sq mile (97 people per sq km)
Total area 91,699 sq. miles (237,500 sq. km)
Languages Romanian, Hungarian (Magyar), Romani, German
Religions Romanian Orthodox 87%, Roman Catholic 5%, Protestant 4%, other 4%
Ethnic mix Romanian 89%, Magyar 7%, Roma 3%, other 1%
Government Presidential system
Currency Romanian leu = 100 bani
Literacy rate 97%
Calorie consumption 3407 calories

SAINT KITTS & NEVIS

Page 33 G3

Separated by a channel, the two islands of Saint Kitts and Nevis are part of the Leeward Islands chain in the Caribbean. Nevis is the less developed of the two.

Official name Federation of Saint Christopher and Nevis
Formation 1983
Capital Basseterre
Population 38,763 / 279 people per sq mile (108 people per sq km)
Total area 101 sq. miles (261 sq. km)
Languages English, English Creole
Religions Anglican 33%, Methodist 29%, Moravian 9%, Roman Catholic 7%, other 22%
Ethnic mix Black 94%, Mixed race 3%, other and Amerindian 2%, White 1%
Government Parliamentary system
Currency Eastern Caribbean dollar = 100 cents
Literacy rate 98%
Calorie consumption 2997 calories

PERU

Page 38 C3

Once the heart of the Inca empire, before the Spanish conquest in the 16th century, Peru lies on the Pacific coast of South America.

Official name Republic of Peru
Formation 1824
Capital Lima
Population 27.2 million / 55 people per sq mile (21 people per sq km)
Total area 496,223 sq. miles (1,285,200 sq. km)
Languages Spanish, Quechua, Aymara
Religions Roman Catholic 95%, other 5%
Ethnic mix Amerindian 50%, Mestizo 40%, White 7%, other 3%
Government Presidential system
Currency New sol = 100 centimos
Literacy rate 85%
Calorie consumption 2610 calories

PORTUGAL

Page 70 B3

Facing the Atlantic on the western side of the Iberian Peninsula, Portugal is the most westerly country on the European mainland.

Official name Republic of Portugal
Formation 1139
Capital Lisbon
Population 10.1 million / 284 people per sq mile (110 people per sq km)
Total area 35,672 sq. miles (92,391 sq. km)
Languages Portuguese
Religions Roman Catholic 97%, Protestant 1%, other 2%
Ethnic mix Portuguese 98%, African and other 2%
Government Parliamentary system
Currency Euro = 100 cents
Literacy rate 93%
Calorie consumption 3751 calories

RUSSIAN FEDERATION

Page 92 D4

Still the world's largest state, despite the breakup of the USSR in 1991, the Russian Federation is struggling to capitalize on its diversity.

Official name Russian Federation
Formation 1480
Capital Moscow
Population 143 million / 22 people per sq mile (8 people per sq km)
Total area 6,592,735 sq. miles (17,075,200 sq. km)
Languages Russian, Tatar, Ukrainian, Chavash, various other national languages
Religions Orthodox Christian 75%, Muslim 10%, other 15%
Ethnic mix Russian 82%, Tatar 4%, Ukrainian 3%, Chavash 1%, other 10%
Government Presidential system
Currency Russian rouble = 100 kopeks
Literacy rate 99%
Calorie consumption 3014 calories

SAINT LUCIA

Page 33 G4

Among the most beautiful of the Caribbean Windward Islands, Saint Lucia retains both French and British influences from its colonial history.

Official name Saint Lucia
Formation 1979
Capital Castries
Population 162,157 / 687 people per sq mile (266 people per sq km)
Total area 239 sq. miles (620 sq. km)
Languages English, French Creole
Religions Roman Catholic 90%, other 10%
Ethnic mix Black 90%, Mulatto (mixed race) 6%, Asian 3%, White 1%
Government Parliamentary system
Currency Eastern Caribbean dollar = 100 cents
Literacy rate 95%
Calorie consumption 2849 calories

PHILIPPINES

Page 117 E1

An archipelago of 7,107 islands between the South China Sea and the Pacific. After 21 years of dictatorship, democracy was restored in 1986.

Official name Republic of the Philippines
Formation 1946
Capital Manila
Population 80 million / 695 people per sq mile (268 people per sq km)
Total area 115,830 sq. miles (300,000 sq. km)
Languages Filipino, Tagalog, Cebuano, Hiligaynon, Samaran, Ilocano, Bicolano, English
Religions Roman Catholic 83%, Protestant 9%, Muslim 5%, other 3%
Ethnic mix Malay 95%, other 5%
Government Presidential system
Currency Peso = 100 centavos
Literacy rate 93%
Calorie consumption 2372 calories

QATAR

Page 98 C4

Projecting north from the Arabian Peninsula into the Persian Gulf, Qatar's reserves of oil and gas make it one of the region's wealthiest states.

Official name State of Qatar
Formation 1971
Capital Doha
Population 610,000 / 144 people per sq mile (55 people per sq km)
Total area 4416 sq. miles (11,437 sq. km)
Languages Arabic
Religions Muslim (mainly Sunni) 95%, other 5%
Ethnic mix Arab 40%, Indian 18%, Pakistani 18%, Iranian 10%, other 14%
Government Monarchy
Currency Qatar riyal = 100 dirhams
Literacy rate 82%
Calorie consumption Not available

RWANDA

Page 51 B6

Rwanda lies just south of the Equator in east central Africa. Since independence from France in 1962, ethnic tensions have dominated politics.

Official name Republic of Rwanda
Formation 1962
Capital Kigali
Population 8.4 million / 872 people per sq mile (337 people per sq km)
Total area 10,169 sq. miles (26,338 sq. km)
Languages Kinyarwanda, French, Kiswahili, English
Religions Roman Catholic 56%, Traditional beliefs 25%, Muslim 10%, Protestant 9%
Ethnic mix Hutu 90%, Tutsi 9%, other (including Twa) 1%
Government Presidential system
Currency Rwanda franc = 100 centimes
Literacy rate 69%
Calorie consumption 2086 calories

SAINT VINCENT & THE GRENADINES

Page 33 G4

Formerly ruled by Britain, these volcanic islands form part of the Caribbean Windward Islands.

Official name Saint Vincent and the Grenadines
Formation 1979
Capital Kingstown
Population 116,812 / 892 people per sq mile (344 people per sq km)
Total area 150 sq. miles (389 sq. km)
Languages English, English Creole
Religions Anglican 47%, Methodist 28%, Roman Catholic 13%, other 12%
Ethnic mix Black 66%, Mulatto (mixed race) 19%, Asian 6%, White 4%, other 5%
Government Parliamentary system
Currency Eastern Caribbean dollar = 100 cents
Literacy rate 83%
Calorie consumption 2609 calories

SAMOA

Page 123 F4

The southern Pacific islands of Samoa gained independence from New Zealand in 1962. Four of the nine islands are inhabited.

Official name Independent State of Samoa
Formation 1962
Capital Apia
Population 178,000 / 163 people per sq mile (63 people per sq km)
Total area 1104 sq. miles (2860 sq. km)
Languages Samoan, English
Religions Christian 99%, other 1%
Ethnic mix Polynesian 90%, Euronesian 9%, other 1%
Government Parliamentary system
Currency Tala = 100 sene
Literacy rate 99%
Calorie consumption Not available

SAN MARINO

Page 74 C3

Perched on the slopes of Monte Titano in the Italian Appennino, San Marino has maintained its independence since the 4th century AD.

Official name Republic of San Marino
Formation 1631
Capital San Marino
Population 28,119 / 1172 people per sq mile (461 people per sq km)
Total area 23.6 sq. miles (61 sq. km)
Languages Italian
Religions Roman Catholic 93%, other and nonreligious 7%
Ethnic mix Sammarinese 80%, Italian 19%, other 1%
Government Parliamentary system
Currency Euro = 100 cents
Literacy rate 99%
Calorie consumption Not available

SAO TOME & PRINCIPE

Page 55 A5

A former Portuguese colony off Africa's west coast, comprising two main islands and smaller islets. The 1991 elections ended 15 years of Marxism.

Official name Democratic Republic of São Tomé and Príncipe
Formation 1975
Capital São Tomé
Population 175,883 / 474 people per sq mile (183 people per sq km)
Total area 386 sq. miles (1001 sq. km)
Languages Portuguese Creole, Portuguese
Religions Roman Catholic 84%, other 16%
Ethnic mix Black 90%, Portuguese and Creole 10%
Government Presidential system
Currency Dobra = 100 centimos
Literacy rate 83%
Calorie consumption 2567 calories

SAUDI ARABIA

Page 99 B5

Occupying most of the Arabian Peninsula, the desert kingdom of Saudi Arabia, rich in oil and gas, covers an area the size of Western Europe.

Official name Kingdom of Saudi Arabia
Formation 1932
Capital Riyadh; Jiddah (administrative)
Population 24.2 million / 30 people per sq mile (11 people per sq km)
Total area 756,981 sq. miles (1,960,582 sq. km)
Languages Arabic
Religions Sunni Muslim 85%, Shi'a Muslim 15%
Ethnic mix Arab 90%, Afro-Asian 10%
Government Monarchy
Currency Saudi riyal = 100 halalat
Literacy rate 78%
Calorie consumption 2841 calories

SENEGAL

Page 52 B3

A former French colony, Senegal achieved independence in 1960. Its capital, Dakar, stands on the westernmost cape of Africa.

Official name Republic of Senegal
Formation 1960
Capital Dakar
Population 10.1 million / 136 people per sq mile (52 people per sq km)
Total area 75,749 sq. miles (196,190 sq. km)
Languages Wolof, Pulaar, Serer, Diola, Mandinka, Malinke, Soninke, French
Religions Sunni Muslim 90%, Traditional beliefs 5%, Christian 5%
Ethnic mix Wolof 43%, Toucouleur 24%, Serer 15%, Diola 4%, Malinke 3%, other 11%
Government Presidential system
Currency CFA franc = 100 centimes
Literacy rate 39%
Calorie consumption 2277 calories

SERBIA & MONTENEGRO (YUGOSLAVIA)

Page 78 D4

Serbia and Montenegro is the successor state to the former Yugoslavia.

Official name Serbia and Montenegro
Formation 1992
Capital Belgrade
Population 10.5 million / 266 people per sq mile (103 people per sq km)
Total area 39,517 sq. miles (102,350 sq. km)
Languages Serbo-Croat, Albanian, Hungarian (Magyar)
Religions Orthodox Christian 65%, other 12%, Muslim 19%, Roman Catholic 4%
Ethnic mix Serb 62%, Albanian 17%, Montenegrin 5%, other 16%
Government Parliamentary system
Currency Dinar (Serbia); euro (Montenegro)
Literacy rate 98%
Calorie consumption 2778 calories

SEYCHELLES

Page 57 G1

A former British colony comprising 115 islands in the Indian Ocean. Under one-party rule for 16 years, it became a multiparty democracy in 1993.

Official name Republic of Seychelles
Formation 1976
Capital Victoria
Population 80,469 / 774 people per sq mile (298 people per sq km)
Total area 176 sq. miles (455 sq. km)
Languages French Creole, English, French
Religions Roman Catholic 90%, Anglican 8%, other (including Muslim) 2%
Ethnic mix Creole 89%, Indian 5%, Chinese 2%, other 4%
Government Presidential system
Currency Seychelles rupee = 100 cents
Literacy rate 92%
Calorie consumption 2461 calories

SIERRA LEONE

Page 52 C4

The West African state of Sierra Leone achieved independence from the British in 1961. Today, it is one of the world's poorest nations.

Official name Republic of Sierra Leone
Formation 1961
Capital Freetown
Population 5 million / 181 people per sq mile (70 people per sq km)
Total area 27,698 sq. miles (71,740 sq. km)
Languages Mende, Temne, Krio, English
Religions Muslim 30%, Traditional beliefs 30%, Christian 10%, other 30%
Ethnic mix Mende 35%, Temne 32%, Limba 8%, Kuranko 4%, other 21%
Government Presidential system
Currency Leone = 100 cents
Literacy rate 36%
Calorie consumption 1913 calories

SINGAPORE

Page 116 A1

A city state linked to the southernmost tip of the Malay Peninsula by a causeway, Singapore is one of Asia's most important commercial centers.

Official name Republic of Singapore
Formation 1965
Capital Singapore
Population 4.3 million / 18220 people per sq mile (7049 people per sq km)
Total area 250 sq. miles (648 sq. km)
Languages Mandarin, Malay, Tamil, English
Religions Buddhist 55%, Taoist 22%, Muslim 16%, Hindu, Christian, and Sikh 7%
Ethnic mix Chinese 77%, Malay 14%, Indian 8%, other 1%
Government Parliamentary system
Currency Singapore dollar = 100 cents
Literacy rate 93%
Calorie consumption Not available

SLOVAKIA

Page 77 C6

Landlocked in Central Europe, Slovakia has been independent since 1993. It is the less developed half of the former Czechoslovakia.

Official name Slovak Republic
Formation 1993
Capital Bratislava
Population 5.4 million / 285 people per sq mile (110 people per sq km)
Total area 18,859 sq. miles (48,845 sq. km)
Languages Slovak, Hungarian (Magyar), Czech
Religions Roman Catholic 60%, Atheist 10%, Protestant 8%, Orthodox Christian 4%, other 18%
Ethnic mix Slovak 85%, Magyar 11%, Roma 1%, Czech 1%, other 2%
Government Parliamentary system
Currency Slovak koruna = 100 halierov
Literacy rate 99%
Calorie consumption 2894 calories

SLOVENIA

Page 73 D8

Northernmost of the former Yugoslav republics, Slovenia has the closest links with Western Europe. In 1991, it gained independence with little violence.

Official name Republic of Slovenia
Formation 1991
Capital Ljubljana
Population 2 million / 256 people per sq mile (99 people er sq km)
Total area 7820 sq. miles 20,253 sq. km)
Languages Slovene, Serbo-Croat
Religions Roman Catholic 96%, Muslim 1%, other 3%
Ethnic mix Slovene 83%, Serb 2%, Croat 2%, Bosniak 1%, other 12%
Government Parliamentary system
Currency Tolar = 100 stotinov
Literacy rate 99%
Calorie consumption 2935 calories

SOLOMON ISLANDS

Page 122 C3

The Solomon archipelago comprises several hundred islands scattered in the southwestern Pacific. Independence from Britain came in 1978.

Official name Solomon Islands
Formation 1978
Capital Honiara
Population 477,000 / 44 people per sq mile (17 people per sq km)
Total area 10,985 sq. miles (28,450 sq. km)
Languages English, Pidgin English, Melanesian Pidgin
Religions Anglican 34%, Roman Catholic 19%, South Seas Evangelical Church 17%, Methodist 11%, other 19%
Ethnic mix Melanesian 94%, other 6%
Government Parliamentary system
Currency Solomon Islands dollar = 100 cents
Literacy rate 77%
Calorie consumption 2272 calories

SOMALIA

Page 51 E5

Italian and British Somaliland were united in 1960 to create this semiarid state occupying the horn of Africa. It has suffered years of civil war.

Official name Somalia
Formation 1960
Capital Mogadishu
Population 9.9 million / 41 people per sq mile (16 people per sq km)
Total area 246,199 sq. miles (637,657 sq. km)
Languages Somali, Arabic, English, Italian
Religions Sunni Muslim 98%, Christian 2%
Ethnic mix Somali 85%, other 15%
Government Transitional regime
Currency Somali shilling = 100 centesimi
Literacy rate 24%
Calorie consumption 1628 calories

SPAIN

Page 70 D2

Lodged between mainland Europe and Africa, the Atlantic and the Mediterranean, Spain has occupied a pivotal position since it was united in 1492.

Official name Kingdom of Spain
Formation 1492
Capital Madrid
Population 41.1 million / 213 people per sq mile (82 people per sq km)
Total area 194,896 sq. miles (504,782 sq. km)
Languages Spanish, Catalan, Galician, Basque
Religions Roman Catholic 96%, other 4%
Ethnic mix Castilian Spanish 72%, Catalan 17%, Galician 6%, Basque 2%, other 2%, Roma 1%
Government Parliamentary system
Currency Euro = 100 cents
Literacy rate 98%
Calorie consumption 3422 calories

SURINAME

Page 37 G3

Suriname is a former Dutch colony on the north coast of South America. Democracy was restored in 1991, after almost 11 years of military rule.

Official name Republic of Suriname
Formation 1975
Capital Paramaribo
Population 436,000 / 7 people per sq mile (3 people per sq km)
Total area 63,039 sq. miles (163,270 sq. km)
Languages Sranan, Dutch, Javanese, Sarnami Hindi, Saramaccan, Chinese
Religions Hindu 27%, Protestant 25%, Roman Catholic 23%, Muslim 20%, Traditional beliefs 5%
Ethnic mix Creole 34%, South Asian 34%, Javanese 18%, Black 9%, other 5%
Government Parliamentary system
Currency Suriname dollar = 100 cents
Literacy rate 94%
Calorie consumption 2643 calories

SWITZERLAND

Page 73 A7

One of the world's most prosperous countries, with a long tradition of neutrality in foreign affairs, it lies at the center of Western Europe.

Official name Swiss Confederation
Formation 1291
Capital Bern
Population 7.2 million / 469 people per sq mile (181 people per sq km)
Total area 15,942 sq. miles (41,290 sq. km)
Languages German, Swiss-German, French, Italian, Romansch
Religions Roman Catholic 46%, Protestant 40%, other, 12%, Muslim 2%
Ethnic mix German 65%, French 18%, Italian 10%, other 6%, Romansch 1%
Government Parliamentary system
Currency Swiss franc = 100 rappen/centimes
Literacy rate 99%
Calorie consumption 3440 calories

SOUTH AFRICA

Page 56 C4

South Africa is the most southerly nation on the African continent. The multiracial elections of 1994 overturned 80 years of white minority rule.

Official name Republic of South Africa
Formation 1934
Capital Pretoria; Cape Town; Bloemfontein
Population 45 million / 95 people per sq mile (37 people per sq km)
Total area 471,008 sq. miles (1,219,912 sq. km)
Languages English, Afrikaans, 9 other African languages
Religions Christian 68%, Traditional beliefs and animist 29%, other 3%
Ethnic mix Black 79%, White 10%, Colored 9%, Asian 2%
Government Presidential system
Currency Rand = 100 cents
Literacy rate 86%
Calorie consumption 2921 calories

SRI LANKA

Page 110 D3

The island republic of Sri Lanka is separated from India by the narrow Palk Strait. Since 1983, the Sinhalese and Tamil population have been in conflict.

Official name Democratic Socialist Republic of Sri Lanka
Formation 1948
Capital Colombo
Population 19.1 million / 764 people per sq mile (295 people per sq km)
Total area 25,332 sq. miles (65,610 sq. km)
Languages Sinhala, Tamil, English
Religions Buddhist 69%, Hindu 15%, Muslim 8%, Christian 8%
Ethnic mix Sinhalese 74%, Tamil 18%, Moor 7%, other 1%
Government Mixed presidential–parliamentary system
Currency Sri Lanka rupee = 100 cents
Literacy rate 92%
Calorie consumption 2274 calories

SWAZILAND

Page 56 D4

The tiny southern African kingdom of Swaziland gained independence from Britain in 1968. It is economically dependent on South Africa.

Official name Kingdom of Swaziland
Formation 1968
Capital Mbabane
Population 1.1 million / 166 people per sq mile (64 people per sq km)
Total area 6704 sq. miles (17,363 sq. km)
Languages English, siSwati, isiZulu, Xitsonga
Religions Christian 60%, Traditional beliefs 40%
Ethnic mix Swazi 97%, other 3%
Government Monarchy
Currency Lilangeni = 100 cents
Literacy rate 81%
Calorie consumption 2593 calories

SYRIA

Page 96 B3

Stretching from the eastern Mediterranean to the River Tigris, Syria's borders were created on its independence from France in 1946.

Official name Syrian Arab Republic
Formation 1941
Capital Damascus
Population 17.8 million / 250 people per sq mile (97 people per sq km)
Total area 71,498 sq. miles (184,180 sq. km)
Languages Arabic, French, Kurdish, Armenian, Circassian
Religions Sunni Muslim 74%, other Muslim 16%, Christian 10%
Ethnic mix Arab 89%, Kurdish 6%, other 3%, Armenian, Turkmen, and Circassian 2%
Government One-party state
Currency Syrian pound = 100 piasters
Literacy rate 83%
Calorie consumption 3038 calories

SOUTH KOREA

Page 106 E4

South Korea occupies the southern half of the Korean peninsula. It was separated from the communist North in 1948.

Official name Republic of Korea
Formation 1948
Capital Seoul
Population 47.7 million / 1251 people per sq mile (483 people per sq km)
Total area 38,023 sq. miles (98,480 sq. km)
Languages Korean, Chinese
Religions Mahayana Buddhist 47%, Protestant 38%, Roman Catholic 11%, Confucianist 3%, other 1%
Ethnic mix Korean 100%
Government Presidential system
Currency South Korean won = 100 chon
Literacy rate 98%
Calorie consumption 3055 calories

SUDAN

Page 50 B4

The largest country in Africa, part of Sudan borders the Red Sea. In 1989, an army coup installed a military Islamic fundamentalist regime.

Official name Republic of the Sudan
Formation 1956
Capital Khartoum
Population 33.6 million / 35 people per sq mile (13 people per sq km)
Total area 967,493 sq. miles (2,505,810 sq. km)
Languages Arabic, Dinka, Nuer, Nubian, Beja, Zande, Bari, Fur, Shilluk
Religions Muslim (mainly Sunni) 70%, Traditional beliefs 20%, other 10%
Ethnic mix Arab 40%, Dinka and Beja 7%, other Black 52%, other 1%
Government Presidential system
Currency Sudanese pound or dinar = 100 piastres
Literacy rate 60%
Calorie consumption 2288 calories

SWEDEN

Page 62 B4

The largest Scandinavian country in both population and area, Sweden's strong industrial base helps to fund its extensive welfare system.

Official name Kingdom of Sweden
Formation 1523
Capital Stockholm
Population 8.9 million / 56 people per sq mile (22 people per sq km)
Total area 173,731 sq. miles (449,964 sq. km)
Languages Swedish, Finnish, Sámi
Religions Evangelical Lutheran 82%, Roman Catholic 2%, Muslim 2%, Orthodox Christian 1%, other 13%
Ethnic mix Swedish 88%, Foreign-born or first-generation immigrant 10%, Finnish and Sámi 2%
Government Parliamentary system
Currency Swedish krona = 100 öre
Literacy rate 99%
Calorie consumption 3164 calories

TAIWAN

Page 107 D6

The island republic of Taiwan lies 130 km (80 miles) off the southeast coast of mainland China. China considers it to be one of its provinces.

Official name Republic of China (ROC)
Formation 1949
Capital Taipei
Population 22.6 million / 1815 people per sq mile (701 people per sq km)
Total area 13,892 sq. miles (35,980 sq. km)
Languages Amoy Chinese, Mandarin Chinese, Hakka Chinese
Religions Buddhist, Confucianist, and Taoist 93%, Christian 5%, other 2%
Ethnic mix Indigenous Chinese 84%, Mainland Chinese 14%, Aboriginal 2%
Government Presidential system
Currency Taiwan dollar = 100 cents
Literacy rate 96%
Calorie consumption Not available

COUNTRY FACTFILE • SAMOA – TAIWAN

149

TAJIKISTAN

Page 101 F3

Tajikistan lies landlocked on the western slopes of the Pamirs in Central Asia. The Tajiks' language and traditions are similar to those of Iran.

Official name Republic of Tajikistan
Formation 1991
Capital Dushanbe
Population 6.2 million / 112 people per sq mile (43 people per sq km)
Total area 55,251 sq. miles (143,100 sq. km)
Languages Tajik, Uzbek, Russian
Religions Sunni Muslim 80%, other 15%, Shi'a Muslim 5%
Ethnic mix Tajik 62%, Uzbek 24%, Russian 8%, Tatar 1%, Kyrgyz 1%, other 4%
Government Presidential system
Currency Somoni = 100 diram
Literacy rate 99%
Calorie consumption 1662 calories

TANZANIA

Page 51 B7

The East African state of Tanzania was formed in 1964 by the union of Tanganyika and Zanzibar. A third of its area is game reserve or national park.

Official name United Republic of Tanzania
Formation 1964
Capital Dodoma
Population 37 million / 108 people per sq mile (42 people per sq km)
Total area 364,898 sq. miles (945,087 sq. km)
Languages Kiswahili, Sukuma, English
Religions Muslim 33%, Christian 33%, Traditional beliefs 30%, other 4%
Ethnic mix Native African (over 120 tribes) 99%, European and Asian 1%
Government Presidential system
Currency Tanzanian shilling = 100 cents
Literacy rate 77%
Calorie consumption 1997 calories

THAILAND

Page 115 C5

Thailand lies at the heart of mainland Southeast Asia. Continuing rapid industrialization has resulted in massive congestion in the capital.

Official name Kingdom of Thailand
Formation 1238
Capital Bangkok
Population 62.8 million / 318 people per sq mile (123 people per sq km)
Total area 198,455 sq. miles (514,000 sq. km)
Languages Thai, Chinese, Malay, Khmer, Mon, Karen, Miao
Religions Buddhist 95%, Muslim 4%, other (including Christian) 1%
Ethnic mix Thai 83%, Chinese 12%, Malay 3%, Khmer and other 2%
Government Parliamentary system
Currency Baht = 100 stang
Literacy rate 93%
Calorie consumption 2486 calories

TOGO

Page 53 F4

Togo lies sandwiched between Ghana and Benin in West Africa. The 1993–94 presidential elections were the first since its independence in 1960.

Official name Republic of Togo
Formation 1960
Capital Lomé
Population 4.9 million / 233 people per sq mile (90 people per sq km)
Total area 21,924 sq. miles (56,785 sq. km)
Languages Ewe, Kabye, Gurma, French
Religions Traditional beliefs 50%, Christian 35%, Muslim 15%
Ethnic mix Ewe 46%, Kabye 27%, other African 26%, European 1%
Government Presidential system
Currency CFA franc = 100 centimes
Literacy rate 60%
Calorie consumption 2287 calories

TONGA

Page 123 E4

Northeast of New Zealand, in the South Pacific, Tonga is an archipelago of 170 islands, 45 of which are inhabited. Politics is effectively controlled by the king.

Official name Kingdom of Tonga
Formation 1970
Capital Nuku'alofa
Population 108,141 / 389 people per sq mile (150 people per sq km)
Total area 289 sq. miles (748 sq. km)
Languages English, Tongan
Religions Free Wesleyan 41%, Roman Catholic 16%, Church of Jesus Christ of Latter-day Saints 14%, Free Church of Tonga 12%, other 17%
Ethnic mix Polynesian 99%, other 1%
Government Monarchy
Currency Pa'anga (Tongan dollar) = 100 seniti
Literacy rate 99%
Calorie consumption Not available

TRINIDAD & TOBAGO

Page 33 H5

The former British colony of Trinidad and Tobago is the most southerly of the West Indies, lying just 15 km (9 miles) off the coast of Venezuela.

Official name Republic of Trinidad and Tobago
Formation 1962
Capital Port-of-Spain
Population 1.3 million / 656 people per sq mile (253 people per sq km)
Total area 1980 sq. miles (5128 sq. km)
Languages English Creole, English, Hindi, French, Spanish
Religions Christian 60%, Hindu 24%, other 16%
Ethnic mix East Indian 40%, Black 40%, Mixed race 19%, other 1%
Government Parliamentary system
Currency Trinidad and Tobago dollar = 100 cents
Literacy rate 99%
Calorie consumption 2756 calories

TUNISIA

Page 49 E2

Tunisia, in North Africa, has traditionally been one of the more liberal Arab states, but is now facing a challenge from Islamic fundamentalists.

Official name Republic of Tunisia
Formation 1956
Capital Tunis
Population 9.8 million / 163 people per sq mile (63 people per sq km)
Total area 63,169 sq. miles (163,610 sq. km)
Languages Arabic, French
Religions Muslim (mainly Sunni) 98%, Christian 1%, Jewish 1%
Ethnic mix Arab and Berber 98%, Jewish 1%, European 1%
Government Presidential system
Currency Tunisian dinar = 1000 millimes
Literacy rate 73%
Calorie consumption 3293 calories

TURKEY

Page 94 B3

Lying partly in Europe, but mostly in Asia, Turkey's position gives it significant influence in the Mediterranean, Black Sea, and Middle East.

Official name Republic of Turkey
Formation 1923
Capital Ankara
Population 71.3 million / 240 people per sq mile (93 people per sq km)
Total area 301,382 sq. miles (780,580 sq. km)
Languages Turkish, Kurdish, Arabic, Circassian, Armenian, Greek, Georgian, Ladino
Religions Muslim (mainly Sunni) 99%, other 1%
Ethnic mix Turkish 70%, Kurdish 20%, Arab 2%, other 8%
Government Parliamentary system
Currency Turkish lira = 100 kurus
Literacy rate 87%
Calorie consumption 3343 calories

TURKMENISTAN

Page 100 B2

Stretching from the Caspian Sea into the deserts of Central Asia, the ex-Soviet state of Turkmenistan has adjusted better than most to independence.

Official name Turkmenistan
Formation 1991
Capital Ashgabat
Population 4.9 million / 26 people per sq mile (10 people per sq km)
Total area 188,455 sq. miles (488,100 sq. km)
Languages Turkmen, Uzbek, Russian, Kazakh, Tatar
Religions Sunni Muslim 87%, Orthodox Christian 11%, other 2%
Ethnic mix Turkmen 77%, Uzbek 9%, Russian 7%, other 4%, Kazakh 2%, Tatar 1%
Government One-party state
Currency Manat = 100 tenga
Literacy rate 98%
Calorie consumption 2738 calories

TUVALU

Page 123 E3

The former Ellice Islands, linked to the Gilbert Islands as a British colony until 1978, Tuvalu is an isolated chain of nine atolls in the Central Pacific.

Official name Tuvalu
Formation 1978
Capital Fongafale, on Funafuti Atoll
Population 11,305 / 1130 people per sq mile (435 people per sq km)
Total area 10 sq. miles (26 sq. km)
Languages Tuvaluan, Kiribati, English
Religions Church of Tuvalu 97%, other 1%, Baha'i 1%, Seventh-day Adventist 1%
Ethnic mix Polynesian 96%, other 4%
Government Nonparty system
Currency Australian dollar and Tuvaluan dollar = 100 cents
Literacy rate 98%
Calorie consumption Not available

UGANDA

Page 51 B6

Uganda lies landlocked in East Africa. It was ruled by one of Africa's more eccentric leaders, the dictator Idi Amin Dada, from 1971–1980.

Official name Republic of Uganda
Formation 1962
Capital Kampala
Population 25.8 million / 335 people per sq mile (129 people per sq km)
Total area 91,135 sq. miles (236,040 sq. km)
Languages Luganda, Nkole, English
Religions Roman Catholic 38%, Protestant 33%, Traditional beliefs 13%, Muslim (mainly Sunni) 8%, other 8%
Ethnic mix Bantu tribes 50%, Sudanese 5%, other 45%
Government Nonparty system
Currency New Uganda shilling = 100 cents
Literacy rate 69%
Calorie consumption 2398 calories

UKRAINE

Page 86 C2

Bordered by seven states, the former "breadbasket of the Soviet Union" balances assertive nationalism with concerns over its relations with Russia.

Official name Ukraine
Formation 1991
Capital Kiev
Population 47.7 million / 205 people per sq mile (79 people per sq km)
Total area 223,089 sq. miles (603,700 sq. km)
Languages Ukrainian, Russian, Tatar
Religions Christian (mainly Orthodox) 95%, Jewish 1%, other 4%
Ethnic mix Ukrainian 73%, Russian 22%, Jewish 1%, other 4%
Government Presidential system
Currency Hryvna = 100 kopiykas
Literacy rate 99%
Calorie consumption 3008 calories

UNITED ARAB EMIRATES

Page 99 D5

Bordering the Persian Gulf on the northern coast of the Arabian Peninsula, is the United Arab Emirates, a working federation of seven states.

Official name United Arab Emirates
Formation 1971
Capital Abu Dhabi
Population 3 million / 93 people per sq mile (36 people per sq km)
Total area 32,000 sq. miles (82,880 sq. km)
Languages Arabic, Farsi, Indian and Pakistani languages, English
Religions Muslim (mainly Sunni) 96%, Christian, Hindu, and other 4%
Ethnic mix Asian 60%, Emirian 25%, other Arab 12%, European 3%
Government Monarchy
Currency UAE dirham = 100 fils
Literacy rate 77%
Calorie consumption 3340 calories

UNITED KINGDOM

Page 67 B5

Separated from continental Europe by the North Sea and the English Channel, the UK comprises England, Wales, Scotland, and Northern Ireland.

Official name United Kingdom of Great Britain and Northern Ireland
Formation 1707
Capital London
Population 59.3 million / 636 people per sq mile (245 people per sq km)
Total area 94,525 sq. miles (244,820 sq. km)
Languages English, Welsh, Scottish Gaelic, Irish Gaelic
Religions Anglican 45%, Roman Catholic 9%, Presbyterian 4%, other 42%
Ethnic mix English 80%, Scottish 9%, Northern Irish 3%, Welsh 3%, other 5%,
Government Parliamentary system
Currency Pound sterling = 100 pence
Literacy rate 99%
Calorie consumption 3368 calories

UNITED STATES OF AMERICA

Page 13 B5

Stretching across the most temperate part of North America, and with many natural resources, the USA is the sole truly global superpower.

Official name United States of America
Formation 1776
Capital Washington D.C.
Population 294 million / 83 people per sq mile (32 people per sq km)
Total area 3,717,792 sq. miles (9,626,091 sq. km)
Languages English, Spanish, Chinese, French, German, Italian, Russian, Polish
Religions Protestant 52%, Roman Catholic 25%, Jewish 2%, other 21%
Ethnic mix White 69%, Hispanic 13%, Black American/African 13%, Asian 4%, Native American 1%
Government Presidential system
Currency US dollar = 100 cents
Literacy rate 99%
Calorie consumption 3766 calories

URUGUAY

Page 42 D4

Uruguay is situated in southeastern South America. It returned to civilian government in 1985, after 12 years of military dictatorship.

Official name Eastern Republic of Uruguay
Formation 1828
Capital Montevideo
Population 3.4 million / 50 people per sq mile (19 people per sq km)
Total area 68,039 sq. miles (176,220 sq. km)
Languages Spanish
Religions Roman Catholic 66%, Jewish 2%, Protestant 2%, other and nonreligious 30%
Ethnic mix White 90%, other 10%
Government Presidential system
Currency Uruguayan peso = 100 centésimos
Literacy rate 98%
Calorie consumption 2848 calories

UZBEKISTAN

Page 100 D2

Sharing the Aral Sea coastline with its northern neighbor, Kazakhstan, Uzbekistan lies on the ancient Silk Road between Asia and Europe.

Official name Republic of Uzbekistan
Formation 1991
Capital Tashkent
Population 26.1 million / 151 people per sq mile (58 people per sq km)
Total area 172,741 sq. miles (447,400 sq. km)
Languages Uzbek, Russian, Tajik, Kazakh
Religions Sunni Muslim 88%, Orthodox Christian 9%, other 3%
Ethnic mix Uzbek 71%, Russian 8%, Tajik 5%, Kazakh 4%, other 12%,
Government Presidential system
Currency Som = 100 tiyin
Literacy rate 99%
Calorie consumption 2197 calories

VANUATU

Page 122 D4

An archipelago of 82 islands and islets in the Pacific Ocean, it was ruled jointly by Britain and France from 1906 until independence in 1980.

Official name Republic of Vanuatu
Formation 1980
Capital Port Vila
Population 212,000 / 45 people per sq mile (17 people per sq km)
Total area 4710 sq. miles (12,200 sq. km)
Languages Bislama, English, French,
Religions Presbyterian 37%, Anglican 15%, Roman Catholic 15%, Traditional beliefs 8%, Seventh-day Adventist 6%, , other 19%
Ethnic mix Melanesian 94%, other 3%, Polynesian 3%
Government Parliamentary system
Currency Vatu = 100 centimes
Literacy rate 34%
Calorie consumption 2565 calories

VATICAN CITY

Page 75 A8

The Vatican City, seat of the Roman Catholic Church, is a walled enclave in the city of Rome. It is the world's smallest fully independent state.

Official name State of the Vatican City
Formation 1929
Capital Vatican City
Population 911 / 5359 people per sq mile (2070 people per sq km)
Total area 0.17 sq. miles (0.44 sq. km)
Languages Italian, Latin
Religions Roman Catholic 100%
Ethnic mix The current pope is Polish, ending nearly 500 years of Italian popes. Cardinals are from many nationalities, but Italians form the largest group. Most of the resident lay persons are Italian.
Government Papal state
Currency Euro = 100 cents
Literacy rate 99%
Calorie consumption Not available

VENEZUELA

Page 36 D2

Located on the north coast of South America, Venezuela has the continent's most urbanized society. Most people live in the northern cities.

Official name Bolivarian Republic of Venezuela
Formation 1830
Capital Caracas
Population 25.7 million / 75 people per sq mile (29 people per sq km)
Total area 352,143 sq. miles (912,050 sq. km)
Languages Spanish, Amerindian languages
Religions Roman Catholic 89%, Protestant and other 11%
Ethnic mix Mestizo 69%, White 20%, Black 9%, Amerindian 2%
Government Presidential system
Currency Bolívar = 100 centimos
Literacy rate 93%
Calorie consumption 2376 calories

VIETNAM

Page 114 D4

Situated in the far east of mainland Southeast Asia, the country is still rebuilding after the devastating 1962–1975 Vietnam War.

Official name Socialist Republic of Vietnam
Formation 1976
Capital Hanoi
Population 81.4 million / 648 people per sq mile (250 people per sq km)
Total area 127,243 sq. miles (329,560 sq. km)
Languages Vietnamese, Chinese, Thai, Khmer, Muong, Nung, Miao, Yao, Jarai
Religions Buddhist 55%, other and nonreligious 38%, Christian 7%
Ethnic mix Vietnamese 88%, Chinese 4%, Thai 2%, other 6%
Government One-party state
Currency Dông = 10 hao = 100 xu
Literacy rate 93%
Calorie consumption 2533 calories

YEMEN

Page 99 C7

Located in southern Arabia, Yemen was formerly two countries – a socialist regime in the south, and a republic in the north. Both united in 1990.

Official name Republic of Yemen
Formation 1990
Capital Sana
Population 20 million / 92 people per sq mile (36 people per sq km)
Total area 203,849 sq. miles (527,970 sq. km)
Languages Arabic
Religions Sunni Muslim 55%, Shi'a Muslim 42%, Christian, Hindu, and Jewish 3%
Ethnic mix Arab 95%, Afro-Arab 3%, Indian, Somali, and European 2%
Government Presidential system
Currency Yemeni rial = 100 sene
Literacy rate 49%
Calorie consumption 2050 calories

ZAMBIA

Page 56 C2

Zambia lies landlocked at the heart of southern Africa. In 1991, it made a peaceful transition from single-party rule to multiparty democracy.

Official name Republic of Zambia
Formation 1964
Capital Lusaka
Population 10 8 million / 38 people per sq mile (15 people per sq km)
Total area 290,584 sq. miles (752,614 sq. km)
Languages Bemba, Tonga, Nyanja, Lozi, Lala-Bisa, Nsenga, English
Religions Christian 63%, Traditional beliefs 36%, Muslim and Hindu 1%
Ethnic mix Bemba 34%, other African 65%, European 1%
Government Presidential system
Currency Zambian kwacha = 100 ngwee
Literacy rate 80%
Calorie consumption 1885 calories

ZIMBABWE

Page 56 D3

The former British colony of Southern Rhodesia became fully independent as Zimbabwe in 1980, after 15 years of troubled white minority rule.

Official name Republic of Zimbabwe
Formation 1980
Capital Harare
Population 12.9 million / 86 people per sq mile (33 people per sq km)
Total area 150,803 sq. miles (390,580 sq. km)
Languages Shona, isiNdebele, English
Religions Syncretic (Christian/traditional beliefs) 50%, Christian 25%, Traditional beliefs 24%, other (including Muslim) 1%
Ethnic mix Shona 71%, Ndebele 16%, other African 11%, White 1%, Asian 1%
Government Presidential system
Currency Zimbabwe dollar = 100 cents
Literacy rate 90%
Calorie consumption 2133 calories

LARGEST COUNTRIES

Russ. Fed.	.6,592,735 sq miles	(17,075,200 sq km)
Canada	.3,855,171 sq miles	(9,984,670 sq km)
USA	.3,717,792 sq miles	(9,629,091 sq km)
China	.3,705,386 sq miles	(9,596,960 sq km)
Brazil	.3,286,470 sq miles	(8,511,965 sq km)
Australia	.2,967,893 sq miles	(7,686,893 sq km)
India	.1,269,339 sq miles	(3,287,590 sq km)
Argentina	.1,068,296 sq miles	(2,766,890 sq km)
Kazakhstan	.1,049,150 sq miles	(2,717,300 sq km)
Sudan	.967,493 sq miles	(2,505,810 sq km)

SMALLEST COUNTRIES

Vatican City	.0.17 sq miles	(0.44 sq km)
Monaco	.0.75 sq miles	(1.95 sq km)
Nauru	.8 sq miles	(21 sq km)
Tuvalu	.10 sq miles	(26 sq km)
San Marino	.24 sq miles	(61 sq km)
Liechtenstein	.62 sq miles	(160 sq km)
Marshall Islands	.70 sq miles	(181 sq km)
St. Kitts & Nevis	.101 sq miles	(261 sq km)
Maldives	.116 sq miles	(300 sq km)
Malta	.122 sq miles	(316 sq km)

LARGEST ISLANDS

(TO THE NEAREST 1,000 - OR 100,000 FOR THE LARGEST)

Greenland	.849,400 sq miles	(2,200,000 sq km)
New Guinea	.312,000 sq miles	(808,000 sq km)
Borneo	.292,222 sq miles	(757,050 sq km)
Madagascar	.229,300 sq miles	(594,000 sq km)
Sumatra	.202,300 sq miles	(524,000 sq km)
Baffin Island	.183,800 sq miles	(476,000 sq km)
Honshu	.88,800 sq miles	(230,000 sq km)
Britain	.88,700 sq miles	(229,800 sq km)

RICHEST COUNTRIES

(GNP PER CAPITA, IN US$)

Liechtenstein	.50,000
Luxembourg	.39,470
Norway	.38,730
Switzerland	.36,170
USA	.35,400
Japan	.34,010
Denmark	.30,260
Iceland	.27,960
Monaco	.27,500
Sweden	.25,970

POOREST COUNTRIES

(GNP PER CAPITA, IN US$)

Congo, Dem. Rep.	.100
Burundi	.100
Ethiopia	.100
Somalia	.120
Guinea-Bissau	.130
Sierra Leone	.140
Liberia	.140
Malawi	.160
Tajikistan	.180
Niger	.180

MOST POPULOUS COUNTRIES

China	.1,304,200,000
India	.1,065,500,000
USA	.294,000,000
Indonesia	.219,900,000
Brazil	.178,500,000
Pakistan	.153,600,000
Bangladesh	.146,700,000

MOST POPULOUS COUNTRIES continued

Russian Federation	.143,200,000
Japan	.127,700,000
Nigeria	.124,000,000

LEAST POPULOUS COUNTRIES

Vatican City	.921
Tuvalu	.11,305
Nauru	.12,570
Palau	.19,717
San Marino	.28,119
Monaco	.32,130
Liechtenstein	.33,145
St. Kitts & Nevis	.38,763
Marshall Islands	.56,429
Antigua & Barbuda	.67,897

MOST DENSELY POPULATED COUNTRIES

Monaco	.42,840 people per sq mile	(16,477 per sq km)
Singapore	18,220 people per sq mile	(7,049 per sq km)
Vatican City	.5,359 people per sq mile	(2,070 per sq km)
Malta	.3,177 people per sq mile	(1,231 per sq km)
Bangladesh	.2,837 people per sq mile	(1,096 per sq km)
Maldives	.2,741 people per sq mile	(1,060 per sq km)
Bahrain	.2,652 people per sq mile	(1,025 per sq km)
Taiwan	.1,815 people per sq mile	(701 per sq km)
Mauritius	.1,671 people per sq mile	(645 per sq km)
Barbados	.1,627 people per sq mile	(628 per sq km)

MOST SPARSELY POPULATED COUNTRIES

Mongolia	.4 people per sq mile	(2 per sq km)
Namibia	.6 people per sq mile	(2 per sq km)
Suriname	.7 people per sq mile	(3 per sq km)
Mauritania	.7 people per sq mile	(3 per sq km)
Iceland	.7 people per sq mile	(3 per sq km)
Australia	.7 people per sq mile	(3 per sq km)
Libya	.8 people per sq mile	(3 per sq km)
Botswana	.8 people per sq mile	(3 per sq km)
Canada	.9 people per sq mile	(3 per sq km)
Guyana	.10 people per sq mile	(4 per sq km)

MOST WIDELY SPOKEN LANGUAGES

1. Chinese (Mandarin)	6. Arabic
2. English	7. Bengali
3. Hindi	8. Portuguese
4. Spanish	9. Malay-Indonesian
5. Russian	10. French

COUNTRIES WITH THE MOST LAND BORDERS

14: China (*Afghanistan, Bhutan, Myanmar, India, Kazakhstan, Kyrgyzstan, Laos, Mongolia, Nepal, North Korea, Pakistan, Russian Federation, Tajikistan, Vietnam*)

14: Russ. Fed. (*Azerbaijan, Belarus, China, Estonia, Finland, Georgia, Kazakhstan, Latvia, Lithuania, Mongolia, North Korea, Norway, Poland, Ukraine*)

10: Brazil (*Argentina, Bolivia, Colombia, French Guiana, Guyana, Paraguay, Peru, Suriname, Uruguay, Venezuela*)

9: Congo, Dem. Rep. (*Angola, Burundi, Central African Republic, Congo, Rwanda, Sudan, Tanzania, Uganda, Zambia*)

9: Germany (*Austria, Belgium, Czech Republic, Denmark, France, Luxembourg, Netherlands, Poland, Switzerland*)

9: Sudan (*Central African Republic, Chad, Congo, Dem. Rep., Egypt, Eritrea, Ethiopia, Kenya, Libya, Uganda*)

8: Austria (*Czech Republic, Germany, Hungary, Italy, Liechtenstein, Slovakia, Slovenia, Switzerland*)

8: France (*Andorra, Belgium, Germany, Italy, Luxembourg, Monaco, Spain, Switzerland*)

8: Tanzania (*Burundi, Congo, Dem. Rep., Kenya, Malawi, Mozambique, Rwanda, Uganda, Zambia*)

8: Turkey (*Armenia, Azerbaijan, Bulgaria, Georgia, Greece, Iran, Iraq, Syria*)

LONGEST RIVERS

Nile (NE Africa)	4,160 miles	(6,695 km)
Amazon (South America)	4,049 miles	(6,516 km)
Yangtze (China)	3,915 miles	(6,299 km)
Mississippi/Missouri (US)	3,710 miles	(5,969 km)
Ob'-Irtysh (Russ. Fed.)	3,461 miles	(5,570 km)
Yellow River (China)	3,395 miles	(5,464 km)
Congo (Central Africa)	2,900 miles	(4,667 km)
Mekong (Southeast Asia)	2,749 miles	(4,425 km)
Lena (Russian Federation)	2,734 miles	(4,400 km)
Mackenzie (Canada)	2,640 miles	(4,250 km)

HIGHEST MOUNTAINS

(HEIGHT ABOVE SEA LEVEL)

Everest	29,035 ft	(8,850 m)
K2	28,253 ft	(8,611 m)
Kanchenjunga I	28,210 ft	(8,598 m)
Makalu I	27,767 ft	(8,463 m)
Cho Oyu	26,907 ft	(8,201 m)
Dhaulagiri I	26,796 ft	(8,167 m)
Manaslu I	26,783 ft	(8,163 m)
Nanga Parbat I	26,661 ft	(8,126 m)
Annapurna I	26,547 ft	(8,091 m)
Gasherbrum I	26,471 ft	(8,068 m)

LARGEST BODIES OF INLAND WATER

(WITH AREA AND DEPTH)

Caspian Sea	143,243 sq miles (371,000 sq km)	3,215 ft (980 m)
Lake Superior	32,151 sq miles (83,270 sq km)	1,289 ft (393 m)
Lake Victoria	26,560 sq miles (68,880 sq km)	328 ft (100 m)
Lake Huron	23,436 sq miles (60,700 sq km)	751 ft (229 m)
Lake Michigan	22,402 sq miles (58,020 sq km)	922 ft (281 m)
Lake Tanganyika	12,703 sq miles (32,900 sq km)	4,700 ft (1,435 m)
Great Bear Lake	12,274 sq miles (31,790 sq km)	1,047 ft (319 m)
Lake Baikal	11,776 sq miles (30,500 sq km)	5,712 ft (1,741 m)
Great Slave Lake	10,981 sq miles (28,440 sq km)	459 ft (140 m)
Lake Erie	9,915 sq miles (25,680 sq km)	197 ft (60 m)

DEEPEST OCEAN FEATURES

Challenger Deep, Marianas Trench (Pacific)	36,201 ft	(11,034 m)
Vityaz III Depth, Tonga Trench (Pacific)	35,704 ft	(10,882 m)
Vityaz Depth, Kurile-Kamchatka Trench (Pacific)	34,588 ft	(10,542 m)
Cape Johnson Deep, Philippine Trench (Pacific)	34,441 ft	(10,497 m)
Kermadec Trench (Pacific)	32,964 ft	(10,047 m)
Ramapo Deep, Japan Trench (Pacific)	32,758 ft	(9,984 m)
Milwaukee Deep, Puerto Rico Trench (Atlantic)	30,185 ft	(9,200 m)
Argo Deep, Torres Trench (Pacific)	30,070 ft	(9,165 m)
Meteor Depth, South Sandwich Trench (Atlantic)	30,000 ft	(9,144 m)
Planet Deep, New Britain Trench (Pacific)	29,988 ft	(9,140 m)

GREATEST WATERFALLS

(MEAN FLOW OF WATER)

Boyoma (Congo, Dem. Rep.)	600,400 cu. ft/sec	(17,000 cu.m/sec)
Khône (Laos/Cambodia)	410,000 cu. ft/sec	(11,600 cu.m/sec)
Niagara (USA/Canada)	195,000 cu. ft/sec	(5,500 cu.m/sec)
Grande (Uruguay)	160,000 cu. ft/sec	(4,500 cu.m/sec)
Paulo Afonso (Brazil)	100,000 cu. ft/sec	(2,800 cu.m/sec)
Urubupunga (Brazil)	97,000 cu. ft/sec	(2,750 cu.m/sec)
Iguaçu (Argentina/Brazil)	62,000 cu. ft/sec	(1,700 cu.m/sec)
Maribondo (Brazil)	53,000 cu. ft/sec	(1,500 cu.m/sec)
Victoria (Zimbabwe)	39,000 cu. ft/sec	(1,100 cu.m/sec)
Kabalega (Uganda)	42,000 cu. ft/sec	(1,200 cu.m/sec)

HIGHEST WATERFALLS

Angel (Venezuela)	3,212 ft	(979 m)
Tugela (South Africa)	3,110 ft	(948 m)
Utigard (Norway)	2,625 ft	(800 m)
Mongefossen (Norway)	2,539 ft	(774 m)
Mtarazi (Zimbabwe)	2,500 ft	(762 m)
Yosemite (USA)	2,425 ft	(739 m)
Ostre Mardola Foss (Norway)	2,156 ft	(657 m)
Tyssestrengane (Norway)	2,119 ft	(646 m)
*Cuquenan (Venezuela)	2,001 ft	(610 m)
Sutherland (New Zealand)	1,903 ft	(580 m)

indicates that the total height is a single leap

LARGEST DESERTS

Sahara	3,450,000 sq miles	(9,065,000 sq km)
Gobi	500,000 sq miles	(1,295,000 sq km)
Ar Rub al Khali	289,600 sq miles	(750,000 sq km)
Great Victorian	249,800 sq miles	(647,000 sq km)
Sonoran	120,000 sq miles	(311,000 sq km)
Kalahari	120,000 sq miles	(310,800 sq km)
Kara Kum	115,800 sq miles	(300,000 sq km)
Takla Makan	100,400 sq miles	(260,000 sq km)
Namib	52,100 sq miles	(135,000 sq km)
Thar	33,670 sq miles	(130,000 sq km)

NB – Most of Antarctica is a polar desert, with only 50 mm of precipitation annually

HOTTEST INHABITED PLACES

Djibouti (Djibouti)	86° F	(30 °C)
Timbouctou (Mali)	84.7° F	(29.3 °C)
Tirunelveli (India)	84.7° F	(29.3 °C)
Tuticorin (India)	84.7° F	(29.3 °C)
Nellore (India)	84.5° F	(29.2 °C)
Santa Marta (Colombia)	84.5° F	(29.2 °C)
Aden (Yemen)	84° F	(28.9 °C)
Madurai (India)	84° F	(28.9 °C)
Niamey (Niger)	84° F	(28.9 °C)
Hodeida (Yemen)	83.8° F	(28.8 °C)

DRIEST INHABITED PLACES

Aswân (Egypt)	0.02 in	(0.5 mm)
Luxor (Egypt)	0.03 in	(0.7 mm)
Arica (Chile)	0.04 in	(1.1 mm)
Ica (Peru)	0.1 in	(2.3 mm)
Antofagasta (Chile)	0.2 in	(4.9 mm)
El Minya (Egypt)	0.2 in	(5.1 mm)
Asyût (Egypt)	0.2 in	(5.2 mm)
Callao (Peru)	0.5 in	(12.0 mm)
Trujillo (Peru)	0.55 in	(14.0 mm)
El Faiyûm (Egypt)	0.8 in	(19.0 mm)

WETTEST INHABITED PLACES

Buenaventura (Colombia)	265 in	(6,743 mm)
Monrovia (Liberia)	202 in	(5,131 mm)
Pago Pago (American Samoa)	196 in	(4,990 mm)
Moulmein (Myanmar)	191 in	(4,852 mm)
Lae (Papua New Guinea)	183 in	(4,645 mm)
Baguio (Luzon Island, Philippines)	180 in	(4,573 mm)
Sylhet (Bangladesh)	176 in	(4,457 mm)
Padang (Sumatra, Indonesia)	166 in	(4,225 mm)
Bogor (Java, Indonesia)	166 in	(4,225 mm)
Conakry (Guinea)	171 in	(4,341 mm)

INDEX

GLOSSARY OF ABBREVIATIONS
This Glossary provides a comprehensive guide to the abbreviations used in this Atlas, and in the Index.

A **abbrev.** abbreviated
Afr. Afrikaans
Alb. Albanian
Amh. Amharic
anc. ancient
Ar. Arabic
Arm. Armenian
Az. Azerbaijani
B **Basq.** Basque
Bel. Belorussian
Ben. Bengali
Bibl. Biblical
Bret. Breton
Bul. Bulgarian
Bur. Burmese
C **Cam.** Cambodian
Cant. Cantonese
Cast. Castilian
Cat. Catalan
Chin. Chinese
Cro. Croat
Cz. Czech
D **Dan.** Danish
Dut. Dutch
E **Eng.** English
Est. Estonian
est. estimated
F **Faer.** Faeroese
Fij. Fijian
Fin. Finnish
Flem. Flemish
Fr. French
Fris. Frisian
G **Geor.** Georgian
Ger. German
Gk. Greek
Guj. Gujarati
H **Haw.** Hawaiian
Heb. Hebrew
Hind. Hindi
hist. historical
Hung. Hungarian
I **Icel.** Icelandic
Ind. Indonesian
Ir. Irish
It. Italian
J **Jap.** Japanese
K **Kaz.** Kazakh
Kir. Kirghiz
Kor. Korean
Kurd. Kurdish
L **Lao.** Laotian
Lapp. Lappish
Lat. Latin
Latv. Latvian
Lith. Lithanian
Lus. Lusatian
M **Mac.** Macedonian
Mal. Malay
Malg. Malagasy
Malt. Maltese
Mong. Mongolian
N **Nepali.** Nepali
Nor. Norwegian
O **off.** officially
P **Pash.** Pashtu
Per. Persian
Pol. Polish
Port. Portuguese
prev. previously
R **Rmsch.** Romansch
Roman. Romanian
Rus. Russian
S **SCr.** Serbo-Croatian
Serb. Serbian
Slvk. Slovak
Slvn. Slovene
Som. Somali
Sp. Spanish
Swa. Swahili
Swe. Swedish
T **Taj.** Tajik
Th. Thai
Tib. Tibetan
Turk. Turkish
Turkm. Turkmenistan
U **Uigh.** Uighur
Ukr. Ukrainian
Uzb. Uzbek
V **var.** variant
Vtn. Vietnamese
W **Wel.** Welsh
X **Xh.** Xhosa
Y **Yugo.** Yugoslavia

154

A

Aachen 72 A4 *Dut.* Aken, *Fr.* Aix-la-Chapelle; *anc.* Aquae Grani, Aquisgranum. Nordrhein-Westfalen, W Germany
Aaiún *see* Laâyoune
Aalborg 58 D3 *var.* Ålborg, Ålborg-Nørresundby; *anc.* Alburgum. Nordjylland, N Denmark
Aalen 73 B6 Baden-Württemberg, S Germany
Aalsmeer 64 C3 Noord-Holland, C Netherlands
Aalst 65 B6 *Fr.* Alost. Oost-Vlaanderen, C Belgium
Aalten 64 E4 Gelderland, E Netherlands
Aalter 65 B5 Oost-Vlaanderen, NW Belgium
Äänekoski 63 D5 Länsi-Suomi, W Finland
Aar *see* Aare
Aare 73 A7 *var.* Aar. *River* W Switzerland
Aarhus *see* Århus
Aat *see* Ath
Aba 53 G5 Abia, S Nigeria
Aba 55 E5 Orientale, NE Dem. Rep. Congo
Abā as Su'ūd *see* Najrān
Abaco Island *see* Great Abaco
Ābādān 98 C4 Khūzestān, SW Iran
Abai *see* Blue Nile
Abakan 92 D4 Respublika Khakasiya, S Russian Federation
Abancay 38 D4 Apurímac, SE Peru
Abariringa *see* Kanton
Abashiri 108 D2 *var.* Abasiri. Hokkaidō, NE Japan
Abasiri *see* Abashiri
Ābaya Hāyk' 51 C5 *Eng.* Lake Margherita, *It.* Abbaia. *Lake* SW Ethiopia
Ābay Wenz *see* Blue Nile
Abbeville 68 C2 *anc.* Abbatis Villa. Somme, N France
Abbeville 20 B3 *var.* Abécher, Abeshr. Ouaddaï, SE Chad
'Abd al 'Azīz, Jabal 96 D2 *mountain range* NE Syria
Abéché 54 C3 *var.* Abécher, Abeshr. Ouaddaï, SE Chad
Abécher *see* Abéché
Abela *see* Ávila
Abemama 122 D2 *var.* Apamama; *prev.* Roger Simpson Island. *Atoll* Tungaru, W Kiribati
Abengourou 53 E5 E Côte d'Ivoire
Aberdeen 66 D3 *anc.* Devana. NE Scotland, UK
Aberdeen 23 E2 South Dakota, C USA
Aberdeen 24 B2 Washington, NW USA
Abergwaun *see* Fishguard
Abertawe *see* Swansea
Aberystwyth 67 C6 W Wales, UK
Abeshr *see* Abéché
Abhā 99 B6 'Asīr, SW Saudi Arabia
Abidavichy 85 D7 *Rus.* Obidovichi. Mahilyowskaya Voblasts', E Belarus
Abidjan 53 E5 S Côte d'Ivoire
Abilene 27 F3 Texas, SW USA
Abingdon *see* Pinta, Isla
Abkhazia 95 E1 *autonomous republic* NW Georgia
Åbo 85 D6 Länsi-Suomi, W Finland
Aboisso 53 E5 SE Côte d'Ivoire
Abo, Massif d' 54 B1 *mountain range* NW Chad
Abomey 53 F5 S Benin
Abou-Déïa 54 C3 Salamat, SE Chad
Abrantes 70 B3 *var.* Abrántes. Santarém, C Portugal
Abrolhos Bank 34 E4 *undersea feature* W Atlantic Ocean
Abrova 85 B6 *Rus.* Obrovo. Brestskaya Voblasts', SW Belarus
Abrud 86 B4 *Ger.* Gross-Schlatten, *Hung.* Abrudbánya. Alba, SW Romania
Abruzzese, Appennino 74 C4 *mountain range* C Italy
Absaroka Range 22 B2 *mountain range* Montana/Wyoming, NW USA
Abū ad Duhūr 96 B3 *Fr.* Aboudouhour. Idlib, NW Syria
Abu Dhabi *see* Abū Ẓaby
Abu Hamed 50 C3 River Nile, N Sudan
Abū Ḥardān 96 E3 *var.* Hajine. Dayr az Zawr, E Syria
Abuja 53 G4 *country capital* (Nigeria) Federal Capital District, C Nigeria
Abū Kamāl 96 E3 *Fr.* Abou Kémal. Dayr az Zawr, E Syria
Abula *see* Ávila
Abunã, Rio 40 C2 *var.* Río Abuná. *River* Bolivia/Brazil
Abut Head 129 B6 *headland* South Island, NZ
Ābuyē Mēda 50 D4 *mountain* C Ethiopia
Abū Ẓabī *see* Abū Ẓaby
Abū Ẓaby 99 C5 *var.* Abū Ẓabī, *Eng.* Abu Dhabi. *Country capital* (UAE) Abū Ẓaby, C UAE
Abyla *see* Ávila
Acalayong 55 A5 SW Equatorial Guinea
Acaponeta 28 D4 Nayarit, C Mexico
Acapulco 29 E5 *var.* Acapulco de Juárez. Guerrero, S Mexico
Acapulco de Juárez *see* Acapulco
Acarai Mountains 37 F4 *Sp.* Serra Acaraí. *Mountain range* Brazil/Guyana
Acarigua 36 D2 Portuguesa, N Venezuela
Accra 53 E5 *country capital* (Ghana) SE Ghana
Achacachi 39 F4 La Paz, W Bolivia
Acklins Island 32 C2 *island* SE Bahamas
Aconcagua, Cerro 42 B4 *mountain* W Argentina

Açores *see* Azores
A Coruña 70 B1 *Cast.* La Coruña, *Eng.* Corunna; *anc.* Caronium. Galicia, NW Spain
Acre 40 C2 *off.* Estado do Acre. *State* W Brazil
Açu 41 G2 *var.* Assu. Rio Grande do Norte, E Brazil
Ada 27 G2 Oklahoma, C USA
Ada 78 D3 Serbia, N Serbia and Montenegro (Yugo.)
Adalia, Gulf of *see* Antalya Körfezi
Adama *see* Nazrēt
Adamawa Highlands 54 B4 *plateau* NW Cameroon
'Adan 99 B7 *Eng.* Aden. SW Yemen
Adana 94 D4 *var.* Seyhan. Adana, S Turkey
Adapazarı 94 B2 *prev.* Ada Bazar. Sakarya, NW Turkey
Adare, Cape 132 B4 *headland* Antarctica
Ad Dahnā 98 C4 *desert* E Saudi Arabia
Ad Dakhla 48 A4 *var.* Dakhla. SW Western Sahara
Ad Dalanj *see* Dilling
Ad Damar *see* Ed Damer
Ad Damazin *see* Ed Damazin
Ad Dāmir *see* Ed Damer
Ad Dammām 98 C4 *var.* Dammām. Ash Sharqīyah, NE Saudi Arabia
Ad Dāmūr *see* Damoûr
Ad Dawḥah 98 C4 *Eng.* Doha. *Country capital* (Qatar) C Qatar
Ad Diffah *see* Libyan Plateau
Addis Ababa *see* Ādīs Ābeba
Addu Atoll 110 A5 *atoll* S Maldives
Adelaide 127 B6 *state capital* South Australia
Aden *see* 'Adan
Aden, Gulf of 99 C7 *gulf* SW Arabian Sea
Adige 74 C2 *Ger.* Etsch. *River* N Italy
Adirondack Mountains 19 F2 *mountain range* New York, NE USA
Adıyaman 95 E4 Adıyaman, SE Turkey
Adjud 86 C4 Vrancea, E Romania
Admiralty Islands 122 B3 *island group* N PNG
Adra 71 E4 Andalucía, S Spain
Adrar 48 D3 C Algeria
Adrar des Iforas *see* Ifôghas, Adrar des
Adrian 18 C3 Michigan, N USA
Adriatic Sea 81 E2 *Alb.* Deti Adriatik, *It.* Mare Adriatico, *SCr.* Jadransko More, *Slvn.* Jadransko Morje. *Sea* N Mediterranean Sea
Adycha 93 F2 *river* NE Russian Federation
Aegean Sea 83 C5 *Gk.* Aigaíon Pélagos, Aigaío Pélagos, *Turk.* Ege Denizi. *Sea* NE Mediterranean Sea
Aegviidu 84 D2 *Ger.* Charlottenhof. Harjumaa, NW Estonia
Aelana *see* Al 'Aqabah
Aelok *see* Ailuk Atoll
Aelönlaplap *see* Ailinglaplap Atoll
Aeolian Islands *see* Eolie, Isole
Afar Depression 87 F4 Zaporiz'ka Oblast', S Ukraine
Afghanistan 100 D4 *off.* Dowlat-e Eslāmī-ye Afghānestān; *prev.* Republic of Afghanistan. *Country* C Asia
Afmadow 51 D6 Jubbada Hoose, S Somalia
Africa 46 *continent*
Africa, Horn of 46 E4 *physical region* Ethiopia/Somalia
Africana Seamount 119 A6 *undersea feature* SW Indian Ocean
'Afrīn 96 B2 Ḥalab, N Syria
Afyon 94 B3 *prev.* Afyonkarahisar. Afyon, W Turkey
Agadez 53 G3 *prev.* Agadès. Agadez, C Niger
Agadir 48 B3 SW Morocco
Agana/Agaña *see* Hagåtña
Āgaro 51 C5 C Ethiopia
Agassiz Fracture Zone 121 G5 *tectonic feature* S Pacific Ocean
Agathónisi 83 D6 *island* Dodekánisos, Greece, Aegean Sea
Agde 69 C6 *anc.* Agatha. Hérault, S France
Agedabia *see* Ajdābiyā
Agen 69 B5 *anc.* Aginnum. Lot-et-Garonne, SW France
Aghri Dagh *see* Büyükağrı Dağı
Agiá 82 B4 *var.* Ayiá. Thessalía, C Greece
Agialoúsa 80 D4 *var.* Yenierenköy. NE Cyprus
Agía Marína 83 E6 Léros, Dodekánisos, Greece, Aegean Sea
Ágios Nikólaos 83 D8 *var.* Áyios Nikólaos. Kríti, Greece, E Mediterranean Sea
Āgra 112 D3 Uttar Pradesh, N India
Agram *see* Zagreb
Ağrı 95 F3 *var.* Karaköse; *prev.* Karakılısse. Ağrı, NE Turkey
Agri Dagi *see* Büyükağrı Dağı
Agrigento 75 C7 *Gk.* Akragas; *prev.* Girgenti. Sicilia, Italy, C Mediterranean Sea
Agriovótano 83 C5 Évvoia, C Greece
Agropoli 75 D5 Campania, S Italy
Aguachica 36 B2 Cesar, N Colombia
Aguadulce 31 F5 Coclé, S Panama
Agua Prieta 28 B1 Sonora, NW Mexico
Aguascalientes 28 D4 Aguascalientes, C Mexico
Aguaytía 38 C3 Ucayali, C Peru
Aguilas 71 E4 Murcia, SE Spain
Aguililla 28 D4 Michoacán de Ocampo, SW Mexico
Agulhas Basin 47 D8 *undersea feature* SW Indian Ocean

Agulhas Plateau 45 D6 *undersea feature* SW Indian Ocean
Ahaggar 53 F2 *high plateau region* SE Algeria
Ahlen 72 B4 Nordrhein-Westfalen, W Germany
Ahmadābād 112 C4 *var.* Ahmedabad. Gujarāt, W India
Ahmadnagar 112 C5 *var.* Ahmednagar. Mahārāshtra, W India
Ahmedabad *see* Ahmadābād
Ahmednagar *see* Ahmadnagar
Ahuachapán 30 B3 Ahuachapán, W El Salvador
Ahvāz 98 C3 *var.* Ahwāz; *prev.* Nāsiri. Khūzestān, SW Iran
Ahvenanmaa *see* Åland
Ahwāz *see* Ahvāz
Aïdin *see* Aydın
Aígina 83 C6 *var.* Aíyina, Egina. Aígina, C Greece
Aígio 83 B5 *var.* Egio; *prev.* Aíyion. Dytikí Ellás, S Greece
Ailigandí 31 G4 San Blas, NE Panama
Ailinglaplap Atoll 122 D2 *var.* Aelönlaplap. *Atoll* Ralik Chain, S Marshall Islands
Ailuk Atoll 122 D1 *var.* Aelok. *Atoll* Ratak Chain, NE Marshall Islands
Ainaži 84 D3 *Est.* Heinaste, *Ger.* Hainasch. Limbaži, N Latvia
'Aïn Ben Tili 52 D1 Tiris Zemmour, N Mauritania
Aintab *see* Gaziantep
Aïoun el Atrous *see* 'Ayoûn el 'Atroûs
Aïoun el Atroûss *see* 'Ayoûn el 'Atroûs
Aiquile 39 F4 Cochabamba, C Bolivia
Aïr *see* Aïr, Massif de l'
Air du Azbine *see* Aïr, Massif de l'
Aïr, Massif de l' 53 G2 *var.* Aïr, Air du Azbine, Asben. *Mountain range* NC Niger
Aiud 86 B4 *Ger.* Strassburg, *Hung.* Nagyenyed; *prev.* Engeten. Alba, SW Romania
Aix *see* Aix-en-Provence
Aix-en-Provence 69 D6 *var.* Aix; *anc.* Aquae Sextiae. Bouches-du-Rhône, SE France
Aíyina *see* Aígina
Aíyion *see* Aígio
Aizkraukle 84 C4 Aizkraukle, S Latvia
Ajaccio 69 E7 Corse, France, C Mediterranean Sea
Ajaria 95 F2 *autonomous republic* SW Georgia
Aj Bogd Uul 104 D2 *mountain* SW Mongolia
Ajdābiyā 49 G2 *var.* Agedabia, Ajdābiyah. NE Libya
Ajdābiyah *see* Ajdābiyā
Ajjinena *see* El Geneina
Ajmer 112 D3 *var.* Ajmere. Rājasthān, N India
Ajmere *see* Ajmer
Ajo 26 A3 Arizona, SW USA
Akaba *see* Al 'Aqabah
Akamagaseki *see* Shimonoseki
Akasha 50 B3 Northern, N Sudan
Akchâr 52 C2 *desert* W Mauritania
Akhalts'ikhe 95 F2 SW Georgia
Akhisar 94 A3 Manisa, W Turkey
Akhmīm 50 B2 *anc.* Panopolis. C Egypt
Akhtubinsk 89 C7 Astrakhanskaya Oblast', SW Russian Federation
Akimiski Island 16 C3 *island* Northwest Territories, C Canada
Akita 108 D4 Akita, Honshū, C Japan
Akjoujt 52 C2 *prev.* Fort-Repoux. Inchiri, W Mauritania
Akkeshi 108 E2 Hokkaidō, NE Japan
Aklavik 14 D3 Northwest Territories, NW Canada
Akmola *see* Astana
Akpatok Island 17 E1 *island* Northwest Territories, E Canada
Akra Dhrepanon *see* Drépano, Akrotírio
Akra Kanestron *see* Palioúri, Akrotírio
Akron 18 D4 Ohio, N USA
Akrotiri *see* Akrotírion
Akrotírion 80 C5 *var.* Akrotiri. *UK air base* S Cyprus
Aksai Chin 102 B2 *Chin.* Aksayqin. *Disputed region* China/India
Aksaray 94 C4 Aksaray, C Turkey
Akşehir 94 B4 Konya, W Turkey
Aktau 92 A4 *Kaz.* Aqtaū; *prev.* Shevchenko. Mangistau, W Kazakhstan
Aktobe 92 B4 *Kaz.* Aqtöbe. *prev.* Aktyubinsk. Aktyubinsk, NW Kazakhstan
Aktsyabrski 85 C7 *Rus.* Oktyabr'skiy; *prev.* Karpilovka. Homyel'skaya Voblasts', SE Belarus
Aktyubinsk *see* Aktobe
Akula 55 C5 Equateur, NW Dem. Rep. Congo
Akureyri 61 E4 Nordhurland Eystra, N Iceland
Akyab *see* Sittwe
Alabama 29 G1 *off.* State of Alabama; also known as Camellia State, Heart of Dixie, The Cotton State, Yellowhammer State. *State* S USA
Alabama River 20 C3 *river* Alabama, S USA
Alaca 94 C3 Çorum, N Turkey
Alacant *see* Alicante
Alagoas 41 G2 *off.* Estado de Alagoas. *State* E Brazil
Alajuela 31 E4 Alajuela, C Costa Rica
Alakanuk 14 C2 Alaska, USA
Al 'Alamayn *see* El 'Alamein
Al 'Amārah 98 C3 *var.* Amara. E Iraq
Alamo 25 D6 Nevada, W USA
Alamogordo 26 D3 New Mexico, SW USA
Alamosa 22 D5 Colorado, C USA
Åland 63 C6 *var.* Aland Islands, *Fin.* Ahvenanmaa. *Island group* SW Finland
Aland Islands *see* Åland
Aland Sea *see* Ålands Hav
Ålands Hav 63 C6 *var.* Aland Sea. *Strait* Baltic Sea/Gulf of Bothnia

Alanya 94 C4 Antalya, S Turkey
Alappuzha *see* Alleppey
Al 'Aqabah 97 B8 *var.* Akaba, Aqaba, 'Aqaba; *anc.* Aelana, Elath. Ma'ān, SW Jordan
Alasca, Golfo de *see* Alaska, Gulf of
Alaşehir 94 A4 Manisa, W Turkey
Al 'Asharah 96 E3 *var.* Ashara. Dayr az Zawr, E Syria
Alaska 14 C3 *off.* State of Alaska; also known as Land of the Midnight Sun, The Last Frontier, Seward's Folly; *prev.* Russian America. *State* NW USA
Alaska, Gulf of 14 C4 *var.* Golfo de Alasca. *Gulf* Canada/USA
Alaska Peninsula 14 C3 *peninsula* Alaska, USA
Alaska Range 12 B2 *mountain range* Alaska, USA
Al-Asnam *see* Chlef
Al Awaynāt *see* Al 'Uwaynāt
Al 'Aynā 97 B7 Al Karak, W Jordan
Alazeya 93 G2 *river* NE Russian Federation
Al Bāb 96 B2 Ḥalab, N Syria
Albacete 71 E3 Castilla-La Mancha, C Spain
Al Baghdādī 98 B3 *var.* Khān al Baghdādī. SW Iraq
Al Bāha *see* Al Bāḩah
Al Bāḩah 99 B5 *var.* Al Bāha. Al Bāḩah, SW Saudi Arabia
Al Bahr al Mayyit *see* Dead Sea
Alba Iulia 86 B4 *Ger.* Weissenburg, *Hung.* Gyulafehérvár; *prev.* Bălgrad, Karlsburg, Károly-Fehérvár. Alba, W Romania
Albania 79 C7 *Alb.* Republika e Shqipërisë, Shqipëria; *prev.* People's Socialist Republic of Albania. *Country* SE Europe
Albany 16 C3 *river* Ontario, S Canada
Albany 19 F3 *state capital* New York, NE USA
Albany 20 D3 Georgia, SE USA
Albany 24 B3 Oregon, NW USA
Albany 125 B7 Western Australia
Al Bāridah 96 C4 *var.* Bāridah. Ḥimṣ, C Syria
Al Başrah 98 C3 *Eng.* Basra; *hist.* Busra, Bussora. SE Iraq
Al Batrūn *see* Batroûn
Al Baydā' 49 G2 *var.* Beida. NE Libya
Albemarle Island *see* Isabela, Isla
Albemarle Sound 21 G1 *inlet* W Atlantic Ocean
Albergaria-a-Velha 70 B2 Aveiro, N Portugal
Albert 68 C3 Somme, N France
Alberta 15 E4 *province* SW Canada
Albert Edward Nyanza *see* Edward, Lake
Albert, Lake 51 B6 *var.* Albert Nyanza, Lac Mobutu Sese Seko. *Lake* Uganda/Dem. Rep. Congo
Albert Lea 23 F3 Minnesota, N USA
Albert Nyanza *see* Albert, Lake
Albi 69 C6 *anc.* Albiga. Tarn, S France
Ålborg *see* Aalborg
Ålborg-Nørresundby *see* Aalborg
Alborz, Reshteh-ye Kūhhā-ye 98 C2 *Eng.* Elburz Mountains. *Mountain range* N Iran
Albuquerque 26 D2 New Mexico, SW USA
Al Burayqah *see* Marsá al Burayqah
Alburgum *see* Aalborg
Albury 127 C7 New South Wales, SE Australia
Alcácer do Sal 70 B4 Setúbal, W Portugal
Alcalá de Henares 71 E3 *Ar.* Alkal'a; *anc.* Complutum. Madrid, C Spain
Alcamo 75 C7 Sicilia, Italy, C Mediterranean Sea
Alcañiz 71 F2 Aragón, NE Spain
Alcántara, Embalse de 70 C3 *reservoir* W Spain
Alcaudete 92 D4 Andalucía, S Spain
Alcázar *see* Ksar-el-Kebir
Alcoi *see* Alcoy
Alcoy 71 F4 *var.* Alcoi. País Valenciano, E Spain
Aldabra Group 57 G2 *island group* SW Seychelles
Aldan 93 F3 *river* NE Russian Federation
al Dar al Baida *see* Rabat
Alderney 68 A2 *island* Channel Islands
Aleg 52 C3 Brakna, SW Mauritania
Aleksandropol' *see* Gyumri
Aleksin 89 B5 Tul'skaya Oblast', W Russian Federation
Aleksinac 78 E4 Serbia, SE Serbia and Montenegro (Yugo.)
Alençon 68 B3 Orne, N France
Alenquer 41 E2 Pará, N Brazil
Aleppo *see* Ḥalab
Alert 15 F1 Ellesmere Island, Nunavut, N Canada
Alès 69 C6 *prev.* Alais. Gard, S France
Aleşd 86 B3 *Hung.* Élesd. Bihor, SW Romania
Alessandria 74 B2 *Fr.* Alexandrie. Piemonte, N Italy
Ålesund 63 A5 Møre og Romsdal, S Norway
Aleutian Basin 91 G3 *undersea feature* Bering Sea
Aleutian Islands 14 A3 *island group* Alaska, USA
Aleutian Range 12 A2 *mountain range* Alaska, USA
Aleutian Trench 91 H3 *undersea feature* S Bering Sea
Alexander Archipelago 14 D4 *island group* Alaska, USA
Alexander City 20 D2 Alabama, S USA
Alexander Island 132 A3 *island* Antarctica
Alexándreia 82 B4 *var.* Alexándria. Kentrikí Makedonía, N Greece
Alexandria 50 B1 *Ar.* Al Iskandarīyah. N Egypt
Alexándria *see* Alexándreia
Alexandria 20 B3 Louisiana, S USA
Alexandria 23 F2 Minnesota, N USA
Alexandria 86 C5 Teleorman, S Romania

Alexandroúpoli – Arabian Basin

Alexandroúpoli *82 D3 var.* Alexandroúpolis, *Turk.* Dedeagaç, Dedeagach. Anatolikí Makedonía kai Thráki, NE Greece
Alexandroúpolis *see* Alexandroúpoli
Al Fāshir *see* El Fasher
Alfatar *82 E1* Silistra, NE Bulgaria
Alfeiós *83 B6 prev.* Alfiós, *anc.* Alpheius, Alpheus. *River* S Greece
Alföld *see* Great Hungarian Plain
Alga *92 B4 Kaz.* Algha. Aktyubinsk, NW Kazakhstan
Algarve *70 B4 cultural region* S Portugal
Algeciras *70 C5* Andalucía, SW Spain
Algemesí *71 F3* País Valenciano, E Spain
Al-Genain *see* El Geneina
Alger *49 E1 var.* Algiers, El Djazaïr, Al Jazair. *Country capital* (Algeria) N Algeria
Algeria *48 C3 Country* N Africa
Algerian Basin *58 C5 var.* Balearic Plain *undersea feature* W Mediterranean Sea
Al Ghābah *99 E5 var.* Ghaba. C Oman
Alghero *75 A5* Sardegna, Italy, C Mediterranean Sea
Al Ghurdaqah *see* Hurghada
Algiers *see* Alger
Al Golea *see* El Goléa
Algona *23 F3* Iowa, C USA
Al Ḥajār al Gharbī *99 D5 mountain range* N Oman
Al Ḥasakah *96 D2 var.* Al Hasijah, El Haseke, *Fr.* Hassetché. Al Ḥasakah, NE Syria
Al Hasijah *see* Al Ḥasakah
Al Ḥillah *98 B3 var.* Hilla. C Iraq
Al Ḥisā *97 B7* Aṭ Ṭafīlah, W Jordan
Al Ḥudaydah *99 B6 Eng.* Hodeida. W Yemen
Al Hufūf *98 C4 var.* Hofuf. Ash Sharqīyah, NE Saudi Arabia
Aliákmonas *82 B4 prev.* Aliákmon, *anc.* Haliacmon. *River* N Greece
Alíartos *83 C5* Stereá Ellás, C Greece
Alicante *71 F4 Cat.* Alacant;. País Valenciano, SE Spain
Alice *27 G5* Texas, SW USA
Alice Springs *126 A4* Northern Territory, C Australia
Aliki *see* Alykí
Alima *55 B6 river* C Congo
Alindao *54 C4* Basse-Kotto, S Central African Republic
Aliquippa *18 D4* Pennsylvania, NE USA
Alistráti *82 C3* Kentrikí Makedonía, NE Greece
Alivéri *83 C5 var.* Alivérion. Évvoia, C Greece
Alivérion *see* Alivéri
Al Jabal al Akhḍar *49 G2 mountain range* NE Libya
Al Jabal ash Sharqī *see* Anti-Lebanon
Al Jafr *97 B7* Ma'ān, S Jordan
Al Jaghbūb *49 H3* NE Libya
Al Jahrā' *98 C4 var.* Al Jahrah, Jahra. C Kuwait
Al Jahrah *see* Al Jahrā'
Al Jawf *98 B4 var.* Jauf. Al Jawf, NW Saudi Arabia
Al Jazair *see* Alger
Al Jazīrah *96 E2 physical region* Iraq/Syria
Al Jīzah *see* El Giza
Al Junaynah *see* El Geneina
Al Karak *97 B7 var.* El Kerak, Karak, Kerak; *anc.* Kir Moab, Kir of Moab. Al Karak, W Jordan
Al-Kasr al-Kebir *see* Ksar-el-Kebir
Al Khalīl *see* Hebron
Al Khārijah *see* El Khârga
Al Khufrah *49 H4* SE Libya
Al Khums *49 F2 var.* Homs, Khoms, Khums. NW Libya
Alkmaar *64 C2* Noord-Holland, NW Netherlands
Al Kūt *98 C3 var.* Kūt al 'Amārah, Kut al Imara. E Iraq
Al-Kuwait *see* Al Kuwayt
Al Kuwayt *98 C4 var.* Al-Kuwait, *Eng.* Kuwait, Kuwait City; *prev.* Qurein. *Country capital* (Kuwait) E Kuwait
Al Lādhiqīyah *96 A3 Eng.* Latakia, *Fr.* Lattaquié; *anc.* Laodicea, Laodicea ad Mare. Al Lādhiqīyah, W Syria
Allahābād *113 E3* Uttar Pradesh, N India
Allanmyo *114 B4* Magwe, C Myanmar
Allegheny Plateau *19 E3 mountain range* New York/Pennsylvania, NE USA
Allentown *19 F4* Pennsylvania, NE USA
Alleppey *110 C3 var.* Alappuzha; *prev.* Alleppi. Kerala, SW India
Alleppi *see* Alleppey
Alliance *22 D3* Nebraska, C USA
Al Līth *99 B5* Makkah, SW Saudi Arabia
Alma-Ata *see* Almaty
Almada *70 B4* Setúbal, W Portugal
Al Madīnah *99 A5 Eng.* Medina. Al Madīnah, W Saudi Arabia
Al Mafraq *97 B6 var.* Mafraq. Al Mafraq, N Jordan
Al Mahdīyah *see* Mahdia
Al Mahrah *99 C6 mountain range* E Yemen
Al Majma'ah *98 B4* Ar Riyāḍ, C Saudi Arabia
Al Mālikīyah *96 E1* Al Ḥasakah, NE Syria
Al Manāmah *98 C4 Eng.* Manama. *Country capital* (Bahrain) N Bahrain
Al Manāṣif *96 E3 mountain range* E Syria
Almansa *71 F4* Castilla-La Mancha, C Spain
Al Marj *49 G2 var.* Barka, *It.* Barce. NE Libya
Almaty *92 C5 var.* Alma-Ata. Almaty, SE Kazakhstan
Al Mawṣil *98 B2 Eng.* Mosul. N Iraq
Al Mayādīn *96 D3 var.* Mayadin, *Fr.* Meyadine. Dayr az Zawr, E Syria
Al Mazra' *see* Al Mazra'ah
Al Mazra'ah *97 B6 var.* Al Mazra', Mazra'a. Al Karak, W Jordan
Almelo *64 E3* Overijssel, E Netherlands
Almendra, Embalse de *70 C2 reservoir* Castilla-León, NW Spain
Almendralejo *70 C4* Extremadura, W Spain
Almere *64 C3 var.* Almere-stad. Flevoland, C Netherlands
Almere-stad *see* Almere
Almería *71 E5 Ar.* Al-Mariyya; *anc.* Unci, *Lat.* Portus Magnus. Andalucía, S Spain
Al'met'yevsk *89 D5* Respublika Tatarstan, W Russian Federation
Al Mīnā' *see* El Mina
Al Minyā *see* El Minya
Almirante *31 E4* Bocas del Toro, NW Panama
Al Mudawwarah *97 B8* Ma'ān, SW Jordan
Al Mukallā *99 C6 var.* Mukalla. SE Yemen
Al Obayyid *see* El Obeid
Alofi *123 F4 dependent territory capital* (Niue) W Niue
Aloja *84 D3* Limbaži, N Latvia
Alónnisos *83 C5 island* Vóreioi Sporádes, Greece, Aegean Sea
Álora *70 D5* Andalucía, S Spain
Alor, Kepulauan *117 E5 island group* E Indonesia
Al Oued *see* El Oued
Alpen *see* Alps
Alpena *18 D2* Michigan, N USA
Alpes *see* Alps
Alpha Cordillera *133 B3 var.* Alpha Ridge. *Undersea feature* Arctic Ocean
Alpha Ridge *see* Alpha Cordillera
Alphen *see* Alphen aan den Rijn
Alphen aan den Rijn *64 C3 var.* Alphen. Zuid-Holland, C Netherlands
Alpi *see* Alps
Alpine *27 E4* Texas, SW USA
Alpi Transilvaniei *see* Carpații Meridionali
Alps *80 C1 Fr.* Alpes, *Ger.* Alpen, *It.* Alpi. *Mountain range* C Europe
Al Qaḍārif *see* Gedaref
Al Qāmishlī *96 E1 var.* Kamishli, Qamishly. Al Ḥasakah, NE Syria
Al Qaṣrayn *see* Kasserine
Al Qayrawān *see* Kairouan
Al-Qsar *see* Ksar-el-Kebir
Al Qubayyāt *see* Qoubaïyât
Alqueva, Barragem do *70 C4 reservoir* S Portugal
Al Qunayṭirah *97 B5 var.* El Kuneitra, El Quneitra, Kuneitra, Qunaytra. Al Qunayṭirah, SW Syria
Al Quṣayr *96 B4 var.* El Quseir, Quṣayr, *Fr.* Kousseir. Ḥimṣ, W Syria
Al Quwayrah *97 B8 var.* El Quweira. Ma'ān, SW Jordan
Alsace *68 E3 cultural region* NE France
Alsdorf *72 A4* Nordrhein-Westfalen, W Germany
Alt *see* Olt
Alta *62 D2 Fin.* Alattio. Finnmark, N Norway
Altai *see* Altai Mountains
Altai Mountains *104 C2 var.* Altai, *Chin.* Altay Shan, *Rus.* Altay. *Mountain range* Asia/Europe
Altamaha River *21 E3 river* Georgia, SE USA
Altamira *41 E2* Pará, NE Brazil
Altamura *75 E5 anc.* Lupatia. Puglia, SE Italy
Altar, Desierto de *28 A1 var.* Sonoran Desert. *Desert* Mexico/USA *see also* Sonoran Desert
Altay *104 C2 Chin.* A-le-t'ai, *Mong.* Sharasume; *prev.* Ch'eng-hua, Chenghwa. Xinjiang Uygur Zizhiqu, NW China
Altay *see* Altai Mountains
Altay *104 D2* Govĭ-Altay, W Mongolia
Altay Shan *see* Altai Mountains
Altin Köprü *98 B3 var.* Altun Kupri. N Iraq
Altiplano *39 F4 physical region* W South America
Alton *18 B5* Illinois, N USA
Alton *18 B4* Missouri, C USA
Altoona *19 E4* Pennsylvania, NE USA
Alto Paraná *see* Paraná
Altun Kupri *see* Altin Köprü
Altun Shan *104 C3 var.* Altyn Tagh. *Mountain range* NW China
Altus *27 F2* Oklahoma, C USA
Altyn Tagh *see* Altun Shan
Al Ubayyiḍ *see* El Obeid
Alūksne *84 D3 Ger.* Marienburg. Alūksne, NE Latvia
Al 'Ulā *98 A4* Al Madīnah, NW Saudi Arabia
Al 'Umarī *97 C6* 'Ammān, E Jordan
Alupka *87 F5* Respublika Krym, S Ukraine
Alushta *87 F5* Respublika Krym, S Ukraine
Al 'Uwaynāt *49 F4 var.* Al Awaynāt. SW Libya
Alva *27 F1* Oklahoma, C USA
Alvarado *29 F4* Veracruz-Llave, E Mexico
Alvin *27 H4* Texas, SW USA
Al Wajh *98 A4* Tabūk, NW Saudi Arabia
Alwar *112 D3* Rājasthān, N India
Al Wari'ah *98 C4* Ash Sharqīyah, N Saudi Arabia
Alykí *82 C4 var.* Aliki. Thásos, N Greece
Alytus *85 B5 Pol.* Olita. Alytus, S Lithuania
Alzette *65 D8 river* S Luxembourg
Amadeus, Lake *125 D5 seasonal lake* Northern Territory, C Australia
Amadi *51 B5* Western Equatoria, SW Sudan
Amadjuak Lake *15 G3 lake* Baffin Island, Nunavut, N Canada
Amakusa-nada *109 A7 gulf* Kyūshū, SW Japan
Åmål *63 B6* Västra Götaland, S Sweden
Amami-guntō *108 A3 island group* SW Japan
Amami-ō-shima *108 A3 island* S Japan
Amantea *75 D6* Calabria, SW Italy
Amapá *41 E1* Amapá, NE Brazil
Amara *see* Al 'Amārah
Amarapura *114 B3* Mandalay, C Myanmar
Amarillo *27 E2* Texas, SW USA
Amay *65 C6* Liège, E Belgium
Amazon *41 E1 Sp.* Amazonas. *River* Brazil/Peru
Amazon Basin *40 D2 basin* N South America
Amazon, Mouths of the *41 F1 delta* NE Brazil
Ambam *55 B5* Sud, S Cameroon
Ambanja *57 G2* Antsirañana, N Madagascar
Ambarchik *93 G2* Respublika Sakha (Yakutiya), NE Russian Federation
Ambato *38 B1* Tungurahua, C Ecuador
Ambérieu-en-Bugey *69 D5* Ain, E France
Amboasary *57 F4* Toliara, S Madagascar
Ambon *117 F4 prev.* Amboina, Amboyna. Pulau Ambon, E Indonesia
Ambositra *57 G3* Fianarantsoa, SE Madagascar
Ambrim *see* Ambrym
Ambriz *56 A1* Bengo, NW Angola
Ambrym *122 D4 var.* Ambrim. *Island* C Vanuatu
Amchitka Island *14 A2 island* Aleutian Islands, Alaska, USA
Amdo *104 C5* Xizang Zizhiqu, W China
Ameland *64 D1 Fris.* It Amelân. *Island* Waddeneilanden, N Netherlands
America-Antarctica Ridge *45 C7 undersea feature* S Atlantic Ocean
American Falls Reservoir *24 E4 reservoir* Idaho, NW USA
American Samoa *123 E4 US unincorporated territory* W Polynesia
Amersfoort *64 D3* Utrecht, C Netherlands
Ames *23 F3* Iowa, C USA
Amfilochía *83 A5 var.* Amfilokhía. Dytikí Elláś, C Greece
Amfilokhía *see* Amfilochía
Amga *93 F3 river* NE Russian Federation
Amherst *17 F4* Nova Scotia, SE Canada
Amida *see* Diyarbakır
Amiens *68 C3 anc.* Ambianum, Samarobriva. Somme, N France
Amíndaion *see* Amýntaio
Amindeo *see* Amýntaio
Amīndīvi Islands *110 A2 island group* Lakshadweep, India, N Indian Ocean
Amirante Islands *57 G1 var.* Amirantes Group. *Island group* C Seychelles
Amirantes Group *see* Amirante Islands
Amistad Reservoir *27 F4 var.* Presa de la Amistad. *Reservoir* Mexico/USA
'Ammān *97 B6 var.* Amman; *anc.* Philadelphia, *Bibl.* Rabbah Ammon, Rabbath Ammon. *Country capital* (Jordan) 'Ammān, NW Jordan
Amman *see* 'Ammān
Ammassalik *60 D4 var.* Angmagssalik. S Greenland
Ammóchostos *80 D5 var.* Famagusta, Gazimağusa. E Cyprus
Āmol *98 D2 var.* Amul. Māzandarān, N Iran
Amorgós *83 D6 island* Kykládes, Greece, Aegean Sea
Amorgós *83 D6* Amorgós, Kykládes, Greece, Aegean Sea
Amos *16 D4* Québec, SE Canada
Amourj *52 D3* Hodh ech Chargui, SE Mauritania
Amoy *see* Xiamen
Ampato, Nevado *39 E4 mountain* S Peru
Amposta *93 F2* Cataluña, NE Spain
Amrāvati *112 D4 prev.* Amraoti. Mahārāshtra, C India
Amritsar *112 D2* Punjab, N India
Amstelveen *64 C3* Noord-Holland, C Netherlands
Amsterdam *64 C3 country capital* (Netherlands) Noord-Holland, C Netherlands
Amsterdam Island *119 C6 island* NE French Southern and Antarctic Territories
Am Timan *54 C3* Salamat, SE Chad
Amu Darya *100 D2 Rus.* Amudar'ya, *Taj.* Dar"yoi Amu, *Turkm.* Amyderya, *Uzb.* Amudaryo; *anc.* Oxus. *River* C Asia
Amu-Dar'ya *see* Amyderýa
Amul *see* Āmol
Amund Ringnes Island *15 F2 island* Nunavut, N Canada
Amundsen Basin *see* Fram Basin
Amundsen Gulf *15 E2 gulf* Northwest Territories, N Canada
Amundsen Plain *132 A4 undersea feature* S Pacific Ocean
Amundsen-Scott *132 B3 US research station* Antarctica
Amundsen Sea *132 A4 sea* S Pacific Ocean
Amuntai *116 D4 prev.* Amoentai. Borneo, C Indonesia
Amur *93 G4 Chin.* Heilong Jiang. *River* China/Russian Federation
Amvrosiyivka *87 H3 Rus.* Amvrosiyevka. Donets'ka Oblast', SE Ukraine
Amyderýa *101 E3 Rus.* Amu-Dar'ya. Lebapskiy Velayat, NE Turkmenistan
Amýntaio *82 B4 var.* Amindeo; *prev.* Amíndaion. Dytikí Makedonía, N Greece
Anabar *93 E2 river* NE Russian Federation
An Abhainn Mhór *see* Blackwater
Anaco *37 E2* Anzoátegui, NE Venezuela
Anaconda *22 B2* Montana, NW USA
Anacortes *24 B1* Washington, NW USA
Anadolu Dağları *see* Doğu Karadeniz Dağları
Anadyr' *93 G1 river* NE Russian Federation
Anadyr' *93 H1* Chukotskiy Avtonomnyy Okrug, NE Russian Federation
Anadyr, Gulf of *see* Anadyrskiy Zaliv
Anadyrskiy Zaliv *93 H1 Eng.* Gulf of Anadyr. *Gulf* NE Russian Federation
Anáfi *83 D7 anc.* Anaphe. *Island* Kykládes, Greece, Aegean Sea
'Ānah *see* 'Annah
Anaheim *24 E2* California, W USA
Anaiza *see* 'Unayzah
Analalava *57 G2* Mahajanga, NW Madagascar
Anamur *94 C5* İçel, S Turkey
Anantapur *110 C2* Andhra Pradesh, S India
Anápolis *41 F3* Goiás, C Brazil
Anār *98 D3* Kermān, C Iran
Anatolia *94 C4 plateau* C Turkey
Anatom *see* Aneityum
Añatuya *42 C3* Santiago del Estero, N Argentina
An Bhearú *see* Barrow
Anchorage *14 C3* Alaska, USA
Ancona *74 C3* Marche, C Italy
Ancud *43 B6 prev.* San Carlos de Ancud. Los Lagos, S Chile
Åndalsnes *63 A5* Møre og Romsdal, S Norway
Andalucía *70 D4 cultural region* S Spain
Andalusia *20 C3* Alabama, S USA
Andaman Islands *102 B4 island group* India, NE Indian Ocean
Andaman Sea *102 C4 sea* NE Indian Ocean
Andenne *65 C6* Namur, SE Belgium
Anderlues *65 B7* Hainaut, S Belgium
Anderson *18 C4* Indiana, N USA
Andes *42 B3 mountain range* W South America
Andhra Pradesh *113 E5 state* E India
Andijon *101 F2 Rus.* Andizhan. Andijon Wiloyati, E Uzbekistan
Andikíthira *see* Antikýthira
Andipaxi *see* Antípaxoi
Andípsara *see* Antípsara
Ándissa *see* Ántissa
Andkhvoy *100 D3* Fāryāb, N Afghanistan
Andorra *69 A7 Cat.* Valls d'Andorra, *Fr.* Vallée d'Andorre. *Country* SW Europe
Andorra *see* Andorra la Vella
Andorra la Vella *69 A8 var.* Andorra, *Fr.* Andorre la Vielle, *Sp.* Andorra la Vieja. *Country capital* (Andorra) C Andorra
Andorra la Vieja *see* Andorra la Vella
Andorre la Vielle *see* Andorra la Vella
Andover *67 D7* S England, UK
Andøya *62 C2 island* C Norway
Andreanof Islands *14 A3 island group* Aleutian Islands, Alaska, USA
Andrews *27 E3* Texas, SW USA
Andrew Tablemount *118 A4 var.* Gora Andryu. *Undersea feature* W Indian Ocean
Andria *75 D5* Puglia, SE Italy
An Droichead Nua *see* Newbridge
Ándros *83 C6 island* Kykládes, Greece, Aegean Sea
Ándros *83 D6* Ándros, Kykládes, Greece, Aegean Sea
Andros Island *32 B2 island* NW Bahamas
Andros Town *32 C1* Andros Island, NW Bahamas
Aneityum *122 D5 var.* Anatom; *prev.* Kéamu. *Island* S Vanuatu
Ānewetak *see* Enewetak Atoll
Angara *93 E4 river* C Russian Federation
Angarsk *93 E4* Irkutskaya Oblast', S Russian Federation
Ånge *63 C5* Västernorrland, C Sweden
Ángel de la Guarda, Isla *28 B2 island* NW Mexico
Angeles *117 E1 off.* Angeles City. Luzon, N Philippines
Angel Falls *see* Ángel, Salto
Ángel, Salto *37 E3 Eng.* Angel Falls. *Waterfall* E Venezuela
Ångermanälven *62 C4 river* N Sweden
Angermünde *72 D3* Brandenburg, NE Germany
Angers *68 B4 anc.* Juliomagus. Maine-et-Loire, NW France
Anglesey *67 C5 island* NW Wales, UK
Anglet *69 A6* Pyrénées-Atlantiques, SW France
Angleton *27 H4* Texas, SW USA
Angmagssalik *see* Ammassalik
Ang Nam Ngum *114 C4 lake* C Laos
Angola *56 B2 prev.* People's Republic of Angola, Portuguese West Africa. *Country* SW Africa
Angola Basin *47 B5 undersea feature* E Atlantic Ocean
Angostura, Presa de la *29 G5 reservoir* SE Mexico
Angoulême *69 B5 anc.* Iculisma. Charente, W France
Angoumois *69 B5 cultural region* W France
Angren *101 F2* Toshkent Wiloyati, E Uzbekistan
Anguilla *33 G3 UK dependent territory* E West Indies
Anguilla Cays *32 B2 islets* SW Bahamas
Anhui *106 C5 var.* Anhui Sheng, Anhwei, Wan. Admin. region *province* E China
Anhui Sheng *see* Anhui
Anhwei *see* Anhui
Anina *86 A4 Ger.* Steierdorf, *Hung.* Stájerlakanina; *prev.* Ştaierdorf-Anina, Steierdorf-Anina, Steyerlak-Anina. Caraş-Severin, SW Romania
Anjou *68 B4 cultural region* NW France
Anjouan *57 F2 var.* Nzwani, Johanna Island. *Island* SE Comoros
Ankara *94 C3 prev.* Angora, *anc.* Ancyra. *Country capital* (Turkey) Ankara, C Turkey
Ankeny *23 F3* Iowa, C USA
Anklam *72 D2* Mecklenburg-Vorpommern, NE Germany
Anykščiai *84 C4* Anykščiai, E Lithuania
An Longfort *see* Longford
An Mhuir Cheilteach *see* Celtic Sea
Annaba *49 E1 prev.* Bône. NE Algeria
An Nafūd *98 B4 desert* NW Saudi Arabia
'Annah *98 B3 var.* 'Ānah. NW Iraq
An Najaf *98 B3 var.* Najaf. S Iraq
Annamitique, Chaîne *114 D4 mountain range* C Laos
Annapolis *19 F4 state capital* Maryland, NE USA
Annapurna *113 E3 mountain* C Nepal
An Nāqūrah *see* En Nâqoûra
Ann Arbor *18 C3* Michigan, N USA
An Nāṣirīyah *98 C3 var.* Nasiriya. SE Iraq
Annecy *69 D5 anc.* Anneciacum. Haute-Savoie, E France
An Nīl al Azraq *see* Blue Nile
Anniston *20 D2* Alabama, S USA
Annotto Bay *32 B4* C Jamaica
An Ómaigh *see* Omagh
Anqing *106 D5* Anhui, E China
Anse La Raye *33 F1* NW Saint Lucia
Anshun *106 B6* Guizhou, S China
Ansongo *53 E3* Gao, E Mali
An Srath Bán *see* Strabane
Antakya *94 D4 anc.* Antioch, Antiochia. Hatay, S Turkey
Antalaha *57 G2* Antsirañana, NE Madagascar
Antalya *94 B4 prev.* Adalia, *anc.* Attaleia, *Bibl.* Attalia. Antalya, SW Turkey
Antalya, Gulf of *see* Antalya Körfezi
Antalya Körfezi *94 B4 var.* Gulf of Adalia, *Eng.* Gulf of Antalya. *Gulf* SW Turkey
Antananarivo *57 G3 prev.* Tananarive. *Country capital* (Madagascar) Antananarivo, C Madagascar
Antarctica *132 B3 continent*
Antarctic Peninsula *132 A2 peninsula* Antarctica
Antep *see* Gaziantep
Antequera *70 D5 anc.* Anticaria, Antiquaria. Andalucía, S Spain
Antequera *see* Oaxaca
Antibes *69 D6 anc.* Antipolis. Alpes-Maritimes, SE France
Anticosti, Île d' *17 F3 Eng.* Anticosti Island. *Island* Québec, E Canada
Antigua *33 G3 island* S Antigua and Barbuda, Leeward Islands
Antigua and Barbuda *33 G3 country* E West Indies
Antikýthira *83 B7 var.* Andikíthira. *Island* S Greece
Anti-Lebanon *96 B4 var.* Jebel esh Sharqi, *Ar.* Al Jabal ash Sharqī, *Fr.* Anti-Liban. *Mountain range* Lebanon/Syria
Anti-Liban *see* Anti-Lebanon
Antípaxoi *83 A5 var.* Andipaxi. *Island* Iónioi Nísoi, Greece, C Mediterranean Sea
Antipodes Islands *120 D5 island group,* S NZ
Antípsara *83 D5 var.* Andípsara. *Island* E Greece
Ántissa *83 D5 var.* Ándissa. Lésvos, E Greece
An tIúr *see* Newry
Antofagasta *42 B2* Antofagasta, N Chile
Antony *68 E2* Hauts-de-Seine, N France
Antserana *see* Antsirañana
An tSionainn *see* Shannon
Antsirañana *57 G2 var.* Antserana; *prev.* Antsirane, Diégo-Suarez. Antsirañana, N Madagascar
Antsirane *see* Antsirañana
Antsohihy *57 G2* Mahajanga, NW Madagascar
An-tung *see* Dandong
Antwerp *see* Antwerpen
Antwerpen *87 C5 Eng.* Antwerp, *Fr.* Anvers. Antwerpen, N Belgium
Anuradhapura *110 D3* North Central Province, C Sri Lanka
Anyang *106 C4* Henan, C China
A'nyêmaqên Shan *104 D4 mountain range* C China
Anzio *75 C5* Lazio, C Italy
Aomen *see* Macao
Aomori *108 D3* Aomori, Honshū, C Japan
Aóos *see* Vjosës, Lumi i
Aoraki *129 B6 prev.* Aorangi, Mount Cook. *Mountain* South Island, NZ
Aorangi *see* Aoraki
Aosta *74 A1 anc.* Augusta Praetoria. Valle d'Aosta, NW Italy
Ao Thai *see* Thailand, Gulf of
Aoukâr *52 D3 var.* Aouker. *Plateau* C Mauritania
Aouk, Bahr *54 C4 river* Central African Republic/Chad
Aouker *see* Aoukâr
Aozou *54 C1* Borkou-Ennedi-Tibesti, N Chad
Apalachee Bay *20 D3 bay* Florida, SE USA
Apalachicola River *20 D3 river* Florida, SE USA
Apamama *see* Abemama
Apaporis, Río *36 C4 river* Brazil/Colombia
Apatity *88 C2* Murmanskaya Oblast', NW Russian Federation
Ape *84 D3* Alūksne, NE Latvia
Apeldoorn *64 D3* Gelderland, E Netherlands
Apennines *see* Appennino
Āpia *123 F4 country capital* (Samoa) Upolu, SE Samoa
Apoera *37 G3* Sipaliwini, NW Suriname
Apostle Islands *18 B1 island group* Wisconsin, N USA
Appalachian Mountains *13 D5 mountain range* E USA
Appennino *74 E2 Eng.* Apennines. *Mountain range* Italy/San Marino
Appingedam *64 E1* Groningen, NE Netherlands
Appleton *18 B2* Wisconsin, N USA
Apure, Río *36 C2 river* W Venezuela
Apurímac, Río *38 D3 river* S Peru
Apuseni, Munții *86 A4 mountain range* W Romania
'Aqaba *see* Al 'Aqabah
Aqaba, Gulf of *98 A4 var.* Gulf of Elat, *Ar.* Khalīj al 'Aqabah; *anc.* Sinus Aelaniticus. *Gulf* NE Red Sea
Āqchah *101 E3 var.* Āqcheh. Jowzjān, N Afghanistan
Āqcheh *see* Āqchah
Aquae Augustae *see* Dax
Aquae Sextiae *see* Aix-en-Provence
Aquae Tarbelicae *see* Dax
Aquidauana *41 E4* Mato Grosso do Sul, S Brazil
Aquila *see* L'Aquila
Aquila degli Abruzzo *see* L'Aquila
Aquitaine *69 B6 cultural region* SW France
'Arabah, Wādī al *135 B7 Heb.* Ha'Arava. *Dry watercourse* Israel/Jordan
Arabian Basin *102 A4 undersea feature* N Arabian Sea

Arabian Desert *see* Eastern Desert
Arabian Peninsula *99 B5 peninsula* SW Asia
Arabian Sea *102 A3 sea* NW Indian Ocean
Aracaju *41 G5 state capital* Sergipe, E Brazil
Araçuaí *41 F3* Minas Gerais, SE Brazil
Arad *86 A4* Arad, W Romania
'Arad *97 B7* Southern, S Israel
Arafura Sea *120 A3 Ind.* Laut Arafuru. *Sea* W Pacific Ocean
Aragón *93 E2 cultural region* E Spain
Araguaia, Río *41 E3 var.* Araguaya. *River* C Brazil
Araguari *41 F3* Minas Gerais, SE Brazil
Araguaya *see* Araguaia, Río
Arāk *98 C3 prev.* Sultānābād. Markazī, W Iran
Arakan Yoma *114 A3 mountain range* W Myanmar
Aral Sea *100 C1 Kaz.* Aral Tengizi, *Rus.* Aral'skoye More, *Uzb.* Orol Dengizi. *Inland sea* Kazakhstan/Uzbekistan
Aral'sk *92 B4 Kaz.* Aral. Kyzylorda, SW Kazakhstan
Aranda de Duero *70 D2* Castilla-León, N Spain
Arandelovac *78 D4 prev.* Arandjelovac. Serbia, C Serbia and Montenegro (Yugo.)
Aranjuez *70 D3 anc.* Ara Jovis. Madrid, C Spain
Araouane *53 E2* Tombouctou, N Mali
'Ar'ar *98 B3* Al Ḥudūd ash Shamālīyah, NW Saudi Arabia
Aras *95 G3 Arm.* Arak's, *Az.* Araz Nehri, *Per.* Rūd-e Aras, *Rus.* Araks; *prev.* Araxes. *River* SW Asia
Arauca *36 C2* Arauca, NE Colombia
Arauca, Río *36 C2 river* Colombia/Venezuela
Arbela *see* Arbīl
Arbīl *98 B2 var.* Erbil, Irbīl, *Kurd.* Hawlēr; *anc.* Arbela. N Iraq
Arbroath *66 D3 anc.* Aberbrothock. E Scotland, UK
Arbyzynka *87 E3 Rus.* Arbuzinka. Mykolayivs'ka Oblast', S Ukraine
Arcachon *69 B5* Gironde, SW France
Arcata *24 A4* California, W USA
Archangel *see* Arkhangel'sk
Archangel Bay *see* Chëshskaya Guba
Archidona *70 D5* Andalucía, S Spain
Archipel des Australes *see* Australes, Îles
Archipel des Tuamotu *see* Tuamotu, Îles
Archipel de Tahiti *see* Société, Archipel de la
Arco *74 C2* Trentino-Alto Adige, N Italy
Arctic-Mid Oceanic Ridge *see* Nansen Cordillera
Arctic Ocean *172 B3 ocean*
Arda *82 C3 var.* Ardhas, *Gk.* Ardas. *River* Bulgaria/Greece *see also* Ardas
Arda *see* Ardas
Ardabīl *98 C2 var.* Ardebil. Ardabīl, NW Iran
Ardakān *98 D3* Yazd, C Iran
Ardas *82 D3 var.* Ardhas, *Bul.* Arda. *River* Bulgaria/Greece *see also* Arda
Ardas *see* Arda
Arḍ aş Şawwān *97 C7 var.* Ardh es Suwwān. *Plain* S Jordan
Ardebil *see* Ardabīl
Ardèche *69 C5 cultural region* E France
Ardennes *65 C8 plateau* W Europe
Ardhas *see* Ardas
Ardh es Suwwān *see* Arḍ aş Şawwān
Ardino *82 D3* Kūrdzhali, S Bulgaria
Ard Mhacha *see* Armagh
Ardmore *27 G2* Oklahoma, C USA
Arelas *see* Arles
Arelate *see* Arles
Arendal *63 A6* Aust-Agder, S Norway
Arenys de Mar *71 G2* Cataluña, NE Spain
Areópoli *83 B7 prev.* Areópolis. Pelopónnisos, S Greece
Arequipa *39 E4* Arequipa, SE Peru
Arezzo *74 C3 anc.* Arretium. Toscana, C Italy
Argalastí *83 C5* Thessalía, C Greece
Argentina *43 B5 Country* S South America
Argentina Basin *see* Argentine Basin
Argentine Basin *35 C7 var.* Argentina Basin. *Undersea feature* SW Atlantic Ocean
Argentine Rise *see* Falkland Plateau
Arghandāb, Daryā-ye *101 E5 river* SE Afghanistan
Argirocastro *see* Gjirokastër
Argo *50 B3* Northern, N Sudan
Argo Fracture Zone *119 C5 tectonic feature* C Indian Ocean
Árgos *83 B6* Pelopónnisos, S Greece
Argostóli *83 A5 var.* Argostólion. Kefallinía, Iónioi Nísoi, Greece, C Mediterranean Sea
Argostólion *see* Argostóli
Argun *103 E1 Chin.* Ergun He, *Rus.* Argun'. *River* China/Russian Federation
Argyrokastron *see* Gjirokastër
Århus *63 B7 var.* Aarhus. Århus, C Denmark
Aria *see* Herāt
Ari Atoll *110 A4 atoll* C Maldives
Arica *42 B1 hist.* San Marcos de Arica. Tarapacá, N Chile
Aridaía *82 B3 var.* Aridea, Aridhaía. Dytikí Makedonía, N Greece
Aridea *see* Aridaía
Aridhaía *see* Aridaía
Arīḥā *96 B3 var.* Arīḥā. Idlib, W Syria
Arīḥā *see* Jericho
Arinsal *69 A7* NW Andorra
Arizona *26 A2 off.* State of Arizona; also known as Copper State, Grand Canyon State. Admin. region *state* SW USA
Arkansas *20 A1 off.* State of Arkansas; also known as The Land of Opportunity. *State* S USA
Arkansas City *23 F5* Kansas, C USA
Arkansas River *22 B2 river* C USA
Arkhangel'sk *92 B2 Eng.* Archangel. Arkhangel'skaya Oblast', NW Russian Federation

Arkoí *83 E6 island* Dodekánisos, Greece, Aegean Sea
Arles *69 D6 var.* Arles-sur-Rhône; *anc.* Arelas, Arelate. Bouches-du-Rhône, SE France
Arles-sur-Rhône *see* Arles
Arlington *27 G2* Texas, SW USA
Arlington *19 E4* Virginia, NE USA
Arlon *65 D8 Dut.* Aarlen, *Ger.* Arel; *Lat.* Orolaunum. Luxembourg, SE Belgium
Armagh *67 B5 Ir.* Ard Mhacha. S Northern Ireland, UK
Armagnac *69 B6 cultural region* S France
Armenia *95 F3 var.* Ajastan, *Arm.* Hayastani Hanrapetut'yun; *prev.* Armenian Soviet Socialist Republic. *Country* SW Asia
Armenia *36 B3* Quindío, W Colombia
Armidale *127 D6* New South Wales, SE Australia
Armstrong *16 C3* Ontario, S Canada
Armyans'k *87 F4 Rus.* Armyansk. Respublika Krym, S Ukraine
Arnaía *82 C4 var.* Arnea. Kentrikí Makedonía, N Greece
Arnaud *60 A3 river* Quebec, E Canada
Arnea *see* Arnaía
Arnedo *71 E2* La Rioja, N Spain
Arnhem *64 D4* Gelderland, SE Netherlands
Arnhem Land *126 A2 physical region* Northern Territory, N Australia
Arno *74 B3 river* C Italy
Arnold *23 G4* Missouri, C USA
Arorae *123 E3 atoll* Tungaru, W Kiribati
Arquipélago da Madeira *see* Madeira
Arquipélago dos Açores *see* Azores
Ar Rahad *see* Er Rahad
Ar Ramādī *98 B3 var.* Ramadi, Rumadiya. SW Iraq
Ar Rāmī *96 C4* Ḥimş, C Syria
Ar Ramthā *97 B5 var.* Ramtha. Irbid, N Jordan
Arran, Isle of *66 C4 island* SW Scotland, UK
Ar Raqqah *96 C2 var.* Rakka; *anc.* Nicephorium. Ar Raqqah, N Syria
Arras *68 C2 anc.* Nemetocenna. Pas-de-Calais, N France
Ar Rawḍatayn *98 C4 var.* Raudhatain. N Kuwait
Arriaga *29 G5* Chiapas, SE Mexico
Ar Riyāḍ *99 C5 Eng.* Riyadh. *Country capital* (Saudi Arabia) Ar Riyāḍ, C Saudi Arabia
Ar Rub 'al Khālī *99 C6 Eng.* Empty Quarter, Great Sandy Desert. *Desert* SW Asia
Ar Rustāq *99 E5 var.* Rostak, Rustaq. N Oman
Ar Ruţbah *98 B3 var.* Rutba. SW Iraq
Árta *83 A5 anc.* Ambracia. Ípeiros, W Greece
Artashat *95 F3* S Armenia
Artemisa *32 B2* La Habana, W Cuba
Artesia *48 D3* New Mexico, SW USA
Arthur's Pass *129 C6 pass* South Island, NZ
Artigas *42 D3 prev.* San Eugenio, San Eugenio del Cuareim. Artigas, N Uruguay
Art'ik *95 F2* W Armenia
Artois *68 C2 cultural region* N France
Artsyz *86 D4 Rus.* Artsiz. Odes'ka Oblast', SW Ukraine
Artvin *95 F2* Artvin, NE Turkey
Arua *51 B6* NW Uganda
Aruângua *see* Luangwa
Aruba *36 C1 var.* Oruba. *Dutch autonomous region* S West Indies
Aru, Kepulauan *117 G4 Eng.* Aru Islands; *prev.* Aroe Islands. *Island group* E Indonesia
Arunāchal Pradesh *113 G3 cultural region* NE India
Arusha *51 C7* Arusha, N Tanzania
Arviat *15 G4 prev.* Eskimo Point. Nunavut, C Canada
Arvidsjaur *62 C4* Norrbotten, N Sweden
Arys' *92 B5 Kaz.* Arys. Yuzhnyy Kazakhstan, S Kazakhstan
Asadābād *101 F4 var.* Asadābād; *prev.* Chaghasarāy. Kunar, E Afghanistan
Asad, Buḩayrat al- *134 C2 Eng.* Lake Assad. *Lake* N Syria
Asahi-dake *108 D2 mountain* Hokkaidō, N Japan
Asahikawa *108 D2* Hokkaidō, N Japan
Asamankese *53 E5* SE Ghana
Āsānsol *113 F4* West Bengal, NE India
Asben *see* Aïr, Massif de l'
Ascension Fracture Zone *47 A5 tectonic feature* C Atlantic Ocean
Ascension Island *63 A5 dependency of St. Helena* C Atlantic Ocean
Ascoli Piceno *74 C4 anc.* Asculum Picenum. Marche, C Italy
Aseb *50 D4 var.* Assab, *Amh.* Āseb. SE Eritrea
Aşgabat *100 C3 Rus.* Ashgabat; *prev.* Ashkhabad, Poltoratsk. *Country capital* (Turkmenistan) Akhalskiy Velayat, C Turkmenistan
Ashara *see* Al 'Ashārah
Ashburton *129 C6* Canterbury, South Island, NZ
Ashburton River *124 A4 river* Western Australia
Ashdod *97 A6 anc.* Azotos, *Lat.* Azotus. Central, C Israel
Asheville *21 E1* North Carolina, SE USA
Ashgabat *see* Aşgabat
Ashkelon *see* Ashqelon
Ashland *18 D2* Ohio, N USA
Ashland *18 B1* Wisconsin, N USA
Ashmore and Cartier Islands *120 A3 Australian external territory* E Indian Ocean
Ashmyany *85 C5 Rus.* Oshmyany. Hrodzyenskaya Voblasts', W Belarus
Ashqelon *97 A6 var.* Ashkelon. Southern, C Israel
Ash Shadādah *96 D2 var.* Ash Shaddādah, Jisr ash Shadadi, Shaddādī, Shedadi, Tell Shedadi. Al Ḥasakah, NE Syria
Ash Shaddādah *see* Ash Shadādah
Ash Shām *see* Dimashq

Ash Sharāh *97 B7 var.* Esh Sharā. *Mountain range* W Jordan
Ash Shāriqah *98 D4 Eng.* Sharjah. Ash Shāriqah, NE UAE
Ash Shawbak *97 B7* Ma'ān, W Jordan
Ash Shiḩr *99 C6* SE Yemen
Asia *25 C2 continent*
Asinara, Isola *74 A4 island* W Italy
Asipovichy *85 D6 Rus.* Osipovichi. Mahilyowskaya Voblasts', C Belarus
Aşkale *95 E3* Erzurum, NE Turkey
Askersund *63 C6* Örebro, C Sweden
Asmara *50 C4 Amh.* Āsmera. *Country capital* (Eritrea) C Eritrea
Assab *see* Aseb
As Sabkhah *96 D2 var.* Sabkha. Ar Raqqah, NE Syria
Assad, Lake *see* Asad, Buḩayrat al-
Aş Şafāwī *97 C6* Al Mafraq, N Jordan
Aş Şaḩrā' al Gharbīyah *see* Sahara el Gharbīya
Aş Şaḩrā' al Lībīyah *see* Libyan Desert
Aş Şaḩrā' ash Sharqīyah *see* Eastern Desert
As Salamīyah *see* Salamīyah
As Salt *97 B6 var.* Salt. Al Balqā', NW Jordan
Assamaka *see* Assamakka
Assamakka *53 F2 var.* Assamaka. Agadez, NW Niger
As Samāwah *98 B3 var.* Samawa. S Iraq
Assen *64 E2* Drenthe, NE Netherlands
Assenede *65 B5* Oost-Vlaanderen, NW Belgium
Assiout *see* Asyūţ
Assiut *see* Asyūţ
Assouan *see* Aswān
Assu *see* Açu
Assuan *see* Aswān
As Sukhnah *96 C3 var.* Sukhne, *Fr.* Soukhné. Ḩimş, C Syria
As Sulaymānīyah *98 C3 var.* Sulaimaniya, *Kurd.* Slēmānī. NE Iraq
As Sulayyil *99 B5* Ar Riyāḍ, S Saudi Arabia
Aş Şuwaydā' *96 M2 var.* Şuwār. Dayr az Zawr, E Syria
As Suwaydā' *97 B5 var.* El Suweida, Es Suweida, Suweida, *Fr.* Soueida. As Suwaydā', SW Syria
Astacus *see* Izmit
Astana *92 C4 prev.* Akmola, Akmolinsk, Tselinograd, Kaz. Aqmola. *country capital* (Kazakhstan) Akmola, N Kazakhstan
Astarabad *see* Gorgān
Asterābād *see* Gorgān
Asti *74 A2 anc.* Asta Colonia, Asta Pompeia, Hasta Colonia, Hasta Pompeia. Piemonte, NW Italy
Astipálaia *see* Astypálaia
Astorga *70 C1 anc.* Asturica Augusta. Castilla-León, N Spain
Astrabad *see* Gorgān
Astrakhan' *89 C7* Astrakhanskaya Oblast', SW Russian Federation
Asturias *70 C1 cultural region* NW Spain
Astypálaia *83 D7 var.* Astipálaia, *It.* Stampalia. *Island* Kykládes, Greece, Aegean Sea
Asunción *42 D2 country capital* (Paraguay) Central, S Paraguay
Aswān *50 B2 var.* Assouan, Assuan; *anc.* Syene. SE Egypt
Asyūţ *50 B2 var.* Assiout, Assiut, Siut; *anc.* Lycopolis. C Egypt
Atacama Desert *see* Atacama, Desierto de
Atacama, Desierto de *42 B2 Eng.* Atacama Desert. *Desert* N Chile
Atafu Atoll *123 E3 island* NW Tokelau
Atamyrat *100 D3 prev.* Kerki. Lebapskiy Velayat, E Turkmenistan
Aţār *52 C2* Adrar, W Mauritania
Atas Bogd *104 D3 mountain* SW Mongolia
Atascadero *25 B7* California, W USA
Atatürk Barajı *95 E4 reservoir* S Turkey
Atbara *50 C3 var.* 'Aṭbārah. River Nile, NE Sudan
'Aṭbārah *see* Atbara
Atbasar *92 C4* Akmola, N Kazakhstan
Atchison *23 F4* Kansas, C USA
Ath *65 B6 var.* Aat. Hainaut, SW Belgium
Athabasca *15 E4* Alberta, SW Canada
Athabasca *15 E5 var.* Athabaska. *River* Alberta, SW Canada
Athabasca, Lake *15 F4 lake* Alberta/Saskatchewan, SW Canada
Athabaska *see* Athabasca
Athens *see* Athína
Athens *21 E2* Georgia, SE USA
Athens *18 D4* Ohio, N USA
Athens *20 D1* Tennessee, S USA
Athens *27 G3* Texas, SW USA
Atherton *126 D3* Queensland, NE Australia
Athína *83 C6 Eng.* Athens; *prev.* Athínai, *anc.* Athenae. *Country capital* (Greece) Attikí, C Greece
Athlone *67 B5 Ir.* Baile Átha Luain. C Ireland
Ath Thawrah *see* Madīnat ath Thawrah
Ati *54 C3* Batha, C Chad
Atikokan *16 B4* Ontario, S Canada
Atka *14 A3* Atka Island, Alaska, USA
Atka *93 G3* Magadanskaya Oblast', E Russian Federation
Atlanta *20 D2 state capital* Georgia, SE USA
Atlanta *27 H2* Texas, SW USA
Atlantic City *19 F4* New Jersey, NE USA
Atlantic-Indian Basin *45 D7 undersea feature* SW Indian Ocean
Atlantic-Indian Ridge *47 B8 undersea feature* SW Indian Ocean
Atlantic Ocean *44 B4 ocean*
Atlas Mountains *48 C2 mountain range* NW Africa
Atlasovo *93 H3* Kamchatskaya Oblast', E Russian Federation
Atlas Saharien *48 D2 var.* Saharan Atlas. *Mountain range* Algeria/Morocco
Atlas Tellien *80 C3 Eng.* Tell Atlas. *Mountain range* N Algeria
Atlin *14 D4* British Columbia, W Canada

Aţ Ţafīlah *97 B7 var.* Et Tafila, Tafila. Aţ Ţafīlah, W Jordan
Aţ Ţā'if *99 B5* Makkah, W Saudi Arabia
At Tall al Abyaḍ *96 C2 var.* Tall al Abyaḍ, Tell Abyad, *Fr.* Tell Abiad. Ar Raqqah, N Syria
Aţ Ţanf *96 D4* Ḩimş, S Syria
Attapu *see* Samakhixai
Attawapiskat *16 C3 river* Ontario, S Canada
Attawapiskat *16 C3* Ontario, C Canada
At Tibnī *96 D2 var.* Tibnī. Dayr az Zawr, NE Syria
Attopeu *see* Samakhixai
Attu Island *14 A2 island* Aleutian Islands, Alaska, USA
Atyrau *92 B4 prev.* Gur'yev. Atyrau, W Kazakhstan
Aubagne *69 D6 anc.* Albania. Bouches-du-Rhône, SE France
Aubange *65 D8* Luxembourg, SE Belgium
Aubervilliers *68 E1* Seine-St-Denis, N France
Auburn *46 B2* Washington, NW USA
Auch *69 B6 Lat.* Augusta Auscorum, Elimberrum. Gers, S France
Auckland *128 D2* Auckland, North Island, N NZ
Auckland Islands *120 C5 island group* S NZ
Audincourt *68 E4* Doubs, E France
Audru *84 D2 Ger.* Audern. Pärnumaa, SW Estonia
Augathella *127 D5* Queensland, E Australia
Augsburg *73 C6 Fr.* Augsbourg; *anc.* Augusta Vindelicorum. Bayern, S Germany
Augusta *19 G2 state capital* Maine, NE USA
Augusta *21 E2* Georgia, SE USA
Augusta *21 A7* Western Australia
Augustów *76 E2 Rus.* Avgustov. Podlaskie, NE Poland
'Aujā et Tahtā *see* Khirbet el 'Aujā et Tahtā
Aulie Ata/Auliye-Ata *see* Taraz
Auob *56 B4 var.* Oup. River Namibia/South Africa
Aurangābād *112 D5* Mahārāshtra, C India
Auray *68 A3* Morbihan, NW France
Aurès, Massif de l' *80 C4 mountain range* NE Algeria
Aurillac *69 C5* Cantal, C France
Aurora *22 D4* Colorado, C USA
Aurora *18 B3* Illinois, N USA
Aurora *23 G5* Missouri, C USA
Aurora *37 F2* var. Vic
Aus *56 B4* Karas, SW Namibia
Ausa *see* Vic
Austin *27 G3 state capital* Texas, S USA
Austin *23 G3* Minnesota, N USA
Austin *124 A4* Western Australia
Australes, Îles *121 F4 var.* Archipel des Australes, Îles Tubuai, Tubuai Islands, *Eng.* Austral Islands. *Island group* SW French Polynesia
Austral Fracture Zone *121 H4 tectonic feature* S Pacific Ocean
Australia *120 A4 Country*
Australian Alps *127 C7 mountain range* SE Australia
Australian Capital Territory *127 D7 prev.* Federal Capital Territory. *Territory* SE Australia
Austral Islands *see* Australes, Îles
Austria *73 D7 Ger.* Österreich. *Country* C Europe
Auvergne *69 C5 cultural region* C France
Auxerre *68 C4 anc.* Autesiodorum, Autissiodorum. Yonne, C France
Avarua *123 G5 dependent territory capital* (Cook Islands) Rarotonga, S Cook Islands
Ávdira *82 C3* Anatolikí Makedonía kai Thráki, NE Greece
Aveiro *70 B2 anc.* Talabriga. Aveiro, W Portugal
Avela *see* Ávila
Avellino *75 D5 anc.* Abellinum. Campania, S Italy
Avesta *63 C6* Kopparberg, C Sweden
Aveyron *69 C5 river* S France
Avezzano *74 C4* Abruzzo, C Italy
Aviemore *66 C3* N Scotland, UK
Avignon *69 D6 anc.* Avenio. Vaucluse, SE France
Ávila *70 D3 var.* Avila; *anc.* Abela, Abula, Abyla, Avela. Castilla-León, C Spain
Avilés *70 C1* Asturias, NW Spain
Avranches *68 B3* Manche, N France
Awaji-shima *109 C6 island* SW Japan
Āwash *51 D5 var.* Hawash. *River* C Ethiopia
Awbārī *49 F3* SW Libya
Ax *see* Dax
Axel *65 B5* Zeeland, SW Netherlands
Axel Heiberg Island *15 E1 var.* Axel Heiburg. *Island* Nunavut, N Canada
Axel Heiberg Island *see* Axel Heiberg Island
Ayacucho *38 D4* Ayacucho, S Peru
Ayagoz *130 C5 var.* Ayaguz, *Kaz.* Ayaköz; *prev.* Sergiopol. Vostochnyy Kazakhstan, E Kazakhstan
Ayaguz *see* Ayagoz
Ayaköz *see* Ayagoz
Ayamonte *70 C4* Andalucía, S Spain
Ayaviri *39 E4* Puno, S Peru
Aydarko'l Ko'li *101 E4 var.* Aydarkül', *Rus.* Ozero Aydarkul'. *Lake* C Uzbekistan
Aydarkül' *see* Aydarko'l Ko'li
Aydın *94 A4 var.* Aïdin; *anc.* Tralles. Aydın, SW Turkey
Ayers Rock *see* Uluru
Ayeyarwady *see* Irrawaddy
Ayiá *see* Agiá
Ayios Evstratios *see* Efstrátios, Ágios
Ayios Nikólaos *see* Ágios Nikólaos
Ayorou *53 E3* Tillabéri, W Niger
'Ayoûn el 'Atroûs *52 D3 var.* Aïoun el Atrous, Aïoun el Atroûss. Hodh el Gharbi, SE Mauritania
Ayr *66 C4* W Scotland, UK
Ayteke Bi *130 B4 . Kaz.* Zhangaqazaly, *prev.* Novokazalinsk Kyzylorda, SW Kazakhstan

Aytos *82 E2* Burgas, E Bulgaria
Ayutthaya *115 C5 var.* Phra Nakhon Si Ayutthaya. Phra Nakhon Si Ayutthaya, C Thailand
Ayvalık *94 A3* Balıkesir, W Turkey
Azahar, Costa del *71 F3 coastal region* E Spain
Azaouâd *53 E3 desert* C Mali
A'zāz *96 B2* Ḥalab, NW Syria
Azerbaijan *95 G2 Az.* Azärbaycan, Azärbaycan Respublikası; *prev.* Azerbaijan SSR. *Country* SE Asia
Azimabad *see* Patna
Azogues *38 B2* Cañar, S Ecuador
Azores *70 A4 var.* Açores, Ilhas dos Açores, *Port.* Arquipélago dos Açores. *Island group* Portugal, NE Atlantic Ocean
Azores-Biscay Rise *58 A3 undersea feature* E Atlantic Ocean
Azoum, Bahr *54 C3 seasonal river* SE Chad
Azov, Sea of *81 H1 Rus.* Azovskoye More, *Ukr.* Azovs'ke More. *Sea* NE Black Sea
Azraq, Wāḩat al *135 C6 oasis* N Jordan
Aztec *26 C1* New Mexico, SW USA
Azuaga *70 C4* Extremadura, W Spain
Azuero, Península de *31 F5 peninsula* S Panama
Azul *43 D5* Buenos Aires, E Argentina
Azur, Côte d' *85 C6 Coastal region* SE France
Az Zaqāzīq *see* Zagazig
Az Zarqā' *97 B6 var.* Zarqa. Az Zarqā', NW Jordan
Az Zāwiyah *49 F2 var.* Zawia. NW Libya
Az Zilfī *98 B4* Ar Riyāḍ, N Saudi Arabia
Æsernia *see* Isernia

B

Ba *78 D3 prev.* Mba. Viti Levu, W Fiji
Baalbek *96 B4 var.* Ba'labakk; *anc.* Heliopolis. E Lebanon
Bá an Daingin *see* Dingle Bay
Baardheere *51 D6 var.* Bardere, *It.* Bardera. Gedo, SW Somalia
Baarle-Hertog *65 C5* Antwerpen, N Belgium
Baarn *64 C3* Utrecht, C Netherlands
Babadag *86 D5* Tulcea, SE Romania
Babahoyo *38 B2 prev.* Bodegas. Los Ríos, C Ecuador
Bābā, Kūh-e *101 E4 mountain range* C Afghanistan
Babayevo *88 B4* Vologodskaya Oblast', NW Russian Federation
Babeldaob *122 A1 var.* Babeldaop, Babelthuap. *Island* N Palau
Babeldaop *see* Babeldaob
Bab el Mandeb *99 B7 strait* Gulf of Aden/Red Sea
Babelthuap *see* Babeldaob
Bá Bheanntraí *see* Bantry Bay
Babruysk *85 D7 Rus.* Bobruysk. Mahilyowskaya Voblasts', E Belarus
Babuyan Channel *117 E1 channel* N Philippines
Babuyan Island *117 E1 island* N Philippines
Bacabal *41 F2* Maranhão, E Brazil
Bacău *86 C4 Hung.* Bákó. Bacău, NE Romania
Bắc Giang *114 D3* Ha Bắc, N Vietnam
Bacheykava *85 D5 Rus.* Bocheykovo. Vitsyebskaya Voblasts', N Belarus
Back *37 F3 river* Nunavut, N Canada
Bačka Palanka *78 D3 prev.* Palanka. Serbia, NW Serbia and Montenegro (Yugo.)
Bačka Topola *78 D3 Hung.* Topolya; *prev.* Hung. Bácstopolya. Serbia, N Serbia and Montenegro (Yugo.)
Bac Liêu *115 D6 var.* Vinh Loi. Minh Hai, S Vietnam
Bacolod *103 E4 off.* Bacolod City. Negros, C Philippines
Bacolod City *see* Bacolod
Bácsszenttamás *see* Srbobran
Badajoz *70 C4 anc.* Pax Augusta. Extremadura, W Spain
Baden-Baden *73 B6 anc.* Aurelia Aquensis. Baden-Württemberg, SW Germany
Bad Freienwalde *72 D3* Brandenburg, NE Germany
Bad Hersfeld *72 B4* Hessen, C Germany
Bad Homburg *see* Bad Homburg vor der Höhe
Bad Homburg vor der Höhe *73 B5 var.* Bad Homburg. Hessen, W Germany
Bá Dhún na nGall *see* Donegal Bay
Bad Ischl *73 D7* Oberösterreich, N Austria
Bad Krozingen *73 A6* Baden-Württemberg, SW Germany
Badlands *22 D2 physical region* North Dakota, N USA
Badu Island *126 C1 island* Queensland, NE Australia
Bad Vöslau *73 E6* Niederösterreich, NE Austria
Baetic Cordillera *see* Béticos, Sistemas
Baetic Mountains *see* Béticos, Sistemas
Bafatá *52 C4* C Guinea-Bissau
Baffin Bay *15 G2 bay* Canada/Greenland
Baffin Island *15 G2 island* Nunavut, NE Canada
Bafing *52 C3 river* W Africa
Bafoussam *54 A4* Ouest, W Cameroon
Bafra *94 D2* Samsun, N Turkey
Bâft *98 D4* Kermān, S Iran
Bagaces *30 D4* Guanacaste, NW Costa Rica
Bagdad *see* Baghdād
Bagé *41 E5* Rio Grande do Sul, S Brazil
Baghdād *98 B3 var.* Bagdad, *Eng.* Baghdad. *Country capital* (Iraq) C Iraq
Baghlān *101 E3* Baghlān, NE Afghanistan
Bago *see* Pegu
Bagoé *52 D4 river* Côte d'Ivoire/Mali
Bagrationovsk *84 A4 Ger.* Preussisch Eylau. Kaliningradskaya Oblast', W Russian Federation
Bagrax Hu *see* Bosten Hu
Baguio *117 E1 off.* Baguio City. Luzon, N Philippines

Bagzane, Monts 53 F3 *mountain* N Niger
Bahama Islands *see* Bahamas
Bahamas 32 C2 *Country* N West Indies
Bahamas 13 D6 *var.* Bahama Islands.
Island group N West Indies
Baharly 100 C3 *var.* Bäherden, *Rus.*
Bakharden; *prev.* Bakherden. Akhalskiy
Velayat, C Turkmenistan
Bahāwalpur 112 C3 Punjab, E Pakistan
Bäherden *see* Baharly
Bahía 41 F3 *off.* Estado da Bahia. *State*
E Brazil
Bahía Blanca 43 C5 Buenos Aires,
E Argentina
Bahía, Islas de la 30 C1 *Eng.* Bay Islands.
Island group N Honduras
Bahir Dar 50 C4 *var.* Bahir Dar, Bahrdar
Giyorgis. NW Ethiopia
Bahraich 113 E3 Uttar Pradesh, N India
Bahrain 98 C4 *Ar.* Al Baḥrayn;
prev. Bahrein, *anc.* Tylos or Tyros.
Country SW Asia
Bahr al Milḥ *see* Razāzah, Buḥayrat ar
Baḥrat Lūt *see* Dead Sea
Bahrat Tabariya *see* Tiberias, Lake
Bahr Dar *see* Bahir Dar
Bahrdar Giyorgis *see* Bahir Dar
Bahr el Azraq *see* Blue Nile
Bahr el Jebel *see* White Nile
Bahret Lut *see* Dead Sea
Bahr Tabariya, Sea of *see* Tiberias, Lake
Bahushewsk 85 E6 *Rus.* Bogushevsk.
Vitsyebskaya Voblasts', NE Belarus
Baia Mare 86 B3 *Ger.* Frauenbach,
Hung. Nagybánya; *prev.* Neustadt.
Maramureş, NW Romania
Baia Sprie 86 B3 *Ger.* Mittelstadt, *Hung.*
Felsőbánya. Maramureş, NW Romania
Baïbokoum 54 B4 Logone-Oriental,
SW Chad
Baidoa *see* Baydhabo
Baie-Comeau 17 E3 Québec, SE Canada
Baikal, Lake *see* Baykal, Ozero
Baile Átha Luain *see* Athlone
Bailén 70 D4 Andalucía, S Spain
Baile na Mainistreach *see* Newtownabbey
Băileşti 86 B5 Dolj, SW Romania
Ba Illi 54 B3 Chari-Baguirmi, SW Chad
Bainbridge 20 D3 Georgia, SE USA
Bā'ir *see* Bāyir
Baireuth *see* Bayreuth
Bairiki 122 D2 *country capital* (Kiribati)
Tarawa, NW Kiribati
Bairnsdale 127 C7 Victoria, SE Australia
Baishan 107 E3 *prev.* Hunjiang. Jilin,
NE China
Baiyin 106 B4 Gansu, C China
Baja 77 C7 Bács-Kiskun, S Hungary
Baja California 26 A4 *Eng.* Lower
California. *Peninsula* NW Mexico
Baja California 28 B2 *state* NW Mexico
Bajo Boquete *see* Boquete
Bajram Curri 79 D5 Kukës, N Albania
Bakala 54 C4 Ouaka,
C Central African Republic
Bakan *see* Shimonoseki
Baker 24 C3 Oregon, NW USA
Baker and Howland Islands 123 E2 *US
unincorporated territory* W Polynesia
Baker Lake 15 F3 Nunavut, N Canada
Bakersfield 25 C7 California, W USA
Bakharden *see* Baharly
Bakhchysaray 87 F5 *Rus.* Bakhchisaray.
Respublika Krym, S Ukraine
Bakhmach 87 F1 Chernihivs'ka Oblast',
N Ukraine
Bākhtarān *see* Kermānshāh
Bakı 95 H2 *Eng.* Baku. *Country capital*
(Azerbaijan) E Azerbaijan
Bakony 77 C7 *Eng.* Bakony Mountains,
Ger. Bakonywald. *Mountain range*
W Hungary
Baku *see* Bakı
Balabac Island 107 C8 *island* W Philippines
Balabac Strait 116 D2 *var.* Selat Balabac.
Strait Malaysia/Philippines
Ba'labakk *see* Baalbek
Balaguer 93 F2 Cataluña, NE Spain
Balakovo 89 C6 Saratovskaya Oblast',
W Russian Federation
Bālā Morghāb 100 D4 Laghmān,
NW Afghanistan
Balashov 89 B6 Saratovskaya Oblast',
W Russian Federation
Balaton C7 *var.* Lake Balaton, *Ger.*
Plattensee. *Lake* W Hungary
Balaton, Lake *see* Balaton
Balbina, Represa 40 D1 *reservoir*
NW Brazil
Balboa 31 G4 Panamá, C Panama
Balcarce 43 D5 Buenos Aires, E Argentina
Balclutha 129 B7 Otago, South Island, NZ
Baldy Mountain 22 C1 *mountain* Montana,
NW USA
Bâle *see* Basel
Baleares, Islas 71 G3 *Eng.* Balearic Islands.
Island group Spain, W Mediterranean Sea
Balearic Islands *see* Baleares, Islas
Balearic Plain *see* Algerian Basin
Baleine, Rivière à la 17 E2 *river* Québec,
E Canada
Balen 65 C5 Antwerpen, N Belgium
Bāleshwar 113 F4 *prev.* Balasore. Orissa,
E India
Bali 116 D5 *island* C Indonesia
Balıkesir 94 A3 Balıkesir, W Turkey
Balīkh, Nahr 96 C2 *river* N Syria
Balikpapan 116 D4 Borneo, C Indonesia
Balkanabat 100 B2 *var.* Nebitdag. Balkanskiy
Velayat, W Turkmenistan
Balkan Mountains 82 C2 *Bul./Scr.* Stara
Planina. *Mountain range* Bulgaria/Serbia
and Montenegro (Yugo.)
Balkh 101 E3 *anc.* Bactra. Balkh,
N Afghanistan
Balkhash 92 C5 *Kaz.* Balqash. Karaganda,
SE Kazakhstan
Balkhash, Lake *see* Balkhash, Ozero

Balkhash, Ozero 92 C5 *Eng.* Lake Balkhash,
Kaz. Balqash. *Lake* SE Kazakhstan
Balladonia 125 C6 Western Australia
Ballarat 127 C7 Victoria, SE Australia
Balleny Islands 132 B5 *island group*
Antarctica
Ballinger 27 F3 Texas, SW USA
Balochistän *see* Baluchistän
Balş 86 B5 Olt, S Romania
Balsas 41 F2 Maranhão, E Brazil
Balsas, Río 41 F2 *var.* Río Mexcala.
River S Mexico
Bal'shavik 85 D7 *Rus.* Bol'shevik.
Homyel'skaya Voblasts', SE Belarus
Balta 86 D3 Odes'ka Oblast', SW Ukraine
Bălţi 86 D3 *Rus.* Bel'tsy. N Moldova
Baltic Sea 63 C7 *Ger.* Ostee, *Rus.* Baltiskoye
More. *Sea* N Europe
Baltimore 19 F4 Maryland, NE USA
Baltkrievija *see* Belarus
Baluchistän 112 B3 *var.* Balochistän,
Beluchistan. Admin. *region province*
SW Pakistan
Balvi 84 D4 Balvi, NE Latvia
Balykchy 101 G2 *Kir.* Ysyk-Köl; *prev.* Issyk-
Kul', Rybach'ye. Issyk-Kul'skaya Oblast',
NE Kyrgyzstan
Balzers 72 E2 S Liechtenstein
Bam 98 E4 Kermän, SE Iran
Bamako 52 D4 *country capital* (Mali)
Capital District, SW Mali
Bambari 54 C4 Ouaka, C Central African
Republic
Bamberg 73 C5 Bayern, SE Germany
Bamenda 54 A4 Nord-Ouest, W Cameroon
Banaba 122 D2 *var.* Ocean Island. *Island*
Tungaru, W Kiribati
Banda Aceh 138 A3 *var.* Banda Atjeh;
prev. Koetaradja, Kutaradja, Kutaraja.
Sumatera, W Indonesia
Banda Atjeh *see* Banda Aceh
Bandama 52 D5 *var.* Bandama Fleuve.
River S Côte d'Ivoire
Bandama Fleuve *see* Bandama
Bandar 'Abbās *see* Bandar-e 'Abbās
Bandarbeyla 51 E5 *var.* Bender Beila, Bender
Beyla. Bari, NE Somalia
Bandar-e 'Abbās 98 D4 *var.* Bandar 'Abbās;
prev. Gombroon. Hormozgän, S Iran
Bandar-e Büshehr 98 C4 *var.* Büshehr, *Eng.*
Bushire. Büshehr, S Iran
Bandar-e Khamīr 98 D4 Hormozgän, S Iran
Bandar-e Langeh 98 D4 *var.* Bandar-e
Lengeh, Lingeh. Hormozgän, S Iran
Bandar-e Lengeh *see* Bandar-e Langeh
Bandar Kassim *see* Boosaaso
Bandarlampung 116 C4 *prev.*
Tanjungkarang, Teloekbetoeng,
Telukbetung. Sumatera, W Indonesia
Bandar Maharani *see* Muar
Bandar Masulipatnam *see* Machilipatnam
Bandar Seri Begawan 116 D3 *prev.* Brunei
Town. *Country capital* (Brunei) N Brunei
Bandar Sri Aman *see* Sri Aman
Banda Sea 117 F5 *var.* Laut Banda. *Sea*
E Indonesia
Bandiagara 53 E3 Mopti, C Mali
Bandırma 94 A3 *var.* Penderma. Balıkesir,
NW Turkey
Bandundu 55 C6 *prev.* Banningville.
Bandundu, W Dem. Rep. Congo
Bandung 116 C5 *prev.* Bandoeng. Jawa,
C Indonesia
Bangalore 110 C2 Karnātaka, S India
Bangassou 54 D4 Mbomou, SE Central
African Republic
Banggai, Kepulauan 117 E4 *island group*
C Indonesia
Banghāzī 49 G2 *Eng.* Bengazi, Benghazi, *It.*
Bengasi. NE Libya
Bangka, Pulau 116 C4 *island* W Indonesia
Bangkok *see* Krung Thep
Bangkok, Bight of *see* Krung Thep, Ao
Bangladesh 113 G3 *prev.* East Pakistan.
Country S Asia
Bangor 67 B5 *Ir.* Beannchar. E Northern
Ireland, UK
Bangor 19 G2 Maine, NE USA
Bangor 67 C6 NW Wales, UK
Bangui 55 B5 *country capital* (Central African
Republic) Ombella-Mpoko, SW Central
African Republic
Bangweulu, Lake 51 B8 *var.* Lake
Bengwelu. *Lake* N Zambia
Ban Hat Yai *see* Hat Yai
Ban Hin Heup 114 C4 Viangchan, C Laos
Ban Houayxay *see* Houayxay
Ban Houei Sai *see* Houayxay
Ban Hua Hin 115 C6 *var.* Hua Hin. Prachuap
Khiri Khan, SW Thailand
Bani 52 D3 *river* S Mali
Banias *see* Bāniyās
Banī Suwayf *see* Beni Suef
Bāniyās 96 B3 *var.* Banias, Baniyas, Paneas.
Tarțūs, W Syria
Baniyas *see* Bāniyās
Banja Luka 78 B3 Republika Srpska,
NW Bosnia and Herzegovina
Banjarmasin 116 D4 *prev.* Bandjarmasin.
Borneo, C Indonesia
Banjul 52 B3 *prev.* Bathurst. *Country capital*
(Gambia) W Gambia
Banks Island 15 E2 *island* Banks Island,
Northwest Territories, NW Canada
Banks Islands 122 D4 *Fr.* Îles Banks.
Island group N Vanuatu
Banks Lake 24 B1 *reservoir* Washington,
NW USA
Banks Peninsula 129 C6 *peninsula* South
Island, NZ
Banks Strait 127 C8 *strait*
SW Tasman Sea
Bānkura 113 F4 West Bengal, NE India
Ban Mak Khaeng *see* Udon Thani
Banmo *see* Bhamo
Bañolas *see* Banyoles
Ban Pak Phanang *see* Pak Phanang
Ban Sichon *see* Sichon

Banská Bystrica 77 C6 *Ger.* Neusohl, *Hung.*
Besztercebánya. Banskobystrický Kraj,
C Slovakia
Bantry Bay 67 A7 *Ir.* Bá Bheanntraí. *Bay*
SW Ireland
Banya 82 E2 Burgas, E Bulgaria
Banyak, Kepulauan 116 A3 *prev.* Kepulauan
Banjak. *Island group* NW Indonesia
Banyo 54 B4 Adamaoua, NW Cameroon
Banyoles 71 G2 *var.* Bañolas. Cataluña,
NE Spain
Banzare Seamounts 119 C7 *undersea feature*
S Indian Ocean
Baoji 106 B4 *var.* Pao-chi, Paoki. Shaanxi,
C China
Baoro 54 B4 Nana-Mambéré, W Central
African Republic
Baoshan 106 A6 *var.* Pao-shan. Yunnan,
SW China
Baotou 105 F3 *var.* Pao-t'ou, Paotow. Nei
Mongol Zizhiqu, N China
Ba'qübah 98 B3 *var.* Qubba. C Iraq
Baquerizo Moreno *see* Puerto Baquerizo
Moreno
Bar 79 C5 *It.* Antivari. Montenegro,
SW Serbia and Montenegro (Yugo.)
Baraawe 51 D6 *It.* Brava. Shabeellaha Hoose,
S Somalia
Baraji, Hirfanli 94 C3 *lake* C Turkey
Bārāmati 112 C5 Mahārāshtra, W India
Baranavichy 85 B6 *Pol.* Baranowicze,
Rus. Baranovichi. Brestskaya Voblasts',
SW Belarus
Barbados 33 G1 *country* SE West Indies
Barbastro 71 F2 Aragón, NE Spain
Barbate de Franco 70 C5 Andalucía,
S Spain
Barbuda 33 G3 *island* N Antigua and
Barbuda
Barcaldine 126 C4 Queensland, E Australia
Barce *see* Al Marj
Barcelona 71 G2 *anc.* Barcino, Barcinona.
Cataluña, E Spain
Barcelona 37 E2 Anzoátegui, NE Venezuela
Barcoo *see* Cooper Creek
Barcs 77 C7 Somogy, SW Hungary
Bardaï 54 C1 Borkou-Ennedi-Tibesti,
N Chad
Bardejov 77 D5 *Ger.* Bartfeld, *Hung.* Bártfa.
Prešovský Kraj, E Slovakia
Bardera *see* Baardheere
Bardere *see* Baardheere
Bareilly 113 E3 *var.* Bareli. Uttar Pradesh,
N India
Bareli *see* Bareilly
Barendrecht 64 C4 Zuid-Holland,
SW Netherlands
Barentin 68 C3 Seine-Maritime, N France
Barentsburg 61 G2 Spitsbergen, W Svalbard
Barentsøya 61 G2 *island* E Svalbard
Barents Sea 82 C2 Nor. Barents Havet,
Rus. Barentsevo More. *Sea* Arctic Ocean
Barents Trough 59 E1 *undersea feature*
SW Barents Sea
Bar Harbor 19 H2 Mount Desert Island,
Maine, NE USA
Bari 75 E5 *var.* Bari delle Puglie; *anc.* Barium.
Puglia, SE Italy
Bāridah *see* Al Bāridah
Bari delle Puglie *see* Bari
Barikot 101 F4 *var.* Barikot. Kunar,
NE Afghanistan
Barīkowt *see* Barikowt
Barillas 30 A2 *var.* Santa Cruz Barillas.
Huehuetenango, NW Guatemala
Barinas 36 C2 Barinas, W Venezuela
Barisal 113 G4 Khulna, S Bangladesh
Barisan, Pegunungan 116 B4 *mountain range*
Sumatera, W Indonesia
Barito, Sungai 116 D4 *river* Borneo,
C Indonesia
Barium *see* Bari
Barka *see* Al Marj
Barkly Tableland 126 B3 *plateau* Northern
Territory/Queensland, N Australia
Bârlad 86 D4 *prev.* Bîrlad. Vaslui, E Romania
Barlavento, Ilhas de 52 A2 *var.* Windward
Islands. *Island group* N Cape Verde
Bar-le-Duc 68 D3 *var.* Bar-sur-Ornain.
Meuse, NE France
Barlee, Lake 125 B6 *lake* Western Australia
Barlee Range 44 A4 *mountain range*
Western Australia
Barletta 75 D5 *anc.* Barduli. Puglia, SE Italy
Barlinek 76 B3 *Ger.* Berlinchen.
Zachodniopomorskie, NW Poland
Barmouth 67 C6 NW Wales, UK
Barnaul 92 D4 Altayskiy Kray,
C Russian Federation
Barnet 67 B8 England, UK
Barnstaple 67 C7 SW England, UK
Baroghil Pass 101 F3 *var.* Kowtal-e
Barowghil. *Pass* Afghanistan/Pakistan
Baron'ki 85 E7 *Rus.* Boron'ki.
Mahilyowskaya Voblasts', E Belarus
Barquisimeto 36 C2 Lara, NW Venezuela
Barra 66 B3 *island* NW Scotland, UK
Barra de Río Grande 31 E3 Región
Autónoma Atlántico Sur, E Nicaragua
Barragem de Sobradinho *see* Sobradinho,
Represa de
Barranca 38 C3 Lima, W Peru
Barrancabermeja 36 B2 Santander,
N Colombia
Barranquilla 36 B1 Atlántico, N Colombia
Barreiro 67 B6 Setúbal, W Portugal
Barrier Range 127 C6 *hill range* New South
Wales, SE Australia
Barrow 67 B6 *Ir.* An Bhearú. *River* SE Ireland
Barrow 14 D2 Alaska, USA
Barrow-in-Furness 67 C5 NW England, UK
Barrow Island 124 A4 *island* Western
Australia
Barstow 25 C7 California, W USA
Bar-sur-Ornain *see* Bar-le-Duc
Bartang 101 F3 *river* SE Tajikistan
Bartica 37 F3 N Guyana
Bartın 94 C2 Bartın NW Turkey

Bartlesville 27 G1 Oklahoma, C USA
Bartoszyce 76 D2 *Ger.* Bartenstein.
Warmińsko-Mazurskie, NE Poland
Baruun-Urt 105 F2 Sühbaatar, E Mongolia
Barú, Volcán 31 E5 *var.* Volcán de Chiriquí.
Volcano W Panama
Barwon River 127 D5 *river* New South
Wales, SE Australia
Barysaw 85 D6 *Rus.* Borisov. Minskaya
Voblasts', NE Belarus
Basarabeasca 86 D4 *Rus.* Bessarabka.
SE Moldova
Basel 73 A7 *Eng.* Basle, *Fr.* Bâle. Basel-Stadt,
NW Switzerland
Basilan 117 E3 *island* SW Philippines
Basle *see* Basel
Basra *see* Al Başrah
Bassano del Grappa 74 C2 Veneto, NE Italy
Bassein 114 A4 *var.* Pathein. Irrawaddy,
SW Myanmar
Basse-Terre 33 G4 *dependent territory capital*
(Guadeloupe) Basse Terre,
SW Guadeloupe
Basse Terre 33 G4 *island* W Guadeloupe
Basseterre 33 G3 *country capital* (Saint Kitts
and Nevis) Saint Kitts, Saint Kitts and
Nevis
Bassikounou 52 D3 Hodh ech Chargui,
SE Mauritania
Bass Strait 127 C7 *strait* SE Australia
Bassum 72 B3 Niedersachsen, NW Germany
Bastia 69 E7 Corse, France, C Mediterranean
Sea
Bastogne 65 D7 Luxembourg, SE Belgium
Bastrop 20 B2 Louisiana, S USA
Bastyn' 85 B7 *Rus.* Bostyn'. Brestskaya
Voblasts', SW Belarus
Basuo *see* Dongfang
Bata 55 A5 NW Equatorial Guinea
Batabanó, Golfo de 32 A2 *gulf* W Cuba
Batajnica 78 D3 Serbia, N Serbia and
Montenegro (Yugo.)
Batangas 117 E2 *off.* Batangas City. Luzon,
N Philippines
Bătdâmbâng 115 C5 *prev.* Battambang.
Bătdâmbâng, NW Cambodia
Batéké, Plateaux 55 B6 *plateau* S Congo
Bath 67 D7 *hist.* Akermanceaster, *anc.* Aquae
Calidae, Aquae Solis. SW England, UK
Bathinda 112 D2 Punjab, NW India
Bathsheba 33 G1 E Barbados
Bathurst 17 F4 New Brunswick, SE Canada
Bathurst 127 D6 New South Wales,
SE Australia
Bathurst Island 124 D2 *island* Northern
Territory, N Australia
Bathurst Island 15 F2 *island* Parry Islands,
Nunavut, N Canada
Bāṭin, Wādī al 136 C4 *dry watercourse*
SW Asia
Batman 95 E4 *var.* İluh. Batman, SE Turkey
Batna 49 E2 NE Algeria
Baton Rouge 20 B3 *state capital* Louisiana,
S USA
Batroûn 96 A4 *var.* Al Batrūn. N Lebanon
Batticaloa 110 D3 Eastern Province,
E Sri Lanka
Bat'umi 95 F2 W Georgia
Batu Pahat 116 B3 *prev.* Bandar Penggaram.
Johor, Peninsular Malaysia
Bauchi 53 G4 Bauchi, NE Nigeria
Bauer Basin 131 F3 *undersea feature*
E Pacific Ocean
Bauska 84 C3 *Ger.* Bauske. Bauska, S Latvia
Bautzen 72 D4 *Lus.* Budyšin. Sachsen,
E Germany
Bavarian Alps 73 C7 *Ger.* Bayrische Alpen.
Mountain range Austria/Germany
Bavispe, Río 28 C2 *river* NW Mexico
Bawītī 50 B2 N Egypt
Bawku 53 E4 N Ghana
Bayamo 32 C3 Granma, E Cuba
Bayan Har Shan 104 D4 *var.* Bayan Khar.
Mountain range C China
Bayanhongor 104 D2 Bayanhongor,
C Mongolia
Bayan Khar *see* Bayan Har Shan
Bayano, Lago 31 G4 *lake* E Panama
Bay City 18 C3 Michigan, N USA
Bay City 27 G4 Texas, SW USA
Baydhabo 51 D6 *var.* Baydhowa, Isha
Baydhabo, It. Baidoa. Bay, SW Somalia
Baydhowa *see* Baydhabo
Bayern 73 C6 *cultural region* SE Germany
Bayeux 68 B3 *anc.* Augustodurum.
Calvados, N France
Bāyir 97 C7 *var.* Bā'ir. Ma'ān, S Jordan
Baykal, Ozero 93 E4 *Eng.* Lake Baikal.
Lake S Russian Federation
Baymak 89 D6 Respublika Bashkortostan,
W Russian Federation
Bayonne 69 A6 *anc.* Lapurdum. Pyrénées-
Atlantiques, SW France
Bayramaly 100 D3 *var.* Bayramaly;
prev. Bayram-Ali. Maryyskiy Velayat,
S Turkmenistan
Bayreuth 73 C5 *var.* Baireuth. Bayern,
SE Germany
Bayrūt *see* Beyrouth
Baytown 27 H4 Texas, SW USA
Baza 71 E4 Andalucía, S Spain
Beagle Channel 43 C8 *channel*
Argentina/Chile
Béal Feirste *see* Belfast
Beannchar *see* Bangor
Bear Lake 24 E4 *lake* Idaho/Utah, NW USA
Beas de Segura 71 E4 Andalucía, S Spain
Beata, Isla 33 E3 *island* SW Dominican
Republic
Beatrice 23 F4 Nebraska, C USA
Beaufort Sea 15 E2 *sea* Arctic Ocean
Beaufort West 56 C5 *Afr.* Beaufort-Wes.
Western Cape, SW South Africa
Beaumont 27 H3 Texas, SW USA
Beaune 68 D4 Côte d'Or, C France
Beauvais 68 C3 *anc.* Bellovacum,
Caesaromagus. Oise, N France

Beaver Island 18 C2 *island* Michigan,
N USA
Beaver Lake 27 H1 *reservoir* Arkansas,
C USA
Beaver River 27 F1 *river* Oklahoma,
C USA
Beāwar 112 C3 Rājasthān, N India
Bečej 78 D3 *Ger.* Altbetsche, *Hung.* Óbecse,
Rácz-Becse; *prev.* Magyar-Becse, Stari
Bečej. Serbia, N Serbia and Montenegro
(Yugo.)
Béchar 48 D2 *prev.* Colomb-Béchar.
W Algeria
Beckley 18 D5 West Virginia, NE USA
Bedford 67 D6 E England, UK
Bedum 64 E1 Groningen, NE Netherlands
Be'ér Menuḥa 97 B7 *var.* Be'er Menukha.
Southern, S Israel
Be'er Menukha *see* Be'ér Menuḥa
Beernem 65 A5 West-Vlaanderen,
NW Belgium
Beersheba *see* Be'ér Sheva'
Be'ér Sheva' 97 A7 *var.* Beersheba,
Ar. Bir es Saba. Southern, S Israel
Beesel 65 D5 Limburg, SE Netherlands
Beeville 27 G4 Texas, SW USA
Bega 127 D7 New South Wales,
SE Australia
Beida *see* Al Bayḍā'
Beihai 106 B6 Guangxi Zhuangzu Zizhiqu,
S China
Beijing 106 C3 *var.* Pei-ching, *Eng.* Peking;
prev. Pei-p'ing. *Country/municipality capital*
(China) Beijing Shi, E China
Beilen 64 E2 Drenthe, NE Netherlands
Beira 57 E3 Sofala, C Mozambique
Beirut *see* Beyrouth
Beit Leḥm *see* Bethlehem
Beiuş 86 B3 *Hung.* Belényes. Bihor,
NW Romania
Beja 70 B4 *anc.* Pax Julia. Beja, SE Portugal
Béjar 70 C3 Castilla-León, N Spain
Bejraburi *see* Phetchaburi
Békéscsaba 77 D7 *Rom.* Bichiş-Ciaba. Békés,
SE Hungary
Bekobod 101 E2 *Rus.* Bekabad; *prev.*
Begovat. Toshkent Wiloyati, E Uzbekistan
Bela Crkva 78 E3 *Ger.* Weisskirchen, *Hung.*
Fehértemplom. Serbia, N Serbia and
Montenegro (Yugo.)
Belarus 85 B6 *var.* Belorussia, *Latv.*
Baltkrievija; *prev.* Belorussian SSR,
Rus. Belorusskaya SSR. *Country* E Europe
Belau *see* Palau
Bełchatów *see* Bełchatów
Bełchatów 76 C4 *var.* Belchatow. Łódzkie,
C Poland
Belcher Islands 16 C2 *Fr.* Îles Belcher.
Island group Northwest Territories,
SE Canada
Beledweyne 51 D5 *var.* Belet Huen, *It.* Belet
Uen. Hiiraan, C Somalia
Belém 41 F1 *var.* Pará. *State capital* Pará,
N Brazil
Belen 26 D2 New Mexico, SW USA
Belén 30 D4 Rivas, SW Nicaragua
Belet Huen *see* Beledweyne
Belet Uen *see* Beledweyne
Belfast 67 B5 *Ir.* Béal Feirste. *Admin capital*
E Northern Ireland, UK
Belfield 22 D2 North Dakota, N USA
Belfort 68 E4 Territoire-de-Belfort, E France
Belgaum 110 B1 Karnātaka, W India
Belgium 65 B6 *Dut.* België, *Fr.* Belgique.
Country NW Europe
Belgorod 89 A6 Belgorodskaya Oblast',
W Russian Federation
Belgrade *see* Beograd
Belgrano II 132 A2 *Argentinian research
station* Antarctica
Belice *see* Belize City
Beligrad *see* Berat
Beli Manastir 78 C3 *Hung.* Pélmonostor;
prev. Monostor. Osijek-Baranja,
NE Croatia
Bélinga 55 B5 Ogooué-Ivindo, NE Gabon
Belitung, Pulau 116 C4 *island* W Indonesia
Belize 30 B1 *Sp.* Belice; *prev.* British
Honduras, Colony of Belize. *Country*
Central America
Belize 30 B1 *river* Belize/Guatemala
Belize *see* Belize City
Belize City 30 C1 *var.* Belize, *Sp.* Belice.
Belize, NE Belize
Belkofski 14 B3 Alaska, USA
Belle Île 68 A4 *island* NW France
Belle Isle, Strait of 17 G3 *strait*
Newfoundland and Labrador, E Canada
Belleville 18 B4 Illinois, N USA
Bellevue 23 F4 Iowa, C USA
Bellevue 24 B2 Washington, NW USA
Bellingham 24 B1 Washington, NW USA
Belling Hausen Mulde *see* Southeast
Pacific Basin
Bellingshausen Abyssal Plain *see*
Bellingshausen Plain
Bellingshausen Plain 131 F5 *var.*
Bellingshausen Abyssal Plain. *Undersea
feature* SE Pacific Ocean
Bellingshausen Sea 132 A3 *sea* Antarctica
Bellinzona 73 B8 *Ger.* Bellenz. Ticino,
S Switzerland
Bello 36 B2 Antioquia, W Colombia
Bellville 56 B5 Western Cape,
SW South Africa
Belmopan 30 C1 *country capital* (Belize)
Cayo, C Belize
Belogradchik 82 B1 Vidin, NW Bulgaria
Belo Horizonte 41 F4 *prev.* Bello Horizonte.
State capital Minas Gerais, SE Brazil
Belomorsk 88 B3 Respublika Kareliya,
NW Russian Federation
Beloretsk 89 D6 Respublika Bashkortostan,
W Russian Federation
Belorussia/Belorussian SSR *see* Belarus
Belorusskaya SSR *see* Belarus
Beloye More 88 C3 *Eng.* White Sea. *Sea*
NW Russian Federation

Belozersk 88 B4 Vologodskaya Oblast', NW Russian Federation
Belton 27 G3 Texas, SW USA
Beluchistan see Baluchistān
Belukha, Gora 92 D3 mountain Kazakhstan/Russian Federation
Belyy, Ostrov 92 D2 island N Russian Federation
Bemaraha 57 F3 var. Plateau du Bemaraha. Mountain range W Madagascar
Bemidji 23 F1 Minnesota, N USA
Bemmel 64 D4 Gelderland, SE Netherlands
Benaco see Garda, Lago di
Benavente 70 D2 Castilla-León, N Spain
Bend 24 B3 Oregon, NW USA
Bender Beila see Bandarbeyla
Bender Beyla see Bandarbeyla
Bender Cassim see Boosaaso
Bendern 72 E1 NW Liechtenstein
Bender Qaasim see Boosaaso
Bendery see Tighina
Bendigo 127 C7 Victoria, SE Australia
Benešov 77 B5 Ger. Beneschau. Středočesky Kraj, W Czech Republic
Benevento 75 D5 anc. Beneventum, Malventum. Campania, S Italy
Bengal, Bay of 102 C4 bay N Indian Ocean
Bengbu 106 D5 var. Peng-pu. Anhui, E China
Benghazi see Banghāzī
Bengkulu 116 B4 prev. Bengkoeloe, Benkoelen, Benkulen. Sumatera, W Indonesia
Benguela 56 A2 var. Benguella. Benguela, W Angola
Benguella see Benguela
Bengweulu, Lake see Bangweulu, Lake
Ben Hope 66 B2 mountain N Scotland, UK
Beni 54 B4 var. El Beni. Admin. region department N Bolivia
Beni 55 E5 Nord Kivu, NE Dem. Rep. Congo
Benidorm 71 F4 País Valenciano, SE Spain
Beni-Mellal 48 C2 C Morocco
Benin 53 F4 prev. Dahomey. Country W Africa
Benin, Bight of 53 F5 gulf W Africa
Benin City 53 F5 Edo, SW Nigeria
Beni, Río 39 E3 river N Bolivia
Beni Suef 50 B2 var. Banī Suwayf. N Egypt
Ben Nevis 66 C3 mountain N Scotland, UK
Benson 26 B3 Arizona, SW USA
Bent Jbaïl 97 A5 var. Bint Jubayl. S Lebanon
Benton 20 B1 Arkansas, C USA
Benue 54 B4 Fr. Bénoué. River Cameroon/Nigeria
Benue 53 G4 state SE Nigeria
Beograd 78 D3 Eng. Belgrade, Ger. Belgrad; anc. Singidunum. Country capital Serbia, N Serbia and Montenegro (Yugo.)
Berane 79 D5 prev. Ivangrad. Montenegro, SW Serbia and Montenegro (Yugo.)
Berat 79 C6 var. Berati, SCr. Beligrad. Berat, C Albania
Berati see Berat
Berau, Teluk 117 G4 var. MacCluer Gulf. Bay Papua, E Indonesia
Berbera 50 D4 Woqooyi Galbeed, NW Somalia
Berbérati 55 B5 Mambéré-Kadéï, SW Central African Republic
Berck-Plage 68 C2 Pas-de-Calais, N France
Berdyans'k 87 G4 Rus. Berdyansk; prev. Osipenko. Zaporiz'ka Oblast', SE Ukraine
Berdychiv 108 D2 Rus. Berdichev. Zhytomyrs'ka Oblast', N Ukraine
Bereket 100 B2 prev. Gazandzhyk, Kazandzhik, Turkm. Gazanjyk. Balkanskiy Velayat, W Turkmenistan
Berehove 86 B3 Cz. Berehovo, Hung. Beregszász, Rus. Beregovo. Zakarpats'ka Oblast', W Ukraine
Berettyó 77 D7 Rom. Barcău; prev. Berătău, Beretău. River Hungary/Romania
Berettyóújfalu 77 D6 Hajdú-Bihar, E Hungary
Berezhany 86 C2 Pol. Brzeżany. Ternopil's'ka Oblast', W Ukraine
Berezniki 89 D5 Permskaya Oblast', NW Russian Federation
Berga 71 G2 Cataluña, NE Spain
Bergamo 74 B2 anc. Bergomum. Lombardia, N Italy
Bergara 71 E1 País Vasco, N Spain
Bergen 63 A5 Hordaland, S Norway
Bergen 72 D2 Mecklenburg-Vorpommern, NE Germany
Bergen 64 C2 Noord-Holland, NW Netherlands
Bergerac 69 B5 Dordogne, SW France
Bergeyk 65 C5 Noord-Brabant, S Netherlands
Bergse Maas 64 D4 river S Netherlands
Beringen 65 C5 Limburg, NE Belgium
Bering Sea 14 A2 sea N Pacific Ocean
Bering Strait 14 C2 Rus. Beringov Proliv. Strait Bering Sea/Chukchi Sea
Berja 71 E5 Andalucía, S Spain
Berkeley 25 B6 California, W USA
Berkner Island 132 A2 island Antarctica
Berkovitsa 82 C2 Montana, NW Bulgaria
Berlin 72 D3 country capital (Germany) Berlin, NE Germany
Berlin 19 G3 New Hampshire, NE USA
Bermejo, Río 42 C2 river N Argentina
Bermeo 71 E1 País Vasco, N Spain
Bermuda 13 D6 var. Bermuda Islands, Bermudas; prev. Somers Islands. UK crown colony NW Atlantic Ocean
Bermuda Islands see Bermuda
Bermuda Rise 13 E6 undersea feature C Sargasso Sea
Bermudas see Bermuda
Bern 73 A7 Fr. Berne. Country capital (Switzerland) Bern, W Switzerland
Bernau 72 D3 Brandenburg, NE Germany
Bernburg 72 C4 Sachsen-Anhalt, C Germany
Berne see Bern

Berner Alpen 73 A7 var. Berner Oberland, Eng. Bernese Oberland. Mountain range SW Switzerland
Berner Oberland see Berner Alpen
Bernese Oberland see Berner Alpen
Bernier Island 125 A5 island Western Australia
Berry 90 C4 cultural region C France
Berry Islands 32 C1 island group N Bahamas
Bertoua 55 B5 Est, E Cameroon
Beru 123 E2 var. Peru. Atoll Tungaru, W Kiribati
Berwick-upon-Tweed 66 D4 N England, UK
Berytus see Beyrouth
Besançon 68 D4 anc. Besontium, Vesontio. Doubs, E France
Beskra see Biskra
Betafo 57 G3 Antananarivo, C Madagascar
Betanzos 70 B1 Galicia, NW Spain
Bethlehem 97 B6 Ar. Beit Laḥm, Heb. Bet Leḥem. C West Bank
Bethlehem 56 D4 Free State, C South Africa
Béticos, Sistemas 70 D4 var. Sistema Penibético, Eng. Baetic Cordillera, Baetic Mountains. Mountain range S Spain
Bet Lehem see Bethlehem
Bétou 55 C5 La Likouala, N Congo
Bette, Picco see Bette, Pic
Bette, Pic 49 G4 var. Bīkkū Bīttī, It. Picco Bette. Mountain S Libya
Bette, Picco see Bette, Pic
Beulah 18 C2 Michigan, N USA
Beuthen see Bytom
Beveren 65 B5 Oost-Vlaanderen, N Belgium
Beverley 67 D5 E England, UK
Bexley 67 B8 SE England, UK
Beyla 52 D4 Guinée-Forestière, SE Guinea
Beyrouth 96 A4 var. Bayrūt, Eng. Beirut; anc. Berytus. Country capital (Lebanon) W Lebanon
Beyşehir 94 B4 Konya, SW Turkey
Beyşehir Gölü 94 B4 lake C Turkey
Béziers 69 C6 anc. Baeterrae, Baeterrae Septimanorum, Julia Beterrae. Hérault, S France
Bhadrāvati 110 C2 Karnātaka, SW India
Bhāgalpur 113 F3 Bihār, NE India
Bhaktapur 113 F3 Central, C Nepal
Bhamo 114 B2 var. Banmo. Kachin State, N Myanmar
Bharūch 112 C4 Gujarāt, W India
Bhāvnagar 112 C4 prev. Bhaunagar. Gujarāt, W India
Bhopāl 112 D4 Madhya Pradesh, C India
Bhubaneshwar 113 F5 prev. Bhubaneswar, Bhuvaneshwar. Orissa, E India
Bhuket see Phuket
Bhusāwal 112 D4 prev. Bhusaval. Mahārāshtra, C India
Bhutan 113 G3 var. Druk-yul. Country S Asia
Biak, Pulau 139 G4 island E Indonesia
Biała Podlaska 76 E3 Lubelskie, E Poland
Białogard 76 B2 Ger. Belgard. Zachodniopomorskie, NW Poland
Białystok 76 E3 Rus. Belostok, Bielostok. Podlaskie, NE Poland
Biarritz 69 A6 Pyrénées-Atlantiques, SW France
Bicaz 86 C3 Hung. Békás. Neamţ, NE Romania
Biddeford 19 G2 Maine, NE USA
Bideford 67 C7 SW England, UK
Biel 73 A7 Fr. Bienne. Bern, W Switzerland
Bielefeld 72 B4 Nordrhein-Westfalen, NW Germany
Bielsko-Biała 77 C5 Ger. Bielitz, Bielitz-Biala. Śląskie, S Poland
Bielsk Podlaski 76 E3 Podlaskie, NE Poland
Bien Bien see Điện Biên
Biên Hoa 115 E6 Đông Nai, S Vietnam
Bienville, Lac 16 D2 lake Québec, C Canada
Bié, Planalto do 56 B2 var. Bié Plateau. Plateau C Angola
Bié Plateau see Bié, Planalto do
Big Cypress Swamp 21 E5 wetland Florida, SE USA
Bigge Island 124 C2 island Western Australia
Bighorn Mountains 22 C2 mountain range Wyoming, C USA
Bighorn River 22 C2 river Montana/Wyoming, NW USA
Bignona 52 B3 SW Senegal
Big Sioux River 23 E2 river Iowa/South Dakota, N USA
Big Spring 27 E3 Texas, SW USA
Bihać 78 B3 Federacija Bosna I Hercegovina, NW Bosnia and Herzegovina
Bihār 113 F3 prev. Behar. Admin. region state N India
Biharamulo 51 B7 Kagera, NW Tanzania
Bihosava 85 D5 Rus. Bigosovo. Vitsyebskaya Voblasts', NW Belarus
Bijeljina 78 C3 Republika Srpska, NE Bosnia and Herzegovina
Bijelo Polje 79 D5 Montenegro, SW Serbia and Montenegro (Yugo.)
Bīkaner 112 C3 Rājasthān, NW India
Bikin 93 G4 Khabarovskiy Kray, SE Russian Federation
Bikini Atoll 122 C1 var. Pikinni. Atoll Ralik Chain, NW Marshall Islands
Bīkkū Bīttī see Bette, Pic
Bilāspur 113 E4 Madhya Pradesh, C India
Biläsuvar 95 H3 Rus. Bilyasuvar; prev. Pushkino. SE Azerbaijan
Bila Tserkva 87 E2 Rus. Belaya Tserkov'. Kyyivs'ka Oblast', N Ukraine
Bilauktaung Range 115 C5 var. Thanintari Taungdan. Mountain range Myanmar/Thailand
Bilbao 71 E1 Basq. Bilbo. País Vasco, N Spain
Bilecik 94 B3 Bilecik, NW Turkey
Billings 22 C2 Montana, NW USA
Bilma, Grand Erg de 53 H3 desert NE Niger
Biloela 126 D4 Queensland, E Australia
Biloxi 20 C3 Mississippi, S USA
Biltine 54 C3 Biltine, E Chad
Bilwi see Puerto Cabezas

Bilzen 87 D6 Limburg, NE Belgium
Bimini Islands 32 C1 island group W Bahamas
Binche 65 B7 Hainaut, S Belgium
Bindloe Island see Marchena, Isla
Binghamton 19 F3 New York, NE USA
Bingöl 95 E3 Bingöl, E Turkey
Bint Jubayl see Bent Jbaïl
Bintulu 116 D3 Sarawak, East Malaysia
Binzhou 106 D4 Shandong, E China
Bío Bío, Río 43 B5 river C Chile
Bioco, Isla de 55 A5 var. Bioko, Eng. Fernando Po, Sp. Fernando Póo; prev. Macías Nguema Biyogo. Island NW Equatorial Guinea
Bioko see Bioco, Isla de
Biratnagar 113 F3 Eastern, SE Nepal
Bir es Saba see Be'ér Sheva'
Birhār Sharīf 113 F3 Bihār, N India
Bīrjand 98 E3 Khorāsān, E Iran
Birkenfeld 73 A5 Rheinland-Pfalz, SW Germany
Birkenhead 67 C5 NW England, UK
Birmingham 20 C2 Alabama, S USA
Birmingham 67 C6 C England, UK
Bir Moghrein see Bîr Mogreïn
Bîr Mogreïn 52 C1 var. Bir Moghrein; prev. Fort-Trinquet. Tiris Zemmour, N Mauritania
Birnie Island 123 E3 atoll Phoenix Islands, C Kiribati
Birni-Nkonni see Birnin Konni
Birnin Konni 53 F3 var. Birni-Nkonni. Tahoua, SW Niger
Birobidzhan 93 G4 Yevreyskaya Avtonomnaya Oblast', SE Russian Federation
Birsk 89 D5 Respublika Bashkortostan, W Russian Federation
Biržai 84 C4 Ger. Birsen. Biržai, NE Lithuania
Biržebbuġa 80 B5 SE Malta
Bisbee 26 B3 Arizona, SW USA
Biscay, Bay of 58 B4 Sp. Golfo de Vizcaya, Port. Baía de Biscaia. Bay France/Spain
Biscay Plain 58 B3 undersea feature SE Bay of Biscay
Bīshah, Wādī 99 B5 dry watercourse C Saudi Arabia
Bishkek 101 G2 var. Pishpek; prev. Frunze. Country capital (Kyrgyzstan) Chuyskaya Oblast', N Kyrgyzstan
Bishop's Lynn see King's Lynn
Bishrī, Jabal 96 D3 mountain range E Syria
Biskara see Biskra
Biskra 49 E2 var. Beskra, Biskara. NE Algeria
Biskupiec 76 D2 Ger. Bischofsburg. Warmińsko-Mazurskie, NE Poland
Bislig 117 F2 Mindanao, S Philippines
Bismarck 23 E2 state capital North Dakota, N USA
Bismarck Archipelago 122 B3 island group NE PNG
Bismarck Sea 122 B3 sea W Pacific Ocean
Bisnulok see Phitsanulok
Bissau 52 B4 country capital (Guinea-Bissau) W Guinea-Bissau
Bistrița 86 B3 Ger. Bistritz, Hung. Beszterce; prev. Nösen. Bistrita-Năsăud, N Romania
Bitam 55 B5 Woleu-Ntem, N Gabon
Bitburg 73 A5 Rheinland-Pfalz, SW Germany
Bitlis 95 F3 Bitlis, SE Turkey
Bitola 79 D6 Turk. Monastir; prev. Bitolj. S FYR Macedonia
Bitonto 75 D5 anc. Butuntum. Puglia, SE Italy
Bitterroot Range 24 D2 mountain range Idaho/Montana, NW USA
Bitung 117 F3 prev. Bitoeng. Sulawesi, C Indonesia
Biu 53 H4 Borno, E Nigeria
Biwa-ko 109 C6 lake Honshū, SW Japan
Bizerte 49 E1 Ar. Banzart, Eng. Bizerta. N Tunisia
Bjelovar 78 B2 Hung. Belovár. Bjelovar-Bilogora, N Croatia
Bjørnøya 61 F3 Eng. Bear Island. Island N Norway
Blackall 126 C4 Queensland, E Australia
Black Drin 79 D6 Alb. Lumi i Drinit të Zi, SCr. Crni Drim. River Albania/FYR Macedonia
Blackfoot 24 E4 Idaho, NW USA
Black Forest see Schwarzwald
Black Hills 22 D3 mountain range South Dakota/Wyoming, N USA
Blackpool 67 C5 NW England, UK
Black Range 26 C2 mountain range New Mexico, SW USA
Black River 114 C3 Chin. Babian Jiang, Lixian Jiang, Fr. Rivière Noire, Vtn. Sông Đa. River China/Vietnam
Black River 32 A5 W Jamaica
Black Rock Desert 25 C5 desert Nevada, W USA
Black Sand Desert see Garagum
Black Sea 94 B1 var. Euxine Sea, Bul. Cherno More, Rom. Marea Neagră, Rus. Chernoye More, Turk. Karadeniz, Ukr. Chorne More. Sea Asia/Europe
Black Sea Lowland 87 E4 Ukr. Prychornomors'ka Nyzovyna. Depression SE Europe
Black Volta 53 E4 var. Borongo, Mouhoun, Moun Hou, Fr. Volta Noire. River W Africa
Blackwater 67 A6 Ir. An Abhainn Mhór. River S Ireland
Blagoevgrad 82 C3 prev. Gorna Dzhumaya. Blagoevgrad, SW Bulgaria
Blagoveshchensk 93 G4 Amurskaya Oblast', SE Russian Federation
Blake Plateau 13 D6 var. Blake Terrace. Undersea feature W Atlantic Ocean
Blake Terrace see Blake Plateau

Blanca, Bahía 43 C5 bay E Argentina
Blanca, Costa 71 F4 physical region SE Spain
Blanche, Lake 127 B5 lake South Australia
Blanc, Mont 69 D5 It. Monte Bianco. Mountain France/Italy
Blanco, Cape 24 A4 headland Oregon, NW USA
Blanes 71 G2 Cataluña, NE Spain
Blankenberge 65 A5 West-Vlaanderen, NW Belgium
Blankenheim 73 A5 Nordrhein-Westfalen, W Germany
Blanquilla, Isla 37 E1 var. La Blanquilla. Island N Venezuela
Blantyre 57 E2 var. Blantyre-Limbe. Southern, S Malawi
Blantyre-Limbe see Blantyre
Blaricum 64 C3 Noord-Holland, C Netherlands
Blenheim 129 C5 Marlborough, South Island, NZ
Blida 48 D2 var. El Boulaida, El Boulaïda. N Algeria
Bloemfontein 56 C4 var. Mangaung. Country capital (South Africa-judicial capital) Free State, C South Africa
Blois 68 C4 anc. Blesae. Loir-et-Cher, C France
Bloomfield 26 C1 New Mexico, SW USA
Bloomington 18 B4 Illinois, N USA
Bloomington 18 C4 Indiana, N USA
Bloomington 23 F2 Minnesota, N USA
Bloomsbury 126 D3 Queensland, NE Australia
Bluefield 18 D5 West Virginia, NE USA
Bluefields 31 E3 Región Autónoma Atlántico Sur, SE Nicaragua
Blue Mountain Peak 32 B5 mountain E Jamaica
Blue Mountains 24 C3 mountain range Oregon/Washington, NW USA
Blue Nile 46 D4 var. Abai, Bahr el Azraq, Amh. Ābay Wenz, Ar. An Nīl al Azraq. River Ethiopia/Sudan
Blue Nile 50 C4 state E Sudan
Blumenau 41 E5 Santa Catarina, S Brazil
Blythe 25 D8 California, W USA
Blytheville 20 C1 Arkansas, C USA
Bo 52 C4 S Sierra Leone
Boaco 30 D3 Boaco, S Nicaragua
Boa Vista 52 A3 island Ilhas de Barlavento, E Cape Verde
Boa Vista 40 D1 state capital Roraima, NW Brazil
Bobaomby, Tanjona 57 G2 Fr. Cap d'Ambre. Headland N Madagascar
Bobigny 68 E1 Seine-St-Denis, N France
Bobo-Dioulasso 52 D4 SW Burkina faso
Bobrynets' 87 E3 Rus. Bobrinets. Kirovohrads'ka Oblast', C Ukraine
Boca Raton 21 F5 Florida, SE USA
Bocay 30 D2 Jinotega, N Nicaragua
Bocche del Po see Po, Foci del
Bocholt 72 A4 Nordrhein-Westfalen, W Germany
Bochum 72 A4 Nordrhein-Westfalen, W Germany
Bocşa 86 A4 Ger. Bokschen, Hung. Boksánbánya. Caraș-Severin, SW Romania
Bodaybo 93 F4 Irkutskaya Oblast', E Russian Federation
Boden 62 D4 Norrbotten, N Sweden
Bodmin 67 C7 SW England, UK
Bodø 62 C3 Nordland, C Norway
Bodrum 94 A4 Muğla, SW Turkey
Boende 55 C5 Equateur, C Dem. Rep. Congo
Boetoeng see Buton, Pulau
Bogale 114 B4 Irrawaddy, SW Myanmar
Bogalusa 20 B3 Louisiana, S USA
Bogatynia 76 B4 Ger. Reichenau. Dolnośląskie, SW Poland
Boğazlıyan 94 D3 Yozgat, C Turkey
Bogor 116 C5 Dut. Buitenzorg. Jawa, C Indonesia
Bogotá 36 B3 prev. Santa Fe, Santa Fe de Bogotá. Country capital (Colombia) Cundinamarca, C Colombia
Bo Hai 106 D4 var. Gulf of Chihli. Gulf NE China
Bohemia 77 A5 Cz. Čechy, Ger. Böhmen. Cultural and historical region W Czech Republic
Bohemian Forest 73 C5 Cz. Český Les, Šumava, Ger. Böhmerwald. Mountain range C Europe
Böhmisch-Krumau see Český Krumlov
Bohol Sea 117 E2 var. Mindanao Sea. Sea S Philippines
Bohoro Shan 104 B2 mountain range NW China
Bohuslav 87 E2 Rus. Boguslav. Kyyivs'ka Oblast', N Ukraine
Boise 24 D3 var. Boise City. State capital Idaho, NW USA
Boise City see Boise
Boise City 27 E1 Oklahoma, C USA
Boizenburg 72 C3 Mecklenburg-Vorpommern, N Germany
Bojador see Boujdour
Bojnūrd 98 D2 var. Bujnurd. Khorāsān, N Iran
Bokāro 113 F4 Bihār, N India
Boké 52 C4 Guinée-Maritime, W Guinea
Bokhara see Buxoro
Boknafjorden 85 A6 fjord S Norway
Bol 54 B3 Lac, W Chad
Bol 55 E3 N Ghana
Bolhrad 86 D4 Rus. Bolgrad. Odes'ka Oblast', SW Ukraine
Bolívar, Pico 36 C2 mountain W Venezuela
Bolivia 39 F3 Country W South America
Bollène 69 D6 Vaucluse, SE France
Bollnäs 85 C5 Gävleborg, C Sweden
Bollon 127 D5 Queensland, C Australia
Bologna 74 C3 Emilia-Romagna, N Italy
Bol'shevik, Ostrov 93 E2 island Severnaya Zemlya, N Russian Federation

Bol'shezemel'skaya Tundra 88 E3 physical region NW Russian Federation
Bol'shoy Lyakhovskiy, Ostrov 93 F2 island NE Russian Federation
Bolton 67 D5 prev. Bolton-le-Moors. NW England, UK
Bolu 94 B3 Bolu, NW Turkey
Bolungarvík 61 E4 Vestfirðhir, NW Iceland
Bolvadin 94 C3 var. Bolvadin. NW Turkey
Bolyarovo 82 D3 prev. Pashkeni. Yambol, E Bulgaria
Bolzano 74 C1 Ger. Bozen; anc. Bauzanum. Trentino-Alto Adige, N Italy
Boma 55 B6 Bas-Zaïre, W Dem. Rep. Congo
Bombay see Mumbai
Bomu 54 D4 var. Mbomou, Mbomu, M'Bomu. River Central African Republic/Dem. Rep. Congo
Bonaire 33 F5 island E Netherlands Antilles
Bonanza 30 D2 Región Autónoma Atlántico Norte, NE Nicaragua
Bonaparte Archipelago 124 C2 island group Western Australia
Bon, Cap 80 D3 headland N Tunisia
Bonda 55 B6 Ogooué-Lolo, C Gabon
Bondoukou 53 E4 E Côte d'Ivoire
Bone see Watampone
Bone, Teluk 117 E4 bay Sulawesi, C Indonesia
Bongaigaon 113 G3 Assam, NE India
Bongo, Massif des 54 D4 var. Chaîne des Mongos. Mountain range NE Central African Republic
Bongor 54 B3 Mayo-Kébbi, SW Chad
Bonifacio 69 E7 Corse, France, C Mediterranean Sea
Bonifacio, Strait of 74 A4 Fr. Bouches de Bonifacio, It. Bocche di Bonifacio. Strait C Mediterranean Sea
Bonn 73 A5 Nordrhein-Westfalen, W Germany
Bononia see Boulogne-sur-Mer
Boosaaso 50 E4 var. Bandar Kassim, Bender Qaasim, Bosaso, It. Bender Cassim. Bari, N Somalia
Boothia, Gulf of 15 F2 gulf Nunavut, NE Canada
Boothia Peninsula 15 F2 prev. Boothia Felix. Peninsula Nunavut, NE Canada
Boppard 73 B5 Rheinland-Pfalz, W Germany
Boquete 31 E5 var. Bajo Boquete. Chiriquí, W Panama
Boquillas 28 D2 var. Boquillas del Carmen. Coahuila de Zaragoza, NE Mexico
Boquillas del Carmen see Boquillas
Bor 81 E5 Jonglei, S Sudan
Bor 78 E4 Serbia, E Serbia and Montenegro (Yugo.)
Borås 63 B7 Västra Götaland, S Sweden
Borborema, Planalto da 34 E3 plateau NE Brazil
Bordeaux 69 B5 anc. Burdigala. Gironde, SW France
Bordj Omar Driss 49 E3 E Algeria
Børgefjell 62 C4 mountain range C Norway
Borger 64 E2 Drenthe, NE Netherlands
Borger 27 E1 Texas, SW USA
Borgholm 63 C7 Kalmar, S Sweden
Borgo Maggiore 74 E1 NW San Marino
Borisoglebsk 89 B6 Voronezhskaya Oblast', W Russian Federation
Borlänge 63 C6 Kopparberg, C Sweden
Borne 64 E3 Overijssel, E Netherlands
Borneo 116 C4 island Brunei/Indonesia/Malaysia
Bornholm 63 B8 island E Denmark
Borohoro Shan 101 H1 mountain range NW China
Borongo see Black Volta
Borovan 82 C2 Vratsa, NW Bulgaria
Borovichi 88 B4 Novgorodskaya Oblast', W Russian Federation
Borovo 78 C3 Vukovar-Srijem, NE Croatia
Borşa 86 C3 Hung. Borsa. Maramureş, N Romania
Boryslav 86 B2 Pol. Borysław, Rus. Borislav. L'vivs'ka Oblast', W Ukraine
Bosanska Dubica 78 B3 var. Kozarska Dubica. Republika Srpska, NW Bosnia and Herzegovina
Bosanska Gradiška 78 B3 var. Gradiška. Republika Srpska, N Bosnia and Herzegovina
Bosanski Novi 78 B3 var. Novi Grad. Republika Srpska, NW Bosnia and Herzegovina
Bosanski Šamac 78 C3 var. Šamac, Republika Srpska, N Bosnia and Herzegovina
Bosaso see Boosaaso
Boskovice 77 B5 Ger. Boskowitz. Brněnský Kraj, SE Czech Republic
Bosna 78 C4 river N Bosnia and Herzegovina
Bosna I Hercegovina, Federacija Admin. region republic Bosnia and Herzegovina
Bosnia and Herzegovina 78 B3 Country SE Europe
Bōsō-hantō 109 D6 peninsula Honshū, S Japan
Bosphorus see İstanbul Boğazı
Bosporus see İstanbul Boğazı
Bosporus Cimmerius see Kerch Strait
Bosporus Thracius see İstanbul Boğazı
Bossangoa 54 C4 Ouham, C Central African Republic
Bossembélé 54 C4 Ombella-Mpoko, C Central African Republic
Bossier City 20 A2 Louisiana, S USA
Bosten Hu 104 C3 var. Bagrax Hu. Lake NW China
Boston 67 E6 prev. St.Botolph's Town. E England, UK
Boston 19 G3 state capital Massachusetts, NE USA
Boston Mountains 20 B1 mountain range Arkansas, C USA

Botany – Caniapiscau, Réservoir de

Botany *126 E2* New South Wales, SE Australia
Botany Bay *126 E2 inlet* New South Wales, SE Australia
Boteti *56 C3 var.* Botletle. *River* N Botswana
Bothnia, Gulf of *63 D5 Fin.* Pohjanlahti, *Swe.* Bottniska Viken. *Gulf* N Baltic Sea
Botletle *see* Boteti
Botoşani *86 C3 Hung.* Botosány. Botoşani, NE Romania
Botou *106 C4 prev.* Bozhen. Hebei, E China
Botrange *65 D6 mountain* E Belgium
Botswana *56 C3 Country* S Africa
Bouar *54 B4* Nana-Mambéré, W Central African Republic
Bou Craa *48 B3 var.* Bu Craa. NW Western Sahara
Bougainville Island *120 B3 island* NE PNG
Bougaroun, Cap *80 C3 headland* NE Algeria
Bougouni *52 D4* Sikasso, SW Mali
Boujdour *48 A3 var.* Bojador. W Western Sahara
Boulder *22 C4* Colorado, C USA
Boulder *22 B2* Montana, NW USA
Boulogne *see* Boulogne-sur-Mer
Boulogne-Billancourt *68 D1 prev.* Boulogne-sur-Seine. Hauts-de-Seine, N France
Boulogne-sur-Mer *68 C2 var.* Boulogne; *anc.* Bononia, Gesoriacum, Gessoriacum. Pas-de-Calais, N France
Boûmdeïd *52 C3 var.* Boumdeït. Assaba, S Mauritania
Boumdeït *see* Boûmdeïd
Boundiali *52 D4* N Côte d'Ivoire
Bountiful *22 B4* Utah, W USA
Bounty Basin *see* Bounty Trough
Bounty Islands *120 D5 island group* S NZ
Bounty Trough *130 C5 var.* Bounty Basin. *Undersea feature* S Pacific Ocean
Bourbonnais *68 C4* Illinois, N USA
Bourg *see* Bourg-en-Bresse
Bourgas *see* Burgas
Bourge-en-Bresse *see* Bourg-en-Bresse
Bourg-en-Bresse *69 D5 var.* Bourg, Bourge-en-Bresse. Ain, E France
Bourges *68 C4 anc.* Avaricum. Cher, C France
Bourgogne *68 C4 Eng.* Burgundy. *Cultural region* E France
Bourke *127 C5* New South Wales, SE Australia
Bournemouth *67 D7* S England, UK
Boutilimit *52 C3* Trarza, SW Mauritania
Bouvet Island *45 D7 Norwegian dependency* S Atlantic Ocean
Bowen *126 D3* Queensland, NE Australia
Bowling Green *18 B5* Kentucky, S USA
Bowling Green *18 C3* Ohio, N USA
Boxmeer *64 D4* Noord-Brabant, SE Netherlands
Boyarka *87 E2* Kyyivs'ka Oblast', N Ukraine
Boysun *101 E3 Rus.* Baysun. Surkhondaryo Wiloyati, S Uzbekistan
Bozeman *22 B2* Montana, NW USA
Bozüyük *94 B3* Bilecik, NW Turkey
Brač *78 B4 var.* Brach, *It.* Brazza; *anc.* Brattia. *Island* S Croatia
Brach *see* Brač
Bradford *67 D5* N England, UK
Brady *27 F3* Texas, SW USA
Braga *70 B2 anc.* Bracara Augusta. Braga, NW Portugal
Bragança *70 C2 Eng.* Braganza; *anc.* Julio Briga. Bragança, NE Portugal
Brahmanbaria *113 G4* Chittagong, E Bangladesh
Brahmapur *113 F5* Orissa, E India
Brahmaputra *113 H3 var.* Padma, Tsangpo, *Ben.* Jamuna, *Chin.* Yarlung Zangbo Jiang, *Ind.* Bramaputra, Dihang, Siang. *River* S Asia
Brăila *86 D4* Brăila, E Romania
Braine-le-Comte *65 B6* Hainaut, SW Belgium
Brainerd *23 F2* Minnesota, N USA
Brak *see* Birāk
Bramaputra *see* Brahmaputra
Brampton *16 D5* Ontario, S Canada
Branco, Rio *34 C3 river* N Brazil
Brandberg *56 A3 mountain* NW Namibia
Brandenburg *72 C3 var.* Brandenburg an der Havel. Brandenburg, NE Germany
Brandenburg an der Havel *see* Brandenburg
Brandon *15 F5* Manitoba, S Canada
Braniewo *76 D2 Ger.* Braunsberg. Warmińsko-Mazurskie, NE Poland
Brasília *41 F3 country capital* (Brazil) Distrito Federal, C Brazil
Braşov *86 C4 Ger.* Kronstadt, *Hung.* Brassó; *prev.* Oraşul Stalin. Braşov, C Romania
Bratislava *77 C6 Ger.* Pressburg, *Hung.* Pozsony. *Country capital* (Slovakia) Bratislavský Kraj, SW Slovakia
Bratsk *93 E4* Irkutskaya Oblast', C Russian Federation
Brattia *see* Brač
Braunschweig *72 C4 Eng./Fr.* Brunswick. Niedersachsen, N Germany
Brava, Costa *71 H2 coastal region* NE Spain
Bravo del Norte *see* Grande, Rio
Bravo del Norte, Río *see* Bravo, Río
Bravo del Norte, Río *see* Bravo, Rio
Bravo del Norte, Río *see* Grande, Rio
Bravo, Río *28 C1 var.* Río Bravo del Norte, Rio Grande. River Mexico/USA
Bravo, Río *see* Grande, Rio
Brawley *25 D8* California, W USA
Brazil *40 C2 Port.* República Federativa do Brasil, *Sp.* Brasil; *prev.* United States of Brazil. *Country* South America
Brazil Basin *45 C5 var.* Brazilian Basin, Brazil'skaya Kotlovina. *Undersea feature* W Atlantic Ocean
Brazilian Basin *see* Brazil Basin
Brazilian Highlands *see* Central, Planalto
Brazil'skaya Kotlovina *see* Brazil Basin
Brazos River *27 G3 river* Texas, SW USA
Brazza *see* Brač
Brazzaville *55 B6 country capital* (Congo) Capital District, S Congo
Brecht *65 C5* Antwerpen, N Belgium
Brecon Beacons *67 C6 mountain range* S Wales, UK
Breda *64 C4* Noord-Brabant, S Netherlands
Bree *65 D5* Limburg, NE Belgium
Bregalnica *79 E6 river* E FYR Macedonia
Bregenz *35 B7 anc.* Brigantium. Vorarlberg, W Austria
Bregovo *82 B1* Vidin, NW Bulgaria
Brčko *78 C3* Republika Srpska, NE Bosnia and Herzegovina
Bremen *72 B3 Fr.* Brême. Bremen, NW Germany
Bremerhaven *72 B3* Bremen, NW Germany
Bremerton *24 B2* Washington, NW USA
Brenham *27 G3* Texas, SW USA
Brenner Pass *74 C1 var.* BrennerSattel, *Fr.* Col du Brenner, *Ger.* Brennerpass, *It.* Passo del Brennero. *Pass* Austria/Italy
Brennerpass *see* Brenner Pass
Brenner Sattel *see* Brenner Pass
Brescia *74 B2 anc.* Brixia. Lombardia, N Italy
Bressanone *74 C1 Ger.* Brixen. Trentino-Alto Adige, N Italy
Brest *85 A6 Pol.* Brześć nad Bugiem, *Rus.* Brest-Litovsk; *prev.* Brześć Litewski. Brestskaya Voblasts', SW Belarus
Brest *68 A3* Finistère, NW France
Bretagne *68 A3 Eng.* Brittany; *Lat.* Britannia Minor. *Cultural region* NW France
Brewton *20 C3* Alabama, S USA
Brezovo *82 D2 prev.* Abrashlare. Plovdiv, C Bulgaria
Bria *54 D4* Haute-Kotto, C Central African Republic
Briançon *69 D5 anc.* Brigantio. Hautes-Alpes, SE France
Bridgeport *19 F3* Connecticut, NE USA
Bridgetown *33 G2 country capital* (Barbados) SW Barbados
Bridlington *67 D5* E England, UK
Bridport *67 D7* S England, UK
Brig *73 A7 Fr.* Brigue, *It.* Briga. Valais, SW Switzerland
Brigham City *22 B3* Utah, W USA
Brighton *22 D4* Colorado, C USA
Brighton *67 E7* SE England, UK
Brindisi *75 E5 anc.* Brundisium, Brundusium. Puglia, SE Italy
Brisbane *127 E5 state capital* Queensland, E Australia
Bristol *67 D7 anc.* Bricgstow. SW England, UK
Bristol *19 F3* Connecticut, NE USA
Bristol *18 D5* Virginia, NE USA
Bristol Bay *14 B3 bay* Alaska, USA
Bristol Channel *67 C7 inlet* England/Wales, UK
Britain *58 C3 var.* Great Britain. *Island* UK
British Columbia *14 D4 Fr.* Colombie-Britannique. *Province* SW Canada
British Indian Ocean Territory *119 B5 UK dependent territory* C Indian Ocean
British Isles *67 island group* NW Europe
British Virgin Islands *33 F3 var.* Virgin Islands. *UK dependent territory* E West Indies
Brive-la-Gaillarde *69 C5 prev.* Brive, *anc.* Briva Curretia. Corrèze, C France
Brno *77 B5 Ger.* Brünn. Brněnský Kraj, SE Czech Republic
Broceni *84 B3* Saldus, SW Latvia
Brodeur Peninsula *15 F2 peninsula* Baffin Island, Nunavut, NE Canada
Brodnica *76 C3 Ger.* Buddenbrock. Kujawski-pomorskie, C Poland
Broek-in-Waterland *64 C3* Noord-Holland, C Netherlands
Broken Arrow *27 G1* Oklahoma, C USA
Broken Bay *126 E1 bay* New South Wales, SE Australia
Broken Hill *127 B6* New South Wales, SE Australia
Broken Ridge *119 D6 undersea feature* S Indian Ocean
Bromley *67 B8* SE England, UK
Brookhaven *20 B3* Mississippi, S USA
Brookings *23 F3* South Dakota, N USA
Brooks Range *14 D2 mountain range* Alaska, USA
Brookton *125 B6* Western Australia
Broome *124 B3* Western Australia
Broomfield *22 D4* Colorado, C USA
Broucsella *see* Brussel
Brovary *87 E2* Kyyivs'ka Oblast', N Ukraine
Brownfield *27 E2* Texas, SW USA
Brownville *27 G5* Texas, SW USA
Brownwood *27 F3* Texas, SW USA
Brozha *85 D7* Mahilyowskaya Voblasts', E Belarus
Brugge *65 A5 Fr.* Bruges. West-Vlaanderen, NW Belgium
Brummen *64 D3* Gelderland, E Netherlands
Brunei *116 D3Mal.* Negara Brunei Darussalam. *Country* SE Asia
Brunner, Lake *129 C5 lake* South Island, NZ
Brunswick *21 E3* Georgia, SE USA
Brusa *see* Bursa
Brus Laguna *30 D2* Gracias a Dios, E Honduras
Brussa *see* Bursa
Brussel *var.* Brussels, *Fr.* Bruxelles, *Ger.* Brüssel; *anc.* Broucsella. *Country capital* (Belgium) Brussels, C Belgium *see also* Bruxelles
Brüssel *see* Brussel
Brussels *see* Brussel
Bruxelles *see* Brussels
Bryan *27 G3* Texas, SW USA
Bryansk *89 A5* Bryanskaya Oblast', W Russian Federation
Brzeg *76 C4 Ger.* Brieg; *anc.* Civitas Altae Ripae. Opolskie, S Poland
Bucaramanga *36 B2* Santander, N Colombia
Buchanan *52 C5 prev.* Grand Bassa. SW Liberia
Buchanan, Lake *27 F3 reservoir* Texas, SW USA
Bucharest *see* Bucureşti
Bu Craa *see* Bou Craa
Bucureşti *86 C5 Eng.* Bucharest, *Ger.* Bukarest; *prev.* Altenburg, *anc.* Cetatea Damboviţei. *Country capital* (Romania) Bucureşti, S Romania
Buda-Kashalyova *85 D7 Rus.* Buda-Koshelëvo. Homyel'skaya Voblasts', SE Belarus
Budapest *77 C6 off.* Budapest Főváros, *SCr.* Budimpešta. *Country capital* (Hungary) Pest, N Hungary
Budaun *112 D3* Uttar Pradesh, N India
Buena Park *46 E2* California, W USA
Buenaventura *36 A3* Valle del Cauca, W Colombia
Buena Vista *71 H5* S Gibraltar
Buena Vista *39 G4* Santa Cruz, C Bolivia
Buenos Aires *42 D4 hist.* Santa Maria del Buen Aire. *Country capital* (Argentina) Buenos Aires, E Argentina
Buenos Aires *31 E5* Puntarenas, SE Costa Rica
Buenos Aires, Lago *43 B6 var.* Lago General Carrera. *Lake* Argentina/Chile
Buffalo *19 E3* New York, NE USA
Buffalo Narrows *15 F4* Saskatchewan, C Canada
Buff Bay *32 B5* E Jamaica
Buftea *86 C5* Bucureşti, S Romania
Bug *59 E3 Bel.* Zakhodni Buh, *Eng.* Western Bug, *Rus.* Zapadnyy Bug, *Ukr.* Zakhidnyy Buh. *River* E Europe
Buga *36 B3* Valle del Cauca, W Colombia
Bughotu *see* Santa Isabel
Buguruslan *89 D6* Orenburgskaya Oblast', W Russian Federation
Buḩayrat Nāşir *see* Nasser, Lake
Buḩeiret Nâşir *see* Nasser, Lake
Bujalance *70 D4* Andalucía, S Spain
Bujanovac *79 E5* Serbia, SE Serbia and Montenegro (Yugo.)
Bujnurd *see* Bojnūrd
Bujumbura *51 B7 prev.* Usumbura. *Country capital* (Burundi) W Burundi
Bukavu *55 E6 prev.* Costermansville. Sud Kivu, E Dem. Rep. Congo
Bukhara *see* Buxoro
Bukhoro *see* Buxoro
Bukoba *51 B6* Kagera, NW Tanzania
Bülach *73 B7* Zürich, NW Switzerland
Bulawayo *56 D3 var.* Buluwayo. Matabeleland North, SW Zimbabwe
Buldur *see* Burdur
Bulgan *105 E2* Bulgan, N Mongolia
Bulgaria *82 C2 Bul.* Bŭlgariya; *prev.* People's Republic of Bulgaria. *Country* SE Europe
Bull Shoals Lake *20 B1 reservoir* Arkansas/Missouri, C USA
Bulukumba *117 E4 prev.* Boeloekoemba. Sulawesi, C Indonesia
Buluwayo *see* Bulawayo
Bumba *55 D5* Equateur, N Dem. Rep. Congo
Bunbury *125 A7* Western Australia
Bundaberg *126 E4* Queensland, E Australia
Bungo-suidō *109 B7 strait* SW Japan
Bunia *55 E5* Orientale, NE Dem. Rep. Congo
Bünyan *94 D3* Kayseri, C Turkey
Buraida *see* Buraydah
Buraydah *98 B4 var.* Buraida. Al Qaşīm, N Saudi Arabia
Burdur *94 B4 var.* Buldur. Burdur, SW Turkey
Burdur Gölü *94 B4 salt lake* SW Turkey
Burē *50 C4* C Ethiopia
Burgas *82 E2 var.* Bourgas. Burgas, E Bulgaria
Burgaski Zaliv *82 E2 gulf* E Bulgaria
Burgos *70 D2* Castilla-León, N Spain
Burhan Budai Shan *104 D4 mountain range* C China
Buri Ram *see* Buriram
Buriram *115 D5 var.* Buri Ram, Puriramya. Buri Ram, E Thailand
Burjassot *71 F3* País Valenciano, E Spain
Burkburnett *27 F2* Texas, SW USA
Burketown *126 B3* Queensland, NE Australia
Burkina *see* Burkina Faso
Burkina Faso *53 E4 var.* Burkina; *prev.* Upper Volta. *Country* W Africa
Burley *24 D4* Idaho, NW USA
Burlington *23 G4* Iowa, C USA
Burlington *19 F2* Vermont, NE USA
Burma *see* Myanmar
Burnie *127 C8* Tasmania, SE Australia
Burns *24 C3* Oregon, NW USA
Burnside *15 F3 river* Nunavut, NW Canada
Burnsville *23 F2* Minnesota, N USA
Burrel *79 D6 var.* Burreli. Dibër, C Albania
Burreli *see* Burrel
Burriana *71 F3* País Valenciano, E Spain
Bursa *94 B3 var.* Brussa; *prev.* Brusa, *anc.* Prusa. Bursa, NW Turkey
Burtnieks *84 C3 var.* Burtnieku Ezers. *Lake* N Latvia
Burtnieku Ezers *see* Burtnieks
Burundi *51 B7 prev.* Kingdom of Burundi, Urundi. *Country* C Africa
Buru, Pulau *117 F4 prev.* Boeroe. *Island* E Indonesia
Buşayrah *96 D3* Dayr az Zawr, E Syria
Būshehr *see* Bandar-e Būshehr
Bushire *see* Bandar-e Būshehr
Busselton *125 A7* Western Australia
Buta *55 D5* Orientale, N Dem. Rep. Congo
Butembo *55 E5* Nord Kivu, NE Dem. Rep. Congo
Butler *19 E4* Pennsylvania, NE USA
Buton, Pulau *117 E4 var.* Pulau Butung; *prev.* Boetoeng. *Island* C Indonesia
Butte *22 B2* Montana, NW USA
Butterworth *116 B3* Pinang, Peninsular Malaysia
Button Islands *17 E1 island group* Northwest Territories, NE Canada
Butuan *117 F2 off.* Butuan City. Mindanao, S Philippines
Buulobarde *51 D5 var.* Buulo Berde. Hiiraan, C Somalia Africa
Buulo Berde *see* Buulobarde
Buur Gaabo *51 D6* Jubbada Hoose, S Somalia
Buxoro *100 D2 var.* Bokhara, Bukhoro, *Rus.* Bukhara. Bukhoro Wiloyati, C Uzbekistan
Buynaksk *89 B8* Respublika Dagestan, SW Russian Federation
Büyükağrı Dağı *95 F3 var.* Aghri Dagh, Agri Dagi, Koh I Noh, Masis, *Eng.* Great Ararat, Mount Ararat. *Mountain* E Turkey
Büyükmenderes Nehri *94 A4 river* SW Turkey
Buzău *86 C4* Buzău, SE Romania
Büzmeýin *100 C3 Rus.* Byuzmeyin; *prev.* Bezmein. Akhalskiy Velayat, C Turkmenistan
Buzuluk *89 D6* Akmola, C Kazakhstan
Byahoml' *85 D5 Rus.* Begoml'. Vitsyebskaya Voblasts', N Belarus
Byalynichy *85 D6 Rus.* Belynichi. Mahilyowskaya Voblasts', E Belarus
Bydgoszcz *76 C3 Ger.* Bromberg. Kujawskie-pomorskie, C Poland
Byelaruskaya Hrada *85 B6 Rus.* Belorusskaya Gryada. *Ridge* N Belarus
Byerezino *85 D6 Rus.* Berezina. *River* C Belarus
Byron Island *see* Nikunau
Bytom *77 C5 Ger.* Beuthen. Śląskie, S Poland
Bytča *77 C5* Žilinský Kraj, N Slovakia
Bytów *76 C2 Ger.* Bütow. Pomorskie, N Poland
Byuzmeyin *see* Büzmeýin
Byval'ki *85 D8* Homyel'skaya Voblasts', SE Belarus
Byzantium *see* İstanbul

C

Caála *56 B2 var.* Kaala, Robert Williams, *Port.* Vila Robert Williams. Huambo, C Angola
Caazapá *42 D3* Caazapá, S Paraguay
Caballo Reservoir *26 C3 reservoir* New Mexico, SW USA
Cabañaquinta *70 D1* Asturias, N Spain
Cabanatuan *117 E1 off.* Cabanatuan City. Luzon, N Philippines
Cabimas *36 C1* Zulia, NW Venezuela
Cabinda *56 A1 var.* Kabinda. Cabinda, NW Angola
Cabinda *56 A1 var.* Kabinda. Admin. region *province* NW Angola
Cabora Bassa, Lake *see* Cahora Bassa, Albufeira de
Caborca *28 B1* Sonora, NW Mexico
Cabot Strait *17 G4 strait* E Canada
Cabras, Ilha das *54 E2 island* S Sao Tome and Principe
Cabrera *71 G3 anc.* Capraria. *Island* Islas Baleares, Spain, W Mediterranean Sea
Cáceres *70 C3 Ar.* Qazris. Extremadura, W Spain
Cachimbo, Serra do *41 E2 mountain range* C Brazil
Caconda *56 B2* Huíla, C Angola
Čadca *77 C5 Hung.* Csaca. Žilinský Kraj, N Slovakia
Cadillac *18 C2* Michigan, N USA
Cadiz *117 E2 off.* Cadiz City. Negros, C Philippines
Cádiz *70 C5 anc.* Gades, Gadier, Gadir, Gadire. Andalucía, SW Spain
Cádiz, Golfo de *70 B5 Eng.* Gulf of Cadiz. *Gulf* Portugal/Spain
Cadiz, Gulf of *see* Cádiz, Golfo de
Caen *68 B3* Calvados, N France
Caene *see* Qena
Caenepolis *see* Qena
Caerdydd *see* Cardiff
Caer Gybi *see* Holyhead
Caesarea Mazaca *see* Kayseri
Cafayate *42 C2* Salta, N Argentina
Cagayan de Oro *117 E2 off.* Cagayan de Oro City. Mindanao, S Philippines
Cagliari *75 A6 anc.* Caralis. Sardegna, Italy, C Mediterranean Sea
Caguas *33 F3* E Puerto Rico
Cahora Bassa, Albufeira de *56 D2 var.* Lake Cabora Bassa. *Reservoir* NW Mozambique
Cahors *69 C5 anc.* Cadurcum. Lot, S France
Cahul *86 D4 Rus.* Kagul. S Moldova
Caicos Passage *32 D2 strait* Bahamas/Turks and Caicos Islands
Caiffa *see* Ḩefa
Cailungo *74 E1* N San Marino
Caiphas *see* Ḩefa
Cairns *126 D3* Queensland, NE Australia
Cairo *50 B2 Ar.* Al Qāhirah, *var.* El Qâhira. *Country capital* (Egypt) N Egypt
Caisleán an Bharraigh *see* Castlebar
Cajamarca *38 B3 prev.* Caxamarca. Cajamarca, NW Peru
Čakovec *78 B2 Ger.* Csakathurn, *Hung.* Csáktornya; *prev. Ger.* Tschakathurn. Medimurje, N Croatia
Calabar *53 G5* Cross River, S Nigeria
Calabozo *36 D2* Guárico, C Venezuela
Calafat *86 B5* Dolj, SW Romania
Calafate *see* El Calafate
Calahorra *71 E2* La Rioja, N Spain
Calais *19 H2* Maine, NE USA
Calais *68 C2* Pas-de-Calais, N France
Calama *42 B2* Antofagasta, N Chile
Calamianes *see* Calamian Group
Calamian Group *107 C7 var.* Calamianes. *Island group* W Philippines
Călăras *see* Călăraşi
Călăraşi *86 D3 var.* Călăras, *Rus.* Kalarash. C Moldova
Călăraşi *86 C5* Călăraşi, SE Romania
Calatayud *71 E2* Aragón, NE Spain
Calbayog *117 E2 off.* Calbayog City. Samar, C Philippines
Calcutta *113 G4 var.* Kolkata. West Bengal, NE India
Caldas da Rainha *70 B3* Leiria, W Portugal
Caldera *42 B3* Atacama, N Chile
Caldwell *24 C3* Idaho, NW USA
Caledonia *30 C1* Corozal, N Belize
Caleta *see* Catalan Bay
Caleta Olivia *43 B6* Santa Cruz, SE Argentina
Calgary *15 E5* Alberta, SW Canada
Cali *36 B3* Valle del Cauca, W Colombia
Calicut *110 C2 var.* Kozhikode. Kerala, SW India
California *25 B7 off.* State of California; also known as El Dorado, The Golden State. *State* W USA
California, Golfo de *28 B2 Eng.* Gulf of California; *prev.* Sea of Cortez. *Gulf* W Mexico
California, Gulf of *see* California, Golfo de
Călimăneşti *86 B4* Vâlcea, SW Romania
Callabonna, Lake *127 B5 lake* South Australia
Callao *38 C4* Callao, W Peru
Callosa de Segura *71 F4* País Valenciano, E Spain
Calmar *see* Kalmar
Caloundra *127 E5* Queensland, E Australia
Caltanissetta *75 C7* Sicilia, Italy, C Mediterranean Sea
Caluula *50 E4* Bari, NE Somalia
Camabatela *56 B1* Cuanza Norte, NW Angola
Camacupa *56 B2 var.* General Machado, *Port.* Vila General Machado. Bié, C Angola
Camagüey *32 C2 prev.* Puerto Príncipe. Camagüey, C Cuba
Camagüey, Archipiélago de *32 C2 island group* C Cuba
Camaná *39 E4* Arequipa, SW Peru
Camargue *69 D6 physical region* SE France
Ca Mau *115 D6 prev.* Quan Long. Minh Hai, S Vietnam
Cambodia *115 D5 var.* Democratic Kampuchea, Roat Kampuchea, *Cam.* Kampuchea; *prev.* People's Democratic Republic of Kampuchea. *Country* SE Asia
Cambrai *68 C2 Flem.* Kambryk; *prev.* Cambray, *anc.* Cameracum. Nord, N France
Cambrian Mountains *67 C6 mountain range* C Wales, UK
Cambridge *67 E6 Lat.* Cantabrigia. E England, UK
Cambridge *19 F4* Maryland, NE USA
Cambridge *18 D4* Ohio, NE USA
Cambridge *32 A4* W Jamaica
Cambridge *128 D3* Waikato, North Island, NZ
Cambridge Bay *15 F3 district capital* Victoria Island, Nunavut, NW Canada
Camden *20 B2* Arkansas, C USA
Cameroon *54 A4 Fr.* Cameroun. *Country* W Africa
Camocim *41 F2* Ceará, E Brazil
Camopi *37 H3* E French Guiana
Campamento *30 C2* Olancho, C Honduras
Campania *75 D5 cultural region* SE Italy
Campbell, Cape *129 D5 headland* South Island, NZ
Campbell Island *120 D5 island* S NZ
Campbell Plateau *120 D5 undersea feature* SW Pacific Ocean
Campbell River *14 D5* Vancouver Island, British Columbia, SW Canada
Campeche *29 G4* Campeche, SE Mexico
Campeche, Bahía de *29 F4 Eng.* Bay of Campeche. *Bay* E Mexico
Cẩm Pha *114 E3* Quang Ninh, N Vietnam
Câmpina *86 C4 prev.* Cîmpina. Prahova, SE Romania
Campina Grande *41 G2* Paraíba, E Brazil
Campinas *41 F4* São Paulo, S Brazil
Campobasso *75 D5* Molise, C Italy
Campo Criptana *see* Campo de Criptana
Campo de Criptana *71 E3 var.* Campo Criptana. Castilla-La Mancha, C Spain
Campo dos Goitacazes *see* Campos
Campo Grande *41 E4 state capital* Mato Grosso do Sul, SW Brazil
Campos *41 F4 var.* Campo dos Goitacazes. Rio de Janeiro, SE Brazil
Câmpulung *86 B4 prev.* Câmpulung-Muşcel, Cîmpulung. Argeş, S Romania
Campus Stellae *see* Santiago
Cam Ranh *115 E6* Khanh Hoa, S Vietnam
Canada *12 B4 country* N North America
Canada Basin *12 C2 undersea feature* Arctic Ocean
Canadian River *27 E2 river* SW USA
Çanakkale *94 A3 var.* Dardanelli; *prev.* Chanak, Kale Sultanie. Çanakkale, W Turkey
Çanakkale Boğazı *94 A2 Eng.* Dardanelles. *Strait* NW Turkey
Cananea *28 B1* Sonora, NW Mexico
Canarias, Islas *48 A2 Eng.* Canary Islands. *Island group* Spain, NE Atlantic Ocean
Canarreos, Archipiélago de los *32 B2 island group* W Cuba
Canary Islands *see* Canarias, Islas
Cañas *30 D4* Guanacaste, NW Costa Rica
Canaveral, Cape *21 E4 headland* Florida, SE USA
Canavieiras *41 G3* Bahia, E Brazil
Canberra *120 C4 country capital* (Australia) Australian Capital Territory, SE Australia
Cancún *29 H3* Quintana Roo, SE Mexico
Candia *see* Irákleio
Canea *see* Chaniá
Cangzhou *106 D4* Hebei, E China
Caniapiscau *17 E2 river* Québec, E Canada
Caniapiscau, Réservoir de *16 D3 reservoir* Québec, C Canada

Canik Dağları 94 D2 mountain range N Turkey

Canillo 69 A7 C Andorra

Çankırı 94 C2 var. Chankiri; anc. Gangra, Germanicopolis. Çankın, N Turkey

Cannanore 110 B2 var. Kananur, Kannur. Kerala, SW India

Cannes 69 D6 Alpes-Maritimes, SE France

Canoas 41 E5 Rio Grande do Sul, S Brazil

Canon City 22 C5 Colorado, C USA

Cantabria 70 D1 cultural region N Spain

Cantábrica, Cordillera 70 C1 mountain range N Spain

Cantaura 37 E2 Anzoátegui, NE Venezuela

Canterbury 67 E7 hist. Cantwaraburh, anc. Durovernum, Lat. Cantuaria. SE England, UK

Canterbury Bight 129 C6 bight South Island, NZ

Canterbury Plains 129 C6 plain South Island, NZ

Cần Thơ 115 E6 Cân Tho, S Vietnam

Canton see Guangzhou

Canton 20 B3 Mississippi, S USA

Canton 18 D4 Ohio, N USA

Canton Island see Kanton

Canyon 27 E2 Texas, SW USA

Cao Bằng 114 D3 var. Caobang. Cao Băng, N Vietnam

Caobang see Cao Bằng

Cape Barren Island 127 C8 island Furneaux Group, Tasmania, SE Australia

Cape Basin 47 B7 undersea feature S Atlantic Ocean

Cape Breton Island 17 G4 Fr. Île du Cap-Breton. Island Nova Scotia, SE Canada

Cape Charles 19 F5 Virginia, USA

Cape Coast 53 E5 prev. Cape Coast Castle. S Ghana

Cape Farewell see Uummannarsuaq

Cape Girardeau 23 H5 Missouri, C USA

Cape Horn see Hornos, Cabo de

Capelle aan den IJssel 64 C4 Zuid-Holland, SW Netherlands

Cape Palmas see Harper

Cape Town 56 B5 var. Ekapa, Afr. Kaapstad, Kapstad. Country capital (South Africa-legislative capital) Western Cape, SW South Africa

Cape Verde 52 A2 Port. Cabo Verde, Ilhas do Cabo Verde. Country E Atlantic Ocean

Cape Verde Basin 44 C4 undersea feature E Atlantic Ocean

Cape Verde Plain 44 C4 undersea feature E Atlantic Ocean

Cape York Peninsula 126 C2 peninsula Queensland, N Australia

Cap-Haïtien 32 D3 var. Le Cap. N Haiti

Capira 31 G5 Panamá, C Panama

Capitán Arturo Prat 132 A2 Chilean research station South Shetland Islands, Antarctica

Capitán Pablo Lagerenza 42 D1 var. Mayor Pablo Lagerenza. Chaco, N Paraguay

Capri, Isola di 75 C5 island S Italy

Caprivi Strip 56 C3 Ger. Caprivizipfel; prev. Caprivi Concession. Cultural region NE Namibia

Caquetá 34 B3 off. Departamanto del Caquetá. Province S Colombia

Caquetá, Río 36 C5 var. Rio Japurá, Yapurá. River Brazil/Colombia see also Japurá, Rio

CAR see Central African Republic

Caracal 86 B5 Olt, S Romania

Caracaraí 40 D1 Rondônia, N Brazil

Caracas 36 D1 country capital (Venezuela) Distrito Federal, N Venezuela

Caratasca, Laguna de 31 E2 lagoon NE Honduras

Carballiño see O Carballiño

Carbondale 18 B5 Illinois, N USA

Carbonia 75 A6 var. Carbonia Centro. Sardegna, Italy, C Mediterranean Sea

Carbonia Centro see Carbonia

Carcassonne 69 C6 anc. Carcaso. Aude, S France

Cárdenas 32 B2 Matanzas, W Cuba

Cardiff 67 C7 Wel. Caerdydd. Admin capital S Wales, UK

Cardigan Bay 67 C6 bay W Wales, UK

Carei 86 B3 Ger. Gross-Karol, Karol, Hung. Nagykároly; prev. Careii-Mari. Satu Mare, NW Romania

Carey, Lake 125 B6 lake Western Australia

Cariaco 37 E1 Sucre, NE Venezuela

Caribbean Sea 32 C4 sea W Atlantic Ocean

Carlisle 66 C4 anc. Caer Luel, Luguvallium, Luguvallum. NW England, UK

Carlow 67 B6 Ir. Ceatharlach. SE Ireland

Carlsbad 26 D3 New Mexico, SW USA

Carlsberg Ridge 118 B4 undersea feature S Arabian Sea

Carlsruhe see Karlsruhe

Carmana see Kermān

Carmarthen 67 C6 SW Wales, UK

Carmaux 69 C6 Tarn, S France

Carmel 18 C4 Indiana, N USA

Carmelita 30 B1 Petén, N Guatemala

Carmen 29 G4 var. Ciudad del Carmen. Campeche, SE Mexico

Carmona 70 C4 Andalucía, S Spain

Carnaro see Kvarner

Carnarvon 125 A5 Western Australia

Carnegie, Lake 125 B5 salt lake Western Australia

Car Nicobar 111 F3 island Nicobar Islands, India, NE Indian Ocean

Caroço, Ilha 54 E1 island N Sao Tome and Principe

Carolina 41 F2 Maranhão, E Brazil

Caroline Island see Millennium Island

Caroline Islands 84 C2 island group C Micronesia

Caroní, Río 37 E3 river E Venezuela

Caronium see A Coruña

Carora 36 C1 Lara, N Venezuela

Carpathian Mountains 59 E4 var. Carpathians, Cz./Pol. Karpaty, Ger. Karpaten. Mountain range E Europe

Carpathians see Carpathian Mountains

Carpații Meridionali 86 B4 var. Alpi Transilvaniei, Carpații Sudici, Eng. South Carpathians, Transylvanian Alps, Ger. Südkarpaten, Transsylvanische Alpen, Hung. Déli-Kárpátok, Erdélyi-Havasok. Mountain range C Romania

Carpații Occidentali 77 E7 Eng. Western Carpathians. Mountain range W Romania

Carpații Sudici see Carpații Meridionali

Carpentaria, Gulf of 126 B2 gulf N Australia

Carpi 74 C2 Emilia-Romagna, N Italy

Carrara 74 B3 Toscana, C Italy

Carson City 25 C5 state capital Nevada, W USA

Carson Sink 25 C5 salt flat Nevada, W USA

Cartagena 71 F4 anc. Carthago Nova. Murcia, SE Spain

Cartagena 36 B1 var. Cartagena de los Indes. Bolívar, NW Colombia

Cartagena de los Indes see Cartagena

Cartago 31 E4 Cartago, C Costa Rica

Carthage 23 F5 Missouri, C USA

Cartwright 17 F2 Newfoundland and Labrador, E Canada

Carúpano 37 E1 Sucre, NE Venezuela

Caruthersville 23 H5 Missouri, C USA

Cary 21 F1 North Carolina, SE USA

Casablanca 48 C2 Ar. Dar-el-Beida. NW Morocco

Casa Grande 26 B2 Arizona, SW USA

Cascade Range 24 B3 mountain range Oregon/Washington, NW USA

Cascadia Basin 12 A4 undersea feature NE Pacific Ocean

Cascais 70 B4 Lisboa, C Portugal

Caserta 75 D5 Campania, S Italy

Casey 132 D4 Australian research station Antarctica

Casino 69 C8 New South Wales, SE Australia

Casper 22 C3 Wyoming, C USA

Caspian Depression 89 B7 Kaz. Kaspīy Mangy Oypaty, Rus. Prikaspiyskaya Nizmennost'. Depression Kazakhstan/Russian Federation

Caspian Sea 92 A4 Az. Xäzär Dänizi, Kaz. Kaspiy Tengizi, Per. Baḥr-e Khazar, Daryā-ye Khazar, Rus. Kaspiyskoye More. Inland sea Asia/Europe

Cassai see Kasai

Castamoni see Kastamonu

Casteggio 96 B2 Lombardia, N Italy

Castelló de la Plana 71 F3 var. Castellón. País Valenciano, E Spain

Castellón see Castelló de la Plana

Castelnaudary 69 C6 Aude, S France

Castelo Branco 70 C3 Castelo Branco, C Portugal

Castelsarrasin 69 B6 Tarn-et-Garonne, S France

Castelvetrano 75 C7 Sicilia, Italy, C Mediterranean Sea

Castilla-La Mancha 71 E3 cultural region NE Spain

Castilla-León 70 C2 cultural region NW Spain

Castlebar 67 A5 Ir. Caisleán an Bharraigh. W Ireland

Castleford 67 D5 N England, UK

Castle Harbour 20 B5 inlet Bermuda, NW Atlantic Ocean

Castricum 64 C3 Noord-Holland, W Netherlands

Castries 33 F1 country capital (Saint Lucia) N Saint Lucia

Castro 43 B6 Los Lagos, W Chile

Castrovillari 75 D6 Calabria, SW Italy

Castuera 70 D4 Extremadura, W Spain

Caswell Sound 129 A7 sound South Island, NZ

Catacamas 30 D3 Olancho, C Honduras

Catacaos 38 B3 Piura, NW Peru

Catalan Bay 71 H4 var. Caleta. Bay E Gibraltar

Cataluña 71 G2 cultural region N Spain

Catamarca see San Fernando del Valle de Catamarca

Catania 75 D7 Sicilia, Italy, C Mediterranean Sea

Catanzaro 75 D6 Calabria, SW Italy

Catarroja 71 F3 País Valenciano, E Spain

Cat Island 32 C1 island C Bahamas

Catskill Mountains 19 F3 mountain range New York, NE USA

Cauca, Río 36 B2 river N Colombia

Caucasia 36 B2 Antioquia, NW Colombia

Caucasus 59 G4 Rus. Kavkaz. Mountain range Georgia/Russian Federation

Caura, Río 37 E3 river C Venezuela

Cavalla 52 D5 var. Cavally, Cavally Fleuve. River Côte d'Ivoire/Liberia

Cavally see Cavalla

Cavally Fleuve see Cavalla

Caviana de Fora, Ilha 41 E1 var. Ilha Caviana. Island N Brazil

Caxito 56 B1 Bengo, NW Angola

Cayenne 37 H3 dépendent territory capital (French Guiana) NE French Guiana

Cayes 32 D3 var. Les Cayes. SW Haiti

Cayman Brac 32 B3 island E Cayman Islands

Cayman Islands 32 B3 UK dependent territory W West Indies

Cay Sal 32 B2 islet SW Bahamas

Cazin 78 B3 Federacija Bosna I Hercegovina, NW Bosnia and Herzegovina

Cazorla 71 E4 Andalucía, S Spain

Ceadâr-Lunga see Ciadîr-Lunga

Ceará 41 F2 off. Estado do Ceará. State C Brazil

Ceará Abyssal Plain see Ceará Plain

Ceará Plain 34 E2 var. Ceara Abyssal Plain. Undersea feature W Atlantic Ocean

Ceatharlach see Carlow

Cébaco, Isla 31 F5 island SW Panama

Cebu 117 E2 off. Cebu City. Cebu, C Philippines

Cebu City see Cebu

Cecina 74 B3 Toscana, C Italy

Cedar City 22 A5 Utah, W USA

Cedar Falls 23 G3 Iowa, C USA

Cedar Lake 16 A2 lake Manitoba, C Canada

Cedar Rapids 23 G3 Iowa, C USA

Cedros, Isla 28 A2 island W Mexico

Ceduna 127 A6 South Australia

Cefalu 75 C7 anc. Cephaloedium. Sicilia, Italy, C Mediterranean Sea

Celebes see Sulawesi

Celebes Sea 117 E3 Ind. Laut Sulawesi. Sea Indonesia/Philippines

Celje 73 E7 Ger. Cilli. C Slovenia

Celldömölk 99 C6 Vas, W Hungary

Celle 72 B3 var. Zelle. Niedersachsen, N Germany

Celtic Sea 67 B7 Ir. An Mhuir Cheilteach. Sea SW British Isles

Celtic Shelf 58 B3 undersea feature E Atlantic Ocean

Cenderawasih, Teluk 117 G4 var. Teluk Irian, Teluk Sarera. Bay W Pacific Ocean

Cenon 69 B5 Gironde, SW France

Central African Republic 54 C4 var. République Centrafricaine, abbrev. CAR; prev. Ubangi-Shari, Oub angui-Chari, Territoire de l'Oubangui-Chari. Country C Africa

Central, Cordillera 33 E3 mountain range C Dominican Republic

Central, Cordillera 31 F5 mountain range C Panama

Central, Cordillera 117 E1 mountain range Luzon, N Philippines

Central, Cordillera 36 B3 mountain range W Colombia

Central Group see Inner Islands

Centralia 24 B2 Washington, NW USA

Central Indian Ridge see Mid-Indian Ridge

Central Makrān Range 112 A3 mountain range W Pakistan

Central Pacific Basin 120 D1 undersea feature C Pacific Ocean

Central, Planalto 41 F3 var. Brazilian Highlands. Mountain range E Brazil

Central Range 122 B3 mountain range NW PNG

Central Russian Upland see Srednerusskaya Vozvyshennost'

Central Siberian Plateau see Srednesibirskoye Ploskogor'ye

Central Siberian Uplands see Srednesibirskoye Ploskogor'ye

Central, Sistema 70 D3 mountain range C Spain

Central Valley 25 B6 valley California, W USA

Cephaloedium see Cefalu

Ceram see Seram, Pulau

Ceram Sea 117 F4 Ind. Laut Seram. Sea E Indonesia

Cerasus see Giresun

Cereté 36 B2 Córdoba, NW Colombia

Cerignola 75 D5 Puglia, SE Italy

Cerigo see Kýthira

Çerkeş 94 C2 Çankın, N Turkey

Cernay 90 E4 Haut-Rhin, NE France

Cerro Chirripó see Chirripó Grande, Cerro

Cerro de Mulhacén see Mulhacén

Cerro de Pasco 38 C3 Pasco, C Peru

Cervera 71 F2 Cataluña, NE Spain

Cesena 74 C3 anc. Caesena. Emilia-Romagna, N Italy

Cēsis 84 D3 Ger. Wenden. Cēsis, C Latvia

České Budějovice 77 B5 Ger. Budweis. Budějovický Kraj, S Czech Republic

Český Krumlov 77 A5 var. Böhmisch-Krumau, Ger. Krummau. Budějovický Kraj, S Czech Republic

Cetinje 79 C5 It. Cettigne. Montenegro, SW Serbia and Montenegro (Yugo.)

Ceuta 48 C2 enclave Spain, N Africa

Cévennes 69 C6 mountain range S France

Ceyhan 94 D4 Adana, S Turkey

Ceylanpinar 95 F4 Şanlıurfa, SE Turkey

Ceylon Plain 102 B4 undersea feature N Indian Ocean

Ceyre to the Caribs see Marie-Galante

Chachapoyas 38 B2 Amazonas, NW Peru

Chachevichy 85 D6 Rus. Chechevichi. Mahilyowskaya Voblasts', E Belarus

Chaco see Gran Chaco

Chad 54 C3 Fr. Tchad. Country C Africa

Chad, Lake 54 B3 Fr. Lac Tchad. Lake C Africa

Chadron 22 D3 Nebraska, C USA

Chadyr-Lunga see Ciadîr-Lunga

Chāgai Hills 112 A2 var. Chāh Gay. Mountain range Afghanistan/Pakistan

Chaghasarāy see Asadābād

Chagos-Laccadive Plateau 102 B4 undersea feature N Indian Ocean

Chagos Trench 119 C5 undersea feature N Indian Ocean

Chāh Gay see Chāgai Hills

Chaillu, Massif du 55 B6 mountain range C Gabon

Chajul 30 B2 Quiché, W Guatemala

Chakhānsūr 100 D5 Nīmrūz, SW Afghanistan

Chalatenango 30 C3 Chalatenango, N El Salvador

Chalcidice see Chalkidikí

Chalcis see Chalkída

Chálki 83 E7 island Dodekánisos, Greece, Aegean Sea

Chalkída 83 C5 var. Halkida; prev. Khalkís, anc. Chalcis. Évvoia, E Greece

Chalkidikí 82 C4 var. Khalkidhikí; anc. Chalcidice. Peninsula NE Greece

Challans 90 B4 Vendée, NW France

Challapata 39 F4 Oruro, SW Bolivia

Challenger Deep 130 B3 undersea feature W Pacific Ocean

Challenger Fracture Zone 131 F4 tectonic feature SE Pacific Ocean

Châlons-en-Champagne 68 D3 prev. Châlons-sur-Marne, hist. Arcae Remorum, anc. Carolopois. Marne, NE France

Chalon-sur-Saône 68 D4 anc. Cabillonum. Saône-et-Loire, C France

Cha Mai see Thung Song

Chaman 112 B2 Baluchistān, SW Pakistan

Chambéry 69 D5 anc. Camberia. Savoie, E France

Champagne 68 D3 Yukon Territory, W Canada

Champaign 18 B4 Illinois, N USA

Champasak 115 D5 Champasak, S Laos

Champotón 29 G4 Campeche, SE Mexico

Chanak see Çanakkale

Chañaral 42 B3 Atacama, N Chile

Chanchiang see Zhanjiang

Chandeleur Islands 20 C3 island group Louisiana, S USA

Chandigarh 112 D2 Punjab, N India

Chandrapur 113 E5 Mahārāshtra, C India

Changan see Xi'an

Changane 57 E3 river S Mozambique

Changchun 106 D3 var. Ch'angch'un, Ch'ang-ch'un; prev. Hsinking. Jilin, NE China

Chang Jiang 106 B5 var. Yangtze Kiang, Eng. Yangtze. River C China

Changkiakow see Zhangjiakou

Chang, Ko 115 C6 island S Thailand

Changsha 106 C5 var. Ch'angsha, Ch'ang-sha. Hunan, S China

Ch'angsha see Changsha

Changzhi 106 C4 Shanxi, C China

Chaniá 83 C7 var. Hania, Khaniá, Eng. Canea; anc. Cydonia. Kríti, Greece, E Mediterranean Sea

Chankiri see Çankırı

Channel Islands 67 C8 Fr. Îles Normandes. Island group S English Channel

Channel Islands 25 B8 island group California, W USA

Channel-Port aux Basques 17 G4 Newfoundland, Newfoundland and Labrador, SE Canada

Channel, The see English Channel

Chantabun see Chanthaburi

Chantaburi see Chanthaburi

Chantada 70 C1 Galicia, NW Spain

Chanthaburi 115 C6 var. Chantabun, Chantaburi. Chantaburi, S Thailand

Chanute 23 F5 Kansas, C USA

Chaouèn see Chefchaouen

Chaoyang 106 D3 Liaoning, NE China

Chapala, Lago de 28 D4 lake C Mexico

Chapan, Gora 100 B3 mountain C Turkmenistan

Chapayevsk 89 C6 Samarskaya Oblast', W Russian Federation

Chaplynka 87 F4 Khersons'ka Oblast', S Ukraine

Charcot Seamounts 58 B3 undersea feature E Atlantic Ocean

Charente 69 B5 cultural region W France

Charente 69 B5 river W France

Chari 54 B3 var. Shari. River Central African Republic/Chad

Chārīkār 101 E4 Parwān, NE Afghanistan

Charity 37 F2 NW Guyana

Charkhlik see Ruoqiang

Charkhliq see Ruoqiang

Charleroi 87 C7 Hainaut, S Belgium

Charlesbourg 17 E4 Québec, SE Canada

Charles de Gaulle 68 E1 international airport (Paris) Seine-et-Marne, N France

Charles Island 16 D1 island Northwest Territories, NE Canada

Charles Island see Santa María, Isla

Charleston 18 D5 state capital West Virginia, NE USA

Charleston 21 F2 South Carolina, SE USA

Charleville 127 D5 Queensland, E Australia

Charleville-Mézières 68 D3 Ardennes, N France

Charlie-Gibbs Fracture Zone 44 C2 tectonic feature N Atlantic Ocean

Charlotte 21 E1 North Carolina, SE USA

Charlotte Amalie 33 F3 prev. Saint Thomas. Dependent territory capital (Virgin Islands (US)) Saint Thomas, N Virgin Islands (US)

Charlotte Harbor 21 E5 inlet Florida, SE USA

Charlottesville 19 E5 Virginia, NE USA

Charlottetown 17 F4 Prince Edward Island, Prince Edward Island, SE Canada

Charsk see Shar

Charters Towers 126 D3 Queensland, NE Australia

Chartres 68 C3 anc. Autricum, Civitas Carnutum. Eure-et-Loir, C France

Charus Nuur 104 D2 NW Mongolia

Chashniki 85 D5 Rus. Chashniki. Vitsyebskaya Voblasts', N Belarus

Châteaubriant 68 B4 Loire-Atlantique, NW France

Châteaudun 68 C3 Eure-et-Loir, C France

Châteauroux 68 C4 prev. Indreville. Indre, C France

Château-Thierry 68 C3 Aisne, N France

Châtelet 65 C7 Hainaut, S Belgium

Châtelherault see Châtellerault

Châtellerault 68 B4 var. Châtelherault. Vienne, W France

Chatham Island see San Cristóbal, Isla

Chatham Island Rise see Chatham Rise

Chatham Islands 121 E5 island group NZ, SW Pacific Ocean

Chatham Rise 120 D5 var. Chatham Island Rise. Undersea feature S Pacific Ocean

Chatkal Range 101 F2 Rus. Chatkal'skiy Khrebet. Mountain range Kyrgyzstan/Uzbekistan

Chattahoochee River 20 D3 river SE USA

Chattanooga 20 D1 Tennessee, S USA

Chatyr-Tash 101 G2 Narynskaya Oblast', C Kyrgyzstan

Châu Độc 115 D6 var. Chauphu, Chau Phu. An Giang, S Vietnam

Chauk 114 A3 Magwe, W Myanmar

Chaumont 68 D4 prev. Chaumont-en-Bassigny. Haute-Marne, N France

Chau Phu see Châu Độc

Chaves 70 C2 anc. Aquae Flaviae. Vila Real, N Portugal

Chávez, Isla see Santa Cruz, Isla

Chavusy 85 E6 Rus. Chausy. Mahilyowskaya Voblasts', E Belarus

Chaykovskiy 89 D5 Permskaya Oblast', NW Russian Federation

Cheb 77 A5 Ger. Eger. Karlovarský Kraj, W Czech Republic

Cheboksary 89 C5 Chuvashskaya Respublika, W Russian Federation

Cheboygan 18 C2 Michigan, N USA

Chechaouèn see Chefchaouen

Chech, Erg 52 D1 desert Algeria/Mali

Che-chiang see Zhejiang

Cheduba Island 114 A4 island W Myanmar

Chefchaouen 48 C2 var. Chaouèn, Chechaouèn, Sp. Xauen. N Morocco

Chefoo see Yantai

Cheju-do 107 E4 Jap. Saishū; prev. Quelpart. Island S South Korea

Cheju Strait 107 E4 strait S South Korea

Chekiang see Zhejiang

Hazar 100 B2 prev. Cheleken. Balkanskiy Velayat, W Turkmenistan

Chelkar see Shalkar

Chełm 76 E4 Rus. Kholm. Lubelskie, E Poland

Chełmno 76 C3 Ger. Culm, Kulm. Kujawski-pomorskie, C Poland

Chełmża 76 C3 Ger. Culmsee, Kulmsee. Kujawski-pomorskie, C Poland

Cheltenham 67 D6 C England, UK

Chelyabinsk 92 C3 Chelyabinskaya Oblast', C Russian Federation

Chemnitz 72 D4 prev. Karl-Marx-Stadt. Sachsen, E Germany

Chenāb 112 C2 river India/Pakistan

Chengchiatun see Liaoyuan

Ch'eng-chou see Zhengzhou

Chengchow see Zhengzhou

Chengde 106 D3 var. Jehol. Hebei, E China

Chengdu 106 B5 var. Chengtu, Ch'eng-tu. Sichuan, C China

Chenghsien see Zhengzhou

Ch'eng-tu see Chengdu

Chennai 110 D2 prev. Madras. Tamil Nādu, S India

Chenxian see Chenzhou

Chen Xian see Chenzhou

Chen Xiang see Chenzhou

Chenzhou 106 C6 var. Chenxian, Chen Xian, Chen Xiang. Hunan, S China

Chepelare 82 C3 Smolyan, S Bulgaria

Chepén 38 B3 La Libertad, C Peru

Cher 68 C4 river C France

Cherbourg 68 B3 anc. Carusbur. Manche, N France

Cherepovets 88 B4 Vologodskaya Oblast', NW Russian Federation

Chergui, Chott ech 48 D2 salt lake NW Algeria

Cherkasy 87 E2 Rus. Cherkassy. Cherkas'ka Oblast', C Ukraine

Cherkessk 89 B7 Karachayevo-Cherkesskaya Respublika, SW Russian Federation

Chernihiv 87 E1 Rus. Chernigov. Chernihivs'ka Oblast', NE Ukraine

Chernivtsi 86 C3 Ger. Czernowitz, Rom. Cernăuți, Rus. Chernovtsy. Chernivets'ka Oblast', W Ukraine

Cherno More see Black Sea

Chernoye More see Black Sea

Chernyakhovsk 84 A4 Ger. Insterburg. Kaliningradskaya Oblast', W Russian Federation

Cherry Hill 19 F4 New Jersey, NE USA

Cherski Range see Cherskogo, Khrebet

Cherskiy 93 G2 Respublika Sakha (Yakutiya), NE Russian Federation

Cherskogo, Khrebet 93 F2 var. Cherski Range. Mountain range NE Russian Federation

Chervonohrad 86 C2 Rus. Chervonograd. L'vivs'ka Oblast', NW Ukraine

Chervyen' 85 D6 Rus. Cherven'. Minskaya Voblasts', C Belarus

Cherykaw 85 E7 Rus. Cherikov. Mahilyowskaya Voblasts', E Belarus

Chesapeake Bay 19 F5 inlet NE USA

Chesha Bay see Chëshskaya Guba

Chëshskaya Guba 172 D5 var. Archangel Bay, Chesha Bay, Dvina Bay. Bay NW Russian Federation

Chester 67 C6 Wel. Caerleon; hist. Legaceaster, Lat. Deva, Devana Castra. C England, UK

Chetumal 29 H4 var. Payo Obispo. Quintana Roo, SE Mexico

Cheviot Hills 66 D4 hill range England/Scotland, UK

Cheyenne 22 D4 state capital Wyoming, C USA

Cheyenne River 22 D3 river South Dakota/Wyoming, N USA

Chhapra 113 F3 prev. Chapra. Bihār, N India

Chhattīsgarh 113 E4 Admin. region state N India

Chiai – Coronado, Bahía de

Chiai 106 D6 *var.* Chia-i, Chiayi, Kiayi, Jiayi, *Jap.* Kagi. C Taiwan
Chia-i *see* Chiai
Chiang-hsi *see* Jiangxi
Chiang Mai 114 B4 *var.* Chiangmai, Chiengmai, Kiangmai. Chiang Mai, NW Thailand
Chiangmai *see* Chiang Mai
Chiang Rai 114 C3 *var.* Chianpai, Chienrai, Muang Chiang Rai. Chiang Rai, NW Thailand
Chiang-su *see* Jiangsu
Chian-ning *see* Nanjing
Chianpai *see* Chiang Rai
Chianti 96 C3 *cultural region* C Italy
Chiapa *see* Chiapa de Corzo
Chiapa de Corzo 29 G5 *var.* Chiapa. Chiapas, SE Mexico
Chiayi *see* Chiai
Chiba 108 B1 *var.* Tiba. Chiba, Honshū, S Japan
Chibougamau 16 D3 Québec, SE Canada
Chicago 18 B3 Illinois, N USA
Ch'i-ch'i-ha-erh *see* Qiqihar
Chickasha 27 G2 Oklahoma, C USA
Chiclayo 38 B3 Lambayeque, NW Peru
Chico 25 B5 California, W USA
Chico, Río 43 B6 *river* S Argentina
Chico, Río 43 B7 *river* SE Argentina
Chicoutimi 17 E4 Québec, SE Canada
Chiengmai *see* Chiang Mai
Chienrai *see* Chiang Rai
Chiesanuova 96 D2 SW San Marino
Chieti 74 D4 *var.* Teate. Abruzzo, C Italy
Chifeng 105 G2 *var.* Ulanhad. Nei Mongol Zizhiqu, N China
Chih-fu *see* Yantai
Chihli *see* Hebei
Chihli, Gulf of *see* Bo Hai
Chihuahua 28 C2 Chihuahua, NW Mexico
Childress 27 F2 Texas, SW USA
Chile 42 B3 *Country* SW South America
Chile Basin 35 A5 *undersea feature* E Pacific Ocean
Chile Chico 43 B6 Aisén, W Chile
Chile Rise 35 A7 *undersea feature* SE Pacific Ocean
Chililabombwe 56 D2 Copperbelt, C Zambia
Chi-lin *see* Jilin
Chillán 43 B5 Bío Bío, C Chile
Chillicothe 18 D4 Ohio, N USA
Chiloé, Isla de 43 A6 *var.* Isla Grande de Chiloé. *Island* W Chile
Chilpancingo 29 E5 *var.* Chilpancingo de los Bravos. Guerrero, S Mexico
Chilpancingo de los Bravos *see* Chilpancingo
Chilung 106 D6 *var.* Keelung, *Jap.* Kirun, Kirun'; *prev. Sp.* Santissima Trinidad. N Taiwan
Chimán 31 G5 Panamá, E Panama
Chimborazo 38 A1 *volcano* C Ecuador
Chimbote 38 C3 Ancash, W Peru
Chimboy 100 D1 *Rus.* Chimbay. Qoraqalpoghiston Respublikasi, NW Uzbekistan
Chimoio 57 E3 Manica, C Mozambique
China 102 C2 *Chin.* Chung-hua Jen-min Kung-ho-kuo, Zhonghua Renmin Gongheguo; *prev.* Chinese Empire. *Country* E Asia
Chi-nan *see* Jinan
Chinandega 30 C3 Chinandega, NW Nicaragua
Chincha Alta 38 D4 Ica, SW Peru
Chin-chiang *see* Quanzhou
Chin-chou *see* Jinzhou
Chinchow *see* Jinzhou
Chindwin 114 B2 *river* N Myanmar
Ch'ing Hai *see* Qinghai Hu
Chingola 56 D2 Copperbelt, C Zambia
Ching-Tao *see* Qingdao
Chinguetti 52 C2 *var.* Chinguetti. Adrar, C Mauritania
Chin Hills 114 A3 *mountain range* W Myanmar
Chinhsien *see* Jinzhou
Chinnereth *see* Tiberias, Lake
Chinook Trough 91 H4 *undersea feature* N Pacific Ocean
Chioggia 74 C2 *anc.* Fossa Claudia. Veneto, NE Italy
Chíos 83 D5 *var.* Hios, Khíos, *It.* Scio, *Turk.* Sakiz-Adasi. Chíos, E Greece
Chíos 83 D5 *var.* Khíos. *Island* E Greece
Chipata 56 D2 *prev.* Fort Jameson. Eastern, E Zambia
Chiquián 38 C3 Ancash, W Peru
Chiquimula 30 B2 Chiquimula, SE Guatemala
Chīrāla 110 D1 Andhra Pradesh, E India
Chirchiq 101 E2 *Rus.* Chirchik. Toshkent Wiloyati, E Uzbekistan
Chiriquí, Golfo de 31 E5 *Eng.* Chiriqui Gulf. *Gulf* SW Panama
Chiriquí, Laguna de 31 E5 *lagoon* NW Panama
Chirripó Grande, Cerro 30 D4 *var.* Cerro Chirripó. *Mountain* SE Costa Rica
Chisec 30 B2 Alta Verapaz, C Guatemala
Chisholm 23 F1 Minnesota, N USA
Chisimaio *see* Kismaayo
Chisimayu *see* Kismaayo
Chişinău 86 D4 *Rus.* Kishinev. *Country capital* (Moldova) C Moldova
Chita 93 F4 Chitinskaya Oblast', S Russian Federation
Chitato 56 C1 Lunda Norte, NE Angola
Chitina 14 D3 Alaska, USA
Chitose 108 D2 *var.* Titose. Hokkaidō, NE Japan
Chitré 31 F5 Herrera, S Panama
Chittagong 113 G4 *Ben.* Chāttagām. Chittagong, SE Bangladesh
Chitungwiza 56 D3 *prev.* Chitangwiza. Mashonaland East, NE Zimbabwe
Chlef 48 D2 *var.* Ech Cheliff, Ech Chleff; *prev.* Al-Asnam, El Asnam, Orléansville. NW Algeria
Chocolate Mountains 25 D8 *mountain range* California, W USA
Chodzież 76 C3 Wielkopolskie, C Poland
Choele Choel 43 C5 Río Negro, C Argentina
Choiseul 122 C3 *var.* Lauru. *Island* NW Solomon Islands
Chojnice 76 C2 *Ger.* Knoitz. Pomorskie, N Poland
Ch'ok'ē 50 C4 *var.* Choke Mountains. *Mountain range* NW Ethiopia
Choke Mountains *see* Ch'ok'ē
Cholet 68 B4 Maine-et-Loire, NW France
Choluteca 30 C3 Choluteca, S Honduras
Choluteca, Río 30 C3 *river* SW Honduras
Choma 56 D2 Southern, S Zambia
Chomutov 76 A4 *Ger.* Komotau. Ústecký Kraj, NW Czech Republic
Chona 91 E2 *river* C Russian Federation
Chon Buri 115 C5 *prev.* Bang Pla Soi. Chon Buri, S Thailand
Chone 38 A1 Manabí, W Ecuador
Ch'ŏngjin 107 E3 NE North Korea
Chongqing 106 B5 *var.* Ch'ung-ching, Ch'ung-ch'ing, Chungking, Pahsien, Tchongking, Yuzhou. Chongqing, C China
Chongqing 106 B5 Admin. region *province* C China
Chonos, Archipiélago de los 43 A6 *island group* S Chile
Chorne More *see* Black Sea
Chornomors'ke 87 E4 *Rus.* Chernomorskoye. Respublika Krym, S Ukraine
Chortkiv 86 C2 *Rus.* Chortkov. Ternopil's'ka Oblast', W Ukraine
Chorum *see* Çorum
Chorzów 77 C5 *Ger.* Königshütte; *prev.* Królewska Huta. Śląskie, S Poland
Chōshi 109 D5 *var.* Tyôsi. Chiba, Honshū, S Japan
Choszczno 76 B3 *Ger.* Arnswalde. Zachodniopomorskie, NW Poland
Chota Nāgpur 113 E4 *plateau* N India
Chott el-Hodna *see* Hodna, Chott El
Chott Melrhir *see* Melghir, Chott
Choûm 52 C2 Adrar, C Mauritania
Choybalsan 105 F2 Dornod, E Mongolia
Christchurch 129 C6 Canterbury, South Island, NZ
Christiana 32 B5 C Jamaica
Christiansand *see* Kristiansand
Christianshåb *see* Qasigiannguit
Christiansund *see* Kristiansund
Christmas Island 119 D5 *Australian external territory* E Indian Ocean
Christmas Ridge 121 E1 *undersea feature* C Pacific Ocean
Chuan *see* Sichuan
Ch'uan-chou *see* Quanzhou
Chubut 35 B7 *off.* Provincia de Chubut. Admin. region *province* S Argentina
Chubut, Río 43 B6 *river* SE Argentina
Ch'u-chiang *see* Shaoguan
Chūgoku-sanchi 109 B6 *mountain range* Honshū, SW Japan
Chuí *see* Chuy
Chukai *see* Cukai
Chukchi Plain 133 B2 *undersea feature* Arctic Ocean
Chukchi Plateau 12 C2 *undersea feature* Arctic Ocean
Chukchi Sea 12 B2 *Rus.* Chukotskoye More. *Sea* Arctic Ocean
Chula Vista 25 C8 California, W USA
Chulucanas 38 B2 Piura, NW Peru
Chulym 92 D4 *river* C Russian Federation
Chumphon 115 C6 *var.* Jumporn. Chumphon, SW Thailand
Ch'unch'ŏn 107 E4 *Jap.* Shunsen. N South Korea
Ch'ung-ching *see* Chongqing
Chungking *see* Chongqing
Chunya 93 E3 *river* C Russian Federation
Chuquicamata 42 B2 Antofagasta, N Chile
Chur 73 B7 *Fr.* Coire, *It.* Coira, *Rmsch.* Cuera, Quera; *anc.* Curia Rhaetorum. Graubünden, E Switzerland
Churchill 16 B2 *river* Manitoba/Saskatchewan, C Canada
Churchill 17 F2 *river* Newfoundland and Labrador, E Canada
Churchill 15 G4 Manitoba, C Canada
Chuska Mountains 26 C1 *mountain range* Arizona/New Mexico, SW USA
Chusovoy 89 D5 Permskaya Oblast', NW Russian Federation
Chuuk Islands 122 B2 *var.* Hogoley Islands; *prev.* Truk Islands. *Island group* Caroline Islands, C Micronesia
Chuy 42 E4 *var.* Chuí. Rocha, E Uruguay
Chyhyryn 87 E2 *Rus.* Chigirin. Cherkas'ka Oblast', N Ukraine
Ciadîr-Lunga 86 D4 *var.* Ceadâr-Lunga, *Rus.* Chadyr-Lunga. S Moldova
Cide 94 C2 Kastamonu, N Turkey
Ciechanów 76 D3 *prev.* Zichenau. Mazowieckie, C Poland
Ciego de Ávila 32 C2 Ciego de Ávila, C Cuba
Ciénaga 36 B1 Magdalena, N Colombia
Cienfuegos 32 B2 Cienfuegos, C Cuba
Cieza 71 E4 Murcia, SE Spain
Cihanbeyli 94 C3 Konya, C Turkey
Cikobia 123 E4 *prev.* Thikombia. *Island* N Fiji
Cilacap 116 C5 *prev.* Tjilatjap. Jawa, C Indonesia
Cill Airne *see* Killarney
Cill Chainnigh *see* Kilkenny
Cill Mhantáin *see* Wicklow
Cincinnati 18 C4 Ohio, N USA
Ciney 65 C7 Namur, SE Belgium
Cinto, Monte 69 E7 *mountain* Corse, France, C Mediterranean Sea
Cipolletti 43 B5 Río Negro, C Argentina
Cirebon 116 C4 *prev.* Tjirebon. Jawa, S Indonesia
Ciro Marino 97 E6 Calabria, S Italy
Cisnădie 86 B4 *Ger.* Heltau, *Hung.* Nagydisznód. Sibiu, SW Romania
Citlaltépetl *see* Orizaba, Volcán Pico de
Citrus Heights 25 B5 California, W USA
Ciudad Bolívar 37 E2 *prev.* Angostura. Bolívar, E Venezuela
Ciudad Acuña *see* Villa Acuña
Cuidad Camargo 28 D2 Chihuahua, N Mexico
Ciudad Cortés *see* Cortés
Ciudad Darío 30 D3 *var.* Dario. Matagalpa, W Nicaragua
Ciudad de Dolores Hidalgo *see* Dolores Hidalgo
Ciudad de Guatemala 30 B2 *var.* Gautemala City *Eng.* Guatemala City; *prev.* Santiago de los Caballeros. *Country capital* (Guatemala) Guatemala, C Guatemala
Ciudad del Carmen *see* Carmen
Ciudad del Este 42 E2 *prev.* Cuidad Presidente Stroessner, Presidente Stroessner, Puerto Presidente Stroessner. Alto Paraná, SE Paraguay
Ciudad Delicias *see* Delicias
Ciudad de México *see* México
Ciudad de Panamá *see* Panamá
Ciudad Guayana 37 E2 *prev.* San Tomé de Guayana, Santo Tomé de Guayana. Bolívar, NE Venezuela
Ciudad Guzmán 28 D4 Jalisco, SW Mexico
Ciudad Hidalgo 29 G5 Chiapas, SE Mexico
Ciudad Juárez 28 C1 Chihuahua, N Mexico
Ciudad Lerdo 28 D3 Durango, C Mexico
Ciudad Madero 29 E3 *var.* Villa Cecilia. Tamaulipas, C Mexico
Ciudad Mante 29 E3 Tamaulipas, C Mexico
Ciudad Miguel Alemán 29 E2 Tamaulipas, C Mexico
Ciudad Obregón 28 B2 Sonora, NW Mexico
Ciudad Ojeda 36 C1 Zulia, NW Venezuela
Ciudad Porfirio Díaz *see* Piedras Negras
Ciudad Quesada *see* Quesada
Ciudad Real 70 D3 Castilla-La Mancha, C Spain
Ciudad-Rodrigo 70 C3 Castilla-León, N Spain
Ciudad Valles 29 E3 San Luis Potosí, C Mexico
Ciudad Victoria 29 E3 Tamaulipas, C Mexico
Ciutadella *see* Ciutadella de Menorca
Ciutadella de Menorca 71 H3 *var.* Ciutadella. Menorca, Spain, W Mediterranean Sea
Civitanova Marche 74 D3 Marche, C Italy
Civitavecchia 74 C4 *anc.* Centum Cellae, Trajani Portus. Lazio, C Italy
Claremore 27 G1 Oklahoma, C USA
Clarence 129 C5 *river* South Island, NZ
Clarence 129 C5 Canterbury, South Island, NZ
Clarence Town 32 D2 Long Island, C Bahamas
Clarinda 23 F4 Iowa, C USA
Clarion Fracture Zone 131 E2 *tectonic feature* NE Pacific Ocean
Clarión, Isla 28 A5 *island* W Mexico
Clark Fork 22 A1 *river* Idaho/Montana, NW USA
Clark Hill Lake 21 E2 *var.* J.Storm Thurmond Reservoir. *Reservoir* Georgia/South Carolina, SE USA
Clarksburg 18 D4 West Virginia, NE USA
Clarksdale 20 B2 Mississippi, S USA
Clarksville 20 C1 Tennessee, S USA
Clayton 27 E1 New Mexico, SW USA
Clearwater 21 E4 Florida, SE USA
Clearwater Mountains 24 D2 *mountain range* Idaho, NW USA
Cleburne 27 G3 Texas, SW USA
Clermont 126 D4 Queensland, E Australia
Clermont-Ferrand 69 C5 Puy-de-Dôme, C France
Cleveland 18 D3 Ohio, N USA
Cleveland 20 D1 Tennessee, S USA
Clifton 26 C2 Arizona, SW USA
Clinton 20 B2 Mississippi, S USA
Clinton 27 F1 Oklahoma, C USA
Clipperton Fracture Zone 131 E3 *tectonic feature* E Pacific Ocean
Clipperton Island 13 A7 *French dependency of French Polynesia* E Pacific Ocean
Cloncurry 126 B3 Queensland, C Australia
Clonmel 67 B6 *Ir.* Cluain Meala. S Ireland
Cloppenburg 72 B3 Niedersachsen, NW Germany
Cloquet 23 G2 Minnesota, N USA
Cloud Peak 22 C3 *mountain* Wyoming, C USA
Clovis 27 E2 New Mexico, SW USA
Cluain Meala *see* Clonmel
Cluj-Napoca 86 B3 *Ger.* Klausenburg, *Hung.* Kolozsvár; *prev.* Cluj. Cluj, NW Romania
Clutha 129 B7 *river* South Island, NZ
Clyde 66 C4 *river* W Scotland, UK
Coari 40 D2 Amazonas, N Brazil
Coast Mountains 14 D4 *Fr.* Chaîne Côtière. *Mountain range* Canada/USA
Coast Ranges 24 A4 *mountain range* W USA
Coats Island 15 G3 *island* Nunavut, NE Canada
Coats Land 132 B2 *physical region* Antarctica
Coatzacoalcos 29 G4 *var.* Quetzalcoalco; *prev.* Puerto México. Veracruz-Llave, E Mexico
Cobán 30 B2 Alta Verapaz, C Guatemala
Cobar 127 C6 New South Wales, SE Australia
Cobija 39 E3 Pando, NW Bolivia
Coburg 73 C5 Bayern, SE Germany
Coca *see* Puerto Francisco de Orellana
Cochabamba 39 F4 *hist.* Oropeza. Cochabamba, C Bolivia
Cochin 110 C3 *var.* Kochi. Kerala, SW India
Cochinos, Bahía de 32 B2 *Eng.* Bay of Pigs. *Bay* SE Cuba
Cochrane 43 B7 Aisén, S Chile
Cochrane 16 C4 Ontario, S Canada
Cocibolca *see* Nicaragua, Lago de
Cockburn Town 33 E2 *var.* Grand *Turk. dependent territory capital* (Turks and Caicos Islands) Grand Turk Island, SE Turks and Caicos Islands
Cockpit Country, The 32 A4 *physical region* W Jamaica
Cocobeach 55 A5 Estuaire, NW Gabon
Coconino Plateau 26 B1 *plain* Arizona, SW USA
Coco, Río 31 E2 *var.* Río Wanki, Segoviao Wangkí. *River* Honduras/Nicaragua
Cocos Basin 102 C5 *undersea feature* E Indian Ocean
Cocos Island Ridge *see* Cocos Ridge
Cocos Islands 119 D5 *island group* E Indian Ocean
Cocos Ridge 13 C8 *var.* Cocos Island Ridge. *Undersea feature* E Pacific Ocean
Cod, Cape 19 G3 *headland* Massachusetts, NE USA
Codfish Island 129 A8 *island* SW NZ
Codlea 86 C4 *Ger.* Zeiden, *Hung.* Feketehalom. Brașov, C Romania
Cody 22 C2 Wyoming, C USA
Coeur d'Alene 24 C2 Idaho, NW USA
Coevorden 64 E2 Drenthe, NE Netherlands
Coffs Harbour 127 E6 New South Wales, SE Australia
Cognac 69 B5 *anc.* Compniacum. Charente, W France
Coiba, Isla de 31 E5 *island* SW Panama
Coihaique 43 B6 *var.* Coyhaique. Aisén, S Chile
Coimbatore 110 C3 Tamil Nādu, S India
Coimbra 70 B3 *anc.* Conimbria, Conimbriga. Coimbra, W Portugal
Coín 70 D5 Andalucía, S Spain
Coirib, Loch *see* Corrib, Lough
Colby 23 E4 Kansas, C USA
Colchester 67 E6 *hist.* Colneceaste, *anc.* Camulodunum. E England, UK
Col du Brenner *see* Brenner Pass
Coleman 27 F3 Texas, SW USA
Coleraine 66 B4 *Ir.* Cúil Raithin. N Northern Ireland, UK
Colesberg 56 C5 Northern Cape, C South Africa
Colima 28 D4 Colima, S Mexico
Coll 66 B3 *island* W Scotland, UK
College Station 27 G3 Texas, SW USA
Collie 125 A7 Western Australia
Colmar 68 E4 *Ger.* Kolmar. Haut-Rhin, NE France
Cöln *see* Köln
Cologne *see* Köln
Colombia 36 B3 *Country* N South America
Colombian Basin 34 A1 *undersea feature* SW Caribbean Sea
Colombo 110 C4 *country capital* (Sri Lanka) Western Province, W Sri Lanka
Colón 31 G4 *prev.* Aspinwall. Colón, C Panama
Colonia Agrippina *see* Köln
Colón Ridge 13 B8 *undersea feature* E Pacific Ocean
Colorado 22 C4 *off.* State of Colorado; also known as Centennial State, Silver State. *State* C USA
Colorado City 27 F3 Texas, SW USA
Colorado Plateau 26 B1 *plateau* W USA
Colorado, Río 43 C5 *river* E Argentina
Colorado, Río *see* Colorado River
Colorado River 13 B5 *var.* Río Colorado. *River* Mexico/USA
Colorado River 27 G4 *river* Texas, SW USA
Colorado Springs 22 D5 Colorado, C USA
Columbia 24 B3 *river* Canada/USA
Columbia 21 E2 *state capital* South Carolina, SE USA
Columbia 19 E4 Maryland, NE USA
Columbia 23 G4 Missouri, C USA
Columbia 20 C1 Tennessee, S USA
Columbia Plateau 24 C3 *plateau* Idaho/Oregon, NW USA
Columbus 18 D4 *state capital* Ohio, N USA
Columbus 20 D2 Georgia, SE USA
Columbus 18 C4 Indiana, N USA
Columbus 20 C2 Mississippi, S USA
Columbus 23 F4 Nebraska, C USA
Colville Channel 128 D2 *channel* North Island, NZ
Colville River 14 D2 *river* Alaska, USA
Comacchio 74 C3 *var.* Commachio; *anc.* Comactium. Emilia-Romagna, N Italy
Comactium *see* Comacchio
Comalcalco 29 G4 Tabasco, SE Mexico
Coma Pedrosa, Pic de 69 A7 *mountain* NW Andorra
Comarapa 39 F4 Santa Cruz, C Bolivia
Comayagua 30 C2 Comayagua, W Honduras
Comer See *see* Como, Lago di
Comilla 113 G4 *Ben.* Kumillā. Chittagong, E Bangladesh
Comino 80 A5 *Malt.* Kemmuna. *Island* C Malta
Comitán 29 G5 *var.* Comitán de Domínguez. Chiapas, SE Mexico
Comitán de Domínguez *see* Comitán
Commachio *see* Comacchio
Commissioner's Point 20 A5 *headland* W Bermuda
Communism Peak *see* Kommunizm, Qullai
Como 74 B2 *anc.* Comum. Lombardia, N Italy
Comodoro Rivadavia 43 B6 Chubut, SE Argentina
Como, Lago di B2 *var.* Lario, *Eng.* Lake Como, *Ger.* Comer See. *Lake* N Italy
Como, Lake *see* Como, Lago di
Comoros 57 F2 *Fr.* République Fédérale Islamique des Comores. *Country* W Indian Ocean
Compiègne 68 C3 Oise, N France
Compostella *see* Santiago
Comrat 86 D4 *Rus.* Komrat. S Moldova
Conakry 52 C4 *country capital* (Guinea) Conakry, SW Guinea
Concarneau 68 A3 Finistère, NW France
Concepción 42 D2 *var.* Villa Concepción. Concepción, C Paraguay
Concepción *see* La Concepción
Concepción 43 B5 Bío Bío, C Chile
Concepción 39 G3 Santa Cruz, E Bolivia
Concepción de la Vega *see* La Vega
Conchos, Río 28 D2 *river* C Mexico
Conchos, Río 26 D4 *river* NW Mexico
Concord 19 G3 *state capital* New Hampshire, NE USA
Concordia 42 D4 Entre Ríos, E Argentina
Concordia 23 E4 Kansas, C USA
Côn Đao 115 E7 *var.* Con Son. *Island* S Vietnam
Condate *see* Cosne-Cours-sur-Loire
Condega 30 D3 Estelí, NW Nicaragua
Congo 55 D5 *Fr.* Moyen-Congo; *prev.* Middle Congo. *Country* C Africa
Congo, Dem. Rep. 55 C6 *prev.* Zaire, Belgian Congo, Congo (Kinshasa). *Country* C Africa
Congo 55 C6 *var.* Kongo, *Fr.* Zaire. *River* C Africa
Congo Basin 55 C6 *drainage basin* W Dem. Rep. Congo
Connacht *see* Connaught
Connaught 67 A5 *var.* Connacht, *Ir.* Chonnacht, Cúige. *Cultural region* W Ireland
Connecticut 19 F3 *off.* State of Connecticut; also known as Blue Law State, Constitution State, Land of Steady Habits, Nutmeg State. *State* NE USA
Connecticut 19 G3 *river* Canada/USA
Conroe 27 G3 Texas, SW USA
Consolación del Sur 32 A2 Pinar del Río, W Cuba
Con Son *see* Côn Đao
Constance *see* Konstanz
Constance, Lake B7 *Ger.* Bodensee. *Lake* C Europe
Constanța 86 D5 *var.* Küstendje, *Eng.* Constanza, *Ger.* Konstanza, *Turk.* Küstence. Constanța, SE Romania
Constantia *see* Konstanz
Constantine 49 E2 *var.* Qacentina, *Ar.* Qoussantîna. NE Algeria
Constantinople *see* İstanbul
Constanz *see* Konstanz
Constanza *see* Constanța
Coober Pedy 127 A5 South Australia
Cookeville 20 D1 Tennessee, S USA
Cook Islands 123 F4 *territory in free association with NZ* S Pacific Ocean
Cook, Mount *see* Aoraki
Cook Strait 129 D5 *var.* Raukawa. *Strait* NZ
Cooktown 126 D2 Queensland, NE Australia
Coolgardie 125 B6 Western Australia
Cooma 127 D7 New South Wales, SE Australia
Coon Rapids 23 F2 Minnesota, N USA
Cooper Creek 126 C4 *var.* Barcoo, Cooper's Creek. *Seasonal river* Queensland/South Australia
Cooper's Creek *see* Cooper Creek
Coos Bay 24 A3 Oregon, NW USA
Cootamundra 127 D6 New South Wales, SE Australia
Copacabana 39 E4 La Paz, W Bolivia
Copenhagen *see* København
Copiapó 42 B3 Atacama, N Chile
Copperas Cove 27 G3 Texas, SW USA
Coppermine *see* Kugluktuk
Coquimbo 42 B3 Coquimbo, N Chile
Corabia 86 B5 Olt, S Romania
Coral Harbour 15 G3 Southampton Island, Nunavut, NE Canada
Coral Sea 120 B3 *sea* SW Pacific Ocean
Coral Sea Islands 122 B4 *Australian external territory* SW Pacific Ocean
Corantijn Rivier *see* Courantyne River
Corcaigh *see* Cork
Corcovado, Golfo 43 B6 *gulf* S Chile
Cordele 20 D3 Georgia, SE USA
Cordillera Ibérica *see* Ibérico, Sistema
Cordoba *see* Córdoba
Córdoba 70 D4 *var.* Cordoba, *Eng.* Cordova; *anc.* Corduba. Andalucía, SW Spain
Córdoba 42 C3 Córdoba, C Argentina
Córdoba 29 F4 Veracruz-Llave, E Mexico
Cordova *see* Córdoba
Cordova 14 C3 Alaska, USA
Corduba *see* Córdoba
Corentyne River *see* Courantyne River
Corfu *see* Kérkyra
Coria 70 C3 Extremadura, W Spain
Corinth *see* Kórinthos
Corinth 20 C1 Mississippi, S USA
Corinth, Gulf of *see* Korinthiakós Kólpos
Corinthiacus Sinus *see* Korinthiakós Kólpos
Corinto 30 C3 Chinandega, NW Nicaragua
Cork 67 A6 *Ir.* Corcaigh. S Ireland
Çorlu 94 A2 Tekirdağ, NW Turkey
Corner Brook 17 G3 Newfoundland, Newfoundland and Labrador, E Canada
Corn Islands *see* Maíz, Islas del
Cornwallis Island 15 F2 *island* Nunavut, N Canada
Coro 36 C1 *prev.* Santa Ana de Coro. Falcón, NW Venezuela
Corocoro 39 F4 La Paz, W Bolivia
Coromandel 128 D2 Waikato, North Island, NZ
Coromandel Coast 110 D2 *coast* E India
Coromandel Peninsula 128 D2 *peninsula* North Island, NZ
Coronado, Bahía de 30 D5 *bay* S Costa Rica

INDEX

Coronel Dorrego 43 C5 Buenos Aires, E Argentina
Coronel Oviedo 42 D2 Caaguazú, SE Paraguay
Corozal 30 C1 Corozal, N Belize
Corpus Christi 27 G4 Texas, SW USA
Corrales 26 D2 New Mexico, SW USA
Corrib, Lough 67 A5 Ir. Loch Coirib. *Lake* W Ireland
Corrientes 42 D3 Corrientes, NE Argentina
Corriza *see* Korçë
Corse 69 E7 *Eng.* Corsica. *Island* France, C Mediterranean Sea
Corsica *see* Corse
Corsicana 27 G3 Texas, SW USA
Cortegana 42 C4 Andalucía, S Spain
Cortés 31 E5 *var.* Ciudad Cortés. Puntarenas, SE Costa Rica
Cortina d'Ampezzo 74 C1 Veneto, NE Italy
Coruche 70 B3 Santarém, C Portugal
Çoruh Nehri 95 E3 *Geor.* Chorokhi, *Rus.* Chorokh. *River* Georgia/Turkey
Çorum 94 D3 *var.* Chorum. Çorum, N Turkey
Corunna *see* A Coruña
Corvallis 24 B3 Oregon, NW USA
Corvo 70 A5 *var.* Ilha do Corvo. *Island* Azores, Portugal, NE Atlantic Ocean
Cosenza 75 D6 *anc.* Consentia. Calabria, SW Italy
Cosne-Cours-sur-Loire 68 C4 *var.* Cosne-sur-Loire; *anc.* Condate. Nièvre, C France
Cosne-sur-Loire *see* Cosne-Cours-sur-Loire
Costa Mesa 24 D2 California, W USA
Costa Rica 31 E4 *Country* Central America
Cotagaita 39 F5 Potosí, S Bolivia
Côte d'Ivoire 52 D4 *Eng.* Ivory Coast, Republic of the Ivory Coast. *Country* W Africa
Côte d'Or 68 D4 *cultural region* C France
Cotonou 53 F5 *var.* Kotonu. S Benin
Cotrone *see* Crotone
Cotswold Hills 67 D6 *var.* Cotswolds. *Hill range* S England, UK
Cotswolds *see* Cotswold Hills
Cottbus 72 D4 *prev.* Kottbus. Brandenburg, E Germany
Council Bluffs 23 F4 Iowa, C USA
Courantyne River 37 G4 *var.* Corantijn Rivier, Corentyne River. *River* Guyana/Suriname
Courland Lagoon 84 A4 *Ger.* Kurisches Haff, *Rus.* Kurskiy Zaliv. *Lagoon* Lithuania/Russian Federation
Coutances 68 B3 *anc.* Constantia. Manche, N France
Couvin 65 C7 Namur, S Belgium
Coventry 67 D6 *anc.* Couentrey. C England, UK
Covilhã 70 C3 Castelo Branco, E Portugal
Cowan, Lake 125 B6 *lake* Western Australia
Coxen Hole *see* Roatán
Coxin Hole *see* Roatán
Coyhaique *see* Coihaique
Cozumel, Isla 29 H3 *island* SE Mexico
Cradock 56 C5 Eastern Cape, S South Africa
Craig 22 C4 Colorado, C USA
Craiova 86 B5 Dolj, SW Romania
Cranbrook 15 E5 British Columbia, SW Canada
Crane *see* The Crane
Crawley 67 E7 SE England, UK
Cremona 74 B2 Lombardia, N Italy
Cres 78 A3 *It.* Cherso; *anc.* Crexa. *Island* W Croatia
Crescent City 24 A4 California, W USA
Crescent Group 106 C7 *island group* C Paracel Islands
Creston 23 F4 Iowa, C USA
Crestview 20 D3 Florida, SE USA
Crete *see* Kríti
Créteil 68 E2 Val-de-Marne, N France
Crete, Sea of *see* Kritikó Pélagos
Creuse 68 B4 *river* C France
Crewe 67 D6 C England, UK
Crikvenica 78 A3 *It.* Cirquenizza; *prev.* Cirkvenica, Crjkvenica. Primorje-Gorski Kotar, NW Croatia
Crimea 59 F4 *var.* Krym, *Eng.* Crimea, Crimean Oblast; *prev. Rus.* Krymskaya ASSR, Krymskaya Oblast'. Admin. region *province* SE Ukraine
Crimean Oblast *see* Crimea
Cristóbal 31 G4 Colón, C Panama
Cristóbal Colón, Pico 36 B1 *mountain* N Colombia
Cristuru Secuiesc 86 C4 *prev.* Cristur, Cristuru Săcuiesc, Sitaş Cristuru, *Ger.* Kreutz, *Hung.* Székelykeresztúr, Szitás-Keresztúr. Harghita, C Romania
Crna Reka 79 D6 *river* S FYR Macedonia
Croatia 78 B3 *Ger.* Kroatien, *SCr.* Hrvatska. *Country* SE Europe
Crocodile *see* Limpopo
Croia *see* Krujë
Croker Island 124 E2 *island* Northern Territory, N Australia
Cromwell 129 B7 Otago, South Island, NZ
Crooked Island 32 D2 *island* SE Bahamas
Crooked Island Passage 32 D2 *channel* SE Bahamas
Crookston 23 F1 Minnesota, N USA
Croton *see* Crotone
Crotona *see* Crotone
Crotone 75 E6 *var.* Cotrone; *anc.* Croton, Crotona. Calabria, SW Italy
Croydon 67 A8 SE England, UK
Crozet Basin 119 B7 *undersea feature* S Indian Ocean
Crozet Islands 119 B7 *island group* French Southern and Antarctic Territories
Crozet Plateau 119 B7 *var.* Crozet Plateaus. *Undersea feature* SW Indian Ocean
Crozet Plateaus *see* Crozet Plateau
Crystal Brook 127 B6 South Australia
Csorna 77 C6 Győr-Moson-Sopron, NW Hungary

Csurgó 99 C7 Somogy, SW Hungary
Cuando 56 C2 *var.* Kwando. *River* S Africa
Cuango 56 B1 *var.* Kwango. *River* Angola/Dem. Rep. Congo *see also* Kwango
Cuan na Gaillimhe *see* Galway Bay
Cuanza 56 B1 *var.* Kwanza. *River* C Angola
Cuauhtémoc 28 C2 Chihuahua, N Mexico
Cuautla 29 E4 Morelos, S Mexico
Cuba 32 B2 *Country* W West Indies
Cubal 56 B2 Benguela, W Angola
Cubango 56 B2 *var.* Kavango, Kavengo, Kubango, Okavango, Okavanggo. *River* S Africa *see also* Okavango
Cubango 56 B2 *var.* Kuvango, *Port.* Vila Artur da Paiva, Vila da Ponte. Huíla, SW Angola
Cúcuta 36 C2 *var.* San José de Cúcuta. Norte de Santander, N Colombia
Cuddapah 110 C2 Andhra Pradesh, S India
Cuenca 71 E3 *anc.* Conca. Castilla-La Mancha, C Spain
Cuenca 38 B2 Azuay, S Ecuador
Cuernavaca 29 E4 Morelos, S Mexico
Cuiabá 41 E3 *prev.* Cuyabá. *State capital* Mato Grosso, SW Brazil
Cúige *see* Connaught
Cúige Laighean *see* Leinster
Cúige Mumhan *see* Munster
Cuijck 64 D4 Noord-Brabant, SE Netherlands
Cuilmsee *see* Chełmża
Cúil Raithin *see* Coleraine
Cuito 56 B2 *var.* Kwito. *River* SE Angola
Cukai 116 B3 *var.* Chukai, Kemaman. Terengganu, Peninsular Malaysia
Culiacán 28 C3 *var.* Culiacán Rosales, Culiacán-Rosales. Sinaloa, C Mexico
Culiacán-Rosales *see* Culiacán
Cullera 71 F3 País Valenciano, E Spain
Cullman 20 C2 Alabama, S USA
Culpepper Island *see* Darwin, Isla
Cumaná 37 E1 Sucre, NE Venezuela
Cumbal, Nevada de 36 A4 *mountain* SW Colombia
Cumberland 19 E4 Maryland, NE USA
Cumberland Plateau 20 D1 *plateau* E USA
Cumberland Sound 15 H3 *inlet* Baffin Island, Nunavut, NE Canada
Cumpas 28 B2 Sonora, NW Mexico
Cunene 47 C6 *var.* Kunene. *River* Angola/Namibia *see also* Kunene
Cunene 56 A3 *province* S Angola
Cuneo 74 A2 *Fr.* Coni. Piemonte, NW Italy
Cunnamulla 127 C5 Queensland, E Australia
Ćuprija 78 E4 Serbia, E Serbia and Montenegro (Yugo.)
Curaçao 33 E5 *island* Netherlands Antilles
Curicó 42 B4 Maule, C Chile
Curitiba 41 E4 *prev.* Curytiba. *State capital* Paraná, S Brazil
Curtea de Argeş 86 C4 *var.* Curtea-de-Arges. Argeş, S Romania
Curtea-de-Arges *see* Curtea de Argeş
Curtici 86 A4 *Ger.* Kurtitsch, *Hung.* Kürtös. Arad, W Romania
Curtis Island 126 E4 *island* Queensland, SE Australia
Cusco 39 E4 *var.* Cuzco. Cusco, C Peru
Cusset 69 C5 Allier, C France
Cutch, Gulf of *see* Kachchh, Gulf of
Cuttack 113 F4 Orissa, E India
Cuvier Plateau 119 E6 *undersea feature* E Indian Ocean
Cuxhaven 72 B2 Niedersachsen, NW Germany
Cuyuni, Río *see* Cuyuni River
Cuyuni River 37 F3 *var.* Río Cuyuni. *River* Guyana/Venezuela
Cuzco *see* Cusco
Cyclades *see* Kykládes
Cydonia *see* Chaniá
Cymru *see* Wales
Cyprus 80 C4 *Gk.* Kypros, *Turk.* Kıbrıs, Kıbrıs Cumhuriyeti. *Country* E Mediterranean Sea
Cythera *see* Kýthira
Cythnos *see* Kýthnos
Czech Republic 77 A5 *Cz.* Česká Republika. *Country* C Europe
Częstochowa 76 C4 *Ger.* Czenstochau, Tschenstochau, *Rus.* Chenstokhov. Śląskie, S Poland
Człuchów 76 C3 *Ger.* Schlochau. Pomorskie, N Poland

D

Dabajuro 36 C1 Falcón, NW Venezuela
Dabeiba 36 B2 Antioquia, NW Colombia
Dąbrowa Tarnowska 77 D5 Małopolskie, S Poland
Dabryn' 85 C8 *Rus.* Dobryn'. Homyel'skaya Voblasts', SE Belarus
Dagana 52 B3 N Senegal
Dagda 84 D4 Krāslava, SE Latvia
Dagenham 67 B8 SE England, UK
Dağlıq Qarabağ *see* Nagorno-Karabakh
Dagupan 117 E1 *off.* Dagupan City. Luzon, N Philippines
Da Hinggan Ling 105 G1 *Eng.* Great Khingan Range. *Mountain range* NE China
Dahm, Ramlat 99 B6 *desert* NW Yemen
Daimiel 70 D3 Castilla-La Mancha, C Spain
Daimoniá 83 B7 Pelopónnisos, S Greece
Dairen *see* Dalian
Dakar 52 B3 *country capital* (Senegal) W Senegal
Dakhla *see* Ad Dakhla
Dakoro 53 G3 Maradi, S Niger
Đakovica 79 D5 *var.* Djakovica, *Alb.* Gjakovë. Serbia, S Serbia and Montenegro (Yugo.)
Đakovo 78 C3 *var.* Djakovo, *Hung.* Diakovár. Osijek-Baranja, E Croatia
Dalai *see* Hulun Nur
Dalain Hob *see* Ejin Qi
Dalaman 94 A4 Muğla, SW Turkey

Dalandzadgad 105 E3 Ömnögovĭ, S Mongolia
Da Lat 115 E6 Lâm Đồng, S Vietnam
Dalby 127 D5 Queensland, E Australia
Dale City 19 E4 Virginia, NE USA
Dalhart 27 E1 Texas, SW USA
Dali 106 A4 *var.* Xiaguan. Yunnan, SW China
Dalian 106 D4 *var.* Dairen, Dalien, Lüda, Ta-lien, *Rus.* Dalny. Liaoning, NE China
Dalien *see* Dalian
Dallas 27 G2 Texas, SW USA
Dalmacija 78 B4 *Eng.* Dalmatia, *Ger.* Dalmatien, *It.* Dalmazia. *Cultural region* S Croatia
Dalny *see* Dalian
Dalton 20 D1 Georgia, SE USA
Daly Waters 126 A2 Northern Territory, N Australia
Damachava 85 A6 *var.* Damachovo, *Pol.* Domaczewo, *Rus.* Domachëvo. Brestskaya Voblasts', SW Belarus
Damachova *see* Damachava
Damān 112 C4 Damān and Diu, W India
Damara 54 C4 Ombella-Mpoko, S Central African Republic
Damas *see* Dimashq
Damasco *see* Dimashq
Damascus *see* Dimashq
Damāvand, Qolleh-ye 98 D3 *mountain* N Iran
Dammām *see* Ad Dammām
Damoûr 97 A5 *var.* Ad Dāmūr. W Lebanon
Dampier 124 A4 Western Australia
Dampier, Selat 117 F4 *strait* Papua, E Indonesia
Damqawt 99 D6 *var.* Damqut. E Yemen
Damqut *see* Damqawt
Damxung 104 C5 Xizang Zizhiqu, W China
Danakil Desert 50 D4 *var.* Afar Depression, Danakil Plain. *Desert* E Africa
Danakil Plain *see* Danakil Desert
Danané 52 D5 W Côte d'Ivoire
Đa Năng 115 E5 *prev.* Tourane. Quang Nam-Đa Nẵng, C Vietnam
Danborg *see* Daneborg
Dandong 106 D3 *var.* Tan-tung; *prev.* An-tung. Liaoning, NE China
Daneborg 61 E3 *var.* Danborg. W Greenland
Dänew *see* Deynau
Dangara *see* Danghara
Danghara 101 E3 *Rus.* Dangara. SW Tajikistan
Danghe Nanshan 104 D3 *mountain range* W China
Dangla *see* Tanggula Shan
Dângrêk, Chuŏr Phnum 115 D5 *var.* Phanom Dang Raek, Phanom Dong Rak, *Fr.* Chaîne des Dangrek. *Mountain range* Cambodia/Thailand
Dangriga 30 C1 *prev.* Stann Creek. Stann Creek, E Belize
Danish West Indies *see* Virgin Islands (US)
Danli 30 D2 El Paraíso, S Honduras
Danmarksstraedet *see* Denmark Strait
Dannenberg 72 C3 Niedersachsen, N Germany
Dannevirke 128 D4 Manawatu-Wanganui, North Island, NZ
Danube 59 E4 *Bul.* Dunav, *Cz.* Dunaj, *Ger.* Donau, *Hung.* Duna, *Rom.* Dunărea. *River* C Europe
Danville 19 E5 Virginia, NE USA
Dan Xian *see* Danzhou
Danxian/Dan Xian *see* Danzhou
Danzhou 106 C7 *prev.* Dan Xian, Danxian, Nada. Hainan, S China
Danziger Bucht *see* Danzig, Gulf of
Danzig, Gulf of 76 C2 *var.* Gulf of Pomorskie, *Ger.* Danziger Bucht, *Pol.* Zatoka Pomorskia, *Rus.* Gdan'skaya Bukhta. *Gulf* N Poland
Daqm *see* Duqm
Dar'ā 97 B5 *var.* Dará, *Fr.* Déraa. Dar'ā, SW Syria
Darabani 86 C3 Botoşani, NW Romania
Daraut-Kurgan *see* Daroot-Korgon
Dardanelli *see* Çanakkale
Dar es Salaam 51 C7 Dar es Salaam, E Tanzania
Darfield 129 C6 Canterbury, South Island, NZ
Darfur 50 A4 *var.* Darfur Massif. *Cultural region* W Sudan
Darfur Massif *see* Darfur
Darhan 105 E2 Selenge, N Mongolia
Darién, Gulf of 36 A2 *Sp.* Golfo del Darién. *Gulf* S Caribbean Sea
Darién, Serranía del 31 H5 *mountain range* Colombia/Panama
Dario *see* Ciudad Darío
Darjeeling *see* Darjiling
Darjiling 113 F3 *prev.* Darjeeling. West Bengal, NE India
Darling River 127 C6 *river* New South Wales, SE Australia
Darlington 67 D5 N England, UK
Darmstadt 73 B5 Hessen, SW Germany
Darnah 49 G2 *var.* Dérna. NE Libya
Darnley, Cape 132 D2 *headland* Antarctica
Daroca 71 E2 Aragón, NE Spain
Daroot-Korgon 101 G2 *var.* Daraut-Kurgan. Oshskaya Oblast', SW Kyrgyzstan
Darvaza *see* Derweze
Darwaza *see* Derweze
Darwin 124 D3 *var.* Palmerston, Port Darwin. *Territory capital* Northern Territory, N Australia
Darwin, Isla 38 A4 *var.* Culpepper Island. *Island* W Ecuador
Daryācheh-ye Hāmūn *see* Şāberī, Hāmūn-e
Daryācheh-ye Sīstān *see* Şāberī, Hāmūn-e
Daryā-ye Morghāb *see* Murgab
Daryā-ye Pāmīr *see* Pamir
Daryoi Pomir *see* Pamir

Dashhowuz *see* Daşoguz
Dashkawka 85 D6 *Rus.* Dashkovka. Mahilyowskaya Voblasts', E Belarus
Dashkhovuz *see* Daşoguz
Daşoguz 100 C2 *var.* Dashhowuz, Dashkhovuz; *prev.* Tashauz. Dashkhovuzskiy Velayat, N Turkmenistan
Datong 106 C3 *var.* Tatung, Ta-t'ung. Shanxi, C China
Daugavpils 84 D4 *Ger.* Dünaburg; *prev. Rus.* Dvinsk. *Municipality* Daugvapils, SE Latvia
Daugpils *see* Daugavpils
Daung Kyun 115 B6 *island* S Myanmar
Dauphiné 69 D5 *cultural region* E France
Dāvangere 110 C2 Karnātaka, W India
Davao 117 F3 *off.* Davao City. Mindanao, S Philippines
Davao Gulf 117 F3 *gulf* Mindanao, S Philippines
Davenport 23 G3 Iowa, C USA
David 31 E5 Chiriquí, W Panama
Davie Ridge 119 A5 *undersea feature* W Indian Ocean
Davis 132 D3 *Australian research station* Antarctica
Davis Sea 132 D3 *sea* Antarctica
Davis Strait 60 D3 *strait* Baffin Bay/Labrador Sea
Dawei *see* Tavoy
Dax 69 B6 *var.* Ax; *anc.* Aquae Augustae, Aquae Tarbelicae. Landes, SW France
Dayr az Zawr 96 D3 *var.* Deir ez Zor. Dayr az Zawr, E Syria
Dayton 18 C4 Ohio, N USA
Daytona Beach 21 E4 Florida, SE USA
De Aar 56 C5 Northern Cape, C South Africa
Dead Sea 97 B6 *var.* Bahret Lut, Lacus Asphaltites, *Ar.* Al Baḩr al Mayyit, Baḩrat Lūt, *Heb.* Yam HaMelaḩ. *Salt lake* Israel/Jordan
Deán Funes 42 C3 Córdoba, C Argentina
Death Valley 25 C7 *valley* California, W USA
Deatnu 62 D2 *Fin.* Tenojoki, *Nor.* Tana. *River* Finland/Norway *see also* Tenojoki
Debar 79 D6 *Ger.* Dibra, *Turk.* Debre. W FYR Macedonia
Debica 77 D5 Podkarpackie, SE Poland
De Bildt *see* De Bilt
De Bilt 64 C3 *var.* De Bildt. Utrecht, C Netherlands
Dębno 76 B3 Zachodniopomorskie, NW Poland
Debrecen 77 D6 *Ger.* Debreczin, *Rom.* Debretin; *prev.* Debreczen. Hajdú-Bihar, E Hungary
Decatur 20 C1 Alabama, S USA
Decatur 18 B4 Illinois, N USA
Deccan 112 D5 *Hind.* Dakshin. *Plateau* C India
Děčín 76 B4 *Ger.* Tetschen. Ústecký Kraj, NW Czech Republic
Dedeagaç *see* Alexandroúpoli
Dedeagach *see* Alexandroúpoli
Dedemsvaart 64 E3 Overijssel, E Netherlands
Dee 66 D3 *river* NE Scotland, UK
Deering 14 C2 Alaska, USA
Deggendorf 73 D6 Bayern, SE Germany
Değirmenlik 80 C5 N Cyprus
Deh Bīd 98 D3 Fārs, C Iran
Dehli *see* Delhi
Deh Shū 100 D5 *var.* Deshu. Helmand, S Afghanistan
Deinze 65 B5 Oost-Vlaanderen, NW Belgium
Deir ez Zor *see* Dayr az Zawr
Deirgeirt, Loch *see* Derg, Lough
Dej 86 B3 *Hung.* Dés; *prev.* Deés. Cluj, NW Romania
Dékoa 54 C4 Kémo, 163C Central African Republic
De Land 21 E4 Florida, SE USA
Delano 25 C7 California, W USA
Delārām 100 D5 Farāh, SW Afghanistan
Delaware 19 F4 *off.* State of Delaware; also known as Blue Hen State, Diamond State, First State. *State* NE USA
Delft 64 B4 Zuid-Holland, W Netherlands
Delfzijl 64 E1 Groningen, NE Netherlands
Delgo 50 B3 Northern, N Sudan
Delhi 112 D3 *var.* Dehli, *Hind.* Dilli; *hist.* Shahjahanabad. Delhi, N India
Delicias 28 D2 *var.* Ciudad Delicias. Chihuahua, N Mexico
Déli-Kárpátok *see* Carpaţii Meridionali
Delmenhorst 72 B3 Niedersachsen, NW Germany
Del Rio 27 E4 Texas, SW USA
Deltona 21 E4 Florida, SE USA
Demba 55 D6 Kasai Occidental, C Dem. Rep. Congo
Dembia 54 D4 Mbomou, SE Central African Republic
Demchok *var.* Dêmqog. *Disputed region* China/India *see also* Dêmqog
Demchok 104 A4 *var.* Dêmqog. China/India *see also* Dêmqog
Demerara Plain 34 C2 *undersea feature* W Atlantic Ocean
Deming 26 C3 New Mexico, SW USA
Demmin 72 C2 Mecklenburg-Vorpommern, NE Germany
Demopolis 20 C2 Alabama, S USA
Dêmqog *var.* Demchok. *Disputed region* China/India *see also* Demchok
Denau *see* Denov
Dender 65 B6 *Fr.* Dendre. *River* W Belgium
Denekamp 64 E3 Overijssel, E Netherlands
Den Haag *see* 's-Gravenhage
Denham 125 A5 Western Australia
Den Helder 64 C2 Noord-Holland, NW Netherlands
Dénia 71 F4 País Valenciano, E Spain

Deniliquin 127 C7 New South Wales, SE Australia
Denison 23 F3 Iowa, C USA
Denison 27 G2 Texas, SW USA
Denizli 94 B4 Denizli, SW Turkey
Denmark 63 A7 *Dan.* Danmark; *anc.* Hafnia. *Country* N Europe
Denmark Strait 60 D4 *var.* Danmarksstraedet. *Strait* Greenland/Iceland
Dennery 33 F1 E Saint Lucia
Denov 101 E3 *var.* Denow, *Rus.* Denau. Surkhondaryo Wiloyati, S Uzbekistan
Denow *see* Denov
Denpasar 116 D5 *prev.* Paloe. Bali, C Indonesia
Denton 27 G2 Texas, SW USA
D'Entrecasteaux Islands 122 B3 *island group* SE PNG
Denver 22 D4 *state capital* Colorado, C USA
Der'a *see* Dar'ā
Déraa *see* Dar'ā
Dera Ghāzi Khān 112 C2 *var.* Dera Ghāzikhān. Punjab, C Pakistan
Dera Ghāzikhān *see* Dera Ghāzi Khān
Đeravica 79 D5 *mountain* S Serbia and Montenegro (Yugo.)
Derbent 89 B8 Respublika Dagestan, SW Russian Federation
Derby 67 D6 C England, UK
Dereli *see* Gönni
Derg, Lough 67 A6 *Ir.* Loch Deirgeirt. *Lake* W Ireland
Derhachi 87 G2 *Rus.* Dergachi. Kharkivs'ka Oblast', E Ukraine
De Ridder 20 A3 Louisiana, S USA
Dérna *see* Darnah
Derry *see* Londonderry
Derventa 78 B3 Republika Srpska, N Bosnia and Herzegovina
Derweze 100 C2 *var.* Darvaza, Darwaza. Akhalskiy Velayat, C Turkmenistan
Deschutes River 24 B3 *river* Oregon, NW USA
Desē 50 C4 *var.* Desse, *It.* Dessie. N Ethiopia
Deseado, Río 43 B7 *river* S Argentina
Desertas, Ilhas 48 A2 *island group* Madeira, Portugal, NE Atlantic Ocean
Deshu *see* Deh Shū
Desierto de Altar *see* Sonoran Desert
Des Moines 23 F3 *state capital* Iowa, C USA
Desna 87 E2 *river* Russian Federation/Ukraine
Dessau 72 C4 Sachsen-Anhalt, E Germany
Desse *see* Desē
Dessie *see* Desē
Detroit 18 D3 Michigan, N USA
Detroit Lakes 23 F2 Minnesota, N USA
Deurne 65 D5 Noord-Brabant, SE Netherlands
Deva 86 B4 *Ger.* Diemrich, *Hung.* Déva. Hunedoara, W Romania
Devdelija *see* Gevgelija
Deventer 64 D3 Overijssel, E Netherlands
Devils Lake 23 E1 North Dakota, N USA
Devoll *see* Devollit, Lumi i
Devollit, Lumi i 79 D6 *var.* Devoll. SE Albania
Devon Island 15 F2 *prev.* North Devon Island. *Island* Parry Islands, Nunavut, NE Canada
Devonport 127 C8 Tasmania, SE Australia
Devrek 94 C2 Zonguldak, N Turkey
Dexter 23 H5 Missouri, C USA
Deynau 100 D3 *var.* Dyanev, *Turkm.* Dänew. Lebapskiy Velayat, NE Turkmenistan
Dezfūl 98 C3 *var.* Dizful. Khūzestān, SW Iran
Dezhou 106 D4 Shandong, E China
Dhaka 113 G4 *prev.* Dacca. *Country capital* (Bangladesh) Dhaka, C Bangladesh
Dhanbād 113 F4 Bihār, NE India
Dhekélia 80 C5 *Eng.* Dhekelia. *Gk.* Dekéleia. *UK air base* SE Cyprus
Dhidhimótikhon *see* Didymóteicho
Dhíkti Ori *see* Dikti
Dhodhekánisos *see* Dodekánisos
Dhomokós *see* Domokós
Dhráma *see* Dráma
Dhrepanon, Akrotírio *see* Drépano Akrotírio
Dhuusa Marreeb 51 E5 *var.* Dusa Marreb, *It.* Dusa Mareb. Galguduud, C Somalia
Diakovár *see* Đakovo
Diamantina, Chapada 41 F3 *mountain range* E Brazil
Diamantina Fracture Zone 119 E6 *tectonic feature* E Indian Ocean
Diarbekr *see* Diyarbakır
Dibrugarh 113 H3 Assam, NE India
Dickinson 22 D2 North Dakota, N USA
Didimotiho *see* Didymóteicho
Didymóteicho 82 D3 *var.* Dhidhimótikhon, Didimotiho. Anatolikí Makedonía kai Thráki, NE Greece
Diégo-Suarez *see* Antsirañana
Diekirch 65 D7 Diekirch, C Luxembourg
Điên Biên 114 D3 *var.* Bien Bien, Dien Bien Phu. Lai Châu, N Vietnam
Dien Bien Phu *see* Điên Biên
Diepenbeek 65 D6 Limburg, NE Belgium
Diepholz 72 B3 Niedersachsen, NW Germany
Dieppe 68 C3 Seine-Maritime, N France
Dieren 64 D4 Gelderland, E Netherlands
Differdange 65 D8 Luxembourg, SW Luxembourg
Digne 69 D6 *var.* Digne-les-Bains. Alpes-de-Haute-Provence, SE France
Digne-les-Bains *see* Digne
Digoin 68 C5 Saône-et-Loire, C France
Digul, Sungai 117 H5 *prev.* Digoel. *River* Papua, E Indonesia
Dihang *see* Brahmaputra
Dijon 68 D4 *anc.* Dibio. Côte d'Or, C France
Dikhil 50 D4 SW Djibouti
Dikson 92 D2 Taymyrskiy (Dolgano-Nenetskiy) Avtonomnyy Okrug, N Russian Federation

Díkti 83 D8 var. Dhíkti Ori. *Mountain range* Kríti, Greece, E Mediterranean Sea
Dili 117 F5 var. Dilli, Dilly. *Country capital* (East Timor), N East Timor
Dilia 53 G3 var. Dillia. *River* SE Niger
Di Linh 115 E6 Lâm Đồng, S Vietnam
Dilli see Delhi
Dilli see Dili
Dillia see Dilia
Dilling 50 B4 var. Ad Dalanj. Southern Kordofan, C Sudan
Dillon 22 B2 Montana, NW USA
Dilly see Dili
Dilolo 55 D7 Ngounié, S Gabon
Dimashq 97 B5 var. Ash Shām, Esh Sham, *Eng.* Damascus, *Fr.* Damas, *It.* Damasco. *Country capital* (Syria) Dimashq, SW Syria
Dimitrovgrad 82 D3 Khaskovo, S Bulgaria
Dimitrovgrad 89 C6 Ul'yanovskaya Oblast', W Russian Federation
Dimovo 82 B1 Vidin, NW Bulgaria
Dinajpur 113 F3 Rajshahi, NW Bangladesh
Dinan 68 B3 Côtes d'Armor, NW France
Dinant 65 C7 Namur, S Belgium
Dinar 94 B4 Afyon, SW Turkey
Dinara see Dinaric Alps
Dinaric Alps 78 C4 var. Dinara. *Mountain range* Bosnia and Herzegovina/Croatia
Dindigul 110 C3 Tamil Nādu, SE India
Dingle Bay 67 A6 Ir. Bá an Daingin. *Bay* SW Ireland
Dinguiraye 52 C4 Haute-Guinée, N Guinea
Diourbel 52 B3 W Senegal
Dirē Dawa 51 D5 E Ethiopia
Dirk Hartog Island 125 A5 *island* Western Australia
Disappointment, Lake 124 C4 *salt lake* Western Australia
Dispur 113 G3 Assam, NE India
Divinópolis 41 F4 Minas Gerais, SE Brazil
Divo 52 D5 S Côte d'Ivoire
Diyarbakır 95 E4 var. Diarbekr; *anc.* Amida. Diyarbakır, SE Turkey
Dizful see Dezful
Djajapura see Jayapura
Djakovica see Đakovica
Djakovo see Đakovo
Djambala 55 B6 Plateaux, C Congo
Djambi see Jambi
Djanet 49 E4 prev. Fort Charlet. SE Algeria
Djéblé see Jablah
Djelfa 48 D2 var. El Djelfa. N Algeria
Djéma 54 D4 Haut-Mbomou, E Central African Republic
Djérablous see Jarābulus
Djerba see Jerba, Île de
Djérem 54 B4 *river* C Cameroon
Djevdjelija see Gevgelija
Djibouti 50 D4 var. Jibuti; *prev.* French Somaliland, French Territory of the Afars and Issas, *Fr.* Côte Française des Somalis, Territoire Français des Afars et des Issas. *Country* E Africa
Djibouti 50 D4 var. Jibuti. *Country capital* (Djibouti) E Djibouti
Djourab, Erg du 54 C2 *dunes* N Chad
Djúpivogur 61 E5 Austurland, SE Iceland
Dnieper 59 F4 Bel. Dnyapro, Rus. Dnepr, Ukr. Dnipro. *River* E Europe
Dnieper Lowland 87 E2 Bel. Prydnyaprowskaya Nizina, Ukr. Prydniprovs'ka Nyzovyna. *Lowlands* Belarus/Ukraine
Dniester 59 E4 Rom. Nistru, Rus. Dnestr, Ukr. Dnister; *anc.* Tyras. *River* Moldova/Ukraine
Dnipro see Dnieper
Dniprodzerzhyns'k 87 F3 Rus. Dneprodzerzhinsk; *prev.* Kamenskoye. Dnipropetrovs'ka Oblast', E Ukraine
Dniprodzerzhyns'ke Vodoskhovyshche 87 F3 Rus. Dneprodzerzhinskoye Vodokhranilishche. *Reservoir* C Ukraine
Dnipropetrovs'k 87 F3 Rus. Dnepropetrovsk; *prev.* Yekaterinoslav. Dnipropetrovs'ka Oblast', E Ukraine
Dniprorudne 87 F3 Rus. Dneprorudnoye. Zaporiz'ka Oblast', SE Ukraine
Doba 54 C4 Logone-Oriental, S Chad
Döbeln 72 D4 Sachsen, E Germany
Doberai, Jazirah 117 G4 Dut. Vogelkop. *Peninsula* Papua, E Indonesia
Doboj 78 C3 Republika Srpska, N Bosnia and Herzegovina
Dobre Miasto 76 D2 Ger. Guttstadt. Warmińsko-Mazurskie, NE Poland
Dobrich 82 E1 Rom. Bazargic; *prev.* Tolbukhin. Dobrich, NE Bulgaria
Dobrush 85 D7 Homyel'skaya Voblasts', SE Belarus
Dodecanese see Dodekánisos
Dodekánisos 83 D6 var. Nóties Sporádes, *Eng.* Dodecanese; *prev.* Dhodhekánisos. *Island group* SE Greece
Dodge City 23 E5 Kansas, C USA
Dodoma 47 D5 *country capital* (Tanzania) Dodoma, C Tanzania
Dodoma 51 C7 *region* C Tanzania
Dogana 74 E1 NE San Marino
Dōgo 109 B6 *island* Oki-shotō, SW Japan
Dogondoutchi 53 F3 Dosso, SW Niger
Doğubayazıt 95 F3 Ağrı, E Turkey
Doğu Karadeniz Dağları 95 E3 *var.* Anadolu Dağları. *Mountain range* NE Turkey
Doha see Ad Dawḩah
Dokkum 64 D1 Friesland, N Netherlands
Dokuchayevs'k 87 G3 var. Dokuchayevsk. Donets'ka Oblast', SE Ukraine
Dokuchayevsk see Dokuchayevs'k
Doldrums Fracture Zone 44 C4 *tectonic feature* W Atlantic Ocean
Dôle 68 D4 Jura, E France
Dolisie 55 B6 prev. Loubomo. Le Niari, S Congo
Dolomites see Dolomitiche, Alpi
Dolomiti see Dolomitiche, Alpi

Dolomitiche, Alpi 74 C1 var. Dolomiti, *Eng.* Dolomites. *Mountain range* NE Italy
Dolores 42 D4 Buenos Aires, E Argentina
Dolores 30 B1 Petén, N Guatemala
Dolores 42 D4 Soriano, SW Uruguay
Dolores Hidalgo 29 E4 var. Ciudad de Dolores Hidalgo. Guanajuato, C Mexico
Dolyna 86 B2 Rus. Dolina. Ivano-Frankivs'ka Oblast', W Ukraine
Dolyns'ka 87 F3 Rus. Dolinskaya. Kirovohrads'ka Oblast', S Ukraine
Domachëvo see Damachava
Domaczewo see Damachava
Dombås 63 B5 Oppland, S Norway
Domel Island see Letsôk-aw Kyun
Domeyko 42 B3 Atacama, N Chile
Dominica 33 H4 *Country* E West Indies
Dominica Channel see Martinique Passage
Dominican Republic 33 E2 *country* C West Indies
Domokós 83 B5 var. Dhomokós. Stereá Ellás, C Greece
Don 89 B6 var. Duna, Tanais. *River* SW Russian Federation
Donau see Danube
Donauwörth 73 C6 Bayern, S Germany
Don Benito 70 C3 Extremadura, W Spain
Doncaster 67 D5 *anc.* Danum. N England, UK
Dondo 56 B1 Cuanza Norte, NW Angola
Donegal 67 B5 Ir. Dún na nGall. NW Ireland
Donegal Bay 67 A5 Ir. Bá Dhún na nGall. *Bay* NW Ireland
Donets 87 G2 var. Sivers'kyy Donets', Rus. Severskiy Donets. Serra Acaraí. *river* Russian Federation/Ukraine
Donets'k 87 G3 Rus. Donetsk; *prev.* Stalino. Donets'ka Oblast', E Ukraine
Dongfang 106 B7 var. Basuo. Hainan, S China
Dongguan 106 C6 Guangdong, S China
Đông Ha 114 E4 Quang Tri, C Vietnam
Đông Hơi 114 D4 Quang Binh, C Vietnam
Dongliao see Liaoyuan
Dongola 50 B3 var. Donqola, Dunqulah. Northern, N Sudan
Dongou 55 C5 La Likouala, NE Congo
Dongting Hu 106 C5 var. Tung-t'ing Hu. *Lake* S China
Donji Vakuf var. Srbobran, Federacija Bosna I Hercegovina, N Serbia and Montenegro (Yugo.)
Donostia-San Sebastián 71 E1 País Vasco, N Spain
Donqola see Dongola
Doolow 51 D5 E Ethiopia
Doornik see Tournai
Door Peninsula 18 C2 *peninsula* Wisconsin, N USA
Dooxo Nugaaleed 51 E5 var. Nogal Valley. *Valley* E Somalia
Dordogne 69 B5 *cultural region* SW France
Dordogne 69 B5 *river* W France
Dordrecht 64 C4 var. Dordt, Dort. Zuid-Holland, SW Netherlands
Dordt see Dordrecht
Dorohoi 86 C3 Botoșani, NE Romania
Dorotea 62 C4 Västerbotten, N Sweden
Dorre Island 125 A5 *island* Western Australia
Dort see Dordrecht
Dortmund 72 A4 Nordrhein-Westfalen, W Germany
Dos Hermanas 70 C4 Andalucía, S Spain
Dospad Dagh see Rhodope Mountains
Dospat 82 C3 Smolyan, S Bulgaria
Dothan 20 D3 Alabama, S USA
Dotnuva 84 B4 Kédainiai, C Lithuania
Douai 68 C2 prev. Douay, *anc.* Duacum. Nord, N France
Douala 55 A5 var. Duala. Littoral, W Cameroon
Douglas 67 C5 *dependent territory capital* (Isle of Man) E Isle of Man
Douglas 26 C3 Arizona, SW USA
Douglas 27 D3 Wyoming, C USA
Douro 70 B2 Sp. Duero. *River* Portugal/Spain *see also* Duero
Dover 67 E7 Fr. Douvres; *Lat.* Dubris Portus. SE England, UK
Dover 19 F4 *state capital* Delaware, NE USA
Dover, Strait of 68 C2 var. Straits of Dover, Fr. Pas de Calais. *Strait* England, UK/France
Dover, Straits of see Dover, Strait of
Dovrefjell 63 B5 *plateau* S Norway
Downpatrick 67 B5 Ir. Dún Pádraig. SE Northern Ireland, UK
Dōzen 109 B6 *island* Oki-shotō, SW Japan
Drachten 64 D2 Friesland, N Netherlands
Drăgășani 86 B5 Vâlcea, SW Romania
Dragoman 82 B2 Sofiya, W Bulgaria
Dra, Hamada du 48 C3 var. Hammada du Drâa, Haut Plateau du Dra. *Plateau* W Algeria
Drahichyn 85 B6 Pol. Drohiczyn Poleski, Rus. Drogichin. Brestskaya Voblasts', SW Belarus
Drakensberg 56 D5 *mountain range* Lesotho/South Africa
Drake Passage 35 B8 *passage* Atlantic Ocean/Pacific Ocean
Dralfa 82 D2 Tŭrgovishte, N Bulgaria
Dráma 82 C3 var. Dhráma. Anatolikí Makedonía kai Thráki, NE Greece
Drammen 63 B6 Buskerud, S Norway
Drau see Drava
Drava 78 C3 var. Drau, *Eng.* Drave, *Hung.* Dráva. *River* C Europe *see also* Drau
Dráva see Drava
Drave see Drava
Drawsko Pomorskie 76 B3 Ger. Dramburg. Zachodniopomorskie, NW Poland
Drépano, Akrotírio 82 C4 var. Akra Dhrepanon. *Headland* N Greece
Dresden 72 D4 Sachsen, E Germany
Drin see Drinit, Lumi i

Drina 78 C3 *river* Bosnia and Herzegovina/Serbia and Montenegro (Yugo.)
Drinit, Lumi i 79 D5 var. Drin. *River* NW Albania
Drobeta-Turnu Severin 86 B5 prev. Turnu Severin. Mehedinţi, SW Romania
Drogheda 67 B5 Ir. Droichead Átha. NE Ireland
Drohobych 86 B2 Pol. Drohobycz, Rus. Drogobych. L'vivs'ka Oblast', NW Ukraine
Droichead Átha see Drogheda
Drôme 69 D5 *cultural region* SE France
Dronning Maud Land 132 B2 *physical region* Antarctica
Drummondville 17 E4 Québec, SE Canada
Druskininkai 85 B5 Pol. Druskienniki. Druskininkai, S Lithuania
Dryden 16 B3 Ontario, C Canada
Drysa 85 D5 Rus. Drissa. *River* N Belarus
Duala see Douala
Dubai see Dubayy
Dubăsari 86 D3 Rus. Dubossary. NE Moldova
Dubawnt 15 F4 *river* Northwest Territories/Nunavut, NW Canada
Dubayy 98 D4 var. Dubai. Dubayy, NE UAE
Dubbo 127 D6 New South Wales, SE Australia
Dublin 67 B5 Ir. Baile Átha Cliath; *anc.* Eblana. *Country capital* (Ireland), E Ireland
Dublin 21 E2 Georgia, SE USA
Dubno 86 C2 Rivnens'ka Oblast', NW Ukraine
Dubrovnik 79 B5 It. Ragusa. Dubrovnik-Neretva, SE Croatia
Dubuque 23 G3 Iowa, C USA
Dudelange 65 D8 var. Forge du Sud, *Ger.* Dudelingen. Luxembourg, S Luxembourg
Dudelingen see Dudelange
Duero 70 D2 Port. Douro. *River* Portugal/Spain *see also* Douro
Duesseldorf see Düsseldorf
Duffel 65 C5 Antwerpen, C Belgium
Dugi Otok 78 A4 var. Isola Grossa, *It.* Isola Lunga. *Island* W Croatia
Duisburg 72 A4 prev. Duisburg-Hamborn. Nordrhein-Westfalen, W Germany
Duiven 64 D4 Gelderland, E Netherlands
Duk Faiwil 51 B5 Jonglei, SE Sudan
Dulan 104 D4 var. Qagan Us. Qinghai, C China
Dulce, Golfo 31 E5 *gulf* S Costa Rica
Dülmen 72 A4 Nordrhein-Westfalen, W Germany
Dulovo 82 E1 Silistra, NE Bulgaria
Duluth 23 G2 Minnesota, N USA
Dūmā 97 B5 Fr. Douma. Dimashq, SW Syria
Dumas 27 E1 Texas, SW USA
Dumfries 66 C4 S Scotland, UK
Dumont d'Urville 132 C4 *French research station* Antarctica
Dumyât 50 B1 *Eng.* Damietta. N Egypt
Duna see Danube
Duna see Don
Dunaj see Danube
Dunaújváros 77 C7 prev. Dunapentele, Sztálinváros. Fejér, C Hungary
Dunav see Danube
Dunavska Ravnina 82 C2 *Eng.* Danubian Plain. *Plain* N Bulgaria
Duncan 27 G2 Oklahoma, C USA
Dundalk 67 B5 Ir. Dún Dealgan. NE Ireland
Dún Dealgan see Dundalk
Dundee 66 C4 E Scotland, UK
Dundee 56 D4 KwaZulu/Natal, E South Africa
Dunedin 129 B7 Otago, South Island, NZ
Dunfermline 88 C4 E Scotland, UK
Dungu 55 E5 Orientale, NE Dem. Rep. Congo
Dungun 116 B3 var. Kuala Dungun. Terengganu, Peninsular Malaysia
Dunkerque 68 C2 Eng. Dunkirk, *Flem.* Duinekerke; *prev.* Dunquerque. Nord, N France
Dún Laoghaire 67 B6 *Eng.* Dunleary; *prev.* Kingstown. E Ireland
Dún na nGall see Donegal
Dún Pádraig see Downpatrick
Dunqulah see Dongola
Dunărea see Danube
Dupnitsa 82 C2 prev. Marek, Stanke Dimitrov. Kyustendil, W Bulgaria
Duqm 99 E5 var. Daqm. E Oman
Durance 69 D6 *river* SE France
Durango 28 D3 var. Victoria de Durango. Durango, W Mexico
Durango 22 C5 Colorado, C USA
Durankulak 82 E1 Rom. Răcari; *prev.* Blatnitsa, Duranulac. Dobrich, NE Bulgaria
Durant 27 G2 Oklahoma, C USA
Durazno see Durrës
Durban 56 D4 var. Port Natal. KwaZulu/Natal, E South Africa
Durbe 84 B3 Ger. Durben. Liepāja, W Latvia
Durg 113 E4 prev. Drug. Madhya Pradesh, C India
Durham 67 D5 *hist.* Dunholme. N England, UK
Durham 21 F1 North Carolina, SE USA
Durocortorum see Reims
Durostorum see Silistra
Durrës 79 C6 var. Durrësi, Dursi, It. Durazzo, SCr. Drač, Turk. Draç; *prev.* Epidamnos, Dyrrhachium. Durrës, W Albania
Durrësi see Durrës
Dursi see Durrës
Durūz, Jabal ad 97 C5 *mountain* SW Syria
D'Urville Island 128 C4 *island* C NZ
Dusa Mareb see Dhuusa Marreeb
Dusa Marreb see Dhuusa Marreeb
Dushanbe 101 E3 var. Dyushambe; *prev.* Stalinabad, Taj. Stalinobod. *Country capital* (Tajikistan) W Tajikistan

Düsseldorf 72 A4 var. Duesseldorf. Nordrhein-Westfalen, W Germany
Dūstī 101 E3 Rus. Dusti. SW Tajikistan
Dutch Harbor 14 B3 Unalaska Island, Alaska, USA
Dutch New Guinea see Papua
Duzdab see Zāhedān
Dvina see Severnaya Dvina
Dvina Bay see Chëshskaya Guba
Dyanev see Deynau
Dyersburg 20 C1 Tennessee, S USA
Dza Chu see Mekong
Dzerzhinsk 89 C5 Nizhegorodskaya Oblast', W Russian Federation
Dzhalal-Abad 101 F2 Kir. Jalal-Abad. Dzhalal-Abadskaya Oblast', W Kyrgyzstan
Dzhambul see Taraz
Dzhankoy 87 F4 Respublika Krym, S Ukraine
Dzhelandy 101 F3 SE Tajikistan
Dzhergalan 101 G2 Kir. Jyrgalan. Issyk-Kul'skaya Oblast', NE Kyrgyzstan
Dzhugdzhur, Khrebet 93 G3 *mountain range* E Russian Federation
Dzhusaly 92 B4 Kaz. Zholsaly. Kyzylorda, SW Kazakhstan
Działdowo 76 D3 Warmińsko-Mazurskie, NE Poland
Dzuunmod 105 E2 Töv, C Mongolia

E

Eagle Pass 27 F4 Texas, SW USA
East Açores Fracture Zone see East Azores Fracture Zone
East Antarctica see Greater Antarctica
East Australian Basin see Tasman Basin
East Azores Fracture Zone 44 C3 var. East Açores Fracture Zone. *Tectonic feature* E Atlantic Ocean
Eastbourne 67 E7 SE England, UK
East Cape 128 E3 *headland* North Island, NZ
East China Sea 103 E2 Chin. Dong Hai. *Sea* W Pacific Ocean
Easter Fracture Zone 131 G4 *tectonic feature* E Pacific Ocean
Easter Island 131 F4 var. Rapa Nui, *island* E Pacific Ocean
Eastern Desert 46 D3 var. Aş Şaḩrā' ash Sharqīyah, *Eng.* Arabian Desert, Eastern Desert. *Desert* E Egypt
Eastern Ghats 102 B3 *mountain range* SE India
Eastern Sayans 93 E4 Mong. Dzüün Soyonī Nuruu, Rus. Vostochnyy Sayan. *Mountain range* Mongolia/Russian Federation
East Falkland 43 D8 var. Isla Soledad. *Island* E Falkland Islands
East Grand Forks 23 E1 Minnesota, N USA
East Indiaman Ridge 119 D6 *undersea feature* E Indian Ocean
East Indies 130 A3 *island group* SE Asia
East Kilbride 66 C4 S Scotland, UK
East Korea Bay 107 E3 *bay* E North Korea
Eastleigh 67 D7 S England, UK
East London 56 D5 Afr. Oos-Londen; *prev.* Emonti, Port Rex. Eastern Cape, S South Africa
Eastmain 16 D3 *river* Québec, C Canada
East Mariana Basin 120 B1 *undersea feature* W Pacific Ocean
East Novaya Zemlya Trench 90 C1 var. Novaya Zemlya Trench. *Undersea feature* W Kara Sea
East Pacific Rise 131 F4 *undersea feature* E Pacific Ocean
East Saint Louis 18 B4 Illinois, N USA
East Scotia Basin 45 C7 *undersea feature* SE Scotia Sea
East Sea 108 A3 var. Sea of Japan Rus. Yapanskoye More. *Sea* NW Pacific Ocean *see also* Japan, Sea of
East Siberian Sea see Vostochno-Sibirskoye More
East Timor 117 F5 var. Loro Sae prev. Portuguese Timor, Timor Timur. *Country,* SE Asia
Eau Claire 18 A2 Wisconsin, N USA
Eauripik Rise 120 B2 *undersea feature* W Pacific Ocean
Ebensee 73 D6 Oberösterreich, N Austria
Eberswalde-Finow 72 D3 Brandenburg, E Germany
Ebetsu 108 D2 var. Ebetu. Hokkaidō, NE Japan
Ebetu see Ebetsu
Ebolowa 55 A5 Sud, S Cameroon
Ebon Atoll 122 D2 var. Epoon. *Atoll* Ralik Chain, S Marshall Islands
Ebro 71 E2 *river* NE Spain
Ebusus see Eivissa
Ech Cheliff see Chlef
Ech Chleff see Chlef
Echo Bay 15 E3 Northwest Territories, NW Canada
Echt 65 D5 Limburg, SE Netherlands
Ecija 70 D4 var. Astigi. Andalucía, SW Spain
Ecuador 38 B1 *Country* NW South America
Ed Da'ein 50 A4 Southern Darfur, W Sudan
Ed Damazin 50 C4 var. Ad Damazīn. Blue Nile, E Sudan
Ed Damer 50 C3 var. Ad Damar, Ad Dāmir. River Nile, NE Sudan
Ed Debba 50 B3 Northern, N Sudan
Ede 64 D4 Gelderland, C Netherlands
Ede 53 F5 Osun, SW Nigeria
Edéa 55 A5 Littoral, SW Cameroon
Edfu see Idfu
Edgeøya 61 G2 *island* E Svalbard
Edgware 67 A7 SE England, UK
Edinburg 27 G5 Texas, SW USA
Edinburgh 66 C4 *admin capital* S Scotland, UK
Edirne 94 A2 *Eng.* Adrianople; *anc.* Adrianopolis, Hadrianopolis. Edirne, NW Turkey

Edmonds 24 B2 Washington, NW USA
Edmonton 15 E5 Alberta, SW Canada
Edmundston 17 E4 New Brunswick, SE Canada
Edna 27 G4 Texas, SW USA
Edolo 74 B1 Lombardia, N Italy
Edremit 94 A3 Balıkesir, NW Turkey
Edward, Lake 55 E5 var. Albert Edward Nyanza, Edward Nyanza, Lac Idi Amin, Lake Rutanzige. *Lake* Uganda/Zaire
Edward Nyanza see Edward, Lake
Edwards Plateau 27 F3 *plain* Texas, SW USA
Eeklo 65 B5 var. Eekloo. Oost-Vlaanderen, NW Belgium
Edzo 15 E4 prev. Rae-Edzo. Northwest Territories, NW Canada
Eekloo see Eeklo
Eersel 65 C5 Noord-Brabant, S Netherlands
Efate 122 D4 var. Éfaté Fr. Vatë; *prev.* Sandwich Island. *Island* C Vanuatu
Effingham 18 B4 Illinois, N USA
Eforie Sud 86 D5 Constanţa, E Romania
Efstrátios, Ágios 82 D4 var. Ayios Evstratios. *Island* E Greece
Egadi, Isole 75 B7 *island group* S Italy
Eger 77 D6 Ger. Erlau. Heves, NE Hungary
Egeria Fracture Zone 119 C5 *tectonic feature* W Indian Ocean
Éghezèe 65 C6 Namur, C Belgium
Egina see Aígina
Egio see Aígio
Egmont, Mount see Taranaki, Mount
Egmont, Cape 128 C4 *headland* North Island, NZ
Egoli see Johannesburg
Egypt 50 B2 Ar. Jumhūrīyah Mişr al 'Arabīyah; *prev.* United Arab Republic, *anc.* Aegyptus. *Country* NE Africa
Eibar 71 E1 País Vasco, N Spain
Eibergen 64 E3 Gelderland, E Netherlands
Eidfjord 63 A5 Hordaland, S Norway
Eier-Berg see Suur Munamägi
Eifel 73 A5 *plateau* W Germany
Eiger 95 B7 *mountain* C Switzerland
Eigg 66 B3 *island* W Scotland, UK
Eight Degree Channel 110 B3 *channel* India/Maldives
Eighty Mile Beach 124 B4 *beach* Western Australia
Eijsden 65 D6 Limburg, SE Netherlands
Eilat see Elat
Eindhoven 65 D5 Noord-Brabant, S Netherlands
Eipel see Ipel'
Eipel see Ipoly
Eisenhüttenstadt 72 D4 Brandenburg, E Germany
Eisenstadt 73 E6 Burgenland, E Austria
Eisleben 72 C4 Sachsen-Anhalt, C Germany
Eivissa 71 G3 var. Ibiza, Cast. Ibiza; *anc.* Ebusus. *Island* Islas Baleares, Spain, W Mediterranean Sea
Eivissa 71 G3 var. Ibiza, Cast. Ibiza; *anc.* Ebusus. Eivissa, Spain, W Mediterranean Sea
Ejea de los Caballeros 71 E2 Aragón, NE Spain
Ejin Qi 104 D3 var. Dalain Hob. Nei Mongol Zizhiqu, N China
Ekapa see Cape Town
Ekiatapskiy Khrebet 93 G1 *mountain range* NE Russian Federation
El 'Alamein 50 B1 var. Al 'Alamayn. N Egypt
El Asnam see Chlef
Elat 97 B8 var. Eilat, Elath. Southern, S Israel
Elat, Gulf of see Aqaba, Gulf of
Elath see Al 'Aqaba
Elath see Elat
El'Atrun 50 B3 Northern Darfur, NW Sudan
Elazığ 95 E3 var. Elâziğ, Elâziz. Elâzığ, E Turkey
Elâziz see Elazığ
Elba, Isola d' 74 B4 *island* Archipelago Toscano, C Italy
Elbasan 79 D6 var. Elbasani. Elbasan, C Albania
Elbasani see Elbasan
Elbe 73 Cz. Labe. *River* Czech Republic/Germany
El Beni see Beni
Elbert, Mount 22 C4 *mountain* Colorado, C USA
Elbing see Elbląg
Elbląg 76 C2 var. Elblag, Ger. Elbing. Warmińsko-Mazurskie, NE Poland
El Boulaida see Blida
El'brus 89 F4 var. Gora El'brus. *Mountain* SW Russian Federation
El Burgo de Osma 71 E2 Castilla-León, C Spain
El Cajon 25 C8 California, W USA
El Calafate 43 B7 var. Calafate. Santa Cruz, S Argentina
El Callao 37 G3 Bolívar, E Venezuela
El Campo 27 G4 Texas, SW USA
El Carmen de Bolívar 36 B2 Bolívar, NW Colombia
El Centro 25 D8 California, W USA
Elche 71 F4 var. Elx; *anc.* Ilici, *Lat.* Illicis. País Valenciano, E Spain
Elda 71 F4 País Valenciano, E Spain
El Djazaïr see Alger
El Djelfa see Djelfa
El Dorado 20 B2 Arkansas, C USA
El Dorado 37 F2 Bolívar, E Venezuela
El Dorado 37 F2 Bolívar, E Venezuela
El Dorado 28 C3 Sinaloa, C Mexico
Eldorado 42 E3 Misiones, NE Argentina
Eldoret 51 C6 Rift Valley, W Kenya
Elektrostal 89 B5 Moskovskaya Oblast', W Russian Federation
Elemi Triangle 51 B5 *disputed region* Kenya/Sudan
Elephant Butte Reservoir 26 C2 *reservoir* New Mexico, SW USA
Eleuthera Island 32 C1 *island* N Bahamas

El Fasher 50 A4 *var.* Al Fāshir. Northern Darfur, W Sudan
El Ferrol *see* Ferrol
El Ferrol del Caudillo *see* Ferrol
El Gedaref *see* Gedaref
El Geneina 50 A4 *var.* Ajjinena, Al-Genain, Al Junaynah. Western Darfur, W Sudan
Elgin 18 B3 Illinois, N USA
Elgin 66 C3 NE Scotland, UK
El Gîza 50 B1 *var.* Al Jīzah, Gîza, Gizeh. N Egypt
El Goléa 48 D3 *var.* Al Golea. C Algeria
El Hank 52 D1 *cliff* N Mauritania
El Haseke *see* Al Ḥasakah
Elista 111 B7 Respublika Kalmykiya, SW Russian Federation
Elizabeth 127 B6 South Australia
Elizabeth City 21 G1 North Carolina, SE USA
Elizabethtown 18 C5 Kentucky, S USA
El-Jadida 48 C2 *prev.* Mazagan. W Morocco
Ełk 76 E2 Ger. Lyck. Warmińsko-Mazurskie, NE Poland
Elk City 27 F1 Oklahoma, C USA
El Kerak *see* Al Karak
El Khalil *see* Hebron
El Khârga 50 B2 *var.* Al Khārijah. C Egypt
Elkhart 18 C3 Indiana, N USA
El Khartûm *see* Khartoum
Elk River 23 F2 Minnesota, N USA
El Kuneitra *see* Al Qunayţirah
Ellef Ringnes Island 15 F1 *island* Nunavut, N Canada
Ellen, Mount 22 B5 *mountain* Utah, W USA
Ellensburg 24 B2 Washington, NW USA
Ellesmere Island 15 F1 *island* Queen Elizabeth Islands, Nunavut, N Canada
Ellesmere, Lake 129 C6 *lake* South Island, NZ
Elliston 127 A6 South Australia
Ellsworth Land 132 A3 *physical region* Antarctica
El Mahbas 48 B3 *var.* Mahbés. SW Western Sahara
El Mina 96 B4 *var.* Al Mînâ'. N Lebanon
El Minya 50 B2 *var.* Al Minyā, Minya. C Egypt
Elmira 19 E3 New York, NE USA
El Mreyyé 52 D2 *desert* E Mauritania
Elmshorn 72 B3 Schleswig-Holstein, N Germany
El Muglad 50 B4 Western Kordofan, C Sudan
El Obeid 50 B4 *var.* Al Obayyid, Al Ubayyiḍ. Northern Kordofan, C Sudan
El Ouâdi *see* El Oued
El Oued 49 E2 *var.* Al Oued, El Ouâdi, El Wad. NE Algeria
Eloy 26 B2 Arizona, SW USA
El Paso 26 D3 Texas, SW USA
El Porvenir 31 G4 San Blas, N Panama
El Progreso 30 C2 Yoro, NW Honduras
El Puerto de Santa María 70 C5 Andalucía, S Spain
El Quds *see* Jerusalem
El Quneitra *see* Al Qunayţirah
El Quseir *see* Al Quşayr
El Quweira *see* Al Quwayrah
El Rama 31 E3 Región Autónoma Atlántico Sur, SE Nicaragua
El Real 31 H5 *var.* El Real de Santa María. Darién, SE Panama
El Real de Santa María *see* El Real
El Reno 27 F1 Oklahoma, C USA
El Salvador 30 B3 *Country* Central America
El Sáuz 28 C2 Chihuahua, N Mexico
El Serrat 69 A7 N Andorra
Elst 64 D4 Gelderland, E Netherlands
El Sueco 28 C2 Chihuahua, N Mexico
El Suweida *see* As Suwaydā'
Eltanin Fracture Zone 131 E5 *tectonic feature* SE Pacific Ocean
El Tigre 37 E2 Anzoátegui, NE Venezuela
Elvas 70 C4 Portalegre, C Portugal
El Vendrell 71 G2 Cataluña, NE Spain
El Vigía 36 C2 Mérida, NW Venezuela
El Wad *see* El Oued
Elwell, Lake 22 B1 *reservoir* Montana, NW USA
Elx *see* Elche
Ely 25 D5 Nevada, W USA
El Yopal *see* Yopal
Emajõgi 84 D3 Ger. Embach. *River* SE Estonia
Emba 92 B4 Kaz. Embi. Aktyubinsk, W Kazakhstan
Emden 72 A3 Niedersachsen, NW Germany
Emerald 126 D4 Queensland, E Australia
Emerald Isle *see* Montserrat
Emesa *see* Ḥimş
Emmaste 84 C2 Hiiumaa, W Estonia
Emmeloord 64 D2 Flevoland, N Netherlands
Emmen 64 E2 Drenthe, NE Netherlands
Emmendingen 73 A6 Baden-Württemberg, SW Germany
Emory Peak 27 E4 *mountain* Texas, SW USA
Empalme 28 B2 Sonora, NW Mexico
Emperor Seamounts 91 G3 *undersea feature* NW Pacific Ocean
Emporia 23 F5 Kansas, C USA
Empty Quarter *see* Ar Rub' al Khālī
Ems 72 A3 Dut. Eems. *River* NW Germany
Encamp 69 A8 C Andorra
Encarnación 42 D3 Itapúa, S Paraguay
Encinitas 25 C8 California, W USA
Encs 77 D6 Borsod-Abaúj-Zemplén, NE Hungary
Endeavour Strait 126 C1 *strait* Queensland, NE Australia
Enderbury Island 123 F3 *atoll* Phoenix Islands, C Kiribati
Enderby Land 132 C2 *physical region* Antarctica
Enderby Plain 132 D2 *undersea feature* S Indian Ocean

Enewetak Atoll 122 C1 *var.* Ânewetak, Eniwetok. *Atoll* Ralik Chain, W Marshall Islands
Enfield 67 A7 SE England, UK
Engannim *see* Jenīn
Enghien 65 B6 Dut. Edingen. Hainaut, SW Belgium
England 67 D5 *Lat.* Anglia. *National region* UK
Englewood 22 D4 Colorado, C USA
English Channel 67 D8 *var.* The Channel, *Fr.* la Manche. *Channel* NW Europe
Engure 81 C3 Tukums, W Latvia
Engures Ezers 84 B3 *lake* NW Latvia
Enguri 95 F1 *Rus.* Inguri. *River* NW Georgia
Enid 27 F1 Oklahoma, C USA
Enikale Strait *see* Kerch Strait
Eniwetok *see* Enewetak Atoll
En Nâqoûra 97 A5 *var.* An Nāqūrah. SW Lebanon
Ennedi 54 D2 *plateau* E Chad
Ennis 67 A6 *Ir.* Inis. W Ireland
Ennis 27 G3 Texas, SW USA
Enniskillen 67 B5 *var.* Inniskilling, *Ir.* Inis Ceithleann. SW Northern Ireland, UK
Enns 73 D6 *river* C Austria
Enschede 64 E3 Overijssel, E Netherlands
Ensenada 28 A1 Baja California, NW Mexico
Entebbe 51 B6 S Uganda
Entroncamento 70 B3 Santarém, C Portugal
Enugu 53 G5 Enugu, S Nigeria
Eolie, Isole 75 C6 *var.* Isole Lipari, *Eng.* Aeolian Islands, Lipari Islands. *Island group* S Italy
Epanomí 82 B4 Kentrikí Makedonía, N Greece
Epéna 55 B5 La Likouala, NE Congo
Eperies *see* Prešov
Eperjes *see* Prešov
Epi 122 D4 *var.* Épi. *Island* C Vanuatu
Épi *see* Epi
Épinal 68 D4 Vosges, NE France
Epiphania *see* Ḥamāh
Epitoli *see* Pretoria
Epoon *see* Ebon Atoll
Epsom 67 A8 SE England, UK
Equatorial Guinea 55 A5 *Country* C Africa
Erautini *see* Johannesburg
Erbil *see* Arbīl
Erciş 95 F3 Van, E Turkey
Erdélyi-Havasok *see* Carpaţii Meridionali
Erdenet 105 E2 Bulgan, N Mongolia
Erdi 54 C2 *plateau* NE Chad
Erdi Ma 54 D2 *desert* NE Chad
Erebus, Mount 132 B4 *mountain* Ross Island, Antarctica
Ereğli 94 C4 Konya, S Turkey
Erenhot 105 F2 *var.* Erlian. Nei Mongol Zizhiqu, NE China
Erevan *see* Yerevan
Erfurt 72 C4 Thüringen, C Germany
Ergene Irmağı 94 A2 *var.* Ergene Irmağı. *River* NW Turkey
Erg Iguidi *see* Iguïdi, 'Erg
Ergun He *see* Argun
Ergun Zuoqi 105 F1 Nei Mongol Zizhiqu, N China
Erie 18 D3 Pennsylvania, NE USA
Erie, Lake 18 D3 Fr. Lac Érié. *Lake* Canada/USA
Eritrea 50 C4 *Tig.* Ērtra. *Country* E Africa
Erivan *see* Yerevan
Erlangen 73 C5 Bayern, S Germany
Erlian *see* Erenhot
Ermelo 64 D3 Gelderland, C Netherlands
Ermióni 83 C6 Pelopónnisos, S Greece
Ermoúpoli 83 D6 *var.* Hermoupolis; *prev.* Ermoúpolis. Sýros, Kykládes, Greece, Aegean Sea
Ermoúpolis *see* Ermoúpoli
Ernākulam 110 C3 Kerala, SW India
Erode 110 C2 Tamil Nādu, SE India
Erquelinnes 65 B7 Hainaut, S Belgium
Er-Rachidia 48 C2 *var.* Ksar al Soule. E Morocco
Er Rahad 50 B4 *var.* Ar Rahad. Northern Kordofan, C Sudan
Erromango 122 D4 *island* S Vanuatu
Ertis *see* Irtysh
Erzgebirge 73 C5 *Cz.* Krušné Hory, *Eng.* Ore Mountains. *Mountain range* Czech Republic/Germany *see also* Krušné Hory
Erzincan 95 E3 *var.* Erzinjan. Erzincan, E Turkey
Erzinjan *see* Erzincan
Erzurum 95 F3 *prev.* Erzerum. Erzurum, NE Turkey
Esbjerg 63 A7 Ribe, W Denmark
Escaldes 69 A8 C Andorra
Escanaba 18 C2 Michigan, N USA
Esch-sur-Alzette 65 D8 Luxembourg, S Luxembourg
Escondido 25 C8 California, W USA
Escuinapa 28 D3 *var.* Escuinapa de Hidalgo. Sinaloa, C Mexico
Escuinapa de Hidalgo *see* Escuinapa
Escuintla 29 G5 Chiapas, SE Mexico
Escuintla 30 B2 Escuintla, S Guatemala
Esenguly 100 B3 *var.* Gasan-Kuli. Balkanskiy Velayat, W Turkmenistan
Eşfahān 98 C3 *Eng.* Isfahan; *anc.* Aspadana. Eşfahān, C Iran
Esh Sham *see* Dimashq
Esh Sharā *see* Ash Sharāh
Eskişehir 94 B3 *var.* Eskishehr. Eskişehir, W Turkey
Eskishehr *see* Eskişehir
Eslāmābād 98 C3 *var.* Eslāmābād-e Gharb; *prev.* Harunabad, Shāhābād. Kermānshāhān, W Iran
Eslāmābād-e Gharb *see* Eslāmābād
Esmeraldas 38 A1 Esmeraldas, N Ecuador
Esna *see* Isna
Espanola 26 D1 New Mexico, SW USA
Esperance 125 C7 Western Australia
Esperanza 132 A2 *Argentinian research station* Antarctica
Esperanza 28 B2 Sonora, NW Mexico

Espinal 36 B3 Tolima, C Colombia
Espinhaço, Serra do 34 D4 *mountain range* SE Brazil
Espírito Santo 41 F4 *off.* Estado do Espírito Santo. *State* E Brazil
Espiritu Santo 122 C4 *var.* Santo. *Island* W Vanuatu
Espoo 63 D6 *Swe.* Esbo. Etelä-Suomi, S Finland
Esquel 43 B6 Chubut, SW Argentina
Essaouira 48 B2 *prev.* Mogador. W Morocco
Es Semara *see* Smara
Essen 72 A4 *var.* Essen an der Ruhr. Nordrhein-Westfalen, W Germany
Essen an der Ruhr *see* Essen
Essen 65 C5 Antwerpen, N Belgium
Essequibo River 37 F3 *river* C Guyana
Es Suweida *see* As Suwaydā'
Estacado, Llano 27 E2 *plain* New Mexico/Texas, SW USA
Estados, Isla de los 43 C8 *prev. Eng.* Staten Island. *Island*, S Argentina
Estância 41 G3 Sergipe, E Brazil
Estelí 30 D3 Estelí, NW Nicaragua
Estella 71 E1 *Bas.* Lizarra. Navarra, N Spain
Estepona 92 D5 Andalucía, S Spain
Estevan 15 F5 Saskatchewan, S Canada
Estonia 84 D2*Est.* Eesti Vabariik, *Ger.* Estland, *Latv.* Igaunija; *prev.* Estonian SSR, *Rus.* Estonskaya SSR. *Country* NE Europe
Estrela, Serra da 70 C3 *mountain range* C Portugal
Estremoz 70 C4 Évora, S Portugal
Esztergom 77 C6 Ger. Gran; *anc.* Strigonium. Komárom-Esztergom, N Hungary
Étalle 65 D8 Luxembourg, SE Belgium
Etāwah 112 D3 Uttar Pradesh, N India
Ethiopia 51 C5 *prev.* Abyssinia, People's Democratic Republic of Ethiopia. *Country* E Africa
Ethiopian Highlands 51 C5 *var.* Ethiopian Plateau. *Upland* E Ethiopia
Ethiopian Plateau *see* Ethiopian Highlands
Etna, Monte 75 C7 *Eng.* Mount Etna. *Volcano* Sicilia, Italy, C Mediterranean Sea
Etna, Mount *see* Etna, Monte
Etosha Pan 56 B3 *salt lake* N Namibia
Etoumbi 55 B5 Cuvette, NW Congo
Et Tafila *see* Aţ Ţafīlah
Ettelbrück 65 D8 Diekirch, C Luxembourg
'Eua 123 F5 *var.* Middleburg Island. *Island* Tongatapu Group, SE Tonga
Euboea *see* Évvoia
Eucla 125 D6 Western Australia
Euclid 18 D3 Ohio, N USA
Eufaula Lake 27 G1 *var.* Eufaula Reservoir. *Reservoir* Oklahoma, C USA
Eufaula Reservoir *see* Eufaula Lake
Eugene 24 B3 Oregon, NW USA
Eupen 65 D6 Liège, E Belgium
Euphrates 90 B4 *Ar.* Al Furāt, *Turk.* Fırat Nehri. *River* SW Asia
Eureka 25 A5 California, W USA
Eureka 22 A1 Montana, NW USA
Europa Point 71 H5 *headland* S Gibraltar
Europe 12 E1 *continent*
Eutin 72 C2 Schleswig-Holstein, N Germany
Euxine Sea *see* Black Sea
Evansdale 23 G3 Iowa, C USA
Evanston 18 B3 Illinois, N USA
Evanston 22 B4 Wyoming, C USA
Evansville 18 B5 Indiana, N USA
Eveleth 23 G1 Minnesota, N USA
Everard, Lake 127 A6 *salt lake* South Australia
Everest, Mount 104 B3 *Chin.* Qomolangma Feng, *Nep.* Sagarmatha. *Mountain* China/Nepal
Everett 24 B2 Washington, NW USA
Everglades, The 21 F5 *wetland* Florida, SE USA
Evje 63 A6 Aust-Agder, S Norway
Évora 70 B4 *anc.* Ebora, *Lat.* Liberalitas Julia.Évora, C Portugal
Évreux 68 C3 *anc.* Civitas Eburovicum. Eure, N France
Évros *see* Maritsa
Évry 68 E2 Essonne, N France
Évvoia 79 E8 *Lat.* Euboea. *Island* C Greece
Ewarton 32 B5 C Jamaica
Excelsior Springs 23 F4 Missouri, C USA
Exe 67 C7 *river* SW England, UK
Exeter 67 C7 *anc.* Isca Damnoniorum. SW England, UK
Exmoor 67 C7 *moorland* SW England, UK
Exmouth 67 C7 SW England, UK
Exmouth 124 A4 Western Australia
Exmouth Gulf 124 A4 *gulf* Western Australia
Exmouth Plateau 119 E5 *undersea feature* E Indian Ocean
Extremadura 70 C3 *cultural region* W Spain
Exuma Cays 32 C1 *islets* C Bahamas
Exuma Sound 32 C1 *sound* C Bahamas
Eyre Mountains 129 A7 *mountain range* South Island, NZ
Eyre North, Lake 127 A5 *salt lake* South Australia
Eyre Peninsula 127 A6 *peninsula* South Australia
Eyre South, Lake 127 A5 *salt lake* South Australia

F

Faadhippolhu Atoll 110 B4 *var.* Fadiffolu, Lhaviyani Atoll. *Atoll* N Maldives
Fabens 26 D3 Texas, SW USA
Fada 54 C2 Borkou-Ennedi-Tibesti, E Chad
Fada-Ngourma 53 E4 E Burkina faso
Fadiffolu *see* Faadhippolhu Atoll
Faenza 74 C3 *anc.* Faventia. Emilia-Romagna, N Italy
Faeroe-Iceland Ridge 58 C1 *undersea feature* NW Norwegian Sea
Faeroe-Shetland Trough 58 C2 *undersea feature* NE Atlantic Ocean
Faeroes Islands 61 E5 *Dan.* Færøerne, *Faer.* Føroyar. *Danish external territory* N Atlantic Ocean
Faetano 74 E2 E San Marino
Făgăraș 86 C4 Ger. Fogarasch, *Hung.* Fogaras. Braşov, C Romania
Fagne 65 C7 *hill range* S Belgium
Faguibine, Lac 53 E3 *var.* Lake Fagibina. *Lake* NW Mali
Fahlun *see* Falun
Fahraj 98 E4 Kermān, SE Iran
Faial 70 A5 *var.* Ilha do Faial. *Island* Azores, Portugal, NE Atlantic Ocean
Fairbanks 14 D3 Alaska, USA
Fairfield 25 B6 California, W USA
Fair Isle 66 D2 *island* NE Scotland, UK
Fairlie 129 B6 Canterbury, South Island, NZ
Fairmont 23 F3 Minnesota, N USA
Faisalābād 112 C2 *prev.* Lyallpur. Punjab, NE Pakistan
Faizābād *see* Feyzābād
Faizābād 113 F3 Uttar Pradesh, N India
Fakaofo Atoll 123 F3 *island* SE Tokelau
Falam 114 A3 Chin State, W Myanmar
Falconara Marittima 74 C3 Marche, C Italy
Falkland Islands 43 D7 *var.* Falklands, Islas Malvinas. *UK dependent territory* SW Atlantic Ocean
Falkland Plateau 35 D7 *var.* Argentine Rise. *Undersea feature* SW Atlantic Ocean
Falklands *see* Falkland Islands
Fallbrook 25 C8 California, W USA
Falmouth 67 C7 SW England, UK
Falmouth 32 A4 W Jamaica
Falster 63 B8 *island* SE Denmark
Fălticeni 86 C3 *Hung.* Falticsén. Suceava, NE Romania
Falun 63 C6 *var.* Fahlun. Kopparberg, C Sweden
Famagusta *see* Ammóchostos
Famagusta Bay *see* Kólpos Ammochóstos
Famenne 65 C7 *physical region* SE Belgium
Fang 114 C3 Chiang Mai, NW Thailand
Fano 74 C3 *anc.* Colonia Julia Fanestris, Fanum Fortunae. Marche, C Italy
Farafangana 57 G4 Fianarantsoa, SE Madagascar
Farāh 100 D4 *var.* Farah, Fararud. Farāh, W Afghanistan
Farāh Rūd 100 D4 *river* W Afghanistan
Faranah 52 C4 Haute-Guinée, S Guinea
Fararud *see* Farāh
Farāsān, Jazā'ir 99 A6 *island group* SW Saudi Arabia
Farewell, Cape 128 C4 *headland* South Island, NZ
Farewell, Cape *see* Nunap Isua
Farghona *see* Farg'ona
Fargo 23 F2 North Dakota, N USA
Farg'ona 101 F2 *var.* Farghona, *Rus.* Fergana; *prev.* Novyy Margilan. Farghona Wiloyati, E Uzbekistan
Faribault 23 F2 Minnesota, N USA
Farīdābād 112 D3 Haryāna, N India
Farkhor 101 E3 *Rus.* Parkhar. SW Tajikistan
Farmington 23 G5 Missouri, C USA
Farmington 26 C1 New Mexico, SW USA
Faro 70 B5 Faro, S Portugal
Farquhar Group 57 G2 *island group* S Seychelles
Farvel, Kap *see* Nunap Isua
Fasil 124 C3 Nordland, C Norway
Faxaflói 60 D5 *Eng.* Faxa Bay. *Bay* W Iceland
Faya 54 C2 *prev.* Faya-Largeau, Largeau. Borkou-Ennedi-Tibesti, N Chad
Fayetteville 20 A1 Arkansas, C USA
Fayetteville 21 F1 North Carolina, SE USA
Fderick *see* Fdérik
Fdérik 52 C2 *var.* Fdérick, *Fr.* Fort Gouraud. Tiris Zemmour, NW Mauritania
Fear, Cape 21 F2 *headland* Bald Head Island, North Carolina, SE USA
Fécamp 68 B3 Seine-Maritime, N France
Federation of the separate territories of *see* Malaysia
Fehérgyarmat 77 E6 Szabolcs-Szatmár-Bereg, E Hungary
Fehmarn 72 C2 *island* N Germany
Fehmarnbelt 72 C2 *var.* Fehmarn Belt, *Dan.* Fehmern Bælt. *Strait* Denmark/Germany
Fehmern Bælt *see* Fehmarnbelt
Feijó 40 C2 Acre, W Brazil
Feilding 128 D4 Manawatu-Wanganui, North Island, NZ
Feira *see* Feira de Santana
Feira de Santana 41 G3 *var.* Feira. Bahia, E Brazil
Felanitx 71 G3 *anc.* Canati, Felaniche. Mallorca, Spain, W Mediterranean Sea
Felidhu Atoll 110 B4 *atoll* C Maldives
Felipe Carrillo Puerto 29 H4 Quintana Roo, SE Mexico
Felixstowe 67 E6 E England, UK
Femunden 63 B5 *lake* S Norway
Fengcheng 106 D3 *var.* Feng-cheng, Fenghwangcheng. Liaoning, NE China
Feng-cheng *see* Fengcheng
Fenghwangcheng *see* Fengcheng
Fengtien *see* Liaoning
Fenoarivo 57 G3 Toamasina, E Madagascar
Fens, The 67 E6 *wetland* E England, UK
Feodosiya 87 F5 *var.* Kefe, It. Kaffa; *anc.* Theodosia. Respublika Krym, S Ukraine
Féres 82 D3 Anatolikí Makedonía kai Thráki, NE Greece
Fergus Falls 23 F2 Minnesota, N USA
Ferkessédougou 53 E4 N Côte d'Ivoire
Ferghana *see* Farg'ona
Fermo 74 C4 *anc.* Firmum Picenum. Marche, C Italy
Fernandina, Isla 38 A5 *var.* Narborough Island. *Island* Galapagos Islands, Ecuador, E Pacific Ocean
Fernando de Noronha 41 H2 *island* E Brazil
Fernando Po *see* Bioco, Isla de
Fernando Póo *see* Bioco, Isla de

Ferrara 74 C2 *anc.* Forum Alieni. Emilia-Romagna, N Italy
Ferreñafe 38 B3 Lambayeque, W Peru
Ferro *see* Hierro
Ferrol 70 B1 *var.* El Ferrol; *prev.* El Ferrol del Caudillo. Galicia, NW Spain
Ferwerd 64 D1 *Fris.* Ferwert. Friesland, N Netherlands
Fès 48 C2 *Eng.* Fez. N Morocco
Feteşti 86 D5 Ialomiţa, SE Romania
Fethiye 94 B4 Muğla, SW Turkey
Fetlar 66 D1 *island* NE Scotland, UK
Feyzābād 101 F3 *var.* Faizabad, Faizābād, Feyzābād, Fyzabad. Badakhshān, NE Afghanistan
Fianarantsoa 57 F3 Fianarantsoa, C Madagascar
Fianga 54 B4 Mayo-Kébbi, SW Chad
Fier 79 C6 *var.* Fieri. Fier, SW Albania
Fieri *see* Fier
Figeac 69 C5 Lot, S France
Figig *see* Figuig
Figueira da Foz 70 B3 Coimbra, W Portugal
Figueres 71 G2 Cataluña, E Spain
Figuig 48 D2 *var.* Figig. E Morocco
Fiji 123 E5 *Fij.* Viti. *Country* SW Pacific Ocean
Filadelfia 30 D4 Guanacaste, W Costa Rica
Filiaşi 86 B5 Dolj, SW Romania
Filipstad 63 B6 Värmland, C Sweden
Finale Ligure 74 A3 Liguria, NW Italy
Finchley 67 A7 SE England, UK
Findlay 18 C4 Ohio, N USA
Finike 94 B4 Antalya, SW Turkey
Finland 62 D4 *Fin.* Suomen Tasavalta, Suomi. *Country* N Europe
Finland, Gulf of 63 D6 *Est.* Soome Laht, *Fin.* Suomenlahti, *Ger.* Finnischer Meerbusen, *Rus.* Finskiy Zaliv, *Swe.* Finska Viken. *Gulf* E Baltic Sea
Finnmarksvidda 62 D2 *physical region* N Norway
Finsterwalde 72 D4 Brandenburg, E Germany
Fiordland 129 A7 *physical region* South Island, NZ
Fiorina 74 E1 NE San Marino
Firenze 74 C3 *Eng.* Florence; *anc.* Florentia. Toscana, C Italy
Fischbacher Alpen 73 E7 *mountain range* E Austria
Fish 56 B4 *var.* Vis. *River* S Namibia
Fishguard 67 C6 *Wel.* Abergwaun. SW Wales, UK
Fisterra, Cabo 70 B1 *headland* NW Spain
Fitzroy Crossing 124 C3 Western Australia
Fitzroy River 124 C3 *river* Western Australia
Flagstaff 26 B2 Arizona, SW USA
Flanders 65 A6 Dut. Vlaanderen, Fr. Flandre. *Cultural region* Belgium/France
Flathead Lake 22 B1 *lake* Montana, NW USA
Flat Island 106 C8 *island* NE Spratly Islands
Flatts Village 20 B5 *var.* The Flatts Village. C Bermuda
Flensburg 72 B2 Schleswig-Holstein, N Germany
Flinders Island 127 C8 *island* Furneaux Group, Tasmania, SE Australia
Flinders Ranges 127 B6 *mountain range* South Australia
Flinders River 126 C3 *river* Queensland, NE Australia
Flin Flon 15 F5 Manitoba, C Canada
Flint 18 C3 Michigan, N USA
Flint Island 123 G4 *island* Line Islands, E Kiribati
Floreana, Isla *see* Santa María, Isla
Florence 20 C1 Alabama, S USA
Florence 21 F2 South Carolina, SE USA
Florencia 36 B4 Caquetá, S Colombia
Florentia *see* Firenze
Flores 70 A5 *island* Azores, Portugal, NE Atlantic Ocean
Flores 117 E5 *island* Nusa Tenggara, C Indonesia
Flores 30 B1 Petén, N Guatemala
Flores Sea 116 D5 *Ind.* Laut Flores. *Sea* C Indonesia
Floriano 41 F2 Piauí, E Brazil
Florianópolis 41 F5 *prev.* Destêrro. *State capital* Santa Catarina, S Brazil
Florida 21 E4 *off.* State of Florida; also known as Peninsular State, Sunshine State. *State* SE USA
Florida 42 D4 Florida, S Uruguay
Florida Bay 21 E5 *bay* Florida, SE USA
Florida Keys 21 E5 *island group* Florida, SE USA
Florida, Straits of 32 B1 *strait* Atlantic Ocean/Gulf of Mexico
Flórina 82 B4 *var.* Phlórina. Dytikí Makedonía, N Greece
Florissant 23 G4 Missouri, C USA
Flouda, Akrotírio 83 D7 *headland* Astypálaia, Kykládes, Greece, Aegean Sea
Foča 78 C4 *var.* Srbinje, Republika Srpska, SE Bosnia and Herzegovina
Focşani 86 C4 Vrancea, E Romania
Foggia 75 D5 Puglia, SE Italy
Fogo 52 A3 *island* Ilhas de Sotavento, SW Cape Verde
Foix 69 B6 Ariège, S France
Folégandros 83 C7 *island* Kykládes, Greece, Aegean Sea
Foleyet 16 C4 Ontario, S Canada
Foligno 74 C4 Umbria, C Italy
Folkestone 67 E7 SE England, UK
Fond du Lac 18 B2 Wisconsin, N USA
Fongafale 123 E3 *var.* Funafuti. *Country capital* (Tuvalu) Funafuti Atoll, SE Tuvalu
Fonseca, Gulf of 30 C3 *Sp.* Golfo de Fonseca. *Gulf* Central America
Fontainebleau 68 C3 Seine-et-Marne, N France
Fontenay-le-Comte 68 B4 Vendée, NW France

Fontvieille – Glasgow

Fontvieille 69 B8 SW Monaco
Fonyód 77 C7 Somogy, W Hungary
Foochow *see* Fuzhou
Forchheim 73 C5 Bayern, SE Germany
Forel, Mont 60 D4 *mountain* SE Greenland
Forfar 66 C3 E Scotland, UK
Forge du Sud *see* Dudelange
Forlì 74 C3 *anc.* Forum Livii. Emilia-Romagna, N Italy
Formentera 93 G4 *anc.* Ophiusa, *Lat.* Frumentum. *Island* Islas Baleares, Spain, W Mediterranean Sea
Formosa 42 D2 Formosa, NE Argentina
Formosa, Serra 41 E3 *mountain range* C Brazil
Formosa Strait *see* Taiwan Strait
Forrest City 20 B1 Arkansas, C USA
Fort Albany 16 C3 Ontario, C Canada
Fortaleza 41 G2 *prev.* Ceará. *State capital* Ceará, NE Brazil
Fortaleza 39 F2 Pando, N Bolivia
Fort-Bayard *see* Zhanjiang
Fort-Cappolani *see* Tîdjikja
Fort Collins 22 D4 Colorado, C USA
Fort Davis 27 E3 Texas, SW USA
Fort-de-France 33 H4 *prev.* Fort-Royal. *Dependent territory capital* (Martinique) W Martinique
Fort Dodge 23 F3 Iowa, C USA
Fortescue River 124 A4 *river* Western Australia
Fort Frances 16 B4 Ontario, S Canada
Fort Good Hope 15 E3 *var.* Good Hope. Northwest Territories, NW Canada
Fort Gouraud *see* Fdérik
Forth 66 C4 *river* C Scotland, UK
Forth, Firth of 66 C4 *estuary* E Scotland, UK
Fort-Lamy *see* Ndjamena
Fort Lauderdale 21 F5 Florida, SE USA
Fort Liard 15 E4 *var.* Liard. Northwest Territories, W Canada
Fort Madison 23 G4 Iowa, C USA
Fort McMurray 15 E4 Alberta, C Canada
Fort McPherson 14 D3 *var.* McPherson. Northwest Territories, NW Canada
Fort Morgan 22 D4 Colorado, C USA
Fort Myers 21 E5 Florida, SE USA
Fort Nelson 15 E4 British Columbia, W Canada
Fort Peck Lake 22 C1 *reservoir* Montana, NW USA
Fort Pierce 21 F4 Florida, SE USA
Fort Providence 15 E4 *var.* Providence. Northwest Territories, W Canada
Fort St.John 15 E4 British Columbia, W Canada
Fort Scott 23 F5 Kansas, C USA
Fort Severn 16 C2 Ontario, C Canada
Fort-Shevchenko 92 A4 Mangistau, W Kazakhstan
Fort Simpson 15 E4 *var.* Simpson. Northwest Territories, W Canada
Fort Smith 15 E4 *district capital* Northwest Territories, W Canada
Fort Smith 20 B1 Arkansas, C USA
Fort Stockton 27 E3 Texas, SW USA
Fort-Trinquet *see* Bîr Mogreïn
Fort Vermilion 15 E4 Alberta, W Canada
Fort Walton Beach 20 C3 Florida, SE USA
Fort Wayne 18 C4 Indiana, N USA
Fort William 66 C3 N Scotland, UK
Fort Worth 27 G2 Texas, SW USA
Fort Yukon 14 D3 Alaska, USA
Fougamou 55 A6 Ngounié, C Gabon
Fougères 68 B3 Ille-et-Vilaine, NW France
Fou-hsin *see* Fuxin
Foulwind, Cape 129 B5 *headland* South Island, NZ
Foumban 54 A4 Ouest, NW Cameroon
Fou-shan *see* Fushun
Foveaux Strait 129 A8 *strait* S NZ
Foxe Basin 15 G3 *sea* Nunavut, N Canada
Fox Glacier 129 B6 West Coast, South Island, NZ
Fox Mine 15 F4 Manitoba, C Canada
Fraga 71 F2 Aragón, NE Spain
Fram Basin 133 C3 *var.* Amundsen Basin. *Undersea feature* Arctic Ocean
France 68 B4 *It./Sp.* Francia; *prev.* Gaul, Gaule, *Lat.* Gallia. *Country* W Europe
Franceville 55 B6 *var.* Massoukou, Masuku. Haut-Ogooué, E Gabon
Francfort prev *see* Frankfurt am Main
Franche-Comté 68 D4 *cultural region* E France
Francis Case, Lake 23 E3 *reservoir* South Dakota, N USA
Francisco Escárcega 29 G4 Campeche, SE Mexico
Francistown 56 D3 North East, NE Botswana
Franconian Jura *see* Fränkische Alb
Frankenalb *see* Fränkische Alb
Frankenstein *see* Ząbkowice Śląskie
Frankenstein in Schlesien *see* Ząbkowice Śląskie
Frankfort 18 C5 *state capital* Kentucky, S USA
Frankfort on the Main *see* Frankfurt am Main
Frankfurt *see* Frankfurt am Main
Frankfurt am Main 73 B5 *var.* Frankfurt, *Fr.* Francfort; prev. *Eng.* Frankfort on the Main. Hessen, SW Germany
Frankfurt an der Oder 72 D3 Brandenburg, E Germany
Fränkische Alb 73 C6 *var.* Frankenalb, *Eng.* Franconian Jura. *Mountain range* S Germany
Franklin 20 C1 Tennessee, S USA
Franklin D.Roosevelt Lake 24 C1 *reservoir* Washington, NW USA
Frantsa-Iosifa, Zemlya 92 D1 *Eng.* Franz Josef Land. *Island group* N Russian Federation
Franz Josef Land *see* Frantsa-Iosifa, Zemlya
Fraserburgh 66 D3 NE Scotland, UK
Fraser Island 126 E4 *var.* Great Sandy Island. *Island* Queensland, E Australia
Fredericksburg 19 E5 Virginia, NE USA
Fredericton 17 F4 New Brunswick, SE Canada
Frederikshåb *see* Paamiut
Fredrikstad 63 B6 Østfold, S Norway
Freeport 32 C1 Grand Bahama Island, N Bahamas
Freeport 27 H4 Texas, SW USA
Freetown 52 C4 *country capital* (Sierra Leone) W Sierra Leone
Freiburg *see* Freiburg im Breisgau
Freiburg im Breisgau 73 A6 *var.* Freiburg, *Fr.* Fribourg-en-Brisgau. Baden-Württemberg, SW Germany
Fremantle 125 A6 Western Australia
Fremont 23 F4 Nebraska, C USA
French Guiana 37 H3 *var.* Guiana, Guyane. *French overseas department* N South America
French Polynesia 121 F4 *French overseas territory* C Polynesia
French Southern and Antarctic Territories 119 B7 *Fr.* Terres Australes et Antarctiques Françaises. *French overseas territory* S Indian Ocean
Fresnillo 28 D3 *var.* Fresnillo de González Echeverría. Zacatecas, C Mexico
Fresnillo de González Echeverría *see* Fresnillo
Fresno 25 C6 California, W USA
Frías 42 C3 Catamarca, N Argentina
Fribourg-en-Brisgau *see* Freiburg im Breisgau
Friedrichshafen 73 B7 Baden-Württemberg, S Germany
Frobisher Bay 60 B3 *inlet* Baffin Island, Northwest Territories, NE Canada
Frohavet 62 B4 *sound* C Norway
Frome, Lake 127 B6 *salt lake* South Australia
Frontera 29 G4 Tabasco, SE Mexico
Frontignan 91 C6 Hérault, S France
Frostviken *see* Kvarnbergsvattnet
Frøya 62 A4 *island* W Norway
Frunze *see* Bishkek
Frýdek-Místek 77 C5 *Ger.* Friedek-Mistek. Ostravský Kraj, E Czech Republic
Fu-chien *see* Fujian
Fu-chou *see* Fuzhou
Fuengirola 70 D5 Andalucía, S Spain
Fuerte Olimpo 42 D2 *var.* Olimpo. Alto Paraguay, NE Paraguay
Fuerte, Río 26 C5 *river* C Mexico
Fuerteventura 48 B3 *island* Islas Canarias, Spain, NE Atlantic Ocean
Fuhkien *see* Fujian
Fu-hsin *see* Fuxin
Fuji 109 D6 *var.* Huzi. Shizuoka, Honshū, S Japan
Fujian 106 D6 *var.* Fu-chien, Fuhkien, Fujian Sheng, Fukien, Min. Admin. region *province* SE China
Fujian Sheng *see* Fujian
Fuji-san 109 C6 *var.* Fujiyama, *Eng.* Mount Fuji. *Mountain* Honshū, SE Japan
Fujiyama *see* Fuji-san
Fukang 104 C2 Xinjiang Uygur Zizhiqu, W China
Fukien *see* Fujian
Fukui 109 C6 *var.* Hukui. Fukui, Honshū, SW Japan
Fukuoka 109 A7 *var.* Hukuoka; *hist.* Najima. Fukuoka, Kyūshū, SW Japan
Fukushima 108 D4 *var.* Hukusima. Fukushima, Honshū, C Japan
Fulda 73 B5 Hessen, C Germany
Funafuti *see* Fongafale
Funafuti Atoll 123 E3 *atoll* C Tuvalu
Funchal 48 A2 Madeira, Portugal, NE Atlantic Ocean
Fundy, Bay of 17 F5 *bay* Canada/USA
Furnes *see* Veurne
Fürth 73 C5 Bayern, S Germany
Furukawa 108 D4 *var.* Hurukawa. Miyagi, Honshū, C Japan
Fushun 106 D3 *var.* Fou-shan, Fu-shun. Liaoning, NE China
Fu-shun *see* Fushun
Fusin *see* Fuxin
Füssen 73 C7 Bayern, S Germany
Futog 78 D3 Serbia, NW Serbia and Montenegro (Yugo.)
Futuna, Île 123 E4 *island* S Wallis and Futuna
Fuxin 106 D3 *var.* Fou-hsin, Fu-hsin, Fusin. Liaoning, NE China
Fuzhou 106 D6 *var.* Foochow, Fu-chou. Fujian, SE China
Fuzhou 106 D5 *prev.* Linchuan. Jiangxi, S China
Fyn 63 B8 *Ger.* Fünen. *Island* C Denmark
Fyzabad *see* Feyẓābād

G

Gaafu Alifu Atoll *see* North Huvadhu Atoll
Gaafu Dhaalu Atoll *see* South Huvadhu Atoll
Gaalkacyo 51 E5 *var.* Galka'yo, *It.* Galcaio. Mudug, C Somalia
Gabela 56 B2 Cuanza Sul, W Angola
Gabès 49 E2 *var.* Qābis. E Tunisia
Gabès, Golfe de 49 F2 *Ar.* Khalīj Qābis. *Gulf* E Tunisia
Gabon 55 B6 *Country* C Africa
Gaborone 56 C4 *prev.* Gaberones. *Country capital* (Botswana) South East, SE Botswana
Gabrovo 82 D2 Gabrovo, N Bulgaria
Gadag 110 C1 Karnātaka, W India
Gadsden 20 D2 Alabama, S USA
Gaeta 75 C5 Lazio, C Italy
Gaeta, Golfo di 75 C5 *var.* Gulf of Gaeta. *Gulf* C Italy
Gaeta, Gulf of *see* Gaeta, Golfo di
Gäfle *see* Gävle
Gafsa 49 E2 *var.* Qafṣah. W Tunisia
Gagnoa 52 D5 C Côte d'Ivoire
Gagra 95 E1 NW Georgia
Gaillac 69 C6 *var.* Gaillac-sur-Tarn. Tarn, S France
Gaillac-sur-Tarn *see* Gaillac
Gaillimh *see* Galway
Gainesville 21 E3 Florida, SE USA
Gainesville 20 D2 Georgia, SE USA
Gainesville 27 G2 Texas, SW USA
Gairdner, Lake 127 A6 *salt lake* South Australia
Gaiziņkalns 84 C3 *var.* Gaizina Kalns. *Mountain* E Latvia
Gaizina Kalns *see* Gaiziņkalns
Galán, Cerro 42 B3 *mountain* NW Argentina
Galanta 77 C6 *Hung.* Galánta. Trnavský Kraj, W Slovakia
Galapagos Fracture Zone 131 E3 *tectonic feature* E Pacific Ocean
Galapagos Islands 131 F3 *var.* Islas de los Galápagos,Tortoise Islands. *Island group* Ecuador, E Pacific Ocean
Galapagos Rise 131 F3 *undersea feature* E Pacific Ocean
Galashiels 66 C4 SE Scotland, UK
Galați 86 D4 *Ger.* Galatz. Galați, E Romania
Galcaio *see* Gaalkacyo
Galesburg 18 B3 Illinois, N USA
Galicia 70 B1 *cultural region* NW Spain
Galicia Bank 58 B4 *undersea feature* E Atlantic Ocean
Galilee, Sea of *see* Tiberias, Lake
Galka'yo *see* Gaalkacyo
Galle 110 D4 *prev.* Point de Galle. Southern Province, SW Sri Lanka
Gallego Rise 131 F3 *undersea feature* E Pacific Ocean
Gallegos *see* Río Gallegos
Gallipoli 75 E6 Puglia, SE Italy
Gällivare 62 C3 Norrbotten, N Sweden
Gallup 26 C1 New Mexico, SW USA
Galtat-Zemmour 48 B3 C Western Sahara
Galveston 27 H4 Texas, SW USA
Galway 67 A5 *Ir.* Gaillimh. W Ireland
Galway Bay 67 A6 *Ir.* Cuan na Gaillimhe. *Bay* W Ireland
Gambell 14 C2 Saint Lawrence Island, Alaska, USA
Gambia 52 C3 *Fr.* Gambie. *River* W Africa
Gambia 52 B3 *Country* W Africa
Gambier, Îles 121 G4 *island group* E French Polynesia
Gamboma 55 B6 Plateaux, E Congo
Gan *see* Gansu
Gan *see* Jiangxi
Gan 110 B5 Addu Atoll, C Maldives
Gäncä 95 G2 *Rus.* Gyandzha; *prev.* Kirovabad, Yelisavetpol. W Azerbaijan
Gandajika 55 D7 Kasai Oriental, S Dem. Rep. Congo
Gander 17 G3 Newfoundland, Newfoundland and Labrador, SE Canada
Gāndhīdhām 112 C4 Gujarāt, W India
Gandía 71 F3 País Valenciano, E Spain
Ganges 113 F3 *Ben.* Padma. *River* Bangladesh/India *see also* Padma
Ganges Cone *see* Ganges Fan
Ganges Fan 118 D3 *var.* Ganges Cone. *Undersea feature* N Bay of Bengal
Ganges, Mouths of the 113 G4 *delta* Bangladesh/India
Gangra *see* Çankırı
Gangtok 113 F3 Sikkim, N India
Gansu 106 B4 *var.* Gan, Gansu Sheng, Kansu. Admin. region *province* N China
Gansu Sheng *see* Gansu
Ganzhou 106 D6 Jiangxi, S China
Gao 53 E3 Gao, E Mali
Gaoual 52 C4 Moyenne-Guinée, N Guinea
Gaoxiong *see* Kaohsiung
Gap 69 D5 *anc.* Vapincum. Hautes-Alpes, SE France
Gaplaňgyr Platosy 100 C2 *Rus.* Kaplangky, Plato. *Ridge* Turkmenistan/Uzbekistan
Gar 104 A4 *var.* Gar Xincun. Xizang Zizhiqu, W China
Garabil Belentligi 100 D3 *Rus.* Karabil', Vozvyshennost'. *Mountain range* S Turkmenistan
Garabogaz Aylagy 100 B2 *Rus.* Zaliv Kara-Bogaz-Gol. *Bay* Balkanskiy Velayat, W Turkmenistan
Garachiné 31 G5 Darién, SE Panama
Garagum 100 C3 *var.* Garagumy, Qara Qum, *Eng.* Black Sand Desert, Kara Kum; *prev.* Peski Karakumy. *Desert* C Turkmenistan
Garagum Kanaly 100 D3 *var.* Kara Kum Canal, Karakumskiy Kanal, *Turkm.* Garagumskiy Kanaly. *Canal* C Turkmenistan
Garagumskiy Kanal *see* Garagum Kanaly
Garagumy *see* Garagum
Gara Khitrino 82 D2 Shumen, NE Bulgaria
Garda, Lago di C2 *var.* Benaco, *Eng.* Lake Garda, *Ger.* Gardasee. *Lake* NE Italy
Garda, Lake *see* Garda, Lago di
Gardasee *see* Garda, Lago di
Garden City 23 E5 Kansas, C USA
Gardeyz *see* Gardēz
Gardēz 101 E4 *var.* Gardeyz, Gordiaz. Paktīā, E Afghanistan
Gargždai 84 B3 Gargždai, W Lithuania
Garissa 51 D6 Coast, E Kenya
Garland 27 G2 Texas, SW USA
Garman, Loch *see* Wexford
Garoe *see* Garoowe
Garonne 69 B5 *anc.* Garumna. *River* S France
Garoowe 51 E5 *var.* Garoe. Nugaal, N Somalia
Garoua 54 B4 *var.* Garua. Nord, N Cameroon
Garrygala 100 C3 *Rus.* Kara-Kala. Balkanskiy Velayat, W Turkmenistan
Garry Lake 15 F3 *lake* Nunavut, N Canada
Garsen 51 D6 Coast, S Kenya
Garua *see* Garoua
Garwolin 76 D4 Mazowieckie, C Poland
Gar Xincun *see* Gar
Gary 18 B3 Indiana, N USA
Garzón 36 B4 Huila, S Colombia
Gasan-Kuli *see* Esenguly
Gascogne 69 B6 *Eng.* Gascony. *Cultural region* S France
Gascoyne River 125 A5 *river* Western Australia
Gaspé 17 F3 Québec, SE Canada
Gaspé, Péninsule de 17 E4 *var.* Péninsule de la Gaspésie. *Peninsula* Québec, SE Canada
Gastonia 21 E1 North Carolina, SE USA
Gastoúni 83 B6 Dytikí Ellás, S Greece
Gatchina 88 B4 Leningradskaya Oblast', NW Russian Federation
Gatineau 16 D4 Québec, SE Canada
Gatún, Lago 31 F4 *reservoir* C Panama
Gauja 84 D3 *Ger.* Aa. *River* Estonia/Latvia
Gauteng *see* Johannesburg
Gāvbandī 98 D4 Hormozgān, S Iran
Gávdos 83 C8 *island* SE Greece
Gavere 65 B6 Oost-Vlaanderen, NW Belgium
Gävle 63 C6 *var.* Gäfle; *prev.* Gefle. Gävleborg, C Sweden
Gawler 127 B6 South Australia
Gaya 113 F3 Bihār, N India
Gayndah 127 E5 Queensland, E Australia
Gaza 97 A6 *Ar.* Ghazzah, *Heb.* 'Azza. NE Gaza Strip
Gaz-Achak *see* Gazojak
Gaza Strip 97 A7 *Ar.* Qiṭā' Ghazzah. *Disputed region* SW Asia
Gazi Antep *see* Gaziantep
Gaziantep 94 D4 *var.* Gazi Antep; *prev.* Aintab, Antep. Gaziantep, S Turkey
Gazimağusa *see* Ammóchostos
Gazimağusa Körfezi *see* Kólpos Ammóchostos
Gazli 100 D2 Bukhoro Wiloyati, C Uzbekistan
Gazojak 100 D2 *var.* Gaz-Achak. Lebapskiy Velayat, NE Turkmenistan
Gbanga 52 D5 *var.* Gbarnga. N Liberia
Gbarnga *see* Gbanga
Gdańsk 76 C2 *Fr.* Dantzig, *Ger.* Danzig. Pomorskie, N Poland
Gdan'skaya Bukhta *see* Danzig, Gulf of
Gdańsk, Gulf of *see* Danzig, Gulf of
Gdynia 76 C2 *Ger.* Gdingen. Pomorskie, N Poland
Gedaref 50 C4 *var.* Al Qaḍārif, El Gedaref. Gedaref, E Sudan
Gediz 94 B3 Kütahya, W Turkey
Gediz Nehri 94 A3 *river* W Turkey
Geel 65 C5 *var.* Gheel. Antwerpen, N Belgium
Geelong 127 C7 Victoria, SE Australia
Ge'e'mu *see* Golmud
Gefle *see* Gävle
Geilo 63 A5 Buskerud, S Norway
Gejiu 106 B6 *var.* Kochiu. Yunnan, S China
Gëkdepe *see* Gökdepe
Gela 75 C7 *prev.* Terranova di Sicilia. Sicilia, Italy, C Mediterranean Sea
Geldermalsen 64 C4 Gelderland, C Netherlands
Geleen 65 D6 Limburg, SE Netherlands
Gelinsoor *see* Gellinsoor
Gellinsoor 51 E5 *var.* Gelinsoor. Mudug, NE Somalia
Gembloux 65 C6 Namur, Belgium
Gemena 55 C5 Equateur, NW Dem. Rep. Congo
Gemona del Friuli 74 D2 Friuli-Venezia Giulia, NE Italy
Genck *see* Genk
General Alvear 42 B4 Mendoza, W Argentina
General Eugenio A.Garay 42 C1 Guairá, S Paraguay
General Machado *see* Camacupa
General Santos 117 F3 *off.* General Santos City. Mindanao, S Philippines
Geneva *see* Genève
Geneva, Lake A7 *Fr.* Lac de Genève, Lac Léman, le Léman, *Ger.* Genfer See. *Lake* France/Switzerland
Genève 73 A7 *Eng.* Geneva, *Ger.* Genf, *It.* Ginevra. Genève, SW Switzerland
Genf *see* Genève
Genk 65 D6 *var.* Genck. Limburg, NE Belgium
Gennep 64 D4 Limburg, SE Netherlands
Genoa *see* Genova
Genova 80 D1 *Eng.* Genoa, *Fr.* Gênes; *anc.* Genua. Liguria, NW Italy
Genova, Golfo di 74 A3 *Eng.* Gulf of Genoa. *Gulf* NW Italy
Genovesa, Isla 38 B5 *var.* Tower Island. *Island* Galapagos Islands, Ecuador, E Pacific Ocean
Gent 65 B5 *Eng.* Ghent, *Fr.* Gand. Oost-Vlaanderen, NW Belgium
Geok-Tepe *see* Gökdepe
George 60 A4 *river* Newfoundland and Labrador/Quebec, E Canada
George 56 C5 Western Cape, S South Africa
George, Lake 21 E3 *lake* Florida, SE USA
Georges Bank 13 D5 *undersea feature* W Atlantic Ocean
George Sound 129 A7 *sound* South Island, NZ
Georges River 126 D2 *river* New South Wales, SE Australia
George Town 32 B3 *var.* Georgetown. *Dependent territory capital* (Cayman Islands) Grand Cayman, SW Cayman Islands
George Town 116 B3 *var.* Penang, Pinang. Pinang, Peninsular Malaysia
George Town 32 C2 Great Exuma Island, C Bahamas
Georgetown 37 F2 *country capital* (Guyana) N Guyana
Georgetown 21 F2 South Carolina, SE USA
George V Land 132 C4 *physical region* Antarctica
Georgia 95 F2 *Geor.* Sak'art'velo, *Rus.* Gruzinskaya SSR, Gruziya; *prev.* Georgian SSR. *Country* SW Asia
Georgia 20 D2 *off.* State of Georgia; also known as Empire State of the South, Peach State. *State* SE USA
Georgian Bay 18 D2 *lake bay* Ontario, S Canada
Georgia, Strait of 24 A1 *strait* British Columbia, W Canada
Georg von Neumayer 132 A2 *German research station* Antarctica
Gera 72 C4 Thüringen, E Germany
Geráki 83 B6 Pelopónnisos, S Greece
Geraldine 129 B6 Canterbury, South Island, NZ
Geraldton 125 A6 Western Australia
Geral, Serra 35 D5 *mountain range* S Brazil
Gerede 94 C2 Bolu, N Turkey
Gereshk 100 D5 Helmand, SW Afghanistan
Gering 22 D3 Nebraska, C USA
Germanicopolis *see* Çankırı
Germany 72 B4 *Ger.* Bundesrepublik Deutschland, Deutschland. *Country* N Europe
Geroliménas 83 B7 Pelopónnisos, S Greece
Gerona *see* Girona
Gerpinnes 65 C7 Hainaut, S Belgium
Gerunda *see* Girona
Gerze 94 D2 Sinop, N Turkey
Gesoriacum *see* Boulogne-sur-Mer
Gessoriacum *see* Boulogne-sur-Mer
Getafe 70 D3 Madrid, C Spain
Gevaş 95 F3 Van, SE Turkey
Gevgeli *see* Gevgelija
Gevgelija 79 E6 *var.* Đevđelija, Djevdjelija, *Turk.* Gevgeli. SE FYR Macedonia
Ghaba *see* Al Ghābah
Ghana 53 E5 *Country* W Africa
Ghanzi 56 C3 *var.* Khanzi. Ghanzi, W Botswana
Gharandal 97 B7 Ma'ān, SW Jordan
Ghardaïa 48 D2 N Algeria
Gharvān *see* Gharyān
Gharyān 49 F2 *var.* Gharvān. NW Libya
Ghaznī 101 E4 *var.* Ghazni. Ghaznī, E Afghanistan
Ghazni *see* Ghaznī
Gheel *see* Geel
Gheorgheni 86 C4 *prev.* Gheorghieni, Sînt-Miclăuş, *Ger.* Niklasmarkt, *Hung.* Gyergyószentmiklós. Harghita, C Romania
Ghijduwon *see* G'ijduvon
Ghŭdara 101 F3 *var.* Gudara, *Rus.* Kudara. SE Tajikistan
Ghurdaqah *see* Hurghada
Ghūrīān 100 D4 Herāt, W Afghanistan
Giannitsá 82 B4 *var.* Yiannitsá. Kentrikí Makedonía, N Greece
Gibraltar 71 G4 *UK dependent territory* SW Europe
Gibraltar, Bay of 71 C5 *bay* Gibraltar/Spain
Gibraltar, Strait of 70 C5 *Fr.* Détroit de Gibraltar, *Sp.* Estrecho de Gibraltar. *Strait* Atlantic Ocean/Mediterranean Sea
Gibson Desert 125 B5 *desert* Western Australia
Giedraičiai 85 C5 Molėtai, E Lithuania
Giessen 95 B5 Hessen, W Germany
Gifu 109 C6 *var.* Gihu. Gifu, Honshū, SW Japan
Giganta, Sierra de la 28 B3 *mountain range* W Mexico
Gihu *see* Gifu
G'ijduvon 100 D2 *var.* Ghijduwon, *Rus.* Gizhduvan. Bukhoro Wiloyati, C Uzbekistan
Gijón 70 D1 *var.* Xixón. Asturias, NW Spain
Gilani *see* Gnjilane
Gila River 26 A2 *river* Arizona, SW USA
Gilbert River 126 C3 *river* Queensland, NE Australia
Gilf Kebir Plateau 50 A2 *Ar.* Haḍabat al Jilf al Kabīr. *Plateau* SW Egypt
Gillette 22 D3 Wyoming, C USA
Gilroy 25 B6 California, W USA
Gimie, Mount 33 F1 *mountain* C Saint Lucia
Gimma *see* Jīma
Ginevra *see* Genève
Gingin 125 A6 Western Australia
Giohar *see* Jawhar
Girardot 36 B3 Cundinamarca, C Colombia
Giresun 95 E2 *var.* Kerasunt; *anc.* Cerasus, Pharnacia. Giresun, NE Turkey
Girin *see* Jilin
Girne *see* Kerýneia
Girona 71 G2 *var.* Gerona; *anc.* Gerunda. Cataluña, NE Spain
Gisborne 128 E3 Gisborne, North Island, NZ
Gissar Range 101 E3 *Rus.* Gissarskiy Khrebet. *Mountain range* Tajikistan/Uzbekistan
Githio *see* Gýtheio
Giulianova 74 D4 Abruzzo, C Italy
Giumri *see* Gyumri
Giurgiu 86 C5 Giurgiu, S Romania
Gîza *see* El Gîza
Gizeh *see* El Gîza
Gizhduvan *see* G'ijduvon
Giżycko 76 D2 Warmiúsko-Mazurskie, NE Poland
Gjakovë *see* Đakovica
Gjilan *see* Gnjilane
Gjinokastër *see* Gjirokastër
Gjirokastër 79 C7 *var.* Gjirokastra; *prev.* Gjinokastër, *Gk.* Argyrokastron, *It.* Argirocastro. Gjirokastër, S Albania
Gjirokastra *see* Gjirokastër
Gjoa Haven 15 F3 King William Island, Nunavut, NW Canada
Gjøvik 63 B5 Oppland, S Norway
Glace Bay 17 G4 Cape Breton Island, Nova Scotia, SE Canada
Gladstone 126 E4 Queensland, E Australia
Glåma 63 B5 *river* SE Norway
Glasgow 66 C4 S Scotland, UK

Glavn'a Morava *see* Velika Morava
Glazov 89 D5 Udmurtskaya Respublika, NW Russian Federation
Glendale 26 B2 Arizona, SW USA
Glendive 22 D2 Montana, NW USA
Glens Falls 19 F3 New York, NE USA
Glina 78 B3 Sisak-Moslavina, NE Croatia
Glittertind 63 A5 *mountain* S Norway
Gliwice 77 C5 *Ger.* Gleiwitz. Śląskie, S Poland
Globe 26 B2 Arizona, SW USA
Głogów 76 B4 *Ger.* Glogau, Glogow. Dolnośląskie
Gloucester 67 D6 *hist.* Caer Glou, *Lat.* Glevum. C England, UK
Głowno 76 D4 Łódź, C Poland
Gniezno 76 C3 *Ger.* Gnesen. Wielkopolskie, C Poland
Gnjilane 79 D5 *var.* Gilani, *Alb.* Gjilan. Serbia, S Serbia and Montenegro (Yugo.)
Goa *see* Panaji
Gobabis 56 B3 Omaheke, E Namibia
Gobi 104 D3 *desert* China/Mongolia
Gobō 109 C6 Wakayama, Honshū, SW Japan
Godāvari 102 B3 *var.* Godavari. *River* C India
Godhavn *see* Qeqertarsuaq
Godhra 112 C4 Gujarāt, W India
Godoy Cruz 42 B4 Mendoza, W Argentina
Godthaab *see* Nuuk
Godthåb *see* Nuuk
Goeree 64 B4 *island* SW Netherlands
Goes 65 B5 Zeeland, SW Netherlands
Goettingen *see* Göttingen
Gogebic Range 18 B1 *hill range* Michigan/Wisconsin, N USA
Goiânia 41 E3 *prev.* Goyania. *State capital* Goiás, C Brazil
Goiás 41 E3 Goiás, C Brazil
Gojōme 108 D4 Akita, Honshū, NW Japan
Gökçeada 82 D4 *var.* Imroz Adası, *Gk.* Imbros. *Island* NW Turkey
Gökdepe 100 C3 *var.* Gëkdepe, Geok-Tepe. Akhalskiy Velayat, C Turkmenistan
Göksun 94 D4 Kahramanmaraş, S Turkey
Gol 63 A5 Buskerud, S Norway
Golan Heights 97 B5 *Ar.* Al Jawlān, *Heb.* HaGolan. *Mountain range* SW Syria
Gołdap 76 E2 *Ger.* Goldap. Warmińsko-Mazurskie, NE Poland
Gold Coast 127 E5 *cultural region* Queensland, E Australia
Golden Bay 128 C4 *bay* South Island, NZ
Goldsboro 21 F1 North Carolina, SE USA
Goleniów 76 B3 *Ger.* Gollnow. Zachodniopomorskie, NW Poland
Golmo *see* Golmud
Golub-Dobrzyń 76 C3 Kujawski-pomorskie, C Poland
Golmud 104 D4 *var.* Ge'e'mu, Golmo, *Chin.* Ko-erh-mu. Qinghai, C China
Goma 55 E6 Nord Kivu, NE Dem. Rep. Congo
Gombi 53 H4 Adamawa, E Nigeria
Gombroon *see* Bandar-e 'Abbās
Gomera 48 A3 *island* Islas Canarias, Spain, NE Atlantic Ocean
Gómez Palacio 28 D3 Durango, C Mexico
Gonaïves 32 D3 *var.* Les Gonaïves. N Haiti
Gonâve, Île de la 32 D3 *island* C Haiti
Gondar *see* Gonder
Gonder 50 C4 *var.* Gondar. N Ethiopia
Gondia 113 E4 Mahārāshtra, C India
Gonggar 104 C5 Xizang Zizhiqu, W China
Gongola 53 G4 *river* E Nigeria
Gonni *see* Gónnoi
Gónnoi 82 B4 *var.* Gonni, Gónnos; *prev.* Dereli. Thessalía, C Greece
Gónnos *see* Gónnoi
Good Hope *see* Fort Good Hope
Good Hope, Cape of 56 B5 *Afr.* Kaap de Goede Hoop, Kaap die Goeie Hoop. *Headland* SW South Africa
Goodland 22 D4 Kansas, C USA
Goondiwindi 127 D5 Queensland, E Australia
Goor 64 E3 Overijssel, E Netherlands
Goose Green 43 D7 *var.* Prado del Ganso. East Falkland, Falkland Islands
Goose Lake 24 B4 *var.* Lago dos Gansos. *Lake* California/Oregon, W USA
Göppingen 73 B6 Baden-Württemberg, SW Germany
Gora Andryu *see* Andrew Tablemount
Gora El'brus *see* El'brus
Góra Kalwaria 114 D4 Mazowieckie, C Poland
Gorakhpur 113 E3 Uttar Pradesh, N India
Goražde 78 C4 Federacija Bosna I Hercegovina, SE Bosnia and Herzegovina
Gordiaz *see* Gardēz
Gore 129 B7 Southland, South Island, NZ
Gorē 51 C5 C Ethiopia
Goré 54 C4 Logone-Oriental, S Chad
Gorgān 98 D2 *var.* Astarabad, Astrabad, Gurgan; *prev.* Asterābād, *anc.* Hyrcania. Golestān, N Iran
Gori 95 F2 C Georgia
Gorinchem 64 C4 *var.* Gorkum. Zuid-Holland, C Netherlands
Goris 95 G3 SE Armenia
Gorkum *see* Gorinchem
Görlitz 72 D4 Sachsen, E Germany
Gornji Milanovac 78 C4 Serbia, C Serbia and Montenegro (Yugo.)
Gorontalo 117 E3 Sulawesi, C Indonesia
Gorontalo, Teluk *see* Tomini, Gulf of
Gorssel 64 D3 Gelderland, E Netherlands
Gory Putorana *see* Putorana, Plato
Gorzów Wielkopolski 76 B3 *Ger.* Landsberg, Landsberg an der Warthe. Lubuskie, W Poland
Gosford 127 D6 New South Wales, SE Australia
Goshogawara 108 D3 *var.* Gosyogawara. Aomori, Honshū, C Japan
Gospić 78 A3 Lika-Senj, C Croatia

Gostivar 79 D6 W FYR Macedonia
Gosyogawara *see* Goshogawara
Göteborg 63 B7 *Eng.* Gothenburg. Västra Götaland, S Sweden
Gotel Mountains 53 G5 *mountain range* E Nigeria
Gotha 72 C4 Thüringen, C Germany
Gothenburg *see* Göteborg
Gothenburg 23 D5 Nebraska, C USA
Gotland 63 C7 *island* SE Sweden
Gotō-rettō 109 A7 *island group* SW Japan
Gotska Sandön 84 B1 *island* SE Sweden
Gōtsu 109 B6 *var.* Gôtu. Shimane, Honshū, SW Japan
Göttingen 72 B4 *var.* Goettingen. Niedersachsen, C Germany
Gôtu *see* Gōtsu
Gouda 64 C4 Zuid-Holland, C Netherlands
Gough Fracture Zone 45 C6 *tectonic feature* S Atlantic Ocean
Gough Island 47 B8 *island* Tristan da Cunha, S Atlantic Ocean
Gouin, Réservoir 16 D4 *reservoir* Québec, SE Canada
Goulburn 127 D6 New South Wales, SE Australia
Goundam 53 E3 Tombouctou, NW Mali
Gouré 53 G3 Zinder, SE Niger
Governador Valadares 41 F4 Minas Gerais, SE Brazil
Govĭ Altayn Nuruu 105 E3 *mountain range* S Mongolia
Goya 42 D3 Corrientes, NE Argentina
Goz Beïda 54 C3 Ouaddaï, SE Chad
Gozo 75 C8 *Malt.* Ghawdex. *Island* N Malta
Graciosa 70 A5 *var.* Ilha Graciosa. *Island* Azores, Portugal, NE Atlantic Ocean
Gradačac 78 C3 Federacija Bosna I Hercegovina, N Bosnia and Herzegovina
Gradaús, Serra dos 41 E3 *mountain range* C Brazil
Gradiška *see* Bosanska Gradiška
Grafton 127 E5 New South Wales, SE Australia
Grafton 23 E1 North Dakota, N USA
Graham Land 132 A2 *physical region* Antarctica
Grajewo 76 E3 Podlaskie, NE Poland
Grampian Mountains 66 C3 *mountain range* C Scotland, UK
Granada 70 D5 Andalucía, S Spain
Granada 30 D3 Granada, SW Nicaragua
Gran Canaria 48 A3 *var.* Grand Canary. *Island* Islas Canarias, Spain, NE Atlantic Ocean
Gran Chaco 42 D2 *var.* Chaco. *Lowland plain* South America
Grand *see* Cockburn Town
Grand Bahama Island 32 B1 *island* N Bahamas
Grand Banks of Newfoundland 12 E4 *undersea feature* NW Atlantic Ocean
Grand Canary *see* Gran Canaria
Grand Canyon 26 A1 *canyon* Arizona, SW USA
Grand Cayman 32 B3 *island* SW Cayman Islands
Grande, Bahía 43 B7 *bay* S Argentina
Grande Comore 57 F2 *var.* Njazidja, Great Comoro. *Island* NW Comoros
Grande de Chiloé, Isla *see* Chiloé, Isla de
Grande Prairie 15 E4 Alberta, W Canada
Grand Erg Occidental 48 D3 *desert* W Algeria
Grand Erg Oriental 49 E3 *desert* Algeria/Tunisia
Grande, Rio 13 B6 *var.* Río Bravo, *Sp.* Río Bravo del Norte, Bravo del Norte. *River* Mexico/USA
Grande, Rio 27 F4 *river* Texas, SW USA
Grande, Rio *see* Bravo, Río
Grande, Río 29 E2 *river* S Mexico
Grande Terre 33 G3 *island* E West Indies
Grand Falls 17 G3 Newfoundland, Newfoundland and Labrador, SE Canada
Grand Forks 23 E1 North Dakota, N USA
Grand Island 23 E4 Nebraska, C USA
Grand Junction 22 C4 Colorado, C USA
Grand Rapids 18 C3 Michigan, N USA
Grand Rapids 23 F1 Minnesota, N USA
Grand-Santi 37 H3 W French Guiana
Gran Lago *see* Nicaragua, Lago de
Gran Malvina, Isla *see* West Falkland
Gran Paradiso 74 A2 *Fr.* Grand Paradis. *Mountain* NW Italy
Gran Santiago *see* Santiago
Grants 26 C2 New Mexico, SW USA
Grants Pass 24 B4 Oregon, NW USA
Granville 68 B3 Manche, N France
Graulhet 69 C6 Tarn, S France
Grave 64 D4 Noord-Brabant, SE Netherlands
Grayling 14 C2 Alaska, USA
Graz 73 E7 *prev.* Gratz. Steiermark, SE Austria
Great Abaco 32 C1 *var.* Abaco Island. *Island* N Bahamas
Great Alfold *see* Great Hungarian Plain
Great Ararat *see* Büyükağrı Dağı
Great Australian Bight 125 D7 *bight* S Australia
Great Barrier Island 128 D2 *island* N NZ
Great Barrier Reef 126 D2 *reef* Queensland, NE Australia
Great Basin 25 C5 *basin* W USA
Great Bear Lake 15 E3 *Fr.* Grand Lac de l'Ours. *Lake* Northwest Territories, NW Canada
Great Belt *see* Storebælt
Great Bend 23 E5 Kansas, C USA
Great Bermuda *see* Bermuda
Great Britain *see* Britain
Great Comoro *see* Grande Comore
Great Dividing Range 126 D4 *mountain range* NE Australia

Greater Antilles 32 D3 *island group* West Indies
Greater Caucasus 95 G2 *Az.* Bas Qafqaz Silsiläsi, *Geor.* Kavkasioni, *Rus.* Bol'shoy Kavkaz. *Mountain range* Asia/Europe
Greater Sunda Islands 102 B5 *var.* Sunda Islands. *Island group* Indonesia
Great Exhibition Bay 128 C1 *inlet* North Island, NZ
Great Exuma Island 32 C2 *island* C Bahamas
Great Falls 22 B1 Montana, NW USA
Great Hungarian Plain 77 C7 *var.* Great Alfold, Plain of Hungary, *Hung.* Alföld. *Plain* SE Europe
Great Inagua 32 D2 *var.* Inagua Islands. *Island* S Bahamas
Great Indian Desert *see* Thar Desert
Great Karoo *see* Great Karoo
Great Lakes 13 C5 *lakes* Ontario, Canada/USA
Great Meteor Seamount *see* Great Meteor Tablemount
Great Meteor Tablemount 44 B3 *var.* Great Meteor Seamount. *Undersea feature* E Atlantic Ocean
Great Nicobar 111 G3 *island* Nicobar Islands, India, NE Indian Ocean
Great Plain of China 103 E2 *plain* E China
Great Plains 23 E3 *var.* High Plains. *Plains* Canada/USA
Great Rift Valley 51 C5 *var.* Rift Valley. *Depression* Asia/Africa
Great Ruaha 51 C7 *river* S Tanzania
Great Saint Bernard Pass 74 A1 *Fr.* Col du Grand-Saint-Bernard, *It.* Passo di Gran San Bernardo. *Pass* Italy/Switzerland
Great Salt Desert *see* Kavīr, Dasht-e
Great Salt Lake 22 A3 *salt lake* Utah, W USA
Great Salt Lake Desert 22 A4 *plain* Utah, W USA
Great Sand Sea 49 H3 *desert* Egypt/Libya
Great Sandy Desert 124 C4 *desert* Western Australia
Great Sandy Island *see* Fraser Island
Great Slave Lake 15 E4 *Fr.* Grand Lac des Esclaves. *Lake* Northwest Territories, NW Canada
Great Sound 20 A5 *bay* Bermuda, NW Atlantic Ocean
Great Victoria Desert 125 C5 *desert* South Australia/Western Australia
Great Wall of China 106 C4 *ancient monument* N China
Great Yarmouth 67 E6 *var.* Yarmouth. E England, UK
Gredos, Sierra de 70 D3 *mountain range* W Spain
Greece 83 A5 *Gk.* Ellás; *anc.* Hellas. *Country* SE Europe
Greece 59 E5 New York, NE USA
Greeley 22 D4 Colorado, C USA
Green Bay 18 B2 *lake bay* Michigan/Wisconsin, N USA
Green Bay 18 B2 Wisconsin, N USA
Greeneville 21 E1 Tennessee, S USA
Greenland 60 D3 *Dan.* Grønland, *Inuit* Kalaallit Nunaat. *Danish external territory* NE North America
Greenland Sea 61 F2 *sea* Arctic Ocean
Green Mountains 19 G2 *mountain range* Vermont, NE USA
Greenock 66 C4 W Scotland, UK
Green River 18 C5 *river* Kentucky, C USA
Green River 22 B4 river Utah, W USA
Green River 22 B3 Wyoming, C USA
Greensboro 21 F1 North Carolina, SE USA
Greenville 20 B2 Mississippi, S USA
Greenville 21 F1 North Carolina, SE USA
Greenville 21 E1 South Carolina, SE USA
Greenville 27 G2 Texas, SW USA
Greenwich 67 B8 SE England, UK
Greenwood 20 B2 Mississippi, S USA
Greenwood 21 E2 South Carolina, SE USA
Gregory Range 126 C3 *mountain range* Queensland, NE Australia
Greifswald 72 D2 Mecklenburg-Vorpommern, NE Germany
Grenada 33 G5 *country* SE West Indies
Grenada 20 C2 Mississippi, S USA
Grenadines, The 33 H4 *island group* Grenada/St Vincent and the Grenadines
Grenoble 69 D5 *anc.* Cularo, Gratianopolis. Isère, E France
Gresham 24 B3 Oregon, NW USA
Grevená 82 B4 Dytikí Makedonía, N Greece
Grevenmacher 65 E8 Grevenmacher, E Luxembourg
Greymouth 129 B5 West Coast, South Island, NZ
Grey Range 127 C5 *mountain range* New South Wales/Queensland, E Australia
Greytown *see* San Juan del Norte
Griffin 20 D2 Georgia, SE USA
Grimari 54 C4 Ouaka, C Central African Republic
Grimsby 67 E5 *prev.* Great Grimsby. E England, UK
Grobiņa 84 B3 *Ger.* Grobin. Liepāja, W Latvia
Grodno *see* Hrodna
Grodzisk Wielkopolski 76 B3 Wielkopolskie, C Poland
Groesbeek 64 D4 Gelderland, SE Netherlands
Grójec 76 D4 Mazowieckie, C Poland
Groningen 64 E1 Groningen, NE Netherlands
Groote Eylandt 126 B2 *island* Northern Territory, N Australia
Grootfontein 56 B3 Otjozondjupa, N Namibia
Groot Karasberge 56 B4 *mountain range* S Namibia
Groot Karoo *see* Great Karoo
Gros Islet 33 F1 N Saint Lucia
Grosse Morava *see* Velika Morava
Grosseto 74 B4 Toscana, C Italy
Grossglockner 73 C7 *mountain* W Austria

Groznyy 89 B8 Chechenskaya Respublika, SW Russian Federation
Grudziądz 76 C3 *Ger.* Graudenz. Kujawski-pomorskie, C Poland
Grums 63 B6 Värmland, C Sweden
Gryazi 89 B6 Lipetskaya Oblast', W Russian Federation
Gryfice 76 B2 *Ger.* Greifenberg, Greifenberg in Pommern. Zachodniopomorskie, NW Poland
Guabito 31 E4 Bocas del Toro, NW Panama
Guadalajara 71 E3 *Ar.* Wad Al-Hajarah; *anc.* Arriaca. Castilla-La Mancha, C Spain
Guadalajara 28 D4 Jalisco, C Mexico
Guadalcanal 122 C3 *island* C Solomon Islands
Guadalquivir 70 D4 *river* W Spain
Guadalupe 28 D3 Zacatecas, C Mexico
Guadalupe Peak 26 D3 *mountain* Texas, SW USA
Guadalupe River 27 G4 *river* SW USA
Guadarrama, Sierra de 71 E2 *mountain range* C Spain
Guadeloupe 33 H3 *French overseas department* E West Indies
Guadiana 70 C4 *river* Portugal/Spain
Guadix 71 E4 Andalucía, S Spain
Guaimaca 30 C2 Francisco Morazán, C Honduras
Guaire 36 D2 Portuguesa, N Venezuela
Guanare, Río 36 D2 *river* W Venezuela
Guangdong 106 C6 *var.* Guangdong Sheng, Kuang-tung, Kwangtung, Yue. *Admin. region province* S China
Guangdong Sheng *see* Guangdong
Guangxi *see* Guangxi Zhuangzu Zizhiqu
Guangxi Zhuangzu Zizhiqu 106 C6 *var.* Guangxi, Gui, Kuang-hsi, Kwangsi, *Eng.* Kwangsi Chuang Autonomous Region. *Admin. region autonomous region* S China
Guangyuan 106 B5 *var.* Kuang-yuan, Kwangyuan. Sichuan, C China
Guangzhou 106 C6 *var.* Kuang-chou, Kwangchow, *Eng.* Canton. Guangdong, S China
Guantánamo 32 D3 Guantánamo, SE Cuba
Guantánamo Bay 32 D3 *US military installation*, SE Cuba
Guaporé, Rio 40 D3 *var.* Río Iténez. *River* Bolivia/Brazil *see also* Iténez, Río
Guarda 70 C3 Guarda, N Portugal
Guarumal 31 F5 Veraguas, S Panama
Guasave 28 C3 Sinaloa, C Mexico
Guatemala 30 A2 *Country* Central America
Guatemala Basin 13 B7 *undersea feature* E Pacific Ocean
Guatemala City *see* Ciudad de Guatemala
Guaviare 34 A2 *off.* Comisaría Guaviare. *Province* S Colombia
Guaviare, Río 36 D3 *river* E Colombia
Guayaquil 38 A2 *var.* Santiago de Guayaquil. Guayas, SW Ecuador
Guayaquil, Golfo de 38 A2 *var.* Gulf of Guayaquil. *Gulf* SW Ecuador
Guaymas 28 B2 Sonora, NW Mexico
Gubadag 100 C2 *Turkm.* Tel'man; *prev.* Tel'mansk. Dashkhovuzskiy Velayat, N Turkmenistan
Guben 72 D4 *var.* Wilhelm-Pieck-Stadt. Brandenburg, E Germany
Gudara *see* Ghūdara
Gudaut'a 95 E1 NW Georgia
Guéret 68 C4 Creuse, C France
Guernsey 67 D8 *UK dependent territory* NW Europe
Guerrero Negro 28 A2 Baja California Sur, NW Mexico
Gui *see* Guangxi Zhuangzu Zizhiqu
Guiana *see* French Guiana
Guiana Highlands 40 D1 *var.* Macizo de las Guayanas. *Mountain range* N South America
Guidder *see* Guider
Guider 54 B4 *var.* Guidder. Nord, N Cameroon
Guidimouni 53 G3 Zinder, S Niger
Guildford 67 D7 SE England, UK
Guilin 106 C6 *var.* Kuei-lin, Kweilin. Guangxi Zhuangzu Zizhiqu, S China
Guimarães 70 B2 *var.* Guimaráes. Braga, N Portugal
Guinea 52 C4 *var.* Guinée; *prev.* French Guinea, People's Revolutionary Republic of Guinea. *Country* W Africa
Guinea Basin 47 A5 *undersea feature* E Atlantic Ocean
Guinea-Bissau 52 B4 *Fr.* Guinée-Bissau, *Port.* Guiné-Bissau; *prev.* Portuguese Guinea. *Country* W Africa
Guinea, Gulf of 46 B4 *Fr.* Golfe de Guinée. *Gulf* E Atlantic Ocean
Güiria 37 E1 Sucre, NE Venezuela
Guiyang 106 B6 *var.* Kuei-Yang, Kuei-yang, Kueyang, Kweiyang; *prev.* Kweichu. Guizhou, S China
Guizhou 106 B6 *var.* Guizhou Sheng, Kuei-chou, Kweichow, Qian. *Admin. region province* S China
Guizhou Sheng *see* Guizhou
Gujarāt 112 C4 *var.* Gujarat. *Admin. region state* W India
Gujerat *see* Gujarāt
Gujrānwāla 112 D2 Punjab, NE Pakistan
Gujrāt 112 D2 Punjab, E Pakistan

Gulbarga 110 C1 Karnātaka, C India
Gulbene 84 D3 *Ger.* Alt-Schwanenburg. Gulbene, NE Latvia
Gulfport 20 C3 Mississippi, S USA
Gulf, The 98 C4 *var.* Persian Gulf, *Ar.* Khalīj al 'Arabī, *Per.* Khalīj-e Fars. *Gulf* SE Asia
Guliston 101 E2 *Rus.* Gulistan. Sirdaryo Wiloyati, E Uzbekistan
Gulja *see* Yining
Gulkana 14 D3 Alaska, USA
Gulu 51 B6 C Uganda
Gulyantsi 82 C1 Pleven, N Bulgaria
Guma *see* Pishan
Gümülcine *see* Komotiní
Gümüljina *see* Komotiní
Gümüşane *see* Gümüşhane
Gümüşhane 95 E3 *var.* Gümüşane, Gumushkhane. Gümüşhane, NE Turkey
Gumushkhane *see* Gümüşhane
Güney Doğu Toroslar 95 E4 *mountain range* SE Turkey
Gunnbjørn Fjeld 60 D4 *var.* Gunnbjörns Bjerge. *Mountain* C Greenland
Gunnbjörns Bjerge *see* Gunnbjørn Fjeld
Gunnedah 127 D6 New South Wales, SE Australia
Gunnison 22 C5 Colorado, C USA
Gurbantünggüt Shamo 104 B2 *desert* W China
Gurgan *see* Gorgān
Guri, Embalse de 37 E2 *reservoir* E Venezuela
Gurktaler Alpen 73 D7 *mountain range* S Austria
Gürün 94 D3 Sivas, C Turkey
Gusau 53 G4 Zamfara, NW Nigeria
Gusev 84 B4 *Ger.* Gumbinnen. Kaliningradskaya Oblast', W Russian Federation
Gustavus 14 D4 Alaska, USA
Güstrow 72 C3 Mecklenburg-Vorpommern, NE Germany
Gütersloh 72 B4 Nordrhein-Westfalen, W Germany
Guwāhāti 113 G3 *prev.* Gauhāti. Assam, NE India
Guyana 37 F3 *prev.* British Guiana. *Country* N South America
Guyane *see* French Guiana
Guymon 27 E1 Oklahoma, C USA
Güzelyurt *see* Mórfou
Gvardeysk 84 A4 *Ger.* Tapaiu. Kaliningradskaya Oblast', W Russian Federation
Gwādar 112 A3 *var.* Gwadur. Baluchistān, SW Pakistan
Gwadur *see* Gwādar
Gwalior 112 D3 Madhya Pradesh, C India
Gwanda 56 D3 Matabeleland South, SW Zimbabwe
Gwy *see* Wye
Gyangzê 104 C5 Xizang Zizhiqu, W China
Gyaring Co 104 C5 *lake* W China
Gympie 127 E5 Queensland, E Australia
Gyomaendrőd 77 D7 Békés, SE Hungary
Gyöngyös 77 D6 Heves, NE Hungary
Győr 77 C6 *Ger.* Raab; *Lat.* Arrabona. Győr-Moson-Sopron, NW Hungary
Gytheio 83 B6 *var.* Githio; *prev.* Yíthion. Pelopónnisos, S Greece
Gyumri 95 F2 *var.* Giumri, *Rus.* Kumayri; *prev.* Aleksandropol', Leninakan. W Armenia

H

Haabai *see* Ha'apai Group
Haacht 65 C6 Vlaams Brabant, C Belgium
Haaksbergen 64 E3 Overijssel, E Netherlands
Ha'apai Group 123 F4 *var.* Haabai. *Island group* C Tonga
Haapsalu 84 D2 *Ger.* Hapsal. Läänemaa, W Estonia
Haarlem 64 C3 *prev.* Harlem. Noord-Holland, W Netherlands
Haast 129 B6 West Coast, South Island, NZ
Hachijō-jima 109 D6 *var.* Hatizyô Zima. *Island* Izu-shotō, SE Japan
Hachinohe 108 D3 Aomori, Honshū, C Japan
Hadama *see* Nazrēt
Haddummati Atoll *see* Hadhdhunmathi Atoll
Hadejia 53 G3 *river* N Nigeria
Hadejia 53 G4 Jigawa, N Nigeria
Hadera 97 A6 *var.* Khadera. Haifa, C Israel
Hadhdhunmathi Atoll 110 A5 *var.* Haddummati Atoll, Laamu Atoll. *Atoll* S Maldives
Ha Đông 114 D3 *var.* Hadong. Ha Tây, N Vietnam
Hadong *see* Ha Đông
Hadramawt 99 C6 *Eng.* Hadhramaut. *Mountain range* S Yemen
Haerbin *see* Harbin
Haerhpin *see* Harbin
Hafren *see* Severn
Hagåtña 160 B1 *var.* Agana/Agaña. *Dependent territory capital* (Guam), NW Guam
Hagerstown 19 E4 Maryland, NE USA
Ha Giang 114 D3 Ha Giang, N Vietnam
Hagondange 68 D3 Moselle, NE France
Haguenau 68 E3 Bas-Rhin, NE France
Haicheng 106 D3 Liaoning, NE China
Haidarabad *see* Hyderābād
Haifa *see* Hefa
Haifong *see* Hai Phong
Haikou 106 C7 *var.* Hai-k'ou, Hoihow, *Fr.* Hoï-Hao. Hainan, S China
Hai-k'ou *see* Haikou
Ḩāʾil 98 B4 *off.* Minṭaqah Ḩāʾil. *Province* N Saudi Arabia
Hai-la-erh *see* Hailar
Hailar 105 F1 *var.* Hai-la-erh; *prev.* Hulun. Nei Mongol Zizhiqu, N China
Hailuoto 62 D4 *Swe.* Karlö. *Island* W Finland

Hainan – Huailai

Hainan 106 B7 var. Hainan Sheng, Qiong. Admin. region province S China
Hainan Dao 106 C7 island S China
Hainan Sheng see Hainan
Haines 14 D4 Alaska, USA
Hainichen 72 D4 Sachsen, E Germany
Hai Phong 114 D3 var. Haifong, Haiphong. N Vietnam
Haiphong see Hai Phong
Haiti 32 D3 C West Indies
Haiya 50 C3 Red Sea, NE Sudan
Hajdúhadház 77 D6 Hajdú-Bihar, E Hungary
Hajîne see Abū Ḩardān
Hajnówka 76 E3 Ger. Hermhausen. Podlaskie, NE Poland
Hakodate 108 D3 Hokkaidō, NE Japan
Ḩalab 96 B2 Eng. Aleppo, Fr. Alep; anc. Beroea. Ḩalab, NW Syria
Ḩalāniyāt, Juzur al 137 D6 var. Jazā'ir Bin Ghalfān, Eng. Kuria Muria Islands. Island group S Oman
Halberstadt 72 C4 Sachsen-Anhalt, C Germany
Halden 63 B6 prev. Fredrikshald. Østfold, S Norway
Halfmoon Bay 129 A8 var. Oban. Stewart Island, Southland, NZ
Halifax 17 F4 Nova Scotia, SE Canada
Halkida see Chalkída
Halle 65 B6 Fr. Hal. Vlaams Brabant, C Belgium
Halle 72 C4 var. Halle an der Saale. Sachsen-Anhalt, C Germany
Halle an der Saale see Halle
Halle-Neustadt 72 C4 Sachsen-Anhalt, C Germany
Halley 132 B2 UK research station Antarctica
Hall Islands 120 B2 island group C Micronesia
Halls Creek 124 C3 Western Australia
Halmahera, Pulau 117 F3 prev. Djailolo, Gilolo, Jailolo. Island E Indonesia
Halmahera Sea 117 F4 Ind. Laut Halmahera. Sea E Indonesia
Halmstad 63 B7 Halland, S Sweden
Hama see Ḩamāh
Hamada 109 B6 Shimane, Honshū, SW Japan
Hamadān 98 C3 anc. Ecbatana. Hamadān, W Iran
Ḩamāh 96 B3 var. Hama; anc. Epiphania, Bibl. Hamath. Ḩamāh, W Syria
Hamamatsu 109 D6 var. Hamamatu. Shizuoka, Honshū, S Japan
Hamamatu see Hamamatsu
Hamar 63 B5 prev. Storhammer. Hedmark, S Norway
Hamath see Ḩamāh
Hamburg 72 B3 Hamburg, N Germany
Ḩamḑ, Wādī al 136 A4 dry watercourse W Saudi Arabia
Hämeenlinna 63 D5 Swe. Tavastehus. Etelä-Suomi, S Finland
Hamersley Range 124 A4 mountain range Western Australia
Hamhŭng 107 E3 C North Korea
Hami 104 C3 var. Ha-mi, Uigh. Kumul, Qomul. Xinjiang Uygur Zizhiqu, NW China
Ha-mi see Hami
Hamilton 20 C2 Alabama, S USA
Hamilton 16 D5 Ontario, S Canada
Hamilton 66 C4 S Scotland, UK
Hamilton 128 D3 Waikato, North Island, NZ
Ḩamīm, Wād'ī al 87 G2 river NE Libya
Hamīs Musait see Khamīs Mushayt
Hamiton 20 A5 dependent territory capital (Bermuda) C Bermuda
Hamm 72 B4 var. Hamm in Westfalen. Nordrhein-Westfalen, W Germany
Hammada du Drâa see Dra, Hamada du
Hammamet, Golfe de 80 D3 Ar. Khalīj al Ḩammāmāt. Gulf NE Tunisia
Ḩammār, Hawr al 136 C3 lake SE Iraq
Hamm in Westfalen see Hamm
Hampden 129 B7 Otago, South Island, NZ
Hampstead 67 A7 SE England, UK
Hamrun 80 B5 C Malta
Hânceşti see Hînceşti
Handan 106 C4 var. Han-tan. Hebei, E China
Haneda 108 A2 international airport (Tōkyō) Tōkyō, Honshū, S Japan
HaNegev 97 A7 Eng. Negev. Desert S Israel
Hanford 25 C6 California, W USA
Hangayn Nuruu 104 D2 mountain range C Mongolia
Hang-chou see Hangzhou
Hangchow see Hangzhou
Hangö see Hanko
Hangzhou 106 D5 var. Hang-chou, Hangchow. Zhejiang, SE China
Hania see Chaniá
Hanka, Lake see Khanka, Lake
Hanko 63 D6 Swe. Hangö. Etelä-Suomi, SW Finland
Han-k'ou see Wuhan
Hankow see Wuhan
Hanmer Springs 129 C5 Canterbury, South Island, NZ
Hannibal 23 G4 Missouri, C USA
Hannover 72 B3 Eng. Hanover. Niedersachsen, NW Germany
Hanöbukten 63 B7 bay S Sweden
Ha Nôi 114 D3 Eng. Hanoi, Fr. Ha noï. Country capital (Vietnam) N Vietnam
Hanoi see Ha Nôi
Han Shui 105 E4 river C China
Han-tan see Handan
Hantsavichy 85 B6 Pol. Hancewicze, Rus. Gantsevichi. Brestskaya Voblasts', SW Belarus
Hanyang see Wuhan
Hanzhong 106 B5 Shaanxi, C China
Hāora 113 F4 prev. Howrah. West Bengal, NE India
Haparanda 62 D4 Norrbotten, N Sweden
Haradok 85 E5 Rus. Gorodok. Vitsyebskaya Voblasts', N Belarus
Haradzyets 85 B6 Rus. Gorodets. Brestskaya Voblasts', SW Belarus
Haramachi 108 D4 Fukushima, Honshū, E Japan
Harany 85 D5 Rus. Gorany. Vitsyebskaya Voblasts', N Belarus
Harare 56 D3 prev. Salisbury. Country capital (Zimbabwe) Mashonaland East, NE Zimbabwe
Harbavichy 85 E6 Rus. Gorbovichi. Mahilyowskaya Voblasts', E Belarus
Harbel 52 C5 W Liberia
Harbin 107 E2 var. Haerbin, Ha-erh-pin, Kharbin; prev. Haerhpin, Pingkiang, Pinkiang. Heilongjiang, NE China
Hardangerfjorden 63 A6 fjord S Norway
Hardangervidda 63 A6 plateau S Norway
Hardenberg 64 E3 Overijssel, E Netherlands
Harelbeke 65 A6 var. Harlebeke. West-Vlaanderen, W Belgium
Harem see Ḩārim
Haren 64 E2 Groningen, NE Netherlands
Hārer 51 D5 E Ethiopia
Hargeisa see Hargeysa
Hargeysa 51 D5 var. Hargeisa. Woqooyi Galbeed, NW Somalia
Hariana see Haryāna
Hari, Batang 116 B4 prev. Djambi. River Sumatera, W Indonesia
Ḩārim 96 B2 var. Harem. Idlib, W Syria
Harima-nada 109 B6 sea S Japan
Harīrūd var. Tedzhen, Turkm. Tejen. River Afghanistan/Iran see also Tedzhen
Harlan 23 F3 Iowa, C USA
Harlebeke see Harelbeke
Harlingen 64 D2 Fris. Harns. Friesland, N Netherlands
Harlingen 27 G5 Texas, SW USA
Harlow 67 E6 E England, UK
Harney Basin 24 B4 basin Oregon, NW USA
Härnösand 63 C5 var. Hernösand. Västernorrland, C Sweden
Har Nuur 104 C2 lake NW Mongolia
Harper 52 D5 var. Cape Palmas. NE Liberia
Harricana 16 D3 river Québec, SE Canada
Harris 66 B3 physical region NW Scotland, UK
Harrisburg 19 E4 state capital Pennsylvania, NE USA
Harrisonburg 19 E4 Virginia, NE USA
Harrison, Cape 17 F2 headland Newfoundland and Labrador, E Canada
Harris Ridge see Lomonosov Ridge
Harrogate 67 D5 N England, UK
Hârşova 86 D5 prev. Hîrşova. Constanţa, SE Romania
Harstad 62 C3 Troms, N Norway
Hartford 19 G3 state capital Connecticut, NE USA
Hartlepool 67 D5 N England, UK
Harunabad see Eslāmābād
Harwich 67 E6 E England, UK
Haryāna 112 D2 var. Hariana. Admin. region state N India
Hasselt 65 C6 Limburg, NE Belgium
Hassetché see Al Ḩasakah
Hastings 128 E4 Hawke's Bay, North Island, NZ
Hastings 23 E4 Nebraska, C USA
Hastings 67 E7 SE England, UK
Haţeg 86 B4 Ger. Wallenthal, Hung. Hátszeg; prev. Hatzeg, Hötzing. Hunedoara, SW Romania
Hatizyô Zima see Hachijō-jima
Hattem 64 D3 Gelderland, E Netherlands
Hatteras, Cape 21 G1 headland North Carolina, SE USA
Hatteras Plain 13 D6 undersea feature W Atlantic Ocean
Hattiesburg 20 C3 Mississippi, S USA
Hatton Bank see Hatton Ridge
Hatton Ridge 58 B2 var. Hatton Bank. Undersea feature N Atlantic Ocean
Hat Yai 115 C7 var. Ban Hat Yai. Songkhla, SW Thailand
Haugesund 63 A6 Rogaland, S Norway
Haukeligrend 63 A6 Telemark, S Norway
Haukivesi 63 E5 lake SE Finland
Hauraki Gulf 128 D2 gulf North Island, NZ
Hauroko, Lake 129 A7 lake South Island, NZ
Haut Atlas 48 C2 Eng. High Atlas. Mountain range C Morocco
Hautes Fagnes 65 D6 Ger. Hohes Venn. Mountain range E Belgium
Haut Plateau du Dra see Dra, Hamada du
Hauts Plateaux 48 D2 plateau Algeria/Morocco
Hauzenberg 73 D6 Bayern, SE Germany
Havana see La Habana
Havana 13 D6 Illinois, N USA
Havant 67 D7 S England, UK
Havelock 21 F1 North Carolina, SE USA
Havelock North 128 E4 Hawke's Bay, North Island, NZ
Haverfordwest 67 C6 SW Wales, UK
Havířov 77 C5 Ostravský Kraj, E Czech Republic
Havre 22 C1 Montana, NW USA
Havre-St-Pierre 17 F3 Québec, E Canada
Hawai'i 25 B8 var. Hawaii. Island Hawaiian Islands, USA, C Pacific Ocean
Hawai'i 25 A8 off. State of Hawaii; also known as Aloha State, Paradise of the Pacific, var. Hawaii. State USA, C Pacific Ocean
Hawaiian Islands 130 D2 prev. Sandwich Islands. Island group Hawaii, USA, C Pacific Ocean
Hawaiian Ridge 91 H4 undersea feature N Pacific Ocean
Hawash see Āwash
Hawea, Lake 129 B6 lake South Island, NZ
Hawera 128 D4 Taranaki, North Island, NZ
Hawick 66 C4 SE Scotland, UK
Hawke Bay 128 E4 bay North Island, NZ
Hawlēr see Arbīl
Hawthorne 25 C6 Nevada, W USA
Hay 127 C6 New South Wales, SE Australia
Hayes 16 B2 river Manitoba, C Canada
Hay River 15 E4 Northwest Territories, W Canada
Hays 23 E5 Kansas, C USA
Haysyn 86 D3 Rus. Gaysin. Vinnyts'ka Oblast', C Ukraine
Hazar 100 B2 prev. Cheleken. Balkanskiy Velayat, W Turkmenistan
Heard and McDonald Islands 119 B7 Australian external territory S Indian Ocean
Hearst 16 C4 Ontario, S Canada
Heathrow 67 A8 international airport (London)SE England, UK
Hebei 106 C4 var. Hebei Sheng, Hopeh, Hopei, Ji; prev. Chihli. Admin. region province E China
Hebei Sheng see Hebei
Hebron 97 A6 var. Al Khalīl, El Khalil, Heb. Ḥevron; anc. Kiriath-Arba. S West Bank
Hebrus see Maritsa
Heemskerk 64 C3 Noord-Holland, W Netherlands
Heerde 64 D3 Gelderland, E Netherlands
Heerenveen 64 D2 Fris. It Hearrenfean. Friesland, N Netherlands
Heerhugowaard 64 C2 Noord-Holland, NW Netherlands
Heerlen 65 D6 Limburg, SE Netherlands
Heerwegen see Polkowice
Ḥefa 97 A5 var. Haifa; hist. Caiffa, Caiphas, anc. Sycaminum. Haifa, N Israel
Ḥefa, Mifraẕ 97 A5 Eng. Bay of Haifa. Bay N Israel
Hefei 106 D5 var. Hofei; hist. Luchow. Anhui, E China
Hegang 107 E2 Heilongjiang, NE China
Hei see Heilongjiang
Heide 72 B2 Schleswig-Holstein, N Germany
Heidelberg 73 B5 Baden-Württemberg, SW Germany
Heidenheim see Heidenheim an der Brenz
Heidenheim an der Brenz 73 B6 var. Heidenheim. Baden-Württemberg, S Germany
Heilbronn 73 B6 Baden-Württemberg, SW Germany
Heilongjiang 106 D2 var. Hei, Heilongjiang Sheng, Hei-lung-chiang, Heilungkiang. Admin. region province NE China
Heilongjiang Sheng see Heilongjiang
Heiloo 64 C3 Noord-Holland, NW Netherlands
Hei-lung-chiang see Heilongjiang
Heilungkiang see Heilongjiang
Heimdal 63 B5 Sør-Trøndelag, S Norway
Hekimhan 94 D3 Malatya, C Turkey
Helena 22 B2 state capital Montana, NW USA
Helensville 128 D2 Auckland, North Island, NZ
Helgoland Bay see Helgoländer Bucht
Helgoländer Bucht 72 A2 var. Helgoland Bay, Heligoland Bight. Bay NW Germany
Heligoland Bight see Helgoländer Bucht
Heliopolis see Baalbek
Hellevoetsluis 64 B4 Zuid-Holland, SW Netherlands
Hellín 71 E4 Castilla-La Mancha, C Spain
Helmand, Daryā-ye var. Rūd-e Hīrmand. River Afghanistan/Iran see also Hīrmand, Rūd-e
Helmond 65 D5 Noord-Brabant, S Netherlands
Helsingborg 63 B7 prev. Hälsingborg. Skåne, S Sweden
Helsinki 63 D6 Swe. Helsingfors. Country capital (Finland) Etelä-Suomi, S Finland
Henan 106 C5 var. Henan Sheng, Honan, Yu. Admin. region province C China
Henan Sheng see Henan
Henderson 18 B5 Kentucky, S USA
Henderson 25 D7 Nevada, W USA
Henderson 27 H3 Texas, SW USA
Hengchow see Hengyang
Hengduan Shan 106 A5 mountain range SW China
Hengelo 64 E3 Overijssel, E Netherlands
Hengnan see Hengyang
Hengyang 106 C6 var. Hengnan, Heng-yang; prev. Hengchow. Hunan, S China
Heng-yang see Hengyang
Heniches'k 87 F4 Rus. Genichesk. Khersons'ka Oblast', S Ukraine
Hennebont 68 A3 Morbihan, NW France
Henzada 114 B4 Irrawaddy, SW Myanmar
Herakleion see Irákleio
Herāt 100 D4 var. Herat; anc. Aria. Herāt, W Afghanistan
Herat see Herāt
Heredia 31 E4 Heredia, C Costa Rica
Hereford 27 E2 Texas, SW USA
Herford 72 B4 Nordrhein-Westfalen, NW Germany
Herk-de-Stad 65 C6 Limburg, NE Belgium
Hermansverk 63 A5 Sogn Og Fjordane, S Norway
Hermhausen see Hajnówka
Hermiston 24 C2 Oregon, NW USA
Hermon, Mount 97 B5 Ar. Jabal ash Shaykh. Mountain S Syria
Hermosillo 28 B2 Sonora, NW Mexico
Hermoupolis see Ermoúpoli
Hernösand see Härnösand
Herrera del Duque 70 D3 Extremadura, W Spain
Herselt 65 C5 Antwerpen, C Belgium
Herstal 65 D6 Fr. Héristal. Liège, E Belgium
Hessen 73 B5 cultural region C Germany
Ḥevron see Hebron
Heydebrech see Kędzierzyn-Kole
Heywood Islands 124 C3 island group Western Australia
Hibbing 23 F1 Minnesota, N USA
Hidalgo del Parral 28 C2 var. Parral. Chihuahua, N Mexico
Hida-sanmyaku 109 C5 mountain range Honshū, S Japan
Hierro 48 A3 var. Ferro. Island Islas Canarias, Spain, NE Atlantic Ocean
High Plains see Great Plains
High Point 21 E1 North Carolina, SE USA
High Veld see Great Karoo
Hiiumaa 84 C2 Ger. Dagden, Swe. Dagö. Island W Estonia
Hikurangi 128 D2 Northland, North Island, NZ
Hildesheim 72 B4 Niedersachsen, N Germany
Hilla see Al Ḩillah
Hillaby, Mount 33 G1 mountain N Barbados
Hill Bank 30 C1 Orange Walk, N Belize
Hillegom 64 C3 Zuid-Holland, W Netherlands
Hilo 25 B8 Hawai'i, USA, C Pacific Ocean
Hilton Head Island 21 E2 South Carolina, SE USA
Hilversum 64 C3 Noord-Holland, C Netherlands
Himalaya see Himalayas
Himalayas 113 E2 var. Himalaya, Chin. Himalaya Shan. Mountain range S Asia
Himalaya Shan see Himalayas
Himeji 109 C6 var. Himezi. Hyōgo, Honshū, SW Japan
Himezi see Himeji
Ḩimş 96 B4 var. Homs; anc. Emesa. Ḩimş, C Syria
Hînceşti 86 D4 var. Hânceşti; prev. Kotovsk. C Moldova
Hinchinbrook Island 126 D3 island Queensland, NE Australia
Hinds 129 C6 Canterbury, South Island, NZ
Hindu Kush 101 F4 Per. Hendū Kosh. Mountain range Afghanistan/Pakistan
Hinesville 21 E3 Georgia, SE USA
Hinnøya 62 C3 island C Norway
Hinson Bay 20 A5 bay W Bermuda
Hios see Chíos
Hirosaki 108 D3 Aomori, Honshū, C Japan
Hiroshima 109 B6 var. Hirosima. Hiroshima, Honshū, SW Japan
Hirosima see Hiroshima
Hirson 68 D3 Aisne, N France
Hispaniola 34 B1 island Dominion Republic/Haiti
Hitachi 109 D5 var. Hitati. Ibaraki, Honshū, S Japan
Hitati see Hitachi
Hitra 62 A4 prev. Hitteren. Island S Norway
Hjälmaren 63 C6 Eng. Lake Hjalmar. Lake C Sweden
Hjørring 63 B7 Nordjylland, N Denmark
Hkakabo Razi 114 B1 mountain Myanmar/China
Hlobyne 87 F2 Rus. Globino. Poltavs'ka Oblast', NE Ukraine
Hlukhiv 87 F1 Rus. Glukhov. Sums'ka Oblast', NE Ukraine
Hlybokaye 85 D5 Rus. Glubokoye. Vitsyebskaya Voblasts', N Belarus
Hoa Binh 114 D3 Hoa Binh, N Vietnam
Hoang Liên Sơn 114 D3 mountain range N Vietnam
Hobart 127 C8 prev. Hobarton, Hobart Town. State capital Tasmania, SE Australia
Hobbs 27 E3 New Mexico, SW USA
Hobro 63 A7 Nordjylland, N Denmark
Hô Chi Minh 115 E6 var. Ho Chi Minh City; prev. Saigon. S Vietnam
Ho Chi Minh City see Hô Chi Minh
Hódmezővásárhely 77 D7 Csongrád, SE Hungary
Hodna, Chott El 118 C4 var. Chott el-Hodna, Ar. Shatt al-Hodna. Salt lake N Algeria
Hodonín 77 C5 Ger. Göding. Brněnský Kraj, SE Czech Republic
Hoë Karoo see Great Karoo
Hof 73 C5 Bayern, SE Germany
Hofei see Hefei
Hōfu 109 B7 Yamaguchi, Honshū, SW Japan
Hofuf see Al Hufūf
Hogoley Islands see Chuuk Islands
Hohe Tauern 73 C7 mountain range W Austria
Hohhot 105 F3 var. Huhehot, Huhuohaote, Mong. Kukukhoto; prev. Kweisui, Kwesui. Nei Mongol Zizhiqu, N China
Hôi An 115 E5 prev. Faifo. Quang Nam-Đa Năng, C Vietnam
Hoï-Hao see Haikou
Hoihow see Haikou
Hokianga Harbour 128 C2 inlet SE Tasman Sea
Hokitika 129 B5 West Coast, South Island, NZ
Hokkaidō 108 C2 prev. Ezo, Yeso, Yezo. Island NE Japan
Hola Prystan' 87 E4 Rus. Golaya Pristan. Khersons'ka Oblast', S Ukraine
Holbrook 26 B2 Arizona, SW USA
Holetown 33 G1 prev. Jamestown. W Barbados
Holguín 32 C2 Holguín, SE Cuba
Hollabrunn 73 E6 Niederösterreich, NE Austria
Hollandia see Jayapura
Holly Springs 20 C1 Mississippi, S USA
Holman 15 E3 Victoria Island, Northwest Territories, N Canada
Holmsund 62 D4 Västerbotten, N Sweden
Ḥolon 97 A6 var. Kholon. Tel Aviv, C Israel
Holovanivs'k 87 E3 Rus. Golovanevsk. Kirovohrads'ka Oblast', C Ukraine
Holstebro 63 A7 Ringkøbing, W Denmark
Holsteinborg see Sisimiut
Holsteinsborg see Sisimiut
Holstenborg see Sisimiut
Holstensborg see Sisimiut
Holyhead 67 C5 Wel. Caer Gybi. NW Wales, UK
Hombori 53 E3 Mopti, S Mali
Homs see Al Khums
Homs see Ḩimş
Homyel' 85 D7 Rus. Gomel'. Homyel'skaya Voblasts', SE Belarus
Honan see Henan
Honan see Luoyang
Hondo see Honshū
Hondo 27 F4 Texas, SW USA
Honduras 30 C2 Country Central America
Honduras, Gulf of 30 C2 Sp. Golfo de Honduras. Gulf W Caribbean Sea
Hønefoss 63 B6 Buskerud, S Norway
Honey Lake 25 B5 lake California, W USA
Hon Gai see Hông Gai
Hongay see Hông Gai
Hông Gai 114 E3 var. Hon Gai, Hongay. Quang Ninh, N Vietnam
Hong Kong 106 A1 Chin. Xianggang. S China
Hong Kong Island 106 B2 Chin. Xianggang. Island S China
Honiara 122 C3 country capital (Solomon Islands) Guadalcanal, C Solomon Islands
Honjō 108 D4 var. Honzyô. Akita, Honshū, C Japan
Honolulu 25 A8 admin capital O'ahu, Hawai'i, USA, C Pacific Ocean
Honshū 109 E5 var. Hondo, Honsyû. Island SW Japan
Honsyû see Honshū
Honzyô see Honjō
Hoogeveen 64 E2 Drenthe, NE Netherlands
Hoogezand-Sappemeer 64 E2 Groningen, NE Netherlands
Hoorn 64 C2 Noord-Holland, NW Netherlands
Hopa 95 E2 Artvin, NE Turkey
Hope 14 C3 British Columbia, SW Canada
Hopedale 17 F2 Newfoundland and Labrador, NE Canada
Hopeh see Hebei
Hopei see Hebei
Hopkinsville 18 B5 Kentucky, S USA
Horasan 95 F3 Erzurum, NE Turkey
Horizon Deep 130 D4 undersea feature W Pacific Ocean
Horki 85 E6 Rus. Gorki. Mahilyowskaya Voblasts', E Belarus
Horlivka 87 G3 Rom. Adâncata, Rus. Gorlovka. Donets'ka Oblast', E Ukraine
Hormuz, Strait of 98 D4 var. Strait of Ormuz, Per. Tangeh-ye Hormoz. Strait Iran/Oman
Hornos, Cabo de 43 C8 Eng. Cape Horn. Headland S Chile
Hornsby 126 E1 New South Wales, SE Australia
Horodnya 87 E1 Rus. Gorodnya. Chernihivs'ka Oblast', NE Ukraine
Horodyshche 87 E2 Rus. Gorodishche. Cherkas'ka Oblast', C Ukraine
Horokok 86 B2 Pol. Gródek Jagielloński, Rus. Gorodok, Gorodok Yagellonski. L'vivs'ka Oblast', NW Ukraine
Horoshiri-dake 108 D2 var. Horosiri Dake. Mountain Hokkaidō, N Japan
Horosiri Dake see Horoshiri-dake
Horsburgh Atoll 110 A4 atoll N Maldives
Horseshoe Bay 20 A5 bay W Bermuda
Horseshoe Seamounts 58 A4 undersea feature E Atlantic Ocean
Horsham 127 B7 Victoria, SE Australia
Horst 65 D5 Limburg, SE Netherlands
Horten 63 B6 Vestfold, S Norway
Horyn' 85 B7 Rus. Goryn. River NW Ukraine
Hosingen 65 D7 Diekirch, NE Luxembourg
Hospitalet see L'Hospitalet de Llobregat
Hotan 104 B4 var. Khotan, Chin. Ho-t'ien. Xinjiang Uygur Zizhiqu, NW China
Ho-t'ien see Hotan
Hoting 62 C4 Jämtland, C Sweden
Hot Springs 20 B1 Arkansas, C USA
Houayxay 114 C3 var. Ban Houayxay, Ban Houei Sai. Bokèo, N Laos
Houghton 18 B1 Michigan, N USA
Houilles 69 B5 Yvelines, N France
Houlton 19 H1 Maine, NE USA
Houma 20 B3 Louisiana, S USA
Houston 27 H4 Texas, SW USA
Hovd 104 C2 var. Khovd. Hovd, W Mongolia
Hove 67 E7 SE England, UK
Hoverla, Hora 86 C3 Rus. Gora Goverla. Mountain W Ukraine
Hovsgol, Lake see Hövsgöl Nuur
Hövsgöl Nuur 104 D1 var. Lake Hovsgol. Lake N Mongolia
Howar, Wādi 50 A3 var. Ouadi Howa. River Chad/Sudan see also Howa, Ouadi
Hoy 66 C2 island N Scotland, UK
Hoyerswerda 72 D4 Sachsen, E Germany
Hradec Králové 77 B5 Ger. Königgrätz. Hradecký Kraj, N Czech Republic
Hrandzichy 85 B5 Rus. Grandichi. Hrodzyenskaya Voblasts', W Belarus
Hranice 77 C5 Ger. Mährisch-Weisskirchen. Olomoucký Kraj, E Czech Republic
Hrebinka 87 E2 Rus. Grebenka. Poltavs'ka Oblast', NE Ukraine
Hrodna 85 B5 Pol. Grodno. Hrodzyenskaya Voblasts', W Belarus
Hsia-men see Xiamen
Hsiang-t'an see Xiangtan
Hsi Chiang see Xi Jiang
Hsing-k'ai Hu see Khanka, Lake
Hsining see Xining
Hsinking see Changchun
Hsin-yang see Xinyang
Hsu-chou see Xuzhou
Huacho 38 C4 Lima, W Peru
Hua Hin see Ban Hua Hin
Huaihua 106 C5 Hunan, S China
Huailai 106 C3 prev. Shacheng. Hebei, E China

Huainan 106 D5 *var.* Huai-nan, Hwainan. Anhui, E China
Huai-nan *see* Huainan
Huajuapan 29 F5 *var.* Huajuapan de León. Oaxaca, SE Mexico
Huajuapan de León *see* Huajuapan
Hualapai Peak 26 A2 *mountain* Arizona, SW USA
Huallaga, Río 38 C3 *river* N Peru
Huambo 56 B2 *Port.* Nova Lisboa. Huambo, C Angola
Huancavelica 38 D4 Huancavelica, SW Peru
Huancayo 38 D3 Junín, C Peru
Huang He 106 C4 *var.* Yellow River. *River* C China
Huangshi 106 C4 *var.* Huang-shih, Hwangshih. Hubei, C China
Huang-shih *see* Huangshi
Huanta 38 D4 Ayacucho, C Peru
Huánuco 38 C3 Huánuco, C Peru
Huanuni 39 F4 Oruro, W Bolivia
Huaral 38 C4 Lima, W Peru
Huarás *see* Huaraz
Huaraz 38 C3 *var.* Huarás. Ancash, W Peru
Huarmey 38 C3 Ancash, W Peru
Huatabampo 28 C2 Sonora, NW Mexico
Hubli 102 B3 Karnātaka, SW India
Huddersfield 89 D5 N England, UK
Hudiksvall 63 C5 Gävleborg, C Sweden
Hudson Bay 15 G4 *bay* NE Canada
Hudson Strait 15 H3 *Fr.* Détroit d'Hudson. *Strait* Nunavut/Québec, NE Canada
Hudur *see* Xuddur
Huê 114 E4 Thua Thiên-Huê, C Vietnam
Huehuetenango 30 A2 Huehuetenango, W Guatemala
Huelva 70 C4 *anc.* Onuba. Andalucía, SW Spain
Huesca 71 F2 *anc.* Osca. Aragón, NE Spain
Huéscar 71 E4 Andalucía, S Spain
Hughenden 126 C3 Queensland, NE Australia
Hugo 27 G2 Oklahoma, C USA
Huhehot *see* Hohhot
Huhuohaote *see* Hohhot
Huíla Plateau 56 B2 *plateau* S Angola
Huixtla 29 G5 Chiapas, SE Mexico
Hukui *see* Fukui
Hukuoka *see* Fukuoka
Hukusima *see* Fukushima
Hulingol 105 G2 *prev.* Huolin Gol. Nei Mongol Zizhiqu, N China
Hull *see* Kingston upon Hull
Hull 16 D4 Québec, SE Canada
Hulst 65 B5 Zeeland, SW Netherlands
Hulun *see* Hailar
Hu-lun Ch'ih *see* Hulun Nur
Hulun Nur 105 F1 *var.* Hu-lun Ch'ih; *prev.* Dalai Nor. *lake* NE China
Humaitá 40 D2 Amazonas, N Brazil
Humboldt River 25 C5 *river* Nevada, W USA
Humphreys Peak 26 B1 *mountain* Arizona, SW USA
Humpolec 77 B5 *Ger.* Gumpolds, Humpoletz. Jihlavský Kraj, C Czech Republic
Hunan 106 C6 *var.* Hunan Sheng, Xiang. Admin. region *province* S China
Hunan ShEng *see* Xiang
Hunedoara 86 B4 *Ger.* Eisenmarkt, *Hung.* Vajdahunyad. Hunedoara, SW Romania
Hünfeld 73 B5 Hessen, C Germany
Hungary 77 C6 *Ger.* Ungarn, *Hung.* Magyarország, *Rom.* Ungaria, *SCr.* Madarska, *Ukr.* Uhorshchyna; *prev.* Hungarian People's Republic. *Country* C Europe
Hungary, Plain of *see* Great Hungarian Plain
Hunter Island 127 B8 *island* Tasmania, SE Australia
Huntington 18 D4 West Virginia, NE USA
Huntington Beach 25 C8 California, W USA
Huntly 128 D3 Waikato, North Island, NZ
Huntsville 20 D1 Alabama, S USA
Huntsville 27 G3 Texas, SW USA
Hurghada 50 C2 *var.* Al Ghurdaqah, Ghurdaqah. E Egypt
Huron 23 E3 South Dakota, N USA
Hurukawa *see* Furukawa
Hurunui 129 C5 *river* South Island, NZ
Húsavík 61 E4 Nordhurland Eystra, NE Iceland
Husum 72 B2 Schleswig-Holstein, N Germany
Hutchinson 23 E5 Kansas, C USA
Hutchinson Island 21 F4 *island* Florida, SE USA
Huy 65 C6 *Dut.* Hoei, Hoey. Liège, E Belgium
Huzi *see* Fuji
Hvannadalshnúkur 61 E5 *mountain* S Iceland
Hvar 78 B4 *It.* Lesina; *anc.* Pharus. *Island* S Croatia
Hwainan *see* Huainan
Hwange 56 D3 *prev.* Wankie. Matabeleland North, W Zimbabwe
Hwangshih *see* Huangshi
Hyargas Nuur 104 C2 *lake* NW Mongolia
Hyderābād 112 D5 *var.* Haidarabad. Andhra Pradesh, C India
Hyderābād 112 B3 *var.* Haidarabad. Sind, SE Pakistan
Hyères 69 D6 Var, SE France
Hyères, Îles d' 69 D6 *island group* S France
Hypanis *see* Kuban'
Hyrcania *see* Gorgān
Hyvinkää 63 D5 *Swe.* Hyvinge. Etelä-Suomi, S Finland

I

Ialomiţa 86 C5 *river* SE Romania
Iaşi 86 D3 *Ger.* Jassy. Iaşi, NE Romania
Ibadan 53 F5 Oyo, SW Nigeria
Ibagué 36 B3 Tolima, C Colombia
Ibar 79 D5 *river* C Serbia and Montenegro (Yugo.)
Ibarra 38 B1 *var.* San Miguel de Ibarra. Imbabura, N Ecuador
Iberian Mountains *see* Ibérico, Sistema
Iberian Peninsula 58 B4 *physical region* Portugal/Spain
Iberian Plain 58 B4 *undersea feature* E Atlantic Ocean
Ibérico, Sistema 71 E2 *var.* Cordillera Ibérica, *Eng.* Iberian Mountains. *Mountain range* NE Spain
Ibiza *see* Eivissa
Ibo *see* Sassandra
Ica 38 D4 Ica, SW Peru
Içá *see* Putumayo, Río
Icaria *see* Ikaría
Içá, Rio 40 C2 *var.* Río Putumayo. *River* NW South America *see also* Putumayo, Río
Iceland 61 E4 *Dan.* Island, *Icel.* Ísland. *Country* N Atlantic Ocean
Iceland Basin 58 B1 *undersea feature* N Atlantic Ocean
Icelandic Plateau *see* Iceland Plateau
Iceland Plateau 172 B5 *var.* Icelandic Plateau. *Undersea feature* S Greenland Sea
Iconium *see* Konya
Idabel 27 H2 Oklahoma, C USA
Idaho 24 D3 *off.* State of Idaho; *also known as* Gem of the Mountains, Gem State. *State* NW USA
Idaho Falls 24 E3 Idaho, NW USA
Idensalmi *see* Iisalmi
Idfu 50 B2 *var.* Edfu. SE Egypt
Ídhra *see* Ýdra
Idi Amin, Lac *see* Edward, Lake
Idini 52 B2 Trarza, W Mauritania
Idlib 96 B3 Idlib, NW Syria
Idre 63 B5 Kopparberg, C Sweden
Iecava 84 C3 Bauska, S Latvia
Ieper 65 A6 *Fr.* Ypres. West-Vlaanderen, W Belgium
Ierápetra 83 D8 Kríti, Greece, E Mediterranean Sea
Ierissós *see* Ierissós
Ierissós 82 C4 *var.* Ierisós. Kentrikí Makedonía, N Greece
Iferouâne 53 G2 Agadez, N Niger
Ifôghas, Adrar des 53 F3 *var.* Adrar des Iforas. *Mountain range* NE Mali
Igarka 92 D3 Krasnoyarskiy Kray, N Russian Federation
Iglesias 75 A5 Sardegna, Italy, C Mediterranean Sea
Igloolik 15 G2 Nunavut, N Canada
Igoumenítsa 82 A4 Ípeiros, W Greece
Iguaçu, Rio 41 E4 *Sp.* Río Iguazú. *River* Argentina/Brazil *see also* Iguazú, Río
Iguaçu, Salto do 41 E4 *Sp.* Cataratas del Iguazú; *prev.* Victoria Falls. *Waterfall* Argentina/Brazil *see also* Iguazú, Cataratas del
Iguala 29 E4 *var.* Iguala de la Independencia. Guerrero, S Mexico
Iguala de la Independencia *see* Iguala
Iguîdi, 'Erg 48 C3 *var.* Erg Iguîd. *Desert* Algeria/Mauritania
Ihavandiffulu Atoll *see* Ihavandippolhu Atoll
Ihavandippolhu Atoll 110 A3 *var.* Ihavandiffulu Atoll. *Atoll* N Maldives
Ihosy 57 F4 Fianarantsoa, S Madagascar
IJmuiden 64 C3 Noord-Holland, W Netherlands
IJssel 64 D3 *var.* Yssel. *River* Netherlands/Germany
IJsselmeer 64 C2 *prev.* Zuider Zee. *Lake* N Netherlands
IJsselmuiden 64 D3 Overijssel, E Netherlands
IJzer 65 A6 *river* W Belgium
Ikaría 83 D6 *var.* Kariot, Nicaria, Nikaria; *anc.* Icaria. *Island* Dodekánisos, Greece, Aegean Sea
Ikela 55 D6 Equateur, C Dem. Rep. Congo
Iki 109 A7 *island* SW Japan
Ilagan 117 E1 Luzon, N Philippines
Ilave 39 E4 Puno, S Peru
Iława 76 D3 *Ger.* Deutsch-Eylau. Warmińsko-Mazurskie, NE Poland
Ilebo 55 C6 *prev.* Port-Francqui. Kasai Occidental, W Dem. Rep. Congo
Île-de-France 68 C3 *cultural region* N France
Îles de la Société *see* Société, Archipel de la
Îles Tubuai *see* Australes, Îles
Ilfracombe 67 C7 SW England, UK
Ilha Caviana *see* Caviana de Fora, Ilha
Ilha da Madeira *see* Madeira
Ilha do Corvo *see* Corvo
Ilha do Faial *see* Faial
Ilha do Pico *see* Pico
Ilha do Porto Santo *see* Porto Santo
Ilha Graciosa *see* Graciosa
Ilhas dos Açores *see* Azores
Ilha Terceira *see* Terceira
Ílhavo 70 B2 Aveiro, N Portugal
Ili 90 C3 *Kaz.* Ile, *Rus.* Reka Ili. *River* China/Kazakhstan
Iliamna Lake 14 C3 *lake* Alaska, USA
Ilici *see* Elche
Iligan 117 E2 *off.* Iligan City. Mindanao, S Philippines
Illapel 42 B4 Coquimbo, C Chile
Illicis *see* Elche
Illinois 18 A4 *off.* State of Illinois; *also known as* Prairie State, Sucker State. *State* C USA

Illinois River 18 B4 *river* Illinois, N USA
Ilo 39 E4 Moquegua, SW Peru
Iloilo 117 E2 *off.* Iloilo City. Panay Island, C Philippines
Ilorin 53 F4 Kwara, W Nigeria
Îlots de Bass *see* Marotiri
Ilovlya 89 B6 Volgogradskaya Oblast', SW Russian Federation
Iluh *see* Batman
Il'yaly *see* Ýylanly
Imatra 63 E5 Etelä-Suomi, S Finland
Imbros *see* Gökçeada
İmişli 95 H3 *Rus.* Imishli. C Azerbaijan
Imola 74 C3 Emilia-Romagna, N Italy
Imperatriz 41 F2 Maranhão, NE Brazil
Imperia 74 A3 Liguria, NW Italy
Impfondo 55 C5 La Likouala, NE Congo
Imphāl 113 H3 Manipur, NE India
Imroz Adası *see* Gökçeada
Inagua Islands *see* Great Inagua
Inagua Islands *see* Little Inagua
Inarijärvi 62 D2 *Lapp.* Aanaarjävri, *Swe.* Enareträsk. *Lake* N Finland
Inawashiro-ko 109 D5 *var.* Inawasiro Ko. *Lake* Honshū, C Japan
Inawasiro Ko *see* Inawashiro-ko
İncesu 94 D3 Kayseri, C Turkey
Inch'ŏn 107 E4 *off.* Inch'ŏn-gwangyŏksi, *Jap.* Jinsen; *prev.* Chemulpo. NW South Korea
Incudine, Monte 69 E7 *mountain* Corse, France, C Mediterranean Sea
Indefatigable Island *see* Santa Cruz, Isla
Independence 23 F4 Missouri, C USA
Independence Fjord 61 E1 *fjord* N Greenland
Independence Mountains 24 C4 *mountain range* Nevada, W USA
India 112 D4 Madhya Pradesh, C India
India 100 B3 *var.* Indian Union, Union of India, *Hind.* Bhārat. *Country* S Asia
Indiana 18 B4 *off.* State of Indiana; *also known as* The Hoosier State. *State* N USA
Indianapolis 18 C4 *state capital* Indiana, N USA
Indian Church 30 C1 Orange Walk, N Belize
Indian Desert *see* Thar Desert
Indianola 23 F4 Iowa, C USA
Indigirka 93 F2 *river* NE Russian Federation
Indija 78 D3 *Hung.* India; *prev.* Indjija. Serbia, N Serbia and Montenegro (Yugo.)
Indira Point 110 E3 *headland* Andaman and Nicobar Islands, India, NE Indian Ocean
Indomed Fracture Zone 119 B6 *tectonic feature* SW Indian Ocean
Indonesia 116 B4 *Ind.* Republik Indonesia; *prev.* Dutch East Indies, Netherlands East Indies, United States of Indonesia. *Country* SE Asia
Indore 112 D4 Madhya Pradesh, C India
Indus 112 C2 *Chin.* Yindu He; *prev.* Yin-tu Ho. *River* S Asia
Indus Cone *see* Indus Fan
Indus Fan 90 C5 *var.* Indus Cone. *Undersea feature* N Arabian Sea
Indus, Mouths of the 112 B4 *delta* S Pakistan
İnebolu 94 C2 Kastamonu, N Turkey
Ineu 86 A4 *Hung.* Borosjenő; *prev.* Inău. Arad, W Romania
Infiernillo, Presa del 29 E4 *reservoir* S Mexico
Inglewood 24 D2 California, W USA
Ingolstadt 73 C6 Bayern, S Germany
Inhambane 57 E4 Inhambane, SE Mozambique
Inhulets' 87 F3 *Rus.* Ingulets. Dnipropetrovs'ka Oblast', E Ukraine
I-ning *see* Yining
Inis *see* Ennis
Inis Ceithleann *see* Enniskillen
Inn 73 C6 *river* C Europe
Innaanganeq 60 C1 *var.* Kap York. *Headland* NW Greenland
Inner Hebrides 66 B4 *island group* W Scotland, UK
Inner Islands 57 H1 *var.* Central Group. *Island group* NE Seychelles
Inner Mongolia 105 F3 *var.* Nei Mongol, *Eng.* Inner Mongolia, Inner Mongolian Autonomous Region; *prev.* Nei Monggol Zizhiqu. Admin. region *autonomous region* N China
Inner Mongolian Autonomous Region *see* Inner Mongolia
Innisfail 126 D3 Queensland, NE Australia
Inniskilling *see* Enniskillen
Innsbruch *see* Innsbruck
Innsbruck 73 C7 *var.* Innsbruch. Tirol, W Austria
Inoucdjouac *see* Inukjuak
Inowrocław 76 C3 *Ger.* Hohensalza; *prev.* Inowraztaw. Kujawski-pomorskie, C Poland
In-Salah 48 D3 *var.* In Salah. C Algeria
In Salah *see* In-Salah
Insula *see* Lille
Inta 88 E3 Respublika Komi, NW Russian Federation
International Falls 23 F1 Minnesota, N USA
Inukjuak 16 D2 *var.* Inoucdjouac; *prev.* Port Harrison. Québec, NE Canada
Inuuvik *see* Inuvik
Inuvik 14 D3 *var.* Inuuvik. District capital Northwest Territories, NW Canada
Invercargill 129 A7 Southland, South Island, NZ
Inverness 66 C3 N Scotland, UK
Investigator Ridge 119 D5 *undersea feature* E Indian Ocean
Investigator Strait 127 B7 *strait* South Australia
Inyangani 56 D3 *mountain* NE Zimbabwe
Ioánnina 82 A4 *var.* Janina, Yannina. Ípeiros, W Greece
Iola 23 F5 Kansas, C USA
Ionia Basin *see* Ionian Basin
Ionian Basin 58 D5 *var.* Ionian Basin. *Undersea feature* Ionian Sea, C Mediterranean Sea

Ionian Islands *see* Iónioi Nísoi
Ionian Sea 81 E3 *Gk.* Iónio Pélagos, *It.* Mar Ionio. *Sea* C Mediterranean Sea
Iónioi Nísoi 83 A5 *Eng.* Ionian Islands. *Island group* W Greece
Íos 83 D6 *var.* Nio. *Island* Kykládes, Greece, Aegean Sea
Íos 83 D6 Íos, Kykládes, Greece, Aegean Sea
Iowa 23 F3 *off.* State of Iowa; *also known as* The Hawkeye State. *State* C USA
Iowa City 23 G3 Iowa, C USA
Iowa Falls 23 G3 Iowa, C USA
Ipel 77 C6 *var.* Ipoly, *Ger.* Eipel. *River* Hungary/Slovakia
Ipiales 36 A4 Nariño, SW Colombia
Ipoh 116 B3 Perak, Peninsular Malaysia
Ipoly 77 C6 *var.* Ipel', *Ger.* Eipel. *River* Hungary/Slovakia
Ippy 54 C4 Ouaka, C Central African Republic
Ipswich 67 E6 *hist.* Gipeswic. E England, UK
Ipswich 127 E5 Queensland, E Australia
Iqaluit 15 H3 *prev.* Frobisher Bay. Baffin Island, Nunavut, NE Canada
Iquique 42 B1 Tarapacá, N Chile
Iquitos 38 C1 Loreto, N Peru
Irákleio 83 D7 *var.* Herakleion, *Eng.* Candia; *prev.* Iráklion. Kríti, Greece, E Mediterranean Sea
Iráklion *see* Irákleio
Iran 98 D3 *off.* Islamic Republic of Iran; *prev.* Persia. *Country* SW Asia
Iranian Plateau 98 D3 *var.* Plateau of Iran. *plateau* N Iran
Iran, Plateau of *see* Iranian Plateau
Irapuato 29 E4 Guanajuato, C Mexico
Iraq 98 B3 *Ar.* 'Irāq. *Country* SW Asia
Irbid 97 B5 Irbid, N Jordan
Irbīl *see* Arbīl
Ireland 58 C3 *Lat.* Hibernia. *Island* Ireland/UK
Ireland 67 A5 *var.* Republic of Ireland, *Ir.* Éire. *Country* NW Europe
Irian Barat *see* Papua
Irian Jaya *see* Papua
Irian, Teluk *see* Cenderawasih, Teluk
Iringa 51 C7 Iringa, C Tanzania
Iriomote-jima 108 A4 *island* Sakishima-shotō, SW Japan
Iriona 30 D2 Colón, NE Honduras
Irish Sea 67 C5 *Ir.* Muir Éireann. *Sea* C British Isles
Irkutsk 93 E4 Irkutskaya Oblast', S Russian Federation
Irminger Basin *see* Reykjanes Basin
Iroise 68 A3 *sea* NW France
Iron Mountain 18 B2 Michigan, N USA
Ironwood 18 B1 Michigan, N USA
Irrawaddy 114 B2 *var.* Ayeyarwady. *River* W Myanmar
Irrawaddy, Mouths of the 115 A5 *delta* SW Myanmar
Irtish *see* Irtysh
Irtysh 92 C4 *var.* Irtish, *Kaz.* Ertis. *River* C Asia
Irún 71 E1 País Vasco, N Spain
Iruña *see* Pamplona
Isabela, Isla 38 A5 *var.* Albemarle Island. *Island* Galapagos Islands, Ecuador, E Pacific Ocean
Isaccea 86 D4 Tulcea, E Romania
Isachsen 15 F1 Ellef Ringnes Island, Nunavut, N Canada
Ísafjördhur 61 E4 Vestfirdhir, NW Iceland
Isbarta *see* Isparta
Ise 109 C6 Mie, Honshū, SW Japan
Isère 69 D5 *river* E France
Isernia 75 D5 *var.* Æsernia. Molise, C Italy
Ise-wan 109 C6 *bay* S Japan
Isha Baydhabo *see* Baydhabo
Ishigaki-jima 108 A4 *var.* Isigaki Zima. *Island* Sakishima-shotō, SW Japan
Ishikari-wan 108 C2 *bay* Hokkaidō, NE Japan
Ishim 92 C4 *Kaz.* Esil. *River* Kazakhstan/Russian Federation
Ishim 92 C4 Tyumenskaya Oblast', C Russian Federation
Ishinomaki 108 D4 *var.* Isinomaki. Miyagi, Honshū, C Japan
Ishkoshim 101 F3 *Rus.* Ishkashim. S Tajikistan
Isigaki Zima *see* Ishigaki-jima
Isinomaki *see* Ishinomaki
Isiro 55 E5 Orientale, NE Dem. Rep. Congo
İskår *see* Iskŭr
İskenderun 94 D4 *Eng.* Alexandretta. Hatay, S Turkey
İskenderun Körfezi 96 A2 *Eng.* Gulf of Alexandretta. *Gulf* S Turkey
Iskŭr 82 C2 *var.* İskăr. *River* NW Bulgaria
Iskŭr, Yazovir 82 C2 *prev.* Yazovir Stalin. *Reservoir* W Bulgaria
Isla Cristina 70 C4 Andalucía, S Spain
Isla Gran Malvina *see* West Falkland
Islāmābād 112 C1 *country capital* (Pakistan) Federal Capital Territory Islāmābād, NE Pakistan
Islas de los Galápagos *see* Galapagos Islands
Islas Malvinas *see* Falkland Islands
Islay 66 B4 *island* SW Scotland, UK
Isle 69 B5 *river* W France
Isle of Man 67 B5 UK *crown dependency* NW Europe
Ismailia *see* Ismâ'ilîya
Ismâ'ilîya 50 B1 *var.* Ismailia. N Egypt
Ismid *see* İzmit
Isna 50 B2 *var.* Esna. SE Egypt
Isoka 56 D1 Northern, NE Zambia
Isola Grossa *see* Dugi Otok
Isola Lunga *see* Dugi Otok
Isole Lipari *see* Eolie, Isole
Isparta 94 B4 *var.* Isbarta. Isparta, SW Turkey
İspir 95 E3 Erzurum, NE Turkey
Israel 97 A7 *var.* Medinat Israel, *Heb.* Yisrael, Yisra'el. *Country* SW Asia

Issiq Köl *see* Issyk-Kul', Ozero
Issoire 69 C5 Puy-de-Dôme, C France
Issyk-Kul', Ozero 101 G2 *var.* Issiq Köl, *Kir.* Ysyk-Köl. *Lake* E Kyrgyzstan
İstanbul 94 B2 *Bul.* Tsarigrad, *Eng.* Istanbul; *prev.* Constantinople, *anc.* Byzantium. İstanbul, NW Turkey
İstanbul Boğazı 94 B2 *var.* Bosporus Thracius, *Eng.* Bosphorus, Bosporus, *Turk.* Karadeniz Boğazı. *Strait* NW Turkey
Istra 78 A3 *Eng.* Istria, *Ger.* Istrien. *Cultural region* NW Croatia
Istra 72 D2 *Eng.* Istria. *Peninsula* NW Croatia
Itabuna 41 G3 Bahia, E Brazil
Itagüí 36 B3 Antioquia, W Colombia
Itaipú, Represa de 41 E4 *reservoir* Brazil/Paraguay
Itaituba 41 E2 Pará, NE Brazil
Italy 74 C3 *It.* Italia, Republica Italiana. *Country* S Europe
Italy 74 C3 *It.* Italia, Republica Italiana. *Country* S Europe
Italy 58 D4 Texas, SW USA
Iténez, Río *see* Guaporé, Rio
Ithaca 19 E3 New York, NE USA
Itoigawa 109 C5 Niigata, Honshū, SW Japan
Itseqqortoormiit *see* Ittoqqortoormiit
Ittoqqortoormiit 61 F3 *var.* Itseqqortoormiit, *Dan.* Scoresbysund, *Eng.* Scoresby Sound. C Greenland
Iturup, Ostrov 108 E1 *island* Kuril'skiye Ostrova, SE Russian Federation
Itzehoe 72 B2 Schleswig-Holstein, N Germany
Ivalo 62 D2 *Lapp.* Avveel, Avvil. Lappi, N Finland
Ivanava 85 B7 *Pol.* Janów, Janów Poleski, *Rus.* Ivanovo. Brestskaya Voblasts', SW Belarus
Ivanhoe 127 C6 New South Wales, SE Australia
Ivano-Frankivs'k 86 C2 *Ger.* Stanislau, *Pol.* Stanisławów, *Rus.* Ivano-Frankovsk; *prev.* Stanislav. Ivano-Frankivs'ka Oblast', W Ukraine
Ivanovo 89 B5 Ivanovskaya Oblast', W Russian Federation
Ivatsevichy 85 B6 *Pol.* Iwacewicze, *Rus.* Ivantsevichi, Ivatsevichi. Brestskaya Voblasts', SW Belarus
Ivigtut *see* Ivittuut
Ivittuut 60 B4 *var.* Ivigtut. S Greenland
Iviza *see* Eivissa
Ivory Coast *see* Côte d'Ivoire
Ivujivik 16 D1 Québec, NE Canada
Iwaki 109 D5 Fukushima, Honshū, N Japan
Iwakuni 109 B7 Yamaguchi, Honshū, SW Japan
Iwanai 108 C2 Hokkaidō, NE Japan
Iwate 108 D3 Iwate, Honshū, N Japan
Ixtapa 29 E5 Guerrero, S Mexico
Ixtepec 29 F5 Oaxaca, SE Mexico
Iyo-nada 109 B7 *sea* S Japan
Izabal, Lago de 30 B2 *prev.* Golfo Dulce. *Lake* E Guatemala
Ízad Khvāst 98 D3 Fārs, C Iran
Izegem 65 A6 *prev.* Iseghem. West-Vlaanderen, W Belgium
Izhevsk 89 D5 *prev.* Ustinov. Udmurtskaya Respublika, NW Russian Federation
Izmail 86 D4 *Rus.* Izmail. Odes'ka Oblast', SW Ukraine
İzmir 94 A3 *prev.* Smyrna. İzmir, W Turkey
İzmit 94 B2 *var.* Ismid; *anc.* Astacus. Kocaeli, NW Turkey
İznik Gölü 94 B3 *lake* NW Turkey
Izu-hantō 109 D6 *peninsula* Honshū, S Japan
Izu Shichito *see* Izu-shotō
Izu-shotō 109 D6 *var.* Izu Shichito. *Island group* S Japan
Izvor 82 B2 Pernik, W Bulgaria
Izyaslav 86 C2 Khmel'nyts'ka Oblast', W Ukraine
Izyum 87 G2 Kharkivs'ka Oblast', E Ukraine

J

Jabal ash Shifā 98 A4 *desert* NW Saudi Arabia
Jabalpur 113 E4 *prev.* Jubbulpore. Madhya Pradesh, C India
Jabbūl, Sabkhat al 134 B2 *salt flat* NW Syria
Jablah 96 A3 *var.* Jeble, *Fr.* Djéblé. Al Lādhiqīyah, W Syria
Jaca 71 F1 Aragón, NE Spain
Jacaltenango 30 A2 Huehuetenango, W Guatemala
Jackson 20 B2 *state capital* Mississippi, S USA
Jackson 23 H5 Missouri, C USA
Jackson 20 C1 Tennessee, S USA
Jackson Head 129 A6 *headland* South Island, NZ
Jacksonville 21 E3 Florida, SE USA
Jacksonville 18 B4 Illinois, N USA
Jacksonville 21 F1 North Carolina, SE USA
Jacksonville 27 G3 Texas, SW USA
Jacmel 32 D3 *var.* Jaquemel. S Haiti
Jacobābād 112 B3 Sind, SE Pakistan
Jaén 70 D4 Andalucía, SW Spain
Jaén 38 B2 Cajamarca, N Peru
Jaffna 110 D3 Northern Province, N Sri Lanka
Jagannath *see* Puri
Jagdalpur 113 E5 Madhya Pradesh, C India
Jagdaqi 105 G1 Nei Mongol Zizhiqu, N China
Jagodina 78 D4 *prev.* Svetozarevo. Serbia, C Serbia and Montenegro (Yugo.)
Jahra *see* Al Jahrā'
Jaipur 112 D3 *prev.* Jeypore. Rājasthān, N India

Jaisalmer – Karakol

Jaisalmer 112 C3 Rājasthān, NW India
Jajce 78 B3 Federacija Bosna I Hercegovina, W Bosnia and Herzegovina
Jakarta 116 C5 prev. Djakarta, Dut. Batavia. Country capital (Indonesia) Jawa, C Indonesia
Jakobstad 62 D4 Fin. Pietarsaari. Länsi-Suomi, W Finland
Jalālābād 101 F4 var. Jalalabad, Jelalabad. Nangarhār, E Afghanistan
Jalandhar 112 D2 prev. Jullundur. Punjab, N India
Jalapa see Xalapa
Jalapa 30 D3 Nueva Segovia, NW Nicaragua
Jalapa Enríquez see Xalapa
Jalpa 28 D4 Zacatecas, C Mexico
Jālū 49 G3 var. Jūlā. NE Libya
Jaluit Atoll 122 D2 var. Jālwōj. Atoll Ralik Chain, S Marshall Islands
Jālwōj see Jaluit Atoll
Jamaame 51 D6 It. Giamame; prev. Margherita. Jubbada Hoose, S Somalia
Jamaica 32 A4 country W West Indies
Jamaica 34 A1 island W West Indies
Jamaica Channel 32 D3 channel Haiti/Jamaica
Jamālpur 113 F3 Bihār, NE India
Jambi 116 B4 var. Telanaipura; prev. Djambi. Sumatera, W Indonesia
James Bay 16 C3 bay Ontario/Québec, E Canada
James River 23 E2 river North Dakota/South Dakota, N USA
James River 19 E5 river Virginia, NE USA
Jamestown 19 E3 New York, NE USA
Jamestown 23 E2 North Dakota, N USA
Jammu 112 D2 prev. Jummoo. Jammu and Kashmir, NW India
Jammu and Kashmīr 112 D1 disputed region India/Pakistan
Jāmnagar 112 C4 prev. Navanagar. Gujarāt, W India
Jamshedpur 113 F4 Bihār, NE India
Jamuna see Brahmaputra
Janaúba 41 F3 Minas Gerais, SE Brazil
Janesville 18 B3 Wisconsin, N USA
Janīn see Jenīn
Janina see Ioánnina
Jan Mayen 61 F4 Norwegian dependency N Atlantic Ocean
Jánoshalma 77 C7 SCr. Jankovac. Bács-Kiskun, S Hungary
Japan 108 C4 var. Nippon, Jap. Nihon. Country E Asia
Japan, Sea of 108 A4 var. East Sea, Rus. Yapanskoye More. Sea NW Pacific Ocean see also East Sea
Japan Trench 103 F1 undersea feature NW Pacific Ocean
Japiim 40 C2 var. Máncio Lima. Acre, W Brazil
Japurá, Rio 40 C2 var. Río Caquetá, Yapurá. River Brazil/Colombia see also Caquetá, Río
Jaqué 31 G5 Darién, SE Panama
Jaquemel see Jacmel
Jarablos see Jarābulus
Jarābulus 96 C2 var. Jarablos, Jerablus, Fr. Djérablous. Ḩalab, N Syria
Jardines de la Reina, Archipiélago de los 32 B2 island group C Cuba
Jarocin 76 C4 Wielkopolskie, C Poland
Jarosław 77 E5 Ger. Jaroslau, Rus. Yaroslav. Podkarpackie, SE Poland
Jarqo'rg'on 101 E3 var. Jarqŭrghon, Rus. Dzharkurgan. Surkhondaryo Wiloyati, S Uzbekistan
Jarqŭrghon see Jarqo'rg'on
Jarvis Island 123 G2 US unincorporated territory C Pacific Ocean
Jasło 77 D5 Podkarpackie, SE Poland
Jastrzębie-Zdrój 77 C5 Śląskie, S Poland
Jataí 41 E3 Goiás, C Brazil
Jativa see Xátiva
Jauf see Al Jawf
Jaunpiebalga 84 D3 Gulbene, NE Latvia
Jaunpur 113 E3 Uttar Pradesh, N India
Java 130 A3 prev. Djawa. Island C Indonesia
Javalambre 93 E3 mountain E Spain
Javari, Rio 40 C2 var. Yavarí. River Brazil/Peru
Java Sea 116 D4 Ind. Laut Jawa. Sea W Indonesia
Java Trench 102 D5 var. Sunda Trench. Undersea feature E Indian Ocean
Jawhar 51 D6 var. Jowhar, It. Giohar. Shabeellaha Dhexe, S Somalia
Jaya, Puncak 139 G4 prev. Puntjak Carstensz, Puntjak Sukarno. Mountain Papua, E Indonesia
Jayapura 117 H4 var. Djajapura, Dut. Hollandia; prev. Kotabaru, Sukarnapura. Papua, E Indonesia
Jazā'ir Bin Ghalfān see Ḩalāniyāt, Juzur al
Jazīrat Jarbah see Jerba, Île de
Jazīreh-ye Qeshm see Qeshm
Jaz Mūrīān, Hāmūn-e 98 E4 lake SE Iran
Jebba 53 F4 Kwara, W Nigeria
Jebel esh Sharqi see Anti-Lebanon
Jebel Uweinat see 'Uwaynāt, Jabal al
Jeble see Jablah
Jedda see Jiddah
Jędrzejów 76 D4 Ger. Endersdorf. Świętokrzyskie, C Poland
Jefferson City 23 G5 state capital Missouri, C USA
Jega 53 F4 Kebbi, NW Nigeria
Jehol see Chengde
Jēkabpils 84 D4 Ger. Jakobstadt. Jēkabpils, S Latvia
Jelalabad see Jalālābād
Jelenia Góra 76 B4 Ger. Hirschberg, Hirschberg im Riesengebirge, Hirschberg in Riesengebirge, Hirschberg in Schlesien. Dolnośląskie, SW Poland
Jelgava 84 C3 Ger. Mitau. Jelgava, C Latvia
Jemappes 87 B6 Hainaut, S Belgium
Jember 116 D5 prev. Djember. Jawa, C Indonesia
Jena 72 C4 Thüringen, C Germany
Jenīn 97 A6 var. Janīn, Jinīn; anc. Engannim. N West Bank
Jerablus see Jarābulus
Jerada 48 D2 NE Morocco
Jerba, Île de 49 F2 var. Djerba, Jazīrat Jarbah. Island E Tunisia
Jérémie 32 D3 SW Haiti
Jerez see Jeréz de la Frontera
Jeréz de la Frontera 92 C5 var. Jerez; prev. Xeres. Andalucía, SW Spain
Jeréz de los Caballeros 70 C4 Extremadura, W Spain
Jericho 97 B6 Ar. Arīḩā, Heb. Yeriḥo. E West Bank
Jerid, Chott el 87 E2 var. Shaţţ al Jarīd. Salt lake SW Tunisia
Jersey 67 D8 UK dependent territory NW Europe
Jerusalem 81 H4 Ar. El Quds, Heb. Yerushalayim; anc. Hierosolyma. Country capital (Israel) Jerusalem, NE Israel
Jerusalem 90 A4 Admin. region district E Israel
Jesenice 73 D7 Ger. Assling. NW Slovenia
Jessore 113 G4 Khulna, W Bangladesh
Jesús María 42 C3 Córdoba, C Argentina
Jhānsi 112 D3 Uttar Pradesh, N India
Jhārkand 113 F4 Admin. region state N India
Jhelum 112 C2 Punjab, NE Pakistan
Ji see Hebei
Ji see Jilin
Jiangmen 106 C6 Guangdong, S China
Jiangsu 106 D4 var. Chiang-su, Jiangsu Sheng, Kiangsu, Su. Admin. region province E China
Jiangsu Sheng see Jiangsu
Jiangxi 106 C6 var. Chiang-hsi, Gan, Jiangxi Sheng, Kiangsi. Admin. region province S China
Jiangxi Sheng see Jiangxi
Jiaxing 106 D5 Zhejiang, SE China
Jiayi see Chiai
Jibuti see Djibouti
Jiddah 99 A5 Eng. Jedda. Country capital (Saudi Arabia) Makkah, W Saudi Arabia
Jih-k'a-tse see Xigazê
Jihlava 99 B5 Ger. Iglau, Pol. Igława. Jihlavský Kraj, C Czech Republic
Jilib 51 D6 It. Gelib. Jubbada Dhexe, S Somalia
Jilin 106 D3 var. Chi-lin, Girin, Ji, Jilin Sheng, Kirin. Admin. region province NE China
Jilin 107 E3 var. Chi-lin, Girin, Kirin; prev. Yungki, Yunki. Jilin, NE China
Jilin Sheng see Jilin
Jīma 51 C5 var. Jimma, It. Gimma. C Ethiopia
Jimbolia 86 A4 Ger. Hatzfeld, Hung. Zsombolya. Timiş, W Romania
Jiménez 28 D2 Chihuahua, N Mexico
Jimma see Jīma
Jimsar 104 C3 Xinjiang Uygur Zizhiqu, NW China
Jin see Shanxi
Jin see Tianjin Shi
Jinan 106 C4 var. Chinan, Chi-nan, Tsinan. Shandong, E China
Jingdezhen 106 C5 Jiangxi, S China
Jinghong 106 A6 var. Yunjinghong. Yunnan, SW China
Jinhua 106 D5 Zhejiang, SE China
Jinīn see Jenīn
Jining 105 F3 Shandong, E China
Jinja 51 C6 S Uganda
Jinotega 30 D3 Jinotega, NW Nicaragua
Jinotepe 30 D3 Carazo, SW Nicaragua
Jinsha Jiang 106 A5 river SW China
Jinzhong 106 C4 var. Yuci. Shanxi, C China
Jinzhou 106 D3 var. Chin-chou, Chinchow; prev. Chinhsien. Liaoning, NE China
Jisr ash Shadadi see Ash Shadādah
Jiu 86 B5 Ger. Schil, Schyl, Hung. Zsil, Zsily. River S Romania
Jiujiang 106 C5 Jiangxi, S China
Jixi 107 E2 Heilongjiang, NE China
Jīzān 99 B6 var. Qīzān. Jīzān, SW Saudi Arabia
Jizzakh 101 E2 Rus. Dzhizak. Jizzakh Wiloyati, C Uzbekistan
Jizzax see Jizzax
João Pessoa 41 G2 prev. Paraíba. State capital Paraíba, E Brazil
Jo'burg see Johannesburg
Jo-ch'iang see Ruoqiang
Jodhpur 112 C3 Rājasthān, NW India
Joensuu 85 E5 Itä-Suomi, E Finland
Jōetsu 109 C5 var. Zyôetu. Niigata, Honshū, C Japan
Johanna Island see Anjouan
Johannesburg 56 D4 var. Egoli, Erautini, Gauteng, abbrev. Jo'burg. Gauteng, NE South Africa
John Day River 24 C3 river Oregon, NW USA
John o'Groats 66 C2 N Scotland, UK
Johnston Atoll 121 E1 US unincorporated territory C Pacific Ocean
Johor Baharu see Johor Bahru
Johor Bahru 116 B3 var. Johor Baharu, Johore Bahru. Johor, Peninsular Malaysia
Johore Bahru see Johor Bahru
Johore Strait 116 A1 Mal. Selat Johor. Strait Malaysia/Singapore
Joinvile see Joinville
Joinville 41 E4 var. Joinvile. Santa Catarina, S Brazil
Jokkmokk 62 C3 Norrbotten, N Sweden
Joliet 18 B3 Illinois, N USA
Jonava 84 B4 Ger. Janow, Pol. Janów. Jonava, C Lithuania
Jonesboro 20 B1 Arkansas, C USA
Joniškis 84 C3 Ger. Janischken. Joniškis, N Lithuania
Jönköping 63 B7 Jönköping, S Sweden
Jonquière 17 E4 Québec, SE Canada
Joplin 23 F5 Missouri, C USA
Jordan 97 B5 Ar. Urdunn, Heb. HaYarden. River SW Asia
Jordan 97 B6 Ar. Al Mamlakah al Urdunīyah al Hāshimīyah, Al Urdunn; prev. Transjordan. Country SW Asia
Jorhāt 113 H3 Assam, NE India
Jos 53 G4 Plateau, C Nigeria
Joseph Bonaparte Gulf 124 D2 gulf N Australia
Jos Plateau 53 G4 plateau C Nigeria
Jotunheimen 63 A5 mountain range S Norway
Joûnié 96 A4 var. Junīyah. W Lebanon
Joure 64 D2 Fris. De Jouwer. Friesland, N Netherlands
Joutseno 63 E5 Etelä-Suomi, S Finland
Jowhar see Jawhar
JStorm Thurmond Reservoir see Clark Hill Lake
Juan Aldama 28 D3 Zacatecas, C Mexico
Juan de Fuca, Strait of 24 A1 strait Canada/USA
Juan Fernández, Islas 35 A6 Eng. Juan Fernandez Islands. Island group W Chile
Juazeiro 41 G2 prev. Joazeiro. Bahia, E Brazil
Juazeiro do Norte 41 G2 Ceará, E Brazil
Juba 51 D6 Amh. Genalē Wenz, It. Guiba, Som. Ganaane, Webi Jubba. River Ethiopia/Somalia
Juba 51 B5 var. Jūbā. Bahr el Gabel, S Sudan
Júcar 71 E3 var. Jucar. River C Spain
Juchitán 29 F5 var. Juchitán de Zaragosa. Oaxaca, SE Mexico
Juchitán de Zaragosa see Juchitán
Judayyidat Hāmir 98 B3 S Iraq
Judenburg 73 D7 Steiermark, C Austria
Juigalpa 30 D3 Chontales, S Nicaragua
Juiz de Fora 41 F4 Minas Gerais, SE Brazil
Jujuy see San Salvador de Jujuy
Jūlā see Jālū
Juliaca 39 E4 Puno, SE Peru
Juliana Top 37 G3 mountain C Suriname
Jumilla 71 E4 Murcia, SE Spain
Jumporn see Chumphon
Junction City 23 F4 Kansas, C USA
Juneau 14 D4 state capital Alaska, USA
Junín 42 C4 Buenos Aires, E Argentina
Junīyah see Joûnié
Junkseylon see Phuket
Jur 51 B5 river C Sudan
Jura 66 B4 island SW Scotland, UK
Jura 73 A7 canton NW Switzerland
Jura 68 D4 department E France
Jurbarkas 84 B4 Ger. Georgenburg, Jurburg. Jurbarkas, W Lithuania
Jūrmala 84 C3 Rīga, C Latvia
Juruá, Rio 40 C2 var. Río Yuruá. River Brazil/Peru
Juruena, Rio 40 D3 river W Brazil
Jutiapa 30 B2 Jutiapa, S Guatemala
Juticalpa 30 D2 Olancho, C Honduras
Juventud, Isla de la 32 A2 var. Isla de Pinos, Eng. Isle of Youth; prev. The Isle of the Pines. Island W Cuba
Južna Morava 79 E5 Ger. Südliche Morava. River SE Serbia and Montenegro (Yugo.)
Juzur Qarqannah see Kerkenah, Îles de
Jwaneng 56 C4 Southern, SE Botswana
Jylland 63 A7 Eng. Jutland. Peninsula W Denmark
Jyväskylä 63 D5 Länsi-Suomi, W Finland

K

K2 104 A4 Chin. Qogir Feng, Eng. Mount Godwin Austen. Mountain China/Pakistan
Kaafu Atoll see Male' Atoll
Kaaimanston 37 G3 Sipaliwini, N Suriname
Kaakhka see Kaka
Kaala see Caála
Kaamanen 62 D2 Lapp. Gámas. Lappi, N Finland
Kaapstad see Cape Town
Kaaresuvanto 62 C3 Lapp. Gárassavon. Lappi, N Finland
Kabale 51 B6 SW Uganda
Kabinda see Cabinda
Kabinda 55 D7 Kasai Oriental, SE Dem. Rep. Congo
Kābol see Kābul
Kabompo 56 C2 river W Zambia
Kābul 101 E4 var. Kabul, Per. Kābol. Country capital (Afghanistan) Kābul, E Afghanistan
Kabul see Kābul
Kabwe 56 D2 Central, C Zambia
Kachchh, Gulf of 112 B4 var. Gulf of Cutch, Gulf of Kutch. Gulf W India
Kachchh, Rann of 112 B4 var. Rann of Kachh, Rann of Kutch. Salt marsh India/Pakistan
Kachh, Rann of see Kachchh, Rann of
Kadan Kyun 115 B5 prev. King Island. Island Mergui Archipelago, S Myanmar
Kadavu 123 E4 prev. Kandavu. Island S Fiji
Kadoma 56 D3 prev. Gatooma. Mashonaland West, C Zimbabwe
Kadugli 50 B4 Southern Kordofan, S Sudan
Kaduna 53 G4 Kaduna, C Nigeria
Kadzhi-Say 101 G2 Kir. Kajisay. Issyk-Kul'skaya Oblast', NE Kyrgyzstan
Kaédi 52 C3 Gorgol, S Mauritania
Kaffa see Feodosiya
Kafue 56 C2 river C Zambia
Kafue 56 D2 Lusaka, SE Zambia
Kaga Bandoro 54 C4 prev. Fort-Crampel. Nana-Grébizi, C Central African Republic
Kâghet 52 D1 var. Karet. Physical region N Mauritania
Kagi see Chiai
Kagoshima 109 B8 var. Kagosima. Kagoshima, Kyūshū, SW Japan
Kagoshima-wan 109 A8 bay SW Japan
Kagosima see Kagoshima
Kahmard, Daryā-ye 101 E4 prev. Darya-i-Surkhab. River NE Afghanistan
Kahraman Maraş see Kahramanmaraş
Kahramanmaraş 94 D4 var. Kahraman Maraş, Maraş, Marash. Kahramanmaraş, S Turkey
Kaiapoi 129 C6 Canterbury, South Island, NZ
Kaifeng 106 C4 Henan, C China
Kai, Kepulauan 117 F4 prev. Kei Islands. Island group Maluku, SE Indonesia
Kaikohe 128 C2 Northland, North Island, NZ
Kaikoura 129 C5 Canterbury, South Island, NZ
Kaikoura Peninsula 129 C5 peninsula South Island, NZ
Kainji Lake see Kainji Reservoir
Kainji Reservoir 53 F4 var. Kainji Lake. Reservoir W Nigeria
Kaipara Harbour 128 C2 harbour North Island, NZ
Kairouan 49 E2 var. Al Qayrawān. E Tunisia
Kaisaria see Kayseri
Kaiserslautern 73 A5 Rheinland-Pfalz, SW Germany
Kaišiadorys 85 B5 Kaišiadorys, S Lithuania
Kaitaia 128 C2 Northland, North Island, NZ
Kajaani 62 E4 Swe. Kajana. Oulu, C Finland
Kaka 100 C2 var. Kaakhka. Dashkhovuzskiy Velayat, N Turkmenistan
Kake 14 D4 Kupreanof Island, Alaska, USA
Kakhovka 87 F4 Khersons'ka Oblast', S Ukraine
Kakhovs'ka Vodoskhovyshche 87 F4 Rus. Kakhovskoye Vodokhranilishche. Reservoir SE Ukraine
Kākināda 110 D1 prev. Cocanada. Andhra Pradesh, E India
Kaktovik 14 D2 Alaska, USA
Kalahari Desert 56 B4 desert Southern Africa
Kalamariá 82 B4 Kentrikí Makedonía, N Greece
Kalámata 83 B6 prev. Kalámai. Pelopónnisos, S Greece
Kalamazoo 18 C3 Michigan, N USA
Kalambaka see Kalampáka
Kálamos 83 C5 Attikí, C Greece
Kalampáka 82 B4 var. Kalambaka. Thessalía, C Greece
Kalanchak 87 F4 Khersons'ka Oblast', S Ukraine
Kalarash see Călăraşi
Kalasin 114 D4 var. Muang Kalasin. Kalasin, E Thailand
Kalāt 101 E5 Per. Qalāt. Zābul, S Afghanistan
Kālat 112 B2 var. Kelat, Khelat. Baluchistān, SW Pakistan
Kalbarri 125 A5 Western Australia
Kalecik 94 C3 Ankara, N Turkey
Kalemie 55 E6 prev. Albertville. Shaba, SE Dem. Rep. Congo
Kale Sultanie see Çanakkale
Kalgan see Zhangjiakou
Kalgoorlie 125 B6 Western Australia
Kalima 55 D6 Maniema, E Dem. Rep. Congo
Kalimantan 116 D4 Eng. Indonesian Borneo. Geopolitical region Borneo, C Indonesia
Kálimnos see Kálymnos
Kaliningrad see Kaliningradskaya Oblast'
Kaliningrad 84 A4 Kaliningradskaya Oblast', W Russian Federation
Kaliningradskaya Oblast' 84 B4 var. Kaliningrad. Admin. region province and enclave W Russian Federation
Kalinkavichy 85 C7 Rus. Kalinkovichi. Homyel'skaya Voblasts', SE Belarus
Kalispell 44 B1 Montana, NW USA
Kalisz 76 C4 Ger. Kalisch, Rus. Kalish; anc. Calisia. Wielkopolskie, C Poland
Kalix 62 D4 Norrbotten, N Sweden
Kalixälven 62 D3 river N Sweden
Kallaste 84 E3 Ger. Krasnogor. Tartumaa, SE Estonia
Kallavesi 63 E5 lake SE Finland
Kalloní 83 D5 Lésvos, E Greece
Kalmar 63 C7 var. Calmar. Kalmar, S Sweden
Kalmthout 65 C5 Antwerpen, N Belgium
Kalpáki 82 A4 Ípeiros, W Greece
Kalpeni Island 110 B3 island Lakshadweep, India, N Indian Ocean
Kaluga 89 B5 Kaluzhskaya Oblast', W Russian Federation
Kalush 86 C2 Pol. Kałusz. Ivano-Frankivs'ka Oblast', W Ukraine
Kalutara 110 D4 Western Province, SW Sri Lanka
Kalvarija 85 B5 Pol. Kalwaria. Marijampolė, S Lithuania
Kalyān 112 C5 Mahārāshtra, W India
Kálymnos 83 D6 var. Kálimnos. Island Dodekánisos, Greece, Aegean Sea
Kama 88 D4 river NW Russian Federation
Kamarang 37 F3 W Guyana
Kamchatka see Kamchatka, Poluostrov
Kamchatka, Poluostrov 93 G3 Eng. Kamchatka. Peninsula E Russian Federation
Kamensk-Shakhtinskiy 89 B6 Rostovskaya Oblast', SW Russian Federation
Kamina 55 D7 Shaba, S Dem. Rep. Congo
Kamishli see Al Qāmishlī
Kamloops 15 E5 British Columbia, SW Canada
Kammu Seamount 130 C2 undersea feature N Pacific Ocean
Kampala 51 B6 country capital (Uganda) S Uganda
Kâmpóng Cham 115 D6 prev. Kompong Cham. Kâmpóng Cham, C Cambodia
Kâmpóng Chhnăng 115 D6 prev. Kompong. Kâmpóng Chhnăng, C Cambodia
Kâmpóng Saôm 115 D6 prev. Kompong Som, Sihanoukville. Kâmpóng Saôm, SW Cambodia
Kâmpóng Spoe 115 D6 prev. Kompong Speu. Kâmpóng Spœ, S Cambodia
Kâmpôt 115 D6 Kâmpôt, SW Cambodia
Kam"yanets'-Podil's'kyy 86 C3 Rus. Kamenets-Podol'skiy. Khmel'nyts'ka Oblast', W Ukraine
Kam"yanka-Dniprovs'ka 87 F3 Rus. Kamenka Dneprovskaya. Zaporiz'ka Oblast', SE Ukraine
Kamyshin 89 B6 Volgogradskaya Oblast', SW Russian Federation
Kanaky see New Caledonia
Kananga 55 D6 prev. Luluabourg. Kasai Occidental, S Dem. Rep. Congo
Kananur see Cannanore
Kanara see Karnātaka
Kanash 89 C5 Chuvashskaya Respublika, W Russian Federation
Kanazawa 109 C5 Ishikawa, Honshū, SW Japan
Kanbe 114 B4 Yangon, SW Myanmar
Kānchīpuram 110 C2 prev. Conjeeveram. Tamil Nādu, SE India
Kandahār 101 E5 Per. Qandahār. Kandahār, S Afghanistan
Kandalakša see Kandalaksha
Kandalaksha 88 B2 var. Kandalakša, Fin. Kantalahti. Murmanskaya Oblast', NW Russian Federation
Kandangan 116 D4 Borneo, C Indonesia
Kandava 84 C3 Ger. Kandau. Tukums, W Latvia
Kandi 53 F4 N Benin
Kandy 110 D3 Central Province, C Sri Lanka
Kane Fracture Zone 44 B4 tectonic feature NW Atlantic Ocean
Kāne'ohe 25 A8 var. Kaneohe. O'ahu, Hawai'i, USA, C Pacific Ocean
Kangān 98 D4 Būshehr, S Iran
Kangaroo Island 127 A7 island South Australia
Kangertittivaq 61 E4 Dan. Scoresby Sund. Fjord E Greenland
Kangikajik 61 E4 var. Kap Brewster. Headland E Greenland
Kaniv 87 E2 Rus. Kanëv. Cherkas'ka Oblast', C Ukraine
Kanivs'ke Vodoskhovyshche 87 E2 Rus. Kanevskoye Vodokhranilishche. Reservoir C Ukraine
Kanjiža 78 D2 Ger. Altkanischa, Hung. Magyarkanizsa, Ókanizsa; prev. Stara Kanjiža. Serbia, N Serbia and Montenegro (Yugo.)
Kankaanpää 63 D5 Länsi-Suomi, W Finland
Kankakee 18 B3 Illinois, N USA
Kankan 52 D4 Haute-Guinée, E Guinea
Kannur see Cannanore
Kano 53 G4 Kano, N Nigeria
Kānpur 113 E3 Eng. Cawnpore. Uttar Pradesh, N India
Kansas 27 F1 off. State of Kansas; also known as Jayhawker State, Sunflower State. State C USA
Kansas 23 F5 Kansas, C USA
Kansas City 23 F4 Kansas, C USA
Kansas City 23 F4 Missouri, C USA
Kansas River 23 F5 river Kansas, C USA
Kansk 93 E4 Krasnoyarskiy Kray, S Russian Federation
Kansu see Gansu
Kantalahti see Kandalaksha
Kántanos 83 C7 Kríti, Greece, E Mediterranean Sea
Kantemirovka 89 B6 Voronezhskaya Oblast', W Russian Federation
Kanton 123 F3 var. Abariringa, Canton Island; prev. Mary Island. Atoll Phoenix Islands, C Kiribati
Kanye 56 C4 Southern, SE Botswana
Kaohsiung 106 D6 var. Gaoxiong, Jap. Takao, Takow. S Taiwan
Kaolack 52 B3 var. Kaolak. W Senegal
Kaolak see Kaolack
Kaolan see Lanzhou
Kaoma 56 C2 Western, W Zambia
Kap Brewster see Kangikajik
Kapelle 65 B5 Zeeland, SW Netherlands
Kapellen 65 C5 Antwerpen, N Belgium
Kap Farvel see Uummannarsuaq
Kapka, Massif du 54 C2 mountain range E Chad
Kaplangky, Plato see Gaplañgyr Platosy
Kapoeta 51 C5 Eastern Equatoria, SE Sudan
Kaposvár 77 C7 Somogy, SW Hungary
Kappeln 72 B2 Schleswig-Holstein, N Germany
Kapstad see Cape Town
Kaptsevichy 85 C7 Rus. Koptsevichi. Homyel'skaya Voblasts', SE Belarus
Kapuas, Sungai 116 C4 prev. Kapoeas. River Borneo, C Indonesia
Kapuskasing 16 C4 Ontario, S Canada
Kapyl' 85 C6 Rus. Kopyl'. Minskaya Voblasts', C Belarus
Kap York see Innaanganeq
Kara-Balta 101 F2 Chuyskaya Oblast', N Kyrgyzstan
Karabil', Vozvyshennost' see Garabil Belentligi
Kara-Bogaz-Gol, Zaliv see Garabogaz Aylagy
Karabük 94 C2 Karabük NW Turkey
Karāchi 112 B3 Sind, SE Pakistan
Karadeniz see Black Sea
Karadeniz Boğazı see İstanbul Boğazı
Karaferiye see Véroia
Karaganda 92 C4 Kaz. Qaraghandy. Karaganda, C Kazakhstan
Karaginskiy, Ostrov 93 H2 island E Russian Federation
Karak see Al Karak
Kara-Kala see Garrygala
Karakax see Moyu
Karakılısse see Ağrı
Karakol 101 G2 prev. Przheval'sk. Issyk-Kul'skaya Oblast', NE Kyrgyzstan

Karakol 101 G2 *var.* Karakolka. Issyk-Kul'skaya Oblast', NE Kyrgyzstan
Karakolka *see* Karakol
Karakoram Range 112 D1 *mountain range* C Asia
Karaköse *see* Ağrı
Kara Kum *see* Garagum
Kara Kum Canal *see* Garagum Kanaly
Karakumskiy Kanal *see* Garagum Kanaly
Karakumy, Peski *see* Garagum
Karamai *see* Karamay
Karaman 94 C4 Karaman, S Turkey
Karamay 104 B2 *var.* Karamai, Kelamayi, *prev. Chin.* K'o-la-ma-i. Xinjiang Uygur Zizhiqu, NW China
Karamea Bight 129 B5 *gulf* South Island, NZ
Karapelit 82 E1 *Rom.* Stejarul. Dobrich, NE Bulgaria
Kara-Say 101 G2 Issyk-Kul'skaya Oblast', NE Kyrgyzstan
Karasburg 56 B4 Karas, S Namibia
Kara Sea *see* Karskoye More
Karatau 92 C5 *Kaz.* Qarataū. Zhambyl, S Kazakhstan
Karavás 83 B7 Kýthira, S Greece
Karbalā' 98 B3 *var.* Kerbala, Kerbela. S Iraq
Kardhítsa *see* Karditsa
Karditsa 83 B5 *var.* Kardhítsa. Thessalía, C Greece
Kärdla 84 C2 *Ger.* Kertel. Hiiumaa, W Estonia
Karet *see* Kâghet
Kargı 94 C2 Çorum, N Turkey
Kargilik *see* Yecheng
Kariba 56 D2 Mashonaland West, N Zimbabwe
Kariba, Lake 56 D3 *reservoir* Zambia/Zimbabwe
Karibib 56 B3 Erongo, C Namibia
Karies *see* Karyés
Karigasniemi 62 D2 *Lapp.* Garegegasnjárga. Lappi, N Finland
Karimata, Selat 116 C4 *strait* W Indonesia
Karīmnagar 112 D5 Andhra Pradesh, C India
Karin 50 D4 Woqooyi Galbeed, N Somalia
Kariot *see* Ikaría
Káristos *see* Kárystos
Karkinits'ka Zatoka 87 E4 *Rus.* Karkinitskiy Zaliv. *Gulf* S Ukraine
Karkük *see* Kirkük
Karlovac 78 B3 *Ger.* Karlstadt, *Hung.* Károlyváros. Karlovac, C Croatia
Karlovy Vary 77 A5 *Ger.* Karlsbad; *prev.* Carlsbad. Karlovarský Kraj, W Czech Republic
Karlskrona 63 C7 Blekinge, S Sweden
Karlsruhe 73 B6 *var.* Carlsruhe. Baden-Württemberg, SW Germany
Karlstad 63 B6 Värmland, C Sweden
Karnāl 112 D2 Haryāna, N India
Karnātaka 110 C1 *var.* Kanara; *prev.* Maisur, Mysore. Admin. region *state* W India
Karnobat 82 D2 Burgas, E Bulgaria
Karnul *see* Kurnool
Karpaten *see* Carpathian Mountains
Kárpathos 83 E7 *It.* Scarpanto; *anc.* Carpathos, Carpathus. Island SE Greece
Kárpathos 83 E7 Kárpathos, SE Greece
Karpaty *see* Carpathian Mountains
Karpenísi 83 B5 *prev.* Karpenísion. Stereá Ellás, C Greece
Kars 95 F2 *var.* Qars. Kars, NE Turkey
Kārsava 84 D4 *Ger.* Karsau; *prev. Rus.* Korsovka. Ludza, E Latvia
Karskiye Vorota, Proliv 88 E2 *Eng.* Kara Strait. *Strait* N Russian Federation
Karskoye More 92 D2 *Eng.* Kara Sea. *Sea* Arctic Ocean
Karyés 82 C4 *var.* Karies. Ágion Óros, N Greece
Kárystos 83 C6 *var.* Káristos. Évvoia, C Greece
Kasai 55 C6 *var.* Cassai, Kassai. *River* Angola/Dem. Rep. Congo
Kasaji 55 D7 Shaba, S Dem. Rep. Congo
Kasama 56 D1 Northern, N Zambia
Kāsaragod 110 B2 Kerala, SW India
Kāshān 98 C3 Eşfahān, C Iran
Kashi 104 A3 *Chin.* Kaxgar, K'o-shih, *Uigh.* Kashgar. Xinjiang Uygur Zizhiqu, NW China
Kasongo 55 D6 Maniema, E Dem. Rep. Congo
Kasongo-Lunda 55 C7 Bandundu, SW Dem. Rep. Congo
Kásos 83 D7 *island* S Greece
Kaspiysk 89 B8 Respublika Dagestan, SW Russian Federation
Kassai *see* Kasai
Kassala 50 C4 Kassala, E Sudan
Kassel 72 B4 *prev.* Cassel. Hessen, C Germany
Kasserine 49 E2 *var.* Al Qaşrayn. W Tunisia
Kastamonu 94 C2 *var.* Castamoni, Kastamuni. Kastamonu, N Turkey
Kastamuni *see* Kastamonu
Kastaneá 82 B4 Kentrikí Makedonía, N Greece
Kastélli 83 C7 Kríti, Greece, E Mediterranean Sea
Kastoría 82 B4 Dytikí Makedonía, N Greece
Kástro 83 C6 Sífnos, Kykládes, Greece, Aegean Sea
Kastsyukovichy 85 E7 *Rus.* Kostyukovichi. Mahilyowskaya Voblasts', E Belarus
Kastsyukowka 85 D7 *Rus.* Kostyukovka. Homyel'skaya Voblasts', SE Belarus
Kasulu 51 B7 Kigoma, W Tanzania
Kasumiga-ura 109 D5 *lake* Honshū, S Japan
Katahdin, Mount 19 G1 *mountain* Maine, NE USA
Katalla 14 C3 Alaska, USA
Katana *see* Qaţanā
Katanning 125 B7 Western Australia
Katawaz *see* Zarghūn Shahr
Katchall Island 111 F3 *island* Nicobar Islands, India, NE Indian Ocean

Kateríni 82 B4 Kentrikí Makedonía, N Greece
Katha 114 B2 Sagaing, N Myanmar
Katherine 126 A2 Northern Territory, N Australia
Kathmandu 102 C3 *prev.* Kantipur. *Country capital* (Nepal) Central, C Nepal
Katikati 128 D3 Bay of Plenty, North Island, NZ
Katima Mulilo 56 C3 Caprivi, NE Namibia
Katiola 52 D4 C Côte d'Ivoire
Káto Achaḯa 83 B5 *var.* Kato Ahaia, Káto Akhaïa. Dytikí Ellás, S Greece
Kato Ahaia *see* Káto Achaḯa
Káto Akhaïa *see* Káto Achaḯa
Katoúna 83 A5 Dytikí Ellás, C Greece
Katowice 77 C5 *Ger.* Kattowitz. Śląskie, S Poland
Katsina 53 G3 Katsina, N Nigeria
Kattaqo'rg'on 101 E2 *var.* Kattaqŭrghon, *Rus.* Kattakurgan. Samarqand Wiloyati, C Uzbekistan
Kattaqŭrghon *see* Kattaqo'rg'on
Kattavía 83 E7 Ródos, Dodekánisos, Greece, Aegean Sea
Kattegat 63 B7 *Dan.* Kattegatt. *Strait* N Europe
Kaua'i 25 A7 *var.* Kauai. *Island* Hawaiian Islands, Hawai'i, USA, C Pacific Ocean
Kaufbeuren 73 C6 Bayern, S Germany
Kaunas 84 B4 *Ger.* Kauen, *Pol.* Kowno; *prev. Rus.* Kovno. Kaunas, C Lithuania
Kavadarci 79 E6 *Turk.* Kavadar. C FYR Macedonia
Kavajë 79 C6 *It.* Cavaia, Kavaja. Tiranë, W Albania
Kavála 82 C3 *prev.* Kaválla. Anatolikí Makedonía kai Thráki, NE Greece
Kāvali 110 D2 Andhra Pradesh, E India
Kavango *see* Cubango
Kavaratti Island 110 A3 *island* Lakshadweep, India, N Indian Ocean
Kavarna 82 E2 Dobrich, NE Bulgaria
Kavengo *see* Cubango
Kavīr, Dasht-e 98 D3 *var.* Great Salt Desert. *Salt pan* N Iran
Kavīr-e Lūt *see* Lūt, Dasht-e
Kawagoe 109 D5 Saitama, Honshū, S Japan
Kawasaki 108 A2 Kanagawa, Honshū, S Japan
Kawerau 128 E3 Bay of Plenty, North Island, NZ
Kaya 53 E3 C Burkina faso
Kayan 114 B4 Yangon, SW Myanmar
Kayan, Sungai 116 D3 *prev.* Kajan. *River* Borneo, C Indonesia
Kayes 52 C3 Kayes, W Mali
Kayseri 94 D3 *var.* Kaisaria; *anc.* Caesarea Mazaca, Mazaca. Kayseri, C Turkey
Kazach'ye 93 F2 Respublika Sakha (Yakutiya), NE Russian Federation
Kazakhskiy Melkosopochnik 92 C4 *Eng.* Kazakh Uplands, Kirghiz Steppe, *Kaz.* Saryarqa. *Uplands* C Kazakhstan
Kazakhstan 92 B4 *var.* Kazakstan, *Kaz.* Qazaqstan, Qazaqstan Respublikasy; *prev.* Kazakh Soviet Socialist Republic, *Rus.* Kazakhskaja SSR. *Country* C Asia
Kazakstan *see* Kazakhskiy Melkosopochnik
Kazan' 89 C5 Respublika Tatarstan, W Russian Federation
Kazanlŭk 82 D2 *prev.* Kazanlik. Stara Zagora, C Bulgaria
Kazbegi *see* Kazbek
Kazbek 95 F1 *var.* Kazbegi, *Geor.* Mqinvartsveri. *Mountain* N Georgia
Kāzerūn 98 D4 Fārs, S Iran
Kazvin *see* Qazvīn
Kéa 83 C6 *prev.* Kéos, *anc.* Ceos. *Island* Kykládes, Greece, Aegean Sea
Kéa 83 C6 Kéa, Kykládes, Greece, Aegean Sea
Kea, Mauna 25 B8 *mountain* Hawai'i, USA, C Pacific Ocean
Kéamu *see* Aneityum
Kearney 23 E4 Nebraska, C USA
Keban Baraji 95 E3 *reservoir* C Turkey
Kebkabiya 50 A4 Northern Darfur, W Sudan
Kebnekaise 62 C3 *mountain* N Sweden
Kecskemét 77 D7 Bács-Kiskun, C Hungary
Kediri 116 D5 Jawa, C Indonesia
Kędzierzyn-Kole 77 C5 *Ger.* Heydebrech. Opolskie, S Poland
Keelung *see* Chilung
Keetmanshoop 56 B4 Karas, S Namibia
Kefallinía 83 A5 *var.* Kefalloniá. *Island* Iónioi Nísoi, Greece, C Mediterranean Sea
Kefalloniá *see* Kefallinía
Kefe *see* Feodosiya
Kehl 73 A6 Baden-Württemberg, SW Germany
Keila 84 D2 *Ger.* Kegel. Harjumaa, NW Estonia
Keïta 53 F3 Tahoua, C Niger
Keitele 62 D4 *lake* C Finland
Keith 127 B7 South Australia
Kёk-Art 101 G2 *prev.* Alaykel', Alay-Kuu. Oshskaya Oblast', SW Kyrgyzstan
Kékes 77 C6 *mountain* N Hungary
Kelamayi *see* Karamay
Kelang *see* Klang
Kelat *see* Kālāt
Kelifskiy Uzboy *see* Kelif Uzboýy
Kelif Uzboýy 100 D3 *var.* Kelifskiy Uzboy. *Salt marsh* E Turkmenistan
Kelkit Çayı 95 E3 *river* N Turkey
Kelmė 84 B4 *var.* Kelmé, C Lithuania
Kélo 54 B4 Tandjilé, SW Chad
Kelowna 15 E5 British Columbia, SW Canada
Kelso 24 B2 Washington, NW USA
Keluang 116 B3 *var.* Kluang. Johor, Peninsular Malaysia
Kem' 88 B3 Respublika Kareliya, NW Russian Federation

Kemah 95 E3 Erzincan, E Turkey
Kemaman *see* Cukai
Kemerovo 92 D4 *prev.* Shcheglovsk. Kemerovskaya Oblast', C Russian Federation
Kemi 62 D4 Lappi, NW Finland
Kemijärvi 62 D3 *Swe.* Kemiträsk. Lappi, N Finland
Kemijoki 62 D3 *river* NW Finland
Kemin 101 G2 *prev.* Bystrovka. Chuyskaya Oblast', N Kyrgyzstan
Kempele 62 D4 Oulu, C Finland
Kempten 73 B7 Bayern, S Germany
Kendal 67 D5 NW England, UK
Kendari 117 E4 Sulawesi, C Indonesia
Kenedy 27 G4 Texas, SW USA
Kenema 52 C4 SE Sierra Leone
Kёneurgench *see* Köneürgenç
Kenge 55 C6 Bandundu, SW Dem. Rep. Congo
Keng Tung 114 C3 *var.* Kentung. Shan State, E Myanmar
Kénitra 48 C2 *prev.* Port-Lyautey. NW Morocco
Kennett 23 H5 Missouri, C USA
Kennewick 24 C2 Washington, NW USA
Kenora 16 A3 Ontario, S Canada
Kenosha 18 B3 Wisconsin, N USA
Kentau 92 B5 Yuzhnyy Kazakhstan, S Kazakhstan
Kentucky 18 C5 *off.* Commonwealth of Kentucky; also known as The Bluegrass State. *State* C USA
Kentucky Lake 18 B5 *reservoir* Kentucky/Tennessee, S USA
Kentung *see* Keng Tung
Kenya 51 C6 *Country* E Africa
Keokuk 23 G4 Iowa, C USA
Kępno 76 C4 Wielkopolskie, C Poland
Keppel Island *see* Niuatoputapu
Kepulauan Sangihe *see* Sangir, Kepulauan
Kerak *see* Al Karak
Kerala 110 C2 *state* S India
Kerasunt *see* Giresun
Keratea *see* Keratéa
Keratéa 83 C6 *var.* Keratea. Attikí, C Greece
Kerbala *see* Karbalā'
Kerbela *see* Karbalā'
Kerch 87 G5 *Rus.* Kerch'. Respublika Krym, SE Ukraine
Kerchens'ka Protska *see* Kerch Strait
Kerchenskiy Proliv *see* Kerch Strait
Kerch Strait 87 G4 *var.* Bosporus Cimmerius, Enikale Strait, *Rus.* Kerchenskiy Proliv, *Ukr.* Kerchens'ka Protska. *Strait* Black Sea/Sea of Azov
Kerguelen 119 C7 *island* C French Southern and Antarctic Territories
Kerguelen Plateau 119 C7 *undersea feature* S Indian Ocean
Kerí 83 A6 Zákynthos, Iónioi Nísoi, Greece, C Mediterranean Sea
Kerikeri 128 D2 Northland, North Island, NZ
Kerkenah, Îles de 80 D4 *var.* Kerkenna Islands, *Ar.* Juzur Qarqannah. *Island group* E Tunisia
Kerkenna Islands *see* Kerkenah, Îles de
Kérkira *see* Kérkyra
Kerkrade 65 D6 Limburg, SE Netherlands
Kerkuk *see* Kirkūk
Kérkyra 82 A4 *var.* Kérkira, *Eng.* Corfu. *Island* Iónioi Nisoi, Greece, C Mediterranean Sea
Kermadec Islands 130 C4 *island group* NZ, SW Pacific Ocean
Kermadec Trench 121 E4 *undersea feature* SW Pacific Ocean
Kermān 98 D3 *var.* Kirman; *anc.* Carmana. Kermān, C Iran
Kermānshāh 98 C3 *var.* Qahremānshahr; *prev.* Bākhtarān. Kermānshāh, W Iran
Kerrville 27 F4 Texas, SW USA
Kerulen 105 E2 *Chin.* Herlen He, *Mong.* Herlen Gol. *River* China/Mongolia
Kerýneia 80 C5 *var.* Girne, Kyrenia. N Cyprus
Kesennuma 108 D4 Miyagi, Honshū, C Japan
Keszthely 77 C7 Zala, SW Hungary
Ketchikan 14 D4 Revillagigedo Island, Alaska, USA
Kętrzyn 76 D2 *Ger.* Rastenburg. Warmiusko-Mazurskie, NE Poland
Kettering 67 D6 C England, UK
Kettering 18 C4 Ohio, N USA
Keuruu 63 D5 Länsi-Suomi, W Finland
Keweenaw Peninsula 18 B1 *peninsula* Michigan, N USA
Key Largo 21 F5 Key Largo, Florida, SE USA
Key West 21 E5 Florida Keys, Florida, SE USA
Khabarovsk 93 G4 Khabarovskiy Kray, SE Russian Federation
Khadera *see* Ḥadera
Khairpur 112 B3 Sind, SE Pakistan
Khalīj al 'Aqabah *see* Aqaba, Gulf of
Khalīj al 'Arabī *see* Gulf, The
Khalīj-e Fārs *see* Gulf, The
Khalkidhikí *see* Chalkidikí
Khalkís *see* Chalkída
Khambhat, Gulf of 112 C4 *Eng.* Gulf of Cambay. *Gulf* W India
Khamīs Mushayt 99 B6 *var.* Hamīs Musait. 'Asīr, SW Saudi Arabia
Khānābād 101 E3 Kunduz, NE Afghanistan
Khān al Baghdādī *see* Al Baghdādī
Khandwa 112 D4 Madhya Pradesh, C India
Khanh *see* Soc Trăng
Khaniá *see* Chaniá
Khanka, Lake 107 E2 *var.* Hsing-k'ai Hu, Lake Hanka, *Chin.* Xingkai Hu, *Rus.* Ozero Khanka. *Lake* China/Russian Federation
Khanthabouli 114 D4 *prev.* Savannakhét. Savannakhét, S Laos

Khanty-Mansiysk 92 C3 *prev.* Ostyako-Vogulsk. Khanty-Mansiyskiy Avtonomnyy Okrug, C Russian Federation
Khân Yûnis 97 A7 *var.* Khān Yūnus. S Gaza Strip
Khān Yūnus *see* Khân Yûnis
Khanzi *see* Ghanzi
Kharagpur 113 F4 West Bengal, NE India
Kharbin *see* Harbin
Kharkiv 87 G2 *Rus.* Khar'kov. Kharkivs'ka Oblast', NE Ukraine
Kharmanli 82 D3 Khaskovo, S Bulgaria
Khartoum 50 B4 *var.* El Khartûm, Khartum. *Country capital* (Sudan) Khartoum, C Sudan
Khartum *see* Khartoum
Khasavyurt 89 B8 Respublika Dagestan, SW Russian Federation
Khash, Dasht-e 100 D5 *Eng.* Khash Desert. *Desert* SW Afghanistan
Khashim Al Qirba *see* Khashm el Girba
Khashm al Qirbah *see* Khashm el Girba
Khashm el Girba 50 C4 *var.* Khashim Al Qirba, Khashm al Qirbah. Kassala, E Sudan
Khaskovo 82 D3 Khaskovo, S Bulgaria
Khaydarkan 101 F2 *var.* Khaidarkan, Oshskaya Oblast', SW Kyrgyzstan
Khaydarken *see* Khaydarkan
Khelat *see* Kālāt
Kherson 87 E4 Khersons'ka Oblast', S Ukraine
Kheta 93 E2 *river* N Russian Federation
Khíos *see* Chíos
Khirbet el 'Aujâ et Tahtâ 119 E7 *var.* 'Aujā et Tahtā. E West Bank
Khiva *see* Xiva
Khiwa *see* Xiva
Khmel'nyts'kyy 86 C2 *Rus.* Khmel'nitskiy; *prev.* Proskurov. Khmel'nyts'ka Oblast', W Ukraine
Khodasy 85 E6 *Rus.* Khodosy. Mahilyowskaya Voblasts', E Belarus
Khodorov 86 C2 *Pol.* Chodorów, *Rus.* Khodorov. L'vivs'ka Oblast', NW Ukraine
Khodzhent *see* Khŭjand
Khoi *see* Khvoy
Khojend *see* Khŭjand
Khokand *see* Qo'qon
Kholm 101 E3 *var.* Tashqurghan, *Pash.* Khulm. Balkh, N Afghanistan
Kholon *see* Holon
Khoms *see* Al Khums
Khong Sedone *see* Muang Khôngxédôn
Khon Kaen 114 D4 *var.* Muang Khon Kaen. Khon Kaen, E Thailand
Khor 93 G4 Khabarovskiy Kray, SE Russian Federation
Khorat *see* Nakhon Ratchasima
Khorugh 101 F3 *Rus.* Khorog. S Tajikistan
Khotan *see* Hotan
Khouribga 48 B2 C Morocco
Khovd *see* Hovd
Khowst 101 F4 Paktiā, E Afghanistan
Khoy *see* Khvoy
Khoyniki 85 D8 *Rus.* Khoyniki. Homyel'skaya Voblasts', SE Belarus
Khrebet Kolymskiy *see* Kolyma Range
Khrebet Kopetdag *see* Koppeh Dāgh
Khrebet Lomonosova *see* Lomonosov Ridge
Khudzhand *see* Khŭjand
Khŭjand 101 E2 *var.* Khodzhent, Khojend, *Rus.* Khudzhand; *prev.* Leninabad, *Taj.* Leninobod. N Tajikistan
Khulm *see* Kholm
Khulna 113 G4 Khulna, SW Bangladesh
Khums *see* Al Khums
Khust 86 B3 *Cz.* Chust, Husté, *Hung.* Huszt. Zakarpats'ka Oblast', W Ukraine
Khvoy 98 C2 *var.* Khoi, Khoy. Āzārbāyjān-e Bākhtarī, NW Iran
Khyber Pass 112 C1 *var.* Kowtal-e Khaybar. *Pass* Afghanistan/Pakistan
Kiangmai *see* Chiang Mai
Kiang-ning *see* Nanjing
Kiangsi *see* Jiangxi
Kiangsu *see* Jiangsu
Kiáto 83 B6 *prev.* Kiáton. Pelopónnisos, S Greece
Kiayi *see* Chiai
Kibangou 55 B6 Le Niari, SW Congo
Kibombo 55 D6 Maniema, E Dem. Rep. Congo
Kičevo 79 D6 SW FYR Macedonia
Kidderminster 67 D6 C England, UK
Kiel 72 B2 Schleswig-Holstein, N Germany
Kielce 76 D4 *Rus.* Keltsy. Świętokrzyskie, C Poland
Kieler Bucht 72 B2 *bay* N Germany
Kiev *see* Kyyiv
Kiffa 52 C3 Assaba, S Mauritania
Kigali 51 B6 *country capital* (Rwanda) C Rwanda
Kigoma 51 B7 Kigoma, W Tanzania
Kihnu 84 C2 *var.* Kihnu Saar, *Ger.* Kühnö. *Island* SW Estonia
Kihnu Saar *see* Kihnu
Kii-suidō 109 C7 *strait* S Japan
Kikinda 78 D3 *Ger.* Grosskikinda, *Hung.* Nagykikinda; *prev.* Velika Kikinda. Serbia, N Serbia and Montenegro (Yugo.)
Kikládhes *see* Kykládes
Kikwit 55 C6 Bandundu, W Dem. Rep. Congo
Kilien Mountains *see* Qilian Shan
Kilimane *see* Quelimane
Kilimanjaro 51 C6 *var.* Uhuru Peak. *Mountain* NE Tanzania
Kilinailau 47 E5 *region* E Tanzania
Kilingi-Nõmme 84 D3 *Ger.* Kurkund. Pärnumaa, SW Estonia
Kilis 94 D4 Kilis S Turkey
Kiliya 86 D4 *Rom.* Chilia-Nouă. Odes'ka Oblast', SW Ukraine
Kilkenny 67 B6 *Ir.* Cill Chainnigh. S Ireland
Kilkís 82 B3 Kentrikí Makedonía, N Greece
Killarney 67 A6 *Ir.* Cill Airne. SW Ireland
Killeen 27 G3 Texas, SW USA

Kilmain *see* Quelimane
Kilmarnock 66 C4 W Scotland, UK
Kilwa *see* Kilwa Kivinje
Kilwa Kivinje 51 C7 *var.* Kilwa. Lindi, SE Tanzania
Kimberley 56 C4 Northern Cape, C South Africa
Kimberley Plateau 124 C3 *plateau* Western Australia
Kimch'aek 107 E3 *prev.* Sŏngjin. E North Korea
Kinabalu, Gunung 116 D3 *mountain* East Malaysia
Kindersley 15 F5 Saskatchewan, S Canada
Kindia 52 C4 Guinée-Maritime, SW Guinea
Kindley Field 20 A4 *air base* E Bermuda
Kindu 55 D6 *prev.* Kindu-Port-Empain. Maniema, C Dem. Rep. Congo
Kineshma 89 C5 Ivanovskaya Oblast', W Russian Federation
King Island 127 B8 *island* Tasmania, SE Australia
Kingman 26 A1 Arizona, SW USA
Kingman Reef 123 E2 *US territory* C Pacific Ocean
Kingsford Smith 126 E2 *international airport* (Sydney) New South Wales, SE Australia
King's Lynn 67 E6 *var.* Bishop's Lynn, Kings Lynn, Lynn, Lynn Regis. E England, UK
King Sound 124 C3 *sound* Western Australia
Kingston 21 E1 Tennessee, S USA
Kingston 32 B5 *country capital* (Jamaica) E Jamaica
Kingston 19 F3 New York, NE USA
Kingston 16 D5 Ontario, SE Canada
Kingston upon Hull 67 D5 *var.* Hull. E England, UK
Kingston upon Thames 67 A8 SE England, UK
Kingstown 33 H4 *country capital* (Saint Vincent and the Grenadines) Saint Vincent, Saint Vincent and the Grenadines
Kingsville 27 G5 Texas, SW USA
King William Island 15 F3 *island* Nunavut, N Canada Arctic Ocean
Kinrooi 65 D5 Limburg, NE Belgium
Kinshasa 55 B6 *prev.* Léopoldville. *Country capital* (Congo (Zaire)) Kinshasa, W Dem. Rep. Congo
Kintyre 66 B4 *peninsula* W Scotland, UK
Kinyeti 51 B5 *mountain* S Sudan
Kiparissía 83 B6 S Greece
Kipili 51 B7 Rukwa, W Tanzania
Kipushi 55 D8 Shaba, SE Dem. Rep. Congo
Kirdzhali *see* Kŭrdzhali
Kirghiz Range 101 F2 *Rus.* Kirgizskiy Khrebet; *prev.* Alexander Range. *Mountain range* Kazakhstan/Kyrgyzstan
Kirghiz Steppe *see* Kazakhskiy Melkosopochnik
Kiriath-Arba *see* Hebron
Kiribati 123 F2 *Country* C Pacific Ocean
Kırıkhan 94 D4 Hatay, S Turkey
Kırıkkale 94 C3 Kırıkkale, C Turkey
Kirin *see* Jilin
Kirinyaga 51 C6 *prev.* Mount Kenya. *Volcano* C Kenya
Kirishi 88 B4 *var.* Kirisi. Leningradskaya Oblast', NW Russian Federation
Kirisi *see* Kirishi
Kiritimati 123 G2 *prev.* Christmas Island. *Atoll* Line Islands, E Kiribati
Kirkenes 62 E2 *var.* Kirkkoniemi. Finnmark, N Norway
Kirkkoniemi *see* Kirkenes
Kirkland Lake 16 D4 Ontario, S Canada
Kırklareli 94 A2 *prev.* Kirk-Kilissa. Kırklareli, NW Turkey
Kirkpatrick, Mount 132 B3 *mountain* Antarctica
Kirksville 23 G4 Missouri, C USA
Kirkūk 98 B3 *var.* Karkūk, Kerkuk. N Iraq
Kirkwall 66 C2 NE Scotland, UK
Kirkwood 23 G4 Missouri, C USA
Kirman *see* Kermān
Kir Moab *see* Al Karak
Kirov 89 C5 *prev.* Vyatka. Kirovskaya Oblast', NW Russian Federation
Kirovo-Chepetsk 89 D5 Kirovskaya Oblast', NW Russian Federation
Kirovohrad 87 E3 *Rus.* Kirovograd; *prev.* Kirovo, Yelizavetgrad, Zinov'yevsk. Kirovohrads'ka Oblast', C Ukraine
Kirthar Range 112 B3 *mountain range* S Pakistan
Kirun *see* Chilung
Kiruna 62 C3 Norrbotten, N Sweden
Kisangani 55 D5 *prev.* Stanleyville. Orientale, NE Dem. Rep. Congo
Kislovodsk 89 B7 Stavropol'skiy Kray, SW Russian Federation
Kismaayo 51 D6 *var.* Chisimayu, Kismayu, *It.* Chisimaio. Jubbada Hoose, S Somalia
Kismayu *see* Kismaayo
Kissidougou 52 C4 Guinée-Forestière, S Guinea
Kissimmee, Lake 21 E4 *lake* Florida, SE USA
Kisumu 51 C6 *prev.* Port Florence. Nyanza, W Kenya
Kisvárda 77 E6 *Ger.* Kleinwardein. Szabolcs-Szatmár-Bereg, E Hungary
Kita 52 D3 Kayes, W Mali
Kitakyūshū 109 A7 *var.* Kitakyūsyū. Fukuoka, Kyūshū, SW Japan
Kitakyūsyū *see* Kitakyūshū
Kitami 108 D2 Hokkaidō, NE Japan
Kitchener 16 C5 Ontario, S Canada
Kíthira *see* Kýthira
Kitimat 14 D4 British Columbia, SW Canada
Kitinen 62 D3 *river* N Finland
Kitob 101 E3 *Rus.* Kitab. Qashqadaryo Wiloyati, S Uzbekistan
Kitwe 56 D2 *var.* Kitwe-Nkana. Copperbelt, C Zambia

Kitwe-Nkana see Kitwe
Kitzbühler Alpen 73 C7 mountain range W Austria
Kivalina 14 C2 Alaska, USA
Kivalo 62 D3 ridge C Finland
Kivertsi 86 C1 Pol. Kiwerce, Rus. Kivertsy. Volyns'ka Oblast', NW Ukraine
Kivu, Lake 55 E6 Fr. Lac Kivu. Lake Rwanda/Dem. Rep. Congo
Kızıl Irmak 94 C3 river C Turkey
Kizil Kum see Kyzyl Kum
Kladno 77 A5 Středočesky Kraj, NW Czech Republic
Klagenfurt 73 D7 Slvn. Celovec. Kärnten, S Austria
Klaipėda 84 B3 Ger. Memel. Klaipėda, NW Lithuania
Klamath Falls 24 B4 Oregon, NW USA
Klamath Mountains 24 A4 mountain range California/Oregon, W USA
Klang 116 B3 var. Kelang; prev. Port Swettenham. Selangor, Peninsular Malaysia
Klarälven 63 B6 river Norway/Sweden
Klatovy 77 A5 Ger. Klattau. Plzeňský Kraj, W Czech Republic
Klazienaveen 64 E2 Drenthe, NE Netherlands
Klein Karas 56 B4 Karas, S Namibia
Kleisoúra 83 A5 Ípeiros, W Greece
Klerksdorp 56 D4 North-West, N South Africa
Klimavichy 85 E7 Rus. Klimovichi. Mahilyowskaya Voblasts', E Belarus
Klintsy 89 A5 Bryanskaya Oblast', W Russian Federation
Klisura 82 C2 Plovdiv, C Bulgaria
Ključ 78 B3 Federacija Bosna I Hercegovina, NW Bosnia and Herzegovina
Kłobuck 76 C4 Śląskie, S Poland
Klosters 73 B7 Graubünden, SE Switzerland
Kluang see Keluang
Kluczbork 76 C4 Ger. Kreuzburg, Kreuzburg in Oberschlesien. Opolskie, S Poland
Klyuchevskaya Sopka, Vulkan 93 H3 volcano E Russian Federation
Knin 78 B4 Šibenik-Knin, S Croatia
Knjaževac 78 E4 Serbia, E Serbia and Montenegro (Yugo.)
Knokke-Heist 65 A5 West-Vlaanderen, NW Belgium
Knoxville 20 D1 Tennessee, S USA
Knud Rasmussen Land 60 D1 physical region N Greenland
Kōbe 109 C6 Hyōgo, Honshū, SW Japan
København 63 B7 Eng. Copenhagen; anc. Hafnia. Country capital (Denmark) Sjælland, København, E Denmark
Kobenni 52 D3 Hodh el Gharbi, S Mauritania
Koblenz 73 A5 prev. Coblenz, Fr. Coblence, anc. Confluentes. Rheinland-Pfalz, W Germany
Kobryn 85 A6 Pol. Kobryn, Rus. Kobrin. Brestskaya Voblasts', SW Belarus
K'obulet'i 95 F2 W Georgia
Kočani 79 E6 NE FYR Macedonia
Kočevje 73 D8 Ger. Gottschee. S Slovenia
Koch Bihār 113 G3 West Bengal, NE India
Kōchi 109 B7 var. Kôti. Kōchi, Shikoku, SW Japan
Kochi see Cochin
Kochiu see Gejiu
Kodiak 14 C3 Kodiak Island, Alaska, USA
Kodiak Island 14 C3 island Alaska, USA
Koeln see Köln
Ko-erh-mu see Golmud
Koetai see Mahakam, Sungai
Koetaradja see Bandaaceh
Kōfu 109 D5 var. Kôhu. Yamanashi, Honshū, S Japan
Kogarah 126 E2 New South Wales, SE Australia
Kogon 100 D2 Rus. Kagan. Bukhoro Wiloyati, C Uzbekistan
Kohīma 113 H3 Nāgāland, E India
Koh I Noh see Büyükağrı Dağı
Kohtla-Järve 84 E2 Ida-Virumaa, NE Estonia
Kōhu see Kōfu
Kokand see Qo'qon
Kokkola 62 D4 Swe. Karleby; prev. Swe. Gamlakarleby. Länsi-Suomi, W Finland
Koko see Qinghai Hu
Koko 53 F4 Kebbi, W Nigeria
Kokomo 18 C4 Indiana, N USA
Koko Nor see Qinghai
Kokrines 14 C2 Alaska, USA
Kokshaal-Tau 101 G2 Rus. Khrebet Kakshaal-Too. Mountain range China/Kyrgyzstan
Kokshetau 92 C4 Kaz. Kökshetaū; prev. Kokchetav. Severnyy Kazakhstan, N Kazakhstan
Koksijde 65 A5 West-Vlaanderen, W Belgium
Koksoak 16 D2 river Québec, E Canada
Kokstad 56 D5 KwaZulu/Natal, E South Africa
Kola see Kol'skiy Poluostrov
Kolaka 117 E4 Sulawesi, C Indonesia
Kolam see Quilon
K'o-la-ma-i see Karamay
Kola Peninsula see Kol'skiy Poluostrov
Kolari 62 D3 Lappi, NW Finland
Kolárovo 77 C6 Ger. Gutta; prev. Guta, Hung. Gúta. Nitriansky Kraj, SW Slovakia
Kolda 52 C3 S Senegal
Kolding 63 A7 Vejle, C Denmark
Kölen 59 E1 Nor. Kjølen. Mountain range Norway/Sweden
Kolguyev, Ostrov 88 C2 island NW Russian Federation
Kolhāpur 110 B1 Mahārāshtra, SW India
Kolhumadulu Atoll 110 A5

Kolín 77 B5 Ger. Kolin. Středočesky Kraj, C Czech Republic

Kolka 84 C2 Talsi, NW Latvia
Kolkasrags 84 C2 var. Eng. Cape Domesnes. Headland NW Latvia
Kolkata see Calcutta
Kollam see Quilon
Köln 72 A4 var. Koeln, Eng./Fr. Cologne; prev. Cöln, anc. Colonia Agrippina, Oppidum Ubiorum. Nordrhein-Westfalen, W Germany
Koło 76 C3 Wielkopolskie, C Poland
Kołobrzeg 76 B2 Ger. Kolberg. Zachodniopomorskie, NW Poland
Kolokani 74 D3 Koulikoro, W Mali
Kolomna 89 B5 Moskovskaya Oblast', W Russian Federation
Kolomyya 86 C3 Ger. Kolomea. Ivano-Frankivs'ka Oblast', W Ukraine
Kolpa 78 A2 Ger. Kulpa, SCr. Kupa. River Croatia/Slovenia
Kolpino 88 B4 Leningradskaya Oblast', NW Russian Federation
Kólpos Ammóchostos 80 C5 var. Famagusta Bay, bay E Cyprus
Kol'skiy Poluostrov 88 C2 Eng. Kola Peninsula. Peninsula NW Russian Federation
Kolumadulu Atoll see Kolhumadulu Atoll
Kolwezi 55 D7 Shaba, S Dem. Rep. Congo
Kolyma 93 G2 river NE Russian Federation
Kolyma Range 91 G2 var. Khrebet Kolymskiy, Eng. Kolyma Range. Mountain range E Russian Federation
Komatsu 109 C5 var. Komatu. Ishikawa, Honshū, SW Japan
Komatu see Komatsu
Kommunizm Pik see Kommunizm, Qullai
Kommunizm, Qullai 101 F3 var. Qullai Garmo, Eng. Communism Peak, Rus. Kommunizma Pik; prev. Stalin Peak. Mountain E Tajikistan
Komoé 52 M4 var. Komoé Fleuve. River E Côte d'Ivoire
Komoé Fleuve see Komoé
Komotiní 82 D3 var. Gümüljina, Turk. Gümülcine. Anatolikí Makedonía kai Thráki, NE Greece
Komsomolets, Ostrov 93 E1 island Severnaya Zemlya, N Russian Federation
Komsomol'sk-na-Amure 93 G4 Khabarovskiy Kray, SE Russian Federation
Kondolovo 82 E3 Burgas, E Bulgaria
Kondopoga 88 B3 Respublika Kareliya, NW Russian Federation
Kondoz see Kunduz
Kondūz see Kunduz
Köneürgenç 100 C2 Rus. Këneurgench; prev. Kunya-Urgench. Dashkhovuzskiy Velayat, N Turkmenistan
Kong Christian IX Land 60 D4 Eng. King Christian IX Land. Physical region SE Greenland
Kong Frederik IX Land 60 C3 Eng. King Frederik IX Land. Physical region SW Greenland
Kong Frederik VIII Land 61 E2 Eng. King Frederik VIII Land. Physical region NE Greenland
Kong Frederik VI Kyst 60 C4 Eng. King Frederik VI Coast. Physical region SE Greenland
Kong Karls Land 61 G2 Eng. King Charles Islands. Island group SE Svalbard
Kongo see Congo
Kongolo 55 D6 Shaba, E Dem. Rep. Congo
Kongor 51 B5 Jonglei, SE Sudan
Kong Oscar Fjord 61 E3 fjord E Greenland
Kongsberg 63 B6 Buskerud, S Norway
Kông, Tônle 115 E5 Lao. Xê Kong. River Cambodia/Laos
Konia see Konya
Konieh see Konya
Konin 76 C3 Ger. Kuhnau. Wielkopolskie, C Poland
Konispol 79 C7 var. Konispoli. Vlorë, S Albania
Konispoli see Konispol
Kónitsa 82 A4 Ípeiros, W Greece
Konitz see Chojnice
Konjic 78 C4 Federacija Bosna I Hercegovina, S Bosnia and Herzegovina
Konosha 88 C4 Arkhangel'skaya Oblast', NW Russian Federation
Konotop 87 F1 Sums'ka Oblast', NE Ukraine
Konstanz 73 B7 var. Constanz, Eng. Constance; hist. Kostnitz, anc. Constantia. Baden-Württemberg, S Germany
Konstanza see Constanţa
Konya 94 C4 var. Konieh; prev. Konia, anc. Iconium. Konya, C Turkey
Koosaanik 79 D5 mountain range S Serbia and Montenegro (Yugo.)
Koper 73 D8 It. Capodistria; prev. Kopar. SW Slovenia
Köpetdag Gershi 100 C3 mountain range Iran/Turkmenistan
Koppeh Dāgh 98 D2 var. Khrebet Kopetdag. Mountain range Iran/Turkmenistan
Koprivnica 78 B2 Ger. Kopreinitz, Hung. Kaproncza. Koprivnica-Križevci, N Croatia
Korat see Nakhon Ratchasima
Korat Plateau 114 D4 plateau E Thailand
Korba 113 E4 Madhya Pradesh, C India
Korça see Korçë
Korçë 79 D6 var. Korça, Gk. Korytsa, It. Corriza; prev. Koritsa. Korçë, SE Albania
Korčula 78 B4 It. Curzola; anc. Corcyra Nigra. Island S Croatia
Korea Bay 105 G3 bay China/North Korea
Korea Strait 109 A7 Jap. Chōsen-kaikyō, Kor. Taehan-haehyŏp. Channel Japan/South Korea
Korhogo 52 D4 N Côte d'Ivoire
Korinthiakós Kólpos 83 B5 Eng. Gulf of Corinth; anc. Corinthiacus Sinus. Gulf C Greece

Kórinthos 83 B6 Eng. Corinth; anc. Corinthus. Pelopónnisos, S Greece
Koritsa see Korçë
Kōriyama 109 D5 Fukushima, Honshū, C Japan
Korla 104 C3 Chin. K'u-erh-lo. Xinjiang Uygur Zizhiqu, NW China
Körmend 77 B7 Vas, W Hungary
Koróni 83 B6 Pelopónnisos, S Greece
Koror 122 A2 var. Oreor. Country capital (Palau) Oreor, N Palau
Korosten' 86 D1 Zhytomyrs'ka Oblast', NW Ukraine
Koro Toro 54 C2 Borkou-Ennedi-Tibesti, N Chad
Kortrijk 65 A6 Fr. Courtrai. West-Vlaanderen, W Belgium
Koryak Range see Koryakskoye Nagor'ye
Koryakskiy Khrebet see Koryakskoye Nagor'ye
Koryakskoye Nagor'ye 93 H2 var. Koryakskiy Khrebet, Eng. Koryak Range. Mountain range NE Russian Federation
Koryazhma 88 C4 Arkhangel'skaya Oblast', NW Russian Federation
Korytsa see Korçë
Kos 83 E6 It. Coo; anc. Cos. Island Dodekánisos, Greece, Aegean Sea
Kos 83 E6 Kos, Dodekánisos, Greece, Aegean Sea
Kō-saki 109 A7 headland Nagasaki, Tsushima, SW Japan
Kościan 76 B4 Ger. Kosten. Wielkopolskie, C Poland
Koscian see Lubań
Kościerzyna 76 C2 Pomorskie, NW Poland
Kosciusko, Mount see Kosciuszko, Mount
Kosciuszko, Mount 127 C7 prev. Mount Kosciusko. Mountain New South Wales, SE Australia
Koshikijima-rettō 109 A8 var. Kosikizima Rettō. Island group SW Japan
Košice 77 D6 Ger. Kaschau, Hung. Kassa. Košický Kraj, E Slovakia
Kosikizima Rettō see Koshikijima-rettō
Koson 101 E3 Rus. Kasan. Qashqadaryo Wiloyati, S Uzbekistan
Kosovo 79 D5 prev. Autonomous Province of Kosovo and Metohija. Region S Serbia and Montenegro (Yugo.)
Kosovo Polje 79 D5 Serbia, S Serbia and Montenegro (Yugo.)
Kosovska Mitrovica 79 D5 Alb. Mitrovicë; prev. Mitrovica, Titova Mitrovica. Serbia, S Serbia and Montenegro (Yugo.)
Kosrae 122 C2 prev. Kusaie. Island Caroline Islands, E Micronesia
Kossou, Lac de 52 D5 lake C Côte d'Ivoire
Kostanay 130 C4 var. Kustanay, Kaz. Qostanay. Kostanay, N Kazakhstan
Kosten see Lubań
Kostenets 82 C2 prev. Georgi Dimitrov. Sofiya, W Bulgaria
Kostnitz see Konstanz
Kostroma 88 B4 Kostromskaya Oblast', NW Russian Federation
Kostyantynivka 87 G3 Rus. Konstantinovka. Donets'ka Oblast', SE Ukraine
Koszalin 76 B2 Ger. Köslin. Zachodniopomorskie, NW Poland
Kota 112 D3 prev. Kotah. Rājasthān, N India
Kota Baharu see Kota Bharu
Kota Bahru see Kota Bharu
Kotabaru see Jayapura
Kota Bharu 116 B3 var. Kota Baharu, Kota Bahru. Kelantan, Peninsular Malaysia
Kotabumi 116 B4 prev. Kotaboemi. Sumatera, W Indonesia
Kota Kinabalu 116 D3 prev. Jesselton. Sabah, East Malaysia
Kotel'nyy, Ostrov 93 E2 island Novosibirskiye Ostrova, N Russian Federation
Kôti see Kōchi
Kotka 63 E5 Kymi, S Finland
Kotlas 88 C4 Arkhangel'skaya Oblast', NW Russian Federation
Kotonu see Cotonou
Kotor 79 C5 It. Cattaro. Montenegro, SW Serbia and Montenegro (Yugo.)
Kotovs'k 86 D3 Rus. Kotovsk. Odes'ka Oblast', SW Ukraine
Kotovsk see Hînceşti
Kotte see Sri Jayawardanapura
Kotto 54 D4 river Central African Republic/Dem. Rep. Congo
Kotuy 93 E2 river N Russian Federation
Koudougou 53 E4 C Burkina faso
Koulamoutou 55 B6 Ogooué-Lolo, C Gabon
Koulikoro 52 D3 Koulikoro, SW Mali
Koumra 54 C4 Moyen-Chari, S Chad
Kourou 37 H3 N French Guiana
Kousseir see Al Quşayr
Kousséri 54 B3 prev. Fort-Foureau. Extrême-Nord, NE Cameroon
Koutiala 52 D4 Sikasso, S Mali
Kouvola 63 E5 Kymi, S Finland
Kovel' 86 C1 Pol. Kowel. Volyns'ka Oblast', NW Ukraine
Kowloon 106 A2 Chin. Jiulong. Hong Kong, S China
Kowtal-e Barowghīl see Baroghil Pass
Kowtal-e Khaybar see Khyber Pass
Kozáni 82 B4 Dytikí Makedonía, N Greece
Kozara 78 B3 mountain range NW Bosnia and Herzegovina
Kozarska Dubica see Bosanska Dubica
Kozhikode see Calicut
Kōzu-shima 109 D6 island E Japan
Kozyatyn 86 D2 Rus. Kazatin. Vinnyts'ka Oblast', C Ukraine
Kpalimé 53 E5 var. Palimé. SW Togo
Krâchéh 115 D6 prev. Kratie. Krâchéh, E Cambodia
Kragujevac 78 D4 Serbia, C Serbia and Montenegro (Yugo.)

Kra, Isthmus of 115 B6 isthmus Malaysia/Thailand
Kraków 77 D5 Eng. Cracow, Ger. Krakau; anc. Cracovia. Małopolskie, S Poland
Krälänh 115 D5 Siĕmréab, NW Cambodia
Kraljevo 78 D4 prev. Rankovićevo. Serbia, C Serbia and Montenegro (Yugo.)
Kramators'k 87 G3 Rus. Kramatorsk. Donets'ka Oblast', SE Ukraine
Kramfors 63 C5 Västernorrland, C Sweden
Kranéa 82 B4 Dytikí Makedonía, N Greece
Kranj 73 D7 Ger. Krainburg. NW Slovenia
Krāslava 84 D4 Krāslava, SE Latvia
Krasnaye 85 C5 Rus. Krasnoye. Minskaya Voblasts', C Belarus
Krasnoarmeysk 89 C6 Saratovskaya Oblast', W Russian Federation
Krasnodar 89 A7 prev. Ekaterinodar, Yekaterinodar. Krasnodarskiy Kray, SW Russian Federation
Krasnodon 87 H3 Luhans'ka Oblast', E Ukraine
Krasnohvardiys'ke 87 F4 Rus. Krasnogvardeyskoye. Respublika Krym, S Ukraine
Krasnokamensk 93 F4 Chitinskaya Oblast', S Russian Federation
Krasnokamsk 89 D5 Permskaya Oblast', W Russian Federation
Krasnoperekops'k 87 F4 Rus. Krasnoperekopsk. Respublika Krym, S Ukraine
Krasnoyarsk 92 D4 Krasnoyarskiy Kray, S Russian Federation
Krasnostav 76 E4 Rus. Krasnostav. Lubelskie, E Poland
Krasnyy Kut 89 C6 Saratovskaya Oblast', W Russian Federation
Krasnyy Luch 87 H3 prev. Krindachevka. Luhans'ka Oblast', E Ukraine
Krâvanh, Chuŏr Phnum 115 C6 Eng. Cardamom Mountains, Fr. Chaîne des Cardamomes. Mountain range W Cambodia
Krefeld 72 A4 Nordrhein-Westfalen, W Germany
Kremenchuk 87 F2 Rus. Kremenchug. Poltavs'ka Oblast', NE Ukraine
Kremenchuts'ke Vodoskhovyshche 87 F2 Eng. Kremenchuk Reservoir, Rus. Kremenchugskoye Vodokhranilishche. Reservoir C Ukraine
Kremenets' 86 C2 Pol. Krzemieniec, Rus. Kremenets. Ternopil'ska Oblast', W Ukraine
Kreminna 87 G2 Rus. Kremennaya. Luhans'ka Oblast', E Ukraine
Kresena see Kresna
Kresna 82 C3 var. Kresena. Blagoevgrad, SW Bulgaria
Kretikon Delagos see Kritikó Pélagos
Kretinga 84 B3 Ger. Krottingen. Kretinga, NW Lithuania
Krishna 110 C1 prev. Kistna. River C India
Krishnagiri 110 C2 Tamil Nādu, SE India
Kristiansand 63 A6 var. Christiansand. Vest-Agder, S Norway
Kristianstad 63 B7 Skåne, S Sweden
Kristiansund 62 A4 var. Christiansund. Møre og Romsdal, S Norway
Kríti 83 C7 Eng. Crete. Island Greece, Aegean Sea
Kritikó Pélagos 83 D7 var. Kretikon Delagos, Eng. Sea of Crete; anc. Mare Creticum. Sea Greece, Aegean Sea
Križevci 78 B2 Ger. Kreuz, Hung. Kőrös. Varaždin, NE Croatia
Krk 78 A3 It. Veglia; anc. Curieta. Island NW Croatia
Krolevets' 87 F1 Rus. Krolevets. Sums'ka Oblast', NE Ukraine
Kronach 73 C5 Bayern, E Germany
Kroonstad 56 D4 Free State, C South Africa
Kropotkin 89 A7 Krasnodarskiy Kray, SW Russian Federation
Krosno 77 D5 Ger. Krossen. Podkarpackie, SE Poland
Krosno Odrzańskie 76 B3 Ger. Crossen, Kreisstadt. Lubuskie, W Poland
Krško 73 E8 Ger. Gurkfeld; prev. Videm-Krško. E Slovenia
Kruhlaye 85 D6 Rus. Krugloye. Mahilyowskaya Voblasts', E Belarus
Kruja see Krujë
Krujë 79 C6 var. Kruja, It. Croia. Durrës, C Albania
Krummau see Český Krumlov
Krung Thep 115 C5 var. Krung Thep Mahanakhon, Eng. Bangkok. Country capital (Thailand) Bangkok, C Thailand
Krung Thep, Ao 115 C5 var. Bight of Bangkok. Bay S Thailand
Krung Thep Mahanakhon see Krung Thep
Krupki 85 D6 Rus. Krupki. Minskaya Voblasts', C Belarus
Krychaw 85 E7 Rus. Krichëv. Mahilyowskaya Voblasts', E Belarus
Krym see Crimea
Krymskaya Oblast' see Crimea
Kryms'ki Hory 87 F5 mountain range S Ukraine
Kryms'kyy Pivostriv 87 F5 peninsula S Ukraine
Krynica 77 D5 Ger. Tannenhof. Małopolskie, S Poland
Kryve Ozero 87 E3 Odes'ka Oblast', SW Ukraine
Kryvyy Rih 87 F3 Rus. Krivoy Rog. Dnipropetrovs'ka Oblast', SE Ukraine
Ksar al Kabir see Ksar-el-Kebir
Ksar al Soule see Er-Rachidia
Ksar-el-Kebir 48 C2 var. Alcázar, Ksar al Kabir, Ksar-el-Kébir, Ar. Al-Qsar al-Kbir, Al-Qsar al-Kebir, Sp. Alcazarquivir. NW Morocco
Ksar-el-Kébir see Ksar-el-Kebir
Kuala Dungun see Dungun

Kuala Lumpur 116 B3 country capital (Malaysia) Kuala Lumpur, Peninsular Malaysia
Kuala Terengganu 116 B3 var. Kuala Trengganu. Terengganu, Peninsular Malaysia
Kuala Trengganu see Kuala Terengganu
Kualatungkal 116 B4 Sumatera, W Indonesia
Kuang-chou see Guangzhou
Kuang-hsi see Guangxi Zhuangzu Zizhiqu
Kuang-tung see Guangdong
Kuang-yuan see Guangyuan
Kuantan 116 B3 Pahang, Peninsular Malaysia
Kuban' 87 G5 var. Hypanis. River SW Russian Federation
Kubango see Cubango
Kuching 116 C3 prev. Sarawak. Sarawak, East Malaysia
Kūchnay Darweyshān 100 D5 Helmand, S Afghanistan
Kuçova see Kuçovë
Kuçovë 79 C6 var. Kuçova; prev. Qyteti Stalin. Berat, C Albania
Kudara see Ghūdara
Kudus 116 C5 prev. Koedoes. Jawa, C Indonesia
Kuei-chou see Guizhou
Kuei-lin see Guilin
Kuei-Yang see Guiyang
Kueyang see Guiyang
Kugluktuk 15 E3 var. Qurlurtuuq; prev. Coppermine. Nunavut, NW Canada
Kuhmo 62 E4 Oulu, E Finland
Kühnö see Kihnu
Kuibyshev see Kuybyshevskoye Vodokhranilishche
Kuito 56 B2 Port. Silva Porto. Bié, C Angola
Kuji 108 D3 var. Kuzi. Iwate, Honshū, C Japan
Kukës 79 D5 var. Kukési. Kukës, NE Albania
Kukési see Kukës
Kukong see Shaoguan
Kukukhoto see Hohhot
Kula Kangri 113 G3 var. Kulhakangri. Mountain Bhutan/China
Kuldīga 84 B3 Ger. Goldingen. Kuldīga, W Latvia
Kuldja see Yining
Kulhakangri see Kula Kangri
Kullorsuaq 60 D2 var. Kuvdlorssuak. C Greenland
Kulmsee see Chełmża
Kŭlob 101 F3 Rus. Kulyab. SW Tajikistan
Kulu 94 C3 Konya, W Turkey
Kulunda Steppe 92 C4 Kaz. Qulyndy Zhazyghy, Rus. Kulundinskaya Ravnina. Grassland Kazakhstan/Russian Federation
Kum see Qom
Kuma 89 B7 river SW Russian Federation
Kumamoto 109 A7 Kumamoto, Kyūshū, SW Japan
Kumanovo 79 E5 Turk. Kumanova. N FYR Macedonia
Kumasi 53 E5 prev. Coomassie. C Ghana
Kumba 55 A5 Sud-Ouest, W Cameroon
Kumertau 89 D6 Respublika Bashkortostan, W Russian Federation
Kumo 53 G4 Gombe, E Nigeria
Kumon Range 114 B2 mountain range N Myanmar
Kumul see Hami
Kunashiri see Kunashir, Ostrov
Kunashir, Ostrov 108 E1 var. Kunashiri. Island Kuril'skiye Ostrova, SE Russian Federation
Kunda 84 E2 Lääne-Virumaa, NE Estonia
Kunduz 101 E3 var. Kondoz, Kundūz, Qondūz, Per. Kondūz. Kunduz, NE Afghanistan
Kuneitra see Al Qunayţirah
Kunene see Cunene
Kungsbacka 63 B7 Halland, S Sweden
Kungur 89 D5 Permskaya Oblast', NW Russian Federation
Kunlun Mountains see Kunlun Shan
Kunlun Shan 104 B4 Eng. Kunlun Mountains. NW China
Kunming 106 B6 var. Yunnan, Yünnan, SW China; prev. Yunnan. Yunnan, Yünnan, SW China; prev. Kunming
K'un-ming see Kunming
Kununurra 124 D3 Western Australia
Kuopio 63 E5 Itä-Suomi, C Finland
Kupang 117 E5 prev. Koepang. Timor, C Indonesia
Kup"yans'k 87 G2 Rus. Kupyansk. Kharkivs'ka Oblast', E Ukraine
Kura 95 H3 Az. Kür, Geor. Mtkvari, Turk. Kura Nehri. River SW Asia
Kurashiki 109 B6 var. Kurasiki. Okayama, Honshū, SW Japan
Kurasiki see Kurashiki
Kurdistan 95 F4 cultural region SW Asia
Kŭrdzhali 82 D3 var. Kirdzhali. Kŭrdzhali, S Bulgaria
Kure 109 B7 Hiroshima, Honshū, SW Japan
Küre Dağları 94 C2 mountain range N Turkey
Kuressaare 84 C2 Ger. Arensburg; prev. Kingissepp. Saaremaa, W Estonia
Kureyka 90 D3 river N Russian Federation
Kuria Muria Islands see Ḩalāniyāt, Juzur al
Kurile Islands see Kuril'skiye Ostrova
Kurile-Kamchatka Depression see Kurile Trench
Kurile Trench 91 F3 var. Kurile-Kamchatka Depression. Undersea feature NW Pacific Ocean
Kuril'sk 108 E1 Kuril'skiye Ostrova, Sakhalinskaya Oblast', SE Russian Federation
Kuril'skiye Ostrova 93 H4 Eng. Kurile Islands. Island group SE Russian Federation

171

Ku-ring-gai 126 E1 New South Wales, SE Australia
Kurnool 110 C1 var. Karnul. Andhra Pradesh, S India
Kursk 89 A6 Kurskaya Oblast', W Russian Federation
Kuršumlija 79 D5 Serbia, S Serbia and Montenegro (Yugo.)
Kuruktag 104 C3 mountain range NW China
Kurume 109 A7 Fukuoka, Kyūshū, SW Japan
Kurupukari 37 F3 C Guyana
Kurzeme 84 B3 Eng. Courland, Ger. Kurland. Former province W Latvia
Kushiro 108 D2 var. Kusiro. Hokkaidō, NE Japan
Kusiro see Kushiro
Kuskokwim Mountains 14 C3 mountain range Alaska, USA
Kuźnica 76 E2 Podlaskie, NE Poland
Kustanay see Kostanay
Küstence see Constanța
Küstendje see Constanța
Kütahya 94 B3 prev. Kutaia. Kütahya, W Turkey
Kutai see Mahakam, Sungai
K'ut'aisi 95 F2 W Georgia
Kūt al 'Amārah see Al Kūt
Kut al Imara see Al Kūt
Kutaradja see Bandaaceh
Kutaraja see Bandaaceh
Kutch, Gulf of see Kachchh, Gulf of
Kutch, Rann of see Kachchh, Rann of
Kutina 78 B3 Sisak-Moslavina, NE Croatia
Kutno 76 C3 Łódzkie, C Poland
Kuujjuaq 17 E2 prev. Fort-Chimo. Québec, E Canada
Kuusamo 62 E3 Oulu, Finland
Kuvango see Cubango
Kuvdlorssuak see Kullorsuaq
Kuwait 98 C4 var. Dawlat al Kuwait, Koweit, Kuwait. Country SW Asia
Kuwait see Al Kuwayt
Kuwait City see Al Kuwayt
Kuwajleen see Kwajalein Atoll
Kuwayt 98 C3 E Iraq
Kuybyshev Reservoir see Kuybyshevskoye Vodokhranilishche
Kuybyshevskoye Vodokhranilishche 89 C5 var. Kuibyshev, Eng. Kuybyshev Reservoir. Reservoir W Russian Federation
Kuytun 104 B2 Xinjiang Uygur Zizhiqu, NW China
Kuzi see Kuji
Kuznetsk 89 B6 Penzenskaya Oblast', W Russian Federation
Kvaløya 62 C2 island N Norway
Kvarnbergsvattnet 62 B4 var. Frostviken. Lake N Sweden
Kvarner 78 A3 var. Carnaro, It. Quarnero. Gulf W Croatia
Kvitøya 61 G1 island NE Svalbard
Kwajalein Atoll 122 C1 var. Kuwajleen. Atoll Ralik Chain, C Marshall Islands
Kwando see Cuando
Kwangchow see Guangzhou
Kwangju 107 E4 off. Kwangju-gwangyŏksi, var. Guangju, Kwangchu, Jap. Kōshū. SW South Korea
Kwango 55 C7 Port. Cuango. River Angola/Dem. Rep. Congo see also Cuango
Kwango see Cuango
Kwangsi see Guangxi Zhuangzu Zizhiqu
Kwangsi Chuang Autonomous Region see Guangxi Zhuangzu Zizhiqu
Kwangtung see Guangdong
Kwangyuan see Guangyuan
Kwanza see Cuanza
Kweichow see Guizhou
Kweichu see Guiyang
Kweilin see Guilin
Kweisui see Hohhot
Kweiyang see Guiyang
Kwekwe 56 D3 prev. Que Que. Midlands, C Zimbabwe
Kwesui see Hohhot
Kwidzyń 76 C2 Ger. Marienwerder. Pomorskie, N Poland
Kwigillingok 14 C3 Alaska, USA
Kwilu 55 C6 river W Dem. Rep. Congo
Kwito see Cuito
Kyabé 54 C4 Moyen-Chari, S Chad
Kyaikkami 115 B5 prev. Amherst. Mon State, S Myanmar
Kyaiklat 114 B4 Irrawaddy, SW Myanmar
Kyaikto 114 B4 Mon State, S Myanmar
Kyakhta 93 E5 Respublika Buryatiya, S Russian Federation
Kyaukse 114 B3 Mandalay, C Myanmar
Kyjov 77 C5 Ger. Gaya. Brněnský Kraj, SE Czech Republic
Kykládes 83 D6 var. Kikládhes, Eng. Cyclades. Island group SE Greece
Kými 83 C5 prev. Kími. Évvoia, C Greece
Kyōto 109 C6 Kyōto, Honshū, SW Japan
Kyparissía 83 B6 var. Kiparissía. Pelopónnisos, S Greece
Kyrá Panagía 83 C5 island Vóreioi Sporádes, Greece, Aegean Sea
Kyrenia see Kerýneia
Kyrgyzstan 101 F2 var. Kirghizia; prev. Kirgizskaya SSR, Kirghiz SSR, Republic of Kyrgyzstan. Country C Asia
Kýthira 83 C7 var. Kíthira, It. Cerigo; Lat. Cythera. Island S Greece
Kýthnos 83 C6 var. Kithnos, Thermiá, It. Termia; anc. Cythnos. Island Kykládes, Greece, Aegean Sea
Kýthnos 83 C6 Kýthnos, Kykládes, Greece, Aegean Sea
Kythréa 80 C5 N Cyprus
Kyūshū 109 B7 var. Kyûsyû. Island SW Japan
Kyushu-Palau Ridge 103 F3 var. Kyusyu-Palau Ridge. Undersea feature W Pacific Ocean
Kyustendil 82 B2 anc. Pautalia. Kyustendil, W Bulgaria

Kyûsyû see Kyūshū
Kyusyu-Palau Ridge see Kyushu-Palau Ridge
Kyyiv 87 E2 Eng. Kiev, Rus. Kiyev. Country capital (Ukraine) Kyyivs'ka Oblast', N Ukraine
Kyyivs'ke Vodoskhovyshche 87 E1 Eng. Kiev Reservoir, Rus. Kiyevskoye Vodokhranilishche. Reservoir N Ukraine
Kyzyl 92 D4 Respublika Tyva, C Russian Federation
Kyzyl Kum 100 D2 var. Kizil Kum, Qizil Qum, Qizilqum. Desert Kazakhstan/Uzbekistan
Kyzylorda 92 B5 var. Kyzyl-orda, Qizil Orda, Kaz. Qyzylorda; prev. Perovsk. Kyzylorda, S Kazakhstan
Kyzyl-Suu 101 G2 prev. Pokrovka. Issyk-Kul'skaya Oblast', NE Kyrgyzstan
Kyzyl-orda see Kyzylorda

L

La Algaba 70 C4 Andalucía, S Spain
Laamu Atoll see Hadhdhunmathi Atoll
Laarne 65 B5 Oost-Vlaanderen, NW Belgium
La Asunción 37 E1 Nueva Esparta, NE Venezuela
Laâyoune 48 B3 var. Aaiún. Dependent territory capital (Western Sahara) NW Western Sahara
la Baule-Escoublac 68 A4 Loire-Atlantique, NW France
Labé 52 C4 Moyenne-Guinée, NW Guinea
La Blanquilla see Blanquilla, Isla
Laborec 77 E5 Hung. Laborca. River E Slovakia
Labrador 17 F2 cultural region Newfoundland and Labrador, SW Canada
Labrador Basin 12 E3 var. Labrador Sea Basin. Undersea feature Labrador Sea
Labrador Sea 60 A4 sea NW Atlantic Ocean
Labrador Sea Basin see Labrador Basin
Labutta 115 A5 Irrawaddy, SW Myanmar
Laç 79 C6 var. Laci. Lezhë, C Albania
La Calera 42 B4 Valparaíso, C Chile
La Carolina 70 D4 Andalucía, S Spain
Laccadive Islands see Lakshadweep
La Ceiba 30 D2 Atlántida, N Honduras
Lachanás 82 B3 Kentrikí Makedonía, N Greece
La Chaux-de-Fonds 73 A7 Neuchâtel, W Switzerland
Lachlan River 127 C6 river New South Wales, SE Australia
Laci see Laç
la Ciotat 69 D6 anc. Citharista. Bouches-du-Rhône, SE France
La Concepción 36 C1 Zulia, NW Venezuela
La Concepción 31 E5 var. Concepción. Chiriquí, W Panama
La Condamine 69 C8 NW Andorra
Laconia 19 G2 New Hampshire, NE USA
La Crosse 40 A2 Wisconsin, N USA
La Cruz 30 D4 Guanacaste, NW Costa Rica
Lacus Asphaltites see Dead Sea
Ladoga, Lake see Ladozhskoye Ozero
Ladozhskoye Ozero 88 B3 Eng. Lake Ladoga, Fin. Laatokka. Lake NW Russian Federation
Ladysmith 18 B2 Wisconsin, N USA
Lae 122 B3 Morobe, W PNG
La Esperanza 30 C2 Intibucá, SW Honduras
Lafayette 18 C4 Indiana, N USA
Lafayette 20 B3 Louisiana, S USA
La Fé 32 A2 Pinar del Río, W Cuba
Lafia 53 G4 Nassarawa, C Nigeria
la Flèche 68 B4 Sarthe, NW France
Lagdo, Lac de 54 B4 lake N Cameroon
Laghouat 48 D2 N Algeria
Lago dos Gansos see Goose Lake
Lago General Carrera see Buenos Aires, Lago
Lago Nyassa see Nyasa, Lake
Lago Pampa Aullagas see Poopó, Lago
Lagos 70 B5 anc. Lacobriga. Faro, S Portugal
Lagos 53 F5 Lagos, SW Nigeria
Lagos de Moreno 29 E4 Jalisco, SW Mexico
Lagouira 48 A5 SW Western Sahara
La Grande 24 C3 Oregon, NW USA
La Guaira 44 B4 Distrito Federal, N Venezuela
Laguna Merín see Mirim Lagoon
Lagunas 42 B1 Tarapacá, N Chile
Lagunillas 39 G4 Santa Cruz, SE Bolivia
La Habana 32 B2 var. Havana. Country capital (Cuba) Ciudad de La Habana, W Cuba
Lahat 116 B4 Sumatera, W Indonesia
La Haye see 's-Gravenhage
Laholm 63 B7 Halland, S Sweden
Lahore 112 D2 Punjab, NE Pakistan
Lahr 73 A6 Baden-Württemberg, S Germany
Lahti 63 D5 Swe. Lahtis. Etelä-Suomi, S Finland
Laï 54 B4 prev. Behagle, De Behagle. Tandjilé, S Chad
Lai Châu 114 D3 Lai Châu, N Vietnam
Laila see Laylá
La Junta 22 D5 Colorado, C USA
Lake Charles 20 A3 Louisiana, S USA
Lake City 21 E3 Florida, SE USA
Lake District 67 C5 physical region NW England, UK
Lake Havasu City 26 A2 Arizona, SW USA
Lake Jackson 27 H4 Texas, SW USA
Lakeland 21 E4 Florida, SE USA
Lakeside 25 C8 California, W USA
Lakewood 22 D4 Colorado, C USA
Lakhnau see Lucknow
Lakonikós Kólpos 83 B7 gulf S Greece
Lakselv 62 D2 Finnmark, N Norway
Lakshadweep 110 A3 Eng. Laccadive Islands. Island group India, N Indian Ocean
la Laon see Laon
Lalibela 50 C4 N Ethiopia

La Libertad 30 B1 Petén, N Guatemala
La Ligua 42 B4 Valparaíso, C Chile
Lalín 70 C1 Galicia, NW Spain
La Louvière 65 B6 Hainaut, S Belgium
Lalitpur 113 F3 Central, C Nepal
La Maçana see La Massana
La Maddalena 74 A4 Sardegna, Italy, C Mediterranean Sea
la Manche see English Channel
Lamar 22 D5 Colorado, C USA
La Marmora, Punta 75 A5 mountain Sardegna, Italy, C Mediterranean Sea
La Massana 69 A8 var. La Maçana. W Andorra
Lambaréné 55 A6 Moyen-Ogooué, W Gabon
Lamego 70 C2 Viseu, N Portugal
Lamesa 27 E3 Texas, SW USA
Lamezia Terme 75 D6 Calabria, SE Italy
Lamía 83 B5 Stereá Ellás, C Greece
Lamoni 23 F4 Iowa, C USA
Lampang 114 C4 var. Muang Lampang. Lampang, NW Thailand
Lámpeia 83 B6 Dytikí Ellás, S Greece
Lanbi Kyun 115 B6 prev. Sullivan Island. Island Mergui Archipelago, S Myanmar
Lancang Jiang see Mekong
Lancaster 25 C7 California, W USA
Lancaster 67 D5 NW England, UK
Lancaster 19 F4 Pennsylvania, NE USA
Lancaster Sound 15 F2 sound Nunavut, N Canada
Lan-chou see Lanzhou
Lan-chow see Lanzhou
Landen 65 C6 Vlaams Brabant, C Belgium
Lander 22 C3 Wyoming, C USA
Landerneau 68 A3 Finistère, NW France
Landes 69 B5 department SW France
Land's End 67 B8 headland SW England, UK
Landshut 73 C6 Bayern, SE Germany
Langar 101 E2 Rus. Lyangar. Nawoiy Wiloyati, C Uzbekistan
Langfang 106 D4 Hebei, E China
Langkawi, Pulau 115 B7 island Peninsular Malaysia
Langres 68 D4 Haute-Marne, N France
Langsa 116 A3 Sumatera, W Indonesia
Lang Shan 105 E3 mountain range N China
Lang Son 114 D3 var. Langson. Lang Son, N Vietnam
Langson see Lang Son
Lang Suan 115 B6 Chumphon, SW Thailand
Languedoc 69 C6 cultural region S France
Länkäran 95 H3 Rus. Lenkoran'. S Azerbaijan
Lansing 18 C3 state capital Michigan, N USA
Lanta, Ko 115 B7 island S Thailand
Lantau Island 106 A2 Cant. Tai Yue Shan, Chin. Landao. Island Hong Kong, S China
Lan-ts'ang Chiang see Mekong
Lanzarote 48 B3 island Islas Canarias, Spain, NE Atlantic Ocean
Lanzhou 106 B4 var. Lan-chou, Lanchow, Lan-chow; prev. Kaolan. Gansu, C China
Lao Cai 114 D3 Lao Cai, N Vietnam
Laojunmiao see Yumen
Laon 68 D3 var. la Laon; anc. Laudunum. Aisne, N France
Laos 114 D4 Country SE Asia
La Orchila, Isla 36 D1 island N Venezuela
La Oroya 38 C3 Junín, C Peru
La Palma 30 C2 Darién, SE Panama
La Palma 48 A3 island Islas Canarias, Spain, NE Atlantic Ocean
La Palma 31 F2 Chalatenango, N El Salvador
La Paz 39 F4 var. La Paz de Ayacucho. Country capital (Bolivia-legislative and administrative capital) La Paz, W Bolivia
La Paz 28 B3 Baja California Sur, NW Mexico
La Paz, Bahía de 28 B3 bay W Mexico
La Paz de Ayacucho see La Paz
La Perouse Strait 108 D1 Jap. Sōya-kaikyō, Rus. Proliv Laperuza. Strait Japan/Russian Federation
Lápithos 80 C5 NW Cyprus
Lapland 63 D5 Fin. Lappi, Swe. Lappland. Cultural region N Europe
La Plata 42 D4 Buenos Aires, E Argentina
Lappeenranta 63 E5 Swe. Villmanstrand. Etelä-Suomi, S Finland
Lappi see Lapland
Lappland see Lapland
Lapta see Lápithos
Laptev Sea see Laptevykh, More
Laptevykh, More 93 E2 Eng. Laptev Sea. Sea Arctic Ocean
Lapua 63 D5 Swe. Lappo. Länsi-Suomi, W Finland
La Puebla see Sa Pobla
Lapy 76 E3 Podlaskie
La Quiaca 42 C2 Jujuy, N Argentina
L'Aquila 74 C4 var. Aquila, Aquila degli Abruzzo. Abruzzo, C Italy
Laracha 70 B1 Galicia, NW Spain
Laramie 22 C4 Wyoming, C USA
Laramie Mountains 22 C3 mountain range Wyoming, C USA
Laredo 71 E1 Cantabria, N Spain
Laredo 27 F5 Texas, SW USA
Largo 21 E4 Florida, SE USA
Largo, Cayo 32 B2 island W Cuba
Lario see Como, Lago di
La Rioja 42 C2 La Rioja, NW Argentina
Lárisa 82 B4 var. Larissa. Thessalía, C Greece
Larissa see Lárisa
Lārkāna 112 B3 var. Larkhana. Sind, SE Pakistan
Larkhana see Lārkāna
Larnaca see Lárnaka
Lárnaka 80 C5 var. Larnaca, Larnax. SE Cyprus
Larnax see Lárnaka
la Rochelle 68 B4 anc. Rupella. Charente-Maritime, W France
la Roche-sur-Yon 68 B4 prev. Bourbon Vendée, Napoléon-Vendée. Vendée, NW France

La Roda 71 E3 Castilla-La Mancha, C Spain
La Romana 33 E3 Dominican Republic
Larvotto 69 C8 N Monaco
La-sa see Lhasa
Las Cabezas de San Juan 70 C5 Andalucía, S Spain
Las Cruces 26 D3 New Mexico, SW USA
La See d'Urgel 71 G1 var. La Seu d'Urgell, Seo de Urgel. Cataluña, NE Spain
La Serena 42 B3 Coquimbo, C Chile
La Seu d'Urgell see La See d'Urgel
La Seyne-sur-Mer 69 D6 Var, SE France
Lashio 114 B3 Shan State, E Myanmar
Lashkar Gāh 100 D5 var. Lash-Kar-Gar'. Helmand, S Afghanistan
Lash-Kar-Gar' see Lashkar Gāh
La Sila 75 D6 mountain range SW Italy
La Sirena 30 D3 Región Autónoma Atlántico Sur, E Nicaragua
Łask 76 C4 Łódzkie, C Poland
Las Lomitas 42 D2 Formosa, N Argentina
La Solana 71 E4 Castilla-La Mancha, C Spain
Las Palmas de Gran Canaria 48 A3 Gran Canaria, Islas Canarias, Spain, NE Atlantic Ocean
La Spezia 74 B3 Liguria, NW Italy
Lassa see Lhasa
Las Tablas 31 F5 Los Santos, S Panama
Las Tunas 32 C2 var. Victoria de las Tunas. Las Tunas, E Cuba
Las Vegas 25 D7 Nevada, W USA
Latacunga 38 B1 Cotopaxi, C Ecuador
la Teste 69 B5 Gironde, SW France
Latina 75 C5 prev. Littoria. Lazio, C Italy
La Tortuga, Isla 37 E1 var. Isla La Tortuga. Island N Venezuela
La Tuque 17 E4 Québec, SE Canada
Latvia 84 C3 Ger. Lettland, Latv. Latvija, Latvijas Republika; prev. Latvian SSR, Rus. Latviyskaya SSR. Country NE Europe
Laudunum see Laon
Lauenburg see Lębork
Lauenburg in Pommern see Lębork
Lau Group 123 E4 island group E Fiji
Launceston 127 C8 Tasmania, SE Australia
La Unión 71 F4 Murcia, SE Spain
La Unión 30 C2 Olancho, C Honduras
Laurel 20 C3 Mississippi, S USA
Laurel 22 C2 Montana, NW USA
Laurentian Highlands see Laurentian Mountains
Laurentian Mountains 17 E3 var. Laurentian Highlands, Fr. Les Laurentides. Plateau Newfoundland and Labrador/Québec, Canada
Lauria 75 D6 Basilicata, S Italy
Laurinburg 21 F1 North Carolina, SE USA
Lauru see Choiseul
Lausanne 73 A7 It. Losanna. Vaud, SW Switzerland
Laut Banda see Banda Sea
Laut, Pulau 116 D4 prev. Laoet. Island Borneo, C Indonesia
Laval 68 B3 Mayenne, NW France
Laval 16 D4 Québec, SE Canada
La Vega 33 E3 var. Concepción de la Vega. C Dominican Republic
La Vila Jojosa see Villajoyosa
Lávrio 83 C6 prev. Lávrion. Attikí, C Greece
Lawrence 19 G3 Massachusetts, NE USA
Lawrenceburg 20 C1 Tennessee, S USA
Lawton 27 F2 Oklahoma, C USA
La Yarada 39 E4 Tacna, SW Peru
Laylá 99 C5 var. Laila. Ar Riyāḍ, C Saudi Arabia
Lazarev Sea 132 B1 sea Antarctica
Lázaro Cárdenas 29 E5 Michoacán de Ocampo, SW Mexico
Læsø 63 B7 island N Denmark
Leamhcán see Lucan
Leamington 16 C5 Ontario, S Canada
Lebak 117 E3 Mindanao, S Philippines
Lebanon 96 A4 Ar. Al Lubnān, Fr. Liban. Country SW Asia
Lebanon 23 G5 Missouri, C USA
Lebanon 19 G2 New Hampshire, NE USA
Lebanon 24 B3 Oregon, NW USA
Lebap 100 D2 Lebapskiy Velayat, NE Turkmenistan
Lebedyn 87 F2 Rus. Lebedin. Sums'ka Oblast', NE Ukraine
Lębork 76 C2 var. Lębórk, Ger. Lauenburg, Lauenburg in Pommern. Pomorskie, N Poland
Lebrija 70 C5 Andalucía, S Spain
Lebu 43 A5 Bío Bío, C Chile
le Cannet 69 D6 Alpes-Maritimes, SE France
Le Cap see Cap-Haïtien
Lecce 75 E6 Puglia, SE Italy
Lechainá 83 B6 var. Lehena, Lekhainá. Dytikí Ellás, S Greece
Leduc 15 E5 Alberta, SW Canada
Leech Lake 23 F2 lake Minnesota, N USA
Leeds 67 D5 N England, UK
Leek 64 E2 Groningen, NE Netherlands
Leer 72 A4 Niedersachsen, NW Germany
Leeuwarden 64 D1 Fris. Ljouwert. Friesland, N Netherlands
Leeuwin, Cape 120 A5 headland Western Australia
Leeward Islands 33 G3 island group E West Indies
Leeward Islands see Sotavento, Ilhas de
Lefkáda 83 A5 prev. Levkás. Lefkáda, Iónioi Nísoi, Greece, C Mediterranean Sea
Lefká Óri 83 C7 mountain range Kríti, Greece, E Mediterranean Sea
Lefkímmi 83 A5 var. Levkímmi. Kérkyra, Iónioi Nísoi, Greece, C Mediterranean Sea
Legaspi 117 E2 off. Legaspi City. Luzon, N Philippines

Legnica 76 B4 Ger. Liegnitz. Dolnośląskie, SW Poland
le Havre 68 B3 Eng. Havre; prev. le Havre-de-Grâce. Seine-Maritime, N France
Lehena see Lechainá
Leicester 67 D6 Lat. Batae Coritanorum. C England, UK
Leiden 64 B3 prev. Leyden, anc. Lugdunum Batavorum. Zuid-Holland, W Netherlands
Leie 68 D2 Fr. Lys. River Belgium/France
Leinster 67 B6 Ir. Cúige Laighean. Cultural region E Ireland
Leipsoí 83 E6 island Dodekánisos, Greece, Aegean Sea
Leipzig 72 C4 Pol. Lipsk; hist. Leipsic, anc. Lipsia. Sachsen, E Germany
Leiria 70 B3 anc. Collipo. Leiria, C Portugal
Leirvik 63 A6 Hordaland, S Norway
Lek 64 C4 river SW Netherlands
Lekhainá see Lechainá
Lekhchevo 82 C2 Montana, NW Bulgaria
Leksand 63 C5 Kopparberg, C Sweden
Lelystad 64 D3 Flevoland, C Netherlands
le Mans 68 B3 Sarthe, NW France
Lemesós 80 C5 var. Limassol. SW Cyprus
Lena 93 F3 river NE Russian Federation
Lena Tablemount 119 B7 undersea feature S Indian Ocean
Len Dao 106 C8 island S Spratly Islands
Lengshuitan 106 C6 Hunan, S China
Leninabad see Khūjand
Leninakan see Gyumri
Lenine 87 G5 Rus. Lenino. Respublika Krym, S Ukraine
Leningorsk 92 D4 Kaz. Leningor. Vostochnyy Kazakhstan, E Kazakhstan
Leningrad see Sankt-Peterburg
Leningradskaya 132 B4 Russian research station Antarctica
Leninobod see Khūjand
Leninpol' 101 F2 Talasskaya Oblast', NW Kyrgyzstan
Lenti 77 B7 Zala, SW Hungary
Leoben 95 E7 Steiermark, C Austria
León 29 E4 var. León de los Aldamas. Guanajuato, C Mexico
León 70 D1 Castilla-León, NW Spain
León 30 C3 León, NW Nicaragua
León de los Aldamas see León
Leonídi 83 B6 Pelopónnisos, S Greece
Lepe 70 C4 Andalucía, S Spain
le Portel 68 C2 Pas-de-Calais, N France
le Puy 69 C5 prev. le Puy-en-Velay, hist. Anicium, Podium Anicensis. Haute-Loire, C France
Léré 54 B4 Mayo-Kébbi, SW Chad
Lerma 29 D2 Castilla-León, N Spain
Léros 83 D6 Dodekánisos, Greece, Aegean Sea
Lerrnayin Gharabakh see Nagorno-Karabakh
Lerwick 66 D1 NE Scotland, UK
Lesbos see Lésvos
Les Cayes see Cayes
Les Gonaïves see Gonaïves
Lesh see Lezhë
Leshan 106 B5 Sichuan, C China
les Herbiers 68 B4 Vendée, NW France
Leshi see Lezhë
Leskovac 79 E5 Serbia, SE Serbia and Montenegro (Yugo.)
Les Laurentides see Laurentian Highlands
Lesnoy 92 C3 Sverdlovskaya Oblast', C Russian Federation
Lesotho 56 D4 prev. Basutoland. Country S Africa
les Sables-d'Olonne 68 B4 Vendée, NW France
Lesser Antarctica 132 A3 var. West Antarctica. Physical region Antarctica
Lesser Antilles 33 G4 island group E West Indies
Lesser Caucasus 95 F2 Rus. Malyy Kavkaz. Mountain range SW Asia
Lesser Sunda Islands see Nusa Tenggara
Lésvos 83 A4 anc. Lesbos. Island E Greece
Leszno 76 B4 Ger. Lissa. Wielkopolskie, C Poland
Lethbridge 15 E5 Alberta, SW Canada
Lethem 37 F3 S Guyana
Leti, Kepulauan 117 F5 island group E Indonesia
Letpadan 114 B4 Pegu, SW Myanmar
Letsôk-aw Kyun 115 B6 var. Letsutan Island; prev. Domel Island. Island Mergui Archipelago, S Myanmar
Letsutan Island see Letsôk-aw Kyun
Leuven 65 C6 Fr. Louvain, Ger. Löwen. Vlaams Brabant, C Belgium
Leuze see Leuze-en-Hainaut
Leuze-en-Hainaut 65 B6 var. Leuze. Hainaut, SW Belgium
Levanger 62 B4 Nord-Trøndelag, C Norway
Levelland 27 E2 Texas, SW USA
Leverkusen 72 A4 Nordrhein-Westfalen, W Germany
Levice 77 C6 Ger. Lewentz, Lewenz, Hung. Léva. Nitriansky Kraj, SW Slovakia
Levin 128 D4 Manawatu-Wanganui, North Island, NZ
Levkímmi see Lefkímmi
Lewis, Isle of 66 B2 island NW Scotland, UK
Lewis Range 22 B1 mountain range Montana, NW USA
Lewiston 24 C2 Idaho, NW USA
Lewiston 19 G2 Maine, NE USA
Lewistown 22 C1 Montana, NW USA
Lexington 18 C5 Kentucky, S USA
Lexington 23 E4 Nebraska, C USA
Leyte 117 F2 island C Philippines
Leżajsk 77 E5 Podkarpackie, SE Poland
Lezha see Lezhë
Lezhë 79 C6 var. Lezha; prev. Lesh, Leshi. Lezhë, NW Albania
Lhasa 104 C5 var. La-sa, Lassa. Xizang Zizhiqu, W China
Lhaviyani Atoll see Faadhippolhu Atoll
Lhazê 104 C5 Xizang Zizhiqu, W China

L'Hospitalet de Llobregat – Machanga

L'Hospitalet de Llobregat 71 G2 var. Hospitalet. Cataluña, NE Spain
Liancourt Rocks 109 A5 Jap. Take-shima, Kor. Tok-Do. Island group Japan/South Korea
Lianyungang 106 D4 var. Xinpu. Jiangsu, E China
Liao see Liaoning
Liaodong Wan 105 G3 Eng. Gulf of Lantung, Gulf of Liaotung. Gulf NE China
Liao He 103 E1 river NE China
Liaoning 106 D3 var. Liao, Liaoning Sheng, Shengking; hist. Fengtien, Shenking. Admin. region province NE China
Liaoyuan 107 E3 var. Dongliao, Shuang-liao, Jap. Chengchiatun. Jilin, NE China
Liard see Fort Liard
Liban, Jebel 96 B4 Ar. Jabal al Gharbt, Jabal Lubnān, Eng. Mount Lebanon. Mountain range C Lebanon
Libby 22 A1 Montana, NW USA
Liberal 23 E5 Kansas, C USA
Liberec 76 B4 Ger. Reichenberg. Liberecký Kraj, N Czech Republic
Liberia 52 C5 Country W Africa
Liberia 30 D4 Guanacaste, NW Costa Rica
Libian Desert see Libyan Desert
Libourne 91 B5 Gironde, SW France
Libreville 55 A5 country capital (Gabon) Estuaire, NW Gabon
Libya 49 F3 Ar. Al Jamāhīrīyah al 'Arabīyah al Lībīyah ash Sha'bīyah al Ishtirākīyah; prev. Libyan Arab Republic. Country N Africa
Libyan Desert 49 H4 var. Libian Desert, Ar. Aş Şahrā' al Lībīyah. Desert N Africa
Libyan Plateau 81 F4 var. Aḍ Diffah. Plateau Egypt/Libya
Lichtenfels 73 C5 Bayern, SE Germany
Lichtenvoorde 64 E4 Gelderland, E Netherlands
Lichuan 106 C5 Hubei, C China
Lida 85 B5 Rus. Lida. Hrodzyenskaya Voblasts', W Belarus
Lidköping 63 B6 Västra Götaland, S Sweden
Lidoríki 83 B5 prev. Lidhorikíon, Lidokhorikion. Stereá Ellás, C Greece
Lidzbark Warmiński 76 D2 Ger. Heilsberg. Warmińsko-Mazurskie, NE Poland
Liechtenstein 72 D1 Country C Europe
Liège 65 D6 Dut. Luik, Ger. Lüttich. Liège, E Belgium
Lienz 73 D7 Tirol, W Austria
Liepāja 84 B3 Ger. Libau. Liepāja, W Latvia
Liezen 95 D7 Steiermark, C Austria
Liffey 67 B6 river E Ireland
Lifou 122 D5 island Îles Loyauté, E New Caledonia
Liger see Loire
Ligure, Appennino 74 A2 Eng. Ligurian Mountains. Mountain range NW Italy
Ligurian Sea 74 A3 Fr. Mer Ligurienne, It. Mar Ligure. Sea N Mediterranean Sea
Līhu'e 25 A7 var. Lihue. Kaua'i, Hawai'i, USA, C Pacific Ocean
Lihula 84 D2 Ger. Leal. Läänemaa, W Estonia
Likasi 55 D7 prev. Jadotville. Shaba, SE Dem. Rep. Congo
Liknes 85 A6 Vest-Agder, S Norway
Lille 68 C2 var. l'Isle, Dut. Rijssel, Flem. Ryssel; prev. Lisle, anc. Insula. Nord, N France
Lillehammer 63 B5 Oppland, S Norway
Lillestrøm 63 B6 Akershus, S Norway
Lilongwe 57 E2 country capital (Malawi) Central, W Malawi
Lima 38 C4 country capital (Peru) Lima, W Peru
Limanowa 77 D5 Małopolskie, S Poland
Limassol see Lemesós
Limerick 67 A6 Ir. Luimneach. SW Ireland
Límnos 81 F3 anc. Lemnos. Island E Greece
Limoges 69 C5 anc. Augustoritum Lemovicensium, Lemovices. Haute-Vienne, C France
Limón 31 E4 var. Puerto Limón. Limón, E Costa Rica
Limón 30 D2 Colón, NE Honduras
Limousin 69 C5 cultural region C France
Limoux 69 C6 Aude, S France
Limpopo 56 D3 var. Crocodile. River S Africa
Linares 70 D4 Andalucía, S Spain
Linares 42 B4 Maule, C Chile
Linares 29 E3 Nuevo León, NE Mexico
Lincoln 67 D5 anc. Lindum, Lindum Colonia. E England, UK
Lincoln 23 F4 state capital Nebraska, C USA
Lincoln 19 H2 Maine, NE USA
Lincoln Sea 12 D2 sea Arctic Ocean
Linden 37 F3 E Guyana
Líndhos see Líndos
Lindi 51 D8 Lindi, SE Tanzania
Líndos 83 E7 var. Líndhos. Ródos, Dodekánisos, Greece, Aegean Sea
Line Islands 123 G3 island group E Kiribati
Lingeh see Bandar-e Langeh
Lingen 72 A3 var. Lingen an der Ems. Niedersachsen, NW Germany
Lingen an der Ems see Lingen
Lingga, Kepulauan 116 B4 island group W Indonesia
Linköping 63 C6 Östergötland, S Sweden
Linz 73 D6 anc. Lentia. Oberösterreich, N Austria
Lion, Golfe du 69 C7 Eng. Gulf of Lion, Gulf of Lions; anc. Sinus Gallicus. Gulf S France
Lipari Islands see Eolie, Isole
Lipari, Isola 75 D6 island Isole Eolie, S Italy
Lipetsk 89 B5 Lipetskaya Oblast', W Russian Federation
Lipno 76 C3 Kujawsko-pomorskie, C Poland
Lipova 86 A4 Hung. Lippa. Arad, W Romania
Liqeni i Ohrit see Ohrid, Lake
Lira 51 B6 N Uganda
Lisala 55 C5 Equateur, N Dem. Rep. Congo
Lisboa 70 B4 Eng. Lisbon; anc. Felicitas Julia, Olisipo. Country capital (Portugal) Lisboa, W Portugal
Lisbon see Lisboa
Lisieux 68 B3 anc. Noviomagus. Calvados, N France
Liski 89 B6 prev. Georgiu-Dezh. Voronezhskaya Oblast', W Russian Federation
Lisle see Lille
l'Isle see Lille
Lismore 127 E5 Victoria, SE Australia
Lisse 64 C3 Zuid-Holland, W Netherlands
Litang 106 A5 Sichuan, C China
Lītani, Nahr el 135 B5 var. Nahr al Litant. River C Lebanon
Lithgow 127 D6 New South Wales, SE Australia
Lithuania 84 B4 Ger. Litauen, Lith. Lietuva, Pol. Litwa, Rus. Litva; prev. Lithuanian SSR, Rus. Litovskaya SSR. Country NE Europe
Litóchoro 82 B4 var. Litohoro, Litókhoron. Kentrikí Makedonía, N Greece
Litohoro see Litóchoro
Litókhoron see Litóchoro
Little Alföld 77 C6 Ger. Kleines Ungarisches Tiefland, Hung. Kisalföld, Slvk. Podunajská Rovina. Plain Hungary/Slovakia
Little Andaman 111 F2 island Andaman Islands, India, NE Indian Ocean
Little Barrier Island 128 D2 island N NZ
Little Bay 71 H5 bay S Gibraltar
Little Cayman 32 B3 island E Cayman Islands
Little Falls 23 F2 Minnesota, N USA
Littlefield 27 E2 Texas, SW USA
Little Inagua 32 D2 var. Inagua Islands. Island S Bahamas
Little Minch, The 66 B3 strait NW Scotland, UK
Little Missouri River 22 D2 river NW USA
Little Nicobar 111 G3 island Nicobar Islands, India, NE Indian Ocean
Little Rock 20 B1 state capital Arkansas, C USA
Little Saint Bernard Pass 69 D5 Fr. Col du Petit St-Bernard, It. Colle di Piccolo San Bernardo. Pass France/Italy
Little Sound 20 A5 bay Bermuda, NW Atlantic Ocean
Littleton 22 D4 Colorado, C USA
Liu-chou see Liuzhou
Liuchow see Liuzhou
Liuzhou 106 C6 var. Liu-chou, Liuchow. Guangxi Zhuangzu Zizhiqu, S China
Livanátes 83 B5 prev. Livanátai. Stereá Ellás, C Greece
Līvāni 84 D4 Ger. Lievenhof. Preiļi, SE Latvia
Liverpool 126 D2 New South Wales, SE Australia
Liverpool 17 F5 Nova Scotia, SE Canada
Liverpool 67 C5 NW England, UK
Livingston 22 B2 Montana, NW USA
Livingstone 56 C3 var. Maramba. Southern, S Zambia
Livingstone 27 H3 Texas, SW USA
Livingstone Mountains 129 A7 mountain range South Island, NZ
Livno 78 B4 Federacija Bosna I Hercegovina, SW Bosnia and Herzegovina
Livojoki 62 D4 river C Finland
Livonia 18 D3 Michigan, N USA
Livorno 74 B3 Eng. Leghorn. Toscana, C Italy
Lixoúri 83 A5 prev. Lixoúrion. Kefallinía, Iónioi Nísoi, Greece, C Mediterranean Sea
Lizarra see Estella
Ljubljana 73 D7 Ger. Laibach, It. Lubiana; anc. Aemona, Emona. Country capital (Slovenia) C Slovenia
Ljungby 63 B7 Kronoberg, S Sweden
Ljusdal 85 C5 Gävleborg, C Sweden
Ljusnan 63 C5 river C Sweden
Llanelli 67 C6 prev. Llanelly. SW Wales, UK
Llanes 70 D1 Asturias, N Spain
Llanos 36 D2 physical region Colombia/Venezuela
Lleida 71 F2 Cast. Lérida; anc. Ilerda. Cataluña, NE Spain
Lluchmayor see Llucmajor
Llucmajor 71 G3 var. Lluchmayor. Mallorca, Spain, W Mediterranean Sea
Loaita Island 106 C8 island W Spratly Islands
Loanda see Luanda
Lobatse 56 C4 var. Lobatsi. Kgatleng, SE Botswana
Lobatsi see Lobatse
Löbau 72 D4 Sachsen, E Germany
Lobito 56 B2 Benguela, W Angola
Lob Nor see Lop Nur
Loburi see Lop Buri
Locarno 73 B8 Ger. Luggarus. Ticino, S Switzerland
Lochem 64 E3 Gelderland, E Netherlands
Lockport 19 E3 New York, NE USA
Lodja 55 D6 Kasai Oriental, C Dem. Rep. Congo
Lodwar 51 C6 Rift Valley, NW Kenya
Łódź 76 D4 Rus. Lodz. Łódzkie, C Poland
Loei 114 C4 var. Loey, Muang Loei. Loei, C Thailand
Loey see Loei
Lofoten 62 B3 var. Lofoten Islands. Island group C Norway
Lofoten Islands see Lofoten
Logan 22 B3 Utah, W USA
Logan, Mount 14 D3 mountain Yukon Territory, W Canada
Logroño 71 E1 anc. Vareia, Lat. Juliobriga. La Rioja, N Spain
Loibl Pass 73 D7 Ger. Loiblpass, Slvn. Ljubelj. Pass Austria/Slovenia
Loi-Kaw 114 B4 Kayah State, C Myanmar
Loire 68 B4 var. Liger. River C France
Loja 38 B2 Loja, S Ecuador
Lokitaung 51 C5 Rift Valley, NW Kenya
Lokoja 53 G4 Kogi, C Nigeria
Loksa 84 E2 Ger. Loxa. Harjumaa, NW Estonia
Lolland 63 B8 prev. Laaland. Island S Denmark
Lom 82 C1 prev. Lom-Palanka. Montana, NW Bulgaria
Lomami 55 D6 river C Dem. Rep. Congo
Lomas 38 D4 Arequipa, SW Peru
Lomas de Zamora 42 D4 Buenos Aires, E Argentina
Lombardia 74 B2 cultural region N Italy
Lombok, Pulau 116 D5 island Nusa Tenggara, C Indonesia
Lomé 53 F5 country capital (Togo) S Togo
Lomela 55 D6 Kasai Oriental, C Dem. Rep. Congo
Lommel 87 C5 Limburg, N Belgium
Lomond, Loch 66 B4 lake C Scotland, UK
Lomonosov Ridge 133 B3 var. Harris Ridge, Rus. Khrebet Lomonsova. Undersea feature Arctic Ocean
Lompoc 25 B7 California, W USA
Lom Sak 114 C4 var. Muang Lom Sak. Phetchabun, C Thailand
Łomża 76 D3 off. Województwo Łomżyńskie, Rus. Lomzha. Podlaskie, NE Poland
Loncoche 43 B5 Araucanía, C Chile
London 67 A7 anc. Augusta, Lat. Londinium. Country capital (UK) SE England, UK
London 18 C5 Kentucky, S USA
London 16 C5 Ontario, S Canada
Londonderry 66 B4 var. Derry, Ir. Doire. NW Northern Ireland, UK
Londonderry, Cape 124 C2 headland Western Australia
Londrina 41 E4 Paraná, S Brazil
Longa, Proliv 93 G1 Eng. Long Strait. Strait NE Russian Federation
Long Bay 21 F2 bay North Carolina/South Carolina, E USA
Long Beach 25 C7 California, W USA
Longford 67 B5 Ir. An Longfort. C Ireland
Long Island 32 D2 island C Bahamas
Long Island 19 G4 island New York, NE USA
Long Island see Bermuda
Longlac 16 C3 Ontario, S Canada
Longmont 22 D4 Colorado, C USA
Longreach 126 C4 Queensland, E Australia
Long Strait see Longa, Proliv
Longview 27 H3 Texas, SW USA
Longview 24 B2 Washington, NW USA
Long Xuyên 115 D6 var. Longxuyen. An Giang, S Vietnam
Longxuyen see Long Xuyên
Longyan 106 D6 Fujian, SE China
Longyearbyen 61 G2 dependent territory capital (Svalbard) Spitsbergen, W Svalbard
Lons-le-Saunier 68 D4 anc. Ledo Salinarius. Jura, E France
Lop Buri 115 C5 var. Loburi. Lop Buri, C Thailand
Lop Nor see Lop Nur
Lop Nur 104 C3 var. Lob Nor, Lop Nor, Lo-pu Po. Seasonal lake NW China
Loppersum 64 E1 Groningen, NE Netherlands
Lo-pu Po see Lop Nur
Lorca 71 E4 Ar. Lurka; anc. Eliocroca, Lat. Illur co. Murcia, S Spain
Lord Howe Island 120 C4 island E Australia
Lord Howe Rise 120 C4 undersea feature SW Pacific Ocean
Loreto 28 B3 Baja California Sur, W Mexico
Lorient 68 A3 prev. l'Orient. Morbihan, NW France
Lorn, Firth of 66 B4 inlet W Scotland, UK
Loro Sae see East Timor
Lörrach 73 A7 Baden-Württemberg, S Germany
Lorraine 68 D3 cultural region NE France
Los Alamos 26 C1 New Mexico, SW USA
Los Amates 30 B2 Izabal, E Guatemala
Los Angeles 25 C7 California, W USA
Los Ángeles 43 B5 Bío Bío, C Chile
Lošinj 78 A3 Ger. Lussin, It. Lussino. Island W Croatia
Los Mochis 28 C3 Sinaloa, C Mexico
Los Roques, Islas 36 D1 island group N Venezuela
Los Testigos, Isla 33 G5 island NE Venezuela
Lost River Range 24 D3 mountain range Idaho, C USA
Lot 69 B5 cultural region C France
Lot 69 B5 river S France
Lotagipi Swamp 51 C5 wetland Kenya/Sudan
Louangnamtha 114 C3 var. Luong Nam Tha. Louang Namtha, N Laos
Louangphabang 102 D3 var. Louangphrabang, Luang Prabang. Louangphabang, N Laos
Louangphrabang see Louangphabang
Loudéac 68 A3 Côtes d'Armor, NW France
Loudi 106 C5 Hunan, S China
Louga 52 B3 NW Senegal
Louisiade Archipelago 122 B4 island group SE PNG
Louisiana 20 A2 off. State of Louisiana; also known as Creole State, Pelican State. State S USA
Louisville 18 C5 Kentucky, S USA
Louisville Ridge 121 E4 undersea feature S Pacific Ocean
Loup River 23 E4 river Nebraska, C USA
Lourdes 69 B6 Hautes-Pyrénées, S France
Louth 67 E5 E England, UK
Loutrá 82 C4 Kentrikí Makedonía, N Greece
Lóuva 56 C1 Lunda Norte, NE Angola
Louvain-la Neuve 65 C6 Wallon Brabant, C Belgium
Louviers 68 C3 Eure, N France
Lovech 82 C2 Lovech, N Bulgaria
Loveland 22 D4 Colorado, C USA
Lovosice 76 A4 Ger. Lobositz. Ústecký Kraj, NW Czech Republic
Lowell 19 G3 Massachusetts, NE USA
Lower California see Baja California
Lower Hutt 129 D5 Wellington, North Island, NZ
Lower Lough Erne 67 A5 lake SW Northern Ireland, UK
Lower Red Lake 23 F1 lake Minnesota, N USA
Lower Tunguska see Nizhnyaya Tunguska
Lowestoft 67 E6 E England, UK
Lo-yang see Luoyang
Loyauté, Îles 122 D5 island group S New Caledonia
Loyew 85 D8 Rus. Loyev. Homyel'skaya Voblasts', SE Belarus
Loznica 78 C3 Serbia, W Serbia and Montenegro (Yugo.)
Lu see Shandong
Lualaba 55 D6 Fr. Loualaba. River SE Dem. Rep. Congo
Luanda 56 A1 var. Loanda, Port. São Paulo de Loanda. Country capital (Angola) Luanda, NW Angola
Luang Prabang see Louangphabang
Luang, Thale 115 C7 lagoon S Thailand
Luangua, Rio see Luangwa
Luangwa 51 B8 var. Aruângua, Rio Luangua. River Mozambique/Zambia
Luanshya 56 D2 Copperbelt, C Zambia
Luarca 70 C1 Asturias, N Spain
Lubaczów 77 E5 var. Lúbaczów. Podkarpackie, SE Poland
Lubań 76 B4 var. Koscian, Ger. Kosten. Dolnośląskie, SW Poland
Lubānas Ezers see Lubāns
Lubango 56 B2 Port. Sá da Bandeira. Huíla, SW Angola
Lubāns 84 D4 var. Lubānas Ezers. Lake E Latvia
Lubao 55 D6 Kasai Oriental, C Dem. Rep. Congo
Lübben 72 D4 Brandenburg, E Germany
Lübbenau 72 D4 Brandenburg, E Germany
Lubbock 27 E2 Texas, SW USA
Lübeck 72 C2 Schleswig-Holstein, N Germany
Lubelska, Wyżyna 76 E4 plateau SE Poland
Lubin 76 B4 Ger. Lüben. Dolnośląskie, W Poland
Lublin 76 E4 Rus. Lyublin. Lubelskie, E Poland
Lubliniec 76 C4 Śląskie, S Poland
Lubny 87 F2 Poltavs'ka Oblast', NE Ukraine
Lubsko 76 B4 Ger. Sommerfeld. Lubuskie, W Poland
Lubumbashi 55 E8 prev. Élisabethville. Shaba, SE Dem. Rep. Congo
Lubutu 55 D6 Maniema, E Dem. Rep. Congo
Lucan 89 B5 Ir. Leamhcán. E Ireland
Lucano, Appennino 75 D5 Eng. Lucanian Mountains. Mountain range S Italy
Lucapa 56 C1 var. Lukapa. Lunda Norte, NE Angola
Lucca 74 B3 anc. Luca. Toscana, C Italy
Lucea 32 A4 W Jamaica
Lucena 117 E1 off. Lucena City. Luzon, N Philippines
Lucena 70 D4 Andalucía, S Spain
Lučenec 77 D6 Ger. Losontz, Hung. Losonc. Banskobystrický Kraj, C Slovakia
Luchow see Hefei
Lucknow 113 E3 var. Lakhnau. Uttar Pradesh, N India
Lüda see Dalian
Luda Kamchiya 82 D2 river E Bulgaria
Lüderitz 56 B4 prev. Angra Pequena. Karas, SW Namibia
Ludhiāna 112 D2 Punjab, N India
Ludington 18 C2 Michigan, N USA
Luduş 86 B4 Ger. Ludasch, Hung. Marosludas. Mureş, C Romania
Ludvika 63 C6 Kopparberg, C Sweden
Ludwiglust 72 C3 Mecklenburg-Vorpommern, N Germany
Ludwigsburg 73 B6 Baden-Württemberg, SW Germany
Ludwigsfelde 72 D3 Brandenburg, NE Germany
Ludwigshafen 73 B5 var. Ludwigshafen am Rhein. Rheinland-Pfalz, W Germany
Ludwigshafen am Rhein see Ludwigshafen
Ludza 84 D4 Ger. Ludsan. Ludza, E Latvia
Luebo 55 C6 Kasai Occidental, SW Dem. Rep. Congo
Luena 56 C2 var. Lwena, Port. Luso. Moxico, E Angola
Lufira 55 E7 river SE Dem. Rep. Congo
Lufkin 27 H3 Texas, SW USA
Luga 88 A4 Leningradskaya Oblast', NW Russian Federation
Lugano 73 B8 Ger. Lauis. Ticino, S Switzerland
Lugenda, Rio 57 E2 river N Mozambique
Lugo 70 C1 anc. Lugus Augusti. Galicia, NW Spain
Lugoj 86 A4 Ger. Lugosch, Hung. Lugos. Timiş, W Romania
Luhans'k 87 H3 Rus. Lugansk; prev. Voroshilovgrad. Luhans'ka Oblast', E Ukraine
Luimneach see Limerick
Lukapa see Lucapa
Lukenie 55 C6 river C Dem. Rep. Congo
Lukovit 82 C2 Lovech, NW Bulgaria
Łuków 76 E4 Ger. Bogendorf. Lubelskie, E Poland
Lukuga 55 D7 river SE Dem. Rep. Congo
Luleå 84 D4 Norrbotten, N Sweden
Luleälven 62 C3 river N Sweden
Lulonga 55 C5 river NW Dem. Rep. Congo
Lulua 55 D7 river S Dem. Rep. Congo
Lumbo 57 F2 Nampula, NE Mozambique
Lumsden 129 A7 Southland, South Island, NZ
Lund 63 B7 Skåne, S Sweden
Lüneburg 72 C3 Niedersachsen, N Germany
Lungkiang see Qiqihar
Lungué-Bungo 56 C2 var. Lungwebungu. River Angola/Zambia see also Lungwebungu
Lungwebungu see Lungué-Bungo
Luninyets 85 B7 Pol. Łuniniec, Rus. Luninets. Brestskaya Voblasts', SW Belarus
Lunteren 64 D4 Gelderland, C Netherlands
Luong Nam Tha see Louangnamtha
Luoyang 106 C4 var. Honan, Lo-yang. Henan, C China
Lúrio 57 F2 Nampula, NE Mozambique
Lúrio, Rio 57 E2 river NE Mozambique
Lusaka 56 D2 country capital (Zambia) Lusaka, SE Zambia
Lushnja see Lushnjë
Lushnjë 79 C6 var. Lushnja. Fier, C Albania
Luso see Luena
Lūt, Dasht-e 98 D3 var. Kavīr-e Lūt. Desert E Iran
Luton 67 D6 SE England, UK
Łutselk'e 15 F4 prev. Snowdrift. Northwest Territories, W Canada
Luts'k 86 C1 Pol. Łuck, Rus. Lutsk. Volyns'ka Oblast', NW Ukraine
Lutzow-Holm Bay see Lützow Holmbukta
Lützow Holmbukta 132 C2 var. Lutzow-Holm Bay. Bay Antarctica
Luuq 51 D6 It. Lugh Ganana. Gedo, SW Somalia
Luvua 55 D7 river SE Dem. Rep. Congo
Luwego 51 C8 river S Tanzania
Luxembourg 87 D8 var. Lëtzebuerg, Luxemburg. Country NW Europe
Luxembourg 65 D8 country capital (Luxembourg) Luxembourg, S Luxembourg
Luxor 50 B2 Ar. Al Uqşur. E Egypt
Luza 88 C4 Kirovskaya Oblast', NW Russian Federation
Luz, Costa de la 70 C5 coastal region SW Spain
Luzern 73 B7 Fr. Lucerne, It. Lucerna. Luzern, C Switzerland
Luzon 117 E1 island N Philippines
Luzon Strait 103 E3 strait Philippines/Taiwan
L'viv 86 B2 Ger. Lemberg, Pol. Lwów, Rus. L'vov. L'vivs'ka Oblast', W Ukraine
Lwena see Luena
Lyakhavichy 85 B6 Rus. Lyakhovichi. Brestskaya Voblasts', SW Belarus
Lycksele 62 C4 Västerbotten, N Sweden
Lycopolis see Asyût
Lyel'chytsy 85 C7 Rus. Lel'chitsy. Homyel'skaya Voblasts', SE Belarus
Lyepyel' 85 D5 Rus. Lepel'. Vitsyebskaya Voblasts', N Belarus
Lyme Bay 67 C7 bay S England, UK
Lynchburg 19 E5 Virginia, NE USA
Lynn Regis see King's Lynn
Lyon 69 D5 Eng. Lyons; anc. Lugdunum. Rhône, E France
Lyozna 85 E6 Rus. Liozno. Vitsyebskaya Voblasts', NE Belarus
Lypovets' 86 D2 Rus. Lipovets. Vinnyts'ka Oblast', C Ukraine
Lysychans'k 87 H3 Rus. Lisichansk. Luhans'ka Oblast', E Ukraine
Lyttelton 129 C6 Canterbury, South Island, NZ
Lyubotyn 87 G2 Rus. Lyubotin. Kharkivs'ka Oblast', E Ukraine
Lyulyakovo 82 E2 prev. Keremitlik. Burgas, E Bulgaria
Lyusina 85 B6 Rus. Lyusino. Brestskaya Voblasts', SW Belarus

M

Ma'ān 97 B7 Ma'ān, SW Jordan
Maardu 84 D2 Ger. Maart. Harjumaa, NW Estonia
Ma'aret-en-Nu'man see Ma'arrat an Nu'mān
Ma'arrat an Nu'mān 96 B3 var. Ma'aret-en-Nu'man, Fr. Maarret enn Naamâne. Idlib, NW Syria
Maarret enn Naamâne see Ma'arrat an Nu'mān
Maaseik 65 D5 prev. Maeseyck. Limburg, NE Belgium
Maastricht 65 D6 var. Maestricht; anc. Traietum ad Mosam, Traiectum Tungorum. Limburg, SE Netherlands
Macao 107 C6 Chin. Aomen, Port. Macao. S China
Macapá 41 E1 state capital Amapá, N Brazil
Macassar see Ujungpandang
MacCluer Gulf see Berau, Teluk
Macdonnell Ranges 124 D4 mountain range Northern Territory, C Australia
Macedonia, FYR 79 D6 var. Macedonia, Mac. Makedonija, abbrev. FYR Macedonia, FYROM. Country SE Europe
Maceió 41 G3 state capital Alagoas, E Brazil
Machachi 38 B1 Pichincha, C Ecuador
Machala 38 B2 El Oro, SW Ecuador
Machanga 57 E3 Sofala, E Mozambique

Machilīpatnam 110 D1 var. Bandar Masulipatnam. Andhra Pradesh, E India
Machiques 36 C2 Zulia, NW Venezuela
Macías Nguema Biyogo see Bioco, Isla de
Măcin 86 D5 Tulcea, SE Romania
Macizo de las Guayanas see Guiana Highlands
Mackay 126 D4 Queensland, NE Australia
Mackay, Lake 124 C4 salt lake Northern Territory/Western Australia
Mackenzie 15 E3 river Northwest Territories, NW Canada
Mackenzie Bay 132 D3 bay Antarctica
Mackenzie Mountains 14 D3 mountain range Northwest Territories, NW Canada
Macleod, Lake 124 A4 lake Western Australia
Macomb 18 A4 Illinois, N USA
Macomer 75 A5 Sardegna, Italy, C Mediterranean Sea
Macon 20 D2 Georgia, SE USA
Macon 23 G4 Missouri, C USA
Mâcon 69 D5 anc. Matisco, Matisco Ædourum. Saône-et-Loire, C France
Macquarie Ridge 132 C5 undersea feature SW Pacific Ocean
Macuspana 29 G4 Tabasco, SE Mexico
Ma'daba 97 B6 var. Mādabā, Madeba; anc. Medeba. 'Ammān, NW Jordan
Madagascar 57 F3 Malg. Madagasikara; prev. Malagasy Republic. Country W Indian Ocean
Madagascar 57 F3 island W Indian Ocean
Madagascar Basin 47 E7 var. Madagascar W Indian Ocean
Madagascar Plateau 47 E7 var. Madagascar Ridge, Madagascar Rise, Rus. Madagaskarskiy Khrebet. Undersea feature W Indian Ocean
Madagascar Ridge see Madagascar Plateau
Madagascar Rise see Madagascar Plateau
Madagaskarskiy Khrebet see Madagascar Plateau
Madang 122 B3 Madang, N PNG
Madanīyīn see Médenine
Made 64 C4 Noord-Brabant, S Netherlands
Madeba see Ma'daba
Madeira 48 A3 var. Ilha de Madeira. Island Portugal, NE Atlantic Ocean
Madeira 48 A2 var. Madeira, Port. Arquipélago da Madeira. Island group Portugal, NE Atlantic Ocean
Madeira Plain 44 C3 undersea feature E Atlantic Ocean
Madeira, Rio 40 D2 Sp. Río Madera. River Bolivia/Brazil see also Madera, Río
Madeleine, Îles de la 17 F4 Eng. Magdalen Islands. Island group Québec, E Canada
Madera 25 B6 California, W USA
Madhya Pradesh 113 E4 prev. Central Provinces and Berar. Admin. region state C India
Madīnat ath Thawrah 96 C2 var. Ath Thawrah. Ar Raqqah, N Syria Asia
Madison 18 B3 state capital Wisconsin, N USA
Madison 23 F3 South Dakota, N USA
Madiun 116 D5 prev. Madioen. Jawa, C Indonesia
Madona 84 D4 Ger. Modohn. Madona, E Latvia
Madras see Tamil Nādu
Madras see Chennai
Madre de Dios 34 B4 off. Departamento de Madre de Dios. Department E Peru
Madre de Dios, Río 39 E3 river Bolivia/Peru
Madre del Sur, Sierra 29 E5 mountain range S Mexico
Madre, Laguna 29 F3 lagoon NE Mexico
Madre, Laguna 27 G5 lake Texas, SW USA
Madre Occidental, Sierra 28 C3 var. Western Sierra Madre. Mountain range C Mexico
Madre Oriental, Sierra 29 E3 var. Eastern Sierra Madre. Mountain range C Mexico
Madrid 70 D3 country capital (Spain) Madrid, C Spain
Madurai 110 C3 prev. Madura, Mathurai. Tamil Nādu, S India
Madura, Pulau 116 D5 prev. Madoera. Island C Indonesia
Maebashi 109 D5 var. Maebasi, Mayebashi. Gunma, Honshū, S Japan
Maebasi see Maebashi
Mae Nam Khong see Mekong
Mae Nam Nan 114 C4 river NW Thailand
Mae Nam Yom 114 C4 river W Thailand
Maestricht see Maastricht
Maéwo 122 D4 prev. Aurora. Island C Vanuatu
Mafia 51 D7 island E Tanzania
Mafraq see Al Mafraq
Magadan 93 G3 Magadanskaya Oblast', E Russian Federation
Magangué 36 B2 Bolívar, N Colombia
Magdalena 34 A2 off. Departamento del Magdalena. Province N Colombia
Magdalena 39 F3 Beni, N Bolivia
Magdalena 28 B1 Sonora, NW Mexico
Magdalena, Isla 28 B3 island W Mexico
Magdalena, Río 36 B2 river C Colombia
Magdeburg 72 C4 Sachsen-Anhalt, C Germany
Magelang 116 C5 Jawa, C Indonesia
Magellan, Strait of 43 B8 Sp. Estrecho de Magallanes. Strait Argentina/Chile
Magerøya see Magerøya
Magerøya 62 D1 var. Magerøy. Island N Norway
Maggiore, Lake 74 B1 It. Lago Maggiore. Lake Italy/Switzerland
Maglaj 78 C3 Federacija Bosna I Hercegovina, N Bosnia and Herzegovina
Maglie 75 E6 Puglia, SE Italy
Magna 22 B4 Utah, W USA
Magnesia see Manisa
Magnitogorsk 92 B4 Chelyabinskaya Oblast', C Russian Federation

Magta' Lahjar 52 C3 var. Magta Lahjar, Magta' Lahjar, Magtâ Lahjar. Brakna, SW Mauritania
Magway see Magwe
Magwe 114 A3 var. Magway. Magwe, W Myanmar
Mahajanga 57 F2 var. Majunga. Mahajanga, NW Madagascar
Mahakam, Sungai 116 D4 var. Koetai, Kutai. River Borneo, C Indonesia
Mahalapye 56 D3 var. Mahalatswe. Central, SE Botswana
Mahalatswe see Mahalapye
Mahān 98 D3 Kermān, E Iran
Mahānadi 113 F4 river E India
Mahārāshtra 112 D5 state W India
Mahbés see El Mahbas
Mahbūbnagar 112 D5 Andhra Pradesh, C India
Mahdia 49 F2 var. Al Mahdīyah, Mehdia. NE Tunisia
Mahé 57 H1 island Inner Islands, NE Seychelles
Mahia Peninsula 128 E4 peninsula North Island, NZ
Mahilyow 85 D6 Rus. Mogilëv. Mahilyowskaya Voblasts', E Belarus
Maḥmūd-e 'Erāqī see Maḥmūd-e Rāqī
Maḥmūd-e Rāqī 101 E4 var. Maḥmūd-e 'Erāqī. Kāpīsā, NE Afghanistan
Mahón 71 H3 Cat. Maó, Eng. Port Mahon; anc. Portus Magonis. Menorca, Spain, W Mediterranean Sea
Maicao 36 C1 La Guajira, N Colombia
Mai Ceu see Maych'ew
Mai Chio see Maych'ew
Maidstone 67 E7 SE England, UK
Maiduguri 53 H4 Borno, NE Nigeria
Maimāna see Meymaneh
Main 73 B5 river C Germany
Mai-Ndombe, Lac 55 C6 prev. Lac Léopold II. Lake W Dem. Rep. Congo
Maine 19 G2 off. State of Maine; also known as Lumber State, Pine Tree State. State NE USA
Maine 68 B3 cultural region NW France
Maine, Gulf of 19 H2 gulf NE USA
Main Island see Bermuda
Mainland 66 C2 island Orkney, N Scotland, UK
Mainland 66 D1 island Shetland, NE Scotland, UK
Mainz 73 B5 Fr. Mayence. Rheinland-Pfalz, SW Germany
Maio 52 A3 var. Mayo. Island Ilhas de Sotavento, SE Cape Verde
Maisur see Karnātaka
Maisur see Mysore
Maizhokunggar 104 C5 Xizang Zizhiqu, W China
Maíz, Islas del 31 E3 var. Corn Islands. Island group SE Nicaragua
Mājro see Majuro Atoll
Majunga see Mahajanga
Majuro Atoll 122 D2 var. Mājro. Atoll Ratak Chain, SE Marshall Islands
Makale see Mek'elē
Makarov Basin 133 B3 undersea feature Arctic Ocean
Makarska 78 B4 It. Macarsca. Split-Dalmacija, SE Croatia
Makassar see Ujungpandang
Makassar see Ujungpandang
Makassar Strait 116 D4 Ind. Selat Makasar. Strait C Indonesia
Makay 57 F3 var. Massif du Makay. Mountain range SW Madagascar
Makeni 52 C4 C Sierra Leone
Makhachkala 92 A4 prev. Petrovsk-Port. Respublika Dagestan, SW Russian Federation
Makin 122 D2 prev. Pitt Island. Atoll Tungaru, W Kiribati
Makira see San Cristobal
Makiyivka 87 G3 Rus. Makeyevka; prev. Dmitriyevsk. Donets'ka Oblast', E Ukraine
Makkah 99 A5 Eng. Mecca. Makkah, W Saudi Arabia
Makkovik 17 F2 Newfoundland and Labrador, NE Canada
Makó 77 D7 Rom. Macău. Csongrád, SE Hungary
Makoua 55 B5 Cuvette, C Congo
Makran Coast 98 E4 coastal region SE Iran
Makrany 85 A6 Rus. Mokrany. Brestskaya Voblasts', SW Belarus
Mākū 98 B2 Āzarbāyjān-e Bākhtarī, NW Iran
Makurdi 53 G4 Benue, C Nigeria
Mala see Malaita
Malabār Coast 110 B3 coast SW India
Malabo 55 A5 prev. Santa Isabel. Country capital (Equatorial Guinea) Isla de Bioco, NW Equatorial Guinea
Malacca see Melaka
Malacca, Strait of 116 B3 Ind. Selat Malaka. Strait Indonesia/Malaysia
Malacky 77 C6 Hung. Malacka. Bratislavský Kraj, W Slovakia
Maladzyechna 85 C5 Pol. Molodeczno, Rus. Molodechno. Minskaya Voblasts', C Belarus
Málaga 70 D5 anc. Malaca. Andalucía, S Spain
Malagarasi River 51 B7 river W Tanzania
Malaita 122 C3 var. Mala. Island N Solomon Islands
Malakal 51 B5 Upper Nile, S Sudan
Malakula see Malekula
Malang 116 D5 Jawa, C Indonesia
Malange see Malanje
Malanje 56 B1 var. Malange. Malanje, NW Angola
Mälaren 63 C6 lake C Sweden
Malatya 95 E4 anc. Melitene. Malatya, SE Turkey

Mala Vyska 87 E3 Rus. Malaya Viska. Kirovohrads'ka Oblast', S Ukraine
Malawi 57 E1 prev. Nyasaland, Nyasaland Protectorate. Country S Africa
Malawi, Lake see Nyasa, Lake
Malay Peninsula 102 D4 peninsula Malaysia/Thailand
Malaysia 116 B3 var. Federation of Malaysia; prev. the separate territories of Federation of Malaya, Sarawak and Sabah (North Borneo) and Singapore. Country SE Asia
Malaysia, Federation of see Malaysia
Malbork 76 C2 Ger. Marienburg, Marienburg in Westpreussen. Pomorskie, N Poland
Malchin 72 C3 Mecklenburg-Vorpommern, N Germany
Malden 23 H5 Missouri, C USA
Malden Island 123 G3 prev. Independence Island. Atoll E Kiribati
Maldives 110 A4 Country N Indian Ocean
Male' 110 B4 Male' Atoll, C Maldives
Male' Atoll 110 B4 var. Kaafu Atoll. Atoll C Maldives
Malekula 122 D4 var. Malakula; prev. Mallicolo. Island W Vanuatu
Malesína 83 C5 Stereá Ellás, E Greece
Malheur Lake 24 C3 lake Oregon, NW USA
Mali 53 E3 Fr. République du Mali; prev. French Sudan, Sudanese Republic. Country W Africa
Malik, Wadi el see Milk, Wadi el
Mali Kyun 115 B5 var. Tavoy Island. Island Mergui Archipelago, S Myanmar
Malindi 51 D7 Coast, SE Kenya
Malko Tŭrnovo 82 E3 Burgas, E Bulgaria
Mallaig 66 B3 N Scotland, UK
Mallawi 50 B2 C Egypt
Mallicolo see Malekula
Mallorca 71 G3 Eng. Majorca; anc. Baleares Major. Island Islas Baleares, Spain, W Mediterranean Sea
Malmberget 62 C3 Norrbotten, N Sweden
Malmédy 65 D6 Liège, E Belgium
Malmö 63 B7 Skåne, S Sweden
Maloelap see Maloelap Atoll
Maloelap Atoll 122 D1 var. Maloelap. Atoll E Marshall Islands
Małopolska 76 D4 plateau S Poland
Malozemel'skaya Tundra 88 D3 physical region NW Russian Federation
Malta 75 C8 Country C Mediterranean Sea
Malta 75 C8 island Malta, C Mediterranean Sea
Malta 22 C1 Montana, NW USA
Malta 84 D4 Rēzekne, SE Latvia
Malta Channel 75 C8 It. Canale di Malta. Strait Italy/Malta
Maluku 117 F4 Dut. Molukken, Eng. Moluccas; prev. Spice Islands. Island group E Indonesia
Malung 63 B6 Kopparberg, C Sweden
Malyn 86 D2 Rus. Malin. Zhytomyrs'ka Oblast', N Ukraine
Mamberamo, Sungai 117 H4 river Papua, E Indonesia
Mambij see Manbij
Mamonovo 84 A4 Ger. Heiligenbeil. Kaliningradskaya Oblast', W Russian Federation
Mamoré, Rio 39 F3 river Bolivia/Brazil
Mamou 52 C4 Moyenne-Guinée, W Guinea
Mamoudzou 57 F2 dependent territory capital (Mayotte) C Mayotte
Mamuno 56 C3 Ghanzi, W Botswana
Manacor 71 G3 Mallorca, Spain, W Mediterranean Sea
Manado 117 F3 prev. Menado. Sulawesi, C Indonesia
Managua 30 D3 country capital (Nicaragua) Managua, W Nicaragua
Managua, Lago de 30 C3 var. Xolotlán. Lake W Nicaragua
Manakara 57 G4 Fianarantsoa, SE Madagascar
Manama see Al Manāmah
Mananjary 57 G3 Fianarantsoa, SE Madagascar
Manapouri, Lake 129 A7 lake South Island, NZ
Manar see Mannar
Manas, Gora 101 E2 mountain Kyrgyzstan/Uzbekistan
Manaus 40 D2 prev. Manáos. State capital Amazonas, NW Brazil
Manavgat 94 B4 Antalya, SW Turkey
Manbij 96 C2 var. Mambij, Fr. Membidj. Ḥalab, N Syria
Manchester 67 D5 Lat. Mancunium. NW England, UK
Manchester 19 G3 New Hampshire, NE USA
Man-chou-li see Manzhouli
Manchuria 103 E1 cultural region NE China
Mâncio Lima see Japiim
Mand see Mand, Rūd-e
Mandalay 114 B3 Mandalay, C Myanmar
Mandan 23 E2 North Dakota, N USA
Mandeville 32 B5 C Jamaica
Mándra 83 C6 Attikí, C Greece
Mand, Rūd-e 98 D4 var. Mand. River S Iran
Mandurah 125 A6 Western Australia
Manduria 75 E5 Puglia, SE Italy
Mandya 110 C2 Karnātaka, C India
Manfredonia 75 D5 Puglia, SE Italy
Mangai 55 C6 Bandundu, W Dem. Rep. Congo
Mangaia 123 G5 island group S Cook Islands
Mangalia 86 D5 anc. Callatis. Constanţa, SE Romania
Mangalmé 54 C3 Guéra, SE Chad
Mangalore 110 B2 Karnātaka, W India
Mangaung see Bloemfontein
Mango see Sansanné-Mango

Mangoky 79 F3 river W Madagascar
Manhattan 23 F4 Kansas, C USA
Manicouagan, Réservoir 16 D3 lake Québec, E Canada
Manihiki 123 G4 atoll N Cook Islands
Manihiki Plateau 121 E3 undersea feature C Pacific Ocean
Maniitsoq 60 C3 var. Manîtsoq, Dan. Sukkertoppen. S Greenland
Manila 117 E1 off. City of Manila. Country capital (Philippines) Luzon, N Philippines
Manisa 94 A3 var. Manissa; prev. Saruhan, anc. Magnesia. Manisa, W Turkey
Manissa see Manisa
Manitoba 15 F5 province S Canada
Manitoba, Lake 15 F5 lake Manitoba, S Canada
Manitoulin Island 16 C4 island Ontario, S Canada
Manîtsoq see Maniitsoq
Manizales 36 B3 Caldas, W Colombia
Manjimup 125 A7 Western Australia
Mankato 23 F3 Minnesota, N USA
Manlleu 71 G2 Cataluña, NE Spain
Manly 126 E1 New South Wales, SE Australia
Manmād 112 C5 Mahārāshtra, W India
Mannar 110 C3 var. Manar. Northern Province, NW Sri Lanka
Mannar, Gulf of 110 C3 gulf India/Sri Lanka
Mannheim 73 B5 Baden-Württemberg, SW Germany
Manono 55 E7 Shaba, SE Dem. Rep. Congo
Manosque 69 D6 Alpes-de-Haute-Provence, SE France
Manra 123 F3 prev. Sydney Island. Atoll Phoenix Islands, C Kiribati
Mansa 56 D2 prev. Fort Rosebery. Luapula, N Zambia
Mansel Island 15 G3 island Nunavut, NE Canada
Mansfield 18 D4 Ohio, N USA
Manta 38 A2 Manabí, W Ecuador
Mantova 74 B2 Eng. Mantua, Fr. Mantoue. Lombardia, NW Italy
Manuae 123 G4 island S Cook Islands
Manurewa 128 D3 var. Manukau. Auckland, North Island, NZ
Manzanares 71 E3 Castilla-La Mancha, C Spain
Manzanillo 28 D4 Colima, SW Mexico
Manzanillo 32 C3 Granma, E Cuba
Manzhouli 105 F1 var. Man-chou-li. Nei Mongol Zizhiqu, N China
Mao 54 B3 Kanem, W Chad
Maoke, Pegunungan 117 H4 Dut. Sneeuw-gebergte, Eng. Snow Mountains. Mountain range Papua, E Indonesia
Maoming 106 C6 Guangdong, S China
Mapmaker Seamounts 103 H2 undersea feature N Pacific Ocean
Maputo 56 D4 prev. Lourenço Marques. Country capital (Mozambique) Maputo, S Mozambique
Marabá 41 F2 Pará, NE Brazil
Maracaibo 36 C1 Zulia, NW Venezuela
Maracaibo, Lago de 36 C2 var. Lake Maracaibo. Inlet NW Venezuela
Maracaibo, Lake see Maracaibo, Lago de
Maracay 36 D2 Aragua, N Venezuela
Marada see Marādah
Marādah 49 G3 var. Marada. N Libya
Maradi 53 G3 Maradi, S Niger
Maragha see Marāgheh
Marāgheh 98 C2 var. Maragha. Āzarbāyjān-e Khāvarī, NW Iran
Marajó, Baía de 41 F1 bay N Brazil
Marajó, Ilha de 41 E1 island N Brazil
Marakesh see Marrakech
Maramba see Livingstone
Maranhão 41 F2 off. Estado do Maranhão. State E Brazil
Marañón, Río 38 B2 river N Peru
Maraş see Kahramanmaraş
Marash see Kahramanmaraş
Marathon 16 C4 Ontario, S Canada
Marathónas 83 C5 prev. Marathón. Attikí, C Greece
Mărăză 95 H2 Rus. Maraza. E Azerbaijan
Marbella 70 D5 Andalucía, S Spain
Marble Bar 124 B4 Western Australia
Marburg an der Lahn 72 B4 hist. Marburg. Hessen, W Germany
March see Morava
Marche 69 C5 cultural region C France
Marche 74 C3 cultural region E Italy
Marche-en-Famenne 65 C7 Luxembourg, SE Belgium
Marchena, Isla 38 B5 var. Bindloe Island. Island Galapagos Islands, Ecuador, E Pacific Ocean
Mar Chiquita, Laguna 42 C3 lake C Argentina
Marcounda see Markounda
Mardān 112 C1 North-West Frontier Province, N Pakistan
Mar del Plata 43 D5 Buenos Aires, E Argentina
Mardin 95 E4 Mardin, SE Turkey
Maré 122 D5 island Îles Loyauté, E New Caledonia
Marea Neagră see Black Sea
Mare Creticum see Kritikó Pélagos
Mareeba 126 D3 Queensland, NE Australia
Margarita, Isla de 37 E1 island N Venezuela
Margate 67 E7 prev. Mergate. SE England, UK
Marghita 86 B3 Hung. Margitta. Bihor, NW Romania
Marhanets' 87 F3 Rus. Marganets. Dnipropetrovs'ka Oblast', E Ukraine

Mangoky 79 F3 river W Madagascar
María Cleofas, Isla 28 C4 island C Mexico
Maria Island 127 C8 island Tasmania, SE Australia
María Madre, Isla 28 C4 island C Mexico
María Magdalena, Isla 28 C4 island C Mexico
Mariana Trench 103 G4 undersea feature W Pacific Ocean
Mariánské Lázně 77 A5 Ger. Marienbad. Karlovarský Kraj, W Czech Republic
Marías, Islas 28 C4 island group C Mexico
Maribor 73 E7 Ger. Marburg. NE Slovenia
Marica see Maritsa
Maridi 51 B5 Western Equatoria, SW Sudan
Marie Byrd Land 132 A3 physical region Antarctica
Marie-Galante 33 G4 var. Ceyre to the Caribs. Island SE Guadeloupe
Mariental 56 B4 Hardap, SW Namibia
Mariestad 63 B6 Västra Götaland, S Sweden
Marietta 20 D2 Georgia, SE USA
Marijampolė 84 B4 prev. Kapsukas. Marijampolė, S Lithuania
Marília 41 E4 São Paulo, S Brazil
Marín 70 B1 Galicia, NW Spain
Mar"ina Horka 85 C6 Rus. Mar'ina Gorka. Minskaya Voblasts', C Belarus
Maringá 41 E4 Paraná, S Brazil
Marion 23 G3 Iowa, C USA
Marion 18 D4 Ohio, N USA
Marion, Lake 21 E2 reservoir South Carolina, SE USA
Mariscal Estigarribia 42 D2 Boquerón, NW Paraguay
Maritsa 82 D3 var. Marica, Gk. Évros, Turk. Meriç; anc. Hebrus. River SW Europe see also Évros/Meriç
Maritzburg see Pietermaritzburg
Mariupol' 87 G4 prev. Zhdanov. Donets'ka Oblast', SE Ukraine
Marka 51 D6 var. Merca. Shabeellaha Hoose, S Somalia
Markham, Mount 132 B4 mountain Antarctica
Markounda 54 C4 var. Marcounda. Ouham, NW Central African Republic
Marktredwitz 73 C5 Bayern, E Germany
Marlborough 126 D4 Queensland, E Australia
Marmande 69 B5 anc. Marmanda. Lot-et-Garonne, SW France
Marmara Denizi 94 B2 Eng. Sea of Marmara. Sea NW Turkey
Marmara, Sea of see Marmara Denizi
Marmaris 94 A4 Muğla, SW Turkey
Marne 68 D3 cultural region N France
Marne 68 D3 river N France
Maro 54 C4 Moyen-Chari, S Chad
Maroantsetra 57 G2 Toamasina, NE Madagascar
Maromokotro 57 G2 mountain N Madagascar
Maroni River 37 G3 Dut. Marowijne. River French Guiana/Suriname
Maros see Mureş
Marosch see Mureş
Marotiri 121 F4 var. Îlots de Bass, Morotiri. Island group Îles Australes, SW French Polynesia
Maroua 54 B3 Extrême-Nord, N Cameroon
Marquesas Fracture Zone 131 E3 tectonic feature E Pacific Ocean
Marquesas Islands 131 E3 island group N French Polynesia
Marquette 18 B1 Michigan, N USA
Marrakech 48 C2 var. Marakesh, Eng. Marrakesh; prev. Morocco. W Morocco
Marrakesh see Marrakech
Marrawah 127 C8 Tasmania, SE Australia
Marree 127 B5 South Australia
Marsá al Burayqah 49 G3 var. Al Burayqah, N Libya
Marsabit 51 C6 Eastern, N Kenya
Marsala 75 B7 anc. Lilybaeum. Sicilia, Italy, C Mediterranean Sea
Marsberg 72 B4 Nordrhein-Westfalen, W Germany
Marseille 69 D6 Eng. Marseilles; anc. Massilia. Bouches-du-Rhône, SE France
Marshall 23 F2 Minnesota, N USA
Marshall 27 H2 Texas, SW USA
Marshall Islands 122 C1 Country W Pacific Ocean
Marshall Seamounts 103 H3 undersea feature SW Pacific Ocean
Marsh Harbour 32 C1 Great Abaco, N Bahamas
Martaban 114 B4 var. Moktama. Mon State, S Myanmar
Martha's Vineyard 19 G3 island Massachusetts, NE USA
Martigues 69 D6 Bouches-du-Rhône, SE France
Martin 77 C5 Ger. Sankt Martin, Hung. Turócszentmárton; prev. Turčiansky Svätý Martin. Žilinský Kraj, N Slovakia
Martinique 33 G4 French overseas department E West Indies
Martinique Channel see Martinique Passage
Martinique Passage 33 G4 var. Dominica Channel, Martinique Channel. Channel Dominica/Martinique
Marton 128 D4 Manawatu-Wanganui, North Island, NZ
Martos 70 D4 Andalucía, S Spain
Marungu 55 E7 mountain range SE Dem. Rep. Congo
Mary 100 D3 prev. Merv. Maryyskiy Velayat, S Turkmenistan
Maryborough see Portlaoise
Maryborough 127 D4 Queensland, E Australia
Mary Island see Kanton

Maryland – Missoula

Maryland *19 E5 off.* State of Maryland; also known as America in Miniature, Cockade State, Free State, Old Line State. *State* NE USA
Maryland *20 D1* Tennessee, S USA
Maryville *23 F4* Missouri, C USA
Masai Steppe *51 C7 grassland* NW Tanzania
Masaka *51 B6* SW Uganda
Masallı *95 H3 Rus.* Masally. S Azerbaijan
Masasi *51 C8* Mtwara, SE Tanzania
Masawa *see* Massawa
Masaya *30 D3* Masaya, W Nicaragua
Mascarene Basin *119 B5 undersea feature* W Indian Ocean
Mascarene Islands *57 H4 island group* W Indian Ocean
Mascarene Plain *119 B5 undersea feature* W Indian Ocean
Mascarene Plateau *119 B5 undersea feature* W Indian Ocean
Maseru *56 D4 country capital* (Lesotho) W Lesotho
Mashhad *98 E2 var.* Meshed. Khorāsān, NE Iran
Mas-ha *97 D7* W Bank
Masindi *51 B6* W Uganda
Masīra *see* Maşīrah, Jazīrat
Masira, Gulf of *see* Maşīrah, Khalīj
Maşīrah, Jazīrat *99 E5 var.* Masīra. *Island* E Oman
Maşīrah, Khalīj *99 E5 var.* Gulf of Masira. *Bay* E Oman
Masis *see* Büyükağrı Dağı
Maskat *see* Masqaţ
Mason City *23 F3* Iowa, C USA
Masqaţ *99 E5 var.* Maskat, *Eng.* Muscat. *Country capital* (Oman) NE Oman
Massa *74 B3* Toscana, C Italy
Massachusetts *19 G3 off.* Commonwealth of Massachusetts; also known as Bay State, Old Bay State, Old Colony State. *State* NE USA
Massawa *50 C4 var.* Masawa, *Amh.* Mits'iwa. E Eritrea
Massenya *54 B3* Chari-Baguirmi, SW Chad
Massif Central *69 C5 plateau* C France
Massif du Makay *see* Makay
Massoukou *see* Franceville
Masterton *129 D5* Wellington, North Island, NZ
Masty *85 B5 Rus.* Mosty. Hrodzyenskaya Voblasts', W Belarus
Masuda *109 B6* Shimane, Honshū, SW Japan
Masuku *see* Franceville
Masvingo *56 D3 prev.* Fort Victoria, Nyanda, Victoria. Masvingo, SE Zimbabwe
Maşyāf *96 B3 Fr.* Misiaf. Ḩamāh, C Syria
Matadi *55 B6* Bas-Zaïre, W Dem. Rep. Congo
Matagalpa *30 D3* Matagalpa, C Nicaragua
Matale *110 D3* Central Province, C Sri Lanka
Matam *52 C3* NE Senegal
Matamata *128 D3* Waikato, North Island, NZ
Matamoros *28 D3* Coahuila de Zaragoza, NE Mexico
Matamoros *29 E2* Tamaulipas, C Mexico
Matane *17 E4* Québec, SE Canada
Matanzas *32 B2* Matanzas, NW Cuba
Matara *110 D4* Southern Province, S Sri Lanka
Mataram *116 D5* Pulau Lombok, C Indonesia
Mataró *71 G2 anc.* Illuro. Cataluña, E Spain
Mataura *129 B7 river* South Island, NZ
Mataura *129 B7* Southland, South Island, NZ
Mata Uta *see* Matā'utu
Matā'utu *123 E4 var.* Mata Uta. *Dependent territory capital* (Wallis and Futuna) Île Uvea, Wallis and Futuna
Matera *75 E5* Basilicata, S Italy
Matías Romero *29 F5* Oaxaca, SE Mexico
Mato Grosso *41 E4 prev.* Vila Bela da Santissima Trindade. Mato Grosso, W Brazil
Mato Grosso do Sul *41 E4 off.* Estado de Mato Grosso do Sul. *State* S Brazil
Mato Grosso, Planalto de *34 C4 plateau* C Brazil
Matosinhos *70 B2 prev.* Matozinhos. Porto, NW Portugal
Matsue *109 B6 var.* Matsuye, Matue. Shimane, Honshū, SW Japan
Matsumoto *109 C5 var.* Matumoto. Nagano, Honshū, S Japan
Matsuyama *109 B7 var.* Matuyama. Ehime, Shikoku, SW Japan
Matsuye *see* Matsue
Matterhorn *73 A8 It.* Monte Cervino. *Mountain* Italy/Switzerland *see also* Cervino, Monte
Matthews Ridge *37 F2* N Guyana
Matthew Town *32 D2* Great Inagua, S Bahamas
Matucana *38 C4* Lima, W Peru
Matue *see* Matsue
Matumoto *see* Matsumoto
Maturín *37 E2* Monagas, NE Venezuela
Matuyama *see* Matsuyama
Mau *113 E3 var.* Maunāth Bhanjan. Uttar Pradesh, N India
Maui *25 B8 island* Hawai'i, USA, C Pacific Ocean
Maulmain *see* Moulmein
Maun *56 C3* Ngamiland, C Botswana
Maunāth Bhanjan *see* Mau
Mauren *72 E1* NE Liechtenstein
Mauritania *52 C2 Ar.* Mūrītānīyah. *Country* W Africa
Mauritius *57 H3 Fr.* Maurice. *Country* W Indian Ocean
Mauritius *119 B5 island* W Indian Ocean
Mawlamyine *see* Moulmein
Mawson *132 D2 Australian research station* Antarctica
Maya *30 B1 river* E Russian Federation
Mayadin *see* Al Mayādīn
Mayaguana *32 D2 island* SE Bahamas
Mayaguana Passage *32 D2 passage* SE Bahamas
Mayagüez *33 F3* W Puerto Rico
Mayamey *98 D2* Semnān, N Iran
Maya Mountains *30 B2 Sp.* Montañas Mayas. *Mountain range* Belize/Guatemala
Maych'ew *50 C4 var.* Mai Chio, *It.* Mai Ceu. N Ethiopia
Maydān Shahr *101 E4* Wardag, E Afghanistan
Mayebashi *see* Maebashi
Mayfield *129 B6* Canterbury, South Island, NZ
Maykop *89 A7* Respublika Adygeya, SW Russian Federation
Maymana *see* Meymaneh
Maymyo *114 B3* Mandalay, C Myanmar
Mayo *see* Maio
Mayor Island *128 D3 island* NE NZ
Mayor Pablo Lagerenza *see* Capitán Pablo Lagerenza
Mayotte *57 F2 French territorial collectivity* E Africa
May Pen *32 B5* C Jamaica
Mazabuka *56 D2* Southern, S Zambia
Mazaca *see* Kayseri
Mazār-e Sharīf *101 E3 var.* Mazār-i Sharif. Balkh, N Afghanistan
Mazār-i Sharif *see* Mazār-e Sharīf
Mazatlán *28 C3* Sinaloa, C Mexico
Mažeikiai *84 B3* Mažeikiai, NW Lithuania
Mazirbe *84 C2* Talsi, NW Latvia
Mazra'a *see* Al Mazra'ah
Mazury *76 D3 physical region* NE Poland
Mazyr *85 C7 Rus.* Mozyr'. Homyel'skaya Voblasts', SE Belarus
Mbabane *56 D4 country capital* (Swaziland) NW Swaziland
Mbacké *see* Mbaké
M'Baiki *see* Mbaïki
Mbaïki *55 C5 var.* M'Baiki. Lobaye, SW Central African Republic
Mbaké *52 B3 var.* Mbacké. W Senegal
Mbala *56 D1 prev.* Abercorn. Northern, NE Zambia
Mbale *51 C6* E Uganda
Mbandaka *55 C5 prev.* Coquilhatville. Equateur, NW Dem. Rep. Congo
M'Banza Congo *56 B1 var.* Mbanza Congo; *prev.* São Salvador, São Salvador do Congo. Zaire, NW Angola
Mbanza-Ngungu *55 B6* Bas-Zaïre, W Dem. Rep. Congo
Mbarara *51 B6* SW Uganda
Mbé *54 B4* Nord, N Cameroon
Mbeya *51 C7* Mbeya, SW Tanzania
Mbomou *see* Bomu
M'Bomu *see* Bomu
Mbour *52 B3* W Senegal
Mbuji-Mayi *55 D7 prev.* Bakwanga. Kasai Oriental, S Dem. Rep. Congo
McAlester *27 G2* Oklahoma, C USA
McAllen *27 G5* Texas, SW USA
McCamey *27 E3* Texas, SW USA
McClintock Channel *15 F2 channel* Nunavut, N Canada
McComb *20 B3* Mississippi, S USA
McCook *23 E4* Nebraska, C USA
McKean Island *123 E3 island* Phoenix Islands, C Kiribati
McKinley, Mount *14 C3 var.* Denali. *Mountain* Alaska, USA
McKinley Park *14 C3* Alaska, USA
McMinnville *24 B3* Oregon, NW USA
McMurdo Base *132 B4 US research station* Antarctica
McPherson *see* Fort McPherson
McPherson *23 E5* Kansas, C USA
Mdantsane *56 D5* Eastern Cape, SE South Africa
Mead, Lake *25 D6 reservoir* Arizona/Nevada, W USA
Meghālaya *91 G3 state*, NE India
Mecca *see* Makkah
Mechelen *65 C5 Eng.* Mechlin, *Fr.* Malines. Antwerpen, C Belgium
Mecklenburger Bucht *72 C2 bay* N Germany
Mecsek *77 C7 mountain range* SW Hungary
Medan *116 B3* Sumatera, E Indonesia
Medeba *see* Ma'dabā
Medellín *36 B3* Antioquia, NW Colombia
Médenine *49 F2 var.* Madanīyīn. SE Tunisia
Medford *24 B4* Oregon, NW USA
Medgidia *86 D5* Constanţa, SE Romania
Mediaş *86 B4 Ger.* Mediasch, *Hung.* Medgyes. Sibiu, C Romania
Medicine Hat *15 F5* Alberta, SW Canada
Medinaceli *71 E2* Castilla-León, N Spain
Medina del Campo *70 D2* Castilla-León, N Spain
Mediterranean Sea *80 D3 Fr.* Mer Méditerranée. *Sea* Africa/Asia/Europe
Médoc *69 B5 cultural region* SW France
Medvezh'yegorsk *88 B3* Respublika Kareliya, NW Russian Federation
Meekatharra *125 B5* Western Australia
Meemu Atoll *see* Mulaku Atoll
Meerssen *65 D6 var.* Mersen. Limburg, SE Netherlands
Meerut *112 D2* Uttar Pradesh, N India
Mehdia *see* Mahdia
Meheso *see* Mī'ēso
Me Hka *see* Nmai Hka
Mehrīz *98 D3* Yazd, C Iran
Mehtar Lām *see* Mehtarlām
Mehtarlām *101 F4 var.* Mehtar Lām, Meterlam, Methariam, Metharlam. Laghmān, E Afghanistan
Meiktila *114 B3* Mandalay, C Myanmar
Mejillones *42 B2* Antofagasta, N Chile
Mek'elē *50 C4 var.* Makale. N Ethiopia
Mékhé *52 B3* NW Senegal
Mekong *102 D3 var.* Lan-ts'ang Chiang, *Cam.* Mékôngk, *Chin.* Lancang Jiang, *Lao.* Mènam Khong, *Th.* Mae Nam Khong, *Tib.* Dza Chu, *Vtn.* Sông Tiên Giang. *River* SE Asia
Mékôngk *see* Mekong
Mekong, Mouths of the *115 E6 delta* S Vietnam
Melaka *116 B3 var.* Malacca. Melaka, Peninsular Malaysia
Melanesia *122 D3 island group* W Pacific Ocean
Melanesian Basin *120 C2 undersea feature* W Pacific Ocean
Melbourne *127 C7 state capital* Victoria, SE Australia
Melbourne *21 E4* Florida, SE USA
Melghir, Chott *49 E2 var.* Chott Melrhir. *Salt lake* E Algeria
Melilla *58 B5 anc.* Rusaddir, Russadir. Melilla, Spain, N Africa
Melilla *48 D2 enclave* Spain, N Africa
Melita *15 F5* Manitoba, S Canada
Melitopol' *87 F4* Zaporiz'ka Oblast', SE Ukraine
Melle *65 B5* Oost-Vlaanderen, NW Belgium
Mellerud *63 B6* Västra Götaland, S Sweden
Mellieha *80 B5* E Malta
Mellizo Sur, Cerro *43 A7 mountain* S Chile
Melo *42 E4* Cerro Largo, NE Uruguay
Melsungen *72 B4* Hessen, C Germany
Melun *68 C3 anc.* Melodunum. Seine-et-Marne, N France
Melville Island *124 D2 island* Northern Territory, N Australia
Melville Island *15 E2 island* Parry Islands, Northwest Territories/Nunavut, NW Canada
Melville, Lake *17 F2 lake* Newfoundland and Labrador, E Canada
Melville Peninsula *15 G3 peninsula* Northwest Territories, NE Canada
Membidj *see* Manbij
Memmingen *73 B6* Bayern, S Germany
Memphis *20 C1* Tennessee, S USA
Ménaka *53 F3* Goa, E Mali
Menaldum *64 D1 Fris.* Menaam. Friesland, N Netherlands
Mènam Khong *see* Mekong
Mendaña Fracture Zone *131 F4 tectonic feature* E Pacific Ocean
Mende *69 C5 anc.* Mimatum. Lozère, S France
Mendeleyev Ridge *133 B2 undersea feature* Arctic Ocean
Mendocino Fracture Zone *130 D2 tectonic feature* NE Pacific Ocean
Mendoza *42 B4* Mendoza, W Argentina
Menemen *94 A3* İzmir, W Turkey
Menengiyn Tal *105 F2 plain* E Mongolia
Menongue *56 B2 var.* Vila Serpa Pinto, *Port.* Serpa Pinto. Cuando Cubango, C Angola
Menorca *71 H3 Eng.* Minorca; *anc.* Balearis Minor. *Island* Islas Baleares, Spain, W Mediterranean Sea
Mentawai, Kepulauan *116 A4 island group* W Indonesia
Meppel *64 D2* Drenthe, NE Netherlands
Merano *74 C1 Ger.* Meran. Trentino-Alto Adige, N Italy
Merca *see* Marka
Mercedes *see* Villa Mercedes
Mercedes *42 D3* Corrientes, NE Argentina
Mercedes *42 D4* Soriano, SW Uruguay
Meredith, Lake *27 E1 reservoir* Texas, SW USA
Merefa *87 G2* Kharkivs'ka Oblast', E Ukraine
Mergui *115 B6* Tenasserim, S Myanmar
Mergui Archipelago *115 B6 island group* S Myanmar
Meriç *see* Maritsa
Mérida *70 C4 anc.* Augusta Emerita. Extremadura, W Spain
Mérida *36 C2* Mérida, W Venezuela
Mérida *29 H3* Yucatán, SW Mexico
Meridian *20 C2* Mississippi, S USA
Mérignac *69 B5* Gironde, SW France
Merkinė *85 B5* Varėna, S Lithuania
Merowe *50 B3 desert* W Sudan
Merredin *125 B6* Western Australia
Mersen *see* Meerssen
Mersey *67 D5 river* NW England, UK
Mersin *94 C4* İçel, S Turkey
Mērsrags *84 C3* Talsi, NW Latvia
Meru *51 C6* Eastern, C Kenya
Merzifon *94 D2* Amasya, N Turkey
Merzig *73 A5* Saarland, SW Germany
Mesa *26 B2* Arizona, SW USA
Meshed *see* Mashhad
Mesopotamia *35 C5 var.* Mesopotamia Argentina. *Physical region* NE Argentina
Mesopotamia Argentina *see* Mesopotamia
Messalo, Rio *57 E2 var.* Mualo. *River* NE Mozambique
Messana *see* Messina
Messene *see* Messina
Messina *75 D7 var.* Messana, Messene; *anc.* Zancle. Sicilia, Italy, C Mediterranean Sea
Messina *see* Musina
Messina, Stretto di *75 D7 Eng.* Strait of Messina. *Strait* SW Italy
Messíni *83 B6* Pelopónnisos, S Greece
Mestghanem *see* Mostaganem
Mestia *95 F1 var.* Mestiya. N Georgia
Mestiya *see* Mestia
Mestre *74 C2* Veneto, NE Italy
Meta *34 B2 off.* Departamento del Meta. *Province* C Colombia
Metairie *20 B3* Louisiana, S USA
Metán *42 C2* Salta, N Argentina
Metapán *30 B2* Santa Ana, NW El Salvador
Meta, Río *36 D3 river* Colombia/Venezuela
Meterlam *see* Mehtarlām
Methariam *see* Mehtarlām
Metharlam *see* Mehtarlām
Metković *78 B4* Dubrovnik-Neretva, SE Croatia
Métsovo *82 B4 prev.* Métsovon. Ípeiros, C Greece
Metz *68 D3 anc.* Divodurum Mediomatricum, Mediomatrica, Metis. Moselle, NE France
Meulaboh *116 A3* Sumatera, W Indonesia
Meuse *65 C6 Dut.* Maas. *River* W Europe *see also* Maas
Meuse *90 D3 department* NE France
Mexcala, Río *see* Balsas, Río
Mexicali *28 A1* Baja California, NW Mexico
Mexico *28 C3 var.* Méjico, México, *Sp.* Estados Unidos Mexicanos. *Country* N Central America
Mexico *23 G4* Missouri, C USA
México *29 E4 var.* Ciudad de México, *Eng.* Mexico City. *Country capital* (Mexico) México, C Mexico
Mexico City *see* México
Mexico, Gulf of *29 F2 Sp.* Golfo de México. *Gulf* W Atlantic Ocean
Meyadine *see* Al Mayādīn
Meymaneh *100 D3 var.* Maimāna, Maymana. Fāryāb, NW Afghanistan
Mezen' *88 D3 river* NW Russian Federation
Mezőtúr *77 D7* Jász-Nagykun-Szolnok, E Hungary
Mġarr *80 A5* Gozo, N Malta
Miahuatlán *29 F5 var.* Miahuatlán de Porfirio Díaz. Oaxaca, SE Mexico
Miahuatlán de Porfirio Díaz *see* Miahuatlán
Miami *21 F5* Florida, SE USA
Miami *27 G1* Oklahoma, C USA
Miami Beach *21 F5* Florida, SE USA
Mīāneh *98 C2 var.* Miyāneh. Āzarbāyjān-e Khāvarī, NW Iran
Mianyang *106 B5* Sichuan, C China
Miastko *76 C2 Ger.* Rummelsburg in Pommern. Pomorskie, N Poland
Mi Chai *see* Nong Khai
Michalovce *77 E5 Ger.* Grossmichel, *Hung.* Nagymihály. Košický Kraj, E Slovakia
Michigan *18 C1 off.* State of Michigan; also known as Great Lakes State, Lake State, Wolverine State. *State* N USA
Michigan, Lake *18 C2 lake* N USA
Michurinsk *89 B5* Tambovskaya Oblast', W Russian Federation
Micoud *33 F2* SE Saint Lucia
Micronesia *122 B1 Country* W Pacific Ocean
Micronesia *122 C1 island group* W Pacific Ocean
Mid-Atlantic Cordillera *see* Mid-Atlantic Ridge
Mid-Atlantic Ridge *44 C3 var.* Mid-Atlantic Cordillera, Mid-Atlantic Rise, Mid-Atlantic Swell. *Undersea feature* Atlantic Ocean
Mid-Atlantic Rise *see* Mid-Atlantic Ridge
Mid-Atlantic Swell *see* Mid-Atlantic Ridge
Middelburg *65 B5* Zeeland, SW Netherlands
Middelharnis *64 B4* Zuid-Holland, SW Netherlands
Middelkerke *65 A5* West-Vlaanderen, W Belgium
Middle America Trench *13 B7 undersea feature* E Pacific Ocean
Middle Andaman *111 F2 island* Andaman Islands, India, NE Indian Ocean
Middlesboro *18 C5* Kentucky, S USA
Middlesbrough *67 D5* N England, UK
Middletown *19 F4* New Jersey, NE USA
Middletown *19 F3* New York, NE USA
Mid-Indian Basin *119 C5 undersea feature* N Indian Ocean
Mid-Indian Ridge *119 C5 var.* Central Indian Ridge. *Undersea feature* C Indian Ocean
Midland *18 C3* Michigan, N USA
Midland *16 D5* Ontario, S Canada
Midland *27 E3* Texas, SW USA
Mid-Pacific Mountains *130 C2 var.* Mid-Pacific Seamounts. *Undersea feature* NW Pacific Ocean
Mid-Pacific Seamounts *see* Mid-Pacific Mountains
Midway Islands *130 D2 US territory* C Pacific Ocean
Miechów *77 D5* Małopolskie, S Poland
Międzyrzec Podlaski *76 E3* Lubelskie, E Poland
Międzyrzecz *76 B3 Ger.* Meseritz. Lubuskie, W Poland
Mielec *77 D5* Podkarpackie, SE Poland
Miercurea-Ciuc *86 C4 Ger.* Szeklerburg, *Hung.* Csíkszereda. Harghita, C Romania
Mieres del Camín *see* Mieres del Camino
Mieres del Camino *108 D1 var.* Mieres del Camín. Asturias, NW Spain
Mieresch *see* Mureş
Mī'ēso *51 D5 var.* Meheso, Miesso. C Ethiopia
Miesso *see* Mī'ēso
Miguel Asua *28 D3 var.* Miguel Auza. Zacatecas, C Mexico
Miguel Auza *see* Miguel Asua
Mijdrecht *64 C3* Utrecht, C Netherlands
Mikashevichy *85 C7 Pol.* Mikaszewicze, *Rus.* Mikashevichi. Brestskaya Voblasts', SW Belarus
Mikhaylovka *89 B6* Volgogradskaya Oblast', SW Russian Federation
Míkonos *see* Mýkonos
Mikre *82 C2* Lovech, N Bulgaria
Mikun' *88 D4* Respublika Komi, NW Russian Federation
Mikuni-sanmyaku *109 D5 mountain range* Honshū, N Japan
Mikura-jima *109 D6 island* E Japan
Milagro *38 B2* Guayas, SW Ecuador
Milan *see* Milano
Milange *57 E2* Zambézia, NE Mozambique
Milano *74 B2 Eng.* Milan, *Ger.* Mailand; *anc.* Mediolanum. Lombardia, N Italy
Milas *94 A4* Muğla, SW Turkey
Milashavichy *85 C7 Rus.* Milashevichi. Homyel'skaya Voblasts', SE Belarus
Mildura *127 C6* Victoria, SE Australia
Mile *see* Mili Atoll
Miles *127 D5* Queensland, E Australia
Miles City *22 C2* Montana, NW USA
Milford Haven *67 C6 prev.* Milford. SW Wales, UK
Milford Sound *129 A6 inlet* South Island, NZ
Milford Sound *129 A6* Southland, South Island, NZ
Mili Atoll *122 D2 var.* Mile. *Atoll* Ratak Chain, SE Marshall Islands
Mil'kovo *93 H3* Kamchatskaya Oblast', E Russian Federation
Milk River *22 C1 river* Montana, NW USA
Milk River *15 E5* Alberta, SW Canada
Milk, Wadi el *88 B4 var.* Wadi al Malik. *River* C Sudan
Milledgeville *21 E2* Georgia, SE USA
Mille Lacs Lake *23 F2 lake* Minnesota, N USA
Millennium Island *160 C8 prev.* Caroline Island, Thornton Island. *Atoll* Line Islands, E Kiribati
Millerovo *89 B6* Rostovskaya Oblast', SW Russian Federation
Mílos *83 C7 island* Kykládes, Greece, Aegean Sea
Mílos *83 C6* Mílos, Kykládes, Greece, Aegean Sea
Milton *129 B7* Otago, South Island, NZ
Milton Keynes *67 D6* SE England, UK
Milwaukee *18 B3* Wisconsin, N USA
Min *see* Fujian
Mīnā' Qābūs *118 B3* NE Oman
Minas Gerais *41 F3 off.* Estado de Minas Gerais. *State* E Brazil
Minatitlán *29 F4* Veracruz-Llave, E Mexico
Minbu *114 A3* Magwe, W Myanmar
Minch, The *66 B3 var.* North Minch. *Strait* NW Scotland, UK
Mindanao *117 F2 island* S Philippines
Mindanao Sea *see* Bohol Sea
Mindelheim *73 C6* Bayern, S Germany
Mindello *see* Mindelo
Mindelo *52 A2 var.* Mindello; *prev.* Porto Grande. São Vicente, N Cape Verde
Minden *72 B4 anc.* Minthun. Nordrhein-Westfalen, NW Germany
Mindoro *117 E2 island* N Philippines
Mindoro Strait *117 E2 strait* W Philippines
Mineral Wells *27 F2* Texas, SW USA
Mingäçevir *95 G2 Rus.* Mingechaur, Mingechevir. C Azerbaijan
Mingāora *112 C1 var.* Mingora, Mongora. North-West Frontier Province, N Pakistan
Mingora *see* Mingāora
Minho *70 B2 former province* N Portugal
Minho, Rio *70 B2 Sp.* Miño. *river* Portugal/Spain *see also* Miño
Minicoy Island *110 B3 island* SW India
Minius *see* Miño
Minna *53 G4* Niger, C Nigeria
Minneapolis *23 F2* Minnesota, N USA
Minnesota *23 F2 off.* State of Minnesota; also known as Gopher State, New England of the West, North Star State. *State* N USA
Miño *70 B2 var.* Mino, Minius, *Port.* Rio Minho. *River* Portugal/Spain *see also* Minho, Rio
Mino *see* Miño
Minot *23 E1* North Dakota, N USA
Minsk *85 C6 country capital* (Belarus) Minskaya Voblasts', C Belarus
Minskaya Wzvyshsha *85 C6 mountain range* C Belarus
Mińsk Mazowiecki *76 D3 var.* Nowo-Minsk. Mazowieckie, C Poland
Minto, Lac *16 D2 lake* Québec, C Canada
Minya *see* El Minya
Miraflores *28 C3* Baja California Sur, W Mexico
Miranda de Ebro *71 E1* La Rioja, N Spain
Miri *116 D3* Sarawak, East Malaysia
Mirim Lagoon *41 E5 var.* Lake Mirim, *Sp.* Laguna Merín. *Lagoon* Brazil/Uruguay
Mirim, Lake *see* Mirim Lagoon
Mírina *see* Mýrina
Mīrjāveh *98 E4* Sīstān va Balūchestān, SE Iran
Mirny *132 C3 Russian research station* Antarctica
Mirnyy *93 F3* Respublika Sakha (Yakutiya), NE Russian Federation
Mīrpur Khās *112 B3* Sind, SE Pakistan
Mirtóo Pélagos *83 C6 Eng.* Mirtoan Sea; *anc.* Myrtoum Mare. *Sea* S Greece
Miskito Coast *see* Mosquito Coast
Miskitos, Cayos *31 E2 island group* NE Nicaragua
Miskolc *77 D6* Borsod-Abaúj-Zemplén, NE Hungary
Misool, Pulau *117 F4 island* Maluku, E Indonesia
Mişrātah *49 F2 var.* Misurata. NW Libya
Mission *27 G5* Texas, SW USA
Mississippi *20 B2 off.* State of Mississippi; also known as Bayou State, Magnolia State. *State* SE USA
Mississippi Delta *20 B4 delta* Louisiana, S USA
Mississippi River *13 C6 river* C USA
Missoula *22 B1* Montana, NW USA

Missouri 23 F5 off. State of Missouri; also known as Bullion State, Show Me State. *State* C USA
Missouri River 23 E3 *river* C USA
Mistassini, Lac 16 D3 lake Québec, SE Canada
Mistelbach an der Zaya 73 E6 Niederösterreich, NE Austria
Misti, Volcán 39 E4 *mountain* S Peru
Misurata *see* Miṣrātah
Mitchell 127 D5 Queensland, E Australia
Mitchell 23 E3 South Dakota, N USA
Mitchell, Mount 21 E1 *mountain* North Carolina, SE USA
Mitchell River 126 C2 *river* Queensland, NE Australia
Mi Tho *see* My Tho
Mitilíni *see* Mytilíni
Mito 109 D5 Ibaraki, Honshū, S Japan
Mits'iwa *see* Massawa
Mitspe Ramon *see* Mizpé Ramon
Mitú 36 C4 Vaupés, SE Colombia
Mitumba, Monts 55 E7 *var.* Chaîne des Mitumba, Mitumba Range. *Mountain range* E Dem. Rep. Congo
Mitumba Range *see* Mitumba, Monts
Miyako 108 D4 Iwate, Honshū, C Japan
Miyako-jima 109 D6 *island* Sakishima-shotō, SW Japan
Miyakonojō 109 B8 *var.* Miyakonzyô. Miyazaki, Kyūshū, SW Japan
Miyakonzyô *see* Miyakonojō
Miyāneh *see* Mīāneh
Miyazaki 109 B8 Miyazaki, Kyūshū, SW Japan
Mizil 86 C5 Prahova, SE Romania
Miziya 82 C1 Vratsa, NW Bulgaria
Mizpé Ramon 97 A7 *var.* Mitspe Ramon, Southern, S Israel
Mjøsa 63 B6 *var.* Mjøsen. *Lake* S Norway
Mjøsen *see* Mjøsa
Mladenovac 78 D4 Serbia, C Serbia and Montenegro (Yugo.)
Mława 76 D3 Mazowieckie, C Poland
Mljet 79 B5 *It.* Meleda; *anc.* Melita. *Island* S Croatia
Mmabatho 56 C4 North-West, N South Africa
Moab 22 B5 Utah, W USA
Moab, Kir of *see* Al Karak
Moa Island 126 C1 *island* Queensland, NE Australia
Moanda 55 B6 *var.* Mouanda. Haut-Ogooué, SE Gabon
Moba 55 E7 Shaba, E Dem. Rep. Congo
Mobay *see* Montego Bay
Mobaye 55 C5 Basse-Kotto, S Central African Republic
Moberly 23 G4 Missouri, C USA
Mobile 20 C3 Alabama, S USA
Mobutu Sese Seko, Lac *see* Albert, Lake
Mochudi 56 C4 Kgatleng, SE Botswana
Mocímboa da Praia 57 F2 *var.* Vila de Mocímboa da Praia. Cabo Delgado, N Mozambique
Môco 56 B2 *var.* Morro de Môco. *Mountain* W Angola
Mocoa 36 A4 Putumayo, SW Colombia
Mocuba 57 E3 Zambézia, NE Mozambique
Modena 74 B3 *anc.* Mutina. Emilia-Romagna, N Italy
Modesto 25 B6 California, W USA
Modica 75 C7 *anc.* Motyca. Sicilia, Italy, C Mediterranean Sea
Modimolle 56 D4 *var.* Nylstroom, NE South Africa
Modriča 78 C3 Republika Srpska, N Bosnia and Herzegovina
Moe 127 C7 Victoria, SE Australia
Moero, Lac *see* Mweru, Lake
Mogadishu *see* Muqdisho
Mogilno 76 C3 Kujawski-pomorskie, C Poland
Mohammedia 48 C2 *prev.* Fédala. NW Morocco
Mohave, Lake 25 D7 *reservoir* Arizona/Nevada, W USA
Mohawk River 19 F3 *river* New York, NE USA
Mohéli 57 F2 *var.* Mwali, Mohilla, Mohila, *Fr.* Moili. *Island* S Comoros
Mohila *see* Mohéli
Mohilla *see* Mohéli
Mohns Ridge 61 F3 *undersea feature* Greenland Sea/Norwegian Sea
Moho 39 E4 Puno, SW Peru
Mohoro 51 C7 Pwani, E Tanzania
Mohyliv-Podil's'kyy 86 D3 *Rus.* Mogilev-Podol'skiy. Vinnyts'ka Oblast', C Ukraine
Moi 63 A6 Rogaland, S Norway
Moili *see* Mohéli
Mo i Rana 62 C3 Nordland, C Norway
Mõisaküla 84 D3 *Ger.* Moiseküll. Viljandimaa, S Estonia
Moissac 69 B6 Tarn-et-Garonne, S France
Mojácar 71 E5 Andalucía, S Spain
Mojave Desert 25 D7 *plain* California, W USA
Moktama *see* Martaban
Mol 65 C5 *prev.* Moll. Antwerpen, N Belgium
Moldavia *see* Moldova
Moldavian SSR/Moldavskaya SSR *see* Moldova
Molde 63 A5 Møre og Romsdal, S Norway
Moldo-Too, Khrebet 101 G2 *prev.* Khrebet Moldotau. *Mountain range* C Kyrgyzstan
Moldova 86 D3 *var.* Moldavia; *prev.* Moldavian SSR, *Rus.* Moldavskaya SSR. *Country* SE Europe
Moldova Nouă 86 A4 *Ger.* Neumoldowa, *Hung.* Újmoldova. Caraş-Severin, SW Romania

Moldoveanul *see* Vârful Moldoveanu
Molfetta 75 E5 Puglia, SE Italy
Mollendo 39 E4 Arequipa, SW Peru
Mölndal 63 B7 Västra Götaland, S Sweden
Molochans'k 87 G4 *Rus.* Molochansk. Zaporiz'ka Oblast', SE Ukraine
Molodezhnaya 132 C2 *Russian research station* Antarctica
Moloka'i 25 B8 *var.* Molokai. *Island* Hawai'i, USA, C Pacific Ocean
Molokai Fracture Zone 131 E2 *tectonic feature* NE Pacific Ocean
Molopo 56 C4 *seasonal river* Botswana/South Africa
Mólos 83 B5 Stereá Ellás, C Greece
Moluccas *see* Maluku
Molucca Sea 117 F4 *Ind.* Laut Maluku. *Sea* E Indonesia
Mombasa 51 D7 *international airport* Coast, SE Kenya
Mombasa 51 D7 Coast, SE Kenya
Mombetsu *see* Monbetsu
Momchilgrad 82 D3 *prev.* Mastanli. Kŭrdzhali, S Bulgaria
Møn 63 B8 *prev.* Möen. *Island* SE Denmark
Monaco 69 E6 *Country* W Europe
Monaco 69 C7 *var.* Monaco-Ville; *anc.* Monoecus. *Country capital* (Monaco) S Monaco
Monaco, Port de 69 C8 *bay* S Monaco
Monaco-Ville *see* Monaco
Monahans 27 E3 Texas, SW USA
Mona, Isla 33 E3 *island* W Puerto Rico
Mona Passage 33 E3 *Sp.* Canal de la Mona. *Channel* Dominican Republic/Puerto Rico
Monbetsu 108 D2 *var.* Mombetsu, Monbetu. Hokkaidō, NE Japan
Monbetu *see* Monbetsu
Moncalieri 74 A2 Piemonte, NW Italy
Monchegorsk 88 C2 Murmanskaya Oblast', NW Russian Federation
Monclova 28 D2 Coahuila de Zaragoza, NE Mexico
Moncton 17 F4 New Brunswick, SE Canada
Mondovì 74 A2 Piemonte, NW Italy
Monfalcone 74 D2 Friuli-Venezia Giulia, NE Italy
Monforte *see* Monforte de Lemos
Monforte de Lemos 92 C1 *var.* Monforte. Galicia, NW Spain
Mongo 54 C3 Guéra, C Chad
Mongolia 104 C2 *Mong.* Mongol Uls. *Country* E Asia
Mongolia, Plateau of 102 D1 *plateau* E Mongolia
Mongora *see* Mingaora
Mongu 56 C2 Western, W Zambia
Monkchester *see* Newcastle upon Tyne
Monkey Bay 57 E2 Southern, SE Malawi
Monkey River *see* Monkey River Town
Monkey River Town 30 C2 *var.* Monkey River. Toledo, SE Belize
Monoecus *see* Monaco
Mono Lake 25 C6 *lake* California, W USA
Monovar 71 F4 *Cat.* Monover. País Valenciano, E Spain
Monover *see* Monovar
Monroe 20 B2 Louisiana, S USA
Monrovia 52 C5 *country capital* (Liberia) W Liberia
Mons 65 B6 *Dut.* Bergen. Hainaut, S Belgium
Monselice 74 C2 Veneto, NE Italy
Montagnes Rocheuses *see* Rocky Mountains
Montana 22 B1 *off.* State of Montana; also known as Mountain State, Treasure State. *State* NW USA
Montana 82 C2 *prev.* Ferdinand, Mikhaylovgrad. Montana, NW Bulgaria
Montargis 68 C4 Loiret, C France
Montauban 69 B6 Tarn-et-Garonne, S France
Montbéliard 90 D4 Doubs, E France
Mont Cenis, Col du 69 D5 *pass* E France
Mont-de-Marsan 69 B6 Landes, SW France
Monteagudo 39 G4 Chuquisaca, S Bolivia
Monte-Carlo 69 C8 NE Monaco
Monte Caseros 42 D3 Corrientes, NE Argentina
Monte Cristi 33 D3 *var.* San Fernando de Monte Cristi. NW Dominican Republic
Montegiardino 74 E2 SE San Marino
Montego Bay 32 A4 *var.* Mobay. W Jamaica
Montélimar 69 D5 *anc.* Acunum Acusio, Montilium Adhemari. Drôme, E France
Montemorelos 29 E3 Nuevo León, NE Mexico
Montenegro 79 C5 *Serb.* Crna Gora. Admin. *region republic* SW Serbia and Montenegro (Yugo.)
Monte Patria 42 B3 Coquimbo, N Chile
Monterey *see* Monterrey
Monterey 25 B6 California, W USA
Monterey Bay 25 A6 *bay* California, W USA
Montería 36 B2 Córdoba, NW Colombia
Montero 39 G4 Santa Cruz, C Bolivia
Monterrey 29 E3 *var.* Monterey. Nuevo León, NE Mexico
Montes Claros 41 F3 Minas Gerais, SE Brazil
Montevideo 42 D4 *country capital* (Uruguay) Montevideo, S Uruguay
Montevideo 23 F2 Minnesota, N USA
Montgenèvre, Col de 69 D5 *pass* France/Italy
Montgomery 20 D2 *state capital* Alabama, S USA
Monthey 73 A7 Valais, SW Switzerland
Montluçon 68 C4 Allier, C France
Montoro 92 D4 Andalucía, S Spain
Montpelier 19 G2 *state capital* Vermont, NE USA
Montpellier 69 C6 Hérault, S France

Montréal 17 E4 *Eng.* Montreal. Québec, SE Canada
Montrose 22 C5 Colorado, C USA
Montrose 66 D3 E Scotland, UK
Montserrat 33 G3 *var.* Emerald Isle. *UK dependent territory* E West Indies
Monywa 114 B3 Sagaing, C Myanmar
Monza 74 B2 Lombardia, N Italy
Monze 56 D2 Southern, S Zambia
Monzón 71 F2 Aragón, NE Spain
Moonie 127 D5 Queensland, E Australia
Moora 125 A6 Western Australia
Moore 27 G1 Oklahoma, C USA
Moore, Lake 125 B6 *lake* Western Australia
Moorhead 23 F2 Minnesota, N USA
Moose 16 C3 *river* Ontario, S Canada
Moosehead Lake 19 G1 *lake* Maine, NE USA
Moosonee 16 C3 Ontario, SE Canada
Mopti 53 E3 Mopti, C Mali
Moquegua 39 E4 Moquegua, SE Peru
Mora 63 C5 Kopparberg, C Sweden
Morales 30 C2 Izabal, E Guatemala
Morant Bay 32 B5 E Jamaica
Moratalla 71 E4 Murcia, SE Spain
Morava 77 C5 *var.* March. *River* C Europe *see also* March
Morava *see* Velika Morava
Moravia 77 B5 Iowa, C USA
Moray Firth 66 C3 *inlet* N Scotland, UK
Morea *see* Pelopónnisos
Moreau River 22 D2 *river* South Dakota, N USA
Moree 127 D5 New South Wales, SE Australia
Morelia 29 E4 Michoacán de Ocampo, S Mexico
Morena, Sierra 70 C4 *mountain range* S Spain
Moreni 86 C5 Dâmboviţa, S Romania
Mórfou 80 C5 W Cyprus
Morgan City 20 B3 Louisiana, S USA
Morghāb, Daryā-ye 100 D3 *var.* Murgab, Murghab, *Turkm.* Murgap, Murgap Deryasy. *River* Afghanistan/Turkmenistan *see also* Murgap
Morioka 108 D4 Iwate, Honshū, C Japan
Morlaix 68 A3 Finistère, NW France
Mornington Abyssal Plain 45 A7 *undersea feature* SE Pacific Ocean
Mornington Island 126 B2 *island* Wellesley Islands, Queensland, N Australia
Morocco 48 B3 *Ar.* Al Mamlakah. *Country* N Africa
Morocco *see* Marrakech
Morogoro 51 C7 Morogoro, E Tanzania
Moro Gulf 117 E3 *gulf* S Philippines
Morón 32 C2 Ciego de Ávila, C Cuba
Mörön 104 D2 Hövsgöl, N Mongolia
Morondava 57 F3 Toliara, W Madagascar
Moroni 57 F2 *country capital* (Comoros) Grande Comore, NW Comoros
Morotai, Pulau 117 F3 *island* Maluku, E Indonesia
Morotiri *see* Marotiri
Morrinsville 128 D3 Waikato, North Island, NZ
Morris 23 F2 Minnesota, N USA
Morris Jesup, Kap 61 E1 *headland* N Greenland
Morro de Môco *see* Môco
Morvan 68 D4 *physical region* C France
Moscow *see* Moskva
Moscow 24 C2 Idaho, NW USA
Mosel 73 A5 *Fr.* Moselle. *River* W Europe *see also* Moselle
Moselle 68 E8 *Ger.* Mosel. *River* W Europe *see also* Mosel
Moselle 68 D3 *department* NE France
Mosgiel 129 B7 Otago, South Island, NZ
Moshi 51 C7 Kilimanjaro, NE Tanzania
Mosjøen 62 B4 Nordland, C Norway
Moskva 89 B5 *Eng.* Moscow. *Country capital* (Russian Federation) Gorod Moskva, W Russian Federation
Moskva 101 E3 *Rus.* Moskvovskiy; *prev.* Chubek. SW Tajikistan
Mosonmagyaróvár 77 C6 *Ger.* Wieselburg-Ungarisch-Altenburg; *prev.* Moson and Magyaróvár, *Ger.* Wieselburg and Ungarisch-Altenburg. Győr-Moson-Sopron, NW Hungary
Mosquito Coast 31 E3 *var.* Miskito Coast. *Coastal region* E Nicaragua
Mosquitos, Golfo de los 31 F4 *Eng.* Mosquito Gulf. *Gulf* N Panama
Moss 63 B6 Østfold, S Norway
Mosselbaai 56 C5 *var.* Mosselbai, *Eng.* Mossel Bay. Western Cape, SW South Africa
Mossendjo 55 B6 Le Niari, SW Congo
Mossoró 41 G2 Rio Grande do Norte, NE Brazil
Most 76 A4 *Ger.* Brüx. Ústecký Kraj, NW Czech Republic
Mosta 80 B5 *var.* Musta. C Malta
Mostaganem 48 D2 *var.* Mestghanem. NW Algeria
Mostar 78 C4 Federacija Bosna I Hercegovina, S Bosnia and Herzegovina
Mosul *see* Al Mawşil
Mota del Cuervo 71 E3 Castilla-La Mancha, C Spain
Motagua, Río 30 B2 *river* Guatemala/Honduras
Motril 70 D5 Andalucía, S Spain
Motru 86 B4 Gorj, SW Romania
Motueka 129 C5 Tasman, South Island, NZ
Motul 29 H3 *var.* Motul de Felipe Carrillo Puerto. Yucatán, SE Mexico
Motul de Felipe Carrillo Puerto *see* Motul
Mouanda *see* Moanda
Mouhoun *see* Black Volta
Mouila 55 A6 Ngounié, C Gabon
Mould Bay 15 E2 Prince Patrick Island, Northwest Territories/Nunavut, N Canada
Moulins 68 C4 Allier, C France

Moulmein 114 B4 *var.* Maulmain, Mawlamyine. Mon State, S Myanmar
Moundou 54 B4 Logone-Occidental, SW Chad
Moŭng Roessei 115 D5 Bătdâmbâng, W Cambodia
Moun Hou *see* Black Volta
Mountain Home 20 B1 Arkansas, C USA
Mount Ara *see* Büyükağrı Dağı
Mount Cook 129 B6 Canterbury, South Island, NZ
Mount Desert Island 19 H2 *island* Maine, NE USA
Mount Fuji *see* Fuji-san
Mount Gambier 127 B7 South Australia
Mount Isa 126 B3 Queensland, C Australia
Mount Magnet 125 B5 Western Australia
Mount Pleasant 23 G4 Iowa, C USA
Mount Pleasant 18 C3 Michigan, N USA
Mount Vernon 18 B5 Illinois, N USA
Mount Vernon 24 B1 Washington, NW USA
Mourdi, Dépression du 54 C2 *desert lowland* Chad/Sudan
Mouscron 65 A6 *Dut.* Moeskroen. Hainaut, W Belgium
Mouse River *see* Souris River
Moussoro 54 B3 Kanem, W Chad
Moyen Atlas 48 C2 *Eng.* Middle Atlas. *Mountain range* N Morocco
Mo'ynoq 100 C1 *var.* Müynoq, *Rus.* Muynak. Qoraqalpogʻiston Respublikasi, NW Uzbekistan
Moyobamba 38 B2 San Martín, NW Peru
Moyu 104 B3 *var.* Karakax. Xinjiang Uygur Zizhiqu, NW China
Moyynkum, Peski 101 F1 *Kaz.* Moyynqum. *Desert* S Kazakhstan
Mozambique 57 E3 *prev.* People's Republic of Mozambique, Portuguese East Africa. *Country* S Africa
Mozambique Basin *see* Natal Basin
Mozambique Channel 57 E3 *Fr.* Canal de Mozambique, *Mal.* Lakandranon' i Mozambika. *Strait* W Indian Ocean
Mozambique Plateau 47 D7 *var.* Mozambique Rise. *Undersea feature* SW Indian Ocean
Mozambique Rise *see* Mozambique Plateau
Mpama 55 B6 *river* C Congo
Mpika 56 D2 Northern, NE Zambia
Mqinvartsveri *see* Kazbek
Mrągowo 76 D2 *Ger.* Sensburg. Olsztyn, NE Poland
Mtwara 51 D8 Mtwara, SE Tanzania
Mualo *see* Messalo, Rio
Muang Chiang Rai *see* Chiang Rai
Muang Kalasin *see* Kalasin
Muang Khon Kaen *see* Khon Kaen
Muang Khôngxédôn 115 D5 *var.* Khong Sedone. Salavan, S Laos
Muang Khong 115 D5 Champasak, S Laos
Muang Lampang *see* Lampang
Muang Loei *see* Loei
Muang Lom Sak *see* Lom Sak
Muang Nakhon Sawan *see* Nakhon Sawan
Muang Namo 114 C3 Oudômxai, N Laos
Muang Nan *see* Nan
Muang Phalan 114 D4 *var.* Muang Phalane. Savannakhét, S Laos
Muang Phalane *see* Muang Phalan
Muang Phayao *see* Phayao
Muang Phitsanulok *see* Phitsanulok
Muang Phrae *see* Phrae
Muang Roi Et *see* Roi Et
Muang Sakon Nakhon *see* Sakon Nakhon
Muang Samut Prakan *see* Samut Prakan
Muang Sing 114 C3 Louang Namtha, N Laos
Muang Ubon *see* Ubon Ratchathani
Muar 116 B3 *var.* Bandar Maharani. Johor, Peninsular Malaysia
Mucojo 57 F2 Cabo Delgado, N Mozambique
Mudanjiang 107 E3 *var.* Mu-tan-chiang. Heilongjiang, NE China
Mudon 115 B5 Mon State, S Myanmar
Muenchen *see* Munich
Muenster *see* Münster
Mufulira 56 D2 Copperbelt, C Zambia
Mughla *see* Muğla
Muğla 94 A4 *var.* Mughla. Muğla, SW Turkey
Mūḩ, Sabkhat al 134 C3 *lake* C Syria
Muir Éireann *see* Irish Sea
Muisne 38 A1 Esmeraldas, NW Ecuador
Mukacheve 86 B3 *Hung.* Munkács, *Rus.* Mukachevo. Zakarpats'ka Oblast', W Ukraine
Mukalla *see* Al Mukallā
Mula 71 E4 Murcia, SE Spain
Mulaku Atoll 110 B4 *var.* Meemu Atoll. *Atoll* C Maldives
Muleshoe 27 E2 Texas, SW USA
Mulhacén 71 E5 *var.* Cerro de Mulhacén. *Mountain* S Spain
Mulhouse 68 E4 *Ger.* Mülhausen. Haut-Rhin, NE France
Muller, Pegunungan 116 D4 *Dut.* Müller-gebergte. *Mountain range* Borneo, C Indonesia
Müllheim 73 A6 Baden-Württemberg, SW Germany
Mull, Isle of 66 B4 *island* W Scotland, UK
Mulongo 55 D7 Shaba, SE Dem. Rep. Congo
Multan 112 C2 Punjab, E Pakistan
Mumbai 112 C5 *prev.* Bombay. Mahārāshtra, W India
Munamägi *see* Suur Munamägi
Münchberg 73 C5 Bayern, E Germany
Muncie 18 C4 Indiana, N USA
Mungbere 55 E5 Orientale, NE Dem. Rep. Congo
Mu Nggava *see* Rennell

Munich 58 D4 *var.* Muenchen, Bayern, SE Germany
Munkhafad al Qaṭṭārah *see* Qaṭṭāra, Monkhafad el
Munster 67 A6 *Ir.* Cúige Mumhan. *Cultural region* S Ireland
Münster 72 A4 *var.* Muenster, Münster in Westfalen. Nordrhein-Westfalen, W Germany
Münster in Westfalen *see* Münster
Muong Xiang Ngeun 114 C4 *var.* Xieng Ngeun. Louangphabang, N Laos
Muonio 62 D3 Lappi, N Finland
Muonioälv 62 D3 *river* Finland/Sweden
Muqāṭ 97 C5 Al Mafraq, E Jordan
Muqdisho 51 D6 *Eng.* Mogadishu, *It.* Mogadiscio. *Country capital* (Somalia) Banaadir, S Somalia
Mur 73 E7 *SCr.* Mura. *River* C Europe
Muradiye 95 F3 Van, E Turkey
Murapara *see* Murupara
Murata 74 E2 S San Marino
Murchison River 125 A5 *river* Western Australia
Murcia 71 E4 *cultural region* SE Spain
Murcia 71 F4 Murcia, SE Spain
Mureş 86 A4 *var.* Maros, Mureşul, *Ger.* Marosch, Mieresch. *River* Hungary/Romania *see also* Maros
Mureşul *see* Mureş
Murfreesboro 20 D1 Tennessee, S USA
Murgab *see* Murgap
Murgab 100 D3 *var.* Morghāb, Daryā-ye/Murgap
Murgap 100 D3 *var.* Murgab, Maryyskiy Velayat, S Turkmenistan
Murgap 100 D3 *var.* Murgab, Murghab, *Pash.* Daryā-ye Morghāb, *Turkm.* Murgap Deryasy. *River* Afghanistan/Turkmenistan *see also* Morghāb, Daryā-ye
Murghab *see* Morghāb, Daryā-ye/Murgap
Murghob 101 F3 *Rus.* Murgab. SE Tajikistan
Murgon 127 E5 Queensland, E Australia
Müritz 72 C3 *var.* Müritzee. *Lake* NE Germany
Müritzee *see* Müritz
Murmansk 88 C2 Murmanskaya Oblast', NW Russian Federation
Murmashi 88 C2 Murmanskaya Oblast', NW Russian Federation
Murom 89 B5 Vladimirskaya Oblast', W Russian Federation
Muroran 108 D3 Hokkaidō, NE Japan
Muros 70 B1 Galicia, NW Spain
Murray Fracture Zone 131 E2 *tectonic feature* NE Pacific Ocean
Murray Range *see* Murray Ridge
Murray Ridge 90 C5 *var.* Murray Range. *Undersea feature* N Arabian Sea
Murray River 127 B6 *river* SE Australia
Murrumbidgee River 127 C6 *river* New South Wales, SE Australia
Murska Sobota 73 E7 *Ger.* Olsnitz. NE Slovenia
Murupara 128 E3 *var.* Murapara. Bay of Plenty, North Island, NZ
Murviedro *see* Sagunto
Murwāra 113 E4 Madhya Pradesh, N India
Murwillumbah 127 E5 New South Wales, SE Australia
Murzuq, Idhān 49 F4 *var.* Edeyin Murzuq. *Desert* SW Libya
Mürzzuschlag 73 E7 Steiermark, E Austria
Muş 95 F3 *var.* Mush. Muş, E Turkey
Mūsa, Gebel 50 C2 *mountain* NE Egypt
Musala 82 B3 *mountain* W Bulgaria
Muscat *see* Masqaṭ
Muscatine 23 G3 Iowa, C USA
Musgrave Ranges 125 D5 *mountain range* South Australia
Mush *see* Muş
Musina 56 D3 *var.* Messina. Northern, NE South Africa
Muskegon 18 C3 Michigan, N USA
Muskogee 27 G1 Oklahoma, C USA
Musoma 51 C6 Mara, N Tanzania
Musta *see* Mosta
Musters, Lago 43 B6 *lake* S Argentina
Muswellbrook 127 D6 New South Wales, SE Australia
Mut 94 C4 İçel, S Turkey
Mu-tan-chiang *see* Mudanjiang
Mutare 57 E3 *var.* Mutari; *prev.* Umtali. Manicaland, E Zimbabwe
Mutari *see* Mutare
Mutsu-wan 108 D3 *bay* N Japan
Muttonbird Islands 129 A8 *island group* SW NZ
Mu Us Shamo 105 E3 *var.* Ordos Desert. *Desert* N China
Muy Muy 30 D3 Matagalpa, C Nicaragua
Müynoq *see* Mo'ynoq
Mužlja 78 D3 *Hung.* Felsőmuzslya; *prev.* Gornja Mužlja. Serbia, N Serbia and Montenegro (Yugo.)
Mwali *see* Mohéli
Mwanza 51 B6 Mwanza, NW Tanzania
Mweka 55 C6 Kasai Occidental, C Dem. Rep. Congo
Mwene-Ditu 55 D7 Kasai Oriental, S Dem. Rep. Congo
Mweru, Lake 55 D7 *var.* Lac Moero. *Lake* Congo (Zaire)/Zambia
Mweru Wantipa, Lake 55 E7 *lake* N Zambia
Myadzyel 85 C5 *Pol.* Miadzioł Nowy, *Rus.* Myadel'. Minskaya Voblasts', N Belarus
Myanmar 114 A3 *var.* Burma. *Country* SE Asia
Myanaung 114 B4 Irrawaddy, SW Myanmar
Myaungmya 114 A4 Irrawaddy, SW Myanmar
Myerkulavichy 85 D7 *Rus.* Merkulovichi. Homyel'skaya Voblasts', SE Belarus

Myingyan – Nikopol'

Myingyan 114 B3 Mandalay, C Myanmar
Myitkyina 114 B2 Kachin State, N Myanmar
Mykolayiv 87 E4 Rus. Nikolayev. Mykolayivs'ka Oblast', S Ukraine
Mýkonos 83 D6 var. Míkonos. Island Kykládes, Greece, Aegean Sea
Myrhorod 87 F2 Rus. Mirgorod. Poltavs'ka Oblast', NE Ukraine
Mýrina 82 D4 var. Mírina. Límnos, SE Greece
Myrtle Beach 21 F2 South Carolina, SE USA
Mýrtos 83 D8 Kríti, Greece, E Mediterranean Sea
Myślibórz 76 B3 Zachodniopomorskie, NW Poland
Mysore 110 C2 var. Maisur. Karnātaka, W India
Mysore see Karnātaka
My Tho 115 E6 var. Mi Tho. Tiên Giang, S Vietnam
Mytilene see Mytilíni
Mytilíni 83 D5 var. Mitilíni; anc. Mytilene. Lésvos, E Greece
Mzuzu 57 E2 Northern, N Malawi

N

Naberezhnyye Chelny 89 D5 prev. Brezhnev. Respublika Tatarstan, W Russian Federation
Nablus 97 A6 var. Nābulus, Heb. Shekhem; anc. Neapolis, Bibl. Shechem. N West Bank
Nābulus see Nablus
Nacala 57 F2 Nampula, NE Mozambique
Nada see Danzhou
Nadi 123 E4 prev. Nandi. Viti Levu, W Fiji
Nadur 80 A5 Gozo, N Malta
Nadvirna 86 C3 Pol. Nadwórna, Rus. Nadvornaya. Ivano-Frankivs'ka Oblast', W Ukraine
Nadvoitsy 88 B3 Respublika Kareliya, NW Russian Federation
Nadym 92 C3 Yamalo-Nenetskiy Avtonomnyy Okrug, N Russian Federation
Náfpaktos 83 B5 var. Návpaktos. Dytikí Ellás, C Greece
Náfplio 83 B6 prev. Návplion. Pelopónnisos, S Greece
Naga 117 E2 off. Naga City; prev. Nueva Caceres. Luzon, N Philippines
Nagano 109 C5 Nagano, Honshū, S Japan
Nagaoka 109 D5 Niigata, Honshū, C Japan
Nagara Pathom see Nakhon Pathom
Nagara Sridharmaraj see Nakhon Si Thammarat
Nagara Svarga see Nakhon Sawan
Nagasaki 109 A7 Nagasaki, Kyūshū, SW Japan
Nagato 109 A7 Yamaguchi, Honshū, SW Japan
Nāgercoil 110 C3 Tamil Nādu, SE India
Nagorno-Karabakh 95 G3 var. Nagorno-Karabakhskaya Avtonomnaya Oblast , Arm. Lerrnayin Gharabakh, Az. Dağliq Qarabağ, Rus. Nagornyy Karabakh. Former autonomous region SW Azerbaijan
Nagorno-Karabakhskaya Avtonomnaya Oblast see Nagorno-Karabakh
Nagornyy Karabakh see Nagorno-Karabakh
Nagoya 109 C6 Aichi, Honshū, SW Japan
Nāgpur 112 D4 Mahārāshtra, C India
Nagqu 104 C5 Chin. Na-ch'ii; prev. Hei-ho. Xizang Zizhiqu, W China
Nagykálló 77 E6 Szabolcs-Szatmár-Bereg, E Hungary
Nagykanizsa 77 C7 Ger. Grosskanizsa. Zala, SW Hungary
Nagykőrös 77 D7 Pest, C Hungary
Nagyszentmiklós see Sânnicolau Mare
Naha 108 A3 Okinawa, Okinawa, SW Japan
Nahariya see Nahariyya
Nahariyya 97 A5 var. Nahariya. Northern, N Israel
Nahr al 'Aṣī see Orantes
Nahr al Litant see Litani, Nahr el
Nahr an Nīl see Nile
Nahr el Aassi see Orantes
Nahuel Huapi, Lago 43 B5 lake W Argentina
Nā'īn 98 D3 Eşfahān, C Iran
Nain 17 F2 Newfoundland and Labrador, NE Canada
Nairobi 47 E5 country capital (Kenya) Nairobi Area, S Kenya
Nairobi 51 C6 international airport Nairobi Area, S Kenya
Najaf see An Najaf
Najima see Fukuoka
Najin 107 E3 NE North Korea
Najrān 99 B6 var. Abā as Su'ūd. Najrān, S Saudi Arabia
Nakambé see White Volta
Nakamura 109 B7 Kōchi, Shikoku, SW Japan
Nakatsugawa 109 C6 var. Nakatugawa. Gifu, Honshū, SW Japan
Nakatugawa see Nakatsugawa
Nakhodka 93 G5 Primorskiy Kray, SE Russian Federation
Nakhon Pathom 115 C5 var. Nagara Pathom, Nakorn Pathom. Nakhon Pathom, W Thailand
Nakhon Ratchasima 115 C5 var. Khorat, Korat. Nakhon Ratchasima, E Thailand
Nakhon Sawan 115 C5 var. Muang Nakhon Sawan, Nagara Svarga. Nakhon Sawan, W Thailand
Nakhon Si Thammarat 115 C7 var. Nagara Sridharmaraj, Nakhon Sithamnaraj. Nakhon Si Thammarat, SW Thailand
Nakhon Sithamnaraj see Nakhon Si Thammarat
Nakorn Pathom see Nakhon Pathom
Nakuru 51 C6 Rift Valley, SW Kenya
Nal'chik 89 B8 Kabardino-Balkarskaya Respublika, SW Russian Federation
Nālūt 49 F2 NW Libya
Namakan Lake 18 A1 lake Canada/USA
Namangan 101 F2 Namangan Wiloyati, E Uzbekistan
Nambala 56 D2 Central, C Zambia
Nam Co 104 C5 lake W China
Nam Ðinh 114 D3 Nam Ha, N Vietnam
Namib Desert 56 B3 desert W Namibia
Namibe 56 A2 Port. Moçâmedes, Mossâmedes. Namibe, SW Angola
Namibia 56 B3 var. South West Africa, Afr. Suidwes-Afrika, Ger. Deutsch-Südwestafrika; prev. German Southwest Africa, South-West Africa. Country S Africa
Namo see Namu Atoll
Nam Ou 114 C3 river N Laos
Nampa 24 D3 Idaho, NW USA
Nampula 57 E2 Nampula, NE Mozambique
Namsos 62 B4 Nord-Trøndelag, C Norway
Nam Tha 114 C4 river N Laos
Namu Atoll 122 D2 var. Namo. Atoll Ralik Chain, C Marshall Islands
Namur 65 C6 Dut. Namen. Namur, SE Belgium
Namyit Island 106 C8 island S Spratly Islands
Nan 114 C4 var. Muang Nan. Nan, NW Thailand
Nanaimo 14 D5 Vancouver Island, British Columbia, SW Canada
Nanchang 106 C5 var. Nan-ch'ang, Nanch'ang-hsien. Jiangxi, S China
Nanch'ang-hsien see Nanchang
Nan-ching see Nanjing
Nancy 68 D3 Meurthe-et-Moselle, NE France
Nandaime 30 D3 Granada, SW Nicaragua
Nānded 112 D5 Mahārāshtra, C India
Nandyāl 110 C1 Andhra Pradesh, E India
Nanjing 106 D5 var. Nan-ching, Nanking; prev. Chianning, Chian-ning, Kiang-ning. Jiangsu, E China
Nanking see Nanjing
Nanning 106 B6 var. Nan-ning; prev. Yung-ning. Guangxi Zhuangzu Zizhiqu, S China
Nan-ning see Nanning
Nanortalik 60 C5 S Greenland
Nanpan Jiang 114 D2 river S China
Nanping 106 D6 var. Nan-p'ing; prev. Yenping. Fujian, SE China
Nansei-Shotō 108 A2 var. Ryukyu Islands. Island group SW Japan
Nansei Syotō Trench see Ryukyu Trench
Nansen Basin 133 C4 undersea feature Arctic Ocean
Nansen Cordillera 133 B3 var. Arctic-Mid Oceanic Ridge, Nansen Ridge. Undersea feature Arctic Ocean
Nansen Ridge see Nansen Cordillera
Nanterre 68 D1 Hauts-de-Seine, N France
Nantes 68 B4 Bret. Naoned; anc. Condivincum, Namnetes. Loire-Atlantique, NW France
Nantucket Island 19 G3 island Massachusetts, NE USA
Nanumaga 123 E3 var. Nanumanga. Atoll NW Tuvalu
Nanumanga see Nanumaga
Nanumea Atoll 123 E3 atoll NW Tuvalu
Nanyang 106 C5 var. Nan-yang. Henan, C China
Napa 25 B6 California, W USA
Napier 128 E4 Hawke's Bay, North Island, NZ
Naples 58 D5 anc. Neapolis. Campania, S Italy
Naples 21 E5 Florida, SE USA
Napo 34 A3 province NE Ecuador
Napo, Río 38 C1 river Ecuador/Peru
Naracoorte 127 B7 South Australia
Naradhivas see Narathiwat
Narathiwat 115 C7 var. Naradhivas. Narathiwat, SW Thailand
Narbada see Narmada
Narbonne 69 C6 anc. Narbo Martius. Aude, S France
Narborough Island see Fernandina, Isla
Nares Abyssal Plain see Nares Plain
Nares Plain 13 E6 var. Nares Abyssal Plain. Undersea feature NW Atlantic Ocean
Nares Strait 60 D1 Dan. Nares Stræde. Strait Canada/Greenland
Narew 76 E3 river E Poland
Narmada 102 B3 var. Narbada. River C India
Narowlya 85 C8 Rus. Narovlya. Homyel'skaya Voblasts', SE Belarus
Närpes 63 D5 Fin. Närpiö. Länsi-Suomi, W Finland
Narrabri 127 D6 New South Wales, SE Australia
Narrogin 125 B6 Western Australia
Narva 84 E2 prev. Narova. River Estonia/Russian Federation
Narva 84 E2 Ida-Virumaa, NE Estonia
Narva Bay 84 E2 Est. Narva Laht, Ger. Narwa-Bucht, Rus. Narvskiy Zaliv. Bay Estonia/Russian Federation
Narva Reservoir 84 E2 Est. Narva Veehoidla, Rus. Narvskoye Vodokhranilishche. Reservoir Estonia/Russian Federation
Narvik 62 C3 Nordland, C Norway
Nar'yan-Mar 88 D3 prev. Beloshchel'ye, Dzerzhinskiy. Nenetskiy Avtonomnyy Okrug, NW Russian Federation
Naryn 101 G2 Narynskaya Oblast', C Kyrgyzstan
Năsăud 86 B3 Ger. Nussdorf, Hung. Naszód. Bistrița-Năsăud, N Romania
Nase see Naze
Nāshik 112 C5 prev. Nāsik. Mahārāshtra, W India
Nashua 19 G3 New Hampshire, NE USA
Nashville 20 C1 state capital Tennessee, S USA
Näsijärvi 63 D5 lake SW Finland
Nāsiri see Ahvāz
Nasiriya see An Nāṣirīyah
Nassau 32 C1 country capital (Bahamas) New Providence, N Bahamas
Nasser, Lake 50 B3 var. Buhayrat Nasir, Buḥayrat Nāṣir, Buḥeiret Nâṣir. Lake Egypt/Sudan
Nata 56 C3 Central, NE Botswana
Natal 41 G2 Rio Grande do Norte, E Brazil
Natal Basin 119 A6 var. Mozambique Basin. Undersea feature W Indian Ocean
Natanya see Netanya
Natchez 20 B3 Mississippi, S USA
Natchitoches 20 A2 Louisiana, S USA
Nathanya see Netanya
Natitingou 53 F4 NW Benin
Natsrat see Nazerat
Natuna Islands 102 D4 island group W Indonesia
Naturaliste Plateau 119 E6 undersea feature E Indian Ocean
Naugard see Nowogard
Naujamiestis 84 C4 Panevėžys, C Lithuania
Nauru 122 D2 prev. Pleasant Island. Country W Pacific Ocean
Nauta 38 C2 Loreto, N Peru
Navahrudak 85 C6 Pol. Nowogródek, Rus. Novogrudok. Hrodzyenskaya Voblasts', W Belarus
Navapolatsk 85 D5 Rus. Novopolotsk. Vitsyebskaya Voblasts', N Belarus
Navarra 71 E2 cultural region N Spain
Navassa Island 32 C3 US unincorporated territory C West Indies
Navoiy 101 E2 var. Nawoiy, Rus. Navoi. Nawoiy Wiloyati, C Uzbekistan
Navojoa 28 C2 Sonora, NW Mexico
Navolat see Navolato
Navolato 66 C3 var. Navolat. Sinaloa, C Mexico
Návpaktos see Náfpaktos
Nawabashah see Nawābshāh
Nawābshāh 112 B3 var. Nawabashah. Sind, S Pakistan
Nawoiy see Navoiy
Naxçıvan 95 G3 Rus. Nakhichevan'. SW Azerbaijan
Náxos 83 D6 var. Naxos. Náxos, Kykládes, Greece, Aegean Sea
Náxos 83 D6 island Kykládes, Greece, Aegean Sea
Nayoro 108 D2 Hokkaidō, NE Japan
Nazca 38 D4 Ica, S Peru
Nazca Ridge 35 A5 undersea feature E Pacific Ocean
Naze 108 B3 var. Nase. Kagoshima, Amami-ōshima, SW Japan
Nazerat 97 A5 var. Natsrat, Ar. En Nazira, Eng. Nazareth. Northern, N Israel
Nazilli 94 A4 Aydın, SW Turkey
Nazrēt 51 C5 var. Adama, Hadama. C Ethiopia
N'Dalatando 56 B1 Port. Salazar, Vila Salazar. Cuanza Norte, NW Angola
Ndélé 54 C4 Bamingui-Bangoran, N Central African Republic
Ndendé 55 B6 Ngounié, S Gabon
Ndindi 55 A6 Nyanga, S Gabon
Ndjamena 54 B3 var. N'Djamena; prev. Fort-Lamy. Country capital (Chad) Chari-Baguirmi, W Chad
Ndjolé 55 A5 Moyen-Ogooué, W Gabon
Ndola 56 D2 Copperbelt, C Zambia
Neagh, Lough 67 B5 lake E Northern Ireland, UK
Néa Moudanía 82 C4 var. Néa Moudhaniá. Kentrikí Makedonía, N Greece
Néa Moudhaniá see Néa Moudanía
Neápoli 82 B4 prev. Neápolis. Dytikí Makedonía, N Greece
Neápoli 83 D8 Kríti, Greece, E Mediterranean Sea
Neápoli 83 C7 Pelopónnisos, S Greece
Neapolis see Nablus
Near Islands 14 A2 island group Aleutian Islands, Alaska, USA
Néa Zíchni 82 C3 var. Néa Zíkhni; prev. Néa Zíkhna. Kentrikí Makedonía, NE Greece
Néa Zíkhna see Néa Zíchni
Néa Zíkhni see Néa Zíchni
Nebaj 30 B2 Quiché, W Guatemala
Neblina, Pico da 40 C1 mountain NW Brazil
Nebraska 22 D4 off. State of Nebraska; also known as Blackwater State, Cornhusker State, Tree Planters State. State C USA
Nebraska City 23 F4 Nebraska, C USA
Neches River 27 H3 river Texas, SW USA
Neckar 73 B6 river SW Germany
Necochea 43 D5 Buenos Aires, E Argentina
Neder Rijn 64 D4 Eng. Lower Rhine. River C Netherlands
Nederweert 65 D5 Limburg, SE Netherlands
Neede 64 E3 Gelderland, E Netherlands
Neerpelt 65 D5 Limburg, NE Belgium
Neftekamsk 89 D5 Respublika Bashkortostan, W Russian Federation
Negēlē 51 D5 var. Negelli, It. Neghelli. C Ethiopia
Negelli see Negēlē
Neghelli see Negēlē
Negomane 57 E2 var. Negomano. Cabo Delgado, N Mozambique
Negomano see Negomane
Negombo 110 C3 Western Province, SW Sri Lanka
Negotin 78 E4 Serbia, E Serbia and Montenegro (Yugo.)
Negra, Punta 38 A3 headland NW Peru
Negrești-Oaș 86 B3 Hung. Avasfelsőfalu; prev. Negrești. Satu Mare, NE Romania
Negro, Río 43 C5 river E Argentina
Negro, Rio 40 D1 river N South America
Negro, Río 42 D4 river Brazil/Uruguay
Negros 117 E2 island C Philippines
Nehbandān 98 E3 Khorāsān, E Iran
Neijiang 106 B5 Sichuan, C China
Nei Monggol Zizhiqu see Inner Mongolia
Nei Mongol see Inner Mongolia
Neiva 36 B3 Huila, S Colombia
Nellore 110 D2 Andhra Pradesh, E India
Nelson 15 G4 river Manitoba, C Canada
Nelson 129 C5 Nelson, South Island, NZ
Néma 52 D3 Hodh ech Chargui, SE Mauritania
Neman 84 A4 Bel. Nyoman, Ger. Memel, Lith. Nemunas, Pol. Niemen, Rus. Neman. River NE Europe
Neman 84 B4 Ger. Ragnit. Kaliningradskaya Oblast', W Russian Federation
Neméa 83 B6 Pelopónnisos, S Greece
Nemours 68 C3 Seine-et-Marne, N France
Nemuro 108 E2 Hokkaidō, NE Japan
Neochóri 83 B5 Dytikí Ellás, C Greece
Nepal 113 E3 Country S Asia
Nereta 84 C4 Aizkraukle, S Latvia
Neretva 78 C4 river Bosnia and Herzegovina/Croatia
Neringa 84 A3 var. Nida, Ger. Nidden. Neringa, SW Lithuania
Neris 85 C5 Bel. Viliya, Pol. Wilia; prev. Pol. Wilja. River Belarus/Lithuania
Nerva 70 C4 Andalucía, S Spain
Neryungri 93 F4 Respublika Sakha (Yakutiya), NE Russian Federation
Neskaupstadhur 61 E5 Austurland, E Iceland
Ness, Loch 66 C3 lake N Scotland, UK
Néstos 82 C3 Bul. Mesta, Turk. Kara Su. River Bulgaria/Greece see also Mesta
Netanya 97 A6 var. Natanya, Nathanya. Central, C Israel
Netherlands 64 C3 var. Holland, Dut. Koninkrijk der Nederlanden, Nederland. Country NW Europe
Netherlands Antilles 33 E5 prev. Dutch West Indies. Dutch autonomous region S Caribbean Sea
Netherlands New Guinea see Papua
Nettilling Lake 15 G3 lake Baffin Island, Nunavut, N Canada
Neubrandenburg 72 D3 Mecklenburg-Vorpommern, NE Germany
Neuchâtel 73 A7 Ger. Neuenburg. Neuchâtel, W Switzerland
Neuchâtel, Lac de 73 A7 Ger. Neuenburger See. Lake W Switzerland
Neufchâteau 65 D8 Luxembourg, SE Belgium
Neumünster 72 B2 Schleswig-Holstein, N Germany
Neunkirchen 73 A5 Saarland, SW Germany
Neuquén 43 B5 Neuquén, SE Argentina
Neuruppin 72 C3 Brandenburg, NE Germany
Neusalz an der Oder see Nowa Sól
Neusiedler See 73 E6 Hung. Fertő. Lake Austria/Hungary
Neustadt an der Weinstrasse 73 B5 prev. Neustadt an der Haardt, hist. Niewenstat, anc. Nova Civitas. Rheinland-Pfalz, SW Germany
Neustrelitz 72 D3 Mecklenburg-Vorpommern, NE Germany
Neu-Ulm 73 B6 Bayern, S Germany
Neuwied 73 A5 Rheinland-Pfalz, W Germany
Neuzen see Terneuzen
Nevada 25 C5 off. State of Nevada; also known as Battle Born State, Sagebrush State, Silver State. State W USA
Nevada, Sierra 70 D5 mountain range S Spain
Nevers 68 C4 anc. Noviodunum. Nièvre, C France
Neves 54 E2 São Tomé, S Sao Tome and Principe
Nevinnomyssk 89 B7 Stavropol'skiy Kray, SW Russian Federation
Nevşehir 94 C3 var. Nevshehr. Nevşehir, C Turkey
Nevshehr see Nevşehir
Newala 73 C8 Mtwara, SE Tanzania
New Albany 18 C5 Indiana, N USA
New Amsterdam 37 G3 E Guyana
Newark 19 F4 New Jersey, NE USA
New Bedford 19 G3 Massachusetts, NE USA
Newberg 24 B3 Oregon, NW USA
New Bern 21 F1 North Carolina, SE USA
New Braunfels 27 G4 Texas, SW USA
Newbridge 67 B6 Ir. An Droichead Nua. C Ireland
New Britain 122 B3 island E PNG
New Brunswick 17 E4 Fr. Nouveau-Brunswick. Province SE Canada
New Caledonia 122 D4 var. Kanaky, Fr. Nouvelle-Calédonie. French overseas territory SW Pacific Ocean
New Caledonia 122 C5 island SW Pacific Ocean
New Caledonia Basin 120 C4 undersea feature W Pacific Ocean
Newcastle see Newcastle upon Tyne
Newcastle 127 D6 New South Wales, SE Australia
Newcastle upon Tyne 66 D4 var. Newcastle; hist. Monkchester, Lat. Pons Aelii. NE England, UK
New Delhi 112 D3 country capital (India) Delhi, N India
Newfoundland 17 G3 Fr. Terre-Neuve. Island Newfoundland, SE Canada
Newfoundland 17 F2 Fr. Terre Neuve. Province SE Canada
Newfoundland Basin 44 B3 undersea feature NW Atlantic Ocean
New Georgia Islands 122 C3 island group NW Solomon Islands
New Glasgow 17 F4 Nova Scotia, SE Canada
New Goa see Pānji
New Guinea 122 A3 Dut. Nieuw Guinea, Ind. Irian. Island Indonesia/PNG
New Hampshire 19 F2 off. State of New Hampshire; also known as The Granite State. State NE USA
New Haven 19 G3 Connecticut, NE USA
New Iberia 20 B3 Louisiana, S USA
New Ireland 122 C3 island NE PNG
New Jersey 19 F4 off. State of New Jersey; also known as The Garden State. State NE USA
Newman 124 B4 Western Australia
Newmarket 67 E6 E England, UK
New Mexico 26 C2 off. State of New Mexico; also known as Land of Enchantment, Sunshine State. State SW USA
New Orleans 20 B3 Louisiana, S USA
New Plymouth 128 C4 Taranaki, North Island, NZ
Newport 18 C4 Kentucky, S USA
Newport 67 D7 S England, UK
Newport 67 C7 SE Wales, UK
Newport 19 G2 Vermont, NE USA
Newport News 19 F5 Virginia, NE USA
New Providence 32 C1 island N Bahamas
Newquay 67 C7 SW England, UK
Newry 67 B5 Ir. An tIúr. SE Northern Ireland, UK
New Sarum see Salisbury
New Siberian Islands see Novosibirskiye Ostrova
New South Wales 127 C6 state SE Australia
Newton 23 G3 Iowa, C USA
Newtownabbey 67 B5 Ir. Baile na Mainistreach. E Northern Ireland, UK
New Ulm 23 F2 Minnesota, N USA
New York 19 F4 New York, NE USA
New York 19 F3 state NE USA
New Zealand 128 A4 abbrev. NZ. Country SW Pacific Ocean
Neyveli 110 C2 Tamil Nādu, SE India
Ngangzê Co 104 B5 lake W China
Ngaoundéré 54 B4 var. N'Gaoundéré. Adamaoua, N Cameroon
N'Giva 56 B3 var. Ondjiva, Port. Vila Pereira de Eça. Cunene, S Angola
Ngo 55 B6 Plateaux, SE Congo
Ngoko 55 B5 river Cameroon/Congo
Ngourti 53 H3 Diffa, E Niger
Nguigmi 53 H3 var. N'Guigmi. Diffa, SE Niger
Nguru 53 G3 Yobe, NE Nigeria
Nha Trang 115 E6 Khanh Hoa, S Vietnam
Niagara Falls 18 D3 waterfall Canada/USA
Niagara Falls 19 E3 New York, NE USA
Niagara Falls 16 D5 Ontario, S Canada
Niamey 53 F3 country capital (Niger) Niamey, SW Niger
Niangay, Lac 53 E3 lake E Mali
Nia-Nia 55 E5 Orientale, NE Dem. Rep. Congo
Nias, Pulau 116 A3 island W Indonesia
Nicaragua 30 D3 Country Central America
Nicaragua, Lago de 30 D4 var. Cocibolca, Gran Lago, Eng. Lake Nicaragua. Lake S Nicaragua
Nicaragua, Lake see Nicaragua, Lago de
Nicaria see Ikaría
Nice 69 D6 It. Nizza; anc. Nicaea. Alpes-Maritimes, SE France
Nicephorium see Ar Raqqah
Nicholas II Land see Severnaya Zemlya
Nicholls Town 32 C1 Andros Island, NW Bahamas
Nicobar Islands 102 B4 island group India, E Indian Ocean
Nicosia 80 C5 Gk. Lefkosía, Turk. Lefkoşa. Country capital (Cyprus) C Cyprus
Nicoya 30 D4 Guanacaste, W Costa Rica
Nicoya, Golfo de 30 D5 gulf W Costa Rica
Nicoya, Península de 30 D4 peninsula NW Costa Rica
Nida see Neringa
Nidden see Neringa
Nidzica 76 D3 Ger. Niedenburg. Warmińsko-Mazurskie, NE Poland
Niedere Tauern 77 A6 mountain range C Austria
Nieuw Amsterdam 37 G3 Commewijne, NE Suriname
Nieuw-Bergen 64 D4 Limburg, SE Netherlands
Nieuwegein 64 C4 Utrecht, C Netherlands
Nieuw Nickerie 37 G3 Nickerie, NW Suriname
Niğde 94 C4 Niğde, C Turkey
Niger 53 F3 Country W Africa
Niger 53 F4 river W Africa
Nigeria 53 F4 Country W Africa
Niger, Mouths of the 53 F5 delta S Nigeria
Nihon see Japan
Niigata 109 D5 Niigata, Honshū, C Japan
Niihama 109 B7 Ehime, Shikoku, SW Japan
Ni'ihau 25 A7 var. Niihau. Island Hawai'i, USA, C Pacific Ocean
Nii-jima 109 D6 island E Japan
Nijkerk 64 D3 Gelderland, C Netherlands
Nijlen 65 C5 Antwerpen, N Belgium
Nijmegen 64 D4 Ger. Nimwegen; anc. Noviomagus. Gelderland, SE Netherlands
Nikaria see Ikaría
Nikel' 88 C2 Murmanskaya Oblast', NW Russian Federation
Nikiniki 117 E5 Timor, S Indonesia
Nikopol' 87 F3 Pleven, N Bulgaria

Nikšić 79 C5 Montenegro, SW Serbia and Montenegro (Yugo.)
Nikumaroro 123 E3 prev. Gardner Island, Kemins Island. Atoll Phoenix Islands, C Kiribati
Nikunau 123 E3 var. Nukunau; prev. Byron Island. Atoll Tungaru, W Kiribati
Nile 46 D3 Ar. Nahr an Nīl. River N Africa
Nile 50 B2 former province NW Uganda
Nile Delta 50 B1 delta N Egypt
Nîmes 69 C6 anc. Nemausus, Nismes. Gard, S France
Nine Degree Channel 110 B3 channel India/Maldives
Ninetyeast Ridge 119 D5 undersea feature E Indian Ocean
Ninety Mile Beach 128 C1 beach North Island, NZ
Ningbo 106 D5 var. Ning-po, Yin-hsien; prev. Ninghsien. Zhejiang, SE China
Ninghsien see Ningbo
Ning-po see Ningbo
Ningxia 106 B4 off. Ningxia Huizu Zizhiqu, var. Ning-hsia, Ningsia, Eng. Ningsia Hui, Ningsia Hui Autonomous Region. Admin. region autonomous region N China
Ningxia Huizu Zizhiqu see Ningxia
Nio see Íos
Niobrara River 23 E3 river Nebraska/Wyoming, C USA
Nioro 52 D3 var. Nioro du Sahel. Kayes, W Mali
Nioro du Sahel see Nioro
Niort 90 B4 Deux-Sèvres, W France
Nipigon 16 B4 Ontario, S Canada
Nipigon, Lake 16 B3 lake Ontario, S Canada
Nippon see Japan
Niš 79 E5 Eng. Nish, Ger. Nisch; anc. Naissus. Serbia, SE Serbia and Montenegro (Yugo.)
Nişāb 98 B4 Al Ḩudūd ash Shamālīyah, N Saudi Arabia
Nisibin see Nusaybin
Nisiros see Nísyros
Nisko 76 E4 Podkarpackie, SE Poland
Nísyros 83 E7 var. Nisiros. Island Dodekánisos, Greece, Aegean Sea
Nitra 77 C6 Ger. Neutra, Hung. Nyitra. River W Slovakia
Nitra 77 C6 Ger. Neutra, Hung. Nyitra. Nitriansky Kraj, SW Slovakia
Niuatobutabu see Niuatoputapu
Niuatoputapu 123 E4 var. Niuatobutabu; prev. Keppel Island. Island N Tonga
Niue 123 F4 self-governing territory in free association with NZ S Pacific Ocean
Niulakita 123 E3 var. Nurakita. Atoll S Tuvalu
Niutao 123 E3 atoll NW Tuvalu
Nivernais 68 C4 cultural region C France
Nizāmābād 112 D5 Andhra Pradesh, C India
Nizhnekamsk 89 C5 Respublika Tatarstan, W Russian Federation
Nizhnevartovsk 92 D3 Khanty-Mansiyskiy Avtonomnyy Okrug, C Russian Federation
Nizhniy Novgorod 89 C5 prev. Gor'kiy. Nizhegorodskaya Oblast', W Russian Federation
Nizhniy Odes 88 D4 Respublika Komi, NW Russian Federation
Nizhnyaya Tunguska 93 E3 Eng. Lower Tunguska. River N Russian Federation
Nizhyn 87 E1 Rus. Nezhin. Chernihivs'ka Oblast', NE Ukraine
Njazidja see Grande Comore
Njombe 51 C8 Iringa, S Tanzania
Nkayi 55 B6 prev. Jacob. La Bouenza, S Congo
Nkongsamba 54 A4 var. N'Kongsamba. Littoral, W Cameroon
Nmai Hka 114 B2 var. Me Hka. River N Myanmar
Nobeoka 109 B7 Miyazaki, Kyūshū, SW Japan
Noboribetsu 108 D3 var. Noboribetu. Hokkaidō, NE Japan
Noboribetu see Noboribetsu
Nogales 26 B3 Arizona, SW USA
Nogales 28 B1 Sonora, NW Mexico
Nogal Valley see Dooxo Nugaaleed
Nokia 63 D5 Länsi-Suomi, W Finland
Nokou 54 B3 Kanem, W Chad
Nola 55 B5 Sangha-Mbaéré, SW Central African Republic
Nolinsk 89 C5 Kirovskaya Oblast', NW Russian Federation
Nongkaya see Nong Khai
Nong Khai 114 C4 var. Mi Chai, Nongkaya. Nong Khai, E Thailand
Nonouti 122 D2 prev. Sydenham Island. Atoll Tungaru, W Kiribati
Noord-Beveland 64 B4 var. North Beveland. Island SW Netherlands
Noordwijk aan Zee 64 C3 Zuid-Holland, W Netherlands
Nora 63 C6 Örebro, C Sweden
Norak 101 E3 Rus. Nurek. W Tajikistan
Nord 61 F1 N Greenland
Nordaustlandet 61 G1 island NE Svalbard
Norden 72 A3 Niedersachsen, NW Germany
Norderstedt 72 B3 Schleswig-Holstein, N Germany
Nordfriesische Inseln see North Frisian Islands
Nordhausen 72 C4 Thüringen, C Germany
Nordhorn 72 A3 Niedersachsen, NW Germany
Nordkapp 62 D1 Eng. North Cape. Headland N Norway
Norfolk 23 E3 Nebraska, C USA
Norfolk 19 F5 Virginia, NE USA
Norfolk Island 120 D4 Australian external territory SW Pacific Ocean

Norfolk Ridge 120 D4 undersea feature W Pacific Ocean
Norias 27 G5 Texas, SW USA
Noril'sk 92 D3 Taymyrskiy (Dolgano-Nenetskiy) Avtonomnyy Okrug, N Russian Federation
Norman 27 G1 Oklahoma, USA
Normandie 68 B3 Eng. Normandy. Cultural region N France
Normandy see Normandie
Normanton 126 C3 Queensland, NE Australia
Norrköping 63 C6 Östergötland, S Sweden
Norrtälje 63 C6 Stockholm, C Sweden
Norseman 125 B6 Western Australia
North Albanian Alps 79 C5 Alb. Bjeshkët e Namuna, SCr. Prokletije. Mountain range Albania/Serbia and Montenegro (Yugo.)
Northallerton 67 D5 N England, UK
Northam 125 A6 Western Australia
North America 12 continent
North Andaman 111 F2 island Andaman Islands, India, NE Indian Ocean
North Australian Basin 119 E5 Fr. Bassin Nord de l' Australie. Undersea feature E Indian Ocean
North Bay 16 D4 Ontario, S Canada
North Beveland see Noord-Beveland
North Cape 44 D1 headland New Ireland, NE PNG
North Cape 128 C1 headland North Island, NZ
North Cape see Nordkapp
North Carolina 21 E1 off. State of North Carolina; also known as Old North State, Tar Heel State, Turpentine State. State SE USA
North Channel 18 D2 lake channel Canada/USA
North Charleston 21 F2 South Carolina, SE USA
North Dakota 22 D2 off. State of North Dakota; also known as Flickertail State, Peace Garden State, Sioux State. State N USA
Northeast Providence Channel 32 C1 channel N Bahamas
Northeim 72 B4 Niedersachsen, C Germany
Northern Cook Islands 123 F4 island group N Cook Islands
Northern Cyprus, Turkish Republic of 80 D5 disputed region N Cyprus
Northern Dvina see Severnaya Dvina
Northern Ireland 66 B4 var. The Six Counties. Political division UK
Northern Mariana Islands 120 B1 US commonwealth territory W Pacific Ocean
Northern Sporades see Vóreioi Sporádes
Northern Territory 122 A5 territory N Australia
North European Plain 59 E3 plain N Europe
Northfield 23 F2 Minnesota, N USA
North Fiji Basin 120 D3 undersea feature N Coral Sea
North Frisian Islands 72 B2 var. Nordfriesische Inseln. Island group N Germany
North Huvadhu Atoll 110 B5 var. Gaafu Alifu Atoll. Atoll S Maldives
North Island 128 B2 island N NZ
North Korea 107 E3 Kor. Chosŏn-minjujuŭi-inmin-kanghwaguk. Country E Asia
North Little Rock 20 B1 Arkansas, C USA
North Minch see Minch, The
North Mole 71 G4 harbour wall NW Gibraltar
North Platte 23 E4 Nebraska, C USA
North Platte River 22 D4 river C USA
North Pole 133 B3 pole Arctic Ocean
North Saskatchewan 15 F5 river Alberta/Saskatchewan, S Canada
North Sea 63 C3 Dan. Nordsøen, Dut. Noordzee, Fr. Mer du Nord, Ger. Nordsee, Nor. Nordsjøen; prev. German Ocean, Lat. Mare Germanicum. Sea NW Europe
North Siberian Lowland see Severo-Sibirskaya Nizmennost'
North Siberian Plain see Severo-Sibirskaya Nizmennost'
North Taranaki Bight 128 C3 gulf North Island, NZ
North Uist 66 B3 island NW Scotland, UK
Northwest Atlantic Mid-Ocean Canyon 12 E4 undersea feature N Atlantic Ocean
North West Highlands 66 C3 mountain range N Scotland, UK
Northwest Pacific Basin 91 G4 undersea feature NW Pacific Ocean
Northwest Providence Channel 32 C1 channel N Bahamas
Northwest Territories 15 E3 Fr. Territoires du Nord-Ouest. Territory NW Canada (the eastern part is now the territory of Nunavut)
Northwind Plain 133 B2 undersea feature Arctic Ocean
Norton Sound 14 C2 inlet Alaska, USA
Norway 63 A5 Nor. Norge. Country N Europe
Norwegian Basin 61 F4 undersea feature NW Norwegian Sea
Norwegian Sea 61 F4 Nor. Norske Havet. Sea NE Atlantic Ocean
Norwich 67 E6 E England, UK
Noshiro 108 D3 var. Nosiro; prev. Noshirominato. Akita, Honshū, C Japan
Noshirominato see Noshiro
Nosiro see Noshiro
Nosivka 87 E1 Rus. Nosovka. Chernihivs'ka Oblast', NE Ukraine

Noşratābād 98 E3 Sīstān va Balūchestān, E Iran
Nossob 56 C4 river E Namibia
Noteć 76 C3 Ger. Netze. River NW Poland
Nótioi Sporádes see Dodekánisos
Nottingham 67 D6 C England, UK
Nouâdhibou 52 B2 prev. Port-Étienne. Dakhlet Nouâdhibou, W Mauritania
Nouakchott 52 B2 country capital (Mauritania) Nouakchott District, SW Mauritania
Nouméa 122 C5 dependent territory capital (New Caledonia) Province Sud, S New Caledonia
Nouvelle-Calédonie see New Caledonia
Nova Gorica 73 D8 W Slovenia
Nova Gradiška 78 C3 Ger. Neugradisk, Hung. Újgradiska. Brod-Posavina, NE Croatia
Nova Iguaçu 41 F4 Rio de Janeiro, SE Brazil
Novara 74 B2 anc. Novaria. Piemonte, NW Italy
Nova Scotia 17 F4 Fr. Nouvelle Écosse. Province SE Canada
Nova Scotia 13 E5 physical region SE Canada
Novaya Sibir', Ostrov 93 F1 island Novosibirskiye Ostrova, NE Russian Federation
Novaya Zemlya 88 D1 island group N Russian Federation
Novaya Zemlya Trench see East Novaya Zemlya Trench
Novgorod see Velikiy Novgorod
Novi Grad see Bosanski Novi
Novi Iskŭr 82 C2 Sofiya-Grad, W Bulgaria
Novi Pazar 79 D5 Turk. Yenipazar. Shumen, NE Bulgaria
Novi Sad 78 D3 Ger. Neusatz, Hung. Újvidék. Serbia, N Serbia and Montenegro (Yugo.)
Novoazovs'k 87 G4 Rus. Novoazovsk. Donets'ka Oblast', SE Ukraine
Novocheboksarsk 89 C5 Chuvashskaya Respublika, W Russian Federation
Novocherkassk 89 B7 Rostovskaya Oblast', SW Russian Federation
Novodvinsk 88 C3 Arkhangel'skaya Oblast', NW Russian Federation
Novohrad-Volyns'kyy 86 D2 Rus. Novograd-Volynskiy. Zhytomyrs'ka Oblast', N Ukraine
Novokazalinsk see Ayteke Bi
Novokuznetsk 92 D4 prev. Stalinsk. Kemerovskaya Oblast', S Russian Federation
Novolazarevskaya 132 C2 Russian research station Antarctica
Novo mesto 73 E8 Ger. Rudolfswert; prev. Ger. Neustadtl. SE Slovenia
Novomoskovs'k 87 F3 Rus. Novomoskovsk. Dnipropetrovs'ka Oblast', E Ukraine
Novomoskovsk 89 B5 Tul'skaya Oblast', W Russian Federation
Novorossiysk 89 A7 Krasnodarskiy Kray, SW Russian Federation
Novoshakhtinsk 89 B6 Rostovskaya Oblast', SW Russian Federation
Novosibirsk 92 D4 Novosibirskaya Oblast', C Russian Federation
Novosibirskiye Ostrova 93 F1 Eng. New Siberian Islands. Island group N Russian Federation
Novotroitsk 89 D6 Orenburgskaya Oblast', W Russian Federation
Novotroyits'ke 87 F4 Rus. Novotroitskoye. Khersons'ka Oblast', S Ukraine
Novovolyns'k 86 C1 Rus. Novovolynsk. Volyns'ka Oblast', NW Ukraine
Novozybkov 89 A5 Bryanskaya Oblast', W Russian Federation
Novyy Buh 87 E3 Rus. Novyy Bug. Mykolayivs'ka Oblast', S Ukraine
Novyy Uzen' see Zhanaozen
Nowa Sól 76 B4 var. Nowasól, Ger. Neusalz an der Oder. Lubuskie, W Poland
Nowogard 76 B2 var. Nowógard, Ger. Naugard. Zachodniopomorskie, NW Poland
Nowógard see Nowogard
Nowo-Minsk see Mińsk Mazowiecki
Nowy Dwór Mazowiecki 76 D3 Mazowieckie, C Poland
Nowy Sącz 77 D5 Ger. Neu Sandec. Małopolskie, S Poland
Nowy Tomyśl 76 B3 var. Nowy Tomysl. Wielkopolskie, C Poland
Noyon 68 C3 Oise, N France
Nsanje 57 E3 Southern, S Malawi
Nsawam 53 E5 SE Ghana
Ntomba, Lac 55 C6 var. Lac Tumba. Lake NW Dem. Rep. Congo
Nu'eima 97 E7 E West Bank
Nueva Gerona 32 B2 Isla de la Juventud, S Cuba
Nueva Rosita 28 D2 Coahuila de Zaragoza, NE Mexico
Nuevitas 32 C2 Camagüey, E Cuba
Nuevo, Bajo 31 G1 island NW Colombia
Nuevo Casas Grandes 28 C1 Chihuahua, N Mexico
Nuevo, Golfo 43 C6 gulf S Argentina
Nuevo Laredo 29 E2 Tamaulipas, NE Mexico
Nui Atoll 123 E3 atoll W Tuvalu
Nûk see Nuuk
Nuku'alofa 123 E5 country capital (Tonga) Tongatapu, S Tonga
Nukufetau Atoll 123 E3 atoll C Tuvalu
Nukulaelae Atoll 123 E3 var. Nukulailai. Atoll E Tuvalu
Nukulailai see Nukulaelae Atoll
Nukunau see Nikunau
Nukunonu Atoll 123 E3 island C Tokelau
Nukus 100 C2 Qoraqalpoghiston Respublikasi, W Uzbekistan

Nullarbor Plain 125 C6 plateau South Australia/Western Australia
Nunap Isua 98 B5 var Uummannarsuaq, Dan. Kap Farvel, Eng. Cape Farewell. Headland S Greenland
Nunavut 37 F3 territory N Canada
Nuneaton 67 D6 C England, UK
Nunivak Island 14 B2 island Alaska, USA
Nunspeet 64 D3 Gelderland, E Netherlands
Nuoro 75 A5 Sardegna, Italy, C Mediterranean Sea
Nuqui 36 A3 Chocó, W Colombia
Nurakita see Niulakita
Nuremberg see Nürnberg
Nurmes 62 E4 Itä-Suomi, E Finland
Nürnberg 73 C5 Eng. Nuremberg. Bayern, S Germany
Nurota 101 E2 Rus. Nurata. Nawoiy Wiloyati, C Uzbekistan
Nusa Tenggara 117 E5 Eng. Lesser Sunda Islands. East Timor / C Indonesia
Nusaybin 95 F4 var. Nisibin. Manisa, SE Turkey
Nuuk 60 C4 var. Nûk, Dan. Godthaab, Godthåb. Dependent territory capital (Greenland) SW Greenland
Nyagan' 92 C3 Khanty-Mansiyskiy Avtonomnyy Okrug, N Russian Federation
Nyala 50 A4 Southern Darfur, W Sudan
Nyamapanda 56 D3 Mashonaland East, NE Zimbabwe
Nyamtumbo 51 C8 Ruvuma, S Tanzania
Nyandoma 88 C4 Arkhangel'skaya Oblast', NW Russian Federation
Nyantakara 51 B7 Kagera, NW Tanzania
Nyasa, Lake 51 B8 var. Lake Malawi; prev. Lago Nyassa. Lake E Africa
Nyasvizh 85 C6 Pol. Nieśwież, Rus. Nesvizh. Minskaya Voblasts', C Belarus
Nyaunglebin 114 B4 Pegu, SW Myanmar
Nyeri 51 C6 Central, C Kenya
Nyima 104 C5 Xizang Zizhiqu, W China
Nyíregyháza 77 D6 Szabolcs-Szatmár-Bereg, NE Hungary
Nykøbing 63 B8 Storstrøm, SE Denmark
Nyköping 63 C6 Södermanland, S Sweden
Nylstroom see Modimolle
Nyngan 127 D6 New South Wales, SE Australia
Nyurba 93 F3 Respublika Sakha (Yakutiya), NE Russian Federation
Nyzhn'ohirs'kyy 87 F4 Rus. Nizhnegorskiy. Respublika Krym, S Ukraine
Nzega 51 C7 Tabora, C Tanzania
Nzérékoré 52 D4 Guinée-Forestière, SE Guinea
Nzwani see Anjouan

O

O'ahu 25 A7 var. Oahu. Island Hawai'i, USA, C Pacific Ocean
Oak Harbor 24 B1 Washington, NW USA
Oakland 25 B6 California, W USA
Oamaru 129 B7 Otago, South Island, NZ
Oaxaca 29 F5 var. Oaxaca de Juárez; prev. Antequera. Oaxaca, SE Mexico
Oaxaca de Juárez see Oaxaca
Ob' 90 C2 river C Russian Federation
Obal' 85 D5 Rus. Obol'. Vitsyebskaya Voblasts', N Belarus
Oban see Halfmoon Bay
Oban 66 C4 W Scotland, UK
Obando see Puerto Inírida
Obeliai 84 C4 Rokiškis, NE Lithuania
Oberhollabrunn see Tulln
Ob, Gulf of see Obskaya Guba
Obihiro 108 D2 Hokkaidō, NE Japan
Obo 54 D4 Haut-Mbomou, E Central African Republic
Obock 50 D4 E Djibouti
Oborniki 76 C3 Wielkopolskie, C Poland
Obskaya Guba 92 D3 Eng. Gulf of Ob'. Gulf N Russian Federation
Ob' Tablemount 119 B7 undersea feature S Indian Ocean
Ocala 21 E4 Florida, SE USA
Ocaña 70 D3 Castilla-La Mancha, C Spain
Ocaña 36 B2 Norte de Santander, N Colombia
O Carballiño 108 C1 var Carballiño. Gallicia, NW Spain
Occidental, Cordillera 39 E4 mountain range W South America
Occidental, Cordillera 36 B2 mountain range W Colombia
Occidental, Cordillera 38 D4 mountain range W Peru
Ocean Falls 14 D5 British Columbia, SW Canada
Ocean Island see Banaba
Oceanside 25 C8 California, W USA
Ochakiv 87 E4 Rus. Ochakov. Mykolayivs'ka Oblast', S Ukraine
Och'amch'ire 95 E2 Rus. Ochamchira. W Georgia
Ocho Rios 32 B4 C Jamaica
Ochrida, Lake see Ohrid, Lake
Ocotal 30 D3 Nueva Segovia, NW Nicaragua
Ocozocuautla 29 G5 Chiapas, SE Mexico
Ocú 31 F5 Herrera, S Panama
Ōdate 108 D3 Akita, Honshū, C Japan
Oddur see Xuddur
Ödemiş 94 A4 İzmir, SW Turkey
Odense 63 B7 C Denmark
Oder 76 B3 Cz./Pol. Odra. River C Europe
Oderhaff see Szczeciński, Zalew
Odesa 87 E4 Rus. Odessa. Odes'ka Oblast', SW Ukraine
Odessa 27 E3 Texas, SW USA
Odienné 52 D4 NW Côte d'Ivoire

Ōdŏngk 115 D6 Kâmpóng Spoe, S Cambodia
Odoorn 64 E2 Drenthe, NE Netherlands
Of 95 E2 Trabzon, NE Turkey
Ofanto 75 D5 river S Italy
Offenbach 73 B5 var. Offenbach am Main. Hessen, W Germany
Offenbach am Main see Offenbach
Offenburg 73 B6 Baden-Württemberg, SW Germany
Ogaden 51 D5 Som. Ogaadeen. Plateau Ethiopia/Somalia
Ōgaki 109 C6 Gifu, Honshū, SW Japan
Ogallala 22 D4 Nebraska, C USA
Ogbomosho 53 F4 Oyo, W Nigeria
Ogden 22 B4 Utah, W USA
Ogdensburg 19 F2 New York, NE USA
Ogulin 78 A3 Karlovac, NW Croatia
Ohio 18 C4 off. State of Ohio; also known as The Buckeye State. State N USA
Ohi o River 18 C4 river N USA
Ohrid 79 D6 Turk. Ochrida, Ohri. SW FYR Macedonia
Ohrid, Lake 79 D6 var. Lake Ochrida, Alb. Liqeni i Ohrit, Mac. Ohridsko Ezero. Lake Albania/FYR Macedonia
Ohridsko Ezero see Ohrid, Lake
Ohura 128 D3 Manawatu-Wanganui, North Island, NZ
Oirschot 65 C5 Noord-Brabant, S Netherlands
Oise 68 C3 river N France
Oistins 33 G2 S Barbados
Ōita 109 B7 Ōita, Kyūshū, SW Japan
Ojinaga 28 C2 Chihuahua, N Mexico
Ojos del Salado, Cerro 42 B3 mountain W Argentina
Okaihau 128 C2 Northland, North Island, NZ
Okāra 112 C2 Punjab, E Pakistan
Okavanggo see Cubango
Okavango see Cubango
Okavango 56 C3 district NW Namibia
Okavango Delta 56 C3 wetland N Botswana
Okayama 109 B6 Okayama, Honshū, SW Japan
Okazaki 109 C6 Aichi, Honshū, C Japan
Okeechobee, Lake 21 E4 lake Florida, SE USA
Okefenokee Swamp 21 E3 wetland Georgia, SE USA
Okhotsk 93 G3 Khabarovskiy Kray, E Russian Federation
Okhotskoye More 93 G3 sea NW Pacific Ocean
Okhotsk, Sea of 91 F3 sea NW Pacific Ocean
Okhtyrka 87 F2 Rus. Akhtyrka. Sums'ka Oblast', NE Ukraine
Oki-guntō see Oki-shotō
Okinawa 108 A3 island SW Japan
Okinawa-shotō 108 A3 island group SW Japan
Oki-shotō 109 B6 var. Oki-guntō. Island group SW Japan
Oklahoma 27 F2 off. State of Oklahoma; also known as The Sooner State. State C USA
Oklahoma City 27 G1 state capital Oklahoma, C USA
Okmulgee 27 G1 Oklahoma, C USA
Oko, Wadi 50 C3 river NE Sudan
Oktyabr'skiy 89 D6 Volgogradskaya Oblast', SW Russian Federation
Oktyabr'skoy Revolyutsii, Ostrov 93 E2 Eng. October Revolution Island. Island Severnaya Zemlya, N Russian Federation
Okulovka see Uglovka
Okushiri-tō 108 C3 var. Okusiri Tô. Island NE Japan
Okusiri Tô see Okushiri-tō
Öland 63 C7 island S Sweden
Olavarría 43 D5 Buenos Aires, E Argentina
Oława 76 C4 Ger. Ohlau. Dolnośląskie, SW Poland
Olbia 75 A5 prev. Terranova Pausania. Sardegna, Italy, C Mediterranean Sea
Oldebroek 64 D3 Gelderland, E Netherlands
Oldenburg 72 B3 Niedersachsen, NW Germany
Oldenburg 72 C2 Schleswig-Holstein, N Germany
Oldenzaal 64 E3 Overijssel, E Netherlands
Old Harbour 32 B5 C Jamaica
Olëkma 93 F4 river C Russian Federation
Olëkminsk 93 F3 Respublika Sakha (Yakutiya), NE Russian Federation
Oleksandrivka 87 E3 Rus. Aleksandrovka. Kirovohrads'ka Oblast', C Ukraine
Oleksandriya 87 F3 Rus. Aleksandriya. Kirovohrads'ka Oblast', C Ukraine
Olenegorsk 88 C2 Murmanskaya Oblast', NW Russian Federation
Olenëk 93 E3 Respublika Sakha (Yakutiya), NE Russian Federation
Olenëk 93 E3 river NE Russian Federation
Oléron, Île d' 69 A5 island W France
Olevs'k 86 D2 Rus. Olevsk. Zhytomyrs'ka Oblast', N Ukraine
Ölgiy 104 C2 Bayan-Ölgiy, W Mongolia
Olhão 70 B5 Faro, S Portugal
Olifa 56 B3 Kunene, NW Namibia
Ólimbos see Ólympos
Olimpo see Fuerte Olimpo
Oliva 71 F4 País Valenciano, E Spain
Olivet 68 C4 Loiret, C France
Olmaliq 101 E2 Rus. Almalyk. Toshkent Wiloyati, E Uzbekistan
Olomouc 77 C5 Ger. Olmütz, Pol. Ołomuniec. Olomoucký Kraj, E Czech Republic
Olonets 88 B3 Respublika Kareliya, NW Russian Federation
Olovyannaya 93 F4 Chitinskaya Oblast', S Russian Federation

Olpe – Paraparaumu

Olpe *72 B4* Nordrhein-Westfalen, W Germany
Olsztyn *76 D2 Ger.* Allenstein. Warmińsko-Mazurskie, NE Poland
Olt *86 B5 var.* Oltul, *Ger. Alt. River* S Romania
Oltenița *86 C5 prev. Eng.* Oltenitsa, *anc.* Constantiola. Călărași, SE Romania
Oltul *see* Olt
Olvera *70 D5* Andalucía, S Spain
Olympia *24 B2 state capital* Washington, NW USA
Olympic Mountains *24 A2 mountain range* Washington, NW USA
Ólympos *82 B4 var.* Olimbos, *Eng.* Mount Olympus. *Mountain* N Greece
Olympus, Mount *see* Ólympos
Omagh *67 B5 Ir.* An Ómaigh. W Northern Ireland, UK
Omaha *23 F4* Nebraska, C USA
Oman *99 D6 Ar.* Salṭanat 'Umān; *prev.* Muscat and Oman. *Country* SW Asia
Oman, Gulf of *98 E4 Ar.* Khalīj 'Umān. *Gulf* N Arabian Sea
Omboué *55 A6* Ogooué-Maritime, W Gabon
Omdurman *50 B4 var.* Umm Durmān. Khartoum, C Sudan
Ometepe, Isla de *30 D4 island* S Nicaragua
Ommen *64 E3* Overijssel, E Netherlands
Omsk *92 C4* Omskaya Oblast', C Russian Federation
Ōmuta *109 A7* Fukuoka, Kyūshū, SW Japan
Onda *71 F3* País Valenciano, E Spain
Ondjiva *see* N'Giva
Öndörhaan *105 E2* Hentiy, E Mongolia
Onega *88 B4 river* NW Russian Federation
Onega *88 C3* Arkhangel'skaya Oblast', NW Russian Federation
Onega, Lake *see* Onezhskoye Ozero
Onex *73 A7* Genève, SW Switzerland
Onezhskoye Ozero *88 B4 Eng.* Lake Onega. *Lake* NW Russian Federation
Ongole *110 D1* Andhra Pradesh, E India
Onitsha *53 G5* Anambra, S Nigeria
Onon Gol *105 E2 river* N Mongolia
Onslow *124 A4* Western Australia
Onslow Bay *21 F1 bay* North Carolina, E USA
Ontario *16 B3 province* S Canada
Ontario, Lake *19 E3 lake* Canada/USA
Onteniente *see* Ontinyent
Ontinyent *71 F4 var.* Onteniente. País Valenciano, E Spain
Ontong Java Rise *103 H4 undersea feature* W Pacific Ocean
Oostakker *65 B5* Oost-Vlaanderen, NW Belgium
Oostburg *65 B5* Zeeland, SW Netherlands
Oostende *65 A5 Eng.* Ostend, *Fr.* Ostende. West-Vlaanderen, NW Belgium
Oosterbeek *64 D4* Gelderland, SE Netherlands
Oosterhout *64 C4* Noord-Brabant, S Netherlands
Opatija *78 A2 It.* Abbazia. Primorje-Gorski Kotar, NW Croatia
Opava *77 C5 Ger.* Troppau. Ostravský Kraj, E Czech Republic
Opelika *20 D2* Alabama, S USA
Opelousas *20 B3* Louisiana, S USA
Opmeer *64 C2* Noord-Holland, NW Netherlands
Opochka *88 A4* Pskovskaya Oblast', W Russian Federation
Opole *76 C4 Ger.* Oppeln. Opolskie, S Poland
Opotiki *128 E3* Bay of Plenty, North Island, NZ
Oppidum Ubiorum *see* Köln
Oqtosh *101 E2 Rus.* Aktash. Samarqand Wiloyati, C Uzbekistan
Oradea *86 B3 prev.* Oradea Mare, *Ger.* Grosswardein, *Hung.* Nagyvárad. Bihor, NW Romania
Orahovac *79 D5 Alb.* Rahovec. Serbia, S Serbia and Montenegro (Yugo.)
Oran *48 D2 var.* Ouahran, Wahran. NW Algeria
Orange *69 D6 anc.* Arausio. Vaucluse, SE France
Orange *127 D6* New South Wales, SE Australia
Orangeburg *21 E2* South Carolina, SE USA
Orange Cone *see* Orange Fan
Orange Fan *47 C7 var.* Orange Cone. *Undersea feature* SW Indian Ocean
Orange Mouth *see* Oranjemund
Orangemund *see* Oranjemund
Orange River *56 B4 Afr.* Oranjerivier. *River* S Africa
Orange Walk *30 C1* Orange Walk, N Belize
Oranienburg *72 D3* Brandenburg, NE Germany
Oranjemund *56 B4 var.* Orangemund; *prev.* Orange Mouth. Karas, SW Namibia
Oranjestad *33 E5 dependent territory capital* (Aruba) W Aruba
Orantes *96 B3 var.* Oronte, *Ar.* Nahr el Aassi, Nahr al 'Aṣī. *River* SW Asia
Oravița *86 A4 Ger.* Orawitza, *Hung.* Oravicabánya. Caraș-Severin, SW Romania
Orbetello *74 B4* Toscana, C Italy
Orcadas *132 A1 Argentinian research station* South Orkney Islands, Antarctica
Orchard Homes *22 B1* Montana, NW USA
Ordino *69 A8* NW Andorra
Ordos Desert *see* Mu Us Shamo
Ordu *94 D2 anc.* Cotyora. Ordu, N Turkey
Ordzhonikidze *87 F3* Dnipropetrovs'ka Oblast', E Ukraine
Orealla *37 G3* E Guyana
Örebro *63 C6* Örebro, C Sweden
Oregon *24 B3 off.* State of Oregon; also known as Beaver State, Sunset State, Valentine State, Webfoot State. *State* NW USA
Oregon City *24 B3* Oregon, NW USA
Orël *89 B5* Orlovskaya Oblast', W Russian Federation
Orem *22 B4* Utah, W USA
Orenburg *89 D6 prev.* Chkalov. Orenburgskaya Oblast', W Russian Federation
Orense *see* Ourense
Oreor *see* Koror
Orestiáda *82 D3 prev.* Orestiás. Anatolikí Makedonía kai Thráki, NE Greece
Organ Peak *26 D3 mountain* New Mexico, SW USA
Orgeyev *see* Orhei
Orhei *86 D3 var.* Orheiu, *Rus.* Orgeyev. N Moldova
Orheiu *see* Orhei
Oriental, Cordillera *38 D3 mountain range* Bolivia/Peru
Oriental, Cordillera *39 F4 mountain range* C Bolivia
Oriental, Cordillera *36 B3 mountain range* C Colombia
Orihuela *71 F4* País Valenciano, E Spain
Orikhiv *87 G3 Rus.* Orekhov. Zaporiz'ka Oblast', SE Ukraine
Orinoco, Río *37 E2 river* Colombia/Venezuela
Orissa *113 F4 state* NE India
Orissaare *84 C2 Ger.* Orissaar. Saaremaa, W Estonia
Oristano *75 A5* Sardegna, Italy, C Mediterranean Sea
Orito *36 A4* Putumayo, SW Colombia
Orizaba, Volcán Pico de *13 C7 var.* Citlaltépetl. *Mountain* S Mexico
Orkney *see* Orkney Islands
Orkney Islands *66 C2 var.* Orkney, Orkneys. *Island group* N Scotland, UK
Orkneys *see* Orkney Islands
Orlando *21 E4* Florida, SE USA
Orléanais *68 C4 cultural region* C France
Orléans *68 C4 anc.* Aurelianum. Loiret, C France
Orléansville *see* Chlef
Orly *68 E2 international airport* (Paris) Essonne, N France
Orlya *85 B6 Rus.* Orlya. Hrodzyenskaya Voblasts', W Belarus
Ormuz, Strait of *see* Hormuz, Strait of
Örnsköldsvik *63 C5* Västernorrland, C Sweden
Oromocto *17 F4* New Brunswick, SE Canada
Orona *123 F3 prev.* Hull Island. *Atoll* Phoenix Islands, C Kiribati
Orosirá Rodhópis *see* Rhodope Mountains
Orpington *67 B8* SE England, UK
Orsha *85 E6 Rus.* Orsha. Vitsyebskaya Voblasts', NE Belarus
Orsk *92 B4* Orenburgskaya Oblast', W Russian Federation
Orșova *86 A4 Ger.* Orschowa, *Hung.* Orsova. Mehedinți, SW Romania
Orthez *69 B6* Pyrénées-Atlantiques, SW France
Ortona *74 D4* Abruzzo, C Italy
Oruba *see* Aruba
Oruro *39 F4* Oruro, W Bolivia
Ōsaka *109 C6 hist.* Naniwa. Ōsaka, Honshū, SW Japan
Osa, Península de *31 E5 peninsula* S Costa Rica
Osborn Plateau *119 D5 undersea feature* E Indian Ocean
Osh *101 F2* Oshskaya Oblast', SW Kyrgyzstan
Oshawa *16 D5* Ontario, SE Canada
Oshikango *56 B3* Ohangwena, N Namibia
Ō-shima *109 D6 island* S Japan
Oshkosh *18 B2* Wisconsin, N USA
Osijek *78 C3 prev.* Osiek, Osjek, *Ger.* Esseg, *Hung.* Eszék. Osijek-Baranja, E Croatia
Oskaloosa *23 G4* Iowa, C USA
Oskarshamn *63 C7* Kalmar, S Sweden
Oskil *87 G2 Rus.* Oskol. *River* Russian Federation/Ukraine
Oslo *63 B6 prev.* Christiania, Kristiania. *Country capital* (Norway) Oslo, S Norway
Osmaniye *94 D4* Osmaniye, admin. region *province* S Turkey
Osnabrück *72 A3* Niedersachsen, NW Germany
Osogov Mountains **120 B3** *var.* Osogovske Planine, Osogovski Planina, *Mac.* Osogovski Planini. *mountain range* Bulgaria/FYR, Macedonia
Osogovske Planine/Osogovski Planina/Osogovski Planini *see* Osogov Mountains
Osorno *43 B5* Los Lagos, C Chile
Oss *64 D4* Noord-Brabant, S Netherlands
Ossa, Serra d' *70 C4 mountain range* SE Portugal
Ossora *93 H2* Koryakskiy Avtonomnyy Okrug, E Russian Federation
Ostend *see* Oostende
Ostende *see* Oostende
Oster *87 E1* Chernihivs'ka Oblast', N Ukraine
Östersund *63 C5* Jämtland, C Sweden
Ostfriesische Inseln *72 A3 Eng.* East Frisian Islands. *Island group* NW Germany
Ostiglia *74 C2* Lombardia, N Italy
Ostrava *77 C5* Ostravský Kraj, E Czech Republic
Ostróda *76 D3 Ger.* Osterode, Osterode in Ostpreussen. Warmińsko-Mazurskie, NE Poland
Ostrołęka *76 D3 Ger.* Wiesenhof, *Rus.* Ostrolenka. Mazowieckie, C Poland
Ostrov *88 A4 Latv.* Austrava. Karlovarský Kraj, W Czech Republic
Ostrovets *see* Ostrowiec Świętokrzyski
Ostrovnoy *88 C2* Murmanskaya Oblast', NW Russian Federation
Ostrów *see* Ostrów Wielkopolski
Ostrowiec *see* Ostrowiec Świętokrzyski
Ostrowiec Świętokrzyski *76 D4 var.* Ostrowiec, *Rus.* Ostrovets. Świętokrzyskie, C Poland
Ostrów Mazowiecka *76 D3 var.* Ostrów Mazowiecki. Mazowieckie, C Poland
Ostrów Mazowiecki *see* Ostrów Mazowiecka
Ostrowo *see* Ostrów Wielkopolski
Ostrów Wielkopolski *76 C4 var.* Ostrów, *Ger.* Ostrowo. Wielkopolskie, C Poland
Osum *see* Osumit, Lumi i
Ōsumi-shotō *109 A8 island group* SW Japan
Osumit, Lumi i *79 D7 var.* Osum. *River* SE Albania
Osuna *70 D4* Andalucía, S Spain
Oswego *19 F2* New York, NE USA
Otago Peninsula *129 B7 peninsula* South Island, NZ
Otaki *128 D4* Wellington, North Island, NZ
Otaru *108 C2* Hokkaidō, NE Japan
Otavalo *38 B1* Imbabura, N Ecuador
Otavi *56 B3* Otjozondjupa, N Namibia
Oțelu Roșu *86 B4 Ger.* Ferdinandsberg, *Hung.* Nándorhgy. Caras-Severin, SW Romania
Otepää *84 D3 Ger.* Odenpäh. Valgamaa, SE Estonia
Oti *53 E4 river* W Africa
Otira *129 C6* West Coast, South Island, NZ
Otjiwarongo *56 B3* Otjozondjupa, N Namibia
Otorohanga *128 D3* Waikato, North Island, NZ
Otranto, Strait of *79 C6 It.* Canale d'Otranto. *Strait* Albania/Italy
Otrokovice *77 C5 Ger.* Otrokowitz. Zlínský Kraj, E Czech Republic
Ōtsu *109 C6 var.* Ōtu. Shiga, Honshū, SW Japan
Ottawa *19 E2 Fr.* Outaouais. Admin. region *river* Ontario/Quebec, SE Canada
Ottawa *16 D5 country capital* (Canada) Ontario, SE Canada
Ottawa *18 B3* Illinois, N USA
Ottawa *23 F5* Kansas, C USA
Ottawa Islands *16 C1 island group* Northwest Territories, C Canada
Ottignies *65 C6* Wallon Brabant, C Belgium
Ottumwa *23 G4* Iowa, C USA
Ōtu *see* Ōtsu
Ouachita Mountains *20 A1 mountain range* Arkansas/Oklahoma, C USA
Ouachita River *20 B2 river* Arkansas/Louisiana, C USA
Ouadi Howa *see* Howar, Wādi
Ouagadougou *53 E4 var.* Wagadugu. *Country capital* (Burkina Faso) C Burkina Faso
Ouahigouya *53 E3* NW Burkina faso
Ouahran *see* Oran
Oualata *see* Oualâta
Oualâta *52 D3 var.* Oualata. Hodh ech Chargui, SE Mauritania
Ouanary *37 H3* E French Guiana
Ouanda Djallé *54 D4* Vakaga, NE Central African Republic
Ouarâne *52 D2 desert* C Mauritania
Ouargla *49 E2 var.* Wargla. NE Algeria
Ouarzazate *48 C3* S Morocco
Oubangui *see* Ubangi
Oubangui-Chari *see* Central African Republic
Ouessant, Île d' *68 A3 Eng.* Ushant. *Island* NW France
Ouésso *55 B5* La Sangha, NW Congo
Oujda *48 D2 Ar.* Oudjda, Ujda. NE Morocco
Oujeft *52 C2* Adrar, C Mauritania
Oulu *62 D4 Swe.* Uleåborg. Oulu, C Finland
Oulujärvi *62 D4 Swe.* Uleträsk. *Lake* C Finland
Oulujoki *62 D4 Swe.* Uleälv. *River* C Finland
Ounasjoki *62 D3 river* N Finland
Ounianga Kébir *54 C2* Borkou-Ennedi-Tibesti, N Chad
Oup *see* Auob
Oupeye *65 D6* Liège, E Belgium
Our *65 D6 river* NW Europe
Ourense *70 C1 var. Cast.* Orense; *Lat.* Aurium. Galicia, NW Spain
Ourique *70 B4* Beja, S Portugal
Ourthe *65 D7 river* E Belgium
Ouse *67 D5 river* N England, UK
Outer Hebrides *66 B3 var.* Western Isles. *Island group* NW Scotland, UK
Outer Islands *57 G1 island group* SW Seychelles
Outes *70 B1* Galicia, NW Spain
Ouvéa *122 D5 island* Îles Loyauté, NE New Caledonia
Ouyen *127 C6* Victoria, SE Australia
Ovalle *42 B3* Coquimbo, N Chile
Ovar *70 B2* Aveiro, N Portugal
Overflakkee *64 B4 island* SW Netherlands
Overijse *65 C6* Vlaams Brabant, C Belgium
Oviedo *70 C1 anc.* Asturias. Asturias, NW Spain
Ovruch *86 D1* Zhytomyrs'ka Oblast', N Ukraine
Owando *55 B5 prev.* Fort-Rousset. Cuvette, C Congo
Owase *109 C6* Mie, Honshū, SW Japan
Owatonna *23 F3* Minnesota, N USA
Owen Fracture Zone *118 B4 tectonic feature* W Arabian Sea
Owen, Mount *129 C5 mountain* South Island, NZ
Owensboro *18 B5* Kentucky, S USA
Owen Stanley Range *122 B3 mountain range* S PNG
Owerri *53 G5* Imo, S Nigeria
Owo *53 F5* Ondo, SW Nigeria
Owyhee River *24 C4 river* Idaho/Oregon, NW USA
Oxford *67 D6 Lat.* Oxonia. S England, UK
Oxford *129 C6* Canterbury, South Island, NZ
Oxkutzcab *29 H4* Yucatán, SE Mexico
Oxnard *25 B7* California, W USA
Oyama *109 D5* Tochigi, Honshū, S Japan
Oyem *55 B5* Woleu-Ntem, N Gabon
Oyo *55 B6* Cuvette, C Congo
Oyo *53 F4* Oyo, W Nigeria
Ozark *20 D3* Alabama, S USA
Ozark Plateau *23 G5 plain* Arkansas/Missouri, C USA
Ozarks, Lake of the *23 F5 reservoir* Missouri, C USA
Ozbourn Seamount *130 D4 undersea feature* W Pacific Ocean
Ózd *77 D6* Borsod-Abaúj-Zemplén, NE Hungary
Ozero Khanka *see* Khanka, Lake
Ozero Ubsu-Nur *see* Uvs Nuur
Ozieri *75 A5* Sardegna, Italy, C Mediterranean Sea

P

Paamiut *60 B4 var.* Pâmiut, *Dan.* Frederikshåb. S Greenland
Pa-an *114 B4* Karen State, S Myanmar
Pabianice *76 C4* Łodz, C Poland
Pabna *113 G4* Rajshahi, W Bangladesh
Pachuca *29 E4 var.* Pachuca de Soto. Hidalgo, C Mexico
Pachuca de Soto *see* Pachuca
Pacific-Antarctic Ridge *132 B5 undersea feature* S Pacific Ocean
Pacific Ocean *130 D3 ocean*
Padalung *see* Phatthalung
Padang *116 B4* Sumatera, W Indonesia
Paderborn *72 B4* Nordrhein-Westfalen, NW Germany
Padma *see* Brahmaputra
Padova *74 C2 Eng.* Padua; *anc.* Patavium. Veneto, NE Italy
Padre Island *27 G5 island* Texas, SW USA
Padua *see* Padova
Paducah *18 B5* Kentucky, S USA
Paeroa *128 D3* Waikato, North Island, NZ
Páfos *80 C5 var.* Paphos. W Cyprus
Pag *78 A3 It.* Pago. *Island* Zadar SW Croatia
Page *26 B1* Arizona, SW USA
Pago Pago *123 F4 dependent territory capital* (American Samoa) Tutuila, W American Samoa
Pahiatua *128 D4* Manawatu-Wanganui, North Island, NZ
Pahsien *see* Chongqing
Paide *84 D2 Ger.* Weissenstein. Järvamaa, N Estonia
Paihia *128 D2* Northland, North Island, NZ
Päijänne *63 D5 lake* S Finland
Paine, Cerro *43 A7 mountain* S Chile
Painted Desert *26 B1 desert* Arizona, SW USA
Paisley *66 C4* W Scotland, UK
País Valenciano *71 F3 cultural region* NE Spain
País Vasco *71 E1 cultural region* N Spain
Paita *38 B3* Piura, NW Peru
Pakanbaru *see* Pekanbaru
Pakaraima Mountains *37 E3 var.* Serra Pacaraim, Sierra Pacaraima. *Mountain range* N South America
Pakistan *112 A2 var.* Islami Jamhuriya e Pakistan. *Country* S Asia
Paknam *see* Samut Prakan
Pakokku *114 A3* Magwe, C Myanmar
Pak Phanang *115 C7 var.* Ban Pak Phanang. Nakhon Si Thammarat, SW Thailand
Pakruojis *84 C4* Pakruojis, N Lithuania
Paks *77 C7* Tolna, S Hungary
Paksé *see* Pakxé
Pakxé *115 D5 var.* Paksé. Champasak, S Laos
Palafrugell *71 G2* Cataluña, NE Spain
Palagruža *79 B5 It.* Pelagosa. *Island* SW Croatia
Palaiá Epídavros *83 C6* Pelopónnisos, S Greece
Palaiseau *68 D2* Essonne, N France
Palamós *71 G2* Cataluña, NE Spain
Palamuse *84 E2 Ger.* Sankt-Bartholomäi. Jõgevamaa, E Estonia
Pālanpur *112 C4* Gujarāt, W India
Palapye *56 D3* Central, SE Botswana
Palau *122 A2 var.* Belau. *Country* W Pacific Ocean
Palawan *117 E2 island* W Philippines
Palawan Passage *116 D2 passage* W Philippines
Paldiski *84 D2 prev.* Baltiski, *Eng.* Baltic Port, *Ger.* Baltischport. Harjumaa, NW Estonia
Palembang *116 B4* Sumatera, W Indonesia
Palencia *70 D2 anc.* Palantia, Pallantia. Castilla-León, NW Spain
Palermo *75 C7 Fr.* Palerme; *anc.* Panhormus, Panormus. Sicilia, Italy, C Mediterranean Sea
Pāli *112 C3* Rājasthān, N India
Palikir *122 C2 country capital* (Micronesia) Pohnpei, E Micronesia
Palimé *see* Kpalimé
Palioúri, Akrotírio *82 C4 var.* Akra Kanestron. *Headland* N Greece
Palk Strait *110 C3 strait* India/Sri Lanka
Palliser, Cape *129 D5 headland* North Island, NZ
Palma *71 G3 var.* Palma de Mallorca. Mallorca, Spain, W Mediterranean Sea
Palma del Río *70 D4* Andalucía, S Spain
Palma de Mallorca *see* Palma
Palmar Sur *31 E5* Puntarenas, SE Costa Rica
Palma Soriano *32 C3* Santiago de Cuba, E Cuba
Palm Beach *126 E1* New South Wales, SE Australia
Palmer *132 A2 US research station* Antarctica
Palmer Land *132 A3 physical region* Antarctica
Palmerston *123 F4 island* S Cook Islands
Palmerston North *128 D4* Manawatu-Wanganui, North Island, NZ
Palmi *75 D7* Calabria, SW Italy
Palmira *36 B3* Valle del Cauca, W Colombia
Palm Springs *25 D7* California, W USA
Palmyra *see* Tudmur
Palmyra Atoll *123 G2 US privately owned unincorporated territory* C Pacific Ocean
Palo Alto *25 B6* California, W USA
Palu *117 E4 prev.* Paloe. Sulawesi, C Indonesia
Pamiers *69 B6* Ariège, S France
Pamir *var.* Daryā-ye Pāmīr, *Taj.* Dar"yoi Pomir. *River* Afghanistan/Tajikistan *see also* Pāmīr, Daryā-ye
Pamirs *101 F3 Pash.* Daryā-ye Pāmīr, *Rus.* Pamir. *Mountain range* C Asia
Pâmiut *see* Paamiut
Pamlico Sound *21 G1 sound* North Carolina, SE USA
Pampa *27 E1* Texas, SW USA
Pampas *42 C4 plain* C Argentina
Pamplona *71 E1 Basq.* Iruña; *prev.* Pampeluna, *anc.* Pompaelo. Navarra, N Spain
Pamplona *36 C2* Norte de Santander, N Colombia
Panaji *see* Pānji
Panama *31 G5 Country* Central America
Panamá *31 G4 var.* Ciudad de Panamá, *Eng.* Panama City. *Country capital* (Panama) Panamá, C Panama
Panama Basin *13 C8 undersea feature* E Pacific Ocean
Panama Canal *31 F4 canal* E Panama
Panama City *see* Panamá
Panama City *20 D3* Florida, SE USA
Panamá, Golfo de *31 G5 var.* Gulf of Panama. *Gulf* S Panama
Panama, Gulf of *see* Panamá, Golfo de
Panamá, Isthmus of *see* Panamá, Istmo de
Panamá, Istmo de *31 G4 Eng.* Isthmus of Panama; *prev.* Isthmus of Darien. *Isthmus* E Panama
Panay Island *117 E2 island* C Philippines
Pančevo *78 D3 Ger.* Pantschowa, *Hung.* Pancsova. Serbia, N Serbia and Montenegro (Yugo.)
Paneas *see* Bāniyās
Panevėžys *84 C4* Panevėžys, C Lithuania
Pangim *see* Pānji
Pangkalpinang *116 C4* Pulau Bangka, W Indonesia
Pang-Nga *see* Phang-Nga
Panjim *see* Pānji
Pānji *110 B1 var.* Pangim, Panaji, Panjim, New Goa. Goa, W India
Pánormos *83 C7* Kríti, Greece, E Mediterranean Sea
Pantanal *41 E3 var.* Pantanalmato-Grossense. *Swamp* SW Brazil
Pantanalmato-Grossense *see* Pantanal
Pantelleria, Isola di *75 B7 island* SW Italy
Pánuco *29 E3* Veracruz-Llave, E Mexico
Pao-chi *see* Baoji
Paoki *see* Baoji
Paola *80 B5* E Malta
Pao-shan *see* Baoshan
Pao-t'ou *see* Baotou
Paotow *see* Baotou
Papagayo, Golfo de *30 C4 gulf* NW Costa Rica
Papakura *128 D3* Auckland, North Island, NZ
Papantla *29 F4 var.* Papantla de Olarte. Veracruz-Llave, E Mexico
Papantla de Olarte *see* Papantla
Papeete *123 H4 dependent territory capital* (French Polynesia) Tahiti, W French Polynesia
Paphos *see* Páfos
Papilė *84 B3* Akmenė, NW Lithuania
Papillion *23 F4* Nebraska, C USA
Papua *117 H4 var.* Irian Barat, Irian Jaya, West Irian, West New Guinea, West Papua; *prev.* Dutch New Guinea, Netherlands New Guinea. Admin. region *province* E Indonesia
Papua, Gulf of *122 B3 gulf* S PNG
Papua New Guinea *122 B3 prev.* Territory of Papua and New Guinea, *abbrev.* PNG. *Country* NW Melanesia
Papuk *78 C3 mountain range* NE Croatia
Pará *41 E2 off.* Estado do Pará. *State* NE Brazil
Pará *see* Belém
Paracel Islands *103 E3 disputed territory* SE Asia
Paraćin *78 D4* Serbia, C Serbia and Montenegro (Yugo.)
Paragua, Río *37 E3 river* SE Venezuela
Paraguay *42 D2 var.* Río Paraguay. *River* C South America
Paraguay *42 C2 country* C South America
Paraguay, Río *see* Paraguay
Paraíba *41 G2 off.* Estado da Paraíba; *prev.* Parahiba, Parahyba. *State* E Brazil
Parakou *53 F4* C Benin
Paramaribo *37 G3 country capital* (Suriname) Paramaribo, N Suriname
Paramushir, Ostrov *93 H3 island* SE Russian Federation
Paraná *41 E5 off.* Estado do Paraná. *State* S Brazil
Paraná *35 C5 var.* Alto Paraná. *River* C South America
Paraná *41 E4* Entre Ríos, E Argentina
Paranéstio *82 C3* Anatolikí Makedonía kai Thráki, NE Greece
Paraparaumu *129 D5* Wellington, North Island, NZ

Parchim 72 C3 Mecklenburg-Vorpommern, N Germany
Parczew 76 E4 Lubelskie, E Poland
Pardubice 77 B5 Ger. Pardubitz. Pardubický Kraj, C Czech Republic
Parechcha 85 B5 Rus. Porech'ye. Hrodzyenskaya Voblasts', NE Belarus
Parecis, Chapada dos 40 D3 var. Serra dos Parecis. Mountain range W Brazil
Parepare 117 E4 Sulawesi, C Indonesia
Párga 83 A5 Ípeiros, W Greece
Paria, Golfo de see Paria, Gulf of
Paria, Gulf of 37 E1 var. Golfo de Paria. Gulf Trinidad and Tobago/Venezuela
Parika 37 F2 NE Guyana
Paris 68 D1 anc. Lutetia, Lutetia Parisiorum, Parisii. Country capital (France) Paris, N France
Paris 27 G2 Texas, SW USA
Parkersburg 18 D4 West Virginia, NE USA
Parkes 127 D6 New South Wales, SE Australia
Parma 74 B2 Emilia-Romagna, N Italy
Parnahyba see Parnaíba
Parnaíba 41 F2 var. Parnahyba. Piauí, E Brazil
Pärnu 84 D2 Ger. Pernau, Latv. Pērnava; prev. Rus. Pernov. Pärnumaa, SW Estonia
Pärnu 84 D2 var. Pärnu Jõgi, Ger. Pernau. River SW Estonia
Pärnu-Jaagupi 84 D2 Ger. Sankt-Jakobi. Pärnumaa, SW Estonia
Pärnu Jõgi see Pärnu
Pärnu Laht 84 D2 Ger. Pernauer Bucht. Bay SW Estonia
Páros 83 C6 island Kykládes, Greece, Aegean Sea
Páros 83 D6 Páros, Kykládes, Greece, Aegean Sea
Parral see Hidalgo del Parral
Parral 42 B4 Maule, C Chile
Parramatta 126 D1 New South Wales, SE Australia
Parras 28 D3 var. Parras de la Fuente. Coahuila de Zaragoza, NE Mexico
Parras de la Fuente see Parras
Parsons 23 F5 Kansas, C USA
Pasadena 25 C7 California, W USA
Pasadena 27 H4 Texas, SW USA
Paşcani 86 C3 Hung. Páskán. Iaşi, NE Romania
Pasco 24 C2 Washington, NW USA
Pas de Calais see Dover, Strait of
Pasewalk 72 D3 Mecklenburg-Vorpommern, NE Germany
Pasinler 95 F3 Erzurum, NE Turkey
Pasłęk 76 D2 Ger. Preußisch Holland. Warmińsko-Mazurskie, NE Poland
Pasni 112 A3 Baluchistan, SW Pakistan
Paso de Indios 43 B6 Chubut, S Argentina
Passau 73 D6 Bayern, SE Germany
Passo del Brennero see Brenner Pass
Passo Fundo 41 E5 Rio Grande do Sul, S Brazil
Pastavy 85 C5 Pol. Postawy, Rus. Postavy. Vitsyebskaya Voblasts', NW Belarus
Pastaza, Río 38 B2 river Ecuador/Peru
Pasto 36 A4 Nariño, SW Colombia
Pasvalys 84 C4 Pasvalys, N Lithuania
Patagonia 35 B7 physical region Argentina/Chile
Patalung see Phatthalung
Patani see Pattani
Patavium see Padova
Patea 128 D4 Taranaki, North Island, NZ
Paterson 19 F3 New Jersey, NE USA
Pathein see Bassein
Pátmos 83 D6 island Dodekánisos, Greece, Aegean Sea
Patna 113 F3 var. Azimabad. Bihār, N India
Patnos 95 F3 Ağrı, E Turkey
Patos, Lagoa dos 41 E5 lagoon S Brazil
Pátra 83 B5 Eng. Patras; prev. Pátrai. Dytikí Ellás, S Greece
Pattani 115 C7 var. Patani. Pattani, SW Thailand
Pattaya 115 C5 Chon Buri, S Thailand
Patuca, Río 30 D2 river E Honduras
Pau 69 B6 Pyrénées-Atlantiques, SW France
Paulatuk 15 E3 Northwest Territories, NW Canada
Paungde 114 B4 Pegu, C Myanmar
Pavia 74 B2 anc. Ticinum. Lombardia, N Italy
Pāvilosta 84 B3 Liepāja, W Latvia
Pavlikeni 82 D2 Veliko Tŭrnovo, N Bulgaria
Pavlodar 92 C4 Pavlodar, NE Kazakhstan
Pavlohrad 87 G3 Rus. Pavlograd. Dnipropetrovs'ka Oblast', E Ukraine
Pawn 114 B3 river C Myanmar
Paxoí 83 A5 island Iónioi Nísoi, Greece, C Mediterranean Sea
Payo Obispo see Chetumal
Paysandú 42 D4 Paysandú, W Uruguay
Pazar 95 E2 Rize, NE Turkey
Pazardzhik 82 C3 prev. Tatar Pazardzhik. Pazardzhik, C Bulgaria
Pearl River 20 B3 river Louisiana/Mississippi, S USA
Pearsall 27 F4 Texas, SW USA
Peć 79 D5 Alb. Pejë, Turk. Ipek. Serbia, S Serbia and Montenegro (Yugo.)
Pechora 88 D3 river NW Russian Federation
Pechora 88 D3 Respublika Komi, NW Russian Federation
Pechorskoye More 88 D2 Eng. Pechora Sea NW Russian Federation
Pecos 27 E3 Texas, SW USA
Pecos River 27 E3 river New Mexico/Texas, SW USA
Pécs 77 C7 Ger. Fünfkirchen; Lat. Sopianae. Baranya, SW Hungary
Pedra Lume 52 A3 Sal, NE Cape Verde
Pedro Cays 32 C3 island group S Jamaica

Pedro Juan Caballero 42 D2 Amambay, E Paraguay
Peer 65 D5 Limburg, NE Belgium
Pegasus Bay 129 C6 bay South Island, NZ
Pegu 114 B4 var. Bago. Pegu, SW Myanmar
Pehuajó 42 C4 Buenos Aires, E Argentina
Pei-ching see Beijing
Peine 72 B3 Niedersachsen, C Germany
Pei-p'ing see Beijing
Peipus, Lake E3 Est. Peipsi Järv, Ger. Peipus-See, Rus. Chudskoye Ozero. Lake Estonia/Russian Federation
Peiraiás 83 C6 prev. Piraiévs, Eng. Piraeus. Attikí, C Greece
Pèk 114 D4 var. Xieng Khouang; prev. Xiangkhoang. Xiangkhoang, N Laos
Pekalongan 116 C4 Jawa, C Indonesia
Pekanbaru 116 B3 var. Pakanbaru. Sumatera, W Indonesia
Pekin 18 B4 Illinois, N USA
Peking see Beijing
Pelagie, Isole 75 B8 island group SW Italy
Pelly Bay 15 G3 Nunavut, N Canada
Peloponnese see Pelopónnisos
Peloponnesus see Pelopónnisos
Pelopónnisos 83 B6 var. Morea, Eng. Peloponnese; anc. Peloponnesus. Peninsula S Greece
Pematangsiantar 116 B3 Sumatera, W Indonesia
Pemba 57 F2 var. Port Amelia. Porto Amélia. Cabo Delgado, NE Mozambique
Pemba 51 D7 island E Tanzania
Pembroke 16 D4 Ontario, SE Canada
Penang see George Town
Penang see Pinang, Pulau
Penas, Golfo de 43 A7 gulf S Chile
Penderma see Bandırma
Pendleton 24 C3 Oregon, NW USA
Pend Oreille, Lake 24 D2 lake Idaho, NW USA
Peneius see Pineiós
Peng-pu see Bengbu
Peniche 70 B3 Leiria, W Portugal
Péninsule de la Gaspésie see Gaspé, Péninsule de
Pennine Alps 73 A8 Fr. Alpes Pennines, It. Alpi Pennine; Lat. Alpes Penninae. Mountain range Italy/Switzerland
Pennine Chain see Pennines
Pennines 67 D5 var. Pennine Chain. Mountain range N England, UK
Pennsylvania 18 D3 off. Commonwealth of Pennsylvania; also known as The Keystone State. State NE USA
Penobscot River 19 G2 river Maine, NE USA
Penong 127 A6 South Australia
Penonomé 31 F5 Coclé, C Panama
Penrhyn 123 G3 atoll N Cook Islands
Penrhyn Basin 121 F3 undersea feature C Pacific Ocean
Penrith 126 D1 New South Wales, SE Australia
Penrith 67 D5 NW England, UK
Pensacola 20 C3 Florida, SE USA
Pentecost 122 D4 Fr. Pentecôte. Island C Vanuatu
Penza 89 C6 Penzenskaya Oblast', W Russian Federation
Penzance 67 C7 SW England, UK
Peoria 18 B4 Illinois, N USA
Perchtoldsdorf 73 E6 Niederösterreich, NE Austria
Percival Lakes 124 C4 lakes Western Australia
Perdido, Monte 71 F1 mountain NE Spain
Perece Vela Basin 120 A2 var. West Mariana Basin
Pereira 36 B3 Risaralda, W Colombia
Pergamino 42 C4 Buenos Aires, E Argentina
Périgueux 69 C5 anc. Vesuna. Dordogne, SW France
Perito Moreno 43 B6 Santa Cruz, S Argentina
Perlas, Archipiélago de las 31 G5 Eng. Pearl Islands. Island group SE Panama
Perlas, Laguna de 31 E3 Eng. Pearl Lagoon. Lagoon E Nicaragua
Perleberg 72 C3 Brandenburg, N Germany
Perm' 92 C3 prev. Molotov. Permskaya Oblast', NW Russian Federation
Pernambuco 41 G2 off. Estado de Pernambuco. State E Brazil
Pernambuco Abyssal Plain see Pernambuco Plain
Pernambuco Plain 45 C5 var. Pernambuco Abyssal Plain. Undersea feature E Atlantic Ocean
Pernau see Pärnu
Pernik 82 B2 prev. Dimitrovo. Pernik, W Bulgaria
Perote 29 F4 Veracruz-Llave, E Mexico
Perovsk see Kyzylorda
Perpignan 69 C6 Pyrénées-Orientales, S France
Perryton 27 F1 Texas, SW USA
Perryville 23 H5 Missouri, C USA
Persian Gulf see Gulf, The
Perth 125 A6 state capital Western Australia
Perth 66 C4 C Scotland, UK
Perth Basin 119 E6 undersea feature SE Indian Ocean
Peru 38 C3 Country W South America
Peru see Beru
Peru Basin 45 A5 undersea feature E Pacific Ocean
Peru-Chile Trench 34 A4 undersea feature E Pacific Ocean
Perugia 74 C4 Fr. Pérouse; anc. Perusia. Umbria, C Italy
Péruwelz 65 B6 Hainaut, SW Belgium
Pervomays'k 87 E3 prev. Ol'viopol'. Mykolayivs'ka Oblast', S Ukraine
Pervyy Kuril'skiy Proliv 93 H3 strait E Russian Federation
Pesaro 74 C3 anc. Pisaurum. Marche, C Italy

Pescara 74 D4 anc. Aternum, Ostia Aterni. Abruzzo, C Italy
Peshāwar 112 C1 North-West Frontier Province, N Pakistan
Peshkopi 79 C6 var. Peshkopia, Peshkopija. Dibër, NE Albania
Peshkopia see Peshkopi
Peshkopija see Peshkopi
Pessac 69 B5 Gironde, SW France
Petach-Tikva see Petah Tiqwa
Petah Tiqwa see Petah Tiqwa
Petah Tiqwa 97 A6 var. Petach-Tikva, Petah Tiqva, Petakh Tikva. Tel Aviv, C Israel
Petakh Tikva see Petah Tiqwa
Pétange 65 D8 Luxembourg, SW Luxembourg
Petchaburi see Phetchaburi
Peterborough 67 E6 prev. Medeshamstede. E England, UK
Peterborough 16 D5 Ontario, SE Canada
Peterborough 127 B6 South Australia
Peterhead 66 D3 NE Scotland, UK
Peter I Island 132 A3 Norwegian dependency Antarctica
Petermann Bjerg 61 E3 mountain C Greenland
Petersburg 19 E5 Virginia, NE USA
Peters Mine 37 F3 var. Peter's Mine. N Guyana
Peto 29 H4 Yucatán, SE Mexico
Petoskey 18 C2 Michigan, N USA
Petra see Wādī Mūsā
Petrich 82 C3 Blagoevgrad, SW Bulgaria
Petrinja 78 B3 Sisak-Moslavina, C Croatia
Petrodvorets 88 A4 Fin. Pietarhovi. Leningradskaya Oblast', NW Russian Federation
Petrograd see Sankt-Peterburg
Petropavl 92 C4 Kaz. Petropavl. Severnyy Kazakhstan, N Kazakhstan
Petropavlovsk 92 C4 Kaz. Petropavl. Severnyy Kazakhstan, N Kazakhstan
Petropavlovsk-Kamchatskiy 93 H3 Kamchatskaya Oblast', E Russian Federation
Petroşani 86 B4 var. Petroșeni, Ger. Petroschen, Hung. Petrozsény. Hunedoara, W Romania
Petroschen see Petroşani
Petroșeni see Petroşani
Petrozavodsk 92 B2 Fin. Petroskoi. Respublika Kareliya, NW Russian Federation
Petrozsény see Petroşani
Pevek 93 G1 Chukotskiy Avtonomnyy Okrug, NE Russian Federation
Pezinok 77 C6 Ger. Bösing, Hung. Bazin. Bratislavský Kraj, W Slovakia
Pforzheim 73 B6 Baden-Württemberg, SW Germany
Pfungstadt 73 B5 Hessen, W Germany
Phangan, Ko 115 C6 island SW Thailand
Phang-Nga 115 B7 var. Pang-Nga, Phangnga. Phangnga, SW Thailand
Phangnga see Phang-Nga
Phanom Dang Raek see Dângrêk, Chuŏr Phnum
Phanom Dong Rak see Dângrêk, Chuŏr Phnum
Phan Rang see Phan Rang-Thap Cham
Phan Rang-Thap Cham 115 E6 var. Phanrang, Phan Rang, Phan Rang Thap Cham. Ninh Thuận, S Vietnam
Phan Thiết 115 E6 Bình Thuận, S Vietnam
Pharnacia see Giresun
Phatthalung 115 C7 var. Padalung, Patalung. Phatthalung, SW Thailand
Phayao 114 C4 var. Muang Phayao. Phayao, NW Thailand
Phenix City 20 D2 Alabama, S USA
Phet Buri see Phetchaburi
Phetchaburi 115 C5 var. Bejraburi, Petchaburi, Phet Buri. Phetchaburi, SW Thailand
Philadelphia see 'Ammān
Philadelphia 19 F4 Pennsylvania, NE USA
Philippine Basin 103 F3 undersea feature W Pacific Ocean
Philippines 117 E1 Country SE Asia
Philippines 117 E1 island group W Pacific Ocean
Philippine Sea 103 F3 sea W Pacific Ocean
Philippine Trench 120 A1 undersea feature W Philippine Sea
Phitsanulok 114 C4 var. Bisnulok, Muang Phitsanulok, Pitsanulok. Phitsanulok, C Thailand
Phlórina see Flórina
Phnom Penh see Phnum Penh
Phnum Penh 115 D6 var. Phnom Penh. Country capital (Cambodia) Phnum Penh, S Cambodia
Phoenix 26 B2 state capital Arizona, SW USA
Phoenix Islands 123 E3 island group C Kiribati
Phôngsali 114 C3 var. Phong Saly. Phôngsali, N Laos
Phong Saly see Phôngsali
Phrae 114 C4 var. Muang Phrae, Prae. Phrae, NW Thailand
Phra Nakhon Si Ayutthaya see Ayutthaya
Phra Thong, Ko 115 B6 island SW Thailand
Phuket 115 B7 var. Bhuket, Puket, Mal. Ujung Salang; prev. Junkseylon, Salang. Phuket, SW Thailand
Phuket, Ko 115 B7 island SW Thailand
Phumĭ Kâmpóng Trâbêk 115 D5 Kâmpóng Chhnăng, C Cambodia
Phumĭ Sâmraông 115 D5 Poŭthisăt, C Cambodia
Phu Vinh see Tra Vinh
Piacenza 74 B2 anc. Placentia. Emilia-Romagna, N Italy
Piatra-Neamţ 86 C3 Hung. Karácsonkő. Neamţ, NE Romania
Piauí 41 F2 off. Estado do Piauí; prev. Piauhy. State E Brazil

Picardie 68 C3 Eng. Picardy. Cultural region N France
Pichilemu 42 B4 Libertador, C Chile
Pico 70 A5 var. Ilha do Pico. Island Azores, Portugal, NE Atlantic Ocean
Picos 41 F2 Piauí, E Brazil
Picton 129 C5 Marlborough, South Island, NZ
Piedras Negras 29 E2 var. Ciudad Porfirio Díaz. Coahuila de Zaragoza, NE Mexico
Pielinen 62 E4 var. Pielisjärvi. Lake E Finland
Pielisjärvi see Pielinen
Piemonte 74 A2 Eng. Piedmont. Cultural region NW Italy
Pierre 23 E3 state capital South Dakota, N USA
Pieštʹany 77 C6 Ger. Pistyan, Hung. Pöstyén. Trnavský Kraj, W Slovakia
Pietermaritzburg 56 C5 var. Maritzburg. KwaZulu/Natal, E South Africa
Pietersburg see Polokwane
Pigs, Bay of see Cochinos, Bahía de
Pijijiapán 29 G5 Chiapas, SE Mexico
Pikes Peak 22 C5 mountain Colorado, C USA
Pikeville 18 D5 Kentucky, S USA
Pikinni see Bikini Atoll
Piła 76 B3 Ger. Schneidemühl. Wielkopolskie, C Poland
Pilar 42 D3 var. Villa del Pilar. Ñeembucú, S Paraguay
Pilcomayo 35 C5 river C South America
Pilos see Pýlos
Pinang see George Town
Pinang, Pulau 116 B3 var. Penang, Pinang; prev. Prince of Wales Island. Island Peninsular Malaysia
Pinar del Río 32 A2 Pinar del Río, W Cuba
Píndhos see Píndos
Píndhos Óros see Píndos
Píndos 82 A4 var. Píndhos Óros, Eng. Pindus Mountains; prev. Píndhos. Mountain range C Greece
Pindus Mountains see Píndos
Pine Bluff 20 B2 Arkansas, C USA
Pine Creek 124 D2 Northern Territory, N Australia
Pinega 88 C3 river NW Russian Federation
Pineiós 82 B4 var. Piniós; anc. Peneius. River C Greece
Pineland 27 H3 Texas, SW USA
Pines, The Isle of the see Juventud, Isla de la
Pingdingshan 106 C4 Henan, C China
Pingkiang see Harbin
Ping, Mae Nam 114 B4 river W Thailand
Piniós see Pineiós
Pinkiang see Harbin
Pínnes, Akrotírio 82 C4 headland N Greece
Pinos, Isla de see Juventud, Isla de la
Pinotepa Nacional 29 F5 var. Santiago Pinotepa Nacional. Oaxaca, SE Mexico
Pinsk 85 B7 Pol. Pińsk. SW Belarus
Pinta, Isla 38 A5 var. Abingdon. Island Galapagos Islands, Ecuador, E Pacific Ocean
Piombino 74 B3 Toscana, C Italy
Pioneer Mountains 24 D3 mountain range Montana, N USA
Pionerskiy 84 A4 Ger. Neukuhren. Kaliningradskaya Oblast', W Russian Federation
Piotrków Trybunalski 76 D4 Ger. Petrikau, Rus. Petrokov. Łódzkie, C Poland
Piraeus see Peiraiás
Pírgos see Pýrgos
Piripiri 41 F2 Piauí, E Brazil
Pirna 72 D4 Sachsen, E Germany
Pirot 79 E5 Serbia, SE Serbia and Montenegro (Yugo.)
Pisa 74 B3 var. Pisae. Toscana, C Italy
Pisae see Pisa
Pisco 38 D4 Ica, SW Peru
Písek 77 A5 Budějovicky Kraj, S Czech Republic
Pishan 104 A3 var. Guma. Xinjiang Uygur Zizhiqu, NW China
Pishpek see Bishkek
Pistoia 74 B3 anc. Pistoria, Pistoriæ. Toscana, C Italy
Pisz 76 D3 Ger. Johannisburg. Warminsko-Mazurskie, NE Poland
Pita 52 C4 Moyenne-Guinée, NW Guinea
Pitalito 36 B4 Huila, S Colombia
Pitcairn Island 121 G4 island S Pitcairn Islands
Pitcairn Islands 121 G4 UK dependent territory C Pacific Ocean
Piteå 62 D4 Norrbotten, N Sweden
Piteşti 86 B5 Argeș, S Romania
Pitsanulok see Phitsanulok
Pittsburg 23 F5 Kansas, C USA
Pittsburgh 19 E4 Pennsylvania, NE USA
Pittsfield 19 F3 Massachusetts, NE USA
Piura 38 B2 Piura, NW Peru
Pivdennyy Buh 87 E3 Rus. Yuzhnyy Bug. River S Ukraine
Placentia 32 B2 Villa Clara, C Cuba
Plainview 27 E2 Texas, SW USA
Planeta Rica 36 B2 Córdoba, NW Colombia
Planken 72 E1 C Liechtenstein
Plano 27 G2 Texas, SW USA
Plasencia 70 C3 Extremadura, W Spain
Plateau du Bemaraha see Bemaraha
Platinum 14 C3 Alaska, USA
Plattensee see Balaton
Platte River 23 E4 river Nebraska, C USA
Plattsburgh 19 F2 New York, NE USA
Plauen 73 C5 var. Plauen im Vogtland. Sachsen, E Germany
Plauen im Vogtland see Plauen

Pļaviņas 84 D4 Ger. Stockmannshof. Aizkraukle, S Latvia
Plây Cu 115 E5 var. Pleiku. Gia Lai, C Vietnam
Pleiku see Plây Cu
Plenty, Bay of 128 E3 bay North Island, NZ
Plérin 68 A3 Côtes d'Armor, NW France
Plesetsk 88 C3 Arkhangel'skaya Oblast', NW Russian Federation
Pleszew 76 C4 Wielkopolskie, C Poland
Pleven 82 C2 prev. Plevna. Pleven, N Bulgaria
Plevlja see Pljevlja
Pljevlja 78 C4 prev. Plevlja, Plevlje. Montenegro, N Serbia and Montenegro (Yugo.)
Ploče 78 B4 It. Plocce; prev. Kardeljevo. Dubrovnik-Neretva, SE Croatia
Płock 76 D3 Ger. Plozk. Mazowieckie, C Poland
Plöcken Pass 73 C7 Ger. Plöckenpass, It. Passo di Monte Croce Carnico. Pass SW Austria
Ploieşti 86 C5 prev. Ploeşti. Prahova, SE Romania
Plomári 83 D5 prev. Plomárion. Lésvos, F. Greece
Płońsk 76 D3 Mazowieckie, C Poland
Plovdiv 82 C3 prev. Eumolpias, anc. Evmolpia, Philippopolis, Lat. Trimontium. Plovdiv, C Bulgaria
Plungė 106 B3 Plungė, W Lithuania
Plyeshchanitsy 85 D5 Rus. Pleshchenitsy. Minskaya Voblasts', N Belarus
Plymouth 113 G3 dependent territory capital (Montserrat) SW Montserrat
Plymouth 67 C7 SW England, UK
Plzeň 77 A5 Ger. Pilsen, Pol. Pilzno. Plzeňský Kraj, W Czech Republic
Po 58 D4 river N Italy
Pobeda Peak see Pobedy, Pik
Pobedy, Pik 104 B3 var. Pobeda Peak, Chin. Tomur Feng. Mountain China/Kyrgyzstan see also Tomur Feng
Pocahontas 20 B1 Arkansas, C USA
Pocatello 24 E4 Idaho, NW USA
Pochinok 89 A5 Smolenskaya Oblast', W Russian Federation
Pocking 73 D6 Bayern, SE Germany
Poděbrady 77 B5 Ger. Podiebrad. Středočeský Kraj, C Czech Republic
Podgorica 79 C5 prev. Titograd. Montenegro, SW Serbia and Montenegro (Yugo.)
Podil's'ka Vysochyna 86 D3 Rus. Podol'skaya Vozvyshennost'. Mountain range SW Ukraine
Podkarpackie admin. region province SE Poland
Podol'sk 89 B5 Moskovskaya Oblast', W Russian Federation
Podravska Slatina see Slatina
Podujevo 79 D5 Serbia, S Serbia and Montenegro (Yugo.)
Po, Foci del 74 C2 var. Bocche del Po. River NE Italy
Pogradec 79 D6 var. Pogradeci. Korçë, SE Albania
Pogradeci see Pogradec
Pohnpei 122 C2 prev. Ponape Ascension Island. Island E Micronesia
Poinsett, Cape 132 D4 headland Antarctica
Pointe-à-Pitre 33 G3 Grande Terre, C Guadeloupe
Pointe-Noire 55 B6 Le Kouilou, S Congo
Point Lay 14 C2 Alaska, USA
Poitiers 68 B4 prev. Poictiers, anc. Limonum. Vienne, W France
Poitou 68 B4 cultural region W France
Pokhara 113 E3 Western, C Nepal
Pokrovs'ke 87 G3 Rus. Pokrovskoye. Dnipropetrovs'ka Oblast', E Ukraine
Pola de Lena 70 D1 Asturias, N Spain
Poland 76 B4 var. Polish, Pol. Polska, Rzeczpospolita Polska; prev. Pol. Polska Rzeczpospolita Ludowa, Polish People's Republic. Country C Europe
Polatlı 94 C3 Ankara, C Turkey
Polatsk 85 D5 Rus. Polotsk. Vitsyebskaya Voblasts', N Belarus
Pol-e Khomrī 101 E4 var. Pul-i-Khumri. Baghlān, NE Afghanistan
Poli see Pólis
Polikastro see Polýkastro
Polikastron see Polýkastro
Polikrayshte 82 D2 Veliko Tŭrnovo, N Bulgaria
Pólis 80 C5 var. Poli. W Cyprus
Polkowice 76 B4 Ger. Heerwegen. Dolnośląskie, SW Poland
Pollença 71 G3 var. Pollensa. Mallorca, Spain, W Mediterranean Sea
Pollensa see Pollença
Polohy 87 G3 Rus. Pologi. Zaporiz'ka Oblast', SE Ukraine
Polokwane 56 D4 Var. Pietersburg, NE South Africa
Polonne 86 D2 Rus. Polonnoye. Khmel'nyts'ka Oblast', NW Ukraine
Polski Kosovo 82 D2 Ruse, N Bulgaria
Poltava 87 F2 Poltavs'ka Oblast', NE Ukraine
Põlva 84 E3 Ger. Pölwe. Põlvamaa, SE Estonia
Polyarnyy 88 C2 Murmanskaya Oblast', NW Russian Federation
Polýkastro 82 B3 var. Polikastro; prev. Polikastron. Kentrikí Makedonía, N Greece
Polynesia 121 F4 island group C Pacific Ocean
Pomeranian Bay 72 D2 Ger. Pommersche Bucht, Pol. Zatoka Pomorska. Bay Germany/Poland

Pomorskiy Proliv 88 D2 *strait* NW Russian Federation
Pompano Beach 21 F5 Florida, SE USA
Ponca City 27 G1 Oklahoma, C USA
Ponce 33 F3 C Puerto Rico
Pondicherry 110 C2 *var.* Puduchcheri, *Fr.* Pondichéry. Pondicherry, SE India
Pondichéry *see* Pondicherry
Ponferrada 70 C1 Castilla-León, NW Spain
Poniatowa 76 E4 Lublin, E Poland
Pons Aelii *see* Newcastle upon Tyne
Ponta Delgada 70 B5 São Miguel, Azores, Portugal, NE Atlantic Ocean
Ponta Grossa 41 E4 Paraná, S Brazil
Pontarlier 68 D4 Doubs, E France
Ponteareas 92 B2 Galicia, NW Spain
Ponte da Barca 70 B2 Viana do Castelo, N Portugal
Pontevedra 70 B1 *anc.* Pons Vetus. Galicia, NW Spain
Pontiac 18 D3 Michigan, N USA
Pontianak 116 C4 Borneo, C Indonesia
Pontivy 68 A3 Morbihan, NW France
Pontoise 68 C3 *anc.* Briva Isarae, Cergy-Pontoise, Pontisarae. Val-d'Oise, N France
Ponziane, Isole 75 C5 *island* C Italy
Poole 67 D7 S England, UK
Poopó, Lago 39 F4 *var.* Lago Pampa Aullagas. Lake W Bolivia
Popayán 36 B4 Cauca, SW Colombia
Poperinge 65 A6 West-Vlaanderen, W Belgium
Poplar Bluff 23 G5 Missouri, C USA
Popocatépetl 29 E4 *volcano* S Mexico
Poprad 77 D5 *Ger.* Deutschendorf, *Hung.* Poprád. Prešovský Kraj, E Slovakia
Poprad 77 D5 *Ger.* Popper, *Hung.* Poprád. *River* Poland/Slovakia
Porbandar 112 B4 Gujarāt, W India
Porcupine Plain 58 B3 *undersea feature* E Atlantic Ocean
Pordenone 74 C2 *anc.* Portenau. Friuli-Venezia Giulia, NE Italy
Poreč 78 A2 *It.* Parenzo. Istra, NW Croatia
Pori 63 D5 *Swe.* Björneborg. Länsi-Suomi, W Finland
Porirua 129 D5 Wellington, North Island, NZ
Porkhov 88 A4 Pskovskaya Oblast', W Russian Federation
Porlamar 37 E1 Nueva Esparta, NE Venezuela
Póros 83 A5 Kefallinía, Iónioi Nísoi, Greece, C Mediterranean Sea
Póros 83 C6 Póros, S Greece
Porsangerfjorden 62 D2 *fjord* N Norway
Porsgrunn 63 B6 Telemark, S Norway
Portachuelo 39 G4 Santa Cruz, C Bolivia
Portadown 67 B5 *Ir.* Port An Dúnáin. N Northern Ireland, UK
Portalegre 70 C3 *anc.* Ammaia, Amoea. Portalegre, E Portugal
Port Alexander 14 D4 Baranof Island, Alaska, USA
Port Alfred 56 D5 Eastern Cape, S South Africa
Port An Dúnáin *see* Portadown
Port Angeles 24 B1 Washington, NW USA
Port Antonio 32 B5 NE Jamaica
Port Arthur 27 H4 Texas, SW USA
Port Augusta 127 B6 South Australia
Port-au-Prince 32 D3 *country capital* (Haiti) C Haiti
Port-au-Prince 13 D7 *international airport* E Haiti
Port Blair 111 F2 Andaman and Nicobar Islands, SE India
Port Charlotte 21 E4 Florida, SE USA
Port d'Envalira 69 B8 E Andorra
Port Douglas 126 D3 Queensland, NE Australia
Port Elizabeth 56 C5 Eastern Cape, S South Africa
Porterville 25 C7 California, W USA
Port-Gentil 55 A6 Ogooué-Maritime, W Gabon
Port Harcourt 53 G5 Rivers, S Nigeria
Port Hardy 14 D5 Vancouver Island, British Columbia, SW Canada
Port Harrison *see* Inukjuak
Port Hedland 124 B4 Western Australia
Port Huron 18 D3 Michigan, N USA
Portimão 70 B4 *var.* Vila Nova de Portimão. Faro, S Portugal
Port Jackson 126 E1 *harbour* New South Wales, SE Australia
Port Láirge *see* Waterford
Portland 19 G2 Maine, NE USA
Portland 24 B3 Oregon, NW USA
Portland 27 G4 Texas, SW USA
Portland 127 B7 Victoria, SE Australia
Portland Bight 32 B5 *bay* S Jamaica
Portlaoighise *see* Portlaoise
Portlaoise 67 B6 *Ir.* Portlaoighise; *prev.* Maryborough. C Ireland
Port Lavaca 27 G4 Texas, SW USA
Port Lincoln 127 A6 South Australia
Port Louis 57 H3 *country capital* (Mauritius) NW Mauritius
Port Macquarie 127 E6 New South Wales, SE Australia
Portmore 32 B5 C Jamaica
Port Moresby 122 B3 *country capital* (PNG) Central/National Capital District, SW PNG
Port Musgrave 127 B9 *bay* Queensland, N Australia
Port Natal *see* Durban
Porto 70 B2 *Eng.* Oporto; *anc.* Portus Cale. Porto, NW Portugal
Porto Alegre 41 E5 *var.* Pôrto Alegre. *State capital* Rio Grande do Sul, S Brazil
Porto Alegre 54 E2 São Tomé, S Sao Tome and Principe
Porto Bello *see* Portobelo

Portobelo 31 G4 *var.* Porto Bello, Puerto Bello. Colón, N Panama
Port O'Connor 27 G4 Texas, SW USA
Porto Edda *see* Sarandë
Portoferraio 74 B4 Toscana, C Italy
Port-of-Spain 33 H5 *country capital* (Trinidad and Tobago) Trinidad, Trinidad and Tobago
Porto Grande *see* Mindelo
Portogruaro 74 C2 Veneto, NE Italy
Porto-Novo 53 F5 *country capital* (Benin) S Benin
Porto Santo 48 A2 *var.* Ilha do Porto Santo. *Island* Madeira, Portugal, NE Atlantic Ocean
Porto Torres 75 A5 Sardegna, Italy, C Mediterranean Sea
Porto Velho 40 D2 *var.* Velho. *State capital* Rondônia, W Brazil
Portoviejo 38 A2 *var.* Puertoviejo. Manabí, W Ecuador
Port Pirie 127 B6 South Australia
Port Said 50 B1 *Ar.* Būr Sa'īd. N Egypt
Portsmouth 19 G3 New Hampshire, NE USA
Portsmouth 18 D4 Ohio, N USA
Portsmouth 67 D7 S England, UK
Portsmouth 19 F5 Virginia, NE USA
Port Stanley *see* Stanley
Port Sudan 50 C3 Red Sea, NE Sudan
Port Swettenham *see* Klang
Port Talbot 67 C7 S Wales, UK
Portugal 70 B3 *Country* SW Europe
Portuguese Timor *see* East Timor
Port-Vila 122 D4 *var.* Vila. *Country capital* (Vanuatu) Éfaté, C Vanuatu
Porvenir 43 B8 Magallanes, S Chile
Porvenir 39 E3 Pando, NW Bolivia
Porvoo 63 E6 *Swe.* Borgå. Etelä-Suomi, S Finland
Posadas 42 D3 Misiones, NE Argentina
Poschega *see* Požega
Posterholt 65 D5 Limburg, SE Netherlands
Postojna 73 D8 *Ger.* Adelsberg, *It.* Postumia. SW Slovenia
Potamós 83 C7 Antikýthira, S Greece
Potenza 75 D5 *anc.* Potentia. Basilicata, S Italy
P'ot'i 95 F2 W Georgia
Potiskum 53 G4 Yobe, NE Nigeria
Potomac River 19 E5 *river* NE USA
Potosí 39 F4 Potosí, S Bolivia
Potsdam 72 D3 Brandenburg, NE Germany
Potwar Plateau 112 C2 *plateau* NE Pakistan
Pouthĭsăt 115 D6 *prev.* Pursat. Poŭthĭsăt, W Cambodia
Po Valley 74 C2 *It.* Valle del Po. *Valley* N Italy
Považská Bystrica 77 C5 *Ger.* Waagbistritz, *Hung.* Vágbeszterce. Trenčiansky Kraj, W Slovakia
Poverty Bay 128 E4 *inlet* North Island, NZ
Póvoa de Varzim 70 B2 Porto, NW Portugal
Powder River 22 D2 *river* Montana/Wyoming, NW USA
Powell 22 C2 Wyoming, C USA
Powell, Lake 22 B5 *lake* Utah, W USA
Požarevac 78 D4 *Ger.* Passarowitz. Serbia, NE Serbia and Montenegro (Yugo.)
Poza Rica 29 F4 *var.* Poza Rica de Hidalgo. Veracruz-Llave, E Mexico
Poza Rica de Hidalgo *see* Poza Rica
Požega 78 D4 *prev.* Slavonska Požega. *Ger.* Poschega, *Hung.* Pozsega. Požega-Slavonija, NE Croatia
Pozsega *see* Požega
Poznań 76 C3 *Ger.* Posen, Posnania. Wielkopolskie, C Poland
Pozoblanco 70 D4 Andalucía, S Spain
Pozzallo 75 C8 Sicilia, Italy, C Mediterranean Sea
Prachatice 77 A5 *Ger.* Prachatitz. Budějovický Kraj, S Czech Republic
Prado del Ganso *see* Goose Green
Prae *see* Phrae
Prague 58 D3 Oklahoma, C USA
Praha 77 A5 *Eng.* Prague, *Ger.* Prag, *Pol.* Praga. *Country capital* (Czech Republic) Středočeský Kraj, NW Czech Republic
Praia 52 A3 *country capital* (Cape Verde) Santiago, S Cape Verde
Prato 74 B3 Toscana, C Italy
Pratt 23 E5 Kansas, C USA
Prattville 20 D2 Alabama, S USA
Pravda 82 D1 *prev.* Drugular. Silistra, NE Bulgaria
Pravia 70 C1 Asturias, N Spain
Prenzlau 72 D3 Brandenburg, NE Germany
Přerov 77 C5 *Ger.* Prerau. Olomoucký Kraj, E Czech Republic
Presa de la Amistad *see* Amistad Reservoir
Preschau *see* Prešov
Prescott 26 B2 Arizona, SW USA
Preševo 79 D5 Serbia, SE Serbia and Montenegro (Yugo.)
Presidente Epitácio 41 E4 São Paulo, S Brazil
Prešov 77 D5 *var.* Preschau, *Ger.* Eperies, *Hung.* Eperjes. Prešovský Kraj, E Slovakia
Prespa, Lake 79 D6 *Alb.* Liqen i Prespës, *Gk.* Límni Megáli Préspa, Limni Prespa, *Mac.* Prespansko Ezero, *Serb.* Prespansko Jezero. *Lake* SE Europe
Presque Isle 19 H1 Maine, NE USA
Preston 67 D5 NW England, UK
Prestwick 66 C4 W Scotland, UK
Pretoria 56 D4 *var.* Epitoli, Tshwane. *Country capital*(South Africa-administrative capital) Gauteng, NE South Africa
Préveza 83 A5 Ípeiros, W Greece
Pribilof Islands 14 A3 *island group* Alaska, USA
Priboj 78 C4 Serbia, W Serbia and Montenegro (Yugo.)
Price 22 B4 Utah, W USA
Prichard 20 C3 Alabama, S USA

Priekulė 84 B3 *Ger.* Prökuls. Gargždai, W Lithuania
Prienai 85 B5 *Pol.* Preny. Prienai, S Lithuania
Prieska 56 C4 Northern Cape, C South Africa
Prijedor 78 B3 Republika Srpska, NW Bosnia and Herzegovina
Prijepolje 78 D4 Serbia, W Serbia and Montenegro (Yugo.)
Prilep 79 D6 *Turk.* Perlepe. S FYR Macedonia
Primorsk 84 A4 *Ger.* Fischhausen. Kaliningradskaya Oblast', W Russian Federation
Primorsko 82 E2 *prev.* Keupriya. Burgas, E Bulgaria
Prince Albert 15 F5 Saskatchewan, S Canada
Prince Edward Island 17 F4 Fr. Île-du-Prince-Édouard. *Province* SE Canada
Prince Edward Islands 47 E8 *island group* S South Africa
Prince George 15 E5 British Columbia, SW Canada
Prince of Wales Island 15 F2 *island* Queen Elizabeth Islands, Nunavut, NW Canada
Prince of Wales Island 126 B1 *island* Queensland, E Australia
Prince Patrick Island 15 E2 *island* Parry Islands, Northwest Territories, NW Canada
Prince Rupert 14 D4 British Columbia, SW Canada
Prince's Island *see* Príncipe
Princess Charlotte Bay 126 C2 *bay* Queensland, NE Australia
Princess Elizabeth Land 132 C3 *physical region* Antarctica
Príncipe 55 A5 *var.* Príncipe Island, *Eng.* Prince's Island. *Island* N Sao Tome and Principe
Príncipe Island *see* Portoviejo
Prinzapolka 31 E3 Región Autónoma Atlántico Norte; NE Nicaragua
Pripet 85 C7 *Bel.* Prypyats', *Ukr.* Pryp"yat'. *River* Belarus/Ukraine
Pripet Marshes 85 B7 *wetland* Belarus/Ukraine
Priština 79 D5 *Alb.* Prishtinë. Serbia, S Serbia and Montenegro (Yugo.)
Privas 69 D5 Ardèche, E France
Prizren 79 D5 *Alb.* Prizreni. Serbia, S Serbia and Montenegro (Yugo.)
Probolinggo 116 D5 Jawa, C Indonesia
Progreso 29 H3 Yucatán, SE Mexico
Prokhladnyy 89 B8 Kabardino-Balkarskaya Respublika, SW Russian Federation
Prokuplje 79 D5 Serbia, SE Serbia and Montenegro (Yugo.)
Prome 114 B4 *var.* Pyè. Pegu, C Myanmar
Promyshlennyy 88 E3 Respublika Komi, NW Russian Federation
Prostějov 77 C5 *Ger.* Prossnitz, *Pol.* Prościejów. Olomoucký Kraj, E Czech Republic
Provence 69 D6 *cultural region* SE France
Providence *see* Fort Providence
Providence 19 G3 *state capital* Rhode Island, NE USA
Providencia, Isla de 31 F3 *island* NW Colombia
Provideniya 172 B1 Chukotskiy Avtonomnyy Okrug, NE Russian Federation
Provo 22 B4 Utah, W USA
Prudhoe Bay 14 D2 Alaska, USA
Prusa *see* Bursa
Pruszków 76 D3 *Ger.* Kaltdorf. Mazowieckie, C Poland
Prut 86 D4 *Ger.* Pruth. *River* E Europe
Pruzhany 85 B6 *Pol.* Pružana. Brestskaya Voblasts', SW Belarus
Prydz Bay 132 D3 *bay* Antarctica
Pryluky 87 E2 *Rus.* Priluki. Chernihivs'ka Oblast', NE Ukraine
Prymors'k 87 G4 *Rus.* Primorsk; *prev.* Primorskoye. Zaporiz'ka Oblast', SE Ukraine
Przemyśl 77 E5 *Rus.* Peremyshl. Podkarpackie, SE Poland
Psará 83 D5 *island* E Greece
Psël 87 F2 *river* Russian Federation/Ukraine
Pskov 92 B2 *Ger.* Pleskau, *Latv.* Pleskava. Pskovskaya Oblast', W Russian Federation
Pskov, Lake 84 E3 *Est.* Pihkva Järv, *Ger.* Pleskauer See, *Rus.* Pskovskoye Ozero. *Lake* Estonia/Russian Federation
Ptich' 85 C7 *Rus.* Ptich'. *River* SE Belarus
Ptsich 85 D7 *Rus.* Ptich'. Homyel'skaya Voblasts', SE Belarus
Ptuj 73 E7 *Ger.* Pettau; *anc.* Poetovio. NE Slovenia
Pucallpa 38 C3 Ucayali, C Peru
Puck 76 C2 Pomorskie, N Poland
Pudasjärvi 62 D4 Oulu, C Finland
Puduchcheri *see* Pondicherry
Puebla 29 F4 *var.* Puebla de Zaragoza. Puebla, S Mexico
Puebla de Zaragoza *see* Puebla
Pueblo 22 D5 Colorado, C USA
Puerto Acosta 39 E4 La Paz, W Bolivia
Puerto Aisén 43 B6 Aisén, S Chile
Puerto Ángel 29 F5 Oaxaca, SE Mexico
Puerto Argentino *see* Stanley
Puerto Ayacucho 36 D3 Amazonas, SW Venezuela
Puerto Baquerizo Moreno 38 B5 *var.* Baquerizo Moreno. Galapagos Islands, Ecuador, E Pacific Ocean
Puerto Barrios 30 C2 Izabal, E Guatemala
Puerto Bello *see* Portobelo
Puerto Berrío 36 B2 Antioquia, C Colombia
Puerto Cabello 36 D1 Carabobo, N Venezuela
Puerto Cabezas 31 E2 *var.* Bilwi. Región Autónoma Atlántico Norte, NE Nicaragua
Puerto Carreño 36 D3 Vichada, E Colombia
Puerto Cortés 30 C2 Cortés, NW Honduras

Puerto Cumarebo 36 C1 Falcón, N Venezuela
Puerto Deseado 43 C7 Santa Cruz, SE Argentina
Puerto Escondido 29 F5 Oaxaca, SE Mexico
Puerto Francisco de Orellana 38 B1 *var.* Coca. Napo, N Ecuador
Puerto Gallegos *see* Río Gallegos
Puerto Inírida 36 D3 *var.* Obando. Guainía, E Colombia
Puerto La Cruz 37 E1 Anzoátegui, NE Venezuela
Puerto Lempira 31 E2 Gracias a Dios, E Honduras
Puerto Limón *see* Limón
Puertollano 70 D4 Castilla-La Mancha, C Spain
Puerto López 36 C1 La Guajira, N Colombia
Puerto Maldonado 39 E3 Madre de Dios, E Peru
Puerto México *see* Coatzacoalcos
Puerto Montt 43 B5 Los Lagos, C Chile
Puerto Natales 43 B7 Magallanes, S Chile
Puerto Obaldía 31 H5 San Blas, NE Panama
Puerto Plata 33 E3 *var.* San Felipe de Puerto Plata. N Dominican Republic
Puerto Princesa 117 E2 *off.* Puerto Princesa City. Palawan, W Philippines
Puerto Rico 33 F3 *off.* Commonwealth of Puerto Rico; *prev.* Porto Rico. *US commonwealth territory* C West Indies
Puerto Rico 34 B1 *island* C West Indies
Puerto Rico Trench 34 B1 *undersea feature* NE Caribbean Sea
Puerto San José *see* San José
Puerto San Julián 43 B7 *var.* San Julián. Santa Cruz, SE Argentina
Puerto Suárez 39 H4 Santa Cruz, E Bolivia
Puerto Vallarta 28 D4 Jalisco, SW Mexico
Puerto Varas 43 B5 Los Lagos, C Chile
Puerto Viejo 31 E4 Heredia, NE Costa Rica
Puertoviejo *see* Portoviejo
Puget Sound 24 B1 *sound* Washington, NW USA
Puglia 75 E5 *Eng.* Apulia. *Cultural region* SE Italy
Pukaki, Lake 129 B6 *lake* South Island, NZ
Pukekohe 128 D3 Auckland, North Island, NZ
Puket *see* Phuket
Pukhavichy 85 C6 *Rus.* Pukhovichi. Minskaya Voblasts', C Belarus
Pula 78 A3 *It.* Pola; *prev.* Pulj. Istra, NW Croatia
Pulaski 18 D5 Virginia, NE USA
Puławy 76 D4 *Ger.* Neu Amerika. Lublin, E Poland
Pul-i-Khumri *see* Pol-e Khomri
Pullman 24 C2 Washington, NW USA
Pułtusk 76 D3 Mazowieckie, C Poland
Puná, Isla 38 A2 *island* SW Ecuador
Pune 112 C5 *prev.* Poona. Mahārāshtra, W India
Punjab 112 C2 *prev.* West Punjab, Western Punjab. *Province* E Pakistan
Puno 39 E4 Puno, SE Peru
Punta Alta 43 C5 Buenos Aires, E Argentina
Punta Arenas 43 B8 *prev.* Magallanes. Magallanes, S Chile
Punta Gorda 31 E4 Región Autónoma Atlántico Sur, SE Nicaragua
Punta Gorda 30 C2 Toledo, SE Belize
Puntarenas 30 D4 Puntarenas, W Costa Rica
Punto Fijo 36 C1 Falcón, N Venezuela
Pupuya, Nevado 39 E4 *mountain* W Bolivia
Puri 113 F5 *var.* Jagannath. Orissa, E India
Puriramya *see* Buriram
Purmerend 64 C3 Noord-Holland, C Netherlands
Purus, Rio 40 C2 *Sp.* Río Purús. *River* Brazil/Peru
Pusan 107 E4 *off.* Pusan-gwangyŏksi, *var.* Busan, *Jap.* Fusan. SE South Korea
Püspökladány 77 D6 Hajdú-Bihar, E Hungary
Putrajaya 116 B3 *country capital* (Malaysia) Kuala Lumpur, Peninsular Malaysia
Puttalam 110 C3 North Western Province, W Sri Lanka
Puttgarden 72 C2 Schleswig-Holstein, N Germany
Putumayo, Río 36 B5 *var.* Río Içá. *River* NW South America *see also* Içá, Rio
Putumayo, Río *see* Içá, Rio
Puurmani 84 D2 Tartu. Jõgevamaa, E Estonia
Pyatigorsk 89 B7 Stavropol'skiy Kray, SW Russian Federation
P"yatykhatky 87 F3 *Rus.* Pyatikhatki. Dnipropetrovs'ka Oblast', E Ukraine
Pyè *see* Prome
Pyetrykaw 85 C7 *Rus.* Petrikov. Homyel'skaya Voblasts', SE Belarus
Pyinmana 114 B4 Mandalay, C Myanmar
Pýlos 83 B6 *var.* Pilos. Pelopónnisos, S Greece
P'yŏngyang 107 E3 *var.* P'yŏngyang-si, *Eng.* Pyongyang. *Country capital* (North Korea) SW North Korea
P'yŏngyang-si *see* P'yŏngyang
Pyramid Lake 25 C5 *lake* Nevada, W USA
Pyrenees 92 B6 *Fr.* Pyrénées, *Sp.* Pirineos; *anc.* Pyrenaei Montes. *Mountain range* SW Europe
Pýrgos 83 B6 *var.* Pírgos. Dytikí Ellás, S Greece
Pyryatyn 87 E2 *Rus.* Piryatin. Poltavs'ka Oblast', NE Ukraine
Pyrzyce 76 B3 *Ger.* Pyritz. Zachodniopomorskie, NW Poland
Pyu 114 B4 Pegu, C Myanmar
Pyuntaza 114 B4 Pegu, SW Myanmar

Q

Qā' al Jafr 97 C7 *lake* S Jordan
Qaanaaq 60 D1 *var.* Qânâq, *Dan.* Thule. N Greenland
Qābātiya 97 E6 N West Bank
Qābis *see* Gabès
Qacentina *see* Constantine
Qafşah *see* Gafsa
Qagan Us *see* Dulan
Qahremānshahr *see* Kermānshāh
Qaidam Pendi 104 C4 *basin* C China
Qal'aikhum 101 F3 *Rus.* Kalaikhum. S Tajikistan
Qal'at Bīshah 99 B5 'Asīr, SW Saudi Arabia
Qalqīlya 97 E6 West Bank
Qamdo 104 D5 Xizang Zizhiqu, W China
Qamishly *see* Al Qāmishlī
Qânâq *see* Qaanaaq
Qaqortoq 60 C4 *Dan.* Julianehåb. S Greenland
Qara Qum *see* Garagum
Qarkilik *see* Ruoqiang
Qarokŭl 101 F3 *Rus.* Karakul'. E Tajikistan
Qars *see* Kars
Qarshi 101 E3 *Rus.* Karshi; *prev.* Bek-Budi. Qashqadaryo Wiloyati, S Uzbekistan
Qasigianguit *see* Qasigiannguit
Qasigiannguit 60 C3 *var.* Qasigianguit, *Dan.* Christianshåb. C Greenland
Qasr Farâfra 50 B2 W Egypt
Qaţanā 97 B5 *var.* Katana. Dimashq, S Syria
Qatar 98 C4 *Ar.* Dawlat Qaţar. *Country* SW Asia
Qattara Depression *see* Qaţţâra, Monkhafad el
Qattâra, Monkhafad el 88 A1 *var.* Munkhafad al Qaţţārah, *Eng.* Qattara Depression. *Desert* NW Egypt
Qazimämmäd 95 H3 *Rus.* Kazi Magomed. SE Azerbaijan
Qazvīn 98 C2 *var.* Kazvin. Qazvin, N Iran
Qena 50 B2 *var.* Qinā; *anc.* Caene, Caenepolis. E Egypt
Qeqertarssuaq *see* Qeqertarsuaq
Qeqertarsuaq 60 C3 *var.* Qeqertarssuaq, *Dan.* Godhavn. S Greenland
Qeqertarsuaq 60 C3 *island* W Greenland
Qeqertarsuup Tunua 60 C3 *Dan.* Disko Bugt. *Inlet* W Greenland
Qerveh *see* Qorveh
Qeshm 98 D4 *var.* Jazīreh-ye Qeshm, Qeshm Island. *Island* S Iran
Qeshm Island *see* Qeshm
Qian *see* Guizhou
Qilian Shan 104 D3 *var.* Kilien Mountains. *Mountain range* N China
Qimusseriarsuaq 60 C2 *Dan.* Melville Bugt, *Eng.* Melville Bay. *Bay* NW Greenland
Qinā *see* Qena
Qing *see* Qinghai
Qingdao 106 D4 *var.* Ching-Tao, Ch'ing-tao, Tsingtao, Tsintao, *Ger.* Tsingtau. Shandong, E China
Qinghai 104 C4 *var.* Chinghai, Koko Nor, Qing, Qinghai Sheng, Tsinghai. Admin. region *province* C China
Qinghai Hu 104 C4 *var.* Ch'ing Hai, Tsing Hai, *Mong.* Koko Nor. *lake* C China
Qinghai Sheng *see* Qinghai
Qingzang Gaoyuan 104 B4 *var.* Xizang Gaoyuan, *Eng.* Plateau of Tibet. *Plateau* W China
Qinhuangdao 106 D3 Hebei, E China
Qinzhou 106 B6 Guangxi Zhuangzu Zizhiqu, S China
Qiong *see* Hainan
Qiqihar 106 D2 *var.* Ch'i-ch'i-ha-erh, Tsitsihar; *prev.* Lungkiang. Heilongjiang, NE China
Qira 104 B4 Xinjiang Uygur Zizhiqu, NW China
Qitai 104 C3 Xinjiang Uygur Zizhiqu, NW China
Qīzān *see* Jīzān
Qizil Orda *see* Kyzylorda
Qizil Qum *see* Kyzyl Kum
Qizilrabot 101 G3 *Rus.* Kyzylrabot. SE Tajikistan
Qom 98 C3 *var.* Kum, Qum. Qom, N Iran
Qomul *see* Hami
Qondūz *see* Kunduz
Qo'qon 101 F2 *var.* Khokand, Qŭqon, *Rus.* Kokand. Farghona Wiloyati, E Uzbekistan
Qorveh 98 C3 *var.* Qerveh, Qurveh. Kordestān, W Iran
Qostanay *see* Kostanay
Qoubaïyât 96 B4 *var.* Al Qubayyāt. N Lebanon
Qoussantina *see* Constantine
Quang Ngai 115 E5 *var.* Quangngai, Quang Nghia. Quang Ngai, C Vietnam
Quangngai *see* Quang Ngai
Quang Nghia *see* Quang Ngai
Quanzhou 106 D6 *var.* Ch'uan-chou, Tsinkiang; *prev.* Chin-chiang. Fujian, SE China
Quanzhou 106 C6 Guangxi Zhuangzu Zizhiqu, S China
Qu'Appelle 15 F5 *river* Saskatchewan, S Canada
Quarles, Pegunungan 117 E4 *mountain range* Sulawesi, C Indonesia
Quarnero *see* Kvarner
Quartu Sant' Elena 75 A6 Sardegna, Italy, C Mediterranean Sea
Quba 95 H2 *Rus.* Kuba. N Azerbaijan
Québec 17 E4 *var.* Quebec. Québec, SE Canada
Quebec 16 D3 *var.* Quebec. Admin. region *province* SE Canada
Queen Charlotte Islands 14 C5 *Fr.* Îles de la Reine-Charlotte. *Island group* British Columbia, SW Canada

Queen Charlotte Sound 14 C5 *sea area* British Columbia, W Canada
Queen Elizabeth Islands 15 E1 *Fr.* Îles de la Reine-Élisabeth. *Island group* Northwest Territories/Nunavut, N Canada
Queensland 126 B4 *state* N Australia
Queenstown 56 D5 Eastern Cape, S South Africa
Queenstown 129 B7 Otago, South Island, NZ
Quelimane 57 E3 *var.* Kilimane, Kilmain, Quilimane. Zambézia, NE Mozambique
Quepos 31 E4 Puntarenas, S Costa Rica
Querétaro 29 E4 Querétaro de Arteaga, C Mexico
Quesada 31 E4 *var.* Ciudad Quesada, San Carlos. Alajuela, N Costa Rica
Quetta 112 B2 Baluchistān, SW Pakistan
Quetzalcoalco *see* Coatzacoalcos
Quetzaltenango *see* Quezaltenango
Quezaltenango 30 A2 *var.* Quezaltenango. Quezaltenango, W Guatemala
Quibdó 36 A3 Chocó, W Colombia
Quilimane *see* Quelimane
Quillabamba 38 D3 Cusco, C Peru
Quilon 110 C3 *var.* Kolam, Kollam. Kerala, SW India
Quimper 68 A3 *anc.* Quimper Corentin. Finistère, NW France
Quimperlé 68 A3 Finistère, NW France
Quincy 18 A4 Illinois, N USA
Qui Nhon *see* Quy Nhơn
Quissico 57 E4 Inhambane, S Mozambique
Quito 38 B1 *country capital* (Ecuador) Pichincha, N Ecuador
Qullai Garmo *see* Kommunizm, Qullai
Qum *see* Qom
Qunaytra *see* Al Qunayṭirah
Qŭqon *see* Qo'qon
Qurein *see* Al Kuwayt
Qūrghonteppa 101 E3 *Rus.* Kurgan-Tyube. SW Tajikistan
Qurlurtuuq *see* Kugluktuk
Qurveh *see* Qorveh
Quşayr *see* Al Quşayr
Quy Nhơn 115 E5 *var.* Quinhon, Qui Nhon. Binh Định, C Vietnam
Qyteti Stalin *see* Kuçovë
Qyzylorda *see* Kyzylorda

R

Raab 78 B1 *Hung.* Rába. *River* Austria/Hungary *see also* Rába
Raahe 62 D4 *Swe.* Brahestad. Oulu, W Finland
Raalte 64 D3 Overijssel, E Netherlands
Raamsdonksveer 64 C4 Noord-Brabant, S Netherlands
Raasiku 84 D2 *Ger.* Rasik. Harjumaa, NW Estonia
Rába 77 B7 *Ger.* Raab. *River* Austria/Hungary *see also* Raab
Rabat 48 C2 *var.* al Dar al Baida. *Country capital* (Morocco) NW Morocco
Rabat *see* Victoria
Rabat 80 B5 W Malta
Rabbah Ammon *see* 'Ammān
Rabbath Ammon *see* 'Ammān
Rabinal 30 B2 Baja Verapaz, C Guatemala
Rabka 99 D5 Małopolskie, S Poland
Rābniţa *see* Rîbniţa
Rabyanāh, Ramlat 49 G4 *var.* Rebiana Sand Sea, *approx.* Rabyanāh. *Desert* SE Libya
Race, Cape 17 H3 *headland* Newfoundland, Newfoundland and Labrador, E Canada
Rach Gia 115 D6 Kiên Giang, S Vietnam
Rach Gia, Vinh 115 D6 *bay* S Vietnam
Racine 18 B3 Wisconsin, N USA
Rădăuţi 86 C3 *Ger.* Radautz, *Hung.* Rádóc. Suceava, N Romania
Radom 76 D4 Mazowieckie, C Poland
Radomsko 76 D4 *Rus.* Novoradomsk. Łódzkie, C Poland
Radomyshl' 86 D2 Zhytomyrs'ka Oblast', N Ukraine
Radoviš 79 E6 *prev.* Radovište. E FYR Macedonia
Radviliškis 84 B4 Radviliškis, N Lithuania
Radzyń Podlaski 76 E4 Lubelskie, E Poland
Rae-Edzo *see* Edzo
Raetihi 128 D4 Manawatu-Wanganui, North Island, NZ
Rafa *see* Rafah
Rafaela 42 C3 Santa Fe, E Argentina
Rafah 97 A7 *var.* Rafa, Rafaḥ, *Heb.* Rafiah, Raphiah. SW Gaza Strip
Rafaḥ *see* Rafah
Rafḥah 98 B4 Al Ḥudūd ash Shamālīyah, N Saudi Arabia
Rafiaḥ *see* Rafah
Raga 51 A5 Western Bahr el Ghazal, SW Sudan
Ragged Island Range 32 C2 *island group* S Bahamas
Ragusa 75 C7 Sicilia, Italy, C Mediterranean Sea
Rahachow 85 D7 *Rus.* Rogachëv. Homyel'skaya Voblasts', SE Belarus
Rahaeng *see* Tak
Raḥaṭ, Ḥarrat 99 B5 *lavaflow* W Saudi Arabia
Rahīmyār Khān 112 C3 Punjab, SE Pakistan
Raiatea 123 G4 *island* Îles Sous le Vent, W French Polynesia
Rāichūr 110 C1 Karnātaka, C India
Rainier, Mount 12 A4 *volcano* Washington, NW USA
Rainy Lake 16 A4 *lake* Canada/USA
Raipur 113 E4 Madhya Pradesh, C India
Rājahmundry 113 E5 Andhra Pradesh, E India
Rajang *see* Rajang, Batang
Rajang, Batang 116 D3 *var.* Rajang. *River* East Malaysia
Rājapālaiyam 110 C3 Tamil Nādu, SE India
Rājasthān 112 C3 *state* NW India
Rājkot 112 C4 Gujarāt, W India

Rāj Nāndgaon 113 E4 Madhya Pradesh, C India
Rajshahi 113 G3 *prev.* Rampur Boalia. Rajshahi, W Bangladesh
Rakahanga 123 F3 *atoll* N Cook Islands
Rakaia 129 B6 *river* South Island, NZ
Rakka *see* Ar Raqqah
Rakke 84 E2 Lääne-Virumaa, NE Estonia
Rakvere 84 E2 *Ger.* Wesenberg. Lääne-Virumaa, N Estonia
Ralik Chain 122 D1 *island group* Ralik Chain, W Marshall Islands
Ramadi *see* Ar Ramādī
Ramlat Ahl Wahībah *see* Wahībah, Ramlat Āl
Ramlat Al Wahaybah *see* Wahībah, Ramlat Āl
Râmnicul Sărat 86 C4 *prev.* Râmnicul-Sărat, Râmnicu-Sărat. Buzău, E Romania
Râmnicu Vâlcea 86 B4 *prev.* Rîmnicu Vîlcea. Vâlcea, C Romania
Ramree Island 114 A4 *island* W Myanmar
Ramtha *see* Ar Ramthā
Rancagua 42 B4 Libertador, C Chile
Rānchi 113 F4 Bihār, N India
Randers 63 B7 Århus, C Denmark
Rangiora 129 C6 Canterbury, South Island, NZ
Rangitikei 128 D4 *river* North Island, NZ
Rangoon *see* Yangon
Rangpur 113 G3 Rajshahi, N Bangladesh
Rankin Inlet 15 G3 Nunavut, C Canada
Ranong 115 B6 Ranong, SW Thailand
Rapa Nui *see* Easter Island
Raphiah *see* Rafah
Rapid City 22 D3 South Dakota, N USA
Räpina 84 E3 *Ger.* Rappin. Põlvamaa, SE Estonia
Rapla 84 D2 *Ger.* Rappel. Raplamaa, NW Estonia
Rarotonga 123 G5 *island* S Cook Islands, C Pacific Ocean
Ras al 'Ain *see* Ra's al 'Ayn
Ra's al 'Ayn 96 D1 *var.* Ras al 'Ain. Al Ḥasakah, N Syria
Ra's an Naqb 97 B7 Ma'ān, S Jordan
Raseiniai 84 B4 Raseiniai, C Lithuania
Ras Hafun *see* Xaafuun, Raas
Rasht 98 C2 *var.* Resht. Gīlān, NW Iran
Râşnov 86 C4 *prev.* Rîşno, Rozsnyó, *Hung.* Barcarozsnyó. Braşov, C Romania
Ratak Chain 122 D1 *island group* Ratak Chain, E Marshall Islands
Rätan 63 C5 *var.* Ratan. Jämtland, C Sweden
Rat Buri *see* Ratchaburi
Ratchaburi 115 C5 *var.* Rat Buri. Ratchaburi, W Thailand
Rastenburg *see* Kętrzyn
Rat Islands 14 A2 *island group* Aleutian Islands, Alaska, USA
Ratlām 112 D4 *prev.* Rutlam. Madhya Pradesh, C India
Ratnapura 110 D4 Sabaragamuwa Province, S Sri Lanka
Raton 26 D1 New Mexico, SW USA
Rättvik 63 C5 Kopparberg, C Sweden
Raudhatain *see* Ar Rawḍatayn
Raufarhöfn 61 E4 Nordhurland Eystra, NE Iceland
Raukawa *see* Cook Strait
Raukumara Range 128 E3 *mountain range* North Island, NZ
Rāulakela 151 F4 *var* Rāurkela, *prev.* Rourkela. Orissa, E India
Rauma 63 D5 *Swe.* Raumo. Länsi-Suomi, W Finland
Raurkela *see* Raulakela
Ravenna 74 C3 Emilia-Romagna, N Italy
Rāvi 112 C2 *river* India/Pakistan
Rāwalpindi 112 C1 Punjab, NE Pakistan
Rawa Mazowiecka 76 D4 Łódzkie, C Poland
Rawicz 76 C4 *Ger.* Rawitsch. Wielkopolskie, C Poland
Rawlins 22 C3 Wyoming, C USA
Rawson 43 C6 Chubut, SE Argentina
Rayak 96 B4 *var.* Rayaq, Riyāq. E Lebanon
Rayaq *see* Rayak
Rayleigh 21 F1 *state capital* North Carolina, SE USA
Rayong 115 C5 Rayong, S Thailand
Razāzah, Buḩayrat ar 98 B3 *var.* Baḩr al Milḥ. *Lake* C Iraq
Razgrad 82 D2 Razgrad, N Bulgaria
Razim, Lacul 86 D5 *prev.* Lacul Razelm. *Lagoon* NW Black Sea
Reading 19 F4 Pennsylvania, NE USA
Reading 67 D7 S England, UK
Realicó 42 C4 La Pampa, C Argentina
Reăng Kesei 115 D5 Bătdâmbâng, W Cambodia
Rebecca, Lake 125 C6 *lake* Western Australia
Rebiana Sand Sea *see* Rabyānah, Ramlat
Rebun-tō 108 C2 *island* NE Japan
Rechytsa 85 D7 *Rus.* Rechitsa. Brestskaya Voblasts', SW Belarus
Recife 41 G2 *prev.* Pernambuco. *State capital* Pernambuco, E Brazil
Recklinghausen 72 A4 Nordrhein-Westfalen, W Germany
Recogne 65 C7 Luxembourg, SE Belgium
Reconquista 42 D3 Santa Fe, C Argentina
Red Deer 15 E5 Alberta, SW Canada
Redding 25 B5 California, W USA
Redon 68 B4 Ille-et-Vilaine, NW France
Red River 42 D4 *var.* Yuan, *Chin.* Yuan Jiang, *Vtn.* Sông Hồng Hà. *River* China/Vietnam
Red River 23 E1 *river* Canada/USA
Red River 20 B3 *river* Louisiana, S USA
Red River 13 C6 *river* S USA
Red Sea 50 C3 *anc.* Sinus Arabicus. *Sea* Africa/Asia
Red Wing 23 G2 Minnesota, N USA
Reefton 129 C5 West Coast, South Island, NZ
Reese River 25 C5 *river* Nevada, USA
Refahiye 95 E3 Erzincan, C Turkey

Regensburg 73 C6 *Eng.* Ratisbon, *Fr.* Ratisbonne; *hist.* Ratisbona, *anc.* Castra Regina, Reginum. Bayern, SE Germany
Regenstauf 73 C6 Bayern, SE Germany
Reggane 48 D3 C Algeria
Reggio *see* Reggio nell' Emilia
Reggio Calabria *see* Reggio di Calabria
Reggio di Calabria 75 D7 *var.* Reggio Calabria, *Gk.* Rhegion; *anc.* Rhegium. Calabria, SW Italy
Reggio Emilia *see* Reggio nell' Emilia
Reggio nell' Emilia 74 B2 *var.* Reggio Emilia, *abbrev.* Reggio; *anc.* Regium Lepidum. Emilia-Romagna, N Italy
Reghin 86 C4 *Ger.* Sächsisch-Reen, *Hung.* Szászrégen; *prev.* Reghinul Săsesc, *Ger.* Sächsisch-Regen. Mureş, C Romania
Regina 15 F5 Saskatchewan, S Canada
Registan *see* Rīgestān
Regium *see* Reggio di Calabria
Regium Lepidum *see* Reggio nell' Emilia
Rehoboth *see* Reḥovot
Rehoboth 56 B3 Hardap, C Namibia
Reḥovot 97 A6 *var.* Rehoboth, Rehovoth, Rekhovot. Central, C Israel
Rehovoth *see* Reḥovot
Reid 125 D6 Western Australia
Reikjavik *see* Reykjavík
Reims 68 D3 *Eng.* Rheims, *anc.* Durocortorum, Remi. Marne, N France
Reindeer Lake 15 F4 *lake* Manitoba/Saskatchewan, C Canada
Reinga, Cape 128 C1 *headland* North Island, NZ
Reinosa 70 D1 Cantabria, N Spain
Rekhovot *see* Reḥovot
Reliance 15 F4 Northwest Territories, C Canada
Rendina *see* Rentína
Rendsburg 72 B2 Schleswig-Holstein, N Germany
Rengat 116 B4 Sumatera, W Indonesia
Reni 86 D4 Odes'ka Oblast', SW Ukraine
Rennell 122 C4 *var.* Mu Nggava. *Island* S Solomon Islands
Rennes 68 B3 *Bret.* Roazon; *anc.* Condate. Ille-et-Vilaine, NW France
Reno 25 C5 Nevada, W USA
Renqiu 106 C4 Hebei, E China
Rentína 83 B5 *var.* Rendina. Thessalía, C Greece
Republika Srpska *Admin. region* republic Bosnia and Herzegovina
République Centrafricaine *see* Central African Republic
Repulse Bay 15 G3 Nunavut, N Canada
Resht *see* Rasht
Resistencia 42 D3 Chaco, NE Argentina
Reşiţa 86 A4 *Ger.* Reschitza, *Hung.* Resicabánya. Caraş-Severin, W Romania
Resolute 15 F2 Cornwallis Island, Nunavut, N Canada
Resolution Island 17 E1 *island* Northwest Territories, NE Canada
Resolution Island 129 A7 *island* SW NZ
Réunion 57 H4 *off.* La Réunion. *French overseas department* W Indian Ocean
Réunion 119 B5 *island* W Indian Ocean
Reus 71 F2 Cataluña, E Spain
Reutlingen 73 B6 Baden-Württemberg, S Germany
Reuver 65 D5 Limburg, SE Netherlands
Revillagigedo Islands *see* Revillagigedo, Islas
Revillagigedo, Islas 28 B5 *Eng.* Revillagigedo Islands. *Island group* W Mexico
Rexburg 24 E3 Idaho, NW USA
Reyes 39 F3 Beni, NW Bolivia
Rey, Isla del 31 G5 *island* Archipiélago de las Perlas, SE Panama
Reykjanes Basin 60 C5 *var.* Irminger Basin. *Undersea feature* N Atlantic Ocean
Reykjanes Ridge 58 A1 *undersea feature* N Atlantic Ocean
Reykjavík 61 E5 *var.* Reikjavik. *Country capital* (Iceland) Höfudhborgarsvaedhi, W Iceland
Reynosa 29 E2 Tamaulipas, C Mexico
Rezé 68 A4 Loire-Atlantique, NW France
Rēzekne 84 D4 *Ger.* Rositten; *prev.* Rus. Rezhitsa. Rēzekne, SE Latvia
Rezovo 82 E3 *Turk.* Rezve. Burgas, E Bulgaria
Rhegion *see* Reggio di Calabria
Rhegium *see* Reggio di Calabria
Rhein *see* Rhine
Rheine 72 A3 *var.* Rheine in Westfalen. Nordrhein-Westfalen, NW Germany
Rheine in Westfalen *see* Rheine
Rheinisches Schiefergebirge 73 A5 *var.* Rhine State Uplands, *Eng.* Rhenish Slate Mountains. *Mountain range* W Germany
Rhenish Slate Mountains *see* Rheinisches Schiefergebirge
Rhine 58 D4 *Dut.* Rijn, *Fr.* Rhin, *Ger.* Rhein. *River* W Europe
Rhinelander 18 B2 Wisconsin, N USA
Rhine State Uplands *see* Rheinisches Schiefergebirge
Rho 74 B2 Lombardia, N Italy
Rhode Island 19 G3 *off.* State of Rhode Island and Providence Plantations; *also known as* Little Rhody, Ocean State. *State* NE USA
Rhodes *see* Ródos
Rhodope Mountains 82 C3 *var.* Rodhópi Óri, *Bul.* Rhodope Planina, *Gk.* Orosirá Rodhópis, *Turk.* Dospad Dagh. *Mountain range* Bulgaria/Greece
Rhodope Planina *see* Rhodope Mountains
Rhodos *see* Ródos
Rhône 58 D4 *var.* Rhône. *River* France/Switzerland
Rhône 69 D6 *department* E France
Rhum 66 B3 *var.* Rum. *Island* W Scotland, UK
Ribble 67 D5 *river* NW England, UK

Ribeira 70 B1 Galicia, NW Spain
Ribeirão Preto 41 F4 São Paulo, S Brazil
Riberalta 39 F2 Beni, N Bolivia
Rîbniţa 86 D3 *var.* Rābniţa, *Rus.* Rybnitsa. NE Moldova
Rice Lake 18 A2 Wisconsin, N USA
Richard Toll 52 B3 N Senegal
Richfield 22 B4 Utah, W USA
Richland 24 C2 Washington, NW USA
Richmond 19 E5 *state capital* Virginia, NE USA
Richmond 18 C5 Kentucky, S USA
Richmond 129 C5 Tasman, South Island, NZ
Richmond Range 129 C5 *mountain range* South Island, NZ
Ricobayo, Embalse de 70 C2 *reservoir* NW Spain
Ried *see* Ried im Innkreis
Ried im Innkreis 73 D6 *var.* Ried. Oberösterreich, NW Austria
Riemst 65 D6 Limburg, NE Belgium
Riesa 72 D4 Sachsen, E Germany
Rift Valley *see* Great Rift Valley
Rīga 84 C3 *Eng.* Riga. *Country capital* (Latvia) Rīga, C Latvia
Riga, Gulf of 84 C3 *Est.* Liivi Laht, *Ger.* Rigaer Bucht, *Latv.* Rīgas Jūras Līcis, *Rus.* Rizhskiy Zaliv; *prev.* Est. Riia Laht. *Gulf* Estonia/Latvia
Rīgān 98 E4 Kermān, SE Iran
Rīgestān 100 D5 *var.* Registan. *Desert region* S Afghanistan
Riihimäki 63 D5 Etelä-Suomi, S Finland
Rijeka 78 A2 *Ger.* Sankt Veit am Flaum, *It.* Fiume, *Slvn.* Reka; *anc.* Tarsatica. Primorje-Gorski Kotar, NW Croatia
Rijssel *see* Lille
Rijssen 64 E3 Overijssel, E Netherlands
Rimah, Wādī ar 98 B4 *var.* Wādī ar Rummah. *Dry watercourse* C Saudi Arabia
Rimini 74 C3 *anc.* Ariminum. Emilia-Romagna, N Italy
Rimouski 39 E4 Québec, SE Canada
Ringebu 63 B5 Oppland, S Norway
Ringkøbing Fjord 63 A7 *fjord* W Denmark
Ringvassøya 62 C2 *island* N Norway
Rio *see* Rio de Janeiro
Riobamba 38 B1 Chimborazo, C Ecuador
Rio Branco 34 B3 *state capital* Acre, W Brazil
Río Bravo 29 E2 Tamaulipas, C Mexico
Río Cuarto 42 C4 Córdoba, C Argentina
Rio de Janeiro 41 F4 *var.* Rio. *State capital* Rio de Janeiro, SE Brazil
Río Gallegos 43 B7 *var.* Gallegos, Puerto Gallegos. Santa Cruz, S Argentina
Rio Grande 41 E5 *var.* São Pedro do Rio Grande do Sul. Rio Grande do Sul, S Brazil
Río Grande 28 D3 Zacatecas, C Mexico
Rio Grande do Norte 41 G2 *off.* Estado do Rio Grande do Norte. *State* E Brazil
Rio Grande do Sul 41 E5 *off.* Estado do Rio Grande do Sul. *State* S Brazil
Rio Grande Plateau *see* Rio Grande Rise
Rio Grande Rise 35 E6 *var.* Rio Grande Plateau. *Undersea feature* SW Atlantic Ocean
Ríohacha 36 B1 La Guajira, N Colombia
Río Lagartos 29 H3 Yucatán, SE Mexico
Riom 69 C5 *anc.* Ricomagus. Puy-de-Dôme, C France
Río San Juan 31 E4 *department* S Nicaragua
Rioverde *see* Río Verde
Río Verde 29 E4 *var.* Rioverde. San Luis Potosí, C Mexico
Ripoll 71 G2 Cataluña, NE Spain
Rishiri-tō 108 C2 *var.* Risiri Tō. *Island* NE Japan
Risiri Tō *see* Rishiri-tō
Risle 84 B2 *Ger.* Kreuz. Läänemaa, W Estonia
Rivas 30 D4 Rivas, SW Nicaragua
Rivera 42 D3 Rivera, NE Uruguay
River Falls 18 A2 Wisconsin, N USA
River Plate *see* Plata, Río de la
Riverside 25 C7 California, W USA
Riverton 129 A7 Southland, South Island, NZ
Riverton 22 C3 Wyoming, C USA
Rivière-du-Loup 17 E4 Québec, SE Canada
Rivne 86 C2 *Pol.* Równe, *Rus.* Rovno. Rivnens'ka Oblast', NW Ukraine
Rivoli 74 A2 Piemonte, NW Italy
Riyadh *see* Ar Riyāḍ
Riyāq *see* Rayak
Rize 95 E2 Rize, NE Turkey
Rizhao 106 D4 Shandong, E China
Rkîz 52 C3 Trarza, W Mauritania
Road Town 33 F3 *dependent territory capital* (British Virgin Islands) Tortola, C British Virgin Islands
Roanne 69 D5 *anc.* Rodunma. Loire, E France
Roanoke 19 E5 Virginia, NE USA
Roanoke River 21 F1 *river* North Carolina/Virginia, SE USA
Roatán 30 C2 *var.* Coxen Hole, Coxin Hole. Islas de la Bahía, N Honduras
Robbie Ridge 121 E3 *undersea feature* W Pacific Ocean
Robert Williams *see* Caála
Robinson Range 125 B5 *mountain range* Western Australia
Robson, Mount 15 E5 *mountain* British Columbia, SW Canada
Robstown 27 G4 Texas, SW USA
Roca Partida, Isla 28 B5 *island* W Mexico
Rocas, Atol das 41 G2 *island* E Brazil
Rochefort 68 B4 *var.* Rochefort sur Mer. Charente-Maritime, W France
Rochefort 65 C7 Namur, SE Belgium
Rochefort sur Mer *see* Rochefort
Rochester 23 G3 Minnesota, N USA
Rochester 19 G2 New Hampshire, NE USA
Rochester 19 E3 New York, NE USA
Rockall Bank 58 B2 *undersea feature* N Atlantic Ocean
Rockall Trough 58 B2 *undersea feature* N Atlantic Ocean

Rockdale 126 E2 New South Wales, SE Australia
Rockford 18 B3 Illinois, N USA
Rockhampton 126 D4 Queensland, E Australia
Rock Hill 21 E1 South Carolina, SE USA
Rockies *see* Rocky Mountains
Rockingham 125 A6 Western Australia
Rock Island 18 B3 Illinois, N USA
Rock Sound 32 C1 Eleuthera Island, C Bahamas
Rock Springs 22 C3 Wyoming, C USA
Rockstone 37 F3 C Guyana
Rocky Mount 21 F1 North Carolina, SE USA
Rocky Mountains 12 B4 *var.* Rockies, *Fr.* Montagnes Rocheuses. *Mountain range* Canada/USA
Roden 64 E2 Drenthe, NE Netherlands
Rodez 69 C5 *anc.* Segodunum. Aveyron, S France
Rodhópi Óri *see* Rhodope Mountains
Rodi *see* Ródos
Rodopi *see* Rhodope Mountains
Ródos 83 E7 *var.* Ródhos, *Eng.* Rhodes, *It.* Rodi; *anc.* Rhodos. *Island* Dodekánisos, Greece, Aegean Sea
Roermond 65 D5 Limburg, SE Netherlands
Roeselare 65 A6 *Fr.* Roulers; *prev.* Rousselaere. West-Vlaanderen, W Belgium
Rogatica 78 C4 Republika Srpska, SE Bosnia and Herzegovina
Rogers 20 A1 Arkansas, C USA
Roger Simpson Island *see* Abemama
Roi Ed *see* Roi Et
Roi Et 115 D5 *var.* Muang Roi Et, Roi Ed. Roi Et, E Thailand
Roja 84 C2 Talsi, NW Latvia
Rokiškis 84 C4 Rokiškis, NE Lithuania
Rokycany 77 A5 *Ger.* Rokytzan. Plzeňský Kraj, W Czech Republic
Rokytzan *see* Rokycany
Rôlas, Ilha das 54 E2 *island* S Sao Tome and Principe
Rolla 23 G5 Missouri, C USA
Roma 74 C4 *Eng.* Rome. *Country capital* (Italy) Lazio, C Italy
Roma 127 D5 Queensland, E Australia
Roman 86 C4 *Hung.* Románvásár. Neamţ, NE Romania
Roman 82 C2 Vratsa, NW Bulgaria
Romania 86 B4 *Bul.* Rumŭniya, *Ger.* Rumänien, *Hung.* Románia, *Rom.* România, *SCr.* Rumunjska, *Ukr.* Rumuniya; *prev.* Republica Socialistă România, Roumania, Rumania, Socialist Republic of Romania, *Rom.* Romînia. *Country* SE Europe
Rome *see* Roma
Rome 20 D2 Georgia, SE USA
Romny 87 F2 Sums'ka Oblast', NE Ukraine
Rømø 63 A7 *Ger.* Röm. *Island* SW Denmark
Roncador, Serra do 34 D4 *mountain range* C Brazil
Ronda 70 D5 Andalucía, S Spain
Rondônia 40 D3 *off.* Estado de Rondônia; *prev.* Território de Rondônia. *State* W Brazil
Rondonópolis 41 E3 Mato Grosso, W Brazil
Rongelap Atoll 122 D1 *var.* Rōnlap. *Atoll* Ralik Chain, N Marshall Islands
Rôngu 84 D3 *Ger.* Ringen. Tartumaa, SE Estonia
Rōnlap *see* Rongelap Atoll
Rønne 63 B8 Bornholm, E Denmark
Roosendaal 65 C5 Noord-Brabant, S Netherlands
Roosevelt Island 132 B4 *island* Antarctica
Roraima 40 D1 *off.* Estado de Roraima; *prev.* Território do Rio Branco, Território de Roraima. *State* N Brazil
Roraima, Mount 37 E3 *mountain* N South America
Røros 63 B5 Sør-Trøndelag, S Norway
Rosa, Lake 32 D2 *lake* Great Inagua, S Bahamas
Rosario 42 D4 Santa Fe, C Argentina
Rosario 28 A1 Baja California, NW Mexico
Roscommon 18 C2 Michigan, N USA
Roseau 33 G4 *prev.* Charlotte Town. *Country capital* (Dominica) SW Dominica
Roseburg 24 B4 Oregon, NW USA
Rosenberg 27 G4 Texas, SW USA
Rosengarten 72 B3 Niedersachsen, N Germany
Rosenheim 73 C6 Bayern, S Germany
Rosia 71 H5 W Gibraltar
Rosia Bay 71 H5 *bay* SW Gibraltar
Roşiori de Vede 86 B5 Teleorman, S Romania
Roslavl' 89 A5 Smolenskaya Oblast', W Russian Federation
Rosmalen 64 C4 Noord-Brabant, S Netherlands
Ross 129 B6 West Coast, South Island, NZ
Rossano 75 E6 *anc.* Roscianum. Calabria, SW Italy
Ross Ice Shelf 132 B4 *ice shelf* Antarctica
Rosso 52 B3 Trarza, SW Mauritania
Rossosh' 89 B6 Voronezhskaya Oblast', W Russian Federation
Ross Sea 132 B4 *sea* Antarctica
Rostak *see* Ar Rustāq
Rostock 72 C2 Mecklenburg-Vorpommern, NE Germany
Rostov *see* Rostov-na-Donu
Rostov-na-Donu 89 B7 *var.* Rostov, *Eng.* Rostov-on-Don. Rostovskaya Oblast', SW Russian Federation
Rostov-on-Don *see* Rostov-na-Donu
Roswell 26 D2 New Mexico, SW USA
Rota 122 B1 *island* S Northern Mariana Islands

Rothera – San Jorge, Golfo

Rothera 132 A2 UK research station Antarctica
Rotorua 128 D3 Bay of Plenty, North Island, NZ
Rotorua, Lake 128 D3 lake North Island, NZ
Rotterdam 64 C4 Zuid-Holland, SW Netherlands
Rottweil 73 B6 Baden-Württemberg, S Germany
Rotuma 123 E4 island NW Fiji
Roubaix 68 C2 Nord, N France
Rouen 68 C3 anc. Rotomagus. Seine-Maritime, N France
Round Rock 27 G3 Texas, SW USA
Rourkela see Răulakela
Roussillon 69 C6 cultural region S France
Rouyn-Noranda 16 D4 Québec, SE Canada
Rovaniemi 84 D3 Lappi, N Finland
Rovigo 74 C2 Veneto, NE Italy
Rovinj 78 A3 It. Rovigno. Istra, NW Croatia
Rovuma, Rio 57 F2 var. Ruvuma. River Mozambique/Tanzania see also Ruvuma
Rovuma, Rio see Ruvuma
Roxas City 117 E2 Panay Island, C Philippines
Royale, Isle 18 B1 island Michigan, N USA
Royan 69 B5 Charente-Maritime, W France
Rozdol'ne 87 F4 Rus. Razdolnoye. Respublika Krym, S Ukraine
Rožňava 99 D6 Ger. Rosenau, Hung. Rozsnyó. Košický Kraj, E Slovakia
Ruapehu, Mount 128 D4 mountain North Island, NZ
Ruapuke Island 129 B8 island SW NZ
Ruatoria 128 E3 Gisborne, North Island, NZ
Ruawai 128 D2 Northland, North Island, NZ
Rubizhne 87 H3 Rus. Rubezhnoye. Luhans'ka Oblast', E Ukraine
Ruby Mountains 25 D5 mountain range Nevada, W USA
Rucava 84 B3 Liepāja, SW Latvia
Rūd-e Hīrmand see Helmand, Daryā-ye
Rūdiškės 85 B5 Trakai, S Lithuania
Rudnik 82 E2 Varna, E Bulgaria
Rudny see Rudnyy
Rudnyy 92 C4 var. Rudny. Kostanay, N Kazakhstan
Rudolf, Lake see Turkana, Lake
Rudolfswert see Novo Mesto
Rudzyensk 85 C6 Rus. Rudensk. Minskaya Voblasts', C Belarus
Rufiji 51 C7 river E Tanzania
Rufino 42 C4 Santa Fe, C Argentina
Rugāji 84 D4 Balvi, E Latvia
Rügen 94 D2 headland NE Germany
Ruggell 72 E1 N Liechtenstein
Ruhnu 84 C2 var. Ruhnu Saar, Swe. Runö. Island SW Estonia
Ruhnu Saar see Ruhnu
Rūjiena 84 D3 Est. Ruhja, Ger. Rujen. Valmiera, N Latvia
Rukwa, Lake 51 B7 lake SE Tanzania
Rum see Rhum
Ruma 78 D3 Serbia, N Serbia and Montenegro (Yugo.)
Rumadiya see Ar Ramādī
Rumbek 51 B5 El Buhayrat, S Sudan
Rum Cay 32 D2 island C Bahamas
Rumia 76 C2 Pomorskie, N Poland
Rummah, Wādī ar see Rimah, Wādī ar
Runanga 129 B5 West Coast, South Island, NZ
Runaway Bay 32 B4 C Jamaica
Rundu 56 C3 var. Runtu. Okavango, NE Namibia
Runö see Ruhnu
Runtu see Rundu
Ruoqiang 104 C3 var. Jo-ch'iang, Uigh. Charkhlik, Charkhliq, Qarkilik. Xinjiang Uygur Zizhiqu, NW China
Rupea 86 C4 Ger. Reps, Hung. Kőhalom; prev. Cohalm. Braşov, C Romania
Rupel 65 B5 river N Belgium
Rupert, Rivière de 16 D3 river Québec, C Canada
Ruschuk see Ruse
Rusçuk see Ruse
Ruse 82 D1 var. Ruschuk, Rustchuk, Turk. Rusçuk. Ruse, N Bulgaria
Rus Krymskaya ASSR see Crimea
Russellville 20 A1 Arkansas, C USA
Russian Federation 90 D2 var. Russia, Latv. Krievija, Rus. Rossiyskaya Federatsiya. Country Asia/Europe
Rustaq see Ar Rustāq
Rust'avi 95 G2 SE Georgia
Rustchuk see Ruse
Ruston 20 B2 Louisiana, S USA
Rutanzige !M, Lake see Edward, Lake
Rutba see Ar Ruţbah
Rutland 19 F2 Vermont, NE USA
Rutög 104 A4 var. Rutog, Rutok. Xizang Zizhiqu, W China
Rutok see Rutog
Ruvuma 47 E5 var. Rio Rovuma. River Mozambique/Tanzania see also Rovuma, Rio
Ruvuma see Rovuma, Rio
Ruwenzori 55 E5 mountain range Uganda/Dem. Rep. Congo
Ruzhany 85 B6 Rus. Ruzhany. Brestskaya Voblasts', SW Belarus
Ružomberok 77 C5 Ger. Rosenberg, Hung. Rózsahegy. Žilinsky Kraj, N Slovakia
Rwanda 51 B6 prev. Ruanda. Country C Africa
Ryazan' 89 B5 Ryazanskaya Oblast', W Russian Federation
Rybinsk 88 B4 prev. Andropov. Yaroslavskaya Oblast', W Russian Federation
Rybnik 77 C5 Śląskie, S Poland
Rybnitsa see Rîbniţa
Ryde 126 E1 New South Wales, SE Australia
Ryki 76 D4 Lublin, E Poland
Rypin 76 C3 Kujawsko-pomorskie, C Poland
Ryssel see Lille
Rysy 77 C5 mountain S Poland
Ryukyu Islands 103 E3 island group SW Japan
Ryukyu Trench 103 F3 var. Nansei Syotō Trench. Undersea feature S East China Sea
Rzeszów 77 E5 Podkarpackie, SE Poland
Rzhev 88 B4 Tverskaya Oblast', W Russian Federation

S

Saale 72 C4 river C Germany
Saalfeld 73 C5 var. Saalfeld an der Saale. Thüringen, C Germany
Saalfeld an der Saale see Saalfeld
Saarbrücken 73 A6 Fr. Sarrebruck. Saarland, SW Germany
Sääre 84 C2 var. Sjar. Saaremaa, W Estonia
Saaremaa 84 C2 Ger. Oesel, Ösel; prev. Saare. Island W Estonia
Saariselkä 62 D2 Lapp. Suoločielgi. Lappi, N Finland
Sab' Ābār 96 C4 var. Sab'a Biyar, Sa'b Bi'ār. Ḩimş, C Syria
Sab'a Biyar see Sab' Ābār
Šabac 78 D3 Serbia, W Serbia and Montenegro (Yugo.)
Sabadell 71 G2 Cataluña, E Spain
Sabah 116 D3 cultural region Borneo, SE Asia
Sabanalarga 36 B1 Atlántico, N Colombia
Sabaneta 36 C1 Falcón, N Venezuela
Sab'atayn, Ramlat as 99 C6 desert C Yemen
Sabaya 39 F4 Oruro, S Bolivia
Sa'b Bi'ār see Sab' Ābār
Şāberī, Hāmūn-e var. Daryācheh-ye Hāmūn, Daryācheh-ye Sīstān. Lake Afghanistan/Iran see also Sīstān, Daryācheh-ye
Sabhā 49 F3 C Libya
Sabi, Rio see Save, Rio
Sabinas 29 E2 Coahuila de Zaragoza, NE Mexico
Sabinas Hidalgo 29 E2 Nuevo León, NE Mexico
Sabine River 27 H3 river Louisiana/Texas, SW USA
Sabkha see As Sabkhah
Sable, Cape 21 E5 headland Florida, SE USA
Sable Island 17 G4 island Nova Scotia, SE Canada
Şabyā 99 B6 Jīzān, SW Saudi Arabia
Sabzawar see Sabzevār
Sabzevār 98 D2 var. Sabzawar. Khorāsān, NE Iran
Sachsen 72 D4 Eng. Saxony, Fr. Saxe. State E Germany
Sachs Harbour 15 E2 Banks Island, Northwest Territories, N Canada
Sacramento 25 B5 state capital California, W USA
Sacramento Mountains 26 D2 mountain range New Mexico, SW USA
Sacramento River 25 B5 river California, W USA
Sacramento Valley 25 B5 valley California, W USA
Şa'dah 99 B6 NW Yemen
Sado 109 C5 var. Sadoga-shima. Island C Japan
Sadoga-shima see Sado
Safad see Zefat
Safed see Zefat
Säffle 63 B6 Värmland, C Sweden
Safford 26 C3 Arizona, SW USA
Safi 48 B2 W Morocco
Safid Kūh, Selseleh-ye 100 D4 Eng. Paropamisus Range. Mountain range W Afghanistan
Sagaing 114 B3 Sagaing, C Myanmar
Sagami-nada 109 D6 inlet SW Japan
Sagan see Żagań
Sāgar 112 D4 prev. Saugor. Madhya Pradesh, C India
Saghez see Saqqez
Saginaw 18 C3 Michigan, N USA
Saginaw Bay 18 D2 lake bay Michigan, N USA
Sagua la Grande 32 B2 Villa Clara, C Cuba
Sagunt see Sagunto
Sagunto 71 F3 var. Sagunt, Ar. Murviedro; anc. Saguntum. País Valenciano, E Spain
Saguntum see Sagunto
Sahara 46 B3 desert Libya/Algeria
Sahara el Gharbîya 50 B2 var. Aş Şaḩrā' al Gharbīyah, Eng. Western Desert. Desert C Egypt
Saharan Atlas see Atlas Saharien
Sahel 52 D3 physical region C Africa
Sāḩilīyah, Jibāl as 96 B3 mountain range NW Syria
Sāhīwāl 112 C2 prev. Montgomery. Punjab, E Pakistan
Şahrā' Rabyanāh see Rabyanāh, Ramlat
Saïda 97 A5 var. Şaydā, Sayida; anc. Sidon. W Lebanon
Saidpur 113 G3 var. Syedpur. Rajshahi, NW Bangladesh
Saigon see Hô Chi Minh
Sai Hun see Syr Darya
Saimaa 63 E5 lake SE Finland
St Albans 67 E6 anc. Verulamium. E England, UK
Saint Albans 18 D5 West Virginia, NE USA
St Andrews 66 C4 E Scotland, UK
Saint Anna Trough see Svyataya Anna Trough
St.Ann's Bay 32 B4 C Jamaica
St.Anthony 17 G3 Newfoundland, Newfoundland and Labrador, SE Canada
Saint Augustine 21 E3 Florida, SE USA
St Austell 67 C7 SW England, UK
St-Brieuc 68 A3 Côtes d'Armor, NW France
St. Catharines 16 D5 Ontario, S Canada
St-Chamond 69 D5 Loire, E France
St.Clair, Lake 18 D3 Fr. Lac à L'Eau Claire. Lake Canada/USA
St-Claude 69 D5 anc. Condate. Jura, E France
Saint Cloud 23 F2 Minnesota, N USA
St Croix 33 F3 island S Virgin Islands (US)
Saint Croix River 18 A2 river Minnesota/Wisconsin, N USA
St David's Island 20 B5 island E Bermuda
St-Denis 57 G4 dependent territory capital (Réunion) NW Réunion
St-Dié 68 E4 Vosges, NE France
St-Egrève 69 D5 Isère, E France
Saintes 69 B5 anc. Mediolanum. Charente-Maritime, W France
St-Étienne 69 D5 Loire, E France
St-Flour 69 C5 Cantal, C France
Saint Gall see Sankt Gallen
St-Gall see Sankt Gallen
StGallen see Sankt Gallen
St-Gaudens 69 B6 Haute-Garonne, S France
St George 20 B4 N Bermuda
Saint George 127 D5 Queensland, E Australia
Saint George 22 A5 Utah, W USA
St.George's 33 G5 country capital (Grenada) SW Grenada
St-Georges 37 H3 E French Guiana
St-Georges 17 E4 Québec, SE Canada
St George's Channel 67 B6 channel Ireland/Wales, UK
St George's Island 20 B4 island E Bermuda
Saint Helena 47 B6 UK dependent territory C Atlantic Ocean
St.Helena Bay 56 B5 bay SW South Africa
St Helier 67 D8 dependent territory capital (Jersey) S Jersey, Channel Islands
Saint Ignace 18 C2 Michigan, N USA
St-Jean, Lac 17 E4 lake Québec, SE Canada
Saint Joe River 24 D2 river Idaho, NW USA
Saint John 19 H1 river Canada/USA
Saint John 17 F4 New Brunswick, SE Canada
St John's 33 G3 country capital (Antigua and Barbuda) Antigua, Antigua and Barbuda
St.John's 17 H3 Newfoundland, Newfoundland and Labrador, E Canada
Saint Joseph 23 F4 Missouri, C USA
St Julian's 80 B5 N Malta
St Kilda 66 A3 island NW Scotland, UK
Saint Kitts and Nevis 33 F3 var. Saint Christopher-Nevis. Country E West Indies
St-Laurent see St-Laurent-du-Maroni
St-Laurent-du-Maroni 37 H3 var. St-Laurent. NW French Guiana
St. Lawrence 17 E4 Fr. Fleuve St-Laurent. River Canada/USA
St. Lawrence, Gulf of 17 F3 gulf NW Atlantic Ocean
Saint Lawrence Island 14 B2 island Alaska, USA
St-Lô 68 B3 anc. Briovera, Laudus. Manche, N France
St-Louis 68 E4 Haut-Rhin, NE France
Saint Louis 23 G4 Missouri, C USA
Saint Louis 52 B3 NW Senegal
Saint Lucia 33 E1 country SE West Indies
Saint Lucia Channel 33 H4 channel Martinique/Saint Lucia
St-Malo 68 B3 Ille-et-Vilaine, NW France
St-Malo, Golfe de 68 A3 gulf NW France
St Matthew's Island see Zadetkyi Kyun
St.Matthias Group 122 B3 island group NE PNG
St-Maur-des-Fossés 68 E2 Val-de-Marne, N France
St.Moritz 73 B7 Ger. Sankt Moritz, Rmsch. San Murezzan. Graubünden, SE Switzerland
St-Nazaire 68 A4 Loire-Atlantique, NW France
St-Omer 68 C2 Pas-de-Calais, N France
Saint Paul 23 F2 state capital Minnesota, N USA
St-Paul, Île 119 C6 var. St.Paul Island. Island NE French Southern and Antarctic Territories
St.Paul Island see St-Paul, Île
St Peter Port 67 D8 dependent territory capital (Guernsey) C Guernsey, Channel Islands
Saint Petersburg see Sankt-Peterburg
Saint Petersburg 21 E4 Florida, SE USA
St-Pierre and Miquelon 17 G4 Fr. Îles St-Pierre et Miquelon. French territorial collectivity NE North America
St-Quentin 68 C3 Aisne, N France
Saint Vincent 33 G4 island N Saint Vincent and the Grenadines
Saint Vincent and the Grenadines 33 H4 country SE West Indies
Saint Vincent Passage 33 H4 passage Saint Lucia/Saint Vincent and the Grenadines
Saipan 120 B1 island country capital (Northern Mariana Islands) S Northern Mariana Islands
Sajama, Nevado 39 F4 mountain W Bolivia
Sajószentpéter 77 D6 Borsod-Abaúj-Zemplén, NE Hungary
Sakākah 98 B4 Al Jawf, NW Saudi Arabia
Sakakawea, Lake 22 D1 reservoir North Dakota, N USA
Sakata 108 D4 Yamagata, Honshū, C Japan
Sakhalin see Sakhalin, Ostrov
Sakhalin, Ostrov 93 G4 var. Sakhalin. Island SE Russian Federation
Sakhon Nakhon see Sakon Nakhon
Şäki 95 G2 Rus. Sheki; prev. Nukha. NW Azerbaijan
Sakishima-shotō 108 A3 var. Sakisima Syotô. Island group SW Japan
Sakisima Syotô see Sakishima-shotō
Sakiz see Saqqez
Sakiz-Adasi see Chíos
Sakon Nakhon 114 D4 var. Muang Sakon Nakhon, Sakhon Nakhon. Sakon Nakhon, E Thailand
Saky 87 F5 Rus. Saki. Respublika Krym, S Ukraine
Sal 52 A3 island Ilhas de Barlavento, NE Cape Verde
Sala 63 C6 Västmanland, C Sweden
Salacgrīva 84 C3 Est. Salatsi. Limbaži, N Latvia
Sala Consilina 75 D5 Campania, S Italy
Salado, Río 42 C3 river C Argentina
Salado, Río 40 D5 river E Argentina
Şalālah 99 D6 SW Oman
Salamá 30 B2 Baja Verapaz, C Guatemala
Salamanca 70 D2 anc. Helmantica, Salmantica. Castilla-León, NW Spain
Salamanca 42 B4 Coquimbo, C Chile
Salamīyah 96 B3 var. As Salamīyah. Ḩamāh, W Syria
Salang see Phuket
Salantai 84 B3 Kretinga, NW Lithuania
Salavan 115 D5 var. Saravan, Saravane. Salavan, S Laos
Salavat 89 D6 Respublika Bashkortostan, W Russian Federation
Sala y Gomez 131 F4 island Chile, E Pacific Ocean
Sala y Gomez Fracture Zone see Sala y Gomez Ridge
Sala y Gomez Ridge 131 G4 var. Sala y Gomez Fracture Zone. Tectonic feature SE Pacific Ocean
Šalčininkai 85 C5 Šalčininkai, SE Lithuania
Saldus 84 B3 Ger. Frauenburg. Saldus, W Latvia
Sale 127 C7 Victoria, SE Australia
Salé 48 C2 NW Morocco
Salekhard 92 D3 prev. Obdorsk. Yamalo-Nenetskiy Avtonomnyy Okrug, N Russian Federation
Salem 24 B3 state capital Oregon, NW USA
Salem 110 C2 Tamil Nādu, SE India
Salerno 75 D5 anc. Salernum. Campania, S Italy
Salerno, Golfo di 75 C5 Eng. Gulf of Salerno. Gulf S Italy
Salihorsk 85 C7 Rus. Soligorsk. Minskaya Voblasts', S Belarus
Salima 57 E2 Central, C Malawi
Salina 23 E5 Kansas, C USA
Salina Cruz 29 F5 Oaxaca, SE Mexico
Salinas 25 B6 California, W USA
Salinas 38 A2 Guayas, W Ecuador
Salisbury 67 D7 var. New Sarum. S England, UK
Sallyana see Salyan
Salmon River 24 D3 river Idaho, NW USA
Salmon River Mountains 24 D3 mountain range Idaho, NW USA
Salo 85 D6 Länsi-Suomi, W Finland
Salon-de-Provence 69 D6 Bouches-du-Rhône, SE France
Salonta 86 A3 Hung. Nagyszalonta. Bihor, W Romania
Sal'sk 89 B7 Rostovskaya Oblast', SW Russian Federation
Salt see As Salţ
Salta 42 C2 Salta, NW Argentina
Saltash 67 C7 SW England, UK
Saltillo 29 E3 Coahuila de Zaragoza, NE Mexico
Salt Lake City 22 B4 state capital Utah, W USA
Salto 42 D4 Salto, N Uruguay
Salton Sea 25 D8 lake California, W USA
Salvador 41 G3 prev. São Salvador. Bahia, E Brazil
Salween 102 C2 Bur. Thanlwin, Chin. Nu Chiang, Nu Jiang. River SE Asia
Salyan 113 E3 var. Sallyana. Mid Western, W Nepal
Salzburg 73 D6 anc. Juvavum. Salzburg, N Austria
Salzgitter 72 C4 prev. Watenstedt-Salzgitter. Niedersachsen, C Germany
Salzwedel 72 C3 Sachsen-Anhalt, N Germany
Šamac see Bosanski Šamac
Samakhixai 115 E5 var. Attapu, Attopeu. Attapu, S Laos
Samalayuca 28 C1 Chihuahua, N Mexico
Samar 117 F2 island C Philippines
Samara 92 B3 prev. Kuybyshev. Samarskaya Oblast', W Russian Federation
Samarang see Semarang
Samarinda 116 D4 Borneo, C Indonesia
Samarqand 101 E2 Rus. Samarkand. Samarqand Wiloyati, C Uzbekistan
Samawa see As Samāwah
Sambalpur 113 F4 Orissa, E India
Sambava 57 G2 Antsiraňana, NE Madagascar
Sambir 86 B2 Rus. Sambor. L'vivs'ka Oblast', NW Ukraine
Sambre 68 D2 river Belgium/France
Samfya 56 D2 Luapula, N Zambia
Saminatal 72 E2 valley Austria/Liechtenstein
Samnān see Semnān
Sam Neua see Xam Nua
Samoa 123 E4 var. Sāmoa; prev. Western Samoa. Country W Polynesia
Samoa Basin 121 E3 undersea feature W Pacific Ocean
Samobor 78 A2 Zagreb, N Croatia
Sámos 83 E6 prev. Limín Vathéos. Sámos, Dodekánisos, Greece, Aegean Sea
Sámos 83 D6 island Dodekánisos, Greece, Aegean Sea
Samosch see Someş
Samothráki 82 C4 anc. Samothrace. Island NE Greece
Samothráki 82 D4 Samothráki, NE Greece
Sampit 116 C4 Borneo, C Indonesia
Samsun 94 D2 anc. Amisus. Samsun, N Turkey
Samtredia 95 F2 W Georgia
Samui, Ko 115 C6 island SW Thailand
Samut Prakan 115 C5 var. Muang Samut Prakan, Paknam. Samut Prakan, C Thailand
San 77 E5 river SE Poland
San 52 D3 Ségou, C Mali
Şan'ā' 99 B6 Eng. Sana. Country capital (Yemen) W Yemen
Sana 78 B3 river NW Bosnia and Herzegovina
Sana see Şan'ā'
Sanae 132 B2 South African research station Antarctica
Sanaga 55 B5 river C Cameroon
San Ambrosio, Isla 35 A5 Eng. San Ambrosio Island. Island W Chile
Sanandaj 98 C3 prev. Sinneh. Kordestān, W Iran
San Andrés, Isla de 31 F3 island NW Colombia
San Andrés Tuxtla 29 F4 var. Tuxtla. Veracruz-Llave, E Mexico
San Angelo 27 F3 Texas, SW USA
San Antonio 27 F4 Texas, SW USA
San Antonio 30 B2 Toledo, S Belize
San Antonio 42 B4 Valparaíso, C Chile
San Antonio Oeste 43 C5 Río Negro, E Argentina
San Antonio River 27 G4 river Texas, SW USA
Sanāw 99 C6 var. Sanaw. NE Yemen
San Benedicto, Isla 28 B4 island W Mexico
San Benito 30 B1 Petén, N Guatemala
San Benito 27 G5 Texas, SW USA
San Bernardino 25 C7 California, W USA
San Blas 28 C3 Sinaloa, C Mexico
San Blas, Cape 20 D3 headland Florida, SE USA
San Blas, Cordillera de 31 G4 mountain range NE Panama
San Carlos see Quesada
San Carlos 26 B2 Arizona, SW USA
San Carlos 30 D4 Río San Juan, S Nicaragua
San Carlos de Bariloche 43 B5 Río Negro, SW Argentina
San Carlos del Zulia 36 C2 Zulia, W Venezuela
San Clemente Island 25 B8 island Channel Islands, California, W USA
San Cristobal 122 C4 var. Makira. Island SE Solomon Islands
San Cristóbal see San Cristóbal de Las Casas
San Cristóbal 36 C2 Táchira, W Venezuela
San Cristóbal de Las Casas 29 G5 var. San Cristóbal. Chiapas, SE Mexico
San Cristóbal, Isla 38 B5 var. Chatham Island. Island Galapagos Islands, Ecuador, E Pacific Ocean
Sancti Spíritus 32 B2 Sancti Spíritus, C Cuba
Sandakan 116 D3 Sabah, East Malaysia
Sandanski 82 C3 prev. Sveti Vrach. Blagoevgrad, SW Bulgaria
Sanday 66 D2 island NE Scotland, UK
Sanders 26 C2 Arizona, SW USA
Sand Hills 22 D3 mountain range Nebraska, C USA
San Diego 25 C8 California, W USA
Sandnes 63 A6 Rogaland, S Norway
Sandomierz 76 D4 Rus. Sandomir. Świętokrzyskie, C Poland
Sandoway 114 A4 Arakan State, W Myanmar
Sandpoint 24 C1 Idaho, NW USA
Sand Springs 27 G1 Oklahoma, C USA
Sandusky 18 D3 Ohio, N USA
Sandvika 63 A6 Akershus, S Norway
Sandviken 63 C6 Gävleborg, C Sweden
Sandy Bay 71 H5 bay E Gibraltar
Sandy City 22 B4 Utah, W USA
Sandy Lake 16 B3 lake Ontario, C Canada
San Esteban 30 D2 Olancho, C Honduras
San Felipe 36 D1 Yaracuy, NW Venezuela
San Felipe de Puerto Plata see Puerto Plata
San Félix, Isla 35 A5 Eng. San Felix Island. Island W Chile
San Fernando 70 C5 prev. Isla de León. Andalucía, S Spain
San Fernando 36 D2 var. San Fernando de Apure. Apure, C Venezuela
San Fernando 24 D1 California, W USA
San Fernando 33 H5 Trinidad, Trinidad and Tobago
San Fernando de Apure see San Fernando
San Fernando del Valle de Catamarca 42 C3 var. Catamarca. Catamarca, NW Argentina
San Fernando de Monte Cristi see Monte Cristi
San Francisco 25 B6 California, W USA
San Francisco del Oro 28 C2 Chihuahua, N Mexico
San Francisco de Macorís 33 E3 C Dominican Republic
San Gabriel 38 B1 Carchi, N Ecuador
San Gabriel Mountains 24 E1 mountain range California, W USA
Sangir, Kepulauan 117 F3 var. Kepulauan Sangihe. Island group N Indonesia
Sāngli 132 B1 Mahārāshtra, W India
Sangmélima 77 B5 Sud, S Cameroon
Sangre de Cristo Mountains 26 D1 mountain range Colorado/New Mexico, C USA
San Ignacio 30 B1 prev. Cayo, El Cayo. Cayo, W Belize
San Ignacio 28 B2 Baja California Sur, W Mexico
San Ignacio 39 F3 Beni, N Bolivia
San Joaquin Valley 25 B7 valley California, W USA
San Jorge, Golfo 43 C6 var. Gulf of San Jorge. Gulf S Argentina

INDEX

San Jorge, Gulf of *see* San Jorge, Golfo
San José *see* San José del Guaviare
San Jose 25 B6 California, W USA
San José 30 B3 *var.* Puerto San José.
Escuintla, S Guatemala
San José 39 G3 *var.* San José de Chiquitos.
Santa Cruz, E Bolivia
San José 31 E4 *country capital* (Costa Rica)
San José, C Costa Rica
San José de Chiquitos *see* San José
San José de Cúcuta 36 C6 *see* Cúcuta
San José del Guaviare 36 C4 *var.* San José.
Guaviare, S Colombia
San Juan 33 F3 *dependent territory capital*
(Puerto Rico) NE Puerto Rico
San Juan *see* San Juan de los Morros
San Juan 42 B4 San Juan, W Argentina
San Juan Bautista 42 D3 Misiones,
S Paraguay
San Juan Bautista Tuxtepec *see* Tuxtepec
San Juan de Alicante 71 F4 País Valenciano,
E Spain
San Juan del Norte 31 E4 *var.* Greytown.
Río San Juan, SE Nicaragua
San Juan de los Morros 36 D2 *var.* San Juan.
Guárico, N Venezuela
San Juanito, Isla 28 C4 *island* C Mexico
San Juan Mountains 26 D1 *mountain range*
Colorado, C USA
San Juan River 26 C1 *river* Colorado/Utah,
W USA
San Julián *see* Puerto San Julián
Sankt Gallen 73 B7 *var.* St.Gallen,
Eng. Saint Gall, *Fr.* St-Gall. Sankt Gallen,
NE Switzerland
Sankt-Peterburg 88 B4 *prev.* Leningrad,
Petrograd, *Eng.* Saint Petersburg,
Fin. Pietari. Leningradskaya Oblast',
NW Russian Federation
Sankt Pölten 73 E6 Niederösterreich,
N Austria
Sankuru 55 D6 *river* C Dem. Rep. Congo
Şanlıurfa 95 E4 *prev.* Sanli Urfa, Urfa,
anc. Edessa. Şanlıurfa, S Turkey
San Lorenzo 38 A1 Esmeraldas,
N Ecuador
San Lorenzo 39 G5 Tarija, S Bolivia
San Lorenzo, Isla 38 B3 *island* W Peru
Sanlúcar de Barrameda 70 C5 Andalucía,
S Spain
San Luis 28 A1 *var.* San Luis Río Colorado.
Sonora, NW Mexico
San Luis 30 B2 Petén, NE Guatemala
San Luis 42 C4 San Luis, C Argentina
San Luis Obispo 25 B7 California, W USA
San Luis Potosí 29 E3 San Luis Potosí,
C Mexico
San Luis Río Colorado *see* San Luis
San Marcos 30 A2 San Marcos,
W Guatemala
San Marcos 27 G4 Texas, SW USA
San Marino 74 E1 *country capital* (San
Marino) C San Marino
San Marino 74 D1 *Country* S Europe
San Martín 132 A2 *Argentinian research
station* Antarctica
San Mateo 37 E2 Anzoátegui, NE Venezuela
San Matías 39 H3 Santa Cruz, E Bolivia
San Matías, Golfo 43 C5 *var.* Gulf of San
Matías. *Gulf* E Argentina
San Matías, Gulf of *see* San Matías, Golfo
Sanmenxia 106 C4 *var.* Shan Xian. Henan,
C China
Sânnicolaul Mare *see* Sânnicolau Mare
Sânnicolau Mare 86 A4
var. Sânnicolaul-Mare, *Hung.*
Nagyszentmiklós; *prev.* Sânnicolăuș Mare,
Sinnicolau Mare. Timiș, W Romania
Sanok 77 E5 Podkarpackie, SE Poland
San Pablo 39 F5 Potosí, S Bolivia
San Pedro 28 D3 *var.* San Pedro de las
Colonias. Coahuila de Zaragoza,
NE Mexico
San Pedro 30 C1 Corozal, NE Belize
San-Pédro 52 D5 S Côte d'Ivoire
San Pedro de la Cueva 28 C2 Sonora,
NW Mexico
San Pedro de las Colonias *see* San Pedro
San Pedro de Lloc 38 B3 La Libertad,
NW Peru
San Pedro Mártir, Sierra 28 A1
mountain range NW Mexico
San Pedro Sula 30 C2 Cortés,
NW Honduras
San Rafael 42 B4 Mendoza, W Argentina
San Rafael Mountains 25 C7 *mountain range*
California, W USA
San Ramón de la Nueva Orán 42 C2 Salta,
S Argentina
San Remo 74 A3 Liguria, NW Italy
San Salvador 30 B3 *country capital* (El
Salvador) San Salvador, SW El Salvador
San Salvador de Jujuy 42 C2 *var.* Jujuy.
Jujuy, N Argentina
San Salvador, Isla 38 A4 *prev.* Watlings
Island. *Island* E Bahamas
Sansanné-Mango 53 E4 *var.* Mango.
N Togo
Sansepolcro 74 C3 Toscana, C Italy
San Severo 75 D5 Puglia, SE Italy
Santa Ana 39 F3 Beni, N Bolivia
Santa Ana 24 D2 California, W USA
Santa Ana 30 B3 Santa Ana,
NW El Salvador
Santa Ana Mountains 24 E2 *mountain range*
California, W USA
Santa Barbara 25 C7 California, W USA

Santa Barbara 28 C2 Chihuahua, N Mexico
Santa Catalina Island 25 B8 *island* Channel
Islands, California, W USA
Santa Catarina 41 E5 *off.* Estado de Santa
Catarina. *State* S Brazil
Santa Clara 32 B2 Villa Clara, C Cuba
Santa Clarita 24 D1 California, W USA
Santa Comba 70 B1 Galicia, NW Spain
Santa Cruz 39 G4 *var.* Santa Cruz de la
Sierra. Santa Cruz, C Bolivia
Santa Cruz 54 E2 São Tomé, C Sao Tome
and Principe
Santa Cruz Barillas *see* Barillas
Santa Cruz de la Sierra *see* Santa Cruz
Santa Cruz del Quiché 30 B2 Quiché,
W Guatemala
Santa Cruz de Tenerife 48 A3 Tenerife,
Islas Canarias, Spain, NE Atlantic Ocean
Santa Cruz, Isla 38 B5 *var.* Indefatigable
Island, Isla Chávez. *Island* Galapagos
Islands, Ecuador, E Pacific Ocean
Santa Cruz Islands 122 D3 *island group*
E Solomon Islands
Santa Cruz, Río 43 B7 *river* S Argentina
Santa Elena 30 B1 Cayo, W Belize
Santa Fe 42 C4 Santa Fe, C Argentina
Santa Fe 26 D1 *state capital* New Mexico,
SW USA
Santa Genoveva 28 B3 *mountain* W Mexico
Santa Isabel 122 C3 *var.* Bughotu. *Island*
N Solomon Islands
Santa Lucia Range 25 B7 *mountain range*
California, W USA
Santa Margarita, Isla 28 B3 *island* W Mexico
Santa Maria 70 A5 *island* Azores, Portugal,
NE Atlantic Ocean
Santa Maria 25 B7 California, W USA
Santa Maria 41 E5 Rio Grande do Sul,
S Brazil
Santa María, Isla 38 A5 *var.* Isla Floreana,
Charles Island. *Island* Galapagos Islands,
Ecuador, E Pacific Ocean
Santa Marta 36 B1 Magdalena, N Colombia
Santa Monica 24 C1 California, W USA
Santana 54 E2 São Tomé, S Sao Tome
and Principe
Santander 70 D1 Cantabria, N Spain
Santanilla, Islas 31 E1 *Eng.* Swan Islands.
Island NE Honduras
Santarém 70 B3 *anc.* Scalabis. Santarém,
W Portugal
Santarém 41 E2 Pará, N Brazil
Santa Rosa *see* Santa Rosa de Copán
Santa Rosa 42 C4 La Pampa, C Argentina
Santa Rosa de Copán 30 C2 *var.* Santa Rosa.
Copán, W Honduras
Santa Rosa Island 25 B8 *island* California,
W USA
Sant Carles de la Rápida *see* Sant Carles de
la Ràpita
Sant Carles de la Ràpita 71 F3 *var.* Sant
Carles de la Ràpida. Cataluña, NE Spain
Santiago 42 B4 *var.* Gran Santiago.
Country capital (Chile) Santiago, C Chile
Santiago 70 B1 *var.* Santiago de Compostela,
Eng. Compostella; *anc.* Campus Stellae.
Galicia, NW Spain
Santiago 33 E3 *var.* Santiago de los
Caballeros. N Dominican Republic
Santiago 52 A3 *var.* São Tiago.
Island Ilhas de Sotavento, S Cape Verde
Santiago *see* Santiago de Cuba
Santiago 31 F5 Veraguas, S Panama
Santiago de Compostela *see* Santiago
Santiago de Cuba 32 C3 *var.* Santiago.
Santiago de Cuba, E Cuba
Santiago de Guayaquil *see* Guayaquil
Santiago del Estero 42 C3 Santiago del
Estero, C Argentina
Santiago de los Caballeros *see* Santiago
Santiago Pinotepa Nacional *see* Pinotepa
Nacional
Santiago, Río 38 B2 *river* N Peru
Santi Quarana *see* Sarandë
Santíssima Trinidad *see* Chilung
Sant Julià la Lòria 69 A8 SW Andorra
Santo *see* Espiritu Santo
Santo Antão 52 A2 *island* Ilhas de
Barlavento, N Cape Verde
Santo António 54 E1 Príncipe, N Sao Tome
and Principe
Santo Domingo 32 D3 *prev.* Ciudad Trujillo.
Country capital (Dominican Republic)
SE Dominican Republic
Santo Domingo de los Colorados 38 B1
Pichincha, NW Ecuador
Santo Domingo Tehuantepec *see*
Tehuantepec
Santos 41 F4 São Paulo, S Brazil
Santos Plateau 35 D5 *undersea feature*
SW Atlantic Ocean
Santo Tomé 42 D3 Corrientes, NE Argentina
San Valentín, Cerro 43 A6 *mountain* S Chile
San Vicente 30 C3 San Vicente,
C El Salvador
São Francisco, Rio 41 F3 *river* E Brazil
Sao Hill 51 C7 Iringa, S Tanzania
São João da Madeira 70 B2 Aveiro,
N Portugal
São Jorge 70 A5 *island* Azores, Portugal,
NE Atlantic Ocean
São Luís 41 F2 *state capital* Maranhão,
NE Brazil
São Mandol *see* São Manuel, Rio
São Manuel, Rio 41 E3 *var.* São Mandol,
Teles Pirés. *River* C Brazil
São Marcos, Baía de 41 F1 *bay* N Brazil
São Miguel 70 A5 *island* Azores, Portugal,
NE Atlantic Ocean
Saona, Isla 33 E3 *island* SE Dominican
Republic
Saône 69 D5 *river* E France
São Nicolau 52 A3 *Eng.* Saint Nicholas.
Island Ilhas de Barlavento, N Cape Verde
São Paulo 41 E4 *off.* Estado de São Paulo.
State S Brazil

São Paulo 41 E4 *state capital* São Paulo,
S Brazil
São Paulo de Loanda *see* Luanda
São Pedro do Rio Grande do Sul *see* Rio
Grande
São Roque, Cabo de 41 G2 *headland* E Brazil
São Salvador *see* M'Banza Congo
São Salvador do Congo *see* M'Banza Congo
São Tiago *see* Santiago
São Tomé 54 E2 *Eng.* Saint Thomas. *Island*
S Sao Tome and Principe
São Tomé 55 C1 *Port.* Henrique de Carvalho,
Vila Henrique de Carvalho. Lunda Sul,
NE Angola
São Tomé 55 A5 *country capital* (Sao Tome
and Principe) São Tomé, S Sao Tome
and Principe
Sao Tome and Principe 54 D1 *Country*
E Atlantic Ocean
São Tomé, Pico de 54 D2 *mountain* São
Tomé, S Sao Tome and Principe
São Vicente 52 A3 *Eng.* Saint Vincent.
Island Ilhas de Barlavento, N Cape Verde
São Vicente, Cabo de 70 B5 *Eng.* Cape Saint
Vincent, *Port.* Cabo de São Vicente.
Headland S Portugal
Sápai *see* Sápes
Sapele 53 F5 Delta, S Nigeria
Sápes 82 D3 *var.* Sápai. Anatolikí Makedonía
kai Thráki, NE Greece
Sapir *see* Sappir
Sa Pobla 71 G3 *var.* La Puebla. Mallorca,
Spain, W Mediterranean Sea
Sappir 97 B7 *var.* Sapir. Southern, S Israel
Sapporo 108 D2 Hokkaidō, NE Japan
Sapri 75 D6 Campania, S Italy
Sapulpa 27 G1 Oklahoma, C USA
Saqqez 98 C2 *var.* Saghez, Sakiz, Saqqiz.
Kordestán, NW Iran
Saqqiz *see* Saqqez
Sara Buri 115 C5 *var.* Saraburi. Saraburi,
C Thailand
Saragt *see* Sarahs
Saraguro 38 B2 Loja, S Ecuador
Sarahs 100 D3 *var.* Saragt, Serakhs.
Akhalskiy Velayat, S Turkmenistan
Sarajevo 78 C4 *country capital* (Bosnia and
Herzegovina). Federacija Bosna I
Hercegovina, SE Bosnia and Herzegovina
Sarakhs 98 E2 Khorāsān, NE Iran
Saraktash 89 D6 Orenburgskaya Oblast',
W Russian Federation
Saran' 92 C4 *Kaz.* Saran. Karaganda,
C Kazakhstan
Saranda *see* Sarandë
Sarandë 79 C7 *var.* Saranda, *It.* Porto Edda;
prev. Santi Quaranta. Vlorë, S Albania
Saransk 89 C5 Respublika Mordoviya,
W Russian Federation
Sarasota 21 E4 Florida, SE USA
Saratov 92 B3 Saratovskaya Oblast',
W Russian Federation
Saravan *see* Salavan
Saravane *see* Salavan
Sarawak 116 D3 *cultural region* Borneo,
SE Asia
**Sarawak and Sabah (North Borneo) and
Singapore** *see* Malaysia
Sarcelles 68 D1 Val-d'Oise, N France
Sardegna 75 A5 *Eng.* Sardinia. *Island* Italy,
C Mediterranean Sea
Sardinia *see* Sardegna
Sarera, Teluk *see* Cenderawasih, Teluk
Sargasso Sea 44 B4 *sea* W Atlantic Ocean
Sargodha 112 C2 Punjab, NE Pakistan
Sarh 54 C4 *prev.* Fort-Archambault.
Moyen-Chari, S Chad
Sārī 98 D2 *var.* Sari, Sāri. Māzandarān,
N Iran
Saría 83 E7 *island* SE Greece
Sarıkamış 95 F3 Kars, NE Turkey
Sarikol Range 101 G3 *Rus.* Sarykol'skiy
Khrebet. *Mountain range* China/Tajikistan
Sark 67 D8 *Fr.* Sercq. *Island* Channel Islands
Şarkışla 94 D3 Sivas, C Turkey
Sarmiento 43 B6 Chubut, S Argentina
Sarnia 16 C5 Ontario, S Canada
Sarny 86 C1 Rivnens'ka Oblast',
NW Ukraine
Sarochyna 85 D5 *Rus.* Sorochino.
Vitsyebskaya Voblasts', N Belarus
Sarov 89 C5 *prev.* Sarova. Respublika
Mordoviya, SW Russian Federation
Sarova *see* Sarov
Sarpsborg 85 B6 Østfold, S Norway
Sartène 69 E7 Corse, France,
C Mediterranean Sea
Sarthe 68 B4 *cultural region* N France
Sárti 82 C4 Kentrikí Makedonía, N Greece
Saruhan *see* Manisa
Saryesik-Atyrau, Peski 101 G1 *desert*
E Kazakhstan
Sary-Tash 101 F2 Oshskaya Oblast',
SW Kyrgyzstan
Sasebo 109 A7 Nagasaki, Kyūshū,
SW Japan
Saskatchewan 15 F5 *river*
Manitoba/Saskatchewan, C Canada
Saskatchewan 15 F5 *province* SW Canada
Saskatoon 15 F5 Saskatchewan, S Canada
Sasovo 89 B5 Ryazanskaya Oblast',
W Russian Federation
Sassandra 52 D5 S Côte d'Ivoire
Sassandra 52 D5 *var.* Ibo, Sassandra Fleuve.
River S Côte d'Ivoire
Sassandra Fleuve *see* Sassandra
Sassari 75 A5 Sardegna, Italy,
C Mediterranean Sea
Sassenheim 64 C3 Zuid-Holland,
W Netherlands
Sassnitz 72 D2 Mecklenburg-Vorpommern,
NE Germany
Sátoraljaújhely 77 D6 Borsod-Abaúj-
Zemplén, NE Hungary
Sátpura Range 112 D4 *mountain range*
C India
Satsunan-shotō 108 A3 *var.* Satunan Syotô.
Island group SW Japan
Sattanen 62 D3 Lappi, NE Finland
Satu Mare 86 B3 *Ger.* Sathmar, *Hung.*
Szatmárnémeti. Satu Mare, NW Romania

Satunan Syotô *see* Satsunan-shotō
Saudi Arabia 99 B5 *Ar.* Al 'Arabīyah as
Su'ūdīyah, Al Mamlakah al 'Arabīyah as
Su'ūdīyah. *Country* SW Asia
Sauer *see* Sûre
Saulkrasti 84 C3 Rīga, C Latvia
Sault Sainte Marie 18 C1 Michigan,
N USA
Sault Ste.Marie 16 C4 Ontario, S Canada
Saumur 68 B4 Maine-et-Loire, NW France
Saurimo 56 C1 *Port.* Henrique de Carvalho,
Vila Henrique de Carvalho. Lunda Sul,
NE Angola
Sava 78 B3 *Eng.* Save, *Ger.* Sau, *Hung.* Száva.
River SE Europe
Sava 65 E6 *Rus.* Save. Sava. Mahilyowskaya
Voblasts', E Belarus
Savá 30 D2 Colón, N Honduras
Savai'i 123 E4 *island* NW Samoa
Savannah 21 E2 Georgia, SE USA
Savannah River 21 E2 *river* Georgia/South
Carolina, SE USA
Savanna-La-Mar 32 A5 W Jamaica
Save, Rio 57 E3 *var.* Rio Sabi. *River*
Mozambique/Zimbabwe
Save *see* Sava
Saverne 68 E3 *var.* Zabern; *anc.* Tres
Tabernae. Bas-Rhin, NE France
Savigliano 74 A2 Piemonte, NW Italy
Savigsivik *see* Savissivik
Savinski *see* Savinskiy
Savinskiy 88 C3
var. Savinski. Arkhangel'skaya Oblast',
NW Russian Federation
Savissivik 60 D1 *var.* Savigsivik.
N Greenland
Savoie 69 D5 *cultural region* E France
Savona 74 A2 Liguria, NW Italy
Savu Sea 117 E5 *Ind.* Laut Sawu. *Sea*
S Indonesia
Sawakin *see* Suakin
Sawdirī *see* Sodiri
Sawhāj *see* Sohâg
Şawqirah 99 D6 *var.* Suqrah. S Oman
Sayanskiy Khrebet 90 D3 *mountain range*
S Russian Federation
Sayat 100 D3 *var.* Sayat. Lebapskiy Velayat,
E Turkmenistan
Sayaxché 52 B2 Petén, N Guatemala
Şaydā *see* Saïda
Sayhūt 99 D6 E Yemen
Sayida *see* Saïda
Saynshand 105 E2 Dornogovĭ, SE Mongolia
Sayre 19 E3 Pennsylvania, NE USA
Say'ūn 99 C6 *var.* Saywūn. C Yemen
Saywūn *see* Say'ūn
Scandinavia 44 D2 *geophysical region*
NW Europe
Scarborough 89 D5 N England, UK
Schaan 72 E1 W Liechtenstein
Schaerbeek 65 C6 Brussels, C Belgium
Schaffhausen 73 B7 *Fr.* Schaffhouse.
Schaffhausen, N Switzerland
Schagen 64 C2 Noord-Holland,
NW Netherlands
Schebschi Mountains *see* Shebshi
Mountains
Scheessel 72 B3 Niedersachsen,
NW Germany
Schefferville 17 E2 Québec, E Canada
Scheldt 65 B5 *Dut.* Schelde, *Fr.* Escaut.
River W Europe
Schell Creek Range 25 D5 *mountain range*
Nevada, W USA
Schenectady 19 F3 New York, NE USA
Schertz 27 G4 Texas, SW USA
Schiermonnikoog 64 D1 *Fris.*
Skiermûntseach. *Island* Waddeneilanden,
N Netherlands
Schijndel 64 D4 Noord-Brabant,
S Netherlands
Schiltigheim 68 E3 Bas-Rhin, NE France
Schleswig 72 B2 Schleswig-Holstein,
N Germany
Schleswig-Holstein 72 B2 *cultural region*
N Germany
Schönebeck 72 C4 Sachsen-Anhalt,
C Germany
Schooten *see* Schoten
Schoten 65 C5 *var.* Schooten. Antwerpen,
N Belgium
Schouwen 64 B4 *island* SW Netherlands
Schwabenalb *see* Schwäbische Alb
Schwäbische Alb 73 B6 *var.* Schwabenalb,
Eng. Swabian Jura. *Mountain range*
S Germany
Schwandorf 73 C5 Bayern, SE Germany
Schwarzwald 73 B6 *Eng.* Black Forest.
Mountain range SW Germany
Schwaz 73 C7 Tirol, W Austria
Schweinfurt 73 B5 Bayern, SE Germany
Schwerin 72 C3 Mecklenburg-Vorpommern,
N Germany
Schwiz *see* Schwyz
Schwyz 73 B7 *var.* Schwiz. Schwyz,
C Switzerland
Scilly, Isles of 67 B8 *island group*
SW England, UK
Scio *see* Chíos
Scoresby Sound *see* Ittoqqortoormiit
Scoresbysund *see* Ittoqqortoormiit
Scotia Sea 35 C8 *sea* SW Atlantic Ocean
Scotland 66 C3 *national region* UK
Scott Base 132 B4 *NZ research station*
Antarctica
Scott Island 132 B5 *island* Antarctica
Scottsbluff 22 D3 Nebraska, C USA
Scottsboro 20 D1 Alabama, S USA
Scottsdale 26 B2 Arizona, SW USA
Scranton 19 F3 Pennsylvania, NE USA
Scupi *see* Skopje
Scutari *see* Shkodër
Scutari, Lake 79 C5 *Alb.* Liqeni i Shkodrës,
SCr. Skadarsko Jezero. *Lake*
Albania/Serbia and Montenegro (Yugo.)
Scyros *see* Skýros
Searcy 20 B1 Arkansas, C USA
Seattle 24 B2 Washington, NW USA
Sébaco 30 D3 Matagalpa, W Nicaragua

Sebastián Vizcaíno, Bahía 28 A2 *bay*
NW Mexico
Sechura, Bahía de 38 A3 *bay* NW Peru
Secunderābād 112 D5 *var.* Sikandarabad.
Andhra Pradesh, C India
Sedan 68 D3 Ardennes, N France
Seddon 129 D5 Marlborough, South
Island, NZ
Seddonville 129 C5 West Coast, South
Island, NZ
Sédhiou 52 B3 SW Senegal
Sedona 26 B2 Arizona, SW USA
Seesen 72 B4 Niedersachsen, C Germany
Segestica *see* Sisak
Segezha 88 B3 Respublika Kareliya,
NW Russian Federation
Ségou 52 D3 *var.* Segu. Ségou, C Mali
Segovia 70 D2 Castilla-León, C Spain
Segoviao Wangki *see* Coco, Río
Segu *see* Ségou
Séguédine 53 H2 Agadez, NE Niger
Seguin 27 G4 Texas, SW USA
Segura 71 E4 *river* S Spain
Seinäjoki 63 D5 *Swe.* Östermyra.
Länsi-Suomi, W Finland
Seine 68 D1 *river* N France
Seine, Baie de la 68 B3 *bay* N France
Sekondi *see* Sekondi-Takoradi
Sekondi-Takoradi 53 E5 *var.* Sekondi.
S Ghana
Selat Balabac *see* Balabac Strait
Selenga 105 E1 *Mong.* Selenge Mörön.
River Mongolia/Russian Federation
Sélestat 68 E4 *Ger.* Schlettstadt. Bas-Rhin,
NE France
Selfoss 61 E5 Sudhurland, SW Iceland
Sélibabi 52 C3 *var.* Sélibaby. Guidimaka,
S Mauritania
Sélibaby *see* Sélibabi
Selma 25 C6 California, W USA
Selway River 24 D2 *river* Idaho, NW USA
Selwyn Range 126 B3 *mountain range*
Queensland, C Australia
Selzaete *see* Zelzate
Semarang 116 C5 *var.* Samarang. Jawa,
C Indonesia
Sembé 55 B5 La Sangha, NW Congo
Semey *see* Semipalatinsk
Seminole 27 E3 Texas, SW USA
Seminole, Lake 20 D3 *reservoir*
Florida/Georgia, SE USA
Semipalatinsk 92 D4 *Kaz.* Semey.
Vostochnyy kazakhstan, E Kazakhstan
Semnān 98 D3 *var.* Samnān. Semnān,
N Iran
Semois 65 C8 *river* SE Belgium
Sendai 109 A8 Kagoshima, Kyūshū,
SW Japan
Sendai 108 D4 Miyagi, Honshū, C Japan
Sendai-wan 108 D4 *bay* E Japan
Senec 77 C6 *Ger.* Wartberg, *Hung.* Szenc;
prev. Szempcz. Bratislavský Kraj,
W Slovakia
Senegal 52 C3 *Fr.* Sénégal. *River* W Africa
Senegal 52 B3 *Fr.* Sénégal. *Country*
W Africa
Senftenberg 72 D4 Brandenburg,
E Germany
Senica 77 C6 *Ger.* Senitz, *Hung.* Szenice.
Trnavský Kraj, W Slovakia
Senj 78 A3 *Ger.* Zengg, *It.* Segna; *anc.* Senia.
Lika-Senj, NW Croatia
Senja 62 C2 *prev.* Senjen. *Island* N Norway
Senkaku-shotō 108 A3 *island group*
SW Japan
Senlis 68 C3 Oise, N France
Sennar 50 C4 *var.* Sannâr. Sinnar, C Sudan
Sens 68 C3 *anc.* Agendicum, Senones.
Yonne, C France
Sên, Stœng 115 D5 *river* C Cambodia
Senta 78 D3 *Hung.* Zenta. Serbia, N Serbia
and Montenegro (Yugo.)
Seo de Urgel *see* La See d'Urgel
Seoul *see* Sŏul
Sept-Îles 17 E3 Québec, SE Canada
Seraing 65 D6 Liège, E Belgium
Serakhs *see* Sarahs
Seram, Pulau 117 F4 *var.* Serang, *Eng.*
Ceram. *Island* Maluku, E Indonesia
Serang *see* Seram, Pulau
Serang 116 C5 Jawa, C Indonesia
Serasan, Selat 116 C3 *strait*
Indonesia/Malaysia
Serbia 78 D4 *Ger.* Serbien, *Serb.* Srbija.
Admin. region *republic* Serbia and
Montenegro (Yugo.)
Serbia and Montenegro (Yugo.) 78 D4
SCr. Jugoslavija, Savezna Republika
Jugoslavija. *Country* SE Europe
Serdar 100 C2 *prev.* Gyzylarbat, Kizyl-Arvat.
Balkanskiy Velayat, W Turkmenistan
Serdica *see* Sofiya
Serenje 56 D2 Central, E Zambia
Seres *see* Sérres
Seret *see* Siret
Sereth *see* Siret
Serhetabat 100 D4 *prev.* Gushgy, Kushka.
Maryyskiy Velayat, S Turkmenistan
Sérifos 83 C6 *anc.* Seriphos. *Island* Kykládes,
Greece, Aegean Sea
Serov 92 D3 Sverdlovskaya Oblast',
C Russian Federation
Serowe 56 D3 Central, SE Botswana
Serpa Pinto *see* Menongue
Serpent's Mouth, The 37 F2 *Sp.* Boca de la
Serpiente. *Strait* Trinidad and
Tobago/Venezuela
Serpukhov 89 B5 Moskovskaya Oblast',
W Russian Federation
Serra dos Parecis *see* Parecis, Chapada dos
Sérrai *see* Sérres
Serrana, Cayo de 31 F2 *island group*
NW Colombia
Serranilla, Cayo de 31 F2 *island group*
NW Colombia
Serra Pacaraim *see* Pakaraima Mountains
Serra Tumucumaque *see* Tumuc Humac
Mountains

Serravalle 74 E1 N San Marino
Sérres 82 C3 var. Seres; prev. Sérrai. Kentrikí Makedonía, NE Greece
Sert see Siirt
Sesto San Giovanni 74 B2 Lombardia, N Italy
Sesvete 78 B2 Zagreb, N Croatia
Setabis see Xátiva
Sète 69 C6 prev. Cette. Hérault, S France
Setesdal 63 A6 valley S Norway
Sétif 49 E2 var. Stif. N Algeria
Setté Cama 55 A6 Ogooué-Maritime, SW Gabon
Setúbal 70 B4 Eng. Saint Ubes, Saint Yves. Setúbal, W Portugal
Setúbal, Baía de 70 B4 bay W Portugal
Seul, Lac 16 B3 lake Ontario, S Canada
Sevan 95 G2 C Armenia
Sevana Lich 95 G3 Eng. Lake Sevan, Rus. Ozero Sevan. E Armenia
Sevastopol' 87 F5 Eng. Sebastopol. Respublika Krym, S Ukraine
Severn 67 D6 Wel. Hafren. River England/Wales, UK
Severn 16 B2 river Ontario, S Canada
Severnaya Dvina 88 C4 var. Northern Dvina. River NW Russian Federation
Severnaya Zemlya 93 E2 var. Nicholas II Land. Island group N Russian Federation
Severnyy 88 E3 Respublika Komi, NW Russian Federation
Severodvinsk 88 C3 prev. Molotov, Sudostroy. Arkhangel'skaya Oblast', NW Russian Federation
Severomorsk 88 C2 Murmanskaya Oblast', NW Russian Federation
Severo-Sibirskaya Nizmennost' 93 E2 var. North Siberian Plain, Eng. North Siberian Lowland. Lowlands N Russian Federation
Seversk 92 D4 Tomskaya Oblast', C Russian Federation
Severskiy Donets see Donets
Sevier Lake 22 A4 lake Utah, W USA
Sevilla 70 C4 Eng. Seville; anc. Hispalis. Andalucía, SW Spain
Seville see Sevilla
Sevlievo 82 D2 Gabrovo, N Bulgaria
Seychelles 57 G1 Country W Indian Ocean
Seydhisfjördhur 61 E5 Austurland, E Iceland
Seýdi 100 D2 var. Seydi; prev. Neftezavodsk. Lebapskiy Velayat, E Turkmenistan
Seyhan see Adana
Sfákia 83 C8 Kriti, Greece, E Mediterranean Sea
Sfântu Gheorghe 86 C4 Ger. Sankt-Georgen, Hung. Sepsiszentgyörgy; prev. Şepsi-Sângeorz, Sfintu Gheorghe. Covasna, C Romania
Sfax 49 F2 Ar. Şafāqis. E Tunisia
's-Gravenhage 64 B4 var. Den Haag, Eng. The Hague, Fr. La Haye. Country capital (Netherlands-seat of government) Zuid-Holland, W Netherlands
's-Gravenzande 64 B4 Zuid-Holland, W Netherlands
Shaan see Shaanxi
Shaanxi 106 B5 var. Shaan, Shaanxi Sheng, Shan-hsi, Shenshi, Shensi. Admin. region province C China
Shaanxi Sheng see Shaanxi
Shache 104 A3 var. Yarkant. Xinjiang Uygur Zizhiqu, NW China
Shackleton Ice Shelf 132 D3 ice shelf Antarctica
Shaddādī see Ash Shadādāh
Shāhābād see Eslāmābād
Shahjahanabad see Delhi
Shahr-e Kord 98 C3 var. Shahr Kord. Chahār Maḥall va Bakhtīārī, C Iran
Shahr Kord see Shahr-e Kord
Shāhrūd 98 D2 prev. Emāmrūd, Emāmshahr. Semnān, N Iran
Shalkar 92 B4 var. Chelkar. Aktyubinsk, W Kazakhstan
Shandī see Shendi
Shandong 106 D4 var. Lu, Shandong Sheng, Shantung. Admin. region province E China
Shandong Sheng see Shandong
Shanghai 106 D5 var. Shang-hai. Shanghai Shi, E China
Shang-hai see Shanghai
Shangrao 106 D5 Jiangxi, S China
Shan-hsi see Shaanxi
Shan-hsi see Shanxi
Shannon 67 A6 Ir. An tSionainn. River W Ireland
Shan Plateau 114 B3 plateau E Myanmar
Shansi see Shanxi
Shantarskiye Ostrova 93 G3 Eng. Shantar Islands. Island group E Russian Federation
Shantou 106 D6 var. Shan-t'ou, Swatow. Guangdong, S China
Shantung see Shandong
Shanxi 106 C4 var. Jin, Shan-hsi, Shansi, Shanxi Sheng. Admin. region province C China
Shan Xian see Sanmenxia
Shanxi Sheng see Shanxi
Shaoguan 106 C6 var. Shao-kuan, Cant. Kukong; prev. Ch'u-chiang. Guangdong, S China
Shao-kuan see Shaoguan
Shaqrā see Shuqrah
Shaqrā' 98 B4 Ar Riyāḍ, C Saudi Arabia
Shar 130 D5 var. Charsk. Vostochnyy Kazakhstan, E Kazakhstan
Shari see Chari
Shari 108 D2 Hokkaidō, NE Japan
Shark Bay 125 A5 bay Western Australia
Shashe 56 D3 var. Shashi. River Botswana/Zimbabwe
Shashi see Shashe
Shatskiy Rise 103 G1 undersea feature N Pacific Ocean

Shatt al-Hodna see Hodna, Chott El
Shaṭṭ al Jarīd see Jerid, Chott el
Shawnee 27 G1 Oklahoma, C USA
Shchadrin 85 D7 Rus. Shchedrin. Homyel'skaya Voblasts', SE Belarus
Shchëkino 89 B5 Tul'skaya Oblast', W Russian Federation
Shchors 87 E1 Chernihivs'ka Oblast', N Ukraine
Shchuchinsk 92 C4 prev. Shchuchye. Severnyy kazakhstan, N Kazakhstan
Shchuchyn 85 B5 Pol. Szczuczyn Nowogródzki, Rus. Shchuchin. Hrodzyenskaya Voblasts', W Belarus
Shebekino 89 A6 Belgorodskaya Oblast', W Russian Federation
Shebeli 51 D5 Amh. Wabē Shebelē Wenz, It. Scebeli, Som. Webi Shabeelle. River Ethiopia/Somalia
Sheberghān 101 E3 var. Shibarghān, Shibarghan, Shiberghān. Jowzjān, N Afghanistan
Sheboygan 18 B2 Wisconsin, N USA
Shebshi Mountains 54 A4 var. Schebschi Mountains. Mountain range E Nigeria
Shechem see Nablus
Shedadi see Ash Shadādāh
Sheffield 67 D5 N England, UK
Shekhem see Nablus
Shelby 22 B1 Montana, NW USA
Sheldon 23 F3 Iowa, C USA
Shelekhov Gulf see Shelikhova, Zaliv
Shelikhova, Zaliv 93 G2 Eng. Shelekhov Gulf. Gulf E Russian Federation
Shendi 50 C4 var. Shandī. River Nile, NE Sudan
Shengking see Liaoning
Shenking see Liaoning
Shenshi see Shaanxi
Shensi see Shaanxi
Shenyang 106 D3 Chin. Shen-yang, Eng. Moukden, Mukden; prev. Fengtien. Liaoning, NE China
Shepetivka 86 D2 Rus. Shepetovka. Khmel'nyts'ka Oblast', NW Ukraine
Shepparton 127 C7 Victoria, SE Australia
Sherbrooke 17 E4 Québec, SE Canada
Shereik 50 C3 River Nile, N Sudan
Sheridan 22 C2 Wyoming, C USA
Sherman 27 G2 Texas, SW USA
's-Hertogenbosch 64 C4 Fr. Bois-le-Duc, Ger. Herzogenbusch. Noord-Brabant, S Netherlands
Shetland Islands 66 D1 island group NE Scotland, UK
Shibarghān see Sheberghān
Shiberghān see Sheberghān
Shibetsu 108 D2 var. Sibetu. Hokkaidō, NE Japan
Shibh Jazīrat Sīnā' see Sinai
Shibushi-wan 109 B8 bay SW Japan
Shigatse see Xigazê
Shih-chia-chuang see Shijiazhuang
Shihezi 104 C2 Xinjiang Uygur Zizhiqu, NW China
Shihmen see Shijiazhuang
Shijiazhuang 106 C4 var. Shih-chia-chuang; prev. Shihmen. Hebei, E China
Shikārpur 112 B3 Sind, S Pakistan
Shikoku 109 C7 var. Sikoku. Island SW Japan
Shikoku Basin 103 F2 var. Sikoku Basin. Undersea feature N Philippine Sea
Shikotan, Ostrov 108 E2 Jap. Shikotan-tō. Island NE Russian Federation
Shilabo 51 D5 E Ethiopia
Shiliguri 113 F3 prev. Siliguri. West Bengal, NE India
Shilka 93 F4 river S Russian Federation
Shillong 113 G3 E India
Shimbir Berris see Shimbiris
Shimbiris 50 E4 var. Shimbir Berris. Mountain N Somalia
Shimoga 110 C2 Karnātaka, W India
Shimonoseki 109 A7 var. Simonoseki; hist. Akamagaseki, Bakan. Yamaguchi, Honshū, SW Japan
Shinano-gawa 109 C5 var. Sinano Gawa. River Honshū, C Japan
Shīndand 100 D4 Farāh, W Afghanistan
Shingū 109 C6 var. Singū. Wakayama, Honshū, SW Japan
Shinjō 108 D4 var. Sinzyô. Yamagata, Honshū, C Japan
Shinyanga 51 C7 Shinyanga, NW Tanzania
Shiprock 26 C1 New Mexico, SW USA
Shīrāz 98 D4 var. Shīrāz. Fārs, S Iran
Shivpuri 112 D3 Madhya Pradesh, C India
Shizugawa 108 D4 Miyagi, Honshū, NE Japan
Shizuoka 109 D6 var. Sizuoka. Shizuoka, Honshū, S Japan
Shklov 85 D6 Rus. Shklov. Mahilyowskaya Voblasts', E Belarus
Shkodër 79 C5 var. Shkodra, It. Scutari, SCr. Skadar. Shkodër, NW Albania
Shkodra see Shkodër
Shkumbinit, Lumi i 79 C6 var. Shkumbi, Shkumbin. River C Albania
Shkumbi see Shkumbinit, Lumi i
Shkumbin see Shkumbinit, Lumi i
Sholāpur see Solāpur
Shostka 87 F1 Sums'ka Oblast', NE Ukraine
Show Low 26 B2 Arizona, SW USA
Shpola 87 E3 Cherkas'ka Oblast', N Ukraine
Shreveport 20 A2 Louisiana, S USA
Shrewsbury 67 D6 hist. Scrobesbyrig'. W England, UK
Shu 92 C5 Kaz. Shū. Zhambyl, SE Kazakhstan
Shuang-liao see Liaoyuan
Shumagin Islands 14 B3 island group Alaska, USA
Shumen 82 D2 Shumen, NE Bulgaria
Shumilina 85 E5 Rus. Shumilino. Vitsyebskaya Voblasts', NE Belarus

Shuqrah 99 B7 var. Shaqrā. SW Yemen
Shwebo 114 B3 Sagaing, C Myanmar
Shyichy 85 C7 Rus. Shiichi. Homyel'skaya Voblasts', SE Belarus
Shymkent 92 B5 prev. Chimkent. Yuzhnyy Kazakhstan, S Kazakhstan
Shyshchytsy 85 C6 Rus. Shishchitsy. Minskaya Voblasts', C Belarus
Si see Xi Jiang
Siam, Gulf of see Thailand, Gulf of
Sian see Xi'an
Siang see Brahmaputra
Siangtan see Xiangtan
Šiauliai 84 B4 Ger. Schaulen. Šiauliai, N Lithuania
Sibay 89 D6 Respublika Bashkortostan, W Russian Federation
Šibenik 116 B4 It. Sebenico. Šibenik-Knin, S Croatia
Siberia see Sibir'
Siberut, Pulau 116 A4 prev. Siberoet. Island Kepulauan Mentawai, W Indonesia
Sibetu see Shibetsu
Sibi 112 B2 Baluchistān, SW Pakistan
Sibir' 93 E3 var. Siberia. Physical region NE Russian Federation
Sibiti 55 B6 La Lékoumou, S Congo
Sibiu 86 B4 Ger. Hermannstadt, Hung. Nagyszeben. Sibiu, C Romania
Sibolga 116 B3 Sumatera, W Indonesia
Sibu 116 D3 Sarawak, East Malaysia
Sibut 54 C4 prev. Fort-Sibut. Kémo, S Central African Republic
Sibuyan Sea 117 E2 sea C Philippines
Sichon 115 C6 var. Ban Sichon, Si Chon. Nakhon Si Thammarat, SW Thailand
Sichuan 106 B5 var. Chuan, Sichuan Sheng, Ssu-ch'uan, Szechuan, Szechwan. Admin. region province C China
Sichuan Pendi 106 B5 depression C China
Sichuan Sheng see Sichuan
Sicilia 75 C7 Eng. Sicily; anc. Trinacria. Island Italy, C Mediterranean Sea
Sicilian Channel see Sicily, Strait of
Sicily see Sicilia
Sicily, Strait of 75 B7 var. Sicilian Channel. Strait C Mediterranean Sea
Sicuani 39 E4 Cusco, S Peru
Sidári 82 A4 Kérkyra, Iónioi Nísoi, Greece, C Mediterranean Sea
Sidas 116 C4 Borneo, C Indonesia
Siderno 75 D7 Calabria, SW Italy
Sîdi Barrâni 50 A1 NW Egypt
Sidi Bel Abbès 48 D2 var. Sidi bel Abbès, Sidi-Bel-Abbès. NW Algeria
Sidirókastro 82 C3 prev. Sidhirókastron. Kentrikí Makedonía, NE Greece
Sidley, Mount 132 B4 mountain Antarctica
Sidney 22 D1 Montana, NW USA
Sidney 22 D4 Nebraska, C USA
Sidney 18 D4 Ohio, N USA
Sidon see Saïda
Sidra see Surt
Siedlce 76 E3 Ger. Sedlez, Rus. Sedlets. Mazowieckie, C Poland
Siegen 72 B4 Nordrhein-Westfalen, W Germany
Siemiatycze 76 E3 Podlaskie, NE Poland
Siena 74 B3 Fr. Sienne; anc. Saena Julia. Toscana, C Italy
Sieradz 76 C4 Łódzkie, C Poland
Sierpc 76 D3 Mazowieckie, C Poland
Sierra de Soconusco see Sierra Madre
Sierra Leone 52 C4 Country W Africa
Sierra Leone Basin 44 C4 undersea feature E Atlantic Ocean
Sierra Leone Ridge see Sierra Leone Rise
Sierra Leone Rise 44 C4 var. Sierra Leone Ridge, Sierra Leone Schwelle. Undersea feature E Atlantic Ocean
Sierra Leone Schwelle see Sierra Leone Rise
Sierra Madre 30 B2 var. Sierra de Soconusco. Mountain range Guatemala/Mexico
Sierra Madre see Madre Occidental, Sierra
Sierra Nevada 25 C6 mountain range W USA
Sierra Pacaraima see Pakaraima Mountains
Sierra Vieja 26 D3 mountain range Texas, SW USA
Sierra Vista 26 B3 Arizona, SW USA
Sífnos 83 C6 anc. Siphnos. Island Kykládes, Greece, Aegean Sea
Sigli 116 A3 Sumatera, W Indonesia
Siglufjördhur 61 E4 Nordhurland Vestra, N Iceland
Signal Peak 26 A2 mountain Arizona, SW USA
Signan see Xi'an
Signy 132 A2 UK research station South Orkney Islands, Antarctica
Siguatepeque 30 C2 Comayagua, W Honduras
Siguiri 52 D4 Haute-Guinée, NE Guinea
Siilinjärvi 62 E4 Itä-Suomi, C Finland
Siirt 95 F4 var. Sert; anc. Tigranocerta. Siirt, SE Turkey
Sikandarabad see Secunderābād
Sikasso 52 D4 Sikasso, S Mali
Sikeston 23 H5 Missouri, C USA
Sikhote-Alin', Khrebet 93 G4 mountain range SE Russian Federation
Siking see Xi'an
Siklós 77 C7 Baranya, SW Hungary
Sikoku see Shikoku
Sikoku Basin see Shikoku Basin
Šilalė 84 B4 Šilalė, W Lithuania
Silchar 113 G3 Assam, NE India
Silesia 76 B4 physical region SW Poland
Silifke 94 C4 anc. Seleucia. İçel, S Turkey
Siling Co 104 C5 lake W China
Silinhot see Xilinhot
Silistra 82 E1 var. Silistria; anc. Durostorum. Silistra, NE Bulgaria
Silistria see Silistra
Siljan 63 C6 lake C Sweden
Sillamäe 84 E2 Ger. Sillamäggi. Ida-Virumaa, NE Estonia
Šilutė 84 B4 Ger. Heydekrug. Šilutė, W Lithuania
Silvan 95 F4 var. Diyarbakır, SE Turkey

Silverek 95 E4 Şanlıurfa, SE Turkey
Simanggang see Sri Aman
Simanichy 85 C7 Rus. Simonichi. Homyel'skaya Voblasts', SE Belarus
Simav 94 B3 Kütahya, W Turkey
Simav Çayı 94 A3 river NW Turkey
Simeto 75 C7 river Sicilia, Italy, C Mediterranean Sea
Simeulue, Pulau 116 A3 island NW Indonesia
Simferopol' 87 F5 Respublika Krym, S Ukraine
Simitli 82 C3 Blagoevgrad, SW Bulgaria
Şimleu Silvaniei 86 B3 Hung. Szilágysomlyó; prev. Şimlǎul Silvaniei, Şimleul Silvaniei. Sǎlaj, NW Romania
Simonoseki see Shimonoseki
Simpelveld 65 D6 Limburg, SE Netherlands
Simplon Pass 73 B8 pass S Switzerland
Simpson see Fort Simpson
Simpson Desert 126 B4 desert Northern Territory/South Australia
Sīnā' see Sinai
Sinai 50 C2 var. Sinai Peninsula, Ar. Shibh Jazīrat Sīnā', Sīnā'. Physical region NE Egypt
Sinaia 86 C4 Prahova, SE Romania
Sinai Peninsula see Sinai
Sinano Gawa see Shinano-gawa
Sincelejo 36 B2 Sucre, NW Colombia
Sind 112 B3 var. Sindh. Admin. region province SE Pakistan
Sindelfingen 73 B6 Baden-Württemberg, SW Germany
Sindh see Sind
Sindi 84 D2 Ger. Zintenhof. Pärnumaa, SW Estonia
Sines 70 B4 Setúbal, S Portugal
Singan see Xi'an
Singapore 116 A1 Country SE Asia
Singapore 116 B3 country capital (Singapore) S Singapore
Singen 73 B6 Baden-Württemberg, S Germany
Singida 51 C7 Singida, C Tanzania
Singkang 117 E4 Sulawesi, C Indonesia
Singkawang 116 C3 Borneo, C Indonesia
Singora see Songkhla
Singū see Shingū
Sining see Xining
Siniscola 75 A5 Sardegna, Italy, C Mediterranean Sea
Sinj 78 B4 Split-Dalmacija, SE Croatia
Sinkiang see Xinjiang Uygur Zizhiqu
Sinkiang Uighur Autonomous Region see Xinjiang Uygur Zizhiqu
Sinnamarie see Sinnamary
Sinnamary 37 H3 var. Sinnamarie. N French Guiana
Sînnicolau Mare see Sânnicolau Mare
Sinoie, Lacul 86 D5 prev. Lacul Sinoe. Lagoon SE Romania
Sinop 94 D2 anc. Sinope. Sinop, N Turkey
Sinsheim 73 B6 Baden-Württemberg, SW Germany
Sint Maarten 33 G3 Eng. Saint Martin. Island N Netherlands Antilles
Sint-Michielsgestel 64 C4 Noord-Brabant, S Netherlands
Sint-Niklaas 65 B5 Fr. Saint-Nicolas. Oost-Vlaanderen, N Belgium
Sint-Pieters-Leeuw 65 B6 Vlaams Brabant, C Belgium
Sintra 70 B3 prev. Cintra. Lisboa, W Portugal
Sinujiif 51 E5 Nugaal, NE Somalia
Sinus Aelaniticus see Aqaba, Gulf of
Sinyang see Xinyang
Sinzyô see Shinjō
Sion 73 A7 Ger. Sitten; anc. Sedunum. Valais, SW Switzerland
Sioux City 23 F3 Iowa, C USA
Sioux Falls 23 F3 South Dakota, N USA
Siping 106 D3 var. Ssu-p'ing, Szeping; prev. Ssu-p'ing-chieh. Jilin, NE China
Siple, Mount 132 A4 mountain Siple Island, Antarctica
Siquirres 31 E4 Limón, E Costa Rica
Siracusa 75 D7 Eng. Syracuse. Sicilia, Italy, C Mediterranean Sea
Sir Darya see Syr Darya
Sir Edward Pellew Group 126 B2 island group Northern Territory, NE Australia
Siret 86 C3 var. Siretul, Ger. Sereth, Rus. Seret, Ukr. Siret. River Romania/Ukraine
Siret see Siret
Siretul see Siret
Sirikit Reservoir 114 C4 lake N Thailand
Sīrjān 98 D4 prev. Sa'īdābād. Kermān, S Iran
Sirna see Sýrna
Şırnak 95 F4 Şırnak, SE Turkey
Síros see Sýros
Sirte see Surt
Sirte, Gulf of see Surt, Khalīj
Siros 116 C4 Borneo, C Indonesia
Sisak 78 B3 var. Siscia, ger. Sissek, Hung. Sziszek; anc. Segestica. Sisak-Moslavina, C Croatia
Siscia see Sisak
Sisimiut 60 C3 var. Holsteinborg, Holsteinsborg, Holstensborg, Holstenborg. S Greenland
Sissek see Sisak
Sistema Penibético see Béticos, Sistemas
Sitas 83 D8 var. Sitía. Kriti, Greece, E Mediterranean Sea
Sitges 71 G2 Cataluña, NE Spain
Sitía see Siteía
Sittang 114 B4 var. Sittoung. River S Myanmar
Sittard 65 D5 Limburg, SE Netherlands
Sittoung see Sittang
Sittwe 114 A3 var. Akyab. Arakan State, W Myanmar
Siuna 30 D3 Región Autónoma Atlántico Norte, NE Nicaragua
Siut see Asyūţ

Sivas 94 D3 anc. Sebastia, Sebaste. Sivas, C Turkey
Sivers'kyy Donets' see Donets
Siwa 50 A2 var. Sīwah. NW Egypt
Sīwah see Siwa
Six-Fours-les-Plages 69 D6 Var, SE France
Siyäzän 95 H2 Rus. Siazan'. NE Azerbaijan
Sizuoka see Shizuoka
Sjar see Sääre
Sjælland B8 Eng. Zealand, Ger. Seeland. Island E Denmark
Sjenica 79 D5 Turk. Seniça. Serbia, SW Serbia and Montenegro (Yugo.)
Skadar see Shkodër
Skagerak see Skagerrak
Skagerrak 63 A6 var. Skagerak. Channel N Europe
Skagit River 24 B1 river Washington, NW USA
Skalka 62 C3 lake N Sweden
Skarżysko-Kamienna 76 D4 Świętokrzyskie, C Poland
Skaudvilė 84 B4 Tauragė, SW Lithuania
Skegness 67 E6 E England, UK
Skellefteå 62 D4 Västerbotten, N Sweden
Skellefteälven 62 C4 river N Sweden
Ski 63 B6 Akershus, S Norway
Skíathos 83 C5 Skíathos, Vóreioi Sporádes, Greece, Aegean Sea
Skidal' 85 B5 Rus. Skidel'. Hrodzyenskaya Voblasts', W Belarus
Skierniewice 76 D3 Łódzkie, C Poland
Skiftet 84 C1 Fin. Kihti. Strait Gulf of Bothnia/Gulf of Finland
Skíros see Skýros
Skópelos 83 C5 Skópelos, Vóreioi Sporádes, Greece, Aegean Sea
Skopje 79 D6 var. Üsküb, Turk. Üsküp; prev. Skoplje, anc. Scupi. Country capital (FYR Macedonia) N FYR Macedonia
Skoplje see Skopje
Skovorodino 93 F4 Amurskaya Oblast', SE Russian Federation
Skuodas 84 B3 Ger. Schoden, Pol. Szkudy. Skuodas, NW Lithuania
Skye, Isle of 66 B3 island NW Scotland, UK
Skýros 83 C5 var. Skíros. Skýros, Vóreioi Sporádes, Greece, Aegean Sea
Skýros 83 C5 var. Skíros; anc. Scyros. Island Vóreioi Sporádes, Greece, Aegean Sea
Slagelse 63 B7 Vestsjælland, E Denmark
Slatina 86 B5 Olt, S Romania
Slatina 78 C3 Hung. Szlatina, prev. Podravska Slatina. Virovtica-Podravina, NE Croatia
Slavonia see Požega
Slavonski Brod 78 C3 Ger. Brod, Hung. Bród; prev. Brod, Brod na Savi. Brod-Posavina, NE Croatia
Slavuta 86 C2 Khmel'nyts'ka Oblast', NW Ukraine
Slawharad 85 E7 Rus. Slavgorod. Mahilyowskaya Voblasts', E Belarus
Sławno 76 C2 Zachodniopomorskie, NW Poland
Sléibhte Chill Mhantáin see Wicklow Mountains
Slēmāní see As Sulaymānīyah
Sliema 80 B5 N Malta
Sligeach see Sligo
Sligo 67 A5 Ir. Sligeach. NW Ireland
Sliven 82 D2 var. Slivno. Sliven, C Bulgaria
Slivnitsa 82 B2 Sofiya, W Bulgaria
Slivno see Sliven
Slobozia 86 C5 Ialomiţa, SE Romania
Slonim 85 B6 Pol. Slonim, Rus. Slonim. Hrodzyenskaya Voblasts', W Belarus
Slovakia 77 C6 Ger. Slowakei, Hung. Szlovákia, Slvk. Slovensko. Country C Europe
Slovak Ore Mountains see Slovenské rudohorie
Slovenia 73 D8 Ger. Slowenien, Slvn. Slovenija. Country SE Europe
Slovenské rudohorie 77 D6 Eng. Slovak Ore Mountains, Ger. Slowakisches Erzgebirge, Ungarisches Erzgebirge. Mountain range C Slovakia
Slov"yans'k 87 G3 Rus. Slavyansk. Donets'ka Oblast', E Ukraine
Slowakisches Erzgebirge see Slovenské rudohorie
Słubice 76 B3 Ger. Frankfurt. Lubuskie, W Poland
Sluch 86 D1 river NW Ukraine
Słupsk 76 C2 Ger. Stolp. Pomorskie, N Poland
Slutsk 85 C6 Rus. Slutsk. Minskaya Voblasts', S Belarus
Smallwood Reservoir 17 F2 lake Newfoundland and Labrador, S Canada
Smara 48 B3 var. Es Semara. N Western Sahara
Smarhon' 85 C5 Pol. Smorgonie, Rus. Smorgon'. Hrodzyenskaya Voblasts', W Belarus
Smederevo 78 D4 Ger. Semendria. Serbia, N Serbia and montenegro (Yugo.)
Smederevska Palanka 78 D4 Serbia, C Serbia and Montenegro (Yugo.)
Smila 87 E2 Rus. Smela. Cherkas'ka Oblast', C Ukraine
Smiltene 84 D3 Ger. Smilten. Valka, N Latvia
Smola 62 A4 island W Norway
Smolensk 89 A5 Smolenskaya Oblast', W Russian Federation
Sněžka 76 B4 Ger. Schneekoppe. Mountain N Czech Republic

INDEX

Śniardwy, Jezioro 114 D2 *Ger.* Spirdingsee. *Lake* NE Poland
Snina 77 E5 *Hung.* Szinna. Prešovský Kraj, E Slovakia
Snowdonia 67 C6 *mountain range* NW Wales, UK
Snyder 27 F3 Texas, SW USA
Sobradinho, Represa de 41 F2 *var.* Barragem de Sobradinho. *Reservoir* E Brazil
Sochi 89 A7 Krasnodarskiy Kray, SW Russian Federation
Société, Archipel de la 123 G4 *var.* Archipel de Tahiti, Îles de la Société, *Eng.* Society Islands. *Island group* W French Polynesia
Society Islands *see* Société, Archipel de la
Socorro 26 D2 New Mexico, SW USA
Socorro, Isla 28 B5 *island* W Mexico
Socotra *see* Suquṭrā
Soc Trăng 115 D6 *var.* Khanh. Soc Trăng, S Vietnam
Socuéllamos 71 E3 Castilla-La Mancha, C Spain
Sodankylä 62 D3 Lappi, N Finland
Sodari *see* Sodiri
Söderhamn 63 C5 Gävleborg, C Sweden
Södertälje 63 C6 Stockholm, C Sweden
Sodiri 50 B4 *var.* Sawdirī, Sodari. Northern Kordofan, C Sudan
Sofia *see* Sofiya
Sofiya 82 C2 *var.* Sophia, *Eng.* Sofia; *Lat.* Serdica. *Country capital* (Bulgaria) Sofiya-Grad, W Bulgaria
Sogamoso 36 B3 Boyacá, C Colombia
Sognefjorden 63 A5 *fjord* NE North Sea
Sohâg 50 B2 *var.* Sawhāj, Suliag. C Egypt
Sohar *see* Şuḩār
Sohm Plain 44 B3 *undersea feature* NW Atlantic Ocean
Sohrau *see* Żory
Sokal' 86 C2 *Rus.* Sokal. L'viv's'ka Oblast', NW Ukraine
Söke 94 A4 Aydın, SW Turkey
Sokhumi 95 E1 *Rus.* Sukhumi. NW Georgia
Sokodé 53 F4 C Togo
Sokol 88 C4 Vologodskaya Oblast', NW Russian Federation
Sokółka 76 E3 Białystok, NE Poland
Sokolov 77 A5 *Ger.* Falkenau an der Eger; *prev.* Falknov nad Ohří. Karlovarský Kraj, W Czech Republic
Sokone 52 B3 W Senegal
Sokoto 53 F4 *river* NW Nigeria
Sokoto 53 F3 Sokoto, NW Nigeria
Sokotra *see* Suquṭrā
Solāpur 102 B3 *var.* Sholāpur. Mahārāshtra, W India
Solca 86 C3 *Ger.* Solka. Suceava, N Romania
Sol, Costa del 70 D5 *coastal region* S Spain
Soldeu 69 B7 NE Andorra
Solec Kujawski 76 C3 Kujawsko-pomorskie, C Poland
Soledad, Isla *see* East Falkland
Soledad 36 B1 Anzoátegui, NE Venezuela
Solikamsk 92 C3 Permskaya Oblast', NW Russian Federation
Solingen 72 A4 Nordrhein-Westfalen, W Germany
Sollentuna 63 C6 Stockholm, C Sweden
Solok 116 B4 Sumatera, W Indonesia
Solomon Islands 122 C3 *prev.* British Solomon Islands Protectorate. *Country* W Pacific Ocean
Solomon Islands 122 C3 *island group* PNG/Solomon Islands
Solomon Sea 122 B3 *sea* W Pacific Ocean
Soltau 72 B3 Niedersachsen, NW Germany
Sol'tsy 88 A4 Novgorodskaya Oblast', W Russian Federation
Solwezi 56 D2 North Western, NW Zambia
Sōma 108 D4 Fukushima, Honshū, C Japan
Somalia 51 D5 *Som.* Jamuuriyada Demuqraadiga Soomaaliyeed, Soomaaliya; *prev.* Italian Somaliland, Somaliland Protectorate. *Country* E Africa
Somali Basin 47 E5 *undersea feature* W Indian Ocean
Sombor 78 C3 *Hung.* Zombor. Serbia, NW Serbia and Montenegro (Yugo.)
Someren 65 D5 Noord-Brabant, SE Netherlands
Somerset 20 A5 *var.* Somerset Village. W Bermuda
Somerset 18 C5 Kentucky, S USA
Somerset Island 15 F2 *island* Queen Elizabeth Islands, Nunavut, NW Canada
Somerset Island 20 A5 *island* W Bermuda
Somerset Village *see* Somerset
Somers Islands *see* Bermuda
Somerton 26 A2 Arizona, SW USA
Someş 86 B3 *var.* Somesch, Someşul, Szamos, *Ger.* Samosch. *River* Hungary/Romania
Somesch *see* Someş
Someşul *see* Someş
Somme 68 C2 *river* N France
Somotillo 30 C3 Chinandega, NW Nicaragua
Somoto 30 D3 Madriz, NW Nicaragua
Songea 51 C8 Ruvuma, S Tanzania
Sông Hông Hà *see* Red River
Songkhla 115 C7 *var.* Songkla, *Mal.* Singora. Songkhla, SW Thailand
Songkla *see* Songkhla
Sông Srepok *see* Srêpôk, Tônle
Sông Tiên Giang *see* Mekong
Sonoran Desert 26 A3 *var.* Desierto de Altar. *Desert* Mexico/USA *see also* Altar, Desierto de
Sonsonate 30 B3 Sonsonate, W El Salvador
Soochow *see* Suzhou
Sop Hao 114 D3 Houaphan, N Laos
Sophia *see* Sofiya
Sopot 76 C2 *Ger.* Zoppot. Plovdiv, C Bulgaria
Sopron 77 B6 *Ger.* Ödenburg. Győr-Moson-Sopron, NW Hungary
Sorgues 69 D6 Vaucluse, SE France
Sorgun 94 D3 Yozgat, C Turkey
Soria 71 E2 Castilla-León, N Spain
Soroca 86 D3 *Rus.* Soroki. N Moldova
Sorong 117 F4 Papua, E Indonesia
Sørøy *see* Sørøya
Sørøya 62 C2 *var.* Sørøy. *Island* N Norway
Sortavala 88 B3 Respublika Kareliya, NW Russian Federation
Sotavento, Ilhas de 52 A3 *var.* Leeward Islands. *Island group* S Cape Verde
Sotkamo 62 E4 Oulu, C Finland
Souanké 55 B5 La Sangha, NW Congo
Soueida *see* As Suwaydā'
Soufli 82 D3 *prev.* Souflíon. Anatolikí Makedonía kai Thráki, NE Greece
Soufrière 33 F2 *volcano* S Dominica
Soukhné *see* As Sukhnah
Sŏul 107 E4 *off.* Sŏul-t'ŭkpyŏlsi, *Eng.* Seoul, *Jap.* Keijō; *prev.* Kyŏngsŏng. *Country capital* (South Korea) NW South Korea
Soûr 97 A5 *var.* Şûr; *anc.* Tyre. SW Lebanon
Souris River 23 E1 *var.* Mouse River. *River* Canada/USA
Sourpi 83 B5 Thessalía, C Greece
Sousse 49 F2 *var.* Sūsah. NE Tunisia
South Africa 56 C4 *Afr.* Suid-Afrika. *Country* S Africa
South America 34 *continent*
Southampton 67 D7 *hist.* Hamwih, *Lat.* Clausentum. S England, UK
Southampton Island 15 G3 *island* Nunavut, NE Canada
South Andaman 111 F2 *island* Andaman Islands, India, NE Indian Ocean
South Australia 127 A5 *state* S Australia
South Australian Basin 120 B5 *undersea feature* SW Indian Ocean
South Bend 18 C3 Indiana, N USA
South Beveland *see* Zuid-Beveland
South Bruny Island 127 C8 *island* Tasmania, SE Australia
South Carolina 21 E2 *off.* State of South Carolina; *also known as* The Palmetto State. *State* SE USA
South Carpathians *see* Carpaţii Meridionali
South China Basin 103 E4 *undersea feature* SE South China Sea
South China Sea 102 D4 *Chin.* Nan Hai, *Ind.* Laut Cina Selatan, *Vtn.* Biền Đông. *Sea* SE Asia
South Dakota 22 D2 *off.* State of South Dakota; *also known as* The Coyote State, Sunshine State. *State* N USA
Southeast Indian Ridge 119 D7 *undersea feature* Indian Ocean/Pacific Ocean
Southeast Pacific Basin 131 E5 *var.* Belling Hausen Mulde. *Undersea feature* SE Pacific Ocean
South East Point 127 C7 *headland* Victoria, S Australia
Southend-on-Sea 67 E6 E England, UK
Southern Alps 129 B6 *mountain range* South Island, NZ
Southern Cook Islands 123 F4 *island group* S Cook Islands
Southern Cross 125 B6 Western Australia
Southern Indian Lake 15 F4 *lake* Manitoba, C Canada
Southern Ocean 45 B7 *ocean*
Southern Uplands 66 C4 *mountain range* S Scotland, UK
South Fiji Basin 120 D4 *undersea feature* S Pacific Ocean
South Geomagnetic Pole 132 B3 *pole* Antarctica
South Georgia 35 D8 *island* South Georgia and the South Sandwich Islands, SW Atlantic Ocean
South Goulburn Island 124 E2 *island* Northern Territory, N Australia
South Huvadhu Atoll 110 A5 *var.* Gaafu Dhaalu Atoll. *Atoll* S Maldives
South Indian Basin 119 D7 *undersea feature* Indian Ocean/Pacific Ocean
South Island 129 C6 *island* S NZ
South Korea 107 E4 *Kor.* Taehan Min'guk. *Country* E Asia
South Lake Tahoe 25 C5 California, W USA
South Orkney Islands 132 A2 *island group* Antarctica
South Ossetia 95 F2 *former autonomous region* SW Georgia
South Pacific Basin *see* Southwest Pacific Basin
South Platte River 22 D4 *river* Colorado/Nebraska, C USA
South Pole 132 B3 *pole* Antarctica
South Sandwich Islands 35 D8 *island group* SE South Georgia and South Sandwich Islands
South Sandwich Trench 35 E8 *undersea feature* SW Atlantic Ocean
South Shetland Islands 132 A2 *island group* Antarctica
South Shields 66 D4 NE England, UK
South Sioux City 23 F3 Nebraska, C USA
South Taranaki Bight 128 C4 *bight* SE Tasman Sea
South Tasmania Plateau *see* Tasman Plateau
South Uist 66 B3 *island* NW Scotland, UK
South West Cape 129 A8 *headland* Stewart Island, NZ
Southwest Indian Ocean Ridge *see* Southwest Indian Ridge
Southwest Indian Ridge 119 B6 *var.* Southwest Indian Ocean Ridge. *Undersea feature* SW Indian Ocean
Southwest Pacific Basin 121 E4 *var.* South Pacific Basin. *Undersea feature* SE Pacific Ocean
Sovereign Base Area 80 C5 *UK military installation* E Cyprus
Sovereign Base Area 80 C5 *UK military installation* S Cyprus
Soweto 56 D4 Gauteng, NE South Africa
Spain 70 D3 *Sp.* España; *anc.* Hispania, Iberia, *Lat.* Hispana. *Country* SW Europe
Spanish Town 32 B5 *hist.* St.Iago de la Vega. C Jamaica
Sparks 25 C5 Nevada, W USA
Spartanburg 21 E1 South Carolina, SE USA
Spárti 83 B6 *Eng.* Sparta. Pelopónnisos, S Greece
Spearfish 22 D2 South Dakota, N USA
Speightstown 33 G1 NW Barbados
Spencer 23 F3 Iowa, C USA
Spencer Gulf 127 B6 *gulf* South Australia
Spey 66 C3 *river* NE Scotland, UK
Spiess Seamount 45 C7 *undersea feature* S Atlantic Ocean
Spijkenisse 64 B4 Zuid-Holland, SW Netherlands
Spíli 83 C8 Kríti, Greece, E Mediterranean Sea
Spīn Būldak 101 E5 Kandahār, S Afghanistan
Spirdingsee *see* Śniardwy, Jezioro
Spitsbergen 61 F2 *island* NW Svalbard
Split 78 B4 *It.* Spalato. Split-Dalmacija, S Croatia
Spokane 24 C2 Washington, NW USA
Spratly Islands 116 B2 *Chin.* Nansha Qundao. *Disputed territory* SE Asia
Spree 72 D4 *river* E Germany
Springfield 18 B4 *state capital* Illinois, N USA
Springfield 19 G3 Massachusetts, NE USA
Springfield 23 G5 Missouri, C USA
Springfield 18 C4 Ohio, N USA
Springfield 24 B3 Oregon, NW USA
Spring Garden 37 F2 NE Guyana
Spring Hill 21 E4 Florida, SE USA
Springs Junction 129 C5 West Coast, South Island, NZ
Springsure 126 D4 Queensland, E Australia
Spruce Knob 19 E4 *mountain* West Virginia, NE USA
Srbinje *see* Foča
Srbobran *see* Donji Vakuf
Srebrenica 78 C4 Republika Srpska, E Bosnia and Herzegovina
Sredets 82 E2 *prev.* Grudovo. Burgas, E Bulgaria
Sredets 82 D2 *prev.* Syulemeshlii. Stara Zagora, C Bulgaria
Srednerusskaya Vozvyshennost' 87 G1 *Eng.* Central Russian Upland. *Mountain range* W Russian Federation
Srednesibirskoye Ploskogor'ye 92 D3 *var.* Central Siberian Uplands, *Eng.* Central Siberian Plateau. *Mountain range* N Russian Federation
Sremska Mitrovica 78 C3 *prev.* Mitrovica, *Ger.* Mitrowitz. Serbia, NW Serbia and Montenegro(Yugo.)
Srêpôk, Tônle 115 E5 *var.* Sông Srepok. *River* Cambodia/Vietnam
Sri Aman 116 C3 *var.* Bandar Sri Aman, Simanggang. Borneo, East Malaysia
Sri Jayawardanapura 110 D3 *var.* Sri Jayawardenepura; *prev.* Kotte. Western Province, W Sri Lanka
Sri Jayawardenepura *see* Sri Jayawardanapura
Srīkākulam 113 F5 Andhra Pradesh, E India
Sri Lanka 110 D3 *prev.* Ceylon. *Country* S Asia
Srpska, Republika 78 B3 *Admin. region republic* NE Bosnia and Herzegovina
Srinagarind Reservoir 115 C5 *reservoir* W Thailand
Ssu-ch'uan *see* Sichuan
Ssu-p'ing *see* Siping
Ssu-p'ing-chieh *see* Siping
Stabroek 65 B5 Antwerpen, N Belgium
Stade 72 B3 Niedersachsen, NW Germany
Stadskanaal 64 E2 Groningen, NE Netherlands
Stafford 67 D6 C England, UK
Staicele 84 D3 Limbaži, N Latvia
Stakhanov 87 H3 Luhans'ka Oblast', E Ukraine
Stalinabad *see* Dushanbe
Stalingrad *see* Volgograd
Stalinobod *see* Dushanbe
Stalin Peak *see* Kommunizm, Qullai
Stalowa Wola 76 E4 Podkarpackie, SE Poland
Stamford 19 F3 Connecticut, NE USA
Stampalia *see* Astypálaia
Stanley 43 D7 *var.* Port Stanley, Puerto Argentino. *Dependent territory capital* (Falkland Islands) East Falkland, Falkland Islands
Stanovoy Khrebet 91 F3 *mountain range* SE Russian Federation
Stanthorpe 127 D5 Queensland, E Australia
Staphorst 64 D2 Overijssel, E Netherlands
Starachowice 76 D4 Świętokrzyskie, C Poland
Stara Pazova 78 D3 *Ger.* Altpasua, *Hung.* Ópazova. Serbia, N Serbia and Montenegro (Yugo.)
Stara Zagora 82 D2 *Lat.* Augusta Trajana. Stara Zagora, C Bulgaria
Starbuck Island 123 G3 *prev.* Volunteer Island. *Island* E Kiribati
Stargard Szczeciński 76 B3 *Ger.* Stargard in Pommern. Zachodniopomorskie, NW Poland
Starobil's'k 87 H2 *Rus.* Starobel'sk. Luhans'ka Oblast', E Ukraine
Starobyn 85 C7 *Rus.* Starobin. Minskaya Voblasts', S Belarus
Starogard Pomorskie 76 C2 *Ger.* Preussisch-Stargard. Pomorskie, N Poland
Starokostyantyniv 86 D2 *Rus.* Starokonstantinov. Khmel'nyts'ka Oblast', NW Ukraine
Starominskaya 89 A7 Krasnodarskiy Kray, SW Russian Federation
Staryya Darohi 85 C6 *Rus.* Staryye Dorogi. Minskaya Voblasts', S Belarus
Staryy Oskol 89 B6 Belgorodskaya Oblast', W Russian Federation
State College 19 E4 Pennsylvania, NE USA
Statesboro 21 E2 Georgia, SE USA
Staunton 19 E5 Virginia, NE USA
Stavanger 63 A6 Rogaland, S Norway
Stavers Island *see* Vostok Island
Stavropol' 89 B7 *prev.* Voroshilovsk. Stavropol'skiy Kray, SW Russian Federation
Steamboat Springs 22 C4 Colorado, C USA
Steenwijk 64 D2 Overijssel, N Netherlands
Steier *see* Steyr
Steinkjer 62 B4 Nord-Trøndelag, C Norway
Stendal 72 C3 Sachsen-Anhalt, C Germany
Stephenville 27 F3 Texas, SW USA
Sterling 22 D4 Colorado, C USA
Sterling 18 B3 Illinois, N USA
Sterlitamak 92 B3 Respublika Bashkortostan, W Russian Federation
Stettiner Haff *see* Szczeciński, Zalew
Stevenage 67 E6 E England, UK
Stevens Point 18 B2 Wisconsin, N USA
Stewart Island 129 A8 *island* S NZ
Steyr 73 D6 *var.* Steier. Oberösterreich, N Austria
Stif *see* Sétif
Stillwater 27 G1 Oklahoma, C USA
Stirling 66 C4 C Scotland, UK
Stjørdalshalsen 62 B4 Nord-Trøndelag, C Norway
Stockach 73 B6 Baden-Württemberg, S Germany
Stockholm 63 C6 *country capital* (Sweden) Stockholm, C Sweden
Stockton 25 B6 California, W USA
Stockton Plateau 27 E4 *plain* Texas, SW USA
Stœng Trêng 115 D5 *prev.* Stung Treng. Stœng Trêng, NE Cambodia
Stoke *see* Stoke-on-Trent
Stoke-on-Trent 67 D6 *var.* Stoke. C England, UK
Stómio 82 B4 Thessalía, C Greece
Stony Tunguska 90 D2 *river* C Russian Federation
Store Bælt *see* Storebælt
Storebælt 63 B8 *var.* Store Bælt, *Eng.* Great Belt, Storebelt. *Channel* Baltic Sea/Kattegat
Storebelt *see* Storebælt
Støren 63 B5 Sør-Trøndelag, S Norway
Storfjorden 61 G2 *fjord* S Norway
Stornoway 88 B2 NW Scotland, UK
Storsjön 63 B5 *lake* C Sweden
Storuman 62 C4 *lake* N Sweden
Storuman 62 C4 Västerbotten, N Sweden
Stowbtsy 85 C6 *Pol.* Stolbce, *Rus.* Stolbtsy. Minskaya Voblasts', C Belarus
Strabane 67 B5 *Ir.* An Srath Bán. N Northern Ireland, UK
Strakonice 77 A5 *Ger.* Strakonitz. Budějovický Kraj, S Czech Republic
Stralsund 72 D2 Mecklenburg-Vorpommern, NE Germany
Stranraer 67 C5 S Scotland, UK
Strasbourg 68 E3 *Ger.* Strassburg; *anc.* Argentoratum. Bas-Rhin, NE France
Strășeni 86 D3 *var.* Strasheny. C Moldova
Strasheny *see* Strășeni
Stratford 128 D4 Taranaki, North Island, NZ
Strathfield 126 E2 New South Wales, SE Australia
Straubing 73 C6 Bayern, SE Germany
Strehaia 86 B5 Mehedinţi, SW Romania
Strelka 92 D4 Krasnoyarskiy Kray, C Russian Federation
Strofilia *see* Strofyliá
Strofyliá 83 C5 *var.* Strofilia. Évvoia, C Greece
Stromboli, Isola 75 D6 *island* Isole Eolie, S Italy
Stromeferry 66 C3 N Scotland, UK
Strömstad 63 B6 Västra Götaland, S Sweden
Strömsund 62 C4 Jämtland, C Sweden
Struga 79 D6 SW FYR Macedonia
Strumica 79 E6 E FYR Macedonia
Strumyani 82 C3 Blagoevgrad, SW Bulgaria
Strymónas 82 C3 *Bul.* Struma. *River* Bulgaria/Greece *see also* Struma
Stryy 86 B2 L'vivs'ka Oblast', NW Ukraine
Studholme 129 B6 Canterbury, South Island, NZ
Sturgis 22 D3 South Dakota, N USA
Stuttgart 73 B6 Baden-Württemberg, SW Germany
Stykkishólmur 61 E4 Vesturland, W Iceland
Styr 86 C1 *Rus.* Styr'. *River* Belarus/Ukraine
Su *see* Jiangsu
Suakin 50 C3 *var.* Sawakin. Red Sea, NE Sudan
Subačius 84 C4 Kupiškis, NE Lithuania
Subaykhān 96 E3 Dayr az Zawr, E Syria
Subotica 78 D2 *Ger.* Maria-Theresiopel, *Hung.* Szabadka. Serbia, N Serbia and Montenegro (Yugo.)
Suceava 86 C3 *Ger.* Suczawa, *Hung.* Szucsava. Suceava, NE Romania
Su-chou *see* Xuzhou
Suchow *see* Xuzhou
Sucre 39 F4 *hist.* Chuquisaca, La Plata. *Country capital* (Bolivia-legal capital) Chuquisaca, S Bolivia
Sudan 50 A4 *Ar.* Jumhuriyat as-Sudan; *prev.* Anglo-Egyptian *Sudan. country* N Africa
Sudbury 16 C4 Ontario, S Canada
Sudd 51 B5 *swamp region* S Sudan
Sudeten 76 B4 *var.* Sudetes, Sudetic Mountains, Cz./Pol. Sudety. *Mountain range* Czech Republic/Poland
Sudetes *see* Sudeten
Sudetic Mountains *see* Sudeten
Sudety *see* Sudeten
Südkarpaten *see* Carpaţii Meridionali
Sue 51 B5 *river* S Sudan
Sueca 71 F3 País Valenciano, E Spain
Sue Wood Bay 20 B5 *bay* W Bermuda
Suez 50 B1 *Ar.* As Suways, El Suweis. NE Egypt
Suez Canal 50 B1 *Ar.* Qanāt as Suways. *Canal* NE Egypt
Suez, Gulf of 50 B2 *Ar.* Khalīj as Suways. *Gulf* NE Egypt
Suğla Gölü 94 C4 *lake* SW Turkey
Şuḩār 99 D5 *var.* Sohar. N Oman
Sühbaatar 105 E1 Selenge, N Mongolia
Suhl 73 C5 Thüringen, C Germany
Suixi 106 C6 Guangdong, S China
Sujāwal 112 B3 Sind, SE Pakistan
Sukabumi 116 C5 *prev.* Soekaboemi. Jawa, C Indonesia
Sukagawa 109 D5 Fukushima, Honshū, C Japan
Sukarnapura *see* Jayapura
Sukhne *see* As Sukhnah
Sukhona 88 C4 *var.* Tot'ma. *River* NW Russian Federation
Sukhumi *see* Sokhumi
Sukkertoppen *see* Maniitsoq
Sukkur 112 B3 Sind, SE Pakistan
Sukumo 109 B7 Kōchi, Shikoku, SW Japan
Sulaimaniya *see* As Sulaymānīyah
Sulaimān Range 112 C2 *mountain range* C Pakistan
Sula, Kepulauan 117 E4 *island group* C Indonesia
Sulawesi 117 E4 *Eng.* Celebes. *Island* C Indonesia
Sulechów 76 B3 *Ger.* Züllichau. Lubuskie, W Poland
Suliag *see* Sohâg
Sullana 38 B2 Piura, NW Peru
Sulphur Springs 27 G2 Texas, SW USA
Sulu Archipelago 117 E3 *island group* SW Philippines
Sulu Sea 117 E2 *Ind.* Laut Sulu. *Sea* SW Philippines
Sulyukta 101 E2 *Kir.* Sülüktü. Oshskaya Oblast', SW Kyrgyzstan
Sumatera 115 B8 *Eng.* Sumatra. *Island* W Indonesia
Sumatra *see* Sumatera
Sumba, Pulau 117 E5 *Eng.* Sandalwood Island; *prev.* Soemba. *Island* Nusa Tenggara, C Indonesia
Sumba, Selat 117 E5 *strait* Nusa Tenggara, S Indonesia
Sumbawanga 51 B7 Rukwa, W Tanzania
Sumbe 56 B2 *prev.* N'Gunza, *Port.* Novo Redondo. Cuanza Sul, W Angola
Sumeih 51 B5 Southern Darfur, S Sudan
Summer Lake 24 B4 *lake* Oregon, NW USA
Summit 93 H5 *mountain* C Gibraltar
Sumqayıt 95 H2 *Rus.* Sumgait. E Azerbaijan
Sumy 87 F2 Sums'ka Oblast', NE Ukraine
Sunbury 127 C7 Victoria, SE Australia
Sunda Islands *see* Greater Sunda Islands
Sunda, Selat 116 B5 *strait* Jawa/Sumatera, SW Indonesia
Sunda Trench *see* Java Trench
Sunderland 66 D4 *var.* Wearmouth. NE England, UK
Sundsvall 63 C5 Västernorrland, C Sweden
Sungaipenuh 116 B4 *prev.* Soengaipenoeh. Sumatera, W Indonesia
Sunnyvale 25 A6 California, W USA
Suntar 93 F3 Respublika Sakha (Yakutiya), NE Russian Federation
Sunyani 53 E5 W Ghana
Suomussalmi 62 E4 Oulu, E Finland
Suŏng 115 D6 Kâmpóng Cham, C Cambodia
Suoyarvi 88 B3 Respublika Kareliya, NW Russian Federation
Supe 38 C3 Lima, W Peru
Superior 18 A1 Wisconsin, N USA
Superior, Lake 18 B1 *Fr.* Lac Supérieur. *Lake* Canada/USA
Suqrah *see* Şawqirah
Suquṭrā 99 C7 *var.* Sokotra, *Eng.* Socotra. *Island* SE Yemen
Şūr 99 E5 NE Oman
Şûr *see* Soûr
Surabaya 116 D5 *prev.* Soerabaja, Surabaja. Jawa, C Indonesia
Surakarta 116 C5 *Eng.* Solo; *prev.* Soerakarta. Jawa, S Indonesia
Šurany 77 C6 *Hung.* Nagysurány. Nitriansky Kraj, SW Slovakia
Sūrat 112 C4 Gujarāt, W India
Suratdhani *see* Surat Thani
Surat Thani 115 C6 *var.* Suratdhani. Surat Thani, SW Thailand
Surazh 85 E5 *Rus.* Surazh. Vitsyebskaya Voblasts', NE Belarus
Surdulica 79 E5 Serbia, SE Serbia and Montenegro (Yugo.)
Süre 65 D7 *var.* Sauer. *River* W Europe *see also* Sauer
Surendranagar 112 C4 Gujarāt, W India
Surfers Paradise 127 E5 Queensland, E Australia
Surgut 92 D3 Khanty-Mansiyskiy Avtonomnyy Okrug, C Russian Federation
Surin 115 D5 Surin, E Thailand
Surinam *see* Suriname
Suriname 37 G3 *var.* Surinam; *prev.* Dutch Guiana, Netherlands Guiana. *Country* N S America
Surkhob 101 F3 *river* C Tajikistan
Surt 49 G2 *var.* Sidra, Sirte. N Libya
Surt, Khalīj 49 F2 *Eng.* Gulf of Sidra, Gulf of Sirti, Sidra. *Gulf* N Libya
Surtsey 61 E5 *island* S Iceland
Suruga-wan 109 D6 *bay* SE Japan
Susa 74 A2 Piemonte, NE Italy
Süsah *see* Sousse
Susanville 25 B5 California, W USA
Susitna 14 C3 Alaska, USA

Susteren 65 D5 Limburg, SE Netherlands
Susuman 93 G3 Magadanskaya Oblast', E Russian Federation
Sutherland 126 E2 New South Wales, SE Australia
Sutlej 112 C2 *river* India/Pakistan
Suur Munamägi 84 D3 *var.* Munamägi, *Ger.* Eier-Berg. *Mountain* SE Estonia
Suur Väin 84 C2 *Ger.* Grosser Sund. *Strait* W Estonia
Suva 123 E4 *country capital* (Fiji) Viti Levu, W Fiji
Suwałki 76 E2 *Lith.* Suvalkai, *Rus.* Suvalki. Podlaskie, NE Poland
Şuwār *see* Aş Şuwār
Suweida *see* As Suwaydā'
Suzhou 106 D5 *var.* Soochow, Su-chou, Suchow; *prev.* Wuhsien. Jiangsu, E China
Svalbard 61 E1 *Norwegian dependency* Arctic Ocean
Svartisen 62 C3 *glacier* C Norway
Svay Riĕng 115 D6 Svay Riĕng, S Cambodia
Sveg 63 B5 Jämtland, C Sweden
Svenstavik 63 C5 Jämtland, C Sweden
Svetlograd 89 B7 Stavropol'skiy Kray, SW Russian Federation
Svilengrad 82 D3 *prev.* Mustafa-Pasha. Khaskovo, S Bulgaria
Svitlovods'k 87 F3 *Rus.* Svetlovodsk. Kirovohrads'ka Oblast', C Ukraine
Svobodnyy 93 G4 Amurskaya Oblast', SE Russian Federation
Svyataya Anna Trough 172 C4 *var.* Saint Anna Trough. *Undersea feature* N Kara Sea
Svyetlahorsk 85 D7 *Rus.* Svetlogorsk. Homyel'skaya Voblasts', SE Belarus
Swabian Jura *see* Schwäbische Alb
Swakopmund 56 B3 Erongo, W Namibia
Swansea 67 C7 *Wel.* Abertawe. S Wales, UK
Swatow *see* Shantou
Swaziland 56 D4 *Country* S Africa
Sweden 62 B4 *Swe.* Sverige. *Country* N Europe
Swed Ormsö *see* Vormsi
Sweetwater 27 G1 Texas, SW USA
Świdnica 76 B4 *Ger.* Schweidnitz. Wałbrzych, SW Poland
Świdwin 76 B2 *Ger.* Schivelbein. Zachodniopomorskie, NW Poland
Świebodzice 76 B4 *Ger.* Freiburg in Schlesien, Swiebodzice. Wałbrzych, SW Poland
Świebodzin 76 B3 *Ger.* Schwiebus. Lubuskie, W Poland
Świecie 76 C3 *Ger.* Schwertberg. Kujawski-pomorskie, C Poland
Swindon 67 D7 S England, UK
Świnoujście 76 B2 *Ger.* Swinemünde. Zachodniopomorskie, NW Poland
Switzerland 73 A7 *Fr.* La Suisse, *Ger.* Schweiz, *It.* Svizzera; *anc.* Helvetia. *Country* C Europe
Sycaminum *see* Hefa
Sydney 126 D1 *state capital* New South Wales, SE Australia
Sydney 17 G4 Cape Breton Island, Nova Scotia, SE Canada
Syedpur *see* Saidpur
Syemyezhava 85 C6 *Rus.* Semezhevo. Minskaya Voblasts', C Belarus
Syene *see* Aswān
Syeverodonets'k 87 H3 *Rus.* Severodonetsk. Luhans'ka Oblast', E Ukraine
Syktyvkar 88 D4 *prev.* Ust'-Sysol'sk. Respublika Komi, NW Russian Federation
Sylhet 113 G3 Chittagong, NE Bangladesh
Synel'nykove 87 G3 Dnipropetrovs'ka Oblast', E Ukraine
Syowa 132 C2 *Japanese research station* Antarctica
Syracuse 19 E3 New York, NE USA
Syrdariya *see* Syr Darya
Syr Darya 92 B4 *var.* Sai Hun, Sir Darya, Syrdarya, *Kaz.* Syrdariya, *Rus.* Syrdar'ya, *Uzb.* Sirdaryo; *anc.* Jaxartes. *River* C Asia
Syria 96 B3 *var.* Siria, Syrie, *Ar.* Al-Jumhūrīyah al-'Arabīyah as-Sūrīyah, Sūrīya. *Country* SW Asia
Syrian Desert 97 D5 *Ar.* Al Hamad, Bādiyat ash Shām. *Desert* SW Asia
Sýrna 83 E7 *var.* Sirna. *Island* Kykládes, Greece, Aegean Sea
Sýros 83 C6 *var.* Síros. *Island* Kykládes, Greece, Aegean Sea
Syvash, Zatoka 87 F4 *Rus.* Zaliv Syvash. *Inlet* S Ukraine
Syzran' 89 C6 Samarskaya Oblast', W Russian Federation
Szamos *see* Someş
Szamotuły 76 B3 Wielkopolskie, C Poland
Szczecin 76 B3 *Eng./Ger.* Stettin. Zachodniopomorskie, NW Poland
Szczecinek 76 B2 *Ger.* Neustettin. Zachodniopomorskie, NW Poland
Szczeciński, Zalew 76 A2 *var.* Stettiner Haff, *Ger.* Oderhaff. *Bay* Germany/Poland
Szczytno 76 D3 *Ger.* Ortelsburg. Olsztyn, NE Poland
Szechuan *see* Sichuan
Szechwan *see* Sichuan
Szeged 77 D7 *Ger.* Szegedin, *Rom.* Seghedin. Csongrád, SE Hungary
Székesfehérvár 77 C6 *Ger.* Stuhlweissenberg; *anc.* Alba Regia. Fejér, W Hungary
Szekszárd 77 C7 Tolna, S Hungary
Szenttamás *see* Srbobran
Szeping *see* Siping
Sziszek *see* Sisak
Szlatina *see* Slatina
Szolnok 77 D6 Jász-Nagykun-Szolnok, C Hungary
Szombathely 77 B6 *Ger.* Steinamanger; *anc.* Sabaria, Savaria. Vas, W Hungary
Szprotawa 76 B4 *Ger.* Sprottau. Lubuskie, W Poland

T

Table Rock Lake 27 G1 *reservoir* Arkansas/Missouri, C USA
Tábor 77 B5 Budějovický Kraj, S Czech Republic
Tabora 51 B7 Tabora, W Tanzania
Tabrīz 98 C2 *var.* Tebriz; *anc.* Tauris. Āzarbāyjān-e Khāvarī, NW Iran
Tabuaeran 123 G2 *prev.* Fanning Island. *Atoll* Line Islands, E Kiribati
Tabūk 98 A4 Tabūk, NW Saudi Arabia
Täby 63 C6 Stockholm, C Sweden
Tachov 77 A5 *Ger.* Tachau. Plzeňský Kraj, W Czech Republic
Tacloban 117 F2 *off.* Tacloban City. Leyte, C Philippines
Tacna 39 E4 Tacna, SE Peru
Tacoma 24 B2 Washington, NW USA
Tacuarembó 42 D4 *prev.* San Fructuoso. Tacuarembó, C Uruguay
Tademaït, Plateau du 48 D3 *plateau* C Algeria
Tadmor *see* Tudmur
Tadmur *see* Tudmur
Tādpatri 110 C2 Andhra Pradesh, E India
Taegu 107 E4 *off.* Taegu-gwangyŏksi, *var.* Daegu, *Jap.* Taikyū. SE South Korea
Taejŏn 107 E4 *off.* Taejŏn-gwangyŏksi, *Jap.* Taiden. C South Korea
Tafassasset, Ténéré du 53 G2 *desert* N Niger
Tafila 97 B7 *var.* Aṭ Ṭafīlah
Taganrog 87 A7 Rostovskaya Oblast', SW Russian Federation
Taganrog, Gulf of 87 G4 *Rus.* Taganrogskiy Zaliv, *Ukr.* Tahanroz'ka Zatoka. *Gulf* Russian Federation/Ukraine
Taguatinga 41 F3 Tocantins, C Brazil
Tagus 70 C3 *Port.* Rio Tejo, *Sp.* Río Tajo. *River* Portugal/Spain
Tagus Plain 58 A4 *undersea feature* E Atlantic Ocean
Tahat 49 E4 *mountain* SE Algeria
Tahiti 123 H4 *island* Îles du Vent, W French Polynesia
Tahlequah 27 G1 Oklahoma, C USA
Tahoe, Lake 25 B5 *lake* California/Nevada, W USA
Tahoua 53 F3 Tahoua, W Niger
T'aichung 106 D6 *Jap.* Taichū; *prev.* Taiwan. C Taiwan
Taieri 129 B7 *river* South Island, NZ
Taihape 128 D4 Manawatu-Wanganui, North Island, NZ
Tailem Bend 127 B7 South Australia
T'ainan 106 D6 *Jap.* Tainan; *prev.* Dainan. S Taiwan
T'aipei 106 D6 *Jap.* Taihoku; *prev.* Daihoku. *Country capital* (Taiwan) N Taiwan
Taiping 116 B3 Perak, Peninsular Malaysia
Taiwan 106 D6 *var.* Formosa, Formo'sa. *Country* E Asia
Taiwan Haihsia *see* Taiwan Strait
Taiwan Strait 106 D6 *var.* Formosa Strait, *Chin.* Taiwan Haihsia, Taiwan Haihsia. *Strait* China/Taiwan
Taiyuan 106 C4 *prev.* T'ai-yuan, T'ai-yüan, Yangku. Shanxi, C China
Ta'izz 99 B7 SW Yemen
Tajikistan 101 E3 *Rus.* Tadzhikistan, *Taj.* Jumhurii Tojikiston; *prev.* Tajik S.S.R. *Country* C Asia
Tak 114 C4 *var.* Rahaeng. Tak, W Thailand
Takao *see* Kaohsiung
Takaoka 109 C5 Toyama, Honshū, SW Japan
Takapuna 128 D2 Auckland, North Island, NZ
Takhiatosh *see* Taxiatosh
Takhtakŭpir *see* Taxtako'pir
Takikawa 108 D2 Hokkaidō, NE Japan
Takla Makan Desert *see* Taklimakan Shamo
Taklimakan Shamo 104 B3 *Eng.* Takla Makan Desert. *Desert* NW China
Takow *see* Kaohsiung
Takutea 123 G4 *island* S Cook Islands
Talachyn 85 D6 *Rus.* Tolochin. Vitsyebskaya Voblasts', NE Belarus
Talamanca, Cordillera de 31 E5 *mountain range* S Costa Rica
Talara 38 B2 Piura, NW Peru
Talas 101 F2 Talasskaya Oblast', NW Kyrgyzstan
Talaud, Kepulauan 117 F3 *island group* E Indonesia
Talavera de la Reina 70 D3 *anc.* Caesarobriga, Talabriga. Castilla-La Mancha, C Spain
Talca 42 B4 Maule, C Chile
Talcahuano 43 B5 Bío Bío, C Chile
Taldykorgan 92 C5 *Kaz.* Taldyqorghan; *prev.* Taldy-Kurgan. Almaty, SE Kazakhstan
Taldy-Kurgan/Taldyqorghan *see* Taldykorgan
Ta-lien *see* Dalian
Taliq-an *see* Tāloqān
Tal'ka 85 C6 *Rus.* Tal'ka. Minskaya Voblasts', C Belarus
Tallahassee 20 D3 *prev.* Muskogean. *State capital* Florida, SE USA
Tall al Abyaḍ *see* At Tall al Abyaḍ
Tallinn 84 D2 *Ger.* Reval, *Rus.* Tallin; *prev.* Revel. *Country capital* (Estonia) Harjumaa, NW Estonia
Tall Kalakh 96 B4 *var.* Tell Kalakh. Ḥimṣ, C Syria
Tallulah 20 B2 Louisiana, S USA
Talnakh 92 D3 Taymyrskiy (Dolgano-Nenetskiy) Avtonomnyy Okrug, N Russian Federation
Tal'ne 87 E3 *Rus.* Tal'noye. Cherkas'ka Oblast', C Ukraine
Taloga 27 F1 Oklahoma, C USA
Tāloqān 101 E3 *var.* Taliq-an. Takhār, NE Afghanistan
Talsi 84 C3 *Ger.* Talsen. Talsi, NW Latvia
Taltal 42 B2 Antofagasta, N Chile
Talvik 62 D2 Finnmark, N Norway

Tamabo, Banjaran 116 D3 *mountain range* East Malaysia
Tamale 53 E4 C Ghana
Tamana 123 E3 *prev.* Rotcher Island. *Atoll* Tungaru, W Kiribati
Tamanrasset 49 E4 *var.* Tamenghest. S Algeria
Tamar 67 C7 *river* SW England, UK
Tamar *see* Tudmur
Tamatave *see* Toamasina
Tamazunchale 29 E4 San Luis Potosí, C Mexico
Tambacounda 52 C3 SE Senegal
Tambov 89 B6 Tambovskaya Oblast', W Russian Federation
Tambura 51 B5 Western Equatoria, SW Sudan
Tamchaket *see* Tâmchekkeṭ
Tâmchekkeṭ 52 C3 *var.* Tamchaket. Hodh el Gharbi, S Mauritania
Tamenghest *see* Tamanrasset
Tamiahua, Laguna de 29 F4 *lagoon* E Mexico
Tamil Nādu 110 C3 *prev.* Madras. *State* SE India
Tam Ky 115 E5 Quang Nam-Đa Nẵng, C Vietnam
Tampa 21 E4 Florida, SE USA
Tampa Bay 21 E4 *bay* Florida, SE USA
Tampere 63 D5 *Swe.* Tammerfors. Länsi-Suomi, W Finland
Tampico 29 E3 Tamaulipas, C Mexico
Tamworth 127 D6 New South Wales, SE Australia
Tana *see* Deatnu/Tenojoki
Tanabe 109 C7 Wakayama, Honshū, SW Japan
Tana Bru 62 D2 Finnmark, N Norway
T'ana Hāyk' 50 C4 *Eng.* Lake Tana. *Lake* NW Ethiopia
Tanais *see* Don
Tanami Desert 124 D3 *desert* Northern Territory, N Australia
Ţăndărei 86 D5 Ialomiţa, SE Romania
Tandil 43 D5 Buenos Aires, E Argentina
Tanega-shima 109 B8 *island* Nansei-shotō, SW Japan
Tane Range 114 B4 *Bur.* Tanen Taunggyi. *Mountain range* W Thailand
Tanezrouft 48 D4 *desert* Algeria/Mali
Ṭanf, Jabal aṭ 96 D4 *mountain* SE Syria
Tanga 47 E5 Tanga, E Tanzania
Tanga 51 C7 *region* E Tanzania
Tangeh-ye Hormoz *see* Hormuz, Strait of
Tanger 48 C2 *var.* Tangiers, Tangier, *Fr./Ger.* Tangerk, *Sp.* Tánger; *anc.* Tingis. NW Morocco
Tangerk *see* Tanger
Tanggula Shan 104 C4 *var.* Dangla, Tangla Range. *Mountain range* W China
Tangier *see* Tanger
Tangiers *see* Tanger
Tangla Range *see* Tanggula Shan
Tangra Yumco 104 B5 *var.* Tangro Tso. *Lake* W China
Tangro Tso *see* Tangra Yumco
Tangshan 106 D3 *var.* T'ang-shan. Hebei, E China
T'ang-shan *see* Tangshan
Tanimbar, Kepulauan 117 F5 *island group* Maluku, E Indonesia
Tanna 122 D4 *island* S Vanuatu
Tannenhof *see* Krynica
Tan-Tan 48 B3 SW Morocco
Tanzania 51 C7 *Swa.* Jamhuri ya Muungano wa Tanzania; *prev.* German East Africa, Tanganyika and Zanzibar. *Country* E Africa
Taoudenit *see* Taoudenni
Taoudenni 52 D2 *var.* Taoudenit. Tombouctou, N Mali
Tapa 84 E2 *Ger.* Taps. Lääne-Virumaa, NE Estonia
Tapachula 29 G5 Chiapas, SE Mexico
Tapajós, Rio 41 E2 *var.* Tapajóz. *River* NW Brazil
Tapajóz *see* Tapajós, Rio
Ţarābulus 49 F2 *var.* Ţarābulus al Gharb, *Eng.* Tripoli. *Country capital* (Libya) NW Libya
Ţarābulus *see* Tripoli
Ţarābulus al Gharb *see* Ţarābulus
Ţarābulus ash Shām *see* Tripoli
Taraclia 86 D4 *Rus.* Tarakliya. S Moldova
Taranaki, Mount 128 C4 *var.* Egmont, Mount. *Mountain* North Island, NZ
Tarancón 71 E3 Castilla-La Mancha, C Spain
Taranto 75 E5 *var.* Tarentum. Puglia, SE Italy
Taranto, Golfo di 75 E6 *Eng.* Gulf of Taranto. *Gulf* S Italy
Tarapoto 38 C2 San Martín, N Peru
Tarare 69 D5 Rhône, E France
Tarascon 69 D6 Bouches-du-Rhône, SE France
Tarawa 122 D2 *atoll* Tungaru, W Kiribati
Taraz 92 C5 *prev.* Aulie Ata, Auliye-Ata, Dzhambul, Zhambyl. Zhambyl, S Kazakhstan
Tarazona 71 E2 Aragón, NE Spain
Tarbes 69 B6 *anc.* Bigorra. Hautes-Pyrénées, S France
Tarcoola 127 A6 South Australia
Taree 127 D6 New South Wales, SE Australia
Tarentum *see* Taranto
Târgovişte 86 C5 *prev.* Tîrgovişte. Dâmboviţa, S Romania
Târgul-Neamţ *see* Târgu-Neamţ
Târgu Mureş 86 B4 *prev.* Oşorhei, Tîrgu Mureş, *Ger.* Neumarkt, *Hung.* Marosvásárhely. Mureş, C Romania
Târgu-Neamţ 86 C3 *var.* Târgul-Neamţ; *prev.* Tîrgu-Neamţ. Neamţ, NE Romania
Târgu Ocna 86 C4 *Hung.* Aknavásár; *prev.* Tîrgu Ocna. Bacău, E Romania

Târgu Secuiesc 86 C4 *Ger.* Neumarkt, Szekler Neumarkt, *Hung.* Kezdivásárhely; *prev.* Chezdi-Oşorheiu, Târgul-Săcuiesc, Tîrgu Secuiesc. Covasna, E Romania
Tarija 39 G5 Tarija, S Bolivia
Tarīm 99 C6 C Yemen
Tarim Basin 102 C2 *basin* NW China
Tarim He 104 B3 *river* NW China
Tarma 38 C3 Junín, C Peru
Tarn 69 C6 *cultural region* S France
Tarn 69 C6 *river* S France
Tarnobrzeg 76 D4 Podkarpackie, SE Poland
Tarnów 77 D5 Małopolskie, S Poland
Tarragona 71 G2 *anc.* Tarraco. Cataluña, E Spain
Tàrrega 71 F2 *var.* Tarrega. Cataluña, NE Spain
Tarsus 94 C4 İçel, S Turkey
Tartu 84 D3 *Ger.* Dorpat; *prev.* Rus. Yurev, Yur'yev. Tartumaa, SE Estonia
Ţarţūs 96 A3 *Fr.* Tartouss; *anc.* Tortosa. Ţarţūs, W Syria
Tarvisio 74 D2 Friuli-Venezia Giulia, NE Italy
Tashi Chho Dzong *see* Thimphu
Tashkent *see* Toshkent
Tash-Kömür 101 F2 *Kir.* Tash-Kömür. Dzhalal-Abadskaya Oblast', W Kyrgyzstan
Tashqurghan *see* Kholm
Tasikmalaya 116 C5 *prev.* Tasikmalaja. Jawa, C Indonesia
Tasman Basin 120 C5 *var.* East Australian Basin. *Undersea feature* S Tasman Sea
Tasman Bay 129 C5 *inlet* South Island, NZ
Tasmania 127 B8 *prev.* Van Diemen's Land. *State* SE Australia
Tasmania 130 B4 *island* SE Australia
Tasman Plateau 120 C5 *var.* South Tasmania Plateau. *Undersea feature* SW Tasman Sea
Tasman Sea 120 C5 *sea* SW Pacific Ocean
Tassili-n-Ajjer 49 E4 *plateau* E Algeria
Tatabánya 77 C6 Komárom-Esztergom, NW Hungary
Tathlīth 99 B5 'Asīr, S Saudi Arabia
Tatra Mountains 77 D5 *Ger.* Tatra, *Hung.* Tátra, *Pol./Slvk.* Tatry. *Mountain range* Poland/Slovakia
Tatvan 95 F3 Bitlis, SE Turkey
Ta'ū 123 F4 *var.* Tau. *Island* Manua Islands, E American Samoa
Tau *see* Ta'ū
Taukum, Peski 101 G1 *desert* SE Kazakhstan
Taumarunui 128 D4 Manawatu-Wanganui, North Island, NZ
Taungdwingyi 114 B3 Magwe, C Myanmar
Taunggyi 114 B3 Shan State, C Myanmar
Taunton 67 C7 SW England, UK
Taupo 128 D3 Waikato, North Island, NZ
Taupo, Lake 128 D3 *lake* North Island, NZ
Tauragė 84 B4 *Ger.* Tauroggen. Tauragė, SW Lithuania
Tauranga 128 D3 Bay of Plenty, North Island, NZ
Tauris *see* Tabrīz
Tavas 94 B4 Denizli, SW Turkey
Tavira 70 C5 Faro, S Portugal
Tavoy 115 B5 *var.* Dawei. Tenasserim, S Myanmar
Tavoy Island *see* Mali Kyun
Tawakoni, Lake 27 G2 *reservoir* Texas, SW USA
Tawau 116 D3 Sabah, East Malaysia
Ţawkar *see* Tokar
Tawzar *see* Tozeur
Taxco 29 E4 *var.* Taxco de Alarcón. Guerrero, S Mexico
Taxco de Alarcón *see* Taxco
Taxiatosh 100 C2 *var.* Takhiatosh, *Rus.* Takhiatash. Qoraqalpoghiston Respublikasi, W Uzbekistan
Taxtako'pir 100 D1 *var.* Takhtakŭpir, *Rus.* Takhtakupyr. Qoraqalpoghiston Respublikasi, NW Uzbekistan
Tay 66 C3 *river* C Scotland, UK
Taylor 27 G3 Texas, SW USA
Taymā' 98 A4 Tabūk, NW Saudi Arabia
Taymyr, Ozero 93 E2 *lake* N Russian Federation
Taymyr, Poluostrov 93 E2 *peninsula* N Russian Federation
Taz 92 D3 *river* N Russian Federation
T'bilisi 95 G2 *Eng.* Tiflis. *Country capital* (Georgia) SE Georgia
T'bilisi 90 B7 *international airport* S Georgia
Tchien *see* Zwedru
Tchongking *see* Chongqing
Tczew 76 C2 *Ger.* Dirschau. Pomorskie, N Poland
Te Anau 129 A7 Southland, South Island, NZ
Te Anau, Lake 129 A7 *lake* South Island, NZ
Teapa 29 G4 Tabasco, SE Mexico
Teate *see* Chieti
Tebingtinggi 116 B3 Sumatera, N Indonesia
Tebriz *see* Tabrīz
Techirghiol 86 D5 Constanţa, SE Romania
Tecomán 28 D4 Colima, SW Mexico
Tecpan 29 E5 *var.* Tecpan de Galeana. Guerrero, S Mexico
Tecpan de Galeana *see* Tecpan
Tecucі 86 C4 Galaţi, E Romania
Tedzhen *see* Tejen
Tedzhen *see* Harīrūd
Tees 67 D5 *river* N England, UK
Tefé 40 D2 Amazonas, N Brazil
Tegal 116 C4 Jawa, C Indonesia
Tegelen 65 D5 Limburg, SE Netherlands
Tegucigalpa 30 C3 *country capital* (Honduras) Francisco Morazán, SW Honduras
Teheran *see* Tehrān
Tehrān 98 C3 *var.* Teheran. *Country capital* (Iran) Tehrān, N Iran
Tehuacán 29 F4 Puebla, S Mexico
Tehuantepec 29 F5 *var.* Santo Domingo Tehuantepec. Oaxaca, SE Mexico

Tehuantepec, Golfo de 29 F5 *var.* Gulf of Tehuantepec. *Gulf* S Mexico
Tehuantepec, Gulf of *see* Tehuantepec, Golfo de
Tehuantepec, Isthmus of *see* Tehuantepec, Istmo de
Tehuantepec, Istmo de 29 F5 *var.* Isthmus of Tehuantepec. *Isthmus* SE Mexico
Tejen 100 C3 *Rus.* Tedzhen. Akhalskiy Velayat, S Turkmenistan
Tejen *see* Harīrūd
Te Kao 128 C1 Northland, North Island, NZ
Tekax 29 H4 *var.* Tekax de Álvaro Obregón. Yucatán, SE Mexico
Tekax de Álvaro Obregón *see* Tekax
Tekeli 92 C5 Almaty, SE Kazakhstan
Tekirdağ 94 A2 *It.* Rodosto; *anc.* Bisanthe, Raidestos, Rhaedestus. Tekirdağ, NW Turkey
Te Kuiti 128 D3 Waikato, North Island, NZ
Tela 30 C2 Atlántida, NW Honduras
Telanaipura *see* Jambi
Tel Aviv-Jaffa *see* Tel Aviv-Yafo
Tel Aviv-Yafo 97 A6 *var.* Tel Aviv-Jaffa. Tel Aviv, C Israel
Teles Pirés *see* São Manuel, Rio
Telish 82 C2 *prev.* Azizie. Pleven, NW Bulgaria
Tell Abiad *see* At Tall al Abyaḍ
Tell Abyad *see* At Tall al Abyaḍ
Tell Kalakh *see* Tall Kalakh
Tell Shedadi *see* Ash Shadādah
Telšiai 84 B3 *Ger.* Telschen. Telšiai, NW Lithuania
Teluk Irian *see* Cenderawasih, Teluk
Teluk Serera *see* Cenderawasih, Teluk
Temerin 78 D3 Serbia, N Serbia and Montenegro (Yugo.)
Temirtau 92 C4 *var.* Samarkandski, Samarkandskoye. Karaganda, C Kazakhstan
Tempio Pausania 75 A5 Sardegna, Italy, C Mediterranean Sea
Temple 27 G3 Texas, SW USA
Temuco 43 B5 Araucanía, C Chile
Temuka 129 B6 Canterbury, South Island, NZ
Tenasserim 115 B6 Tenasserim, S Myanmar
Ténenkou 52 D3 Mopti, C Mali
Ténéré 53 G3 *physical region* C Niger
Tenerife 48 A3 *island* Islas Canarias, Spain, NE Atlantic Ocean
Tengger Shamo 105 E3 *desert* N China
Tengréla 52 D4 *var.* Tingréla. N Côte d'Ivoire
Tenkodogo 53 E4 S Burkina faso
Tennant Creek 126 A3 Northern Territory, C Australia
Tennessee 20 C1 *off.* State of Tennessee; *also known as* The Volunteer State. *State* SE USA
Tennessee River 20 C1 *river* S USA
Tenojoki *see* Deatnu/Tana
Tepelena *see* Tepelenë
Tepelenë 79 C7 *var.* Tepelena, *It.* Tepeleni. Gjirokastër, S Albania
Tepeleni *see* Tepelenë
Tepic 28 D4 Nayarit, C Mexico
Teplice 76 A4 *Ger.* Teplitz; *prev.* Teplice-Sanov, Teplitz-Schönau. Ústecký Kraj, NW Czech Republic
Tequila 28 D4 Jalisco, SW Mexico
Teraina 123 G2 *prev.* Washington Island. *Atoll* Line Islands, E Kiribati
Teramo 74 C4 *anc.* Interamna. Abruzzo, C Italy
Tercan 95 F3 Erzincan, NE Turkey
Terceira 70 A5 *var.* Ilha Terceira. *Island* Azores, Portugal, NE Atlantic Ocean
Teresina 41 F2 *var.* Therezina. *State capital* Piauí, NE Brazil
Termia *see* Kýthnos
Términos, Laguna de 29 G4 *lagoon* SE Mexico
Termiz 101 E3 *Rus.* Termez. Surkhondaryo Wiloyati, S Uzbekistan
Termoli 74 D4 Molise, C Italy
Terneuzen 65 B5 *var.* Neuzen. Zeeland, SW Netherlands
Terni 74 C4 *anc.* Interamna Nahars. Umbria, C Italy
Ternopil' 86 C2 *Pol.* Tarnopol, *Rus.* Ternopol'. Ternopil's'ka Oblast', W Ukraine
Terracina 75 C5 Lazio, C Italy
Terrassa 71 G2 *Cast.* Tarrasa. Cataluña, E Spain
Terre Adélie 132 C4 *disputed region* SE Antarctica
Terre Haute 18 B4 Indiana, N USA
Territoire du Yukon *see* Yukon Territory
Terschelling 64 C1 *Fris.* Skylge. *Island* Waddeneilanden, N Netherlands
Teruel 71 F3 *anc.* Turba. Aragón, E Spain
Tervel 82 E1 *prev.* Kurtbunar, *Rom.* Curtbunar. Dobrich, NE Bulgaria
Tervueren *see* Tervuren
Tervuren 65 C6 *var.* Tervueren. Vlaams Brabant, C Belgium
Teseney 50 C4 *var.* Tesseneï. W Eritrea
Tessalit 53 E2 Kidal, NE Mali
Tessaoua 53 G3 Maradi, S Niger
Tessenderlo 65 C5 Limburg, NE Belgium
Tesseneï *see* Teseney
Testigos, Islas los 37 E1 *island group* N Venezuela
Tete 57 E2 Tete, NW Mozambique
Teterow 72 C3 Mecklenburg-Vorpommern, NE Germany
Tétouan 48 C2 *var.* Tetouan, Tetuán. N Morocco
Tetouan *see* Tétouan
Tetovo 79 D5 *Alb.* Tetova, Tetovë, *Turk.* Kalkandelen. Razgrad, N Bulgaria
Tetuán *see* Tétouan
Tevere 74 C4 *Eng.* Tiber. *River* C Italy
Teverya 97 B5 *var.* Tiberias. Tverya. Northern, N Israel
Te Waewae Bay 129 A7 *bay* South Island, NZ
Texarkana 20 A2 Arkansas, C USA

Texarkana 27 H2 Texas, SW USA
Texas 27 F3 *off.* State of Texas; also known as The Lone Star State. *State* S USA
Texas City 27 H4 Texas, SW USA
Texel 64 C2 *island* Waddeneilanden, NW Netherlands
Texoma, Lake 27 G2 *reservoir* Oklahoma/Texas, C USA
Teziutlán 29 F4 Puebla, S Mexico
Thaa Atoll *see* Kolhumadulu Atoll
Thai Bình 114 D3 Thai Binh, N Vietnam
Thailand 115 C5 *Th.* Prathet Thai; *prev.* Siam. *Country* SE Asia
Thailand, Gulf of 115 C6 *var.* Gulf of Siam, *1h.* Ao Thai, *Vtn.* Vinh Thai Lan. *Gulf* SE Asia
Thai Nguyên 114 D3 Băc Thai, N Vietnam
Thakhèk 114 D4 *prev.* Muang Khammouan. Khammouan, C Laos
Thamarïd *see* Thamarît
Thamarît 99 D6 *var.* Thamarïd, Thumrayt. SW Oman
Thames 67 B8 *river* S England, UK
Thames 128 D4 Waikato, North Island, NZ
Thanh Hoa 114 D3 Vinh Phu, N Vietnam
Thanintari Taungdan *see* Bilauktaung Range
Thar Desert 112 C3 *var.* Great Indian Desert, Indian Desert. *Desert* India/Pakistan
Tharthâr, Buhayrat ath 98 B3 *lake* C Iraq
Thásos 82 C4 *island* E Greece
Thásos 82 C4 Thásos, E Greece
Thaton 114 B4 Mon State, S Myanmar
Thayetmyo 114 A4 Magwe, C Myanmar
The Crane 33 H2 *var.* Crane. S Barbados
The Dalles 24 B3 Oregon, NW USA
The Flatts Village *see* Flatts Village
The Hague *see* 's-Gravenhage
Theodosia *see* Feodosiya
The Pas 15 F5 Manitoba, C Canada
Therezina *see* Teresina
Thérma 83 D6 Ikaría, Dodekánisos, Greece, Aegean Sea
Thermaïkós Kólpos 82 B4 *Eng.* Thermaic Gulf; *anc.* Thermaicus Sinus. *Gulf* N Greece
Thermiá *see* Kýthnos
Thérmo 83 B5 Dytikí Ellás, C Greece
The Rock 71 H4 E Gibraltar
The Six Counties *see* Northern Ireland
Thessaloníki 82 C3 *Eng.* Salonica, Salonika, *SCr.* Solun, *Turk.* Selânik. Kentrikí Makedonía, N Greece
The Valley 33 G3 *dependent territory capital* (Anguilla) E Anguilla
The Village 27 G1 Oklahoma, C USA
Thiamis *see* Thýamis
Thibet *see* Xizang Zizhiqu
Thief River Falls 23 F1 Minnesota, N USA
Thienen *see* Tienen
Thiers 69 C5 Puy-de-Dôme, C France
Thiès 52 B3 W Senegal
Thimbu *see* Thimphu
Thimphu 113 G3 *var.* Thimbu; *prev.* Tashi Chho Dzong. *Country capital* (Bhutan) W Bhutan
Thionville 68 D3 *Ger.* Diedenhofen. Moselle, NE France
Thíra 83 D7 *prev.* Santorin, Santoríni, *anc.* Thera. Kykládes, Greece, Aegean Sea
Thíra 83 D7 Thíra, Kykládes, Greece, Aegean Sea
Thiruvanathapuram *see* Trivandrum
Thitu Island 106 C8 *island* NW Spratly Islands
Tholen 64 B4 *island* SW Netherlands
Thomasville 20 D3 Georgia, SE USA
Thompson 15 F4 Manitoba, C Canada
Thonon-les-Bains 69 D5 Haute-Savoie, E France
Thorlákshöfn 61 E5 Sudhurland, SW Iceland
Thornton Island *see* Millennium Island
Thouars 68 B4 Deux-Sèvres, W France
Thracian Sea 82 D4 *Gk.* Thrakikó Pélagos; *anc.* Thracium Mare. *Sea* Greece/Turkey
Three Kings Islands 128 C1 *island group* N NZ
Thrissur *see* Trichûr
Thuin 65 B7 Hainaut, S Belgium
Thule *see* Qaanaaq
Thumrayt *see* Thamarît
Thun 73 A7 *Fr.* Thoune. Bern, W Switzerland
Thunder Bay 16 B4 Ontario, S Canada
Thuner See 73 A7 *lake* C Switzerland
Thung Song 115 C7 *var.* Cha Mai. Nakhon Si Thammarat, SW Thailand
Thurso 66 C2 N Scotland, UK
Thýamis 82 A4 *var.* Thiamis. *River* W Greece
Tianjin 106 D4 *var.* Tientsin. Tianjin Shi, E China
Tianjin *see* Tianjin Shi
Tianjin Shi 106 D4 *var.* Jin, Tianjin, T'ien-ching, Tientsin. Admin. region *municipality* E China
Tianshui 106 B4 Gansu, C China
Tiba *see* Chiba
Tiberias *see* Teverya
Tiberias, Lake 97 B5 *var.* Chinnereth, Sea of Bahr Tabariya, Sea of Galilee, *Ar.* Bahrat Tabariya, *Heb.* Yam Kinneret. *Lake* N Israel
Tibesti 54 C2 *var.* Tibesti Massif, *Ar.* Tîbistî. *Mountain range* N Africa
Tibesti Massif *see* Tibesti
Tibet *see* Xizang Zizhiqu
Tibetan Autonomous Region *see* Xizang Zizhiqu
Tibet, Plateau of *see* Qingzang Gaoyuan
Tîbistî *see* Tibesti
Tibni *see* At Tibnî
Tiburón 28 A2 *var.* Isla del Tiburón. *Island* NW Mexico
Tiburón, Isla del *see* Tiburón, Isla
Tichît 52 D2 *var.* Tichitt. Tagant, C Mauritania

Tichitt *see* Tîchît
Ticul 29 H3 Yucatán, SE Mexico
Tidjikdja *see* Tidjikja
Tidjikja 52 C2 *var.* Tidjikdja; *prev.* Fort-Cappolani. Tagant, C Mauritania
T'ien-ching 64 C4 var. Thienen, *Fr.* Tirlemont. Vlaams Brabant, C Belgium
Tienen 65 C6 *var.* Thienen, *Fr.* Tirlemont. Vlaams Brabant, C Belgium
Tien Shan 104 B3 *Chin.* Thian Shan, Tian Shan, T'ien Shan, *Rus.* Tyan'-Shan'. *Mountain range* C Asia
Tientsin *see* Tianjin Shi
Tierp 63 C6 Uppsala, C Sweden
Tierra del Fuego 43 B8 *off.* Provincia de la Tierra del Fuego. Admin. region *province* S Argentina
Tierra del Fuego 35 B8 *island* Argentina/Chile
Tifton 20 D3 Georgia, SE USA
Tifu 117 F4 Pulau Buru, E Indonesia
Tighina 86 D4 *Rus.* Bendery; *prev.* Bender. E Moldova
Tigranocerta *see* Siirt
Tigris 98 B2 *Ar.* Dijlah, *Turk.* Dicle. *River* Iraq/Turkey
Tiguentourine 49 E3 E Algeria
Ti-hua *see* Ürümqi
Tihwa *see* Ürümqi
Tijuana 28 A1 Baja California, NW Mexico
Tikhoretsk 89 A7 Krasnodarskiy Kray, SW Russian Federation
Tikhvin 88 B4 Leningradskaya Oblast', NW Russian Federation
Tiki Basin 121 G3 *undersea feature* S Pacific Ocean
Tiksi 93 F2 Respublika Sakha (Yakutiya), NE Russian Federation
Tilburg 64 C4 Noord-Brabant, S Netherlands
Tilimsen *see* Tlemcen
Tillabéri 53 F3 *var.* Tillabéry. Tillabéri, W Niger
Tillabéry *see* Tillabéri
Tílos 83 E7 *island* Dodekánisos, Greece, Aegean Sea
Timanskiy Kryazh 88 D3 *Eng.* Timan Ridge. *Ridge* NW Russian Federation
Timaru 129 B6 Canterbury, South Island, NZ
Timbaki *see* Tympáki
Timbákion *see* Tympáki
Timbedgha 52 D3 *var.* Timbédra. Hodh ech Chargui, SE Mauritania
Timbédra *see* Timbedgha
Timbuktu *see* Tombouctou
Timiş 86 A4 *river* W Romania
Timişoara 86 A4 *Ger.* Temeschwar, Temeswar, *Hung.* Temesvár; *prev.* Temeschburg. Timiş, W Romania
Timmins 16 C4 Ontario, S Canada
Timor 103 F5 *island* Nusa Tenggara, East Timor/Indonesia
Timor Timur *see* East Timor
Timor Sea 103 F5 *sea* E Indian Ocean
Timor Trench *see* Timor Trough
Timor Trough 103 F5 *var.* Timor Trench. *Undersea feature* NE Timor Sea
Timrå 63 C5 Västernorrland, C Sweden
Tindouf 48 C3 W Algeria
Tineo 70 C1 Asturias, N Spain
Tingis *MM* *see* Tanger
Tingo María 38 C3 Huánuco, C Peru
Tingréla *see* Tengréla
Tinhosa Grande 54 E2 *island* N Sao Tome and Principe
Tinhosa Pequena 54 E1 *island* N Sao Tome and Principe
Tinian 122 B1 *island* S Northern Mariana Islands
Tínos 83 D6 *anc.* Tenos. *Island* Kykládes, Greece, Aegean Sea
Tínos 83 D6 Tínos, Kykládes, Greece, Aegean Sea
Tip 79 E6 Papua, E Indonesia
Tipitapa 30 D3 Managua, W Nicaragua
Tip Top Mountain 16 C4 *mountain* Ontario, S Canada
Tirana *see* Tiranë
Tiranë 79 C6 *var.* Tirana. *Country capital* (Albania) Tiranë, C Albania
Tiraspol 86 D4 *Rus.* Tiraspol'. E Moldova
Tiree 66 B3 *island* W Scotland, UK
Tîrgu-Neamţ *see* Târgu-Neamţ
Tîrlemont *see* Tienen
Tîrnavos *see* Týrnavos
Tirol 73 C7 *cultural region* Austria/Italy
Tiruchchirāppalli 110 C3 *prev.* Trichinopoly. Tamil Nādu, SE India
Tiruppattūr 110 C2 Tamil Nādu, SE India
Tisza 81 F1 *Ger.* Theiss, *Rom./Slvn./SCr.* Tisa, *Rus.* Tissa, *Ukr.* Tysa. *River* SE Europe *see also* Tisa
Tiszakécske 77 D7 Bács-Kiskun, C Hungary
Titano, Monte 74 E1 *mountain* C San Marino
Titicaca, Lake 39 E4 *lake* Bolivia/Peru
Titose *see* Chitose
Titu 86 C5 Dâmbovita, S Romania
Titule 55 D5 Orientale, N Dem. Rep. Congo
Tiverton 67 C7 SW England, UK
Tivoli 74 C4 *anc.* Tibur. Lazio, C Italy
Tizimín 29 H3 Yucatán, SE Mexico
Tizi Ouzou 49 E1 *var.* Tizi-Ouzou. N Algeria
Tiznit 48 B3 SW Morocco
Tlaquepaque 28 C4 Jalisco, C Mexico
Tlaxcala 29 F4 *var.* Tlascala, Tlaxcala de Xicohténcatl. Tlaxcala, C Mexico
Tlaxcala de Xicohténcatl *see* Tlaxcala
Tlemcen 48 D2 *var.* Tilimsen, Tlemsen. NW Algeria
Tlemsen *see* Tlemcen
Toamasina 57 G3 *var.* Tamatave. Toamasina, E Madagascar
Toba, Danau 116 B3 *lake* Sumatera, W Indonesia
Tobago 33 H5 *island* NE Trinidad and Tobago
Tobol 92 C4 *Kaz.* Tobyl. *River* Kazakhstan/Russian Federation

Tobol'sk 92 C3 Tyumenskaya Oblast', C Russian Federation
Tocantins 41 E3 *off.* Estado do Tocantins. *State* C Brazil
Tocantins, Rio 41 F2 *river* N Brazil
Tocoa 30 D2 Colón, N Honduras
Tocopilla 42 B2 Antofagasta, N Chile
Todi 74 C4 Umbria, C Italy
Todos os Santos, Baía de 41 G3 *bay* E Brazil
Toetoes Bay 129 B8 *bay* South Island, NZ
Tofua 123 E4 *island* Ha'apai Group, C Tonga
Togo 53 E4 *French Togoland*. *Country* W Africa
Tokanui 129 B7 Southland, South Island, NZ
Tokar 50 D3 *var.* Tawkar. Red Sea, NE Sudan
Tokat 94 D3 Tokat, N Turkey
Tokelau 123 E3 *NZ overseas territory* W Polynesia
Tokio *see* Tōkyō
Tokmak 101 G2 *Kir.* Tokmok. Chuyskaya Oblast', N Kyrgyzstan
Tokmak 87 G4 *var.* Velykyy Tokmak. Zaporiz'ka Oblast', SE Ukraine
Tokoroa 128 D3 Waikato, North Island, NZ
Tokounou 52 C4 Haute-Guinée, C Guinea
Tokushima 109 C6 *var.* Tokusima. Tokushima, Shikoku, SW Japan
Tokusima *see* Tokushima
Tōkyō 108 A1 *var.* Tokio. *Country capital* (Japan) Tōkyō, Honshū, S Japan
Tōkyō Bay 108 A2 *bay* SW Japan
Toledo 70 D3 *anc.* Toletum. Castilla-La Mancha, C Spain
Toledo 18 D3 Ohio, N USA
Toledo Bend Reservoir 27 G3 *reservoir* Louisiana/Texas, SW USA
Toliara 57 F4 *var.* Toliary; *prev.* Tuléar. Toliara, SW Madagascar
Toliary *see* Toliara
Tolmin 73 D7 *Ger.* Tolmein, *It.* Tolmino. W Slovenia
Tolna 77 C7 *Ger.* Tolnau. Tolna, S Hungary
Tolosa 71 E1 País Vasco, N Spain
Toluca 29 E4 *var.* Toluca de Lerdo. México, S Mexico
Toluca de Lerdo *see* Toluca
Tol'yatti 89 C6 *prev.* Stavropol'. Samarskaya Oblast', W Russian Federation
Tomah 18 B2 Wisconsin, N USA
Tomakomai 108 D2 Hokkaidō, NE Japan
Tomar 70 B3 Santarém, W Portugal
Tomaschow *see* Tomaszów Mazowiecki
Tomaszów Lubelski 76 E4 *Ger.* Tomaschow. Lubelskie, E Poland
Tomaszów Mazowiecka *see* Tomaszów Mazowiecki
Tomaszów Mazowiecki 76 D4 *var.* Tomaszów Mazowiecka; *prev.* Tomaszów, *Ger.* Tomaschow. Łódzkie, C Poland
Tombigbee River 20 C3 *river* Alabama/Mississippi, S USA
Tombouctou 53 E3 *Eng.* Timbuktu. Tombouctou, N Mali
Tombua 56 A2 *Port.* Porto Alexandre. Namibe, SW Angola
Tomelloso 71 E3 Castilla-La Mancha, C Spain
Tomini, Gulf of 117 E4 *var.* Teluk Tomini; *prev.* Teluk Gorontalo. *Bay* Sulawesi, C Indonesia
Tomini, Teluk *see* Tomini, Gulf of
Tomsk 92 D4 Tomskaya Oblast', C Russian Federation
Tomur Feng *see* Pobedy, Pik
Tonga 123 E4 *var.* Friendly Islands. *Country* SW Pacific Ocean
Tongatapu 123 E5 *island* Tongatapu Group, S Tonga
Tonga Trench 121 E3 *undersea feature* S Pacific Ocean
Tongchuan 106 C4 Shaanxi, C China
Tongeren 65 D6 *Fr.* Tongres. Limburg, NE Belgium
Tongking, Gulf of 106 B7 *Chin.* Beibu Wan, *Vtn.* Vinh Băc Bô. *Gulf* China/Vietnam
Tongliao 105 G2 Nei Mongol Zizhiqu, N China
Tongshan *see* Xuzhou
Tongtian He 104 C4 *river* C China
Tonj 51 B5 Warab, SW Sudan
Tônlé Sap 115 D5 *Eng.* Great Lake. *Lake* W Cambodia
Tonopah 25 C6 Nevada, W USA
Tonyezh 85 C7 *Rus.* Tonezh. Homyel'skaya Voblasts', SE Belarus
Tooele 22 B4 Utah, W USA
Toowoomba 127 E5 Queensland, E Australia
Topeka 23 F4 *state capital* Kansas, C USA
Topliţa 86 C3 *Ger.* Töplitz, *Hung.* Maroshévíz; *prev.* Topliţa Română, *Hung.* Oláh-Toplicza, Toplicza. Harghita, C Romania
Topol'čany 77 C6 *Hung.* Nagytapolcsány. Nitriansky Kraj, SW Slovakia
Topolovgrad 82 D3 *prev.* Kavakli. Khaskovo, S Bulgaria
Top Springs Roadhouse 124 D3 Northern Territory, N Australia
Torez 87 H3 Donets'ka Oblast', SE Ukraine
Torgau 72 D4 Sachsen, E Germany
Torhout 65 A5 West-Vlaanderen, W Belgium
Torino 74 A2 *Eng.* Turin. Piemonte, NW Italy
Tornacum *see* Tournai
Torneälven *see* Torniojoki
Torneträsk 62 C3 *lake* N Sweden
Tornio 62 D4 *Swe.* Torneå. Lappi, NW Finland
Torniojoki *see* Torniojoki
Torniojoki 62 D3 *var.* Torniojoki, *Swe.* Torneälven. *River* Finland/Sweden
Toro 70 D2 Castilla-León, N Spain
Toronto 16 D5 Ontario, S Canada
Toros Dağları 94 C4 *Eng.* Taurus Mountains. *Mountain range* S Turkey
Torquay 67 C7 SW England, UK

Torrance 24 D2 California, W USA
Torre, Alto da 70 B3 *mountain* C Portugal
Torre del Greco 75 D5 Campania, S Italy
Torrejón de Ardoz 71 E3 Madrid, C Spain
Torrelavega 70 D1 Cantabria, N Spain
Torrens, Lake 127 A6 *salt lake* South Australia
Torrent 71 F3 *var.* Torrent de l'Horta, *Cas.* Torrente. País Valenciano, E Spain
Torrent de l'Horta *see* Torrent
Torrente *see* Torrent
Torreón 28 D3 Coahuila de Zaragoza, NE Mexico
Torres Strait 126 C1 *strait* Australia/PNG
Torres Vedras 70 B3 Lisboa, C Portugal
Torrington 22 D3 Wyoming, C USA
Tórshavn 61 F5 *Dan.* Thorshavn. *Dependent territory capital* (Faeroe Islands) N Faeroe Islands
To'rtko'l 100 D2 *var.* Türtkül, *Rus.* Turtkul'; *prev.* Petroaleksandrovsk. Qoraqalpoghiston Respublikasi, W Uzbekistan
Tortoise Islands *see* Galapagos Islands
Tortosa 71 F2 *anc.* Dertosa. Cataluña, E Spain
Tortue, Montagne 37 H3 *mountain range* C French Guiana
Tortuga, Isla *see* La Tortuga, Isla
Toruń 76 C3 *Ger.* Thorn. Kujawskie-pomorskie, C Poland
Tõrva 84 D3 *Ger.* Törwa. Valgamaa, S Estonia
Torzhok 88 B4 Tverskaya Oblast', W Russian Federation
Tosa-wan 109 B7 *bay* SW Japan
Toscana 74 B3 *Eng.* Tuscany. *Cultural region* C Italy
Toscano, Archipelago 74 B4 *Eng.* Tuscan Archipelago. *Island group* C Italy
Toshkent 101 E2 *Eng./Rus.* Tashkent. *Country capital* (Uzbekistan) Toshkent Wiloyati, E Uzbekistan
Totana 71 E4 Murcia, SE Spain
Tot'ma *see* Sukhona
Totness 37 G3 Coronie, N Suriname
Tottori 109 B6 Tottori, Honshū, SW Japan
Touâjil 52 C2 Tiris Zemmour, N Mauritania
Touggourt 49 E2 NE Algeria
Toukoto 52 C3 Kayes, W Mali
Toul 68 D3 Meurthe-et-Moselle, NE France
Toulon 69 D6 *anc.* Telo Martius, Tilio Martius. Var, SE France
Toulouse 69 B6 *anc.* Tolosa. Haute-Garonne, S France
Toungoo 114 B4 Pegu, C Myanmar
Touraine 68 B4 *cultural region* C France
Tourcoing 68 C2 Nord, N France
Tournai 65 A6 *var.* Tournay, *Dut.* Doornik; *anc.* Tornacum. Hainaut, SW Belgium
Tournay *see* Tournai
Tours 68 B4 *anc.* Caesarodunum, Turoni. Indre-et-Loire, C France
Tovarkovskiy 89 B5 Tul'skaya Oblast', W Russian Federation
Tower Island *see* Genovesa, Isla
Townsville 126 D3 Queensland, NE Australia
Towraghoudī 100 D4 Herât, NW Afghanistan
Towson 19 F4 Maryland, NE USA
Towuti, Danau 117 E4 *Dut.* Towoeti Meer. *Lake* Sulawesi, C Indonesia
Toyama 109 C5 Toyama, Honshū, SW Japan
Toyama-wan 109 B5 *bay* W Japan
Toyota 109 C6 Aichi, Honshū, SW Japan
Tozeur 49 E2 *var.* Tawzar. W Tunisia
Trâblous *see* Tripoli
Trabzon 95 E2 *Eng.* Trebizond; *anc.* Trapezus. Trabzon, NE Turkey
Traiectum Tungrorum *see* Maastricht
Traietum ad Mosam *see* Maastricht
Traiskirchen 73 E6 Niederösterreich, NE Austria
Trakai 85 C5 *Ger.* Traken, *Pol.* Troki. Trakai, SE Lithuania
Tralee 67 A6 *Ir.* Trá Lí. SW Ireland
Trá Lí *see* Tralee
Tralles *see* Aydın
Trang 115 C7 Trang, S Thailand
Transantarctic Mountains 132 B3 *mountain range* Antarctica
Transsylvanische Alpen *see* Carpaţii Meridionali
Transylvania 86 B4 *Eng.* Ardeal, Transilvania, *Ger.* Siebenbürgen, *Hung.* Erdély. *Cultural region* NW Romania
Transylvanian Alps *see* Carpaţii Meridionali
Trapani 75 B7 *anc.* Drepanum. Sicilia, Italy, C Mediterranean Sea
Traralgon 127 C7 Victoria, SE Australia
Trasimeno, Lago 74 C4 *Eng.* Lake of Perugia, *Ger.* Trasimenischersee. *Lake* C Italy
Traverse City 18 C2 Michigan, N USA
Tra Vinh 115 D6 *var.* Phu Vinh. Tra Vinh, S Vietnam
Travis, Lake 27 F3 *reservoir* Texas, SW USA
Travnik 78 C4 Federacija Bosna I Hercegovina, C Bosnia and Herzegovina
Trbovlje 73 E7 *Ger.* Trifail. C Slovenia
Třebíč 77 B5 *Ger.* Trebitsch. Jihlavský Kraj, C Czech Republic
Trebinje 79 C5 Republika Srpska, S Bosnia and Herzegovina
Trebišov 77 D6 *Hung.* Tőketerebes. Košický Kraj, E Slovakia
Trélazé 68 B4 Maine-et-Loire, NW France
Trelew 43 C6 Chubut, SE Argentina
Tremelo 65 C5 Vlaams Brabant, C Belgium
Trenčín 77 C5 *Ger.* Trentschin, *Hung.* Trencsén. Trenčiansky Kraj, W Slovakia
Trenque Lauquen 42 C4 Buenos Aires, E Argentina

Trento 74 C2 *Eng.* Trent, *Ger.* Trient; *anc.*Tridentum. Trentino-Alto Adige, N Italy
Trenton 19 F4 *state capital* New Jersey, NE USA
Tres Arroyos 43 D5 Buenos Aires, E Argentina
Treskavica 78 C4 *mountain range* SE Bosnia and Herzegovina
Tres Tabernae *see* Saverne
Treviso 74 C2 *anc.* Tarvisium. Veneto, NE Italy
Trichūr 110 C3 *var.* Thrissur. Kerala, SW India
Trier 73 A5 *Eng.* Treves, *Fr.* Trèves; *anc.* Augusta Treverorum. Rheinland-Pfalz, SW Germany
Triesen 72 E2 SW Liechtenstein
Triesenberg 94 E2 SW Liechtenstein
Trieste 74 D2 *Slvn.* Trst. Friuli-Venezia Giulia, NE Italy
Tríkala 82 B4 *prev.* Trikkala. Thessalía, C Greece
Trikkala *see* Tríkala
Trincomalee 110 D3 *var.* Trinkomali. Eastern Province, NE Sri Lanka
Trindade, Ilha da 45 C5 *island* Brazil, W Atlantic Ocean
Trinidad 33 H5 *island* C Trinidad and Tobago
Trinidad 39 F3 Beni, N Bolivia
Trinidad 22 D5 Colorado, C USA
Trinidad 42 D4 Flores, S Uruguay
Trinidad and Tobago 33 H5 *Country* SE West Indies
Trinité, Montagnes de la 37 H3 *mountain range* C French Guiana
Trinity River 27 G3 *river* Texas, SW USA
Trinkomali *see* Trincomalee
Tripoli 96 B4 *var.* Tarābulus, Ţarābulus ash Shām, Trâblous; *anc.* Tripolis. N Lebanon
Tripoli *see* Ţarābulus
Trípoli 83 B6 *prev.* Trípolis. Pelopónnisos, S Greece
Tripolis *see* Tripoli
Tristan da Cunha 47 B7 *dependency of Saint Helena* SE Atlantic Ocean
Triton Island 106 B7 *island* S Paracel Islands
Trivandrum 110 C3 *var.* Thiruvanathapuram. Kerala, SW India
Trnava 77 C6 *Ger.* Tyrnau, *Hung.* Nagyszombat. Trnavský Kraj, W Slovakia
Trogir 78 B4 *It.* Traù. Split-Dalmacija, S Croatia
Troglav 78 B4 *mountain* Bosnia and Herzegovina/Croatia
Trois-Rivières 17 E4 Québec, SE Canada
Trollhättan 63 B6 Västra Götaland, S Sweden
Tromsø 62 C2 *Fin.* Tromssa. Troms, N Norway
Trondheim 62 B4 *Ger.* Drontheim; *prev.* Nidaros, Trondhjem. Sør-Trøndelag, S Norway
Trondheimsfjorden 62 B4 *fjord* S Norway
Troödos 80 C5 *var.* Troodos Mountains. *Mountain range* C Cyprus
Troodos Mountains *see* Troödos
Troy 20 D3 Alabama, S USA
Troy 19 F3 New York, NE USA
Troyan 82 C2 Lovech, N Bulgaria
Troyes 68 D3 *anc.* Augustobona Tricassium. Aube, N France
Trstenik 78 E4 Serbia, C Serbia and Montenegro (Yugo.)
Trujillo 30 D2 Colón, NE Honduras
Trujillo 70 C3 Extremadura, W Spain
Trujillo 38 B3 La Libertad, NW Peru
Truk Islands *see* Chuuk Islands
Trün 82 B2 Pernik, W Bulgaria
Truro 17 G4 Nova Scotia, SE Canada
Truro 67 C7 SW England, UK
Trzcianka 76 B3 *Ger.* Schönlanke. Wielkopolskie, C Poland
Trzebnica 76 C4 *Ger.* Trebnitz. Dolnoślaskie, SW Poland
Tsalka 95 F2 S Georgia
Tsamkong *see* Zhanjiang
Tsangpo *see* Brahmaputra
Tsarevo 82 E2 *prev.* Michurin. Burgas, E Bulgaria
Tsaritsyn *see* Volgograd
Tsefat *see* Zefat
Tsetserleg 104 D2 Arhangay, C Mongolia
Tsevat *see* Zefat
Tshela 55 B6 Bas-Zaïre, W Dem. Rep. Congo
Tshikapa 55 C7 Kasai Occidental, SW Dem. Rep. Congo
Tshuapa 55 D6 *river* C Dem. Rep. Congo
Tshwane *see* Pretoria
Tsinan *see* Jinan
Tsing Hai *see* Qinghai Hu
Tsingtao *see* Qingdao
Tsingtau *see* Qingdao
Tsinkiang *see* Quanzhou
Tsintao *see* Qingdao
Tsitsihar *see* Qiqihar
Tsu 109 C6 *var.* Tu. Mie, Honshū, SW Japan
Tsugaru-kaikyō 108 D3 *strait* N Japan
Tsumeb 56 B3 Otjikoto, N Namibia
Tsuruga 109 C6 *var.* Turuga. Fukui, Honshū, SW Japan
Tsuruoka 108 D4 *var.* Turuoka. Yamagata, Honshū, C Japan
Tsushima 109 A7 *var.* Tsushima-tō, Tusima. *Island group* SW Japan
Tsushima-tō *see* Tsushima
Tsyelakhova 85 D8 *Rus.* Terekhovka. Homyel'skaya Voblasts', SE Belarus
Tsyurupyns'k 87 E4 *Rus.* Tsyurupinsk. Khersons'ka Oblast', S Ukraine
Tu *see* Tsu
Tuamotu Fracture Zone 121 H3 *tectonic feature* E Pacific Ocean
Tuamotu, Îles 123 H4 *var.* Archipel des Tuamotu, Dangerous Archipelago, Tuamotu Islands. *Island group* N French Polynesia

Tuamotu Islands *see* Tuamotu, Îles
Tuapi 31 F2 Región Autónoma Atlántico Norte, NE Nicaragua
Tuapse 89 A7 Krasnodarskiy Kray, SW Russian Federation
Tuba City 26 B1 Arizona, SW USA
Tubbergen 64 E3 Overijssel, E Netherlands
Tubize 65 B6 Dut. Tubeke. Wallon Brabant, C Belgium
Tubmanburg 52 C5 NW Liberia
Ţubruq 49 H2 Eng. Tobruk, It. Tobruch. NE Libya
Tubuai Islands *see* Australes, Îles
Tucker's Town 20 B5 E Bermuda
Tucson 26 B3 Arizona, SW USA
Tucumán *see* San Miguel de Tucumán
Tucumcari 27 E2 New Mexico, SW USA
Tucupita 37 E2 Delta Amacuro, NE Venezuela
Tucuruí, Represa de 41 F2 *reservoir* NE Brazil
Tudela 71 E2 Basq. Tutera; anc. Tutela. Navarra, N Spain
Tudmur 96 C3 var. Tadmur, Tamar, Gk. Palmyra; Bibl. Tadmor. Ḥimṣ, C Syria
Tuguegarao 117 E1 Luzon, N Philippines
Tuktoyaktuk 15 E3 Northwest Territories, NW Canada
Tukums 84 C3 Ger. Tuckum. Tukums, W Latvia
Tula 89 B5 Tul'skaya Oblast', W Russian Federation
Tulancingo 29 E4 Hidalgo, C Mexico
Tulare Lake Bed 25 C7 salt flat California, W USA
Tulcán 38 B1 Carchi, N Ecuador
Tulcea 86 D5 Tulcea, E Romania
Tul'chyn 86 D3 Rus. Tul'chin. Vinnyts'ka Oblast', C Ukraine
Tuléar *see* Toliara
Tulia 27 E2 Texas, SW USA
Tulle 69 C5 anc. Tutela. Corrèze, C France
Tulln 73 E6 var. Oberhollabrunn. Niederösterreich, NE Austria
Tully 126 D3 Queensland, NE Australia
Tulsa 27 G1 Oklahoma, C USA
Tuluá 36 B3 Valle del Cauca, W Colombia
Tulun 93 E4 Irkutskaya Oblast', S Russian Federation
Tumaco 36 A4 Nariño, SW Colombia
Tumba, Lac *see* Ntomba, Lac
Tumbes 38 A2 Tumbes, NW Peru
Tumkūr 132 C2 Karnātaka, W India
Tumuc Humac Mountains 41 E1 var. Serra Tumucumaque. Mountain range N South America
Tunduru 51 C8 Ruvuma, S Tanzania
Tundzha 82 D3 Turk. Tunca Nehri. River Bulgaria/Turkey see also Tunca Nehri
Tungabhadra Reservoir 110 C2 lake S India
Tungaru 123 E2 prev. Gilbert Islands. Island group W Kiribati
T'ung-shan see Xuzhou
Tungsten 14 D4 Northwest Territories, W Canada
Tung-t'ing Hu see Dongting Hu
Tunis 49 E1 var. Tūnis. Country capital (Tunisia) NE Tunisia
Tūnis see Tunis
Tunis, Golfe de 80 D3 Ar. Khalīj Tūnis. Gulf NE Tunisia
Tunisia 49 F2 Ar. Al Jumhūrīyah at Tūnisīyah, Fr. République Tunisienne. Country N Africa
Tunja 36 B3 Boyacá, C Colombia
Tuong Buong see T,ong Đ,ong
Tupelo 20 C2 Mississippi, S USA
Tupiza 39 G5 Potosí, S Bolivia
Turabah 99 B5 Makkah, W Saudi Arabia
Turangi 128 D4 Waikato, North Island, NZ
Turan Lowland 100 C2 var. Turan Plain, Kaz. Turan Oypaty, Rus. Turanskaya Nizmennost', Turk. Turan Pesligi, Uzb. Turon Pasttekisligi. Plain C Asia
Turan Oypaty see Turan Lowland
Turan Pesligi see Turan Lowland
Turan Plain see Turan Lowland
Turanskaya Nizmennost' see Turan Lowland
Ţurayf 98 A3 Al Ḩudūd ash Shamālīyah, NW Saudi Arabia
Turbat 112 A3 Baluchistān, SW Pakistan
Turda 86 B4 Ger. Thorenburg, Hung. Torda. Cluj, NW Romania
Turek 76 C3 Wielkopolskie, C Poland
Turfan see Turpan
Turin see Torino
Turkana, Lake 89 C6 var. Lake Rudolf. Lake N Kenya
Turkish Republic of Northern Cyprus 80 D5 Ger. Dependent territory, disputed territory. Cyprus
Turkestan 92 B5 Kaz. Türkistan. Yuzhnyy Kazakhstan, S Kazakhstan
Turkey 94 B3 Turk. Türkiye Cumhuriyeti. Country SW Asia
Türkmenabat 100 D3 prev. Chardzhev, Chardzhou, Chardzhui, Leninsk-Turkmenski, Turkm. Chärjew. Lebapskiy Velayat, E Turkmenistan
Turkmen Aylagy 100 B2 Rus. Turkmenskiy Zaliv. Lake gulf W Turkmenistan
Turkmenbashi see Türkmenbaşy
Türkmenbaşy 100 B2 var. Turkmenbashi; prev. Krasnovodsk. Balkanskiy Velayat, W Turkmenistan
Türkmenbaşy Aylagy 100 A2 prev. Krasnovodskiy Zaliv, Krasnovodsk Aylagy. Lake gulf W Turkmenistan
Turkmenistan 100 B2 prev. Turkmenskaya Soviet Socialist Republic. Country C Asia
Turkmenskiy Zaliv see Türkmen Aylagy
Turks and Caicos Islands 33 E2 UK dependent territory N West Indies
Turlock 25 B6 California, W USA
Turnagain, Cape 128 D4 headland North Island, NZ
Turnhout 65 C5 Antwerpen, N Belgium

Turnov 76 B4 Ger. Turnau. Liberecký Kraj, N Czech Republic
Turnu Măgurele 86 B5 var. Turnu-Măgurele. Teleorman, S Romania
Turon Pasttekisligi see Turan Lowland
Turpan 104 C3 var. Turfan. Xinjiang Uygur Zizhiqu, NW China
Turpan Pendi 104 C3 Eng. Turpan Depression. Depression NW China
Türtkül see To'rtko'l
Turuga see Tsuruga
Turuoka see Tsuruoka
Tuscaloosa 20 C2 Alabama, S USA
Tusima see Tsushima
Tuticorin 110 C3 Tamil Nādu, SE India
Tutrakan 82 D1 Silistra, NE Bulgaria
Tutuila 123 F4 island W American Samoa
Tuvalu 123 E3 prev. Ellice Islands. Country SW Pacific Ocean
Ţuwayq, Jabal 99 C5 mountain range C Saudi Arabia
Tuxpán 29 F4 var. Tuxpán de Rodríguez Cano. Veracruz-Llave, E Mexico
Tuxpan 28 C4 Jalisco, C Mexico
Tuxpan 28 D4 Nayarit, C Mexico
Tuxpán de Rodríguez Cano see Tuxpán
Tuxtepec 29 F4 var. San Juan Bautista Tuxtepec. Oaxaca, S Mexico
Tuxtla 29 G5 var. Tuxtla Gutiérrez. Chiapas, SE Mexico
Tuxtla see San Andrés Tuxtla
Tuxtla Gutiérrez see Tuxtla
Tuy Hoa 115 E5 Phu Yên, S Vietnam
Tuz Gölü 94 C3 lake C Turkey
Tuzla 78 C3 Federacija Bosna I Hercegovina, NE Bosnia and Herzegovina
Tver' 88 B4 prev. Kalinin. Tverskaya Oblast', W Russian Federation
Tverya see Teverya
Twin Falls 24 D4 Idaho, NW USA
Tychy 77 D5 Ger. Tichau. Śląskie, S Poland
Tyler 27 G3 Texas, SW USA
Tympáki 83 C8 var. Timbaki; prev. Timbákion. Kríti, Greece, E Mediterranean Sea
Tynda 93 F4 Amurskaya Oblast', SE Russian Federation
Tyne 66 D4 river N England, UK
Tyósi see Chōshi
Tyre see Soûr
Týrnavos 82 B4 var. Tírnavos. Thessalía, C Greece
Tyrrhenian Sea 75 B6 It. Mare Tirreno. Sea N Mediterranean Sea
Tyumen' 92 C3 Tyumenskaya Oblast', C Russian Federation
Tyup 101 G2 Kir. Tüp. Issyk-Kul'skaya Oblast', NE Kyrgyzstan
Tywyn 67 C6 W Wales, UK
Tzekung see Zigong
T,ong Đ,ong 114 D4 var. Tuong Buong. Nghệ An, N Vietnam

U

Uanle Uen see Wanlaweyn
Uaupés, Rio see Vaupés, Río
Ubangi 55 C5 Fr. Oubangui. River C Africa
Ubangi-Shari see Central African Republic
Ube 109 B7 Yamaguchi, Honshū, SW Japan
Úbeda 71 E4 Andalucía, S Spain
Uberaba 41 F4 Minas Gerais, SE Brazil
Uberlândia 41 F4 Minas Gerais, SE Brazil
Ubol Rajadhani see Ubon Ratchathani
Ubol Ratchathani see Ubon Ratchathani
Ubon Ratchathani 115 D5 var. Muang Ubon, Ubol Rajadhani, Ubol Ratchathani, Udon Ratchathani. Ubon Ratchathani, E Thailand
Ubrique 70 D5 Andalucía, S Spain
Ucayali, Río 38 D3 river C Peru
Uchiura-wan 108 D3 bay NW Pacific Ocean
Uchquduq 100 D2 Rus. Uchkuduk. Nawoiy Wiloyati, N Uzbekistan
Uchtagan, Peski see Uçtagan Gumy
Uçtagan Gumy 100 C2 Rus. Peski Uchtagan. Desert NW Turkmenistan
Udaipur 112 C3 prev. Oodeypore. Rājasthān, N India
Uddevalla 63 B6 Västra Götaland, S Sweden
Udine 74 D2 anc. Utina. Friuli-Venezia Giulia, NE Italy
Udintsev Fracture Zone 132 A5 tectonic feature S Pacific Ocean
Udipi see Udupi
Udon Ratchathani see Ubon Ratchathani
Udon Thani 114 C4 var. Ban Mak Khaeng, Udorndhani. Udon Thani, N Thailand
Udorndhani see Udon Thani
Udupi 110 B2 var. Udipi. Karnātaka, SW India
Uele 55 D5 var. Welle. River NE Dem. Rep. Congo
Uelzen 72 C3 Niedersachsen, N Germany
Ufa 89 D6 Respublika Bashkortostan, W Russian Federation
Ugâle 84 C2 Ventspils, NW Latvia
Uganda 51 B6 Country E Africa
Uglovka 88 B4 var. Okulovka. Novgorodskaya Oblast', W Russian Federation
Uhuru Peak see Kilimanjaro
Uíge 56 B1 Port. Carmona, Vila Marechal Carmona. Uíge, NW Angola
Uinta Mountains 22 B4 mountain range Utah, W USA
Uitenhage 56 C5 Eastern Cape, S South Africa
Uithoorn 64 C3 Noord-Holland, C Netherlands
Ujelang Atoll 122 C1 var. Wujlān. Atoll Ralik Chain, W Marshall Islands
Ujungpandang 117 E4 var. Macassar, Makassar; prev. Makasar. Sulawesi, C Indonesia
Ujung Salang see Phuket
Ukhta 92 C3 Respublika Komi, NW Russian Federation

Ukiah 25 B5 California, W USA
Ukmergė 84 C4 Pol. Wiłkomierz. Ukmergė, C Lithuania
Ukraine 86 C2 Ukr. Ukrayina; prev. Ukrainian Soviet Socialist Republic, Ukrainskaya S.S.R. Country SE Europe
Ulaanbaatar 105 E2 Eng. Ulan Bator. Country capital (Mongolia) Töv, C Mongolia
Ulaangom 104 C2 Uvs, NW Mongolia
Ulan Bator see Ulaanbaatar
Ulanhad see Chifeng
Ulan-Ude 93 E4 prev. Verkhneudinsk. Respublika Buryatiya, S Russian Federation
Ulft 64 E4 Gelderland, E Netherlands
Ullapool 66 C3 N Scotland, UK
Ulm 73 B6 Baden-Württemberg, S Germany
Ulsan 107 E4 Jap. Urusan. SE South Korea
Ulster 67 B5 cultural region N Ireland
Ulungur Hu 104 B2 lake NW China
Uluru 125 D5 var. Ayers Rock. Rocky outcrop Northern Territory, C Australia
Ulyanivka 87 E3 Rus. Ul'yanovka. Kirovohrads'ka Oblast', C Ukraine
Ul'yanovsk 89 C5 prev. Simbirsk. Ul'yanovskaya Oblast', W Russian Federation
Uman' 87 E3 Rus. Uman. Cherkas'ka Oblast', C Ukraine
Umán 29 H3 Yucatán, SE Mexico
Umanak see Uummannaq
Umanaq see Uummannaq
Umbro-Marchigiano, Appennino 74 C3 Eng. Umbrian-Machigian Mountains. Mountain range C Italy
Umeå 62 C4 Västerbotten, N Sweden
Umeälven 62 C4 river N Sweden
Umiat 14 D2 Alaska, USA
Umm Buru 50 A4 Western Darfur, W Sudan
Umm Durman see Omdurman
Umm Ruwaba 50 C4 var. Umm Ruwābah, Um Ruwāba. Northern Kordofan, C Sudan
Umm Ruwābah see Umm Ruwaba
Umnak Island 14 A3 island Aleutian Islands, Alaska, USA
Um Ruwāba see Umm Ruwaba
Umtali see Mutare
Umtata 56 D5 Eastern Cape, SE South Africa
Una 78 B3 river Bosnia and Herzegovina/Croatia
Unac 78 B3 river W Bosnia and Herzegovina
Unalaska Island 14 A3 island Aleutian Islands, Alaska, USA
'Unayzah 98 B4 var. Anaiza. Al Qaşīm, C Saudi Arabia
Uncía 39 F4 Potosí, C Bolivia
Uncompahgre Peak 22 B5 mountain Colorado, C USA
Ungarisches Erzgebirge see Slovenské rudohorie
Ungava Bay 17 E1 bay Québec, E Canada
Ungava, Péninsule d' 16 D1 peninsula Québec, SE Canada
Ungheni 86 D3 Rus. Ungeny. W Moldova
Üngüz Angyrsyndaky Garagum 122 C2 Rus. Zaunguzskiye Garagumy. Desert N Turkmenistan
Unimak Island 14 B3 island Aleutian Islands, Alaska, USA
Union 21 E1 South Carolina, SE USA
Union City Tennessee, S USA
United Arab Emirates 99 C5 Ar. Al Imārāt al 'Arabīyah al Muttaḥidah, abbrev. UAE; prev. Trucial States. Country SW Asia
United Kingdom 67 B5 abbrev. UK. Country NW Europe
United States of America 13 B5 var. America, The States, abbrev. U.S., USA. Country
Unst 66 D1 island NE Scotland, UK
Ünye 94 D2 Ordu, W Turkey
Upala 30 D4 Alajuela, NW Costa Rica
Upata 37 E2 Bolívar, E Venezuela
Upemba, Lac 55 D7 lake SE Dem. Rep. Congo
Upernavik 60 C2 var. Upernivik. C Greenland
Upernivik see Upernavik
Upington 56 C4 Northern Cape, W South Africa
Upolu 123 F4 island SE Samoa
Upper Klamath Lake 24 A4 lake Oregon, NW USA
Upper Lough Erne 67 A5 lake SW Northern Ireland, UK
Upper Red Lake 23 F1 lake Minnesota, N USA
Uppsala 63 C6 Uppsala, C Sweden
Ural 90 B3 Kaz. Zayyq. River Kazakhstan/Russian Federation
Ural Mountains see Ural'skiye Gory
Ural'sk 92 B3 Kaz. Oral. Zapadnyy Kazakhstan, NW Kazakhstan
Ural'skiy Gory 92 C3 var. Ural'skiy Khrebet, Eng. Ural Mountains. Mountain range Kazakhstan/Russian Federation
Ural'skiy Khrebet see Ural'skiye Gory
Uraricoera 40 D1 Roraima, N Brazil
Urbandale 23 F3 Iowa, C USA
Uren' 89 C5 Nizhegorodskaya Oblast', W Russian Federation
Urganch 100 D2 Rus. Urgench; prev. Novo-Urgench. Khorazm Wiloyati, W Uzbekistan
Urgut 101 E3 Samarqand Wiloyati, C Uzbekistan
Uroševac 79 D5 Alb. Ferizaj. Serbia, S Serbia and Montenegro (Yugo.)
Ürötegup 101 E2 Rus. Ura-Tyube. NW Tajikistan
Uruapan 29 E4 var. Uruapan del Progreso. Michoacán de Ocampo, SW Mexico
Uruapan del Progreso see Uruapan
Uruguai, Rio see Uruguay
Uruguay 42 D4 prev. La Banda Oriental. Country E South America
Uruguay 42 D3 var. Rio Uruguai, Río Uruguay. River E South America
Uruguay, Río see Uruguay

Urmchi see Ürümqi
Urumqi see Ürümqi
Ürümqi 104 C3 var. Tihwa, Urumchi, Urumqi, Urumtsi, Wu-lu-k'o-mu-shi, Wu-lu-mu-ch'i; prev. Ti-hua. Autonomous region capital Xinjiang Uygur Zizhiqu, NW China
Urumtsi see Ürümqi
Urup, Ostrov 93 H4 island Kuril'skiye Ostrova, SE Russian Federation
Urziceni 86 C5 Ialomiţa, SE Romania
Usa 88 E3 river NW Russian Federation
Uşak 94 B3 prev. Ushak. Uşak, W Turkey
Ushuaia 43 B8 Tierra del Fuego, S Argentina
Usinsk 88 E3 Respublika Komi, NW Russian Federation
Üsküb see Skopje
Üsküp see Skopje
Usmas Ezers 84 B3 lake NW Latvia
Usol'ye-Sibirskoye 93 E4 Irkutskaya Oblast', C Russian Federation
Ussel 69 C5 Corrèze, C France
Ussuriysk 93 G5 prev. Nikol'sk, Nikol'sk-Ussuriyskiy, Voroshilov. Primorskiy Kray, SE Russian Federation
Ust'-Ilimsk 93 E4 Irkutskaya Oblast', C Russian Federation
Ústí nad Labem 76 A4 Ger. Aussig. Ústecký Kraj, NW Czech Republic
Ustka 76 C2 Ger. Stolpmünde. Pomorskie, N Poland
Ust'-Kamchatsk 93 H2 Kamchatskaya Oblast', E Russian Federation
Ust'-Kamenogorsk 92 D5 Kaz. Öskemen. Vostochnyy Kazakhstan, E Kazakhstan
Ust'-Kut 93 E4 Irkutskaya Oblast', C Russian Federation
Ust'-Olenëk 93 E3 Respublika Sakha (Yakutiya), NE Russian Federation
Ustrzyki Dolne 77 E5 Podkarpackie, SE Poland
Ust Urt see Ustyurt Plateau
Ustyurt Plateau 100 B1 var. Ust Urt, Uzb. Ustyurt Platosi. Plateau Kazakhstan/Uzbekistan
Ustyurt Platosi see Ustyurt Plateau
Usulután 30 C3 Usulután, SE El Salvador
Usumacinta, Río 30 B1 river Guatemala/Mexico
Utah 26 A1 off. State of Utah; also known as Beehive State, Mormon State. State W USA
Utah Lake 22 B4 lake Utah, W USA
Utena 84 C4 Utena, E Lithuania
Utica 19 F3 New York, NE USA
Utrecht 64 C4 Lat. Trajectum ad Rhenum. Utrecht C Netherlands
Utsunomiya 109 D5 var. Utunomiya. Tochigi, Honshū, S Japan
Uttaranchal 113 E2 Admin. region state N India
Uttar Pradesh 113 E3 prev. United Provinces, United Provinces of Agra and Oudh. State N India
Utunomiya see Utsunomiya
Uulu 84 D2 Pärnumaa, SW Estonia
Uummannaq 60 C3 var. Umanak, Umanaq. C Greenland
Uummannarsuaq see Nunap Isua
Uvalde 27 F4 Texas, SW USA
Uvaravichy 85 D7 Rus. Uvarovichi. Homyel'skaya Voblasts', SE Belarus
Uvea, Île 123 E4 island N Wallis and Futuna
Uvs Nuur 104 C1 var. Ozero Ubsu-Nur. Lake Mongolia/Russian Federation
'Uwaynāt, Jabal 88 A3 var. Jebel Uweinat. Mountain Libya/Sudan
Uyo 53 G5 Akwa Ibom, S Nigeria
Uyuni 39 F5 Potosí, W Bolivia
Uzbekistan 100 D2 Country C Asia
Uzhhorod 86 B2 Rus. Uzhgorod; prev. Ungvár. Zakarpats'ka Oblast', W Ukraine
Užice 78 D4 prev. Titovo Užice. Serbia, W Serbia and Montenegro (Yugo.)

V

Vaal 56 D4 river C South Africa
Vaals 65 D6 Limburg, SE Netherlands
Vaasa 63 D5 Swe. Vasa; prev. Nikolainkaupunki. Länsi-Suomi, W Finland
Vaassen 64 D3 Gelderland, E Netherlands
Vác 77 C6 Ger. Waitzen. Pest, N Hungary
Vadodara 112 C4 prev. Baroda. Gujarāt, W India
Vaduz 72 E2 country capital (Liechtenstein) W Liechtenstein
Váh 77 C5 Ger. Waag, Hung. Vág. River W Slovakia
Väinameri 84 C2 prev. Muhu Väin, Ger. Moon-Sund. Sea E Baltic Sea
Valachia see Wallachia
Valday 88 B4 Novgorodskaya Oblast', W Russian Federation
Valdecañas, Embalse de 70 D3 reservoir W Spain
Valdepeñas 71 E4 Castilla-La Mancha, C Spain
Valdés, Península 43 C6 peninsula SE Argentina
Valdez 14 C3 Alaska, USA
Valdia see Weldiya
Valdivia 43 B5 Los Lagos, C Chile
Val-d'Or 16 D4 Québec, SE Canada
Valdosta 21 E3 Georgia, SE USA
Valence 69 D5 anc. Valentia, Valentia Julia, Ventia. Drôme, E France
Valencia 25 D1 California, W USA
Valencia 36 D1 Carabobo, N Venezuela
Valencia 71 F3 País Valenciano, E Spain
Valencia, Golfo de 71 F3 var. Gulf of Valencia. Gulf E Spain
Valencia, Gulf of see Valencia, Golfo de
Valenciennes 90 D2 Nord, N France
Valera 36 C2 Trujillo, NW Venezuela

Valga 84 D3 Ger. Walk, Latv. Valka. Valgamaa, S Estonia
Valira 69 A8 river Andorra/Spain
Valjevo 78 C4 Serbia, W Serbia and Montenegro (Yugo.)
Valjok see Válljohka
Valka 84 D3 Ger. Walk. Valka, N Latvia
Valkenswaard 65 D5 Noord-Brabant, S Netherlands
Valladolid 70 D2 Castilla-León, NW Spain
Valladolid 29 H3 Yucatán, SE Mexico
Vall d'Uxó 71 F3 País Valenciano, E Spain
Valle de la Pascua 36 D2 Guárico, N Venezuela
Valledupar 36 B1 Cesar, N Colombia
Vallejo 25 B6 California, W USA
Vallenar 42 B3 Atacama, N Chile
Valletta 75 C8 var. Valleta. Country capital (Malta) E Malta
Valley City 23 E2 North Dakota, N USA
Válljohka 62 D2 var. Valjok. Finnmark, N Norway
Valls 71 G2 Cataluña, NE Spain
Valmiera 84 D3 Est. Volmari, Ger. Wolmar. Valmiera, N Latvia
Valozhyn 85 C5 Pol. Wołożyn, Rus. Volozhin. Minskaya Voblasts', C Belarus
Valparaiso 18 C3 Indiana, N USA
Valparaíso 42 B4 Valparaíso, C Chile
Valverde del Camino 70 C4 Andalucía, S Spain
Van 95 F3 Van, E Turkey
Vanadzor 95 F2 prev. Kirovakan. N Armenia
Vancouver 14 D5 British Columbia, SW Canada
Vancouver 24 B3 Washington, NW USA
Vancouver Island 14 D5 island British Columbia, SW Canada
Van Diemen Gulf 124 D2 gulf Northern Territory, N Australia
Vänern 63 B6 Eng. Lake Vaner; prev. Lake Vener. Lake Sweden
Vangaindrano 57 G4 Fianarantsoa, SE Madagascar
Van Gölü 95 F3 Eng. Lake Van; anc. Thospitis. Salt lake E Turkey
Van Horn 26 D3 Texas, SW USA
Van, Lake see Van Gölü
Vannes 68 A3 anc. Dariorigum. Morbihan, NW France
Vantaa 63 D6 Swe. Vanda. Etelä-Suomi, S Finland
Vanua Levu 123 E4 island N Fiji
Vanuatu 122 C4 prev. New Hebrides. Country SW Pacific Ocean
Van Wert 18 C4 Ohio, N USA
Varakļāni 84 D4 Madona, C Latvia
Vārānasi 113 E3 prev. Banaras, Benares, hist. Kasi. Uttar Pradesh, N India
Varangerfjorden 62 E2 fjord N Norway
Varangerhalvøya 62 D2 peninsula N Norway
Varannó see Vranov nad Topl'ou
Varaždin 78 B2 Ger. Warasdin, Hung. Varasd. Varaždin, N Croatia
Varberg 63 B7 Halland, S Sweden
Vardar 79 E6 Gk. Axiós. River FYR Macedonia/Greece see also Axiós
Varde 63 A7 Ribe, W Denmark
Varёna 85 B5 Pol. Orany. Varёna, S Lithuania
Varese 74 B2 Lombardia, N Italy
Vârful Moldoveanu 86 B4 var. Moldoveanul; prev. Vîrful Moldoveanu. Mountain C Romania
Varkaus 85 E5 Itä-Suomi, C Finland
Varna 82 E2 prev. Stalin, anc. Odessus. Varna, E Bulgaria
Varnenski Zaliv 82 E2 prev. Stalinski Zaliv. Bay E Bulgaria
Vasilíki 83 A5 Lefkáda, Iónioi Nísoi, Greece, C Mediterranean Sea
Vasilishki 85 B5 Pol. Wasiliszki, Rus. Vasilishki. Hrodzyenskaya Voblasts', W Belarus
Vaslui 86 D4 Vaslui, C Romania
Västerås 63 C6 Västmanland, C Sweden
Vasyl'kiv 87 E2 Rus. Vasil'kov. Kyyivs'ka Oblast', N Ukraine
Vaté see Efate
Vatican City 75 A7 Country S Europe
Vatnajökull 61 E5 glacier SE Iceland
Vättern 63 B6 Eng. Lake Vatter; prev. Lake Vetter. Lake S Sweden
Vaughn 26 D2 New Mexico, SW USA
Vaupés, Río 36 C4 var. Rio Uaupés. River Brazil/Colombia see also Uaupés, Rio
Vava'u Group 123 E4 island group N Tonga
Vavuniya 110 D3 Northern Province, N Sri Lanka
Vawkavysk 85 B6 Pol. Wołkowysk, Rus. Volkovysk. Hrodzyenskaya Voblasts', W Belarus
Växjö 63 C7 var. Vexiö. Kronoberg, S Sweden
Vaygach, Ostrov 88 E2 island NW Russian Federation
Veendam 64 E2 Groningen, NE Netherlands
Veenendaal 64 D4 Utrecht, C Netherlands
Vega 62 B4 island C Norway
Veisiejai 85 B5 Lazdijai, S Lithuania
Vejer de la Frontera 70 C5 Andalucía, S Spain
Veldhoven 65 D5 Noord-Brabant, S Netherlands
Velebit 78 A3 mountain range C Croatia
Velenje 73 E7 Ger. Wöllan. N Slovenia
Veles 79 E6 Turk. Köprülü. C FYR Macedonia
Velho see Porto Velho
Velika Morava 78 D4 var. Glavn'a Morava, Morava, Ger. Grosse Morava. River C Serbia and Montenegro (Yugo.)
Velikaya 91 G2 river NE Russian Federation

Velikiye Luki 88 A4 Pskovskaya Oblast', W Russian Federation
Velikiy Novgorod 88 B4 prev. Novgorod. Novgorodskaya Oblast', W Russian Federation
Veliko Tŭrnovo 82 D2 prev. Tirnovo, Trnovo, Tŭrnovo. Veliko Tŭrnovo, N Bulgaria
Velingrad 82 C3 Pazardzhik, C Bulgaria
Vel'ký Krtíš 77 D6 Banskobystrický Kraj, C Slovakia
Vellore 110 C2 Tamil Nādu, SE India
Velobriga see Viana do Castelo
Velsen see Velsen-Noord
Velsen-Noord 64 C3 var. Velsen. Noord-Holland, W Netherlands
Vel'sk 88 C4 var. Velsk. Arkhangel'skaya Oblast', NW Russian Federation
Velsk see Vel'sk
Velvendos see Velvendós
Velvendós 82 B4 var. Velvendos. Dytikí Makedonía, N Greece
Velykyy Tokmak see Tokmak
Vendôme 68 C4 Loir-et-Cher, C France
Venezia 74 C2 Eng. Venice, Fr. Venise, Ger. Venedig; anc.Venetia. Veneto, NE Italy
Venezuela 36 D2 prev. Estados Unidos de Venezuela, United States of Venezuela. Country N South America
Venezuela, Golfo de 36 C1 Eng. Gulf of Maracaibo, Gulf of Venezuela. Gulf NW Venezuela
Venezuelan Basin 34 B1 undersea feature E Caribbean Sea
Venice see Venezia
Venice 20 C4 Louisiana, S USA
Venice, Gulf of 74 C2 It. Golfo di Venezia, Slvn. Beneški Zaliv. Gulf N Adriatic Sea
Venlo 65 D5 prev. Venloo. Limburg, SE Netherlands
Venta 84 B3 Ger. Windau. River Latvia/Lithuania
Ventimiglia 74 A3 Liguria, NW Italy
Ventspils 84 B2 Ger. Windau. Ventspils, NW Latvia
Vera 42 D3 Santa Fe, C Argentina
Veracruz 29 F4 var. Veracruz Llave. Veracruz-Llave, E Mexico
Veracruz Llave see Veracruz
Vercelli 74 A2 anc. Vercellae. Piemonte, NW Italy
Verdal see Verdalsøra
Verdalsøra 62 B4 var. Verdal. Nord-Trøndelag, C Norway
Verde, Costa 70 D1 coastal region N Spain
Verden 72 B3 Niedersachsen, NW Germany
Veria see Véroia
Verkhoyanskiy Khrebet 93 F3 mountain range NE Russian Federation
Vermillion 23 F3 South Dakota, N USA
Vermont 19 F2 off. State of Vermont; also known as The Green Mountain State. State NE USA
Vernal 22 B4 Utah, W USA
Vernon 27 F2 Texas, SW USA
Véroia 82 B4 var. Veria, Vérroia, Turk. Karaferiye. Kentrikí Makedonía, N Greece
Verona 74 C2 Veneto, NE Italy
Vérroia see Véroia
Versailles 90 D1 Yvelines, N France
Verviers 65 D6 Liège, E Belgium
Vesdre 65 D6 river E Belgium
Veselinovo 82 D2 Shumen, NE Bulgaria
Vesoul 68 D4 anc. Vesulium, Vesulum. Haute-Saône, E France
Vesterålen 62 B2 island group N Norway
Vestfjorden 62 C3 fjord C Norway
Vestmannaeyjar 61 E5 Suðurland, S Iceland
Vesuvio 75 D5 Eng. Vesuvius. Volcano S Italy
Veszprém 77 C7 Ger. Veszprim. Veszprém, W Hungary
Vetrino 82 E2 Varna, E Bulgaria
Veurne 65 A5 var. Furnes. West-Vlaanderen, W Belgium
Vexiö see Växjö
Viacha 39 F4 La Paz, W Bolivia
Viana de Castelo see Viana do Castelo
Viana do Castelo 70 B2 var. Viana de Castelo; anc. Velobriga. Viana do Castelo, NW Portugal
Vianen 64 C4 Zuid-Holland, C Netherlands
Viangchan 114 C4 Eng./Fr. Vientiane. Country capital (Laos) C Laos
Viangphoukha 114 C3 var. Vieng Pou Kha. Louang Namtha, N Laos
Viareggio 74 B3 Toscana, C Italy
Viborg 85 A7 Viborg, NW Denmark
Vic 71 G2 var. Vich; anc. Ausa, Vicus Ausonensis. Cataluña, NE Spain
Vicenza 74 C2 anc. Vicentia. Veneto, NE Italy
Vich see Vic
Vichy 69 C5 Allier, C France
Vicksburg 20 B2 Mississippi, S USA
Victoria 80 A5 var. Rabat. Gozo, NW Malta
Victoria 57 H1 country capital (Seychelles) Mahé, SW Seychelles
Victoria 27 G4 Texas, SW USA
Victoria 14 D5 Vancouver Island, British Columbia, SW Canada
Victoria 127 C7 state SE Australia
Victoria Bank see Vitória Seamount
Victoria de Durango see Durango
Victoria de las Tunas see Las Tunas
Victoria Falls 56 C2 waterfall Zambia/Zimbabwe
Victoria Falls 56 C2 Matabeleland North, W Zimbabwe
Victoria Island 15 F3 island Northwest Territories/Nunavut, NW Canada
Victoria, Lake 51 B6 var. Victoria Nyanza. Lake E Africa
Victoria Land 132 C4 physical region Antarctica
Victoria Nyanza see Victoria, Lake

Victoria River 124 D3 river Northern Territory, N Australia
Victorville 25 C7 California, W USA
Vicus Ausonensis see Vic
Vidalia 21 E2 Georgia, SE USA
Vidin 82 B1 anc. Bononia. Vidin, NW Bulgaria
Vidzy 85 C5 Rus. Vidzy. Vitsyebskaya Voblasts', NW Belarus
Viedma 43 C5 Río Negro, E Argentina
Vieng Pou Kha see Viangphoukha
Vienna see Wien
Vienne 69 D5 anc. Vienna. Isère, E France
Vienne 68 B4 river W France
Vientiane see Viangchan
Vierzon 68 C4 Cher, C France
Viesīte 84 C4 Ger. Eckengraf. Jēkabpils, S Latvia
Vietnam 114 D4 Vtn. Công Hoa Xa Hôi Chu Nghia Viêt Nam. Country SE Asia
Vietri see Vietri Tri
Viêt Tri 114 D3 var. Vietri. Vinh Phu, N Vietnam
Vieux Fort 33 F2 S Saint Lucia
Vigo 70 B2 Galicia, NW Spain
Vijayawāda 110 D1 prev. Bezwada. Andhra Pradesh, SE India
Vijosa see Vjosës, Lumi i
Vijosë see Vjosës, Lumi i
Vila see Port-Vila
Vila Artur de Paiva see Cubango
Vila da Ponte see Cubango
Vila de Mocímboa da Praia see Mocímboa da Praia
Vila do Conde 70 B2 Porto, NW Portugal
Vila do Zumbo 56 D2 prev. Vila do Zumbu, Zumbo. Tete, NW Mozambique
Vilafranca del Penedès 71 G2 var. Villafranca del Panadés. Cataluña, NE Spain
Vila General Machado see Camacupa
Vilaka 84 D4 Ger. Marienhausen. Balvi, NE Latvia
Vilalba 70 C1 Galicia, NW Spain
Vila Nova de Gaia 70 B2 Porto, NW Portugal
Vila Nova de Portimão see Portimão
Vila Pereira de Eça see N'Giva
Vila Real 70 C2 var. Vila Rial. Vila Real, N Portugal
Vila Rial see Vila Real
Vila Robert Williams see Caála
Vila Serpa Pinto see Menongue
Vilhelmina 62 C4 Västerbotten, N Sweden
Vilhena 40 D3 Rondônia, W Brazil
Vília 83 C5 Attikí, C Greece
Viliya 85 C5 Lith. Neris, Rus. Viliya. River W Belarus
Viljandi 84 D2 Ger. Fellin. Viljandimaa, S Estonia
Vilkaviškis 84 B4 Pol. Wyłkowyszki. Vilkaviškis, SW Lithuania
Villa Acuña 28 D2 var. Cuidad Acuña. Coahuila de Zaragoza, NE Mexico
Villa Bella 39 F2 Beni, N Bolivia
Villacarrillo 71 E4 Andalucía, S Spain
Villa Cecilia see Ciudad Madero
Villach 73 D7 Slvn. Beljak. Kärnten, S Austria
Villacidro 75 A5 Sardegna, Italy, C Mediterranean Sea
Villa Concepción see Concepción
Villa del Pilar see Pilar
Villafranca de los Barros 70 C4 Extremadura, W Spain
Villafranca del Panadés see Vilafranca del Penedès
Villahermosa 29 G4 prev. San Juan Bautista. Tabasco, SE Mexico
Villajoyosa 71 F4 var. La Vila Jojosa. País Valenciano, E Spain
Villa María 42 C4 Córdoba, C Argentina
Villa Martín 39 F5 Potosí, SW Bolivia
Villa Mercedes 42 C4 prev. Mercedes. San Luis, C Argentina
Villanueva 28 D3 Zacatecas, C Mexico
Villanueva de la Serena 70 C3 Extremadura, W Spain
Villanueva de los Infantes 71 E4 Castilla-La Mancha, C Spain
Villarrica 42 D2 Guairá, SE Paraguay
Villavicencio 36 B3 Meta, C Colombia
Villaviciosa 70 D1 Asturias, N Spain
Villazón 39 G5 Potosí, S Bolivia
Villena 71 F4 País Valenciano, E Spain
Villeurbanne 69 D5 Rhône, E France
Villingen-Schwenningen 73 B6 Baden-Württemberg, S Germany
Vilnius 85 C5 Pol. Wilno, Ger. Wilna; prev. Rus. Vilna. Country capital (Lithuania) Vilnius, SE Lithuania
Vil'shanka 87 E3 Rus. Olshanka. Kirovohrads'ka Oblast', C Ukraine
Vilvoorde 65 C6 Fr. Vilvorde. Vlaams Brabant, C Belgium
Vilyeyka 85 C5 Pol. Wilejka, Rus. Vileyka. Minskaya Voblasts', NW Belarus
Vilyuy 93 F3 river NE Russian Federation
Viña del Mar 42 B4 Valparaíso, C Chile
Vinaròs 71 F3 País Valenciano, E Spain
Vincennes 18 B4 Indiana, N USA
Vindhya Mountains see Vindhya Range
Vindhya Range 112 D4 var. Vindhya Mountains. Mountain range N India
Vineland 19 F4 New Jersey, NE USA
Vinh 114 D4 Nghê An, N Vietnam
Vinh Loi see Bac Liêu
Vinh Thai Lan see Thailand, Gulf of
Vinishte 82 C2 Montana, NW Bulgaria
Vinita 27 G1 Oklahoma, C USA
Vinkovci 78 C3 Ger. Winkowitz, Hung. Vinkovcze. Vukovar-Srijem, E Croatia
Vinnytsya 86 D2 Rus. Vinnitsa. Vinnyts'ka Oblast', C Ukraine
Vinson Massif 132 A3 mountain Antarctica
Vîranşehir 95 E4 Şanlıurfa, SE Turkey
Vîrful Moldoveanu see Vârful Moldoveanu

Virginia 19 E5 off. Commonwealth of Virginia; also known as Mother of Presidents, Mother of States, Old Dominion. State NE USA
Virginia 23 G1 Minnesota, N USA
Virginia Beach 19 F5 Virginia, NE USA
Virgin Islands see British Virgin Islands
Virgin Islands (US) 33 F3 var. Virgin Islands of the United States; prev. Danish West Indies. US unincorporated territory E West Indies
Virgin Islands of the United States see Virgin Islands (US)
Virôchey 115 E5 Rôtânôkiri, NE Cambodia
Virovitica 78 C2 Ger. Virovititz, Hung. Verôcze; prev. Ger. Werowitz. Virovitica-Podravina, NE Croatia
Virton 65 D8 Luxembourg, SE Belgium
Virtsu 84 D2 Ger. Werder. Läänemaa, W Estonia
Vis 78 B4 It. Lissa; anc. Issa. Island S Croatia
Vis see Fish
Visaginas 84 C4 prev. Sniečkus. Ignalina, E Lithuania
Visākhapatnam 113 E5 Andhra Pradesh, SE India
Visalia 25 C6 California, W USA
Visby 63 C7 Ger. Wisby. Gotland, SE Sweden
Viscount Melville Sound 15 F2 prev. Melville Sound. Sound Northwest Territories/Nunavut, N Canada
Visé 65 D6 Liège, E Belgium
Viseu 70 C2 prev. Vizeu. Viseu, N Portugal
Visoko 78 C4 Federacija Bosna I Hercegovina, C Bosnia and Herzegovina
Visttasjohka 62 D3 Swe. Kalixälven. River N Sweden
Vistula see Wisła
Vistula Lagoon 76 C2 Ger. Frisches Haff, Pol. Zalew Wiślany, Rus. Vislinskiy Zaliv. Lagoon Poland/Russian Federation
Viterbo 74 C4 anc. Vicus Elbii. Lazio, C Italy
Viti Levu 123 E4 island W Fiji
Vitim 93 F4 river C Russian Federation
Vitória 41 F4 Espírito Santo, SE Brazil
Vitória Bank see Vitória Seamount
Vitória da Conquista 41 F3 Bahia, E Brazil
Vitoria-Gasteiz 71 E1 var. Vitoria, Eng. Vittoria. País Vasco, N Spain
Vitória Seamount 45 B5 var. Victoria Bank, Vitoria Bank. Undersea feature C Atlantic Ocean
Vitré 68 B3 Ille-et-Vilaine, NW France
Vitsyebsk 85 E5 Rus. Vitebsk. Vitsyebskaya Voblasts', NE Belarus
Vittoria see Vitoria-Gasteiz
Vittoria 75 C7 Sicilia, Italy, C Mediterranean Sea
Vizianagaram 113 E5 var. Vizianagram. Andhra Pradesh, E India
Vizianagram see Vizianagaram
Vjosës, Lumi i 79 C7 var. Vijosa, Vijosë, Gk. Aóos. River Albania/Greece see also Aóos
Vlaardingen 64 B4 Zuid-Holland, SW Netherlands
Vladikavkaz 89 B8 prev. Dzaudzhikau, Ordzhonikidze. Severnaya Osetiya-Alaniya, SW Russian Federation
Vladimir 89 B5 Vladimirskaya Oblast', W Russian Federation
Vladivostok 93 G5 Primorskiy Kray, SE Russian Federation
Vlagtwedde 64 E2 Groningen, NE Netherlands
Vlasotince 79 E5 Serbia, SE Serbia and Montenegro (Yugo.)
Vlieland 64 C1 Fris. Flylân. Island Waddeneilanden, N Netherlands
Vlijmen 64 C4 Noord-Brabant, S Netherlands
Vlissingen 65 B5 Eng. Flushing, Fr. Flessingue. Zeeland, SW Netherlands
Vlorë 79 C7 prev. Vlonë, It. Valona, Vlora. Vlorë, SW Albania
Vöcklabruck 73 D6 Oberösterreich, NW Austria
Vohimena, Tanjona 57 F4 Fr. Cap Sainte Marie. Headland S Madagascar
Voiron 69 D5 Isère, E France
Vojvodina 78 D3 Ger. Wojwodina. Region N Serbia and Montenegro (Yugo.)
Volcán de Chiriquí see Barú, Volcán
Volga 89 B7 river NW Russian Federation
Volga Delta 59 G4 delta Astrakhanskaya Oblast', SW Russian Federation
Volga Uplands 59 G3 Rus. Privolzhskaya Vozvyshennost' mountain range W Russian Federation
Volgodonsk 89 B7 Rostovskaya Oblast', SW Russian Federation
Volgograd 89 B7 prev. Stalingrad, Tsaritsyn. Volgogradskaya Oblast', SW Russian Federation
Volkhov 88 B4 Leningradskaya Oblast', NW Russian Federation
Volnovakha 87 G3 Donets'ka Oblast', SE Ukraine
Volodymyr-Volyns'kyy 86 C1 Pol. Włodzimierz, Rus. Vladimir-Volynskiy. Volyns'ka Oblast', NW Ukraine
Vólos 83 B5 Thessalía, C Greece
Vol'sk 89 C6 Saratovskaya Oblast', W Russian Federation
Volta 53 E5 river SE Ghana
Volta Blanche see White Volta
Volta, Lake 53 E5 reservoir SE Ghana
Volta Noire see Black Volta
Volturno 75 D5 river S Italy
Volzhskiy 89 B6 Volgogradskaya Oblast', SW Russian Federation
Võnnu 84 E3 Ger. Wendau. Tartumaa, SE Estonia
Voorst 64 D3 Gelderland, E Netherlands

Voranava 85 C5 Pol. Werenów, Rus. Voronovo. Hrodzyenskaya Voblasts', W Belarus
Vorderrhein 73 B7 river SE Switzerland
Vóreioi Sporádes 83 C5 var. Vórioi Sporádhes, Eng. Northern Sporades. Island group E Greece
Vórioi Sporádhes see Vóreioi Sporádes
Vorkuta 92 C2 Respublika Komi, NW Russian Federation
Vormsi 84 C2 var. Vormsi Saar, Ger. Worms, Swed. Ormsö. Island W Estonia
Vormsi Saar see Vormsi
Voronezh 89 B6 Voronezhskaya Oblast', W Russian Federation
Võru 84 D3 Ger. Werro. Võrumaa, SE Estonia
Vosges 68 E4 mountain range NE France
Vostochno-Sibirskoye More 93 F1 Eng. East Siberian Sea. Sea Arctic Ocean
Vostok 132 C3 Russian research station Antarctica
Vostok Island 123 G3 var. Vostock Island; prev. Stavers Island. Island Line Islands, SE Kiribati
Voznesens'k 87 E3 Rus. Voznesensk. Mykolayivs'ka Oblast', S Ukraine
Vrangelya, Ostrov 93 F1 Eng. Wrangel Island. Island NE Russian Federation
Vranje 79 E5 Serbia, SE Serbia and Montenegro (Yugo.)
Vranov see Vranov nad Topl'ou
Vranov nad Topl'ou 77 D5 var. Vranov, Hung. Varannó. Prešovský Kraj, E Slovakia
Vratsa 82 C2 Vratsa, NW Bulgaria
Vrbas 78 C3 river N Bosnia and Herzegovina
Vrbas 78 C3 Serbia, NW Serbia and Montenegro (Yugo.)
Vsetín 77 C5 Ger. Wsetin. Zlínský Kraj, E Czech Republic
Vučitrn 79 D5 Serbia, S Serbia and Montenegro (Yugo.)
Vukovar 78 C3 Hung. Vukovár. Vukovar-Srijem, E Croatia
Vulcano, Isola 75 C7 island Isole Eolie, S Italy
Vung Tau 115 E6 prev. Fr. Cape Saint Jacques, Cap Saint-Jacques. Ba Ria-Vung Tau, S Vietnam
Vyatka 89 C5 river NW Russian Federation
Vyborg 88 B3 Fin. Viipuri. Leningradskaya Oblast', NW Russian Federation
Vyerkhnyadzvinsk 85 D5 Rus. Verkhnedvinsk. Vitsyebskaya Voblasts', N Belarus
Vyetryna 85 D5 Rus. Vetrino. Vitsyebskaya Voblasts', N Belarus
Vynohradiv 86 B3 Cz. Sevluš, Hung. Nagyszőllős, Rus. Vinogradov; prev. Sevlyush. Zakarpats'ka Oblast', W Ukraine

W

Wa 53 E4 NW Ghana
Waal 64 C4 river S Netherlands
Wabash 18 C4 Indiana, N USA
Wabash River 18 B5 river N USA
Waco 27 G3 Texas, SW USA
Waddān 49 F3 NW Libya
Waddeneilanden 64 C1 Eng. West Frisian Islands. Island group N Netherlands
Waddenzee 64 C1 var. Wadden Zee. Sea SE North Sea
Waddington, Mount 14 D5 mountain British Columbia, SW Canada
Wādī as Sīr 97 B6 var. Wadi es Sir. 'Ammān, NW Jordan
Wadi es Sir see Wādī as Sīr
Wadi Halfa 50 B3 var. Wādī Ḥalfā'. Northern, N Sudan
Wādī Mūsā 97 B7 var. Petra. Ma'ān, S Jordan
Wad Madanī see Wad Medani
Wad Medani 50 C4 var. Wad Madanī. Gezira, C Sudan
Waflia 117 F4 Pulau Buru, E Indonesia
Wagadugu see Ouagadougou
Wagga Wagga 127 C7 New South Wales, SE Australia
Wagin 125 B7 Western Australia
Wāh 112 C1 Punjab, NE Pakistan
Wahai 117 F4 Pulau Seram, E Indonesia
Wahiawā 25 A8 var. Wahiawa. O'ahu, Hawai'i, USA, C Pacific Ocean
Wahībah, Ramlat Āl 99 E5 var. Ramlat Ahl Wahībah, Ramlat Al Wahaybah, Eng. Wahibah Sands. Desert N Oman
Wahibah Sands see Wahībah, Ramlat Āl
Wahpeton 89 B7 North Dakota, N USA
Wahran see Oran
Waiau 129 A7 river South Island, NZ
Waigeo, Pulau 117 G4 island Maluku, E Indonesia
Waikaremoana, Lake 128 E4 lake North Island, NZ
Wailuku 25 B8 Maui, Hawai'i, USA, C Pacific Ocean
Waimate 129 B6 Canterbury, South Island, NZ
Waiouru 128 D4 Manawatu-Wanganui, North Island, NZ
Waipara 129 C6 Canterbury, South Island, NZ
Waipawa 128 E4 Hawke's Bay, North Island, NZ
Waipukurau 128 D4 Hawke's Bay, North Island, NZ
Wairau 129 C5 river South Island, NZ
Wairoa 128 D2 river North Island, NZ
Wairoa 128 E4 Hawke's Bay, North Island, NZ
Waitaki 129 B6 river South Island, NZ
Waitara 128 D4 Taranaki, North Island, NZ
Waiuku 128 D3 Auckland, North Island, NZ
Wakasa-wan 109 C6 bay C Japan
Wakatipu, Lake 129 A7 lake South Island, NZ

Wakayama 109 C6 Wakayama, Honshū, SW Japan
Wake Island 120 D1 atoll NW Pacific Ocean
Wake Island 130 C2 US unincorporated territory NW Pacific Ocean
Wakkanai 108 D1 Hokkaidō, NE Japan
Walachei see Wallachia
Walachia see Wallachia
Wałbrzych 76 B4 Ger. Waldenburg, Waldenburg in Schlesien. Dolnośląskie, SW Poland
Walcourt 65 C7 Namur, S Belgium
Wałcz 76 B3 Ger. Deutsch Krone. Zachodniopomorskie, NW Poland
Waldia see Weldiya
Wales 67 C6 Wel. Cymru. National region UK
Wales 14 C2 Alaska, USA
Wales Island, Prince of see Pinang, Pulau
Walgett 127 D5 New South Wales, SE Australia
Walker Lake 25 C5 lake Nevada, W USA
Wallachia 86 B5 var. Walachia, Ger. Walachei, Rom. Valachia. Cultural region S Romania
Walla Walla 24 C2 Washington, NW USA
Wallis and Futuna 123 E4 Fr. Territoire de Wallis et Futuna. French overseas territory C Pacific Ocean
Walnut Ridge 20 B1 Arkansas, C USA
Walthamstow 67 B7 SE England, UK
Walvis Bay 56 A4 Afr. Walvisbaai. Erongo, NW Namibia
Walvis Ridge see Walvis Ridge
Walvis Ridge 47 B7 var. Walvish Ridge. Undersea feature E Atlantic Ocean
Wan see Anhui
Wanaka 129 B6 Otago, South Island, NZ
Wanaka, Lake 129 A6 lake South Island, NZ
Wanchuan see Zhangjiakou
Wandel Sea 61 E1 sea Arctic Ocean
Wandsworth 89 A8 SE England, UK
Wanganui 128 D4 Manawatu-Wanganui, North Island, NZ
Wangaratta 127 C7 Victoria, SE Australia
Wanki, Río see Coco, Río
Wanlaweyn 51 D6 var. Wanle Weyn, It. Uanle Uen. Shabeellaha Hoose, SW Somalia
Wanle Weyn see Wanlaweyn
Wanxian 106 B5 Chongqing, C China
Warangal 113 E5 Andhra Pradesh, C India
Warburg 72 B4 Nordrhein-Westfalen, W Germany
Ware 15 E4 British Columbia, W Canada
Waremme 65 C6 Liège, E Belgium
Waren 72 C3 Mecklenburg-Vorpommern, NE Germany
Wargla see Ouargla
Warkworth 128 D2 Auckland, North Island, NZ
Warnemünde 72 C2 Mecklenburg-Vorpommern, NE Germany
Warner 27 G1 Oklahoma, C USA
Warnes 39 G4 Santa Cruz, C Bolivia
Warrego River 127 C5 seasonal river New South Wales/Queensland, E Australia
Warren 18 D3 Michigan, N USA
Warren 18 D3 Ohio, N USA
Warren 19 E3 Pennsylvania, NE USA
Warri 53 F5 Delta, S Nigeria
Warrnambool 127 B7 Victoria, SE Australia
Warsaw see Mazowieckie
Warszawa 76 D3 Eng. Warsaw, Ger. Warschau, Rus. Varshava. Country capital (Poland) Mazowieckie, C Poland
Warta 76 B3 Ger. Warthe. River W Poland
Warwick 127 E5 Queensland, E Australia
Washington 22 A2 off. State of Washington; also known as Chinook State, Evergreen State. State NW USA
Washington D. C. 19 E4 country capital (USA) District of Columbia, NE USA
Washington, Mount 19 G2 mountain New Hampshire, NE USA
Wash, The 67 E6 inlet E England, UK
Waspam 31 E2 var. Waspán. Región Autónoma Atlántico Norte, NE Nicaragua
Waspán see Waspam
Watampone 117 E4 var. Bone. Sulawesi, C Indonesia
Waterbury 19 F3 Connecticut, NE USA
Waterford 67 B6 Ir. Port Láirge. S Ireland
Waterloo 23 G3 Iowa, C USA
Watertown 19 F2 New York, NE USA
Watertown 23 F2 South Dakota, N USA
Waterville 19 G2 Maine, NE USA
Watford 67 A7 SE England, UK
Watsa 55 E5 Orientale, NE Dem. Rep. Congo
Watts Bar Lake reservoir Tennessee, S USA
Wau 51 B5 var. Wāw. Western Bahr el Ghazal, S Sudan
Waukegan 18 B3 Illinois, N USA
Waukesha 18 B3 Wisconsin, N USA
Wausau 18 B2 Wisconsin, N USA
Waverly 23 G3 Iowa, C USA
Wavre 65 C6 Wallon Brabant, C Belgium
Wāw see Wau
Wawa 16 C4 Ontario, S Canada
Waycross 21 E3 Georgia, SE USA
Wearmouth see Sunderland
Webster City 23 F3 Iowa, C USA
Weddell Plain 132 A2 undersea feature SW Atlantic Ocean
Weddell Sea 132 A2 sea SW Atlantic Ocean
Weener 72 A3 Niedersachsen, NW Germany
Weert 65 D5 Limburg, SE Netherlands
Weesp 64 C3 Noord-Holland, C Netherlands
Węgorzewo 76 D2 Ger. Angerburg. Warmińsko-Mazurskie, NE Poland
Weimar 72 C4 Thüringen, C Germany
Weissenburg see Weissenburg in Bayern
Weissenburg in Bayern 73 C6 var. Weissenburg. Bayern, SE Germany
Weiswampach 65 D7 Diekirch, N Luxembourg
Wejherowo 76 C2 Pomorskie, NW Poland

Welchman Hall *33 G1* C Barbados
Weldiya *50 C4 var.* Waldia, *It.* Valdia.
  N Ethiopia
Welkom *56 D4* Free State, C South Africa
Welle *see* Uele
Wellesley Islands *126 B2* island group
  Queensland, N Australia
Wellington *129 D5* country capital (NZ)
  Wellington, North Island, NZ
Wellington *see* Wellington, Isla
Wellington *23 F3* Kansas, C USA
Wellington, Isla *43 A7 var.* Wellington.
  Island S Chile
Wells *24 D4* Nevada, W USA
Wellsford *128 D2* Auckland, North
  Island, NZ
Wells, Lake *125 C5 lake* Western Australia
Wels *73 D6 anc.* Ovilava. Oberösterreich,
  N Austria
Wembley *67 A8* SE England, UK
Wemmel *65 B6* Vlaams Brabant, C Belgium
Wenatchee *24 B2* Washington, NW USA
Wenchi *53 E4* W Ghana
Wen-chou *see* Wenzhou
Wenchow *see* Wenzhou
Wenmen Island *see* Wolf, Isla
Wenzhou *106 D5 var.* Wen-chou, Wenchow.
  Zhejiang, SE China
Werda *56 C4* Kgalagadi, S Botswana
Werkendam *64 C4* Noord-Brabant,
  S Netherlands
Weser *72 B3 river* NW Germany
Wessel Islands *126 B1* island group
  Northern Territory, N Australia
West Antarctica *see* Lesser Antarctica
West Bank *97 A6 disputed region* SW Asia
West Bend *18 B3* Wisconsin, N USA
West Bengal *113 F4 state* NE India
West Cape *129 A7 headland* South Island, NZ
West Des Moines *23 F3* Iowa, C USA
Westerland *72 B2* Schleswig-Holstein,
  N Germany
Western Australia *124 B4 state* W Australia
Western Desert *see* Sahara el Gharbîya
Western Dvina *63 E7 Bel.* Dzvina,
  Ger. Düna, *Latv.* Daugava, *Rus.* Zapadnaya
  Dvina. *River* W Europe
Western Ghats *112 C5 mountain range*
  SW India
Western Isles *see* Outer Hebrides
Western Sahara *48 B3 UK disputed territory*
  N Africa
Western Samoa *see* Samoa
Westerschelde *65 B5 Eng.* Western Scheldt;
  prev. Honte. *Inlet* S North Sea
West Falkland *43 C7 var.* Isla Gran Malvina.
  Island W Falkland Islands
West Fargo *23 F2* North Dakota, N USA
West Irian *see* Papua
West Mariana Basin *120 B1*
  var. Perece Vela Basin. *Undersea feature*
  W Pacific Ocean
West Memphis *20 B1* Arkansas, C USA
West New Guinea *see* Papua
West Palm Beach *21 F4* Florida, SE USA
West Papua *see* Papua
Weston-super-Mare *67 D7* SW England, UK
Westport *129 C5* West Coast, South
  Island, NZ
West River *see* Xi Jiang
West Siberian Plain *see*
  Zapadno-Sibirskaya Ravnina
West Virginia *18 D4 off.* State of West
  Virginia; also known as The Mountain
  State. *State* NE USA
Wetar, Pulau *117 F5 island* Kepulauan
  Damar, E Indonesia
Wetzlar *73 B5* Hessen,
  W Germany
Wevok *14 C2 var.* Wewuk. Alaska, USA
Wewuk *see* Wevok
Wexford *67 B6 Ir.* Loch Garman.
  SE Ireland
Weyburn *15 F5* Saskatchewan, S Canada
Weymouth *67 D7* S England, UK
Wezep *64 D3* Gelderland, E Netherlands
Whakatane *128 E3* Bay of Plenty, North
  Island, NZ
Whale Cove *15 G3* Nunavut, C Canada
Whangarei *128 D2* Northland, North Island,
  NZ
Wharton Basin *119 D5 var.* West Australian
  Basin. *Undersea feature* E Indian Ocean
Whataroa *129 B6* West Coast, South Island,
  NZ
Wheatland *22 D3* Wyoming, C USA
Wheeler Peak *26 D1 mountain* New Mexico,
  SW USA
Wheeling *18 D4* West Virginia, NE USA
Whitby *67 D5* N England, UK
Whitefish *22 B1* Montana, NW USA
Whitehaven *67 C5* NW England, UK
Whitehorse *14 D4 territory capital* Yukon
  Territory, W Canada
White Nile *50 B4 Ar.* Al Bahr al Abyaḍ, An
  Nîl al Abyaḍ, Bahr el Jebel. *River* SE Sudan
White Nile *50 B4 var.* Bahr el Jebel. *River*
  S Sudan
White River *22 D3 river* South Dakota,
  N USA
White Sea *see* Beloye More
White Volta *53 E4 var.* Nakambé, *Fr.* Volta
  Blanche. *River* Burkina faso/Ghana
Whitianga *128 D2* Waikato, North
  Island, NZ
Whitney, Mount *25 C6 mountain* California,
  W USA
Whitsunday Group *126 D3 island group*
  Queensland, E Australia
Whyalla *127 B6* South Australia
Wichita *23 F5* Kansas, C USA
Wichita Falls *27 F2* Texas, SW USA
Wichita River *27 F2 river* Texas, SW USA
Wickenburg *26 B2* Arizona, SW USA
Wicklow *67 B6 Ir.* Cill Mhantáin. *Cultural*
  region E Ireland
Wicklow Mountains *67 B6 Ir.* Sléibhte Chill
  Mhantáin. *Mountain range* E Ireland

Wieliczka *77 D5* Małopolskie, S Poland
Wieluń *76 C4* Łódzkie, C Poland
Wien *73 E6 Eng.* Vienna, *Hung.* Bécs,
  Slvk. Vídeň, *Slvn.* Dunaj; *anc.* Vindobona.
  Country capital (Austria) Wien, NE Austria
Wiener Neustadt *73 E6* Niederösterreich,
  E Austria
Wierden *64 E3* Overijssel, E Netherlands
Wiesbaden *73 B5* Hessen, W Germany
Wight, Isle of *67 D7 island* S England, UK
Wijchen *64 D4* Gelderland, SE Netherlands
Wijk bij Duurstede *64 D4* Utrecht,
  C Netherlands
Wilcannia *127 C6* New South Wales,
  SE Australia
Wilhelm, Mount *122 B3 mountain* C PNG
Wilhelm-Pieck-Stadt *see* Guben
Wilhelmshaven *72 B3* Niedersachsen,
  NW Germany
Wilkes Barre *19 F3* Pennsylvania, NE USA
Wilkes Land *132 C4 physical region*
  Antarctica
Willard *26 D2* New Mexico, SW USA
Willcox *26 C3* Arizona, SW USA
Willebroek *65 B5* Antwerpen, C Belgium
Willemstad *33 E5 dependent territory capital*
  (Netherlands Antilles) Curaçao,
  Netherlands Antilles
Williston *22 D1* North Dakota, N USA
Wilmington *19 F4* Delaware, NE USA
Wilmington *21 F2* North Carolina,
  SE USA
Wilmington *18 C4* Ohio, N USA
Wilrijk *65 C5* Antwerpen, N Belgium
Winchester *67 D7 hist.* Wintancaester, *Lat.*
  Venta Belgarum. S England, UK
Winchester *19 E4* Virginia, NE USA
Windhoek *56 B3 Ger.* Windhuk.
  Country capital (Namibia) Khomas,
  C Namibia
Windorah *126 C4* Queensland, C Australia
Windsor *19 G3* Connecticut, NE USA
Windsor *126 D1* New South Wales,
  SE Australia
Windsor *16 C5* Ontario, S Canada
Windsor *67 D7* SE England, UK
Windward Islands *33 H4 island group*
  E West Indies
Windward Islands *see* Barlavento, Ilhas de
Windward Passage *32 D3 Sp.* Paso de los
  Vientos. *Channel* Cuba/Haiti
Winisk *16 C2 river* Ontario, S Canada
Winisk *16 C2* Ontario, C Canada
Winnebago, Lake *18 B2 lake* Wisconsin,
  N USA
Winnemucca *25 C5* Nevada, W USA
Winnipeg *15 G5* Manitoba, S Canada
Winnipeg, Lake *15 G5 lake* Manitoba,
  C Canada
Winnipegosis, Lake *16 A3 lake* Manitoba,
  C Canada
Winona *23 G3* Minnesota, N USA
Winschoten *64 E2* Groningen,
  NE Netherlands
Winsen *72 B3* Niedersachsen, N Germany
Winston Salem *21 E1* North Carolina,
  SE USA
Winsum *64 D1* Groningen, NE Netherlands
Winterswijk *64 E4* Gelderland,
  E Netherlands
Winterthur *73 B7* Zürich, NE Switzerland
Winton *126 C4* Queensland, E Australia
Winton *129 A7* Southland, South Island, NZ
Wisconsin *18 A2 off.* State of Wisconsin;
  also known as The Badger State. *State*
  N USA
Wisconsin Rapids *18 B2* Wisconsin, N USA
Wisconsin River *18 B3 river* Wisconsin,
  N USA
Wisła *76 C2 Eng.* Vistula, *Ger.* Weichsel.
  River Śląskie, S Poland
Wismar *72 C2* Mecklenburg-Vorpommern,
  N Germany
Wittenberge *72 C3* Brandenburg,
  N Germany
Wittlich *73 A5* Rheinland-Pfalz,
  SW Germany
Wittstock *72 C3* Brandenburg,
  NE Germany
W.J. van Blommesteinmeer *37 G3 reservoir*
  E Suriname
Władysławowo *76 C2* Pomorskie, N Poland
Włocławek *76 C3 Ger./Rus.* Vlotslavsk.
  Kujawsko-pomorskie, C Poland
Włodawa *76 E4 Rus.* Vlodava. Lubelskie,
  E Poland
Wlotzkasbaken *56 B3* Erongo, W Namibia
Wodonga *127 C7* Victoria, SE Australia
Wodzisław Śląski *77 C5 Ger.* Loslau. Śląskie,
  S Poland
Wōjjā *see* Wotje Atoll
Woking *67 D7* SE England, UK
Wolf, Isla *38 A4 var.* Wenmen Island. *Island*
  W Ecuador
Wolfsberg *73 D7* Kärnten, SE Austria
Wolfsburg *72 C3* Niedersachsen,
  N Germany
Wolgast *72 D2* Mecklenburg-Vorpommern,
  NE Germany
Wollaston Lake *15 F4* Saskatchewan,
  C Canada
Wollongong *127 D6* New South Wales,
  SE Australia
Wolvega *64 D2 Fris.* Wolvegea. Friesland,
  N Netherlands
Wolverhampton *67 D6* C England, UK
Wönsan *107 E3* SE North Korea
Woodburn *24 B3* Oregon, NW USA
Woodland *25 B5* California, W USA
Woodruff *18 B2* Wisconsin, N USA
Woods, Lake of the *16 A3 Fr.* Lac des Bois.
  Lake Canada/USA
Woodville *128 D4* Manawatu-Wanganui,
  North Island, NZ
Woodward *27 F1* Oklahoma, C USA
Worcester *67 D6 hist.* Wigorna Ceaster.
  W England, UK
Worcester *19 G3* Massachusetts, NE USA

Worcester *56 C5* Western Cape, SW South
  Africa
Workington *67 C5* NW England, UK
Worland *22 C3* Wyoming, C USA
Worms *73 B5 anc.* Augusta
  Vangionum, Borbetomagus, Wormatia.
  Rheinland-Pfalz, SW Germany
Worms *see* Vormsi
Worthington *23 F3* Minnesota, N USA
Wotje Atoll *122 D1 var.* Wōjjā. *Atoll* Ratak
  Chain, E Marshall Islands
Woudrichem *64 C4* Noord-Brabant,
  S Netherlands
Wrangel Island *see* Vrangelya, Ostrov
Wrangel Plain *133 B2 undersea feature*
  Arctic Ocean
Wrocław *76 C4 Eng./Ger.* Breslau.
  Dolnośląskie, SW Poland
Września *76 C3* Wielkopolskie, C Poland
Wuchang *see* Wuhan
Wuday 'ah *99 C6* Najrān, S Saudi Arabia
Wuhai *105 E3* Nei Mongol Zizhiqu,
  N China
Wuhan *106 C5 var.* Han-kou, Han-k'ou,
  Hanyang, Wuchang, Wu-han; *prev.*
  Hankow. Hubei, C China
Wuhsi *see* Wuxi
Wuhsien *see* Suzhou
Wuhu *106 D5 var.* Wu-na-mu. Anhui,
  E China
Wujlān *see* Ujelang Atoll
Wukari *53 G4* Taraba, E Nigeria
Wuliang Shan *106 A6 mountain range*
  SW China
Wu-lu-k'o-mu-shi *see* Ürümqi
Wu-lu-mu-ch'i *see* Ürümqi
Wu-na-mu *see* Wuhu
Wuppertal *72 A4 prev.* Barmen-Elberfeld.
  Nordrhein-Westfalen, W Germany
Würzburg *73 B5* Bayern, SW Germany
Wusih *see* Wuxi
Wuxi *106 D5 var.* Wuhsi, Wu-hsi, Wusih.
  Jiangsu, E China
Wuyi Shan *103 E3 mountain range* SE China
Wye *67 C6 Wel.* Gwy. *River* England/
  Wales, UK
Wyndham *124 D3* Western Australia
Wyoming *22 B3 off.* State of Wyoming;
  also known as The Equality State. *State*
  C USA
Wyoming *18 C3* Michigan, N USA
Wyszków *76 D3 Ger.* Probstberg.
  Mazowieckie, C Poland

X

Xaafuun, Raas *50 E4 var.* Ras Hafun.
  Headland NE Somalia
Xaçmaz *95 H2 Rus.* Khachmas. N Azerbaijan
Xaignabouli *114 C4 prev.* Muang
  Xaignabouri, *Fr.* Sayaboury. Xaignabouli,
  N Laos
Xai-Xai *57 E4 prev.* João Belo, Vila de João
  Bel. Gaza, S Mozambique
Xalapa *29 F4 var.* Jalapa, Jalapa Enríquez.
  Veracruz-Llave, SE Mexico
Xam Nua *114 D3 var.* Sam Neua. Houaphan,
  N Laos
Xankändi *95 G3 Rus.* Khankendi; *prev.*
  Stepanakert. SW Azerbaijan
Xánthi *82 C3* Anatolikí Makedonía kai
  Thráki, NE Greece
Xátiva *71 F3 var.* Jativa;*anc.* Setabis. País
  Valenciano, E Spain
Xauen *see* Chefchaouen
Xeres *see* Jeréz de la Frontera
Xiaguan *see* Dali
Xiamen *106 D6 var.* Hsia-men; *prev.* Amoy.
  Fujian, SE China
Xi'an *106 C4 var.* Changan, Sian, Signan,
  Siking, Singan, Xian. Shaanxi, C China
Xian *see* Xi'an
Xiangkhoang *see* Pèk
Xiangtan *106 C5 var.* Hsiang-t'an, Siangtan.
  Hunan, S China
Xiao Hinggan Ling *106 D2 Eng.* Lesser
  Khingan Range. *Mountain range* NE China
Xichang *106 B5* Sichuan, C China
Xieng Khouang *see* Pèk
Xieng Ngeun *see* Muong Xiang Ngeun
Xigaze *see* Xigazê
Xigazê *104 C5 var.* Jih-k'a-tse, Shigatse,
  Xigaze. Xizang Zizhiqu, W China
Xi Jiang *106 C6 var.* Hsi Chiang,
  Eng. West River. *River* S China
Xilinhot *105 F2 var.* Silinhot. Nei Mongol
  Zizhiqu, N China
Xilokastro *see* Xylókastro
Xin *see* Xinjiang Uygur Zizhiqu
Xingkai Hu *see* Khanka, Lake
Xingu, Rio *41 E2 river* C Brazil
Xingxingxia *104 D3* Xinjiang Uygur
  Zizhiqu, NW China
Xining *105 D4 var.* Hsining, Hsi-ning, Sining.
  Province capital Qinghai, C China
Xinjiang *see* Xinjiang Uygur Zizhiqu
Xinjiang Uygur Zizhiqu *104 B3*
  var. Sinkiang, Sinkiang Uighur
  Autonomous Region, Xin, Xinjiang.
  Admin. region *autonomous region*
  NW China
Xinpu *see* Lianyungang
Xinxiang *106 C4* Henan, C China
Xinyang *106 C5 var.* Hsin-yang, Sinyang.
  Henan, C China
Xinzo de Limia *70 C2* Galicia, NW Spain
Xiqing Shan *102 D2 mountain range* C China
Xiva *100 D2 var.* Khiwa, Rus. Khiva.
  Khorazm Wiloyati, W Uzbekistan
Xixón *see* Gijón
Xizang *see* Xizang Zizhiqu
Xizang Gaoyuan *see* Qingzang Gaoyuan
Xizang Zizhiqu *104 B4 var.* Thibet, Tibetan
  Autonomous Region, Xizang, *Eng.* Tibet.
  Admin. region *autonomous region* W China
Xolotlán *see* Managua, Lago de
Xuddur *51 D5 var.* Hudur, *It.* Oddur. Bakool,
  SW Somalia

Xuwen *106 C7* Guangdong, S China
Xuzhou *106 D4 var.* Hsu-chou, Suchow,
  Tongshan; *prev.* T'ung-shan. Jiangsu,
  E China
Xylókastro *83 B5 var.* Xilokastro.
  Pelopónnisos, S Greece

Y

Ya'an *106 B5 var.* Yaan. Sichuan, C China
Yabēlo *51 C5* C Ethiopia
Yablis *31 E2* Región Autónoma Atlántico
  Norte, NE Nicaragua
Yablonovyy Khrebet *93 F4 mountain range*
  S Russian Federation
Yabrai Shan *105 E3 mountain range*
  NE China
Yafran *49 F2* NW Libya
Yaghan Basin *45 B7 undersea feature*
  SE Pacific Ocean
Yahotyn *87 E2 Rus.* Yagotin. Kyyivs'ka
  Oblast', N Ukraine
Yahualica *28 D4* Jalisco, SW Mexico
Yakima *24 B2* Washington, NW USA
Yakima River *24 B2 river* Washington,
  NW USA
Yakoruda *82 C3* Blagoevgrad, SW Bulgaria
Yaku-shima *109 B8 island* Nansei-shotō,
  SW Japan
Yakutat *14 D4* Alaska, USA
Yakutsk *93 F3* Respublika Sakha (Yakutiya),
  NE Russian Federation
Yala *115 C7* Yala, SW Thailand
Yalizava *85 D6 Rus.* Yelizovo.
  Mahilyowskaya Voblasts', E Belarus
Yalong Jiang *106 A5 river* C China
Yalova *94 B3* Yalova, NW Turkey
Yalpuh, Ozero *86 D4 Rus.* Ozero Yalpug.
  Lake SW Ukraine
Yalta *87 F5* Respublika Krym, S Ukraine
Yalu *106 D3 var.* Yalu Jiang,
  Jap. Oryoko, *Kor.* Amnok-kang. *River*
  China/North Korea
Yamaguchi *109 B7 var.* Yamaguti.
  Yamaguchi, Honshū, SW Japan
Yamaguti *see* Yamaguchi
Yamal, Poluostrov *92 D2 peninsula*
  N Russian Federation
Yambio *51 B5 var.* Yambiyo. Western
  Equatoria, S Sudan
Yambiyo *see* Yambio
Yambol *82 D2 Turk.* Yanboli. Yambol,
  E Bulgaria
Yamdena, Pulau *117 G5 prev.* Jamdena.
  Island Kepulauan Tanimbar, E Indonesia
Yam HaMelah *see* Dead Sea
Yam Kinneret *see* Tiberias, Lake
Yamoussoukro *52 D5 country capital*
  (Côte d'Ivoire) C Côte d'Ivoire
Yamuna *112 D3 prev.* Jumna. *River* N India
Yana *93 F2 river* NE Russian Federation
Yanbu 'al Bahr *99 A5* Al Madīnah,
  W Saudi Arabia
Yangambi *55 D5* Orientale,
  N Dem. Rep. Congo
Yangchow *see* Yangzhou
Yangiyo'l *101 E2 var.* Yangiyŭl,
  Rus. Yangiyul'. Toshkent Wiloyati,
  E Uzbekistan
Yangiyŭl *see* Yangiyo'l
Yangon *114 B4 Eng.* Rangoon. *Country capital*
  (Myanmar) Yangon, S Myanmar
Yangtze *see* Chang Jiang
Yangtze Kiang *see* Chang Jiang
Yangzhou *106 D5 var.* Yangchow. Jiangsu,
  E China
Yankton *23 E3* South Dakota, N USA
Yannina *see* Ioánnina
Yanskiy Zaliv *91 F2 bay* N Russian
  Federation
Yantai *106 D4 var.* Yan-t'ai; *prev.* Chefoo,
  Chih-fu. Shandong, E China
Yan-t'ai *see* Yantai
Yaoundé *55 B5 var.* Yaunde. *Country capital*
  (Cameroon) Centre, S Cameroon
Yap *122 A1 island* Caroline Islands,
  W Micronesia
Yapanskoye More *see* East Sea/Japan, Sea of
Yapen, Pulau *117 G4 prev.* Japen. *Island*
  E Indonesia
Yap Trench *120 B2 var.* Yap Trough. *Undersea*
  feature SE Philippine Sea
Yap Trough *see* Yap Trench
Yapurá *see* Caquetá, Río
Yapurá *see* Japurá, Rio
Yaqui, Río *28 C2 river* NW Mexico
Yaransk *89 C5* Kirovskaya Oblast',
  NW Russian Federation
Yarega *88 D4* Respublika Komi,
  NW Russian Federation
Yarkant *see* Shache
Yarlung Zangbo Jiang *see* Brahmaputra
Yarmouth *see* Great Yarmouth
Yarmouth *17 F5* Nova Scotia, SE Canada
Yaroslavl' *88 B4* Yaroslavskaya Oblast',
  W Russian Federation
Yarumal *36 B2* Antioquia, NW Colombia
Yasel'da *85 B7 river* SW Belarus
Yatsushiro *109 A7 var.* Yatusiro. Kumamoto,
  Kyūshū, SW Japan
Yatusiro *see* Yatsushiro
Yaunde *see* Yaoundé
Yavarí *see* Javari, Rio
Yaviza *31 H5* Darién, SE Panama
Yavoriv *86 B2 Pol.* Jaworów, *Rus.* Yavorov.
  L'vivs'ka Oblast', NW Ukraine
Yazd *98 D3 var.* Yezd. Yazd, C Iran
Yazoo City *20 B2* Mississippi, S USA
Yding Skovhøj *63 A7 hill* C Denmark
Ýdra *83 C6 var.* Ídhra. *Island* S Greece
Ye *115 B5* Mon State, S Myanmar
Yecheng *104 A3 var.* Kargilik. Xinjiang
  Uygur Zizhiqu, NW China
Yefremov *89 B5* Tul'skaya Oblast',
  W Russian Federation
Yekaterinburg *92 C3*
  prev. Sverdlovsk. Sverdlovskaya Oblast',
  C Russian Federation

Yelets *89 B5* Lipetskaya Oblast',
  W Russian Federation
Yell *66 D1 island* NE Scotland, UK
Yellowknife *15 E4 territory capital*
  Northwest Territories, W Canada
Yellow River *see* Huang He
Yellow Sea *106 D4 Chin.* Huang Hai,
  Kor. Hwang-Hae. *Sea* E Asia
Yellowstone River *22 C2 river*
  Montana/Wyoming, NW USA
Yel'sk *85 C7 Rus.* Homyel'skaya
  Voblasts', SE Belarus
Yelwa *53 F4* Kebbi, W Nigeria
Yemen *99 C7 Ar.* Al Jumhūrīyah
  al Yamanīyah, Al Yaman. *Country*
  SW Asia
Yemva *88 D4 prev.* Zheleznodorozhnyy.
  Respublika Komi, NW Russian Federation
Yenakiyeve *87 G3 Rus.* Yenakiyevo;
  prev. Ordzhonikidze, Rykovo. Donets'ka
  Oblast', E Ukraine
Yenangyaung *114 A3* Magwe, W Myanmar
Yendi *53 E4* NE Ghana
Yengisar *104 A3* Xinjiang Uygur Zizhiqu,
  NW China
Yenierenköy *see* Agialoúsa
Yenisey *92 D3 river* Mongolia/Russian
  Federation
Yenping *see* Nanping
Yeovil *67 D7* SW England, UK
Yeppoon *126 D4* Queensland, E Australia
Yerevan *95 F3 var.* Erevan, *Eng.* Erivan.
  Country capital (Armenia) C Armenia
Yeriho *see* Jericho
Yerushalayim *see* Jerusalem
Yeu, Île d' *68 A4 island* NW France
Yevlax *95 G2 Rus.* Yevlakh. C Azerbaijan
Yevpatoriya *87 F5* Respublika Krym,
  S Ukraine
Yeya *87 H4 river* SW Russian Federation
Yezd *see* Yazd
Yezyaryshcha *85 E5 Rus.* Yezerishche.
  Vitsyebskaya Voblasts', NE Belarus
Yiannitsá *see* Giannitsá
Yichang *106 C5* Hubei, C China
Yıldızeli *94 D3* Sivas, N Turkey
Yinchuan *106 B4 var.* Yinch'uan, Yin-ch'uan,
  Yinchwan. Ningxia, N China
Yinchwan *see* Yinchuan
Yin-hsien *see* Ningbo
Yining *104 B2 var.* I-ning, *Uigh.* Gulja,
  Kuldja. Xinjiang Uygur Zizhiqu,
  NW China
Yíthion *see* Gýtheio
Yogyakarta *116 C5 prev.* Djokjakarta,
  Jogjakarta, Jokyakarta. Jawa, C Indonesia
Yokohama *109 D5* Aomori, Honshū,
  C Japan
Yokohama *108 D4* Kanagawa, Honshū,
  S Japan
Yokote *108 D4* Akita, Honshū, C Japan
Yola *53 H4* Adamawa, E Nigeria
Yonago *109 B6* Tottori, Honshū,
  SW Japan
Yong'an *106 D6 var.* Yongan. Fujian,
  SE China
Yonkers *19 F3* New York, NE USA
Yonne *68 C4 river* C France
Yopal *36 C3 var.* El Yopal. Casanare,
  C Colombia
York *67 D5 anc.* Eboracum, Eburacum.
  N England, UK
York *23 E4* Nebraska, C USA
York, Cape *126 C1 headland* Queensland,
  NE Australia
Yorkton *15 F5* Saskatchewan,
  S Canada
Yoro *30 C2* Yoro, C Honduras
Yoshkar-Ola *89 C5* Respublika Mariy El,
  W Russian Federation
Youngstown *18 D4* Ohio, N USA
Youth, Isle of *see* Juventud, Isla de la
Yreka *24 B4* California, W USA
Yssel *see* IJssel
Ysyk-Köl *see* Issyk-Kul', Ozero
Yu *see* Henan
Yuan *see* Red River
Yuan Jiang *see* Red River
Yuba City *25 B5* California, W USA
Yucatan Channel *29 H3 Sp.* Canal de
  Yucatán. *Channel* Cuba/Mexico
Yucatan Peninsula *13 C7 peninsula*
  Guatemala/Mexico
Yuci *see* Jinzhong
Yue *see* Guangdong
Yueyang *106 C5* Hunan, S China
Yukhavichy *85 D5 Rus.* Yukhovichi.
  Vitsyebskaya Voblasts', N Belarus
Yukon *14 C2 river* Canada/USA
Yukon *see* Yukon Territory
Yukon Territory *14 D3 var.* Yukon,
  Fr. Territoire du Yukon. Admin. region
  territory NW Canada
Yulin *106 C6* Guangxi Zhuangzu Zizhiqu,
  S China
Yuma *26 A2* Arizona, SW USA
Yumen *106 A3 var.* Laojunmiao, Yümen.
  Gansu, N China
Yun *see* Yunnan
Yungki *see* Jilin
Yung-ning *see* Nanning
Yunjinghong *see* Jinghong
Yunki *see* Jilin
Yunnan *106 A6 var.* Yun, Yunnan Sheng,
  Yünnan, Yun-nan. Admin. region *province*
  SW China
Yunnan *see* Kunming
Yunnan Sheng *see* Yunnan
Yurúa, Río *see* Juruá, Rio
Yushu *104 D4* Qinghai, C China
Yuty *42 D3* Caazapá, S Paraguay
Yuzhno-Sakhalinsk *93 H4 Jap.* Toyohara;
  prev. Vladimirovka. Ostrov Sakhalin,
  Sakhalinskaya Oblast', SE Russian
  Federation
Yuzhou *see* Chongqing
Ýylanly *100 C2 var.* Il'yaly. Dashkhovuzskiy
  Velayat, N Turkmenistan

Z

Zaanstad 64 C3 *prev.* Zaandam. Noord-Holland, C Netherlands
Zabaykal'sk 93 F5 Chitinskaya Oblast', S Russian Federation
Zabern *see* Saverne
Zabīd 99 B7 W Yemen
Ząbkowice *see* Ząbkowice Śląskie
Ząbkowice Śląskie 76 B4 *var.* Ząbkowice, *Ger.* Frankenstein, Frankenstein in Schlesien. Wałbrzych, SW Poland
Zábřeh 77 C5 *Ger.* Hohenstadt. Olomoucký Kraj, E Czech Republic
Zacapa 30 B2 Zacapa, E Guatemala
Zacatecas 28 D3 Zacatecas, C Mexico
Zacatepec 29 E4 Morelos, S Mexico
Zacháro 83 B6 *var.* Zaharo, Zakháro. Dytikí Ellás, S Greece
Zadar 78 A3 *It.* Zara; *anc.* Iader. Zadar, SW Croatia
Zadetkyi Kyun 115 B6 *var.* St. Matthew's Island. *Island* Mergui Archipelago, S Myanmar
Zafra 70 C4 Extremadura, W Spain
Żagań 76 B4 *var.* Zagań, Żegań; *Ger.* Sagan. Lubuskie, W Poland
Zagazig 50 B1 *var.* Az Zaqāziq. N Egypt
Zágráb *see* Zagreb
Zagreb 78 B2 *Ger.* Agram, *Hung.* Zágráb. *Country capital* (Croatia) Zagreb, N Croatia
Zāgros, Kūhhā-ye 98 C3 *Eng.* Zagros Mountains. *Mountain range* W Iran
Zāgros Mountains *see* Zāgros, Kūhhā-ye
Zaharo *see* Zacháro
Zāhedān 98 E4 *var.* Zahidan; *prev.* Duzdab. Sīstān va Balūchestān, SE Iran
Zahidan *see* Zāhedān
Zaḥlah *see* Zahlé
Zahlé 96 B4 *var.* Zaḥlah. C Lebanon
Záhony 77 E6 Szabolcs-Szatmár-Bereg, NE Hungary
Zaire *see* Congo
Zaječar 78 E4 Serbia, E Serbia and Montenegro (Yugo.)
Zakhárov *see* Zacháro
Zākhō 98 B2 *var.* Zākhū. N Iraq
Zākhū *see* Zākhō
Zákinthos *see* Zákynthos
Zakopane 77 D5 Małopolskie, S Poland
Zakota Pomorskiea *see* Danzig, Gulf of
Zákynthos 83 A6 *var.* Zákinthos, *It.* Zante. *Island* Iónioi Nísoi, Greece, C Mediterranean Sea
Zalaegerszeg 77 B7 Zala, W Hungary
Zalău 86 B3 *Ger.* Waltenberg, *Hung.* Zilah; *prev. Ger.* Zillenmarkt. Sălaj, NW Romania
Zalim 99 B5 Makkah, W Saudi Arabia
Zambeze *see* Zambezi
Zambeze *see* Zambezi
Zambezi 76 B4 *var.* Zambesi, *Port.* Zambeze. *River* S Africa
Zambezi 56 C2 North Western, W Zambia
Zambia 56 C2 *off.* Republic of Zambia; *prev.* Northern Rhodesia. *Country* S Africa
Zamboanga 117 E3 *off.* Zamboanga City. Mindanao, S Philippines

Zambrów 76 E3 Podlaskie, E Poland
Zamora 70 D2 Castilla-León, NW Spain
Zamora de Hidalgo 28 D4 Michoacán de Ocampo, SW Mexico
Zamość 76 E4 *Rus.* Zamoste. Lubelskie, E Poland
Zancle *see* Messina
Zanda 104 A4 Xizang Zizhiqu, W China
Zanesville 18 D4 Ohio, N USA
Zanjān 98 C2 *var.* Zenjan, Zinjan. Zanjān, NW Iran
Zante *see* Zákynthos
Zanthus 125 C6 Western Australia
Zanzibar 51 C7 *Swa.* Unguja. *Island* E Tanzania
Zanzibar 51 D7 Zanzibar, E Tanzania
Zaozhuang 106 D4 Shandong, E China
Zapadna Morava 78 D4 *Ger.* Westliche Morava. *River* C Serbia and Montenegro (Yugo.)
Zapadnaya Dvina 88 A4 Tverskaya Oblast', W Russian Federation
Zapadno-Sibirskaya Ravnina 92 C3 *Eng.* West Siberian Plain. *Plain* C Russian Federation
Zapadnyy Sayan 92 D4 *Eng.* Western Sayans. *Mountain range* S Russian Federation
Zapala 43 B5 Neuquén, W Argentina
Zapiola Ridge 45 B6 *undersea feature* SW Atlantic Ocean
Zapolyarnyy 88 C2 Murmanskaya Oblast', NW Russian Federation
Zaporizhzhya 87 F3 *Rus.* Zaporozh'ye; *prev.* Aleksandrovsk. Zaporiz'ka Oblast', SE Ukraine
Zapotiltic 28 D4 Jalisco, SW Mexico
Zaqatala 95 G2 *Rus.* Zakataly. NW Azerbaijan
Zara 94 D3 Sivas, C Turkey
Zarafshon 100 D2 *Rus.* Zarafshan. Nawoiy Wiloyati, N Uzbekistan
Zaragoza 71 F2 *Eng.* Saragossa; *anc.* Caesaraugusta, Salduba. Aragón, NE Spain
Zarand 98 D3 Kermān, C Iran
Zaranj 100 D5 Nīmrūz, SW Afghanistan
Zarasai 84 C4 Zarasai, E Lithuania
Zárate 42 D4 *prev.* General José F.Uriburu. Buenos Aires, E Argentina
Zarautz 71 E1 *var.* Zarauz. País Vasco, N Spain
Zarauz *see* Zarautz
Zaraza 37 E2 Guárico, N Venezuela
Zarghūn Shahr 101 E4 *var.* Katawaz. Paktīkā, SE Afghanistan
Zaria 53 G4 Kaduna, C Nigeria
Zarós 83 D8 Kríti, Greece, E Mediterranean Sea
Zarqa *see* Az Zarqā'
Żary 76 B4 *Ger.* Sorau, Sorau in der Niederlausitz. Lubulskie, W Poland
Zaunguzskiye Garagumy *see* Üngüz Angyrsyndaky Garagum
Zavet 82 D1 Razgrad, N Bulgaria
Zavidovići 78 C3 Federacija Bosna I Hercegovina, N Bosnia and Herzegovina

Zawia *see* Az Zāwiyah
Zawiercie 76 D4 *Rus.* Zavertse. Śląskie, S Poland
Zawīlah 49 F3 *var.* Zuwaylah, *It.* Zueila. C Libya
Zaysan, Ozero 92 D5 *Kaz.* Zaysan Köl. *Lake* E Kazakhstan
Zbarazh 86 C2 Ternopil's'ka Oblast', W Ukraine
Zduńska Wola 76 C4 Łódzkie, C Poland
Zeebrugge 65 A5 West-Vlaanderen, NW Belgium
Zeewolde 64 D3 Flevoland, C Netherlands
Żegań *see* Żagań
Zefat 97 B5 *var.* Safed, Tsefat, *Ar.* Safad. Northern, N Israel
Zeist 64 C4 Utrecht, C Netherlands
Zele 65 B5 Oost-Vlaanderen, NW Belgium
Zelenoborskiy 88 B2 Murmanskaya Oblast', NW Russian Federation
Zelenograd 89 B5 Moskovskaya Oblast', W Russian Federation
Zelenogradsk 84 A4 *Ger.* Cranz, Kranz. Kaliningradskaya Oblast', W Russian Federation
Zelle *see* Celle
Zel'va 85 B6 *Pol.* Zelwa. Hrodzyenskaya Voblasts', W Belarus
Zelzate 65 B5 *var.* Selzaete. Oost-Vlaanderen, NW Belgium
Žemaičių Aukštumas 84 B4 *physical region* W Lithuania
Zemst 65 C5 Vlaams Brabant, C Belgium
Zemun 78 D3 Serbia, N Serbia and Montenegro (Yugo.)
Zenica 78 C4 Federacija Bosna I Herzegovina, C Bosnia and Herzegovina
Zenjan *see* Zanjān
Zeravshan 101 E3 *Taj./Uzb.* Zarafshon. *River* Tajikistan/Uzbekistan
Zevenaar 64 D4 Gelderland, SE Netherlands
Zevenbergen 64 C4 Noord-Brabant, S Netherlands
Zeya 91 E3 *river* SE Russian Federation
Zgierz 76 C4 *Ger.* Neuhof, *Rus.* Zgerzh. Łódź, C Poland
Zgorzelec 76 B4 *Ger.* Görlitz. Dolnośląskie, SW Poland
Zhabinka 85 A6 *Pol.* Żabinka, *Rus.* Zhabinka. Brestskaya Voblasts', SW Belarus
Zhambyl *see* Taraz
Zhanaozen 92 A4 *Kaz.* Zhangaözen, *prev.* Novyy Uzen'. Mangistau, W Kazakhstan
Zhangaözen *see* Zhanaozen
Zhangaqazaly *see* Ayteke Bi
Zhang-chia-k'ou *see* Zhangjiakou
Zhangdian *see* Zibo
Zhangjiakou 106 C3 *var.* Changkiakow, Zhang-chia-k'ou, *Eng.* Kalgan; *prev.* Wanchuan. Hebei, E China
Zhangzhou 106 D6 Fujian, SE China
Zhanjiang 106 C7 *var.* Chanchiang, Chan-chiang, *Cant.* Tsamkong, *Fr.* Fort-Bayard. Guangdong, S China
Zhaoqing 106 C6 Guangdong, S China

Zhe *see* Zhejiang
Zhejiang 106 D5 *var.* Che-chiang, Chekiang, Zhe, Zhejiang Sheng. Admin. region *province* SE China
Zhejiang Sheng *see* Zhejiang
Zheleznodoroznyy 84 A4 *Ger.* Gerdauen. Kaliningradskaya Oblast', W Russian Federation
Zheleznogorsk 89 A5 Kurskaya Oblast', W Russian Federation
Zhengzhou 106 C4 *var.* Ch'eng-chou, Chengchow; *prev.* Chenghsien. Henan, C China
Zhezkazgan 92 C4 *Kaz.* Zhezqazghan; *prev.* Dzhezkazgan. Karaganda, C Kazakhstan
Zhlobin 85 D7 Homyel'skaya Voblasts', SE Belarus
Zhmerynka 86 D2 *Rus.* Zhmerinka. Vinnyts'ka Oblast', C Ukraine
Zhodzina 85 D6 *Rus.* Zhodino. Minskaya Voblasts', C Belarus
Zhovkva 86 B2 *Pol.* Żółkiew, *Rus.* Zholkev, Zholkva; *prev.* Nesterov. L'vivs'ka Oblast', NW Ukraine
Zhovti Vody 87 F3 *Rus.* Zhëltyye Vody. Dnipropetrovs'ka Oblast', E Ukraine
Zhovtneve 87 E4 *Rus.* Zhovtnevoye. Mykolayivs'ka Oblast', S Ukraine
Zhydachiv 86 B2 *Pol.* Żydaczów, *Rus.* Zhidachov. L'vivs'ka Oblast', NW Ukraine
Zhytkavichy 85 C7 *Rus.* Zhitkovichi. Homyel'skaya Voblasts', SE Belarus
Zhytomyr 86 D2 *Rus.* Zhitomir. Zhytomyrs'ka Oblast', NW Ukraine
Zibo 106 D4 *var.* Zhangdian. Shandong, E China
Zielona Góra 76 B4 *Ger.* Grünberg, Grünberg in Schlesien, Grüneberg. Lubuskie, W Poland
Zierikzee 64 B4 Zeeland, SW Netherlands
Zigong 106 B5 *var.* Tzekung. Sichuan, C China
Ziguinchor 52 B3 SW Senegal
Žilina 77 C5 *Ger.* Sillein, *Hung.* Zsolna. Žilinský Kraj, N Slovakia
Zimbabwe 56 D3 *prev.* Rhodesia. *Country* S Africa
Zimnicea 86 C5 Teleorman, S Romania
Zimovniki 89 B7 Rostovskaya Oblast', SW Russian Federation
Zinder 53 G3 Zinder, S Niger
Zinjan *see* Zanjān
Zipaquirá 36 B3 Cundinamarca, C Colombia
Zittau 72 D4 Sachsen, E Germany
Zlatni Pyasŭtsi 82 E2 Dobrich, NE Bulgaria
Zlín 77 C5 *prev.* Gottwaldov. Zlínský Kraj, E Czech Republic
Złotów 76 C3 Wielkopolskie, C Poland
Znam"yanka 87 F3 *Rus.* Znamenka. Kirovohrads'ka Oblast', C Ukraine
Żnin 76 C3 Kujawski-pomorskie, C Poland
Znojmo 77 B5 *Ger.* Znaim. Brněnský Kraj, SE Czech Republic
Zoetermeer 64 C4 Zuid-Holland, W Netherlands

Zolochiv 86 C2 *Pol.* Złoczów, *Rus.* Zolochev. L'vivs'ka Oblast', W Ukraine
Zolochiv 87 G2 *Rus.* Zolochev. Kharkivs'ka Oblast', E Ukraine
Zolote 87 H3 *Rus.* Zolotoye. Luhans'ka Oblast', E Ukraine
Zolotonosha 87 E2 Cherkas'ka Oblast', C Ukraine
Zomba 57 E2 Southern, S Malawi
Zongo 55 C5 Equateur, N Dem. Rep. Congo
Zonguldak 94 C2 Zonguldak, NW Turkey
Zonhoven 65 D6 Limburg, NE Belgium
Żory 77 C5 *var.* Zory, *Ger.* Sohrau. Śląskie, S Poland
Zouar 54 C2 Borkou-Ennedi-Tibesti, N Chad
Zouérat 52 C2 *var.* Zouérate, Zouîrât. Tiris Zemmour, N Mauritania
Zouérate *see* Zouérat
Zouîrât *see* Zouérat
Zrenjanin 78 D3 *prev.* Petrovgrad, Veliki Bečkerek, *Ger.* Grossbetschkerek, *Hung.* Nagybecskerek. Serbia, N Serbia and Montenegro (Yugo.)
Zubov Seamount 45 D5 *undersea feature* E Atlantic Ocean
Zueila *see* Zawīlah
Zug 73 B7 *Fr.* Zoug. Zug, C Switzerland
Zugspitze 73 C7 *mountain* S Germany
Zuid-Beveland 65 B5 *var.* South Beveland. *Island* SW Netherlands
Zuidhorn 64 E1 Groningen, NE Netherlands
Zuidlaren 64 E2 Drenthe, NE Netherlands
Zula 50 C4 E Eritrea
Züllichau *see* Sulechów
Zundert 65 C5 Noord-Brabant, S Netherlands
Zunyi 106 B5 Guizhou, S China
Županja 78 C3 *Hung.* Zsupanya. Vukovar-Srijem, E Croatia
Zürich 73 B7 *Eng./Fr.* Zurich, *It.* Zurigo. Zürich, N Switzerland
Zürichsee 73 B7 *Eng.* Lake Zurich. *Lake* NE Switzerland
Zutphen 64 D3 Gelderland, E Netherlands
Zuwārah 49 F2 NW Libya
Zuwaylah *see* Zawīlah
Zuyevka 89 D5 Kirovskaya Oblast', NW Russian Federation
Zvenyhorodka 87 E2 *Rus.* Zvenigorodka. Cherkas'ka Oblast', C Ukraine
Zvishavane 56 D3 *prev.* Shabani. Matabeleland South, S Zimbabwe
Zvolen 77 C6 *Ger.* Altsohl, *Hung.* Zólyom. Banskobystricky Kraj, C Slovakia
Zvornik 78 C4 E Bosnia and Herzegovina
Zwedru 52 D5 *var.* Tchien. E Liberia
Zwettl 73 E6 Wien, NE Austria
Zwevegem 65 A6 West-Vlaanderen, W Belgium
Zwickau 73 C5 Sachsen, E Germany
Zwolle 64 D3 Overijssel, E Netherlan
Zyôetu *see* Jōetsu
Żyardów 76 D3 Mazowieckie, C Poland
Zyryanovsk 92 D5 Vostochnyy Kazakhstan, E Kazakhstan